The Winter Missal of Arnold of Rummen

Library of the Written Word

VOLUME 124

The Manuscript World

Editor-in-Chief

Richard Gameson (*Durham University*)

Editorial Board

Martin Kauffmann (*The Bodleian Library, Oxford*)
Kathryn Rudy (*University of St Andrews*)
Roger S. Wieck (*The Morgan Library & Museum, New York*)

VOLUME 15

The titles published in this series are listed at *brill.com/lww*

The Winter Missal of Arnold of Rummen

Huis van het boek, Ms. 10 A 14

By

Carolyn Coker Joslin Watson

BRILL

LEIDEN | BOSTON

FRONTISPIECE   The Crucifixion (Artist 2) and the opening of the Canon of the Mass (Artist 1). Winter Missal of Arnold of Rummen, Sint-Truiden (text), Ghent (decoration and illumination), *c.*1345–1366. The Hague, Huis van het boek, Ms. MMW 10 A 14, fols. 143v–144r
PHOTO: HUIS VAN HET BOEK

Te igitur clementissi-
me pater p ihesum
xpristum dominū
nrm supplices roga-
mus ac petimus.
uti accepta habeas
et benedicas hec ✠
dona. hec ✠ mune-
ra. hec sancta ✠ sa-
crificia illibata.
In primis que tibi
offerimus pro eccl-
tua sancta catholi-

ca. quam pacifica-
re. custodire. aduna-
re. et regere digneris
toto orbe terrarum
una cum famulo
tuo papa nro. N
et antistite nro. N.
et rege nro. N. necn
et omnibus ortho-
doxis atq; catholi-
ce et apostolice fidi
cultoribus
Memento dñe
famulorum
famularumq; tua-
rum. N. Et om-
nium circumstā-
tium quorum tibi
fides cognita est et

Cover illustration: Ad te levavi. Detail from Introit for the First Sunday of Advent. Artist 2. Winter missal of Arnold of Rummen, Sint-Truiden (text), Ghent (decoration and illumination), c.1345–1366, fol. 7r. The Hague, Huis van het boek, MMW 10 A 14. Photo: Huis van het boek.

The Library of Congress Cataloging-in-Publication Data is available online at https://catalog.loc.gov

Typeface for the Latin, Greek, and Cyrillic scripts: "Brill". See and download: brill.com/brill-typeface.

ISSN 1874-4834
ISBN 978-90-04-42712-9 (hardback)
ISBN 978-90-04-42713-6 (e-book)
DOI 10.1163/9789004427136

Copyright 2025 by Koninklijke Brill BV, Leiden, The Netherlands.
Koninklijke Brill BV incorporates the imprints Brill, Brill Nijhoff, Brill Schöningh, Brill Fink, Brill mentis, Brill Wageningen Academic, Vandenhoeck & Ruprecht, Böhlau and V&R unipress.
All rights reserved. No part of this publication may be reproduced, translated, stored in a retrieval system, or transmitted in any form or by any means, electronic, mechanical, photocopying, recording or otherwise, without prior written permission from the publisher. Requests for re-use and/or translations must be addressed to Koninklijke Brill BV via brill.com or copyright.com.

This book is printed on acid-free paper and produced in a sustainable manner.

This book is dedicated to St. Joseph: Father, Guardian, Tecton, Dreamer

∴

Contents

Acknowledgements XIII
List of Figures and Tables XIV
Abbreviations for Repositories XXVII

1 **Introduction** 1
  1 Purpose and Contributions 1
  2 Why Study Flourishing? 3
  3 Flourisher-Illuminators and the Relationship of Flourishing and Painting 4
  4 Identities of Flourisher-Illuminators 5
  5 Models of Production 5
  6 Method 6
  7 The Colophons 6
  8 Fourteenth-Century Flanders 8
  9 The Historical Context of 10 A 14 10
  10 Overpaints and Heraldry 13
  11 Overpaints and Heraldry in KBR 9427 and KBR 9217 15

2 **Contents, Codicology, and Script** 17
  1 The Calendar 17
  2 Quires and Contents 17
  3 Ruling 18
  4 Script 20
  5 Rubrics and Directives 21
  6 Decoration 21

3 **Penwork Initials and Borders** 22
  1 One-Line Initials 22
  2 Two-Line Initials 22
  3 The Initial *I* 23
  4 Initials in Musical Notation and Three- and Four-Line Penwork Initials 23
  5 Penwork Borders and Their Flourishing 24
  6 Terminal Complexes 25
  7 Conclusion 25

4 **The Flourisher-Illuminators of the Two Campaigns** 27
  1 Two Campaigns and an Addendum 27
  2 Scholarship on Illumination and Decoration 27
  3 The First Campaign, *c.*1345–1355 29
  4 The First Campaign: Artist 1 30
    4.1 *Two-Line Penwork Initials* 30
    4.2 I-*Initials* 31
    4.3 *Puns, Play, and Challenges to Boundaries* 31
    4.4 *Style of Illumination* 31
    4.5 *Minor Illumination* 32
    4.6 *Artist 1: Conclusion* 32
  5 The First Campaign: Artist 2 32
    5.1 *Two-Line Penwork Initials* 33
    5.2 *Five Cycles of Flourishing* 34

		5.3	*Style of Illumination* 36
		5.4	*Minor Illumination* 37
		5.5	*Incompletions* 37
		5.6	*Artist 2: Conclusion* 38
	6	Collaboration between Artists 1 and 2 39
	7	The Second Campaign, *c.*1366 40
	8	The Second Campaign: Artist 3 40
	9	Were Artist 2 and Artist 3 the Same Person? Evidence from Penwork 41
	10	The Second Campaign: Artist 4 42
		10.1	*Two-Line Penwork Initials and Border Bars* 42
		10.2	*Minor Illumination* 42
		10.3	*Style of Illumination* 42
	11	Parallels between the First and Second Campaigns 43
	12	Conclusion 43

5 The Miniatures: Style and Iconography 44

1   Fol. 7r: the First Sunday in Advent, *Ad te levavi*. First Campaign, Artist 2   44

2   Fol. 22r: the Nativity of Christ. Second Campaign, Artist 3   45

3   Fol. 26r: the Circumcision of Christ. Second Campaign, Artist 4;
Some Preliminary Drawing by Artist 2, First Campaign   47

4   Fol. 27v: the Epiphany. Second Campaign, Artist 3   48

5   Fol. 106v: Palm Sunday: Christ Entering Jerusalem. First Campaign, Artist 2   51

6   Fol. 139r: the Preface of the Canon for Easter. First Campaign, Artist 1   53

7   Fol. 143v: the Crucifixion. First Campaign, Artist 2   54

     7.1   *The Sources for 10 A 14's Crucifixion: 9217*   56

     7.2   *Connections to Cologne*   57

     7.3   *The Scourge Wounds*   58

8   Fol. 144r: the Opening of the Canon of the Mass. First Campaign, Artist 1   58

     8.1   *The Crucifixion-*Te igitur *Pairing and the Feast of Corpus Christi*   59

9   Fol. 151r: the Feast of St. Lucy. First Campaign, Artist 1   63

10   Fol. 167r: the Presentation in the Temple. First Campaign, Artist 1   64

11   Fol. 176v: the Annunciation. First Campaign, Artist 1   64

12   Fol. 192v: the Dedication of a Church. First Campaign, Artist 1   65

13   Were Artist 2 and Artist 3 the Same Person? Evidence from Illumination 65

14   Conclusion 67

6 The Calendar 69

1   Liège and the Mosan Region 69

2   Sint-Truiden 70

3   Ghent 70

4   Gallican Elements 71

5   England 72

6   Brussels 72

7   Cologne and Münster 72

8   The Illustration of the Calendar 72

9   Conclusion 73

CONTENTS

XI

7 The Origins and Formation of the Flourisher-Illuminators   75

1   Artist 1: the Loppem-Bruges Antiphonal, Tournai, Perhaps Cologne   75

2   Artist 2: Sint-Truiden   77

2.1   *The Evidence from Penwork*   78

2.2   *The Evidence from Illumination*   80

3   Artist 3   82

4   Artist 4: a Follower of Artist 3   84

5   Conclusion   84

8 The Place of Production   85

1   Brabant/Brussels   85

2   Cologne   86

3   Sint-Truiden   86

4   Ghent   87

5   Conclusion   92

9 Conclusions   93

Appendices   97

Appendix 1: Heraldry of Oreye, Loon, Chiny, Somerghem, Perweis, Flanders, and Brabant   99

Appendix 2: Transcription of Calendar of 10 A 14   101

Appendix 3: Artist 2's Penwork Flourishing in Cycle 1 of 10 A 14 and Its Relation to Other Rummen-Group Manuscripts   105

Appendix 4: Rummen-Group Manuscripts: Flourishing, Illumination, Artistic Hands, and Sources, Pts. 1–5   107

Appendix 5: Comparative Iconography of Labors of the Months   116

Appendix 6: Gorgons   117

Appendix 7: The Contents of 10 A 14 and Summary Description of Illumination, by Quire   119

Inventories   126

Inventory 1: Flourishing by Quire and Artist   126

Inventory 2: Penwork Border Bars of Types 1–4 by Quire and Artist   130

Inventory 3: *I*-Initials by Quire and Artist   134

Inventory 4: Minor Illumination: Painted Initials, Partial Borders   139

Inventory 5: Faces in the Penwork of Artist 1   139

Inventory 6: Combinations of Penwork Elements in the *Passionarium 1*, BUL, Ms. 57   140

Inventory 7: Miscellaneous Penwork Initials   141

Tables   144

Bibliography   151

Index   158

Index of Manuscripts Cited   161

Figures   163

Full pages   165

Details   309

Acknowledgements

This book was more than three decades in the making. Many scholars, teachers, librarians, and friends have helped me along the way, to say nothing of family. To Jos van Heel of The Hague's Huis van het boek (at that time, the Rijksmuseum Meermanno-Westreenianum) I owe my introduction to Ms. 10 A 14. Rickey Tax, Head of Collections at the Huis van het boek, most graciously granted me access to the manuscript and facilitated my work on many days during the years of my research. Likewise, Petra Luijkx of the Huis van het boek assisted me on multiple occasions. Anne Korteweg assisted me in my work in the Koninklijke Bibliotheek, The Hague. Others at many libraries in Europe, the United Kingdom, and the United States also have assisted me over the years; however, I am especially grateful to the staff of the James B. Duke Library at Furman University, in particular, to Elaina Griffith, Robyn Andrews, and Jimmy Quinn, for invaluable help over the years in facilitating my access to materials essential to this project. The expertise of my colleague Mary Wolinski, who shared with me her musicological research on manuscripts of the Rummen group, greatly helped to contextualize, expand, and correct my ideas. Barbara Haggh-Huglo offered helpful commentary on the Rummen group's two antiphonals. Daniel Sheerin helped with the colophons and inscriptions. Celia Chazelle and Eric Palazzo answered questions related to the Eucharistic dimensions of iconography. Furman University has generously supported this project through grants awarded me by the Committee for Research and Professional Growth, the Humanities Center, and the Office of Academic Affairs. To Richard Gameson, editor-in-chief of Brill's Manuscript World series, I am deeply indebted for advice and comments and for his professional, careful, and patient editorial work. I am truly grateful to the specialist readers (identities unknown to me) who read and commented extensively on the earlier draft of my manuscript. Their perspectives helped me to broaden my own.

From very early on, I benefited greatly from Jaroslav Folda's example of high excellence in scholarship. I owe to Mary Coker Joslin, my mother now deceased, the introduction to fourteenth-century illumination through my collaborative work with her on the Egerton Genesis. And finally, Ann Killough, Nell Joslin, Stella Self, and Snowy Albright for their support of this project and for their work in proofreading; and I thank my husband Randal Watson for his consistent and patient support and encouragement.

Figures and Tables

Figures

Frontispiece   The Crucifixion (Artist 2) and the opening of the Canon of the Mass (Artist 1). Winter Missal of Arnold of Rummen, Sint-Truiden (text), Ghent (decoration and illumination), *c.*1345–1366. The Hague, Huis van het boek, Ms. MMW 10 A 14, fols. 143v–144r   iv–v

1   Front cover, calfskin. 18th c. Winter Missal of Arnold of Rummen, Sint-Truiden (text), Ghent (decoration and illumination), *c.*1345–1366. The Hague, Huis van het boek, Ms. MMW 10 A 14   167

1a   Spine of calfskin cover with gold stippling and filigree, 18th c. Winter Missal of Arnold of Rummen, Sint-Truiden (text), Ghent (decoration and illumination), *c.*1345–1366. The Hague, Huis van het boek, Ms. MMW 10 A 14   167

2   Inside of front cover. Winter Missal of Arnold of Rummen, Sint-Truiden (text), Ghent (decoration and illumination), *c.*1345–1366. The Hague, Huis van het boek, Ms. MMW 10 A 14   168

3   Calendar for January. Artist 1. Winter Missal of Arnold of Rummen, Sint-Truiden (text), Ghent (decoration and illumination), *c.*1345–1366. The Hague, Huis van het boek, Ms. MMW 10 A 14, fol. 1r   169

4   Calendar for February. Artist 1. Winter Missal of Arnold of Rummen, Sint-Truiden (text), Ghent (decoration and illumination), *c.*1345–1366. The Hague, Huis van het boek, Ms. MMW 10 A 14, fol. 1v   170

5   Calendar for March. Artist 1. Winter Missal of Arnold of Rummen, Sint-Truiden (text), Ghent (decoration and illumination), *c.*1345–1366. The Hague, Huis van het boek, Ms. MMW 10 A 14, fol. 2r   171

6   Calendar for April. Artist 1. Winter Missal of Arnold of Rummen, Sint-Truiden (text), Ghent (decoration and illumination), *c.*1345–1366. The Hague, Huis van het boek, Ms. MMW 10 A 14, fol. 2v   172

7   Calendar for May. Artist 1. Winter Missal of Arnold of Rummen, Sint-Truiden (text), Ghent (decoration and illumination), *c.*1345–1366. The Hague, Huis van het boek, Ms. MMW 10 A 14, fol. 3r   173

8   Calendar for June. Artist 1. Winter Missal of Arnold of Rummen, Sint-Truiden (text), Ghent (decoration and illumination), *c.*1345–1366. The Hague, Huis van het boek, Ms. MMW 10 A 14, fol. 3v   174

9   Calendar for July. Artist 1. Winter Missal of Arnold of Rummen, Sint-Truiden (text), Ghent (decoration and illumination), *c.*1345–1366. The Hague, Huis van het boek, Ms. MMW 10 A 14, fol. 4r   175

10   Calendar for August. Artist 1. Winter Missal of Arnold of Rummen, Sint-Truiden (text), Ghent (decoration and illumination), *c.*1345–1366. The Hague, Huis van het boek, Ms. MMW 10 A 14, fol. 4v   176

11   Calendar for September. Artist 1. Winter Missal of Arnold of Rummen, Sint-Truiden (text), Ghent (decoration and illumination), *c.*1345–1366. The Hague, Huis van het boek, Ms. MMW 10 A 14, fol. 5r   177

12   Calendar for October. Artist 1. Winter Missal of Arnold of Rummen, Sint-Truiden (text), Ghent (decoration and illumination), *c.*1345–1366. The Hague, Huis van het boek, Ms. MMW 10 A 14, fol. 5v   178

13   Calendar for November. Artist 1. Winter Missal of Arnold of Rummen, Sint-Truiden (text), Ghent (decoration and illumination), *c.*1345–1366. The Hague, Huis van het boek, Ms. MMW 10 A 14, fol. 6r   179

14   Calendar for December. Artist 1. Winter Missal of Arnold of Rummen, Sint-Truiden (text), Ghent (decoration and illumination), *c.*1345–1366. The Hague, Huis van het boek, Ms. MMW 10 A 14, fol. 6v   180

15   *Ad te levavi*, First Sunday of Advent. Artist 2. Winter Missal of Arnold of Rummen, Sint-Truiden (text), Ghent (decoration and illumination), *c.*1345–1366. The Hague, Huis van het boek, Ms. MMW 10 A 14, fol. 7r   181

15a   Initial *A*(*d te*). Artist 2. Winter Missal of Arnold of Rummen, Sint-Truiden (text), Ghent (decoration and illumination), *c.*1345–1366. The Hague, Huis van het boek, Ms. MMW 10 A 14, fol. 7r, detail   311

16   Silver stains from overpainted shields. Winter Missal of Arnold of Rummen, Sint-Truiden (text), Ghent (decoration and illumination), *c.*1345–1366. The Hague, Huis van het boek, Ms. MMW 10 A 14, fol. 7v   182

16a   Initial *H*(*ec*) with tufted grotesque. Artist 2. Winter Missal of Arnold of Rummen, Sint-Truiden (text), Ghent (decoration and illumination), *c.*1345–1366. The Hague, Huis van het boek, Ms. MMW 10 A 14, fol. 7v, detail   311

17   Penwork with a variety of foliate types. Artist 2. Winter Missal of Arnold of Rummen, Sint-Truiden (text), Ghent (decoration and illumination), *c.*1345–1366. The Hague, Huis van het boek, Ms. MMW 10 A 14, fol. 8r   183

18   Initial *P*(*opulus*) with tonsured head. Artist 2. Winter Missal of Arnold of Rummen, Sint-Truiden (text), Ghent (decoration and illumination), *c.*1345–1366. The Hague, Huis van het boek, Ms. MMW 10 A 14, fol. 8v, detail   312

19   Penwork of Cycle 1A. Artist 2. Winter Missal of Arnold of Rummen, Sint-Truiden (text), Ghent (decoration and illumination), *c.*1345–1366. The Hague, Huis van het boek, Ms. MMW 10 A 14, fol. 9r   184

FIGURES AND TABLES   XV

19a Lower terminal bar. Artist 2. Winter Missal of Arnold of Rummen, Sint-Truiden (text), Ghent (decoration and illumination), *c*.1345–1366. The Hague, Huis van het boek, Ms. MMW 10 A 14, fol. 9r detail   312

20 Lower terminal complex; hooked penwork tendril supporting a head; lateral extensions of lower terminal complex. Artist 2. Winter Missal of Arnold of Rummen, Sint-Truiden (text), Ghent (decoration and illumination), *c*.1345–1366. The Hague, Huis van het boek, Ms. MMW 10 A 14, fol. 9v   185

21 Initial *I*(*hesus*) with elongated grotesque pressed into panel beside initial. Artist 2. Winter Missal of Arnold of Rummen, Sint-Truiden (text), Ghent (decoration and illumination) *c*.1345–1366. The Hague, Huis van het boek, Ms. MMW 10 A 14, fol. 10r   186

22 Penwork with a variety of foliate types. Artist 2. Winter Missal of Arnold of Rummen, Sint-Truiden (text), Ghent (decoration and illumination), *c*.1345–1366. The Hague, Huis van het boek, Ms. MMW 10 A 14, fol. 10v, detail   313

23 Penwork with a variety of foliate types. Artist 2. Winter Missal of Arnold of Rummen, Sint-Truiden (text), Ghent (decoration and illumination), *c*.1345–1366. The Hague, Huis van het boek, Ms. MMW 10 A 14, fol. 11r   187

24 Diagonal alignment of elements in lower terminal complex; extension of border bar into terminal complex. Artist 2. Winter Missal of Arnold of Rummen, Sint-Truiden (text), Ghent (decoration and illumination), *c*.1345–1366. The Hague, Huis van het boek, Ms. MMW 10 A 14, fol. 11v   188

24a Graphite asterisk in margin beside initial *R*(*orate*). Winter Missal of Arnold of Rummen, Sint-Truiden (text), Ghent (decoration and illumination), *c*.1345–1366. The Hague, Huis van het boek, Ms. MMW 10 A 14, fol. 11v, detail   313

25 Penwork Cycle 1C. Artist 2. Winter Missal of Arnold of Rummen, Sint-Truiden (text), Ghent (decoration and illumination), *c*.1345–1366. The Hague, Huis van het boek, Ms. MMW 10 A 14, fol. 12r   189

26 Anchored and floating rosettes; symmetries in penwork of upper terminal complex echoed in lower partial border. Artist 2. Winter Missal of Arnold of Rummen, Sint-Truiden (text), Ghent (decoration and illumination), *c*.1345–1366. The Hague, Huis van het boek, Ms. MMW 10 A 14, fol. 12v   190

27 Initial *D*(*eus*) with beardless man. Artist 2. Winter Missal of Arnold of Rummen, Sint-Truiden (text), Ghent (decoration and illumination), *c*.1345–1366. The Hague, Huis van het boek, Ms. MMW 10 A 14, fol. 13v   191

28 Penwork of Cycle 1A. Artist 2. Winter Missal of Arnold of Rummen, Sint-Truiden (text), Ghent (decoration and

illumination), *c*.1345–1366. The Hague, Huis van het boek, Ms. MMW 10 A 14, fol. 14r   192

29 Floating and anchored rosettes. Artist 2. Winter Missal of Arnold of Rummen, Sint-Truiden (text), Ghent (decoration and illumination), *c*.1345–1366. The Hague, Huis van het boek, Ms. MMW 10 A 14, fol. 14v   193

30 Convex *I*. Artist 3. Winter Missal of Arnold of Rummen, Sint-Truiden (text), Ghent (decoration and illumination), *c*.1345–1366. The Hague, Huis van het boek, Ms. MMW 10 A 14, fol. 15r   194

31 Penwork trilobes grouped as pairs of pairs; bubble-like pearls. Artist 3. Winter Missal of Arnold of Rummen, Sint-Truiden (text), Ghent (decoration and illumination), *c*.1345–1366. The Hague, Huis van het boek, Ms. MMW 10 A 14, fol. 15v   195

32 Type 1 border bar; beginning of penwork Cycle 2. Artist 2. Winter Missal of Arnold of Rummen, Sint-Truiden (text), Ghent (decoration and illumination), *c*.1345–1366. The Hague, Huis van het boek, Ms. MMW 10 A 14, fol. 21r   196

33 Beginning of penwork Cycle 2. Artist 2. Winter Missal of Arnold of Rummen, Sint-Truiden (text), Ghent (decoration and illumination), *c*.1345–1366. The Hague, Huis van het boek, Ms. MMW 10 A 14, fol. 21v   197

34 Introit for Christmas. Artist 3. Winter Missal of Arnold of Rummen, Sint-Truiden (text), Ghent (decoration and illumination), *c*.1345–1366. The Hague, Huis van het boek, Ms. MMW 10 A 14, fol. 22r   198

34a Miniature with the Nativity of Christ. Artist 3. Winter Missal of Arnold of Rummen, Sint-Truiden (text), Ghent (decoration and illumination), *c*.1345–1366. The Hague, Huis van het boek, Ms. MMW 10 A 14, fol. 22r, detail   314

34b Overpainted shield in upper section of intercolumniation. Winter Missal of Arnold of Rummen, Sint-Truiden (text), Ghent (decoration and illumination), *c*.1345–1366. The Hague, Huis van het boek, Ms. MMW 10 A 14, fol. 22r, detail   314

34c Initial *P*(*uer*), Artist 3; overpainted shield in lower section of intercolumniation; initial *C*(*oncede*) with head of Christ, Artist 3. Winter Missal of Arnold of Rummen, Sint-Truiden (text), Ghent (decoration and illumination), *c*.1345–1366. The Hague, Huis van het boek, Ms. MMW 10 A 14, fol. 22r, detail   315

34d Overpainted helmet in lower right corner. Winter Missal of Arnold of Rummen, Sint-Truiden (text), Ghent (decoration and illumination), *c*.1345–1366. The Hague, Huis van het boek, Ms. MMW 10 A 14, fol. 22r, detail   315

35 Silver stains from overpainted shields. Winter Missal of Arnold of Rummen, Sint-Truiden (text), Ghent (decoration and illumination), *c*.1345–1366. The Hague, Huis van het boek, Ms. MMW 10 A 14, fol. 22v   199

36 Page with flourishing begun by Artist 2 (red ink in upper margin) and completed by Artist 4. Winter Missal of Arnold of Rummen, Sint-Truiden (text), Ghent (decoration and illumination), c.1345–1366. The Hague, Huis van het boek, Ms. MMW 10 A 14, fol. 23r   200

37 Introit for the Circumcision of Christ. Artist 4, painting; Artist 3, flourishing. Winter Missal of Arnold of Rummen, Sint-Truiden (text), Ghent (decoration and illumination), c.1345–1366. The Hague, Huis van het boek, Ms. MMW 10 A 14, fol. 26r   201

37a Graphite sketches of figures in margin. Artist 2. Winter Missal of Arnold of Rummen, Sint-Truiden (text), Ghent (decoration and illumination), c.1345–1366. The Hague, Huis van het boek, Ms. MMW 10 A 14, fol. 26r, detail   316

37b Initial P(uer) with Circumcision of Christ. Artist 4. Winter Missal of Arnold of Rummen, Sint-Truiden (text), Ghent (decoration and illumination), c.1345–1366. The Hague, Huis van het boek, Ms. MMW 10 A 14, fol. 26r, detail   316

38 Silver stains from overpainted shields. Winter Missal of Arnold of Rummen, Sint-Truiden (text), Ghent (decoration and illumination), c.1345–1366. The Hague, Huis van het boek, Ms. MMW 10 A 14, fol. 27r   202

39 Introit for Epiphany. Artist 3. Winter Missal of Arnold of Rummen, Sint-Truiden (text), Ghent (decoration and illumination), c.1345–1366. The Hague, Huis van het boek, Ms. MMW 10 A 14, fol. 27v   203

39a Miniature with Adoration of the Magi and donors; initial E(cce). Artist 3. Heraldic lions with overpaints. Winter Missal of Arnold of Rummen, Sint-Truiden (text), Ghent (decoration and illumination), c.1345–1366. The Hague, Huis van het boek, Ms. MMW 10 A 14, fol. 27v, detail   317

40 Minor illumination begun by Artist 2, completed by Artist 4. Winter Missal of Arnold of Rummen, Sint-Truiden (text), Ghent (decoration and illumination), c.1345–1366. The Hague, Huis van het boek, Ms. MMW 10 A 14, fol. 29v   204

40a Initials E(cce) with trilobe decoration, Artist 2; initial D(eus) with trilobe decoration, Artist 4. Winter Missal of Arnold of Rummen, Sint-Truiden (text), Ghent (decoration and illumination), c.1345–1366. The Hague, Huis van het boek, Ms. MMW 10 A 14, fol. 29v, detail   318

41 Figural initial I(n excell'o) as human-headed grotesque. Artist 4. Winter Missal of Arnold of Rummen, Sint-Truiden (text), Ghent (decoration and illumination), c.1345–1366. The Hague, Huis van het boek, Ms. MMW 10 A 14, fol. 30v, detail   318

42 Grotesque overflows initial A(dorate). Artist 2. Winter Missal of Arnold of Rummen, Sint-Truiden (text), Ghent (decoration and illumination), c.1345–1366. The Hague, Huis van het boek, Ms. MMW 10 A 14, fol. 34r   205

43 Free-floating partial border with threatening grotesques. Artist 4. Winter Missal of Arnold of Rummen, Sint-Truiden (text), Ghent (decoration and illumination), c.1345–1366. The Hague, Huis van het boek, Ms. MMW 10 A 14, fol. 36r   206

43a Initial C(ircumdederunt) in gold frame with black internal detail. Artist 4. Winter Missal of Arnold of Rummen, Sint-Truiden (text), Ghent (decoration and illumination), c.1345–1366. The Hague, Huis van het boek, Ms. MMW 10 A 14, fol. 36r, detail   319

44 Initial E(xurge) with tonsured head behind initial arm. Artist 2. Winter Missal of Arnold of Rummen, Sint-Truiden (text), Ghent (decoration and illumination), c.1345–1366. The Hague, Huis van het boek, Ms. MMW 10 A 14, fol. 38v, detail   319

45 Type 2 border bar. Artist 2. Winter Missal of Arnold of Rummen, Sint-Truiden (text), Ghent (decoration and illumination), c.1345–1366. The Hague, Huis van het boek, Ms. MMW 10 A 14, fol. 39r   207

46 Artist 2's sweeping curves and reverse curves in lower terminal complex. Winter Missal of Arnold of Rummen, Sint-Truiden (text), Ghent (decoration and illumination), c.1345–1366. The Hague, Huis van het boek, Ms. MMW 10 A 14, fol. 39v, detail   320

47 Type 3 border bar. Artist 2. Winter Missal of Arnold of Rummen, Sint-Truiden (text), Ghent (decoration and illumination), c.1345–1366. The Hague, Huis van het boek, Ms. MMW 10 A 14, fol. 40v   208

48 Artist 4's corkscrews. Winter Missal of Arnold of Rummen, Sint-Truiden (text), Ghent (decoration and illumination), c.1345–1366. The Hague, Huis van het boek, Ms. MMW 10 A 14, fol. 42v, detail   321

49 Artist 4's corkscrews. Winter Missal of Arnold of Rummen, Sint-Truiden (text), Ghent (decoration and illumination), c.1345–1366. The Hague, Huis van het boek, Ms. MMW 10 A 14, fol. 43r, detail   322

50 Initial D(omine) with double profile. Artist 2. Winter Missal of Arnold of Rummen, Sint-Truiden (text), Ghent (decoration and illumination), c.1345–1366. The Hague, Huis van het boek, Ms. MMW 10 A 14, fol. 45r, detail   322

51 Initial D(eus) with Christ bruised and crowned with thorns. Artist 2. Winter Missal of Arnold of Rummen, Sint-Truiden (text), Ghent (decoration and illumination), c.1345–1366. The Hague, Huis van het boek, Ms. MMW 10 A 14, fol. 46r, detail   322

52 Initial A(udiunt) with leonine grotesque. Artist 2. Winter Missal of Arnold of Rummen, c.1345–1366. Sint-Truiden (text), Ghent (decoration and illumination), The Hague, Huis van het boek, Ms. MMW 10 A 14, fol. 47r, detail   322

53 Type 3 border bar. Artist 3. Winter Missal of Arnold of Rummen, Sint-Truiden (text), Ghent (decoration and

illumination), *c.*1345–1366. The Hague, Huis van het boek, Ms. MMW 10 A 14, fol. 48v   209

54   Grotesque as figural initial *I*(*nvocavit*). Artist 2. Winter Missal of Arnold of Rummen, Sint-Truiden (text), Ghent (decoration and illumination), *c.*1345–1366. The Hague, Huis van het boek, Ms. MMW 10 A 14, fol. 49v, detail   323

55   Type 2 border bar along column b. Artist 2. Winter Missal of Arnold of Rummen, Sint-Truiden (text), Ghent (decoration and illumination), *c.*1345–1366. The Hague, Huis van het boek, Ms. MMW 10 A 14, fol. 50v   210

56   Lower terminal complex with pairs of pairs, complex symmetry. Artist 2. Winter Missal of Arnold of Rummen, Sint-Truiden (text), Ghent (decoration and illumination), *c.*1345–1366. The Hague, Huis van het boek, Ms. MMW 10 A 14, fol. 51r, detail   323

57   Penwork bird in lower margin. Artist 2. Winter Missal of Arnold of Rummen, Sint-Truiden (text), Ghent (decoration and illumination), *c.*1345–1366. The Hague, Huis van het boek, Ms. MMW 10 A 14, fol. 52v, detail   324

58   Initial *D*(*evotionem*) with woman in ruffled hood. Artist 2. Winter Missal of Arnold of Rummen, Sint-Truiden (text), Ghent (decoration and illumination), *c.*1345–1366. The Hague, Huis van het boek, Ms. MMW 10 A 14, fol. 54va, detail   324

58a   Initial *D*(*e necessitatibus*) with woman in ruffled hood. Artist 2. Winter Missal of Arnold of Rummen, Sint-Truiden (text), Ghent (decoration and illumination), *c.*1345–1366. The Hague, Huis van het boek, Ms. MMW 10 A 14, fol. 54vb, detail   324

59   Initial *C*(*onfessio*) with trilobes as decoration and extensions. Artist 2. Winter Missal of Arnold of Rummen, Sint-Truiden (text), Ghent (decoration and illumination), *c.*1345–1366. The Hague, Huis van het boek, Ms. MMW 10 A 14, fol. 55v, detail   325

60   Type 3 border bar; penwork Cycle 2. Artist 2. Winter Missal of Arnold of Rummen, Sint-Truiden (text), Ghent (decoration and illumination), *c.*1345–1366. The Hague, Huis van het boek, Ms. MMW 10 A 14, fol. 57r   211

60a   Initial *D*(*e necessitatibus*) with tonsured head. Artist 2. Winter Missal of Arnold of Rummen, Sint-Truiden (text), Ghent (decoration and illumination), *c.*1345–1366. The Hague, Huis van het boek, Ms. MMW 10 A 14, fol. 57r, detail   325

61   Artist 2's plethora of foliate types; penwork Cycle 2. Winter Missal of Arnold of Rummen, Sint-Truiden (text), Ghent (decoration and illumination), *c.*1345–1366. The Hague, Huis van het boek, Ms. MMW 10 A 14, fol. 58v   212

61a   Figural initial *I*(*ntret*) with human-headed grotesques. Artist 2. Winter Missal of Arnold of Rummen, Sint-Truiden (text), Ghent (decoration and illumination),

*c.*1345–1366. The Hague, Huis van het boek, Ms. MMW 10 A 14, fol. 58v, detail   325

62   Initial *P*(*reces*) with triple profile. Artist 2. Winter Missal of Arnold of Rummen, Sint-Truiden (text), Ghent (decoration and illumination), *c.*1345–1366. The Hague, Huis van het boek, Ms. MMW 10 A 14, fol. 60r, detail   326

63   Initial *R*(*eminiscere*) and extension with graphite sk etch lines for cusping and tendrils. Artist 2. Winter Missal of Arnold of Rummen, Sint-Truiden (text), Ghent (decoration and illumination), *c.*1345–1366. The Hague, Huis van het boek, Ms. MMW 10 A 14, fol. 61v, detail   326

64   Initial *R*(*edime*) with woman's head in grisaille. Artist 4. Winter Missal of Arnold of Rummen, Sint-Truiden (text), Ghent (decoration and illumination), *c.*1345–1366. The Hague, Huis van het boek, Ms. MMW 10 A 14, fol. 63r, detail   327

65   Free-floating partial border with threatening grotesque. Artist 4. Winter Missal of Arnold of Rummen, Sint-Truiden (text), Ghent (decoration and illumination), *c.*1345–1366. The Hague, Huis van het boek, Ms. MMW 10 A 14, fol. 64r, detail   327

66   Initial *N*(*e derelinquas*) with tonsured head; foliage comparable to that on fol. 26r. Artist 4. Winter Missal of Arnold of Rummen, Sint-Truiden (text), Ghent (decoration and illumination), *c.*1345–1366. The Hague, Huis van het boek, Ms. MMW 10 A 14, fol. 65v, detail   328

67   Face behind arm of initial *E*(*go*). Artist 4. Winter Missal of Arnold of Rummen, Sint-Truiden (text), Ghent (decoration and illumination), *c.*1345–1366. The Hague, Huis van het boek, Ms. MMW 10 A 14, fol. 68r, detail   328

68   Upside down initial *I*(*llumina*). Artist 2. Winter Missal of Arnold of Rummen, Sint-Truiden (text), Ghent (decoration and illumination), *c.*1345–1366. The Hague, Huis van het boek, Ms. MMW 10 A 14, fol. 72r   213

69   Mid-page extension into the left margin. Artist 2. Winter Missal of Arnold of Rummen, Sint-Truiden (text), Ghent (decoration and illumination), *c.*1345–1366. The Hague, Huis van het boek, Ms. MMW 10 A 14, fol. 73v   214

70   Tiered blossoms. Artist 2. Winter Missal of Arnold of Rummen, Sint-Truiden (text), Ghent (decoration and Illumination), *c.*1345–1366. The Hague, Huis van het boek, Ms. MMW 10 A 14, fol. 76r   215

70a   Type 4 border bar with small urns; initial *P*(*er*) with humanoid grotesque having recurved neck. Artist 2. Winter Missal of Arnold of Rummen, Sint-Truiden (text), Ghent (decoration and Illumination), *c.*1345–1366. The Hague, Huis het boek, Ms. MMW 10 A 14, fol. 76r, detail   329

70b   Initial *T*(*ua*) with tufted grotesque and lower terminal complex. Artist 2. Winter Missal of Arnold of Rummen, Sint-Truiden (text), Ghent (decoration and Illumination), c.1345–1366. The Hague, Huis van het boek, Ms. MMW 10 A 14, fol. 76r, detail   329

71   Tiered blossoms. Artist 2. Winter Missal of Arnold of Rummen, Sint-Truiden (text), Ghent (decoration and Illumination), c.1345–1366. The Hague, Huis van het boek, Ms. MMW 10 A 14, fol. 76v   216

72   Type 4 border bars with varied buttons, pearls, rosettes. Artist 2. Winter Missal of Arnold of Rummen, Sint-Truiden (text), Ghent (decoration and Illumination), c.1345–1366. The Hague, Huis van het boek, Ms. MMW 10 A 14, fol. 77v   217

73   Green and blue border bar. Artist 2. Winter Missal of Arnold of Rummen, Sint-Truiden (text), Ghent (decoration and illumination), c.1345–1366. The Hague, Huis van het boek, Ms. MMW 10 A 14, fol. 78r   218

74   Border bars with extension into the lower margin. Artist 2. Winter Missal of Arnold of Rummen, Sint-Truiden (text), Ghent (decoration and illumination), c.1345–1366. The Hague, Huis van het boek, Ms. MMW 10 A 14, fol. 78v   219

74a   Initial D(eus) with head of Christ. Artist 2. Winter Missal of Arnold of Rummen, Sint-Truiden (text), Ghent (decoration and illumination), c.1345–1366. The Hague, Huis van het boek, Ms. MMW 10 A 14, fol. 78v, detail   330

75   Initial I(deo) projects into lower margin and pushes terminal bar downward. Artist 2. Winter Missal of Arnold of Rummen, Sint-Truiden (text), Ghent (decoration and illumination), c.1345–1366. The Hague, Huis van het boek, Ms. MMW 10 A 14, fol. 79v, detail   330

76   Rosettes, circle-complexes, corkscrews. Artist 2. Winter Missal of Arnold of Rummen, Sint-Truiden (text), Ghent (decoration and illumination), c.1345–1366. The Hague, Huis van het boek, Ms. MMW 10 A 14, fol. 83v   220

77   Plummet asterisk in margin marks location of initial; portrait-like head in initial D(eus). Winter Missal of Arnold of Rummen, Sint-Truiden (text), Ghent (decoration and illumination), c.1345–1366. The Hague, Huis van het boek, Ms. MMW 10 A 14, fol. 85v, detail   331

78   Penwork with ball-and-squiggle trilobes, maple leaves, ivy leaves. Artist 2. Winter Missal of Arnold of Rummen, Sin t-Truiden (text), Ghent (decoration and illumination), c.1345–1366. The Hague, Huis van het boek, Ms. MMW 10 A 14, fol. 86r   221

79   Initial S(umptis) with connection to border bar; spiked pearls; initials O(blatum) with mitred head and D(eprecationem) with crowned head. Artist 2. Winter Missal of Arnold of Rummen, Sint-Truiden (text), Ghent (decoration and illumination), c.1345–1366. The Hague, Huis van het boek, Ms. MMW 10 A 14, fol. 86v, detail   331

80   Hatched border bar. Initials H(uius) with profile hooded head and D(um) with three-quarters head. Artist 2.

Winter Missal of Arnold of Rummen, Sint-Truiden (text), Ghent (decoration and illumination), c.1345–1366. The Hague, Huis van het boek, Ms. MMW 10 A 14, fol. 88r, detail   332

81   Oak leaves, acorns, and lilies. Artist 2. Winter Missal of Arnold of Rummen, Sint-Truiden (text), Ghent (decoration and illumination), c.1345–1366. The Hague, Huis van het boek, Ms. MMW 10 A 14, fol. 90v   222

82   Penwork butterflies in left margin. Artist 2. Winter Missal of Arnold of Rummen, Sint-Truiden (text), Ghent (decoration and illumination), c.1345–1366. The Hague, Huis van het boek, Ms. MMW 10 A 14, fol. 91v   223

83   Lower terminal complex with corkscrews. Artist 2. Winter Missal of Arnold of Rummen, Sint-Truiden (text), Ghent (decoration and illumination), c.1345–1366. The Hague, Huis van het boek, Ms. MMW 10 A 14, fol. 95r, detail   333

84   Cracked I in lower terminal complex. Artist 2. Winter Missal of Arnold of Rummen, Sint-Truiden (text), Ghent (decoration and illumination), c.1345–1366. The Hague, Huis van het boek, Ms. MMW 10 A 14, fol. 96r   224

85   Pearl spirals. Artist 2. Winter Missal of Arnold of Rummen, Sint- Truiden (text), Ghent (decoration and illumination), c.1345–1366. The Hague, Huis van het boek, Ms. MMW 10 A 14, fol. 100r, detail   333

86   Type 4 border bar; large and varied leaves. Artist 2. Winter Missal of Arnold of Rummen, Sint-Truiden (text), Ghent (decoration and illumination), c.1345–1366. The Hague, Huis van het boek, Ms. MMW 10 A 14, fol. 100v   225

86a   Initial C(elestis) with soldier in helmet and chain mail. Artist 2. Winter Missal of Arnold of Rummen, Sint-Truiden (text), Ghent (decoration and illumination), c.1345–1366. The Hague, Huis van het boek, Ms. MMW 10 A 14, fol. 100v, detail   334

86b   Grotesque echoes appearance of head in initial O(mnia). Artist 2. Winter Missal of Arnold of Rummen, Sint-Truiden (text), Ghent (decoration and illumination), c.1345–1366. The Hague, Huis van het boek, Ms. MMW 10 A 14, fol. 100v, detail   334

87   Artist 3's corkscrews. Winter Missal of Arnold of Rummen, Sint-Truiden (text), Ghent (decoration and illumination), c.1345–1366. The Hague, Huis van het boek, Ms. MMW 10 A 14, fol. 104v   226

87a   Artist 3's corkscrews. Winter Missal of Arnold of Rummen, Sint-Truiden (text), Ghent (decoration and illumination), c.1345–1366. The Hague, Huis van het boek, Ms. MMW 10 A 14, fol. 104v, detail   335

88   Penwork trilobes with tremulous outline. Artist 3. Winter Missal of Arnold of Rummen, Sint-Truiden (text), Ghent (decoration and illumination), c.1345–1366.

The Hague, Huis van het boek, Ms. MMW 10 A 14, fol. 105r, detail   335

89   Type 4 border bar. Artist 3. Winter Missal of Arnold of Rummen, Sint-Truiden (text), Ghent (decoration and illumination), c.1345–1366. The Hague, Huis van het boek, Ms. MMW 10 A 14, fol. 105v   227

89a   Pearls. Artist 3. Winter Missal of Arnold of Rummen, Sint-Truiden (text), Ghent (decoration and illumination), c.1345–1366. The Hague, Huis van het boek, 10 A 14, fol. 105v, detail   336

90   Initial C(um) with face washed in grisaille. Artist 3. Winter Missal of Arnold of Rummen, Sint-Truiden (text), Ghent (decoration and illumination), c.1345–1366. The Hague, Huis van het boek, Ms. MMW 10 A 14, fol. 106r, detail   336

91   Introit for Palm Sunday. Artist 2. Winter Missal of Arnold of Rummen, Sint-Truiden (text), Ghent (decoration and illumination), c.1345–1366. The Hague, Huis van het boek, Ms. MMW 10 A 14, fol. 106v   228

91a   Miniature and initial D(omine) with woman pointing to Christ. Artist 2. Winter Missal of Arnold of Rummen, Sint-Truiden (text), Ghent (decoration and illumination), c.1345–1366. The Hague, Huis van het boek, Ms. MMW 10 A 14, fol. 106v, detail   337

91b   Vignette of rabbits, burrows, and trees. Artist 2. Winter Missal of Arnold of Rummen, Sint-Truiden (text), Ghent (decoration and illumination), c.1345–1366. The Hague, Huis van het boek, Ms. MMW 10 A 14, fol. 106v, detail   338

92   Initial D(eus) with head of Christ. Artist 3. Winter Missal of Arnold of Rummen, Sint-Truiden (text), Ghent (decoration and illumination), 1345–1366. The Hague, Huis van het boek, Ms. MMW 10 A 14, fol. 107r, detail   338

93   Penwork head at upper left. Artist 3. Winter Missal of Arnold of Rummen, Sint-Truiden (text), Ghent (decoration and illumination), c.1345–1366. The Hague, Huis van het boek, Ms. MMW 10 A 14, fol. 107v, detail   338

94   Page with all painting and penwork by Artist 1. Winter Missal of Arnold of Rummen, Sint-Truiden (text), Ghent (decoration and illumination), c.1345–1366. The Hague, Huis van het boek, Ms. MMW 10 A 14, fol. 112v   229

94a   Penwork face beside initial D(a quesumus). Artist 1. Winter Missal of Arnold of Rummen, Sint-Truiden (text), Ghent (decoration and illumination), c.1345–1366. The Hague, Huis van het boek, Ms. MMW 10 A 14, fol. 112v, detail   339

95   Painterly application of green inkwash. Artist 2. Winter Missal of Arnold of Rummen, Sint-Truiden (text), Ghent (decoration and illumination), c.1345–1366. The Hague, Huis van het boek, Ms. MMW 10 A 14, fol. 119r   230

96   Simian face in penwork beside initial D(omine). Artist 2. Winter Missal of Arnold of Rummen, Sint-Truiden (text), Ghent (decoration and illumination), c.1345–1366. The Hague, Huis van het boek, Ms. MMW 10 A 14, fol. 121r, detail   340

97   Initial H(anc) with grotesque. Artist 2. Winter Missal of Arnold of Rummen, Sint-Truiden (text), Ghent (decoration and illumination), c.1345–1366. The Hague, Huis van het boek, Ms. MMW 10 A 14, fol. 127v, detail   340

98   Initial P(ostquam) with humanoid-avian-mammalian grotesque. Artist 2. Winter Missal of Arnold of Rummen, Sint-Truiden (text), Ghent (decoration and illumination), c.1345–1366. The Hague, Huis van het boek, Ms. MMW 10 A 14, fol. 128r, detail   340

99   Painted initial H(ec) and extensions by Artist 1; penwork by Artist 2. Winter Missal of Arnold of Rummen, Sint-Truiden (text), Ghent (decoration and illumination), c.1345–1366. The Hague, Huis van het boek, Ms. MMW 10 A 14, fol. 128v   231

99a   Initial H(ec) with bearded, cowled monk. Artist 1. Winter Missal of Arnold of Rummen, Sint-Truiden (text), Ghent (decoration and illumination), c.1345–1366. The Hague, Huis van het boek, Ms. MMW 10 A 14, fol. 128v, detail   340

100   Three initials with bearded men. Artist 2. Winter Missal of Arnold of Rummen, Sint-Truiden (text), Ghent (decoration and illumination), c.1345–1366. The Hague, Huis van het boek, Ms. MMW 10 A 14, fol. 133v   232

101   Border bar with lavender-pink sections. Artist 2. Winter Missal of Arnold of Rummen, Sint-Truiden (text), Ghent (decoration and illumination), c.1345–1366. The Hague, Huis van het boek, Ms. MMW 10 A 14, fol. 134v   233

102   Initial O(mnipotens) with tonsured head. Artist 2. Winter Missal of Arnold of Rummen, Sint-Truiden (text), Ghent (decoration and illumination), c.1345–1366. The Hague, Huis van het boek, Ms. MMW 10 A 14, fol. 135r, detail   341

102a   Initial O(mnipotens) with tonsured head. Artist 2. Winter Missal of Arnold of Rummen, Sint-Truiden (text), Ghent (decoration and illumination), c.1345–1366. The Hague, Huis van het boek, Ms. MMW 10 A 14, fol. 135r, detail   341

103   Preface for the Ordinary of the Mass. Initial and borders, Artist 1; penwork, Artist 2. Winter Missal of Arnold of Rummen, Sint-Truiden (text), Ghent (decoration and illumination), c.1345–1366. The Hague, Huis van het boek, Ms. MMW 10 A 14, fol. 139r   234

103a   Miniature and initial for the Preface of the Ordinary of the Mass; donor portraits. Artist 1. Winter Missal of Arnold of Rummen, Sint-Truiden (text), Ghent (decoration and illumination), *c.*1345–1366. The Hague, Huis van het boek, Ms. MMW 10 A 14, fol. 139r, detail   341

104   *AE(terne)* with cross-inscribed *A* and cadel *E.* Winter Missal of Arnold of Rummen, Sint-Truiden (text), Ghent (decoration and illumination), *c.*1345–1366. The Hague, Huis van het boek, Ms. MMW 10 A 14, fol. 140r   235

105   Leaves with yellow-beige inkwash. Artist 2. Winter Missal of Arnold of Rummen, Sint-Truiden (text), Ghent (decoration and illumination), *c.*1345–1366. The Hague, Huis van het boek, Ms. MMW 10 A 14, fol. 141v   236

105a   Initial *Q(ui)* with softly modeled, grisaille figure. Artist 2. Winter Missal of Arnold of Rummen, Sint-Truiden (text), Ghent (decoration and illumination), *c.*1345–1366. The Hague, Huis van het boek, Ms. MMW 10 A 14, fol. 141v, detail   341

106   The Crucifixion. Artist 2. Winter Missal of Arnold of Rummen, Sint-Truiden (text), Ghent (decoration and illumination), *c.*1345–1366. The Hague, Huis van het boek, Ms. MMW 10 A 14, fol. 143v   237

106a   Donor portrait of Elisabeth of Lierde. Artist 2. Overpaint of Arnold of Rummen. Winter Missal of Arnold of Rummen, Sint-Truiden (text), Ghent (decoration and illumination), *c.*1345–1366. The Hague, Huis van het boek, Ms. MMW 10 A 14, fol. 143v, detail   342

106b   St. John supporting the Virgin; streaky modeling. Artist 2. Winter Missal of Arnold of Rummen, Sint-Truiden (text), Ghent (decoration and illumination), *c.*1345–1366. The Hague, Huis van het boek, Ms. MMW 10 A 14, fol. 143v, detail   342

106c   Crucified Christ; use of line in modeling the body of Christ. Artist 2. Winter Missal of Arnold of Rummen, Sint-Truiden (text), Ghent (decoration and illumination), *c.*1345–1366. The Hague, Huis van het boek, Ms. MMW 10 A 14, fol. 143v, detail   343

107   *Te igitur,* opening of the Canon of the Mass. Artist 1. Winter Missal of Arnold of Rummen, Sint-Truiden (text), Ghent (decoration and illumination), *c.*1345–1366. The Hague, Huis van het boek, Ms. MMW 10 A 14, fol. 144r   238

107a   Miniature with priest and acolyte at the altar, and initial *T(e igitur)* with grotesques. Artist 1. Winter Missal of Arnold of Rummen, Sint-Truiden (text), Ghent (decoration and illumination), *c.*1345–1366. The Hague, Huis van het boek, Ms. MMW 10 A 14, fol. 144r, detail   344

107b   Bas-de-page with wild pigs and hares. Artist 1. Winter Missal of Arnold of Rummen, Sint-Truiden (text),

Ghent (decoration and illumination), *c.*1345–1366. The Hague, Huis van het boek, Ms. MMW 10 A 14, fol. 144r, detail   345

108   Grandest effects in decoration; initials *P(er)* with Arnold's castle and *P(ater)* with his helmet. Artist 2. Winter Missal of Arnold of Rummen, Sint-Truiden (text), Ghent (decoration and illumination), *c.*1345–1366. The Hague, Huis van het boek, Ms. MMW 10 A 14, fol. 147v   239

109   Grandest effects in decoration. Artist 2. Winter Missal of Arnold of Rummen, Sint-Truiden (text), Ghent (decoration and illumination), *c.*1345–1366. The Hague, Huis van het boek, Ms. MMW 10 A 14, fol. 149r   240

109a   Grotesque, curling tendrils to compare with those in *Passionarium 1,* BUL, Ms. 57. Artist 2. Winter Missal of Arnold of Rummen, Sint-Truiden (text), Ghent (decoration and illumination), *c.*1345–1366. The Hague, Huis van het boek, Ms. MMW 10 A 14, fol. 149r, detail   345

110   Introit for the Feast of St. Lucy. Artist 1. Winter Missal of Arnold of Rummen, Sint-Truiden (text), Ghent (decoration and illumination), *c.*1345–1366. The Hague, Huis van het boek, Ms. MMW 10 A 14, fol. 151r   241

110a   Initial *D(ilexisti)* with St. Lucy and Eutychia at the tomb of St. Agatha. Artist 1. Winter Missal of Arnold of Rummen, Sint-Truiden (text), Ghent (decoration and illumination), *c.*1345–1366. The Hague, Huis van het boek, Ms. MMW 10 A 14, fol. 151r, detail   346

111   Penwork with fish face and ruffled maple leaves. Artist 1. Winter Missal of Arnold of Rummen, Sint-Truiden (text), Ghent (decoration and illumination), *c.*1345–1366. The Hague, Huis van het boek, Ms. MMW 10 A 14, fol. 153v   242

112   Terminal complexes and corkscrews. Artist 1. Winter Missal of Arnold of Rummen, Sint-Truiden (text), Ghent (decoration and illumination), *c.*1345–1366. The Hague, Huis van het boek, Ms. MMW 10 A 14, fol. 154r   243

112a   Human face and oak leaves in lower terminal complex. Artist 1. Winter Missal of Arnold of Rummen, Sint-Truiden (text), Ghent (decoration and illumination), *c.*1345–1366. The Hague, Huis van het boek, Ms. MMW 10 A 14, fol. 154r, detail   347

113   The sequence of prayers written in scripts of alternating sizes. Decoration by Artist 1. Winter Missal of Arnold of Rummen, Sint-Truiden (text), Ghent (decoration and illumination), *c.*1345–1366. The Hague, Huis van het boek, Ms. MMW 10 A 14, fol. 154v   244

113a   Knobby faces beside initial *R(efecti)* and in lower terminal complex. Artist 1. Winter Missal of Arnold of Rummen, Sint-Truiden (text), Ghent (decoration and

FIGURES AND TABLES | XXI

illumination), *c*.1345–1366. The Hague, Huis van het boek, Ms. MMW 10 A 14, fol. 154v, detail 347

113b Initial *I*(*n diebus*) with knobby face and pearl clusters. Artist 1. Winter Missal of Arnold of Rummen, Sint-Truiden (text), Ghent (decoration and illumination), *c*.1345–1366. The Hague, Huis van het boek, Ms. MMW 10 A 14, fol. 154v, detail 348

114 Four types of foliate initial decoration. Artist 1. Winter Missal of Arnold of Rummen, Sint-Truiden (text), Ghent (decoration and illumination), *c*.1345–1366. The Hague, Huis van het boek, Ms. MMW 10 A 14, fol. 155v 245

115 One-line initial and human face in penwork of lower margin; fish face in penwork of upper margin. Artist 1. Winter Missal of Arnold of Rummen, Sint-Truiden (text), Ghent (decoration and illumination), *c*.1345–1366. The Hague, Huis van het boek, Ms. MMW 10 A 14, fol. 156r 246

116 Initial *B*(*eate*)with humanoid grotesque. Artist 1. Winter Missal of Arnold of Rummen, Sint-Truiden (text), Ghent (decoration and illumination), *c*.1345–1366. The Hague, Huis van het boek, Ms. MMW 10 A 14, fol. 156v, detail 348

117 Two-line penwork initial *H*(*ostias*)with bearded male head. Artist 1. Winter Missal of Arnold of Rummen, Sint-Truiden (text), Ghent (decoration and illumination), *c*.1345–1366. The Hague, Huis van het boek, Ms. MMW 10 A 14, fol. 157v, detail 349

118 Penwork face above ivy leaves, lower terminal complex. Artist 1. Winter Missal of Arnold of Rummen, Sint-Truiden (text), Ghent (decoration and illumination), *c*.1345–1366. The Hague, Huis van het boek, Ms. MMW 10 A 14, fol. 158r, detail 350

119 Initial *D*(*eus*) with face-like form in adjacent penwork. Artist 1. Winter Missal of Arnold of Rummen, Sint-Truiden (text), Ghent (decoration and illumination), *c*.1345–1366. The Hague, Huis van het boek, Ms. MMW 10 A 14, fol. 160r, detail 350

120 Penwork rosettes hovering before faces adjacent to initials *V*(*otiva*) and *D*(*omine*). Artist 1. Winter Missal of Arnold of Rummen, Sint-Truiden (text), Ghent (decoration and illumination), *c*.1345–1366. The Hague, Huis van het boek, Ms. MMW 10 A 14, fol. 165r, detail 351

121 Introit for the Presentation of Christ. Artist 1. Winter Missal of Arnold of Rummen, Sint-Truiden (text), Ghent (decoration and illumination), *c*.1345–1366. The Hague, Huis van het boek, Ms. MMW 10 A 14, fol. 167r 247

121a Introit for the Presentation of Christ: initial *S*(*uscepimus*) with the Presentation. Artist 1. Winter Missal of Arnold of Rummen, Sint-Truiden (text), Ghent (decoration and illumination), *c*.1345–1366. The Hague, Huis van het boek, Ms. MMW 10 A 14, fol. 167r, detail 351

122 Initial *D*(*iffusa*): Penwork face beside the initial echoes face in the initial. Artist 1. Winter Missal of Arnold of Rummen, Sint-Truiden (text), Ghent (decoration and illumination), *c*.1345–1366. The Hague, Huis van het boek, Ms. MMW 10 A 14, fol. 167v, detail 352

123 Penwork initial *P*(*reces*) with Jew. Artist 1. Winter Missal of Arnold of Rummen, Sint-Truiden (text), Ghent (decoration and illumination), *c*.1345–1366. The Hague, Huis van het boek, Ms. MMW 10 A 14, fol. 170r, detail 352

124 Penwork border bars, corkscrews, and ball-and-squiggle trilobes. Artist 1. Winter Missal of Arnold of Rummen, Sint-Ttruiden (text), Ghent (decoration and illumination), *c*.1345–1366. The Hague, Huis van het boek, Ms. MMW 10 A 14, fol. 175r 248

124a Corkscrews. Artist 1. Winter Missal of Arnold of Rummen, Sint-Truiden (text), Ghent (decoration and illumination), *c*.1345–1366. The Hague, Huis van het boek, Ms. MMW 10 A 14, fol. 175r, detail 353

125 Introit for the Annunciation. Artist 1. Winter Missal of Arnold of Rummen, Sint-Truiden (text), Ghent (decoration and illumination), *c*.1345–1366. The Hague, Huis van het boek, Ms. MMW 10 A 14, fol. 176v 249

125a Introit for the Annunciation: initial *R*(*orate*) with the Annunciation. Artist 1. Winter Missal of Arnold of Rummen, Sint-Truiden (text), Ghent (decoration and illumination), *c*.1345–1366. The Hague, Huis van het boek, Ms. MMW 10 A 14, fol. 176v, detail 353

126 Upside-down *I*. Artist 1. Winter Missal of Arnold of Rummen, Sint-Truiden (text), Ghent (decoration and illumination), Sint-Truiden (text), Ghent (decoration and illumination), *c*.1345–1366. The Hague, Huis van het boek, Ms. MMW 10 A 14, fol. 177r 250

127 Introit for Vigil of an Apostle. Artist 1. Winter Missal of Arnold of Rummen, Sint-Truiden (text), Ghent (decoration and illumination), *c*.1345–1366. The Hague, Huis van het boek, Ms. MMW 10 A 14, fol. 178r 251

127a Initial *C*(*oncede*) with beardless male head. Artist 1. Winter Missal of Arnold of Rummen, Sint-Truiden (text), Ghent (decoration and illumination), *c*.1345–1366. The Hague, Huis van het boek, Ms. MMW 10 A 14, fol. 178r, detail 354

127b Initial *E*(*go*) with St. Andrew. Artist 1. Winter Missal of Arnold of Rummen, Sint-Truiden (text), Ghent (decoration and illumination), *c*.1345–1366. The Hague, Huis van het boek, Ms. MMW 10 A 14, fol. 178r, detail 354

127c Initial *D*(*a nobis*) with winged profile head. Artist 1. Winter Missal of Arnold of Rummen, Sint-Truiden (text), Ghent (decoration and illumination), *c*.1345–1366. The Hague, Huis van het boek, Ms. MMW 10 A 14, fol. 178r, detail 354

128 Profile heads in penwork of lower terminal complex. Artist 1. Winter Missal of Arnold of Rummen, Sint-Truiden (text), Ghent (decoration and illumination), c.1345–1366. The Hague, Huis van het boek, Ms. MMW 10 A 14, fol. 178v, detail 355

129 Penwork face adjacent to initial N(imis) with profile head. Artist 1. Winter Missal of Arnold of Rummen, Sint-Truiden (text), Ghent (decoration and illumination), c.1345–1366. The Hague, Huis van het boek, Ms. MMW 10 A 14, fol. 179r, detail 355

129a Initial P(resta) with head of woman wearing a hood. Artist 1. Winter Missal of Arnold of Rummen, Sint-Truiden (text), Ghent (decoration and illumination), c.1345–1366. The Hague, Huis van het boek, Ms. MMW 10 A 14, fol. 179r, detail 355

130 Initial O(mnipotens) with woman's head. Artist 1. Winter Missal of Arnold of Rummen, Sint-Truiden (text), Ghent (decoration and illumination), c.1345–1366. The Hague, Huis van het boek, Ms. MMW 10 A 14, fol. 186r, detail 356

131 Whiplash penwork in lower terminal complex. Artist 1. Winter Missal of Arnold of of Rummen, Sint-Truiden (text), Ghent (decoration and illumination), c.1345–1366. The Hague, Huis van het boek, Ms. MMW 10 A 14, fol. 189v 252

132 Introit for dedication of a church. Artist 1. Winter Missal of Arnold of Rummen, Sint-Truiden (text), Ghent (decoration and illumination), c.1345–1366. The Hague, Huis van het boek, Ms. MMW 10 A 14, fol. 192v 253

132a Initial T(erribilis) with bishop asperging church and acolyte with situla. Artist 1. Winter Missal of Arnold of Rummen, Sint-Truiden (text), Ghent (decoration and illumination), c.1345–1366. The Hague, Huis van het boek, Ms. MMW 10 A 14, fol. 192v, detail 356

133 Decoration in Quire 27. Artist 2. Winter Missal of Arnold of Rummen, Sint-Truiden (text), Ghent (decoration and illumination), c.1345–1366. The Hague, Huis van het boek, Ms. MMW 10 A 14, fol. 199v 254

134 Decoration in Quire 27: Synthesis of features from earlier quires. Artist 2. Winter Missal of Arnold of Rummen, Sint-Truiden (text), Ghent (decoration and illumination), c.1345–1366. The Hague, Huis van het boek, Ms. MMW 10 A 14, fol. 200r 255

134a Initial D(eus) with head in grisaille. Artist 2. Winter Missal of Arnold of Rummen, Sint-Truiden (text), Ghent (decoration and illumination), c.1345–1366. The Hague, Huis van het boek, Ms. MMW 10 A 14, fol. 200r, detail 356

135 Decoration in Quire 27. Synthesis of features from earlier quires. Artist 2. Winter Missal of Arnold of Rummen, Sint-Truiden (text), Ghent (decoration and illumination), c.1345–1366. The Hague, Huis van het boek, Ms. MMW 10 A 14, fol. 200v 256

135a Upper terminal complex; pearls. Artist 2. Winter Missal of Arnold of Rummen, Sint-Truiden (text), Ghent (decoration and illumination), c.1345–1366. The Hague, Huis van het boek, Ms. MMW 10 A 14, fol. 200v, detail 357

135b Initial D(eus) with tonsured head. Artist 2. Winter Missal of Arnold of Rummen, Sint-Truiden (text), Ghent (decoration and illumination), c.1345–1366. The Hague, Huis van het boek, Ms. MMW 10 A 14, fol. 200v, detail 357

135c Initial O(mnipotens) with head of Christ. Artist 2. Winter Missal of Arnold of Rummen, Sint-Truiden (text), Ghent (decoration and illumination), c.1345–1366. The Hague, Huis van het boek, Ms. MMW 10 A 14, fol. 200v, detail 357

136 Penwork head in upper margin. Artist 2. Winter Missal of Arnold of Rummen, Sint-Truiden (text), Ghent (decoration and illumination), c.1345–1366. The Hague, Huis van het boek, Ms. MMW 10 A 14, fol. 201r, detail 357

137 Decoration in Quire 27: Synthesis of features from earlier quires. Artist 2. Winter Missal of Arnold of Rummen, Sint-Truiden (text), Ghent (decoration and illumination), c.1345–1366. The Hague, Huis van het boek, Ms. MMW 10 A 14, fol. 203v 257

138 Colophon decoration. Artists 1 and 4. Winter Missal of Arnold of Rummen, Sint-Truiden (text), Ghent (decoration and illumination), c.1345–1366. The Hague, Huis van het boek, Ms. MMW 10 A 14, fol. 204r 258

138a First and second colophons. Winter Missal of Arnold of Rummen, Sint-Truiden (text), Ghent (decoration and illumination), c.1345–1366. The Hague, Huis van het boek, Ms. MMW 10 A 14, fol. 204r, detail 358

139 Faces with thick white highlights. Decretals of Gregory IX, Bologna, 1330s or 1340s. Vatican City, Biblioteca Apostolica Vaticana, Ms. Vat. lat. 1389, fol. 3v 259

140 The Crucifixion: flattened converging ribs; proportion of figures to space compared to 10 A 14's Crucifixion. Fitzwarin Psalter, East Anglia or Diocese of Ely (?), c.1345–1350. Paris, Bibliothèque nationale de France, Ms. lat. 765, fol. 14r 260

141 Christ in Majesty: weight, support, symmetry. Leaf of added bifolium. Fitzwarin Psalter, East Anglia or Diocese of Ely (?), c.1345–1350. Paris, Bibliothèque nationale de France, Ms. lat. 765, fol. 21v 261

142 The Crucifixion: weight, support, symmetry. Leaf of added bifolium. Fitzwarin Psalter, East Anglia or Diocese of Ely (?), c.1345–1350. Paris, Bibliothèque nationale de France, Ms. lat. 765, fol. 22r 262

FIGURES AND TABLES

143 Second battle of Alexander and Porus: colored masonry; spectators. *The Romance of Alexander*, Tournai, 1338–1344. Oxford, Bodleian Library, Ms. Bodley 264, fol. 58r 263

144 Initial *U(ns)* with gorgonesque head in initial body. *The Romance of Alexander*, Tournai, 1338–1344. Oxford, Bodleian Library, Ms. Bodley 264, fol. 79v 359

145 Alexander's aerial adventure: colored masonry, initial *E(n viele)* with gorgonesque head in initial body. *The Romance of Alexander*, Tournai, 1338–1344. Oxford, Bodleian Library, Ms. Bodley 264, fol. 80v 264

146 Scenes from the *La prise de Defur*: border strip with gold balls; music in superstructure; oversized foliate capitals. *The Romance of Alexander*, Tournai, 1338–1344. Oxford, Bodleian Library, Ms. Bodley 264, fol. 101v 265

147 The Nativity: modeling with creamy white; spindly architectural supports. Psalter, Ghent, *c.*1330–1335. Oxford, Bodleian Library, Ms. Douce 5, fol. 14v 266

148 Christ's Entry into Jerusalem: lower border with confronted grotesques. Psalter, Ghent, *c.*1330–1335. Oxford, Bodleian Library, Ms. Douce 5, fol. 16v 267

149 Man of Sorrows. Psalter, Ghent, *c.*1330–1335. Oxford, Bodleian Library, Ms. Douce 5, fol. 60v 268

150 Incipit for Psalm 51 (52): border strip with gold balls. Psalter, Ghent, *c.*1330–1335. Oxford, Bodleian Library, Ms. Douce 6, fol. 143r 269

151 Penwork flourishing. Psalter, Ghent, *c.*1330–1335. Oxford, Bodleian Library, Ms. Douce 6, fol. 59v 270

152 Jeanne d'Evreux at the Tomb of St. Louis. Hours of Jeanne d'Evreux, Paris, 1325–1328. New York, Cloisters Collection, Metropolitan Museum of Art, Ms. 54.1.2, fol. 102v 271

153 Wildman. *Les voeux du paon*, Tournai, *c.*1348–1350. New York, The Morgan Library & Museum, Ms. G. 24, fol. 81r, detail. Gift of the Trustees of the William S. Glazier Collection, 1984 359

154 Initial *P(arabolae)*, with streaky, white modeling. Bible, Palermo (?), *c.*1325. New York, The Morgan Library & Museum, Ms. G. 60, fol. 293v, detail. Gift of the Trustees of the William S. Glazier Collection, 1984 360

155 Page with border at far left comparable to those of Ms. 10 A 14. Bible, Padua, *c.*1287–1300. New York, The Morgan Library & Museum, Ms. M. 436, fol. 4r. Purchased by J. Pierpont Morgan (1837–1913), 1910 272

156 Single leaf with borders comparable to those of Ms. 10 A 14. The Laudario of the Compagnia di Sant' Agnese, Florence, *c.*1340. New York, The Morgan Library & Museum, Ms. M. 742. Purchased in 1929 360

157 The Crucifixion. Missal of Conrad of Rennenberg, Cologne, *c.*1350–1357. Cologne, Diözesan- und Dombibliothek, Cod. 149, fol. 51v 273

158 *Ad te levavi*, First Sunday of Advent: stem of initial *A(d te)* with confronted grotesques. Missal for St. Cunibert, Cologne, *c.*1330. Darmstadt, Universitäts- und Landesbibliothek, Ms. 876, fol. 12r 274

159 The Crucifixion: Compare to Rummen-group Crucifixions. Missal for St. Cunibert, Cologne, *c.*1330. Darmstadt, Universitäts- und Landesbibliothek, Ms. 876, fol. 223v 275

160 The Crucifixion: St. John supports the Virgin. Missal of St. Peter's Abbey, Ghent, *c.*1275–1285. Ghent, STAM—Ghent City Museum, Inv. A60.01, fol. 7v 276

161 Penwork resembling curled shavings. Missal of St. Peter's Abbey, Ghent, *c.*1275–1285. Ghent, STAM—Ghent City Museum, Inv. A60.01, fols. 120v–121r 277

162 Frizzy penwork. Ghent Ceremonial, Ghent or Tournai, 1322. Ghent, Universiteit Gent Universiteitsbibliotheek, Ms. 233, fol. 66v 278

163 The Crucifixion: St. John supports the Virgin. Ghent Ceremonial, Ghent or Tournai, 1322. Ghent, Universiteit Gent Universiteitsbibliotheek, Ms. 233, fol. 70v 279

164 Border strip with attached gold balls. Ghent Ceremonial, Ghent or Tournai, 1322. Ghent, Universiteit Gent Universiteitsbibliotheek, Ms. 233, fol. 93v 280

164a Initial *N(on)* with monks praying at a draped coffin. Ghent Ceremonial, Ghent or Tournai, 1322. Ghent, Universiteit Gent Universiteitsbibliotheek, Ms. 233, fol. 93v, detail 361

165 Spare, nervous penwork flourishing. Ceremonial, Ghent, 1st half of the 14th c. Ghent, Universiteit Gent Universiteitsbibliotheek, Ms. 114, fols. 30v–31r 281

166 Penwork flourishing like that of Artist 1 in the Winter Missal of Arnold of Rummen. Breviary from St. Peter's Abbey, Ghent, 1373. Ghent, Universiteit Gent Universiteitsbibliotheek, Ms. 3381, fol. 4v 282

167 Initial *A(spiciens)* with gorgon mouth enclosing man in combat. Antiphonal, Ghent (?), *c.*1345. Brussels, Koninklijke Bibliotheek/Bibliothèque royale de Belgique, Ms. 6426, fol. 2r, detail 362

168 Penwork flourishing with stiff arcs and recurves, barbed corkscrews, and other motifs. Artist 2. Antiphonal, Ghent (?), *c.*1345. Brussels, Koninklijke Bibliotheek/Bibliothèque royale de Belgique, Ms. 6426, fol. 106v, detail 363

169 Penwork flourishing with stiff arcs and recurves, barbed corkscrews. Artist 2. Antiphonal, Ghent (?), *c.*1345. Brussels, Koninklijke Bibliotheek/Bibliothèque royale de Belgique, Ms. 6426, fol. 119v 283

170 Complex symmetry in design of lower border. Artist 2. Antiphonal, Ghent (?), *c.*1345. Brussels, Koninklijke Bibliotheek/Bibliothèque royale de Belgique, Ms. 6426, fol. 147v 284

171 Introit to Easter Sunday: bas-de-page vignettes with human figures. Summer Missal of Arnold of Rummen, Sint-Truiden (text), Ghent (decoration and illumination), *c.*1345–1350. Brussels, Koninklijke Bibliotheek/Bibliothèque royale de Belgique, Ms. 9217, fol. 11v   285

171a Initial *R*(*esurrexi*) with sturdy architecture. Summer Missal of Arnold of Rummen, Sint-Truiden (text), Ghent (decoration and illumination), *c.*1345–1350. Brussels, Koninklijke Bibliotheek/Bibliothèque royale de Belgique, Ms. 9217, fol. 11v, detail   364

172 Penwork flourishing. Summer Missal of Arnold of Rummen, Sint-Truiden (text), Ghent (decoration and illumination), *c.*1345–1350. Brussels, Koninklijke Bibliotheek/Bibliothèque royale de Belgique, Ms. 9217, fol. 22v   286

173 Introit for the Ascension. Summer Missal of Arnold of Rummen, Sint-Truiden (text), Ghent (decoration and illumination), *c.*1345–1350. Brussels, Koninklijke Bibliotheek/Bibliothèque royale de Belgique, Ms. 9217, fol. 33r   287

173a Initial *V*(*iri*) with sturdy architecture; fluent application of paint; oblivious man in gorgon's mouth. Summer Missal of Arnold of Rummen, Sint-Truiden (text), Ghent (decoration and illumination), *c.*1345–1350. Brussels, Koninklijke Bibliotheek/Bibliothèque royale de Belgique, Ms. 9217, fol. 33r, detail   364

174 Musical notation with penwork flourishing. Summer Missal of Arnold of Rummen, Sint-Truiden (text), Ghent (decoration and illumination), *c.*1345–1350. Brussels, Koninklijke Bibliotheek/Bibliothèque royale de Belgique, Ms. 9217, fol. 112r   288

175 The Crucifixion. Summer Missal of Arnold of Rummen, Sint-Truiden (text), Ghent (decoration and illumination), *c.*1345–1350. Brussels, Koninklijke Bibliotheek/Bibliothèque royale de Belgique, Ms. 9217, fol. 115v   289

175a Quadrant 1 of the Crucifixion, with traces of arms beneath overpaints. Summer Missal of Arnold of Rummen, Sint-Truiden (text), Ghent (decoration and illumination), *c.*1345–1350. Brussels, Koninklijke Bibliotheek/Bibliothèque royale de Belgique, Ms. 9217, fol. 115v, detail   365

175b Quadrant 4 of the Crucifixion, with traces of arms beneath overpaints. Summer Missal of Arnold of Rummen, Sint-Truiden (text), Ghent (decoration and illumination), *c.*1345–1350. Brussels, Koninklijke Bibliotheek/Bibliothèque royale de Belgique, Ms. 9217, fol. 115v, detail   365

176 Penwork flourishing of Artist 9217-2. Summer Missal of Arnold of Rummen, Sint-Truiden (text), Ghent

(decoration and illumination), *c.*1345–1350. Brussels, Koninklijke Bibliotheek /Bibliothèque royale de Belgique, Ms. 9217, fol. 130r   290

177 Overpainted arms. Liturgical psalter, Sint-Truiden (text), Ghent (decoration and illumination), *c.*1345–1350. Brussels, Koninklijke Bibliotheek/Bibliothèque royale de Belgique, Ms. 9427, fol. 14r   291

177a David harping: Compare to David in initial *A*(*d te*) on fol. 7r, Ms. 10 A 14. Artist 2. Liturgical psalter, Sint-Truiden (text), Ghent (decoration and illumination), *c.*1345–1350. Brussels, Koninklijke Bibliotheek/Bibliothèque royale de Belgique, Ms. 9427, fol. 14r, detail   366

178 Initial *D*(*ixit*). Artist 2. Liturgical psalter, Sint-Truiden (text), Ghent (decoration and illumination), *c.*1345–1350. Brussels, Koninklijke Bibliotheek/Bibliothèque royale de Belgique, Ms. 9427, fol. 25r, detail   367

179 Flourishing with tension and opposition. Artist 2. Liturgical psalter, Sint-Truiden (text), Ghent (decoration and illumination), *c.*1345–1350. Brussels, Koninklijke Bibliotheek/Bibliothèque royale de Belgique, Ms. 9427, fol. 40v   292

180 Overpainted arms; paired elements above and below border bar. Liturgical psalter, Sint-Truiden (text), Ghent (decoration and illumination), *c.*1345–1350. Brussels, Koninklijke Bibliotheek/Bibliothèque royale de Belgique, Ms. 9427, fol. 43r   293

181 Type 1 border bars and corkscrews; diagonal alignment of penwork elements. Artist 2. Liturgical psalter, Sint-Truiden (text), Ghent (decoration and illumination), *c.*1345–1350. Brussels, Koninklijke Bibliotheek/Bibliothèque de Belgique, Ms. 9427, fol. 45r   294

181a Stiff, barbed corkscrews. Artist 2. Liturgical psalter, Sint-Truiden (text), Ghent (decoration and illumination), *c.*1345–1350. Brussels, Koninklijke Bibliotheek/Bibliothèque royale de Belgique, Ms. 9427, fol. 45r, detail   368

182 Overpainted arms. Liturgical psalter, Sint-Truiden (text), Ghent (decoration and illumination), *c.*1345–1350. Brussels, Koninklijke Bibliotheek/Bibliothèque royale de Belgique, Ms. 9427, fol. 100v   295

182a Initial *S*(*alvum*): divided image field. Liturgical psalter, Sint-Truiden (text), Ghent (decoration and illumination), *c.*1345–1350. Brussels, Koninklijke Bibliotheek/Bibliothèque royale de Belgique, Ms. 9427, fol. 100v, detail   369

183 Incipit of Psalm 80 (81). Liturgical psalter, Sint-Truiden (text), Ghent (decoration and illumination), *c.*1345–1350. Brussels, Koninklijke Bibliotheek/Bibliothèque royale de Belgique, Ms. 9427, fol. 124r   296

FIGURES AND TABLES

183a Initial *E(xultate)*: architecture of throne. Liturgical psalter, Sint-Truiden (text), Ghent (decoration and illumination), *c.*1345–1350. Brussels, Koninklijke Bibliotheek/Bibliothèque royale de Belgique, Brussels, Ms. 9427, fol. 124r, detail 370

184 Initial *V(ix)* with humpbacked grotesque. *Dialogues of Gregory the Great*, Sint-Truiden, *c.*1350 (?)–1366. Liège, Bibliothèque de l'Université de Liège, Ms. 43, fol. 57r, detail 371

185 Initial *C(unctorum)* with John the Baptist in grisaille. *Passionarium 1*, Sint-Truiden, completed 1366. Liège, Bibliothèque de l'Université de Liège, Ms. 57, fol. 4r, detail 371

186 Truncated penwork extensions in lower margin. *Passionarium 1*, Sint-Truiden, completed 1366. Liège, Bibliothèque de l'Université de Liège, Ms. 57, fol. 14v 297

187 Initial *T(empore)* with humpbacked grotesque. *Passionarium 1*, Sint-Truiden, completed 1366. Liège, Bibliothèque de l'Université de Liège, Ms. 57, fol. 33v, detail 372

188 Initial *T(empore)* with humpbacked grotesque. *Passionarium 1*, Sint-Truiden, completed 1366. Liège, Bibliothèque de l'Université de Liège, Ms. 57, fol. 63v, detail 372

189 Initial *R(egnante)* with profile and ¾ heads in body of initial. *Passionarium 1*, Sint-Truiden, completed 1366. Liège, Bibliothèque de l'Université de Liège, Ms. 57, fol. 67v, detail 373

190 Flourishing in lower terminal complex. *Passionarium 1*, Sint-Truiden, completed 1366. Liège, Bibliothèque de l'Université de Liège, Ms. 57, fol. 220r, detail 373

191 Flourishing in lower terminal complex. *Passionarium 1*, Sint-Truiden, completed 1366. Liège, Bibliothèque de l'Université de Liège, Ms. 57, fol. 254v, detail 374

192 Flourishing in upper terminal complex. *Passionarium 1*, Sint-Truiden, completed 1366. Liège, Bibliothèque de l'Université de Liège, Ms. 57, fol. 256v, detail 374

193 Prologue to passion of St. Dionysius, historiated initials *G(loriose)* and *P(ost)* and full borders. *Passionarium 2*, Sint-Truiden, completed *c.*1366. Liège, Bibliothèque de l'Université de Liège, Ms. 58, fol. 2r 298

193a Initial *G(loriose)*. *Passionarium 2*, Sint-Truiden, completed *c.*1366. Liège, Bibliothèque de l'Université de Liège, Ms. 58, fol. 2r, detail 375

194 Initial *Q(uartus)*, *littera duplex*. *Passionarium 2*, Sint-Truiden, completed *c.*1366. Liège, Bibliothèque de l'Université de Liège, Ms. 58, fol. 12r, detail 375

195 Parisian-influenced penwork flourishing. *Speculum historiale 1*, Sint-Truiden, completed 1350. Liège,

Bibliothèque de l'Université de Liège, Ms. 60, fol. 60r 299

196 Decorated initial and partial borders. *Speculum historiale 1*, Sint-Truiden, completed 1350. Liège, Bibliothèque de l'Université de Liège, Ms. 60, fol. 1r 300

196a Initial *Q(uoniam)* with leaf face. *Speculum historiale 1*, Sint-Truiden, completed 1350. Liège, Bibliothèque de l'Université de Liège, Ms. 60, fol. 1r, detail 376

197 Historiated initial *D(eus)*, with van Myrle and St Trudo, and partial borders. *Speculum historiale 1*, Sint-Truiden, completed 1350. Liège, Bibliothèque de l'Université de Liège, Ms. 60, fol. 17r 301

197a Initial *D(eus)* with van Myrle and St. Trudo. *Speculum historiale 1*, Sint-Truiden, completed 1350. Liège, Bibliothèque de l'Université de Liège, Ms.60, fol. 17r, detail 376

198 Initial *A(b anno)*, with van Myrle and St. Trudo, and partial border. *Speculum historiale 2*, Sint-Truiden, completed 1352. Liège, Bibliothèque de l'Université de Liège, Ms. 61, fol. 1r 302

198a Initial *A(b anno)* with van Myrle and St. Trudo; gorgon in initial body. *Speculum historiale 2*, Sint-Truiden, completed 1352. Liège, Bibliothèque de l'Université de Liège, Ms. 61, fol. 1r, detail 377

199 Initial *D(ubitare)* with humpback grotesque. Gregory the Great, *Homilies on the Gospels*, Sint-Truiden, 1350 (?)–1366. Liège, Bibliothèque de l'Université de Liège, Ms. 138, fol. 36r, detail 377

200 End of Trinity and beginning of Corpus Christi, with historiated initial and partial borders. Loppem/Bruges Antiphonal, Ghent (?), *c.*1345. Bruges, Openbare Bibliotheek, Ms. svc 10a, fol. [3r]. On loan from Stichting Jean van Caloen 303

200a Initial *S(acerdos)* with priest at the elevation. Loppem/Bruges Antiphonal, Ghent (?), *c.*1345. Bruges, Openbare Bibliotheek, Ms. svc 10a, fol. [3r], detail. On loan from Stichting Jean van Caloen 378

201 Continuation of Third Sunday after the Octave of Easter, with historiated initial and partial borders. Loppem/Bruges Antiphonal, Ghent (?), *c.*1345. Bruges, Openbare Bibliotheek, Ms. svc 10a, fol. [4r]. On loan from Stichting Jean van Caloen 304

201a Initial *S(i oblitus)* with two clerics. Loppem/Bruges Antiphonal, Ghent (?), *c.*1345. Bruges, Openbare Bibliotheek, Ms. svc 10a, fol. [4r], detail. On loan from Stichting Jean van Caloen 379

202 Initial *N(otam)* with pen flourishing. Loppem/Bruges Antiphonal, Ghent (?), *c.*1345. Bruges, Openbare Bibliotheek, Ms. svc 10a, fol. [5v], detail. On loan from Stichting Jean van Caloen 379

203 Initial *D*(*Cum* [sic]) with Descent of the Holy Spirit. Loppem/Bruges Antiphonal, Ghent (?), *c.*1345. Bruges, Openbare Bibliotheek, Ms. svc 10a, fol. [6r], detail. On loan from Stichting Jean van Caloen 380

204 Initial *S*(*cio*) with pen flourishing. Loppem/Bruges Antiphonal, Ghent (?), *c.*1345. Bruges, Openbare Bibliotheek, Ms. svc 10a, fol. [8v], detail. On loan from Stichting Jean van Caloen 380

205 Initials with pen flourishing. Loppem/Bruges Antiphonal, Ghent (?), *c.*1345. Bruges, Openbare Bibliotheek, Ms. svc 10a, fol. [11v], detail. On loan from Stichting Jean van Caloen 381

206 Incipit of letter of St. Jerome to Paulinus, with historiated initial, pen-flourished lettering, and borders. *Biblia*, Latin text with *Epistole* and *Prologi Hieronymi* and *Interpretationes*, Paris, *c.*1350. Stockholm, National Library of Sweden, Ms. A 165, fol. 2r 305

206a Initial *F*(*rater*), with St. Jerome; frizzy pen flourishing. *Biblia*, Latin text with *Epistole* and *Prologi Hieronymi* and *Interpretationes*, Paris, *c.*1350. Stockholm, National Library of Sweden, Ms. A 165, fol. 2r, detail 381

207 Incipit of Leviticus, with Moses kneeling before the Lord in initial *V*(*ocavit*) and gorgonesque grotesques in initial stem and bowl. *Biblia*, Latin text with *Epistole* and *Prologi Hieronymi* and *Interpretationes*, Paris, *c.*1350. Stockholm, National Library of Sweden, Ms. A 165, fol. 45v, detail 382

208 Incipit of Psalm 38 (39) with King David in initial *D*(*ixi*) and gorgonesque conjoined heads in initial stem. *Biblia*, Latin text with *Epistole* and *Prologi Hieronymi* and *Interpretationes*, Paris, *c.*1350. Stockholm, National Library of Sweden, Ms. A 165, fol. 278r, detail 383

209 Alexander's siege tower before Tyre; architecture comparable to some in KBR 9217. *The Romance of Alexander*, Tournai, 1338–1344. Oxford, Bodleian Library, Ms. Bodley 264, fol. 20v 306

209a Soldier with facial rendering comparable to rendering in KBR 9217. *The Romance of Alexander*, Tournai, 1338–1344. Oxford, Bodleian Library, Ms. Bodley 264, fol. 20v, detail 384

210 Incipit of Christmas with gorgonesque grotesques in body of initial *H*(*odie*). Loppem/Bruges Antiphonal, Ghent (?), *c.*1345. Bruges, Openbare Bibliotheek, Ms. svc 10a, fol. [2r], detail. On loan from Stichting Jean van Caloen 385

211 The Crucifixion: Compare to Rummen-group Crucifixions. Missal for St. Cunibert, Cologne, *c.*1330. Darmstadt, Universitäts- und Landesbibliothek, Ms. 837, fol. 145v 307

Tables

1 Quires and contents 17

2 Number of two-line penwork initials by each artist in each quire 144

3 Iconography of two-line penwork initials by subject, in the work of each artist 145

4 Percent of two-line penwork initials by subject in the work of each artist 145

5 *I*-initials by artist and type 145

6 Frequency of each type of border bar in the quires of artists 1, 2, 3, and 4 (*type abbreviated* T) 145

7 Iconography of minor illumination 147

8 Iconography of large penwork initials 148

Abbreviations for Repositories

BAV   Vatican City, Biblioteca Apostolica Vaticana

BNF   Paris, Bibliothèque nationale de France

BOB   Bruges, Openbare Bibliotheek

BUL   Liège, Bibliothèque de l'Université de Liège

CKB   Copenhagen, Kongelige Bibliothek

CMM   Cambrai, Médiathèque municipale

CDD   Cologne, Diözesan- und Dombibliothek

DUL   Darmstadt, Universitäts-und Landesbibliothek

HKB   The Hague, Koninklijke Bibliotheek

KBR   Brussels, Koninklijke Bibliotheek/Bibliothèque royale de Belgique

LBL   London, British Library

MSV   Arras, Médiathèque de l'abbaye Saint-Vaast

MMA   New York, Metropolitan Museum of Art

MLM   New York, The Morgan Library & Museum

NLW   Aberystwyth, National Library of Wales

OBL   Oxford, Bodleian Library

SMG   Ghent, Stadsmuseum Gent

SPK   Berlin, Staatsbibliothek Preussischer Kulturbesitz

TBM   Tournai, Bibliothèque municipale

UGU   Ghent, Universiteit Gent Universiteitsbibliotheek

VON   Vienna, Österreichische Nationalbibliothek

WAG   Baltimore, Walters Art Gallery

WRM   Vienna, Österreichische Nationalbibliothek

CHAPTER 1

Introduction

The Winter Missal of Arnold of Rummen, The Hague, Huis van het boek, Ms. MMW 10 A 14, is the winter portion of a large, beautifully decorated mid-fourteenth-century Roman missal of 204 folios, in near-pristine condition, probably written in Sint-Truiden and decorated in Ghent by three artists in two campaigns dating between 1345 and 1366. The missal is an artifact of considerable historical interest, for its production was marked by notable events and persons in mid-fourteenth-century Flanders. The early years of the Hundred Years' War, in which Ghent was a pivotal city; the bloody civic upheaval in Ghent in the era of the populist leader James of Artevelde; and the Black Death immediately preceded the main campaign of illumination and may have overlapped it. The very wealthy banker Simon of Mirabello, counselor of James of Artevelde, and the ruthless and crafty Louis of Male, Count of Flanders, both imprinted, the one indirectly and the other directly, the manuscript's iconography. Arnold of Rummen himself presided over the demise of the County of Loon (Looz) as an independent political entity and its definitive subordination to the prince-bishops of Liège. The writing of the manuscript's colophon was embedded in this catastrophic event.

Difficulties around 10 A 14 attach to the site of its production, its patronage, the number of its flourishers and/or artists, and the number and dating of its campaigns of illumination. Jarring disjunctions in design; marked changes in style; erasures, overpaints, and incompletions all greatly complicate research on the manuscript. This study addresses these difficulties and the scholarly discussions they have engendered, as well as important aspects of decoration and iconography that have not yet been considered. The Winter Missal is related in style to a summer missal, KBR, Ms. 9217 and to a liturgical psalter, KBR, Ms. 9427, both commissioned by Arnold of Rummen; it is also stylistically related to two antiphonals of unknown patronage, KBR, Ms. 6426 and BOB, Ms. SVC 10a/b, the Loppem-Bruges antiphonal.[1]

1 Purpose and Contributions

The purpose of this study is to examine the manuscript's flourishing, illumination, calendar, patronage, and historical context, with the intention of broadening and deepening understanding in all these areas. The manuscript's varied and abundant penwork flourishing and its curious disruptions, erasures, and overpaints first drew my attention. As all aspects of the book's decoration are interconnected, the inquiry expanded to include the book's production and illumination, but the emphasis on flourishing, and by extension on the flourishers, remained.

The study of this missal has resulted in nine principal contributions, listed here not necessarily in order of importance but, loosely, from the more specific and developed to the more conceptual and conjectural. The first is to elucidate the role and possibilities of penwork flourishing in the missal's decoration. The second, related to the first, is to demonstrate that the flourishers were the illuminators, to identify their oeuvre in both kinds, and to recognize them as individuals with various artistic gifts, interests, habits, and paths of development. The third is to present the case for Ghent as the city in which the manuscript was illuminated. The fourth contribution is explication of the iconography, above all, that of the Crucifixion-*Te igitur* imagery. The importance of the Feast of Corpus Christi and the associated concept of sacrifice is on display in the iconography of the Crucifixion-*Te igitur*. The curious paired beasts with conjoined jaws or snouts, here termed gorgons, that decorate initial stems (e.g., figs. 15a, 132a), and a magnificent display of columbines (figs. 91) are also considered. The fifth is to analyze some of the collaborations, discontinuities, disruptions, and overpaints in the decoration and to suggest possible causes for them. The sixth is to examine the implications of patronage for the manuscript's date, its calendar, its donor portraits, and its erasures and overpaints. The seventh is to elucidate what can be termed, abstractly, the Eucharistic

---

1 The terms *Rummen group* and *Rummen cohort* are used here to designate this stylistic group. For KBR 9217, 9427, and 6426, see Camille Gaspar and Frédéric Lyna, *Les principaux manuscrits à peintures de la Bibliothèque Royale de Belgique* (Paris: La Société Française de Reproductions de Manuscrits à Peintures, 1937; repr., Brussels: Bibliothèque Royale Albert 1er, 1984), 1:344–346, 346–349, and 341–343; for the second antiphonal, BOB, Ms. SVC 10a/b, see Maurits Smeyers, "64. Fragmenten van een antifonarium.—Maasland, 3de

kwart 14de eeuw, en Kanalstil, ca. 1400," Provinciaal Museum voor Religieuze Kunst, *Handschriften uit de abdij van Sint-Truiden*, exhib. cat., Provinciaal Museum voor Religieuze Kunst, Begijnhofkerk, Sint-Truiden, 1986 (Leuven: Uitgeverij Peeters, 1986), 275–278. This manuscript, herein termed the Loppem-Bruges antiphonal, was in the collection of Baron Jean van Caloen at Loppem Castle for many years prior to its recent transfer to Bruges. For further bibliography and discussion of the Rummen-group manuscripts, see Appendix 4.

principle, or, more organically, *eucharisma*, as manifested in this missal. The eighth is to consider the manuscript's illumination in the context of the pivotal shifts towards realism in the rendering of surfaces and, beyond that, in the rendering of spatial depth that marked Northern fourteenth-century pictorialism. A final contribution is to make available the riches of the manuscript for consideration in the context of broader art historical issues.

Each of these contributions can be explained further. The first two, about which there is much to say, are discussed in two separate sections entitled "Flourisher-illuminators and the Relationship of Flourishing and Painting" and "Why Study Flourishing?" immediately following the last of the seven entries below.

Ghent as the site of flourishing and illumination: Ghent, Sint-Truiden, and Brussels have all been suggested as sites of the Winter Missal's production. The manuscript's text was likely written in Sint-Truiden, but the case for illumination in Ghent is supported by stylistic and iconographical evidence, by the circumstances of Ghent's history as a site of illumination and patronage, and by the connections to the city of Arnold of Rummen's wife Elisabeth of Lierde.

Iconography: The theology of Corpus Christi informs the central iconographical display of the Winter Missal, the Crucifixion-*Te igitur* opening on fols. 143v–144r. (See frontispiece.) Corpus Christi was declared a universal feast by Pope Urban IV in 1264, but the office was not widely assimilated into liturgical texts until the following century. The Winter Missal's iconography exemplifies the significance of the feast for reworking and interpreting Eucharistic imagery at a key liturgical text, the Canon of the Mass. Components of the imagery are not new in themselves, but they are combined in ways that lead to new emphases in meaning. The gorgons in initial stems and the columbines speak, respectively, to Ghent as the city of the manuscript's origin and to a theology of sacrifice related to Corpus Christi.

Collaborations, discontinuities, disruptions, and overpaints: These are of heterogeneous sorts, some difficult to understand; causal attributions are thus conjectural. On some pages the manuscript's two main artists worked together; why? Some discontinuities and disruptions may have occurred in consequence of external events; can these events be identified? Mistakes in design and the personal habits of the illuminators may have been contributory also. Shields and helmets were concealed by paint, probably at the point of a change of ownership in 1366, but none was replaced with the arms of Louis of Male, the new owner.

Patronage: The Winter Missal's second colophon names Arnold of Rummen as the commissioner, but the site of production, the calendar, and the imagery all indicate that Arnold's wife Elisabeth was more than an adjunct to her husband in the project and that she was esteemed by the manuscript's subsequent owner. The donor portraits on fols. 27v, 139r, and 143v (figs. 39, 103, 106) are significant both historically with respect to the question of ownership and art historically for the future of the donor portrait.

The Eucharistic principle or eucharisma: An illuminated missal in the Middle Ages was not only an object—a thing dazzling with gold and color, crafted with skill and at great expense to serve social, political, or ideological purposes, a thing produced to impress and persuade. It might indeed have functioned in these ways, but it was fundamentally more, other.[2] A missal, illuminated or not, was a sort of spiritual organism; it functioned as a midwife to the Eucharist, the living Christ. The psalter, the book of hours, and the breviary, which facilitate and direct liturgical prayer, did not share the missal's purpose of miraculously mediating the real presence of the Divine person. Among these liturgical manuscripts, a missal was thus unique. The Winter Missal of Arnold of Rummen—or any illuminated missal—is not fully comprehensible without recognition of this singular purpose. Purpose is voiced in expression. In the case of 10 A 14, I argue that a sense of *eucharisma*, of Eucharistic life, animates the missal's extraordinary penwork and its painted decoration and that the Eucharistic principle was a factor in decisions relevant to design and production.

The shift from the planar to the spatial in pictorialism: The manuscript's two campaigns mark a major change in concepts of surface, volume, and space. In the first campaign, Italianate techniques are applied mainly to the modeling of surfaces; in the second campaign these techniques are refined and, further, are synthesized with Northern ideas of creating volume through construction of surfaces.

---

2 For the idea that the spiritual character of late medieval Flemish devotional and liturgical texts powers the creativity of pictorial design, see James H. Marrow, "Scholarship on Flemish Manuscript Illumination of the Renaissance: Remarks on Past, Present, and Future," in *Flemish Manuscript Painting in Context: Recent Research*, ed. Elizabeth Morrison and Thomas Kren (Los Angeles: The J. Paul Getty Museum, 2006), 163–176. Marrow notes that the illumination of secular books of the Northern Renaissance is on the whole less creative than that of books of hours and liturgical books (pp. 165–166). See also Eric Palazzo, *Le souffle de Dieu. L'énergie de la liturgie et l'art au Moyen Age*, (Paris: Éditions du Cerf, 2020), p. 139–158, for the idea that the eucharistic liturgy is informed by a creative energy that manifests in decoration.

The missal and broader art historical questions: The study of the Winter Missal generates rich contributions to a range of art historical questions. What is the relationship between brush painting and penwork flourishing in fourteenth-century manuscripts? How did flourisher-illuminators interact and collaborate? How and when do additions to liturgy impact imagery? What circumstances and passions fueled the practice of overpainting heraldry and figures after a manuscript's initial completion? What might a calendar—both its entries and its iconography—reveal about the balance of interests in a marital relationship? How are Italianate ideas of space and volume absorbed and transformed in fourteenth-century Netherlandish painting? How is the iconography of Netherlandish manuscript illumination used and transformed in fifteenth-century panel painting?

2   Why Study Flourishing?

Penwork flourishing in fourteenth-century manuscripts from centers in Paris, the upper Rhine, the northern Netherlands, and England has been the object of study, but more often with the intention of describing motifs and tracing the development of forms rather than with the intention of identifying and personalizing artistic hands, as is the case with the study of illumination.[3]

Studies of penwork are few in number compared with those of illumination. However, reasons to attend to flourishing are many.

Why study styles of flourishing? First, because these embellishments were intended to beautify, and beauty in the Middle Ages was, among other things, an end in itself. It is not my aim, nor my interest, to argue Classical versus political notions of beauty but to acknowledge the conceptual lens of the fourteenth century. The Classical conception of beauty, adopted and modified by the medieval scholastics, ranked beauty among the highest values, with goodness, truth, and justice.[4] Aquinas's definition of beauty included both the subjective and the objective. He saw beauty as a relation between subject and object, thus establishing a subjective element in the perception of beauty. On the other hand, the qualities perceived—integrity or perfection, proportion or harmony, and clarity—were inherent to the object rather than inventions of the viewer.[5] Philosophy shapes culture; this idea of beauty was integral to the cultural framework within which the artists of 10 A 14 functioned. It is appropriate and profitable to consider flourishing and illumination in the context of the ideas that shaped the time, though these arts are not reducible to illustrations of philosophical concepts. In 10 A 14 the intrinsic beauty and great abundance of the flourishing make this medium worthy of attention for its own sake. The truly remarkable penwork decoration in 10 A 14 is a major aesthetic statement of its genre. The penwork virtually dances from page after page of the manuscript, enhancing and framing initials, enlivening text columns, spilling into margins.

Second, the penwork in 10 A 14 manifests several styles and an impressive array of motifs. These differences give evidence of the identity of different illuminator-flourishers, of their oeuvre, of their particular interests, and of their interactions and collaborations, and add to

---

3   One important exception is the study by François Avril, "Un enlumineur ornemaniste parisien de la première moitié du XIVe siècle: Jacobus Mathey (Jaquet Maci?)," *Bulletin monumental* 129 (1971): 249–264. Avril discusses Mathey's style as a flourisher; see p. 256, n.4, for the use of the term *enlumineur* to designate flourishers in the fifteenth century. For Paris, see Patricia Stirnemann, "Dating, Placement, and Illumination," *Journal of the Early Book Society for the Study of Manuscripts and Printing History* 11 (2008): 155–166. For penwork in the upper Rhine in the fourteenth century, see Ellen J. Beer, *Beiträge zur oberrheinischen Buchmalerei in der ersten Hälfte des 14. Jahrhunderts unter besonderer Berücksichtigung der Initialornamentik* (Basel: Birkhäuser Verlag, 1959). For analysis of form and use of penwork decoration in fifteenth-century illumination in the northern Netherlands, see Anne S. Korteweg, ed., *Kriezels, aubergines en takkenbossen: randversiering in Noordnederlandse handschriften uit de vijftiende eeuw*, exhib. cat., The Hague, Rijksmuseum Meermanno Westreenianum/Museum van het Boek and Koninklijke Bibliotheek, 1992–1993 (Zutphen: Walburg Pers, 1992). For England, see Lynda Dennison, "The Significance of Ornamental Penwork in Illuminated and Decorated Manuscripts of the Second Half of the Fourteenth Century," in *Tributes to Kathleen L. Scott: English Medieval Manuscripts: Readers, Makers and Illuminators*, ed. Marlene Villalobos-Hennessey (London: Harvey Miller, 2009), 31–64. This study has much to say about the identities of artists and flourishers in mid- and later fourteenth-century English manuscripts. For typology and nomenclature of penwork forms in English and French manuscripts of the thirteenth century, see Sonia Scott-Fleming, *The Analysis of Pen Flourishing in Thirteenth-Century*

Manuscripts (Leiden: E. J. Brill, 1989). For application of typology to the question of identifying hands in flourishing, see Sonia Patterson, "Comparison of Minor Initial Decoration: A Possible Method of Showing the Place of Origin of 13th-Century Manuscripts," *The Library*, 5th ser., 27 (1972): 23–30.

4   Crispin Sartwell, "Beauty," *The Stanford Encyclopedia of Philosophy* (Summer 2022 Edition), ed. Edward N. Zalta. https://plato.stanford .edu/archives/sum2022/entries/beauty/. Accessed 29 March 2022.

5   *Summa Theologiae*, I, question 39, article 8, objection 5. *The Summa Theologiae of St. Thomas Aquinas: Part I*, trans. Fathers of the English Dominican Province, 2nd rev. ed., 1920. https://www.newadvent.org/summa. Accessed 29 March 2022. A readable and short explanation of Aquinas's statements on beauty, with attention to their implications for the visual, is in Mosche Barasch, *Theories of Art: From Plato to Winckelmann* (New York: New York University Press, 1985), 98–101.

our understanding of the operations of fourteenth-century manuscript production.

Third, flourishing is valuable in identifying artistic hands between as well as within manuscripts and expands the usual categories of study, keyed to figures, architecture, and space. An understanding of styles, development, and interactions in penwork makes it possible to hypothesize certain workshop practices and to identify the workshop's aesthetic.[6]

Fourth, identification of the artists and of their workshops can provide evidence for determining the site of the manuscript's production.

Fifth, the medium has a unique character, combining translucence, immediacy, and the potential for improvisation with pattern and structure. Flourishing is neither sketch nor finished line drawing. It is friendly to insights into the process and dynamics of execution. As a vehicle of personal artistic expression, flourishing invites exploration of areas beyond the conventions of illumination. Flourishing is fertile ground for play, for displays of humor, and for exploration of the psychologically suggestive and subliminal. It is a window into the creativity and expressive impulses of its practitioners and into their particular abilities, tastes, and habits, a supplement to artistic identities often weighted by the *gravitas* of the religious subjects in miniatures.

Thus, although it does not lend itself to making the specific social, religious, or political statements that are congenial to the figural-spatial imagery of major illumination, flourishing is nonetheless more than a self-contained product of mannerism and rote, disconnected from painted and figural decoration and entitled to status merely as a footnote to other forms of decoration. It brings substantial evidence—much of it not duplicated in the illumination—to central art historical issues and questions. It is worthy of study, not only in its own right as beautiful, but also as a source of potential contributions to the scholarly enterprise.

3 Flourisher-Illuminators and the Relationship of Flourishing and Painting

The term *flourishing* refers to decoration with pen and ink. It is here used of both the internal decoration of penwork initials and the external decorative attachments to initials and border bars. Flourishing is primarily linear rather than planar; its forms are both abstract and figural.

My study of 10 A 14 shows that the flourishers were in fact the illuminators.[7] The main evidence for identifying flourishers with illuminators is twofold: First, evidence is in the simultaneity of shifts in style which often happen between and within quires. Abrupt, coordinated changes in styles of illumination and penwork in this context must either be attributed to a change in the identity of the one person who both illuminates and flourishes, or to choreographed simultaneous changes between two pairs of craftsmen. The latter is possible, but the former provides a simpler and more likely explanation. A second reason for identifying flourishers with illuminators is a kinship of attitudes towards structure, expression, and experimentation in both flourishing and illumination. If the same attitudes permeate a specified body of work, which might include both penwork and painting and a variety of formats from large miniatures to initials and border bars, it is likely that the same person was responsible for all species of decoration.

Flourishing and painting are differentiated by tools and material, but the two media share techniques and motifs in ways that are at once complex and commonsensical. Flourishing requires a pen and translucent water-based ink colored with organic pigments; painting requires a brush and at least some opaque inorganic pigments. However, the boundary between flourishing and illumination is not always clear because the two media can produce similar effects. A brush of a few hairs might produce a line similar to that produced by a pen. An initial brushed in gold wash might have extensions of the same wash drawn in pen. Multiple blended strokes of the pen might produce the effect of a brush.

In 10 A 14, two-line initials and their extensions are the site of parallels, combinations, and crossovers between the two media. Many two-line penwork initials are flatly washed in ink or gold—and thus already an inorganic pigment is introduced into a medium otherwise dominated by

---

6 The term *workshop* here refers to artists who work on a common project of illumination, probably in the same city or other shared location, but not necessarily in the same building.

7 Stirnemann "Dating, Placement, and Illumination," 155, characterizes flourishers as a separate class of workers, an intermediate layer in the pyramid of craftsmen, in which the many illuminators fill the bottom, a moderate number of flourishers occupy the middle level and miniaturists, the least in number, occupy the top. Certainly, in different eras and regions the numbers of craftsmen associated with manuscript production, the relationships among occupations, and the degree of segregation or integration of practitioners of the different functions involved in production varied greatly. Dennison's "Significance of Ornamental Penwork" considers manuscripts whose production was associated with monastic centers and concludes that illuminators often flourished their manuscripts; see especially p. 46.

organic colorants. The letterform has no decorative overlay, and its internal decoration consists of line drawing in pen. A painted initial's letterform, by contrast, is enhanced with modeling and is embellished with various motifs; its internal decoration is likewise modeled. Generally, both the two-line initial and its decoration are executed in pen, or both are painted. This difference in media can be seen in the two initials on fol. 29v (fig. 40a). However, initials of both kinds draw from a common repertoire of decorative motifs, including trilobes, heads, and grotesques. In some instances, elements of the two initial types are combined. On fol. 22r, a painted, three-dimensionalized head of Christ is enclosed in a flat goldwash initial (fig. 34c). Exceptionally fine linear detailing suggests use of the pen along with the brush. Some imagery, structures, and motifs typically found in painted decoration, or even in metalwork, appear as novelties in penwork in what can be termed transmedial migration. (See discussion of penwork borders in Chapter 3.) It seems likely that the decorators of 10 A 14 were equipped with both pen and brush, ink and paint, and that they were flexible, adaptive, and practical in working with the tools and materials of both media; the aim was to facilitate production and enliven the product. Hierarchical-typological distinctions in media and categories of decoration (i.e., miniature, large initial, two-line initial, etc.), however useful they may be as organizational tools for the researcher, are nonetheless of limited value in understanding the flourisher-illuminator's approach to design and decoration.

4 Identities of Flourisher-Illuminators

Artistic hands are distinguished primarily by some sort of connoisseurship, whether of the intuitive variety fathered by Roger de Piles or the supposedly more scientific Morellian connoisseurship, itself dependent on unprovable assumptions about the adoption and distribution of *Grundformen*. Products of the post-medieval era, both methods should be employed with caution. In either case, an element of subjective choice on the part of the artist and of subjective judgment on the part of the art historian and the reader cannot be avoided. Criteria for distinguishing artists include a wide range of features, from the most quantifiable and concrete to the most qualitative and abstract, and include both stylistic and iconographical elements. Details and motifs, patterns of handling the elements and principles of design, aesthetic and expressive qualities, conceptual and intellectual choices, attitudes towards absorbing external influences, artistic

purposes and intentions, intrinsic capacity for change and growth—these can all be criteria for identifying artists.[8]

Definitive proof in the determination of hands is hampered by difficult questions. Are differences in style the result of an artist's development and exposure to new influences, or to the advent of a different artist?[9] Are differences in quality attributable to different hands—master and assistant—or to a single artist working under different conditions and circumstances, some more conducive to excellence than others? To what degree does an artist adapt his style or choice and his rendering of motifs to the tastes and demands of his patrons? Whatever the organizational structure and relationships, pressures of time, money, and events must at times have engendered improvised or ad hoc measures in the execution of a commission: Everyone in the workshop did what was necessary to facilitate production of the work.

5 Models of Production

Although we have a general understanding of the activities that were required to write and decorate a manuscript and of the sequence of these steps, much about the functions of fourteenth-century manuscript workshops in the Low Countries and elsewhere is not known. There does not seem to have been anything like a uniform system of

---

8 Dennison relies primarily on selected motifs, mannerisms, and details in the treatment of figures, architecture, initials, and borders. See, for example, her use of many specific motifs and mannerisms for identifying the work of artists in the Rummen group in "The Dating and Localisation of the Hague Missal (Meermanno-Westreenianum MS 10A14 and the Connection Between English and Flemish Miniature Painting in the Mid-fourteenth Century," in *"Als Ich Can": Liber Amicorum in Memory of Professor Dr. Maurits Smeyers*, ed. Bert Cardon, Jan Van der Stock, and Dominique Vanwijnsberghe, Corpus of Illuminated Manuscripts 11 (Leuven: Uitgeverij Peeters, 2002), 505–510. Carlvant's criteria are based primarily on general distinctions in quality, in expression, and in aesthetics of style and composition rather than on specific motifs, though some of the latter are also cited. She characterizes the Ghent Master of the later century in terms of his able combination of realism, emotional expression, delicacy and refinement of drawing, and gentleness. See Kerstin Carlvant, *Manuscript Painting in Thirteenth-Century Flanders: Bruges, Ghent and the Circle of the Counts* (London: Harvey Miller, 2012), Chapter 7 and especially pp. 102–105; see also her discussions of the Ghent Master's work in MLM, Ms. 72, pp. 249–253, and in the missal of *c.*1275–1285 from St. Peter's Abbey, SMG, inv. A60.01, p. 261.

9 This question is front and center in Scot McKendrick, "Between Flanders and Normandy: Collaboration among Miniaturists or a Case of Influence?" in *Under the Influence: The Concept of Influence and the Study of Illuminated Manuscripts*, ed. John Lowden and Alixe Bovey (Turnhout: Brepols Publishers, 2007), 139–149.

production. Different scholars have developed different conceptual models for production depending on the relevant manuscripts' particularities, and on their particular philosophical predispositions and analytical aptitudes. Rarely is a conceptual scenario entirely satisfactory; questions about patterns of collaboration between and among masters and between masters and assistants arise in close study of most illuminated manuscripts.

In an integrated model, a single artist completes essentially all elements of given illumination. In scholarship relevant to 10 A 14, Dennison's discussions of hands in the manuscripts of the Rummen group as well as in related English manuscripts presume an essentially integrated model but with some uncertainties about the identity of artists who made particular images.[10]

In a stratified or hierarchical model, different workers, presumably grouped according to ability or experience, direct their efforts to certain tasks—initial underpainting or gilding, for example—perhaps using the preparatory drawings of a master, who may also execute final painting and overdrawing. In a hybridization of the integrated and the stratified, the lesser illumination and decoration—execution of secondary initials, borders or marginalia—are assigned in their entirety to assistants, while primary miniatures and initials are the work of the masters. Carlvant sees elements of the hierarchical and hybridized models of production in thirteenth-century psalters of Bruges and Ghent, in which she identifies and differentiates masters and assistants, though often citing little evidence for attributions and often with bewildering complexities in artistic interactions.[11]

6 Method

I presume both the possibility and the inherent value of searching for and understanding, to some degree, what happened in the past through examination of the past's artifacts and art. My method is essentially inductive rather than deductive and has the strengths and weaknesses inherent in such an approach. I employ close visual study

and follow the evidence thus uncovered, in the belief that events leave evidence, and that the former can be reconstructed to some degree from the latter. This method has the virtue of immediacy, of staying close to the pen of the flourisher and the brush of the painter. Patterns and processes, characteristic forms, combinations, and placements are accessible through close observation. A sense of the flourisher's or painter's particular aesthetic and of his interests coalesces from close study of many details and of the patterns that organize them. The drawback of this method is the tendency to over-immersion in the profusion of detail at the expense of analysis and interpretation. To counter the latter tendency, I have moved much description to appendices and have included a number of tables and inventories as a step towards organizing the material. Some understanding of processes and interactions, of sequencing and development, emerges from the functions of observing, intuiting, judging, and reasoning. Of course, all conclusions are open to correction and clarification. This method is not exercised to the exclusion of considering broader social and historical questions; indeed, it should eventuate in illuminating these; but they are not the primary engines of inquiry.

7 The Colophons

The manuscript's two colophons are written in gold, one below the other and in two different hands, on fol. 204r (figs. 138, 138a).[12] They provide information on the date and place of illumination, on the identity of one illuminator, and on the patronage.

---

10 See Lynda Dennison's discussion of artists throughout "Dating and Localisation" and in "The Technical Mastery of the Macclesfield Psalter: A Preliminary Stylistic Appraisal of the Illuminators and Their Suggested Origin," in *Transactions of the Cambridge Bibliographical Society* 13, no. 3 (2006): 253–288.

11 See Carlvant, *Manuscript Painting*, Chapters 7 and 8, on the Ghent Master and the Dampierre Master and her discussion of hands and style in manuscripts associated with these two artists in her catalogue. For an example of complexities and difficulties of specifying interactions and identities, see her discussion of illuminators in MLM, Ms. M. 72, pp. 250–251.

---

12 The transcription resolves abbreviations, notably *pbro* in line seven of the first colophon as *presbytero*, and transcribes according to common-sense reading the rubbed letters towards the end of each line in the first colophon. My thanks to Dr. Daniel Sheerin for his generous help with questions about the colophons. I rely heavily on his phrasing for the translation of the second colophon. The colophons are also transcribed, with some slight differences in form, in A. W. Byvanck, *Les principaux manuscrits à peintures de la Bibliothèque Royale des Pays-Bas et du Musée Meermanno-Westreenianum à la Haye* (Paris: Société française de reproductions de manuscrits à peintures, 1924), 99; G. I. Lieftinck, "No. 118—La Haye, Mus. Meerm.-Westr. 10 A 14 (60)," *Manuscrits datés conservés dans les Pays-Bas* (Amsterdam: North-Holland Publishing Company, 1964), vol. 1, pt. 1, p. 50; P. C. Boeren, *Catalogus van de handschriften van het Rijksmuseum Meermanno-Westreenianum* (The Hague: Rijksmuseum Meermanno-Westreenianum, 1979), 17; Dennison, "Dating and Localisation," 510, and Lynda Eileen Dennison, "The Stylistic Sources, Dating and Development of the Bohun Workshop, ca. 1340–1400" (PhD diss., Westfield College, University of London, 1988), 120. Dennison provides an English translation.

INTRODUCTION

Colophon 1: *Anno domini · M · CCC · LXVI · sabbato post nativitatem beate marie virginis fuit perfectus liber iste a laurentio illuminatore presbytero de andwerpia commoranti gandavi. deo gratias.*

"In the year of the Lord 1366 on the Saturday after the Nativity of the Blessed Virgin Mary, this book was completed by Laurence the illuminator, priest of Antwerp residing in Ghent. Thanks be to God."[13]

Colophon 2: *Sic scribi · et · illuminandi · ob · laudem · dei · et · ecclesie · sancte · fecit · nobilis · arnoldus · dominus · de · rimmen · et · de · quaetbeecke · Baro · orate · pro · eo.*

"That it be so written and illuminated unto the praise of God and Holy Church was brought about by Arnold, Lord of Rummen and Quaetbeecke, Baron. Pray for him."

The first colophon identifies 1366 as the date of completion and Laurence the Priest of Antwerp as the illuminator who completed the manuscript. Laurence's self-identification as illuminator and priest testify that both his artistry and his priestly vocation were important to him; this twin vocation is an interpretive key for the missal's decoration. Ghent is named as the location of the final work on the missal. The second colophon names Arnold, Lord of Rummen and Quaetbeecke, Baron, as the commissioner of the manuscript. All four nuggets of information bear further study; none is entirely without problems. In the second colophon, one finds the future passive participle *illuminandi*, where one expects the present passive infinitive *illuminari*, "to be illuminated," analogous to *scribi*, "to be written." The future passive participle is very likely a scribal error.[14] The manuscript's text, exclusive of the colophons, was written in its entirety by one scribe.[15] The two colophons are more problematic. Both are in gold ink, but the second is written in a slightly less regular hand than the first.

Differences in the flourishing of the two colophons likewise suggest that the decoration of the second colophon, though not necessarily its text, postdates that of the

first.[16] The blue inner element of the penwork border originates as an extension from the initial *A(nno)* of the first colophon and edges the left side of the page.[17] However, neither the initial *S(ic)* of the second colophon, nor the penwork framing the initial is connected to the extension; rather, both are placed against the text side of the border. This lack of continuity between initial and border runs counter to the designs elsewhere in the manuscript; the usual practice was to merge the lower terminal of the letter S with the penwork border (fig. 79).

Another feature differentiating the two colophons is the use of penwork line-fillers. The first of these, a fillet-and-button strip, is inserted after the last word of the first colophon. A floating rosette appears at the end of the third line of the second colophon and a leaf at the end of the sixth line. A second fillet-and-button appears at the end of the eighth line, after the last word of the second colophon. All four line-endings appear to be by the same hand and are inferior in deftness of execution to the penwork of the border bar; they do not appear to be by the hand of the artist who produced the latter. Elsewhere in the manuscript line endings are all but non-existent; the text almost everywhere fills out the ruled lines; where the text does not reach the end of a line, the space is left blank, as on fol. 145rb. The line fillers on fol. 204r may have been intended to create consistency in the text block's width in order to link the two colophons more closely, but the effect was just the opposite; the line fillers draw attention to the twoness of the inscriptions, making the differences in penmanship between first and second colophons more noticeable.

Sheerin proposed that the same scribe wrote both colophons but that the second was written later, with a thicker point and less control, than the first.[18] It could also be that the first colophon was written by Laurence, the priest-illuminator named therein, and that the second colophon was by a co-worker of Father Laurence, someone who wrote in a slightly less certain script. Presumably, the second colophon need not have postdated the first by a prolonged interval, perhaps only by a few days or weeks, as it reads almost as an afterthought to the first. In response to Byvanck, who dated the second colophon to the fifteenth century, Dennison proposed that both colophons were products of the second campaign, which

---

13 The Feast of the Nativity of the Blessed Virgin Mary, 8 September, is noted in the calendar for 10 A 14. In 1366, 8 September fell on a Tuesday (Julian calendar); the following Saturday was the twelfth, as noted by Lieftinck, *Manuscrits datés*, 50, and Boeren, *Catalogus van de handschriften* 18. Patrick M. de Winter, *La bibliothèque de Philippe le Hardi, Duc de Bourgogne (1364–1404): Étude sur les manuscrits à peintures d'une collection princière à l'époque du "style gothique international"* (Paris: Éditions du Centre National de la Recherche Scientifique 1985), 229, identifies the day of completion as 5 September.

14 Lieftinck, *Manuscrits datés*, 50, and Boeren, *Catalogus van de handschriften*, 17, in effect noted this anomaly. Sheerin finds it inexplicable except as an error.

15 This point is not in dispute: Boeren, *Catalogus van de handschriften*, 17; Haagdorens, "Sint-Truidense handschriften," 270.

16 Dennison, "Stylistic Sources," 123–124, discusses the differences in the initials and flourishing of the two colophons.

17 The initial, its decoration, the border bar, and the terminal complex at the top of the page are all the work of Artist 1, whose penwork is discussed in Chapter 4.

18 Daniel Sheerin, email message of 6 August 2020.

ended in 1366.[19] It seems indeed very likely that both colophons date to 1366.

The initial *A* and its border-extension likely date to the campaign of *c*.1345–55. These are the work of Artist 1, discussed at length in Chapter 4. The colophon's site was thus prepared but left uninscribed until the manuscript was finally completed in 1366. The first colophon gives information about artist, location, and date of completion. The purpose of the second colophon is the memorialization of Arnold, who was engulfed in a series of financial, personal, and social catastrophes in 1365 and 1366, as recounted below. The final blow was the surrender of his claim to the County of Loon to the bishop of Liège on 21 September 1366, less than two weeks after the completion of the manuscript. Perhaps his financial collapse brought loss of the manuscript in its train and the second inscription was an empathetic tribute to his part in the creation of a work he was not, in the end, to enjoy.

8 Fourteenth-Century Flanders

In Flanders, new texts were composed in the vernacular during the mid- and later fourteenth century, and translation of older texts, already well underway in the thirteenth century, continued.[20] New texts reflected the tastes and interests of the wealthy merchant class, rather than those of the aristocracy. Although the illumination of manuscripts in the southern Netherlands never ceased—in

Tournai, Jehan de Grise, Pierart dou Tielt and their associates produced illuminated books through the 1330s and 1340s—production declined, towards the end of the thirteenth century in Bruges and Liège and by about 1335 in Ghent. The decades-long prolific output of illuminated romances, poetry, didactic compositions, histories, scientific works and especially of psalters and books of hours, tapered off; the lesser number of surviving manuscripts of mid-century date indicates that fewer illuminated books were made at that time in Ghent and elsewhere in the region.[21] The production of illuminated manuscripts in Flanders began again in quantity towards the end of the fourteenth century.

For centuries prior to the very turbulent fourteenth, Flanders was commercially vibrant. Its economy, powered primarily by the manufacture of woolen cloth, was distinguished by its orientation, from the beginning, not only to a healthy local market but also to export.[22] The development of this trade was in turn enabled by the geographical terrain and the situation of Flanders, within easy reach across the English Channel of the sheep-raising districts of England and richly supplied with navigable rivers. Development was encouraged first by the policies of able twelfth-century counts, such as Philip of Alsace (1157–1191) and Baldwin IX (1194–1206), and in the thirteenth century by the initiatives of leaders in the increasingly powerful cities, especially Ghent, Bruges, and Ypres.

Nonetheless, Flanders was much troubled economically, politically, and socially through most of the fourteenth century. Crop failures in consequence of heavy rains and flooding in 1315 and the peasant revolt in

---

19 Byvanck, *Les principaux manuscrits*, 99; Dennison, "Stylistic Sources," 123–124.

20 For Arthurian literature in the thirteenth and fourteenth centuries, see Norris J. Lacy et al., eds., *The New Arthurian Encyclopedia*, 3rd ed. (New York: Garland, 1991). For Jacob van Maerlant's works, see F. P. van Oostrom, *Maerlant's Wereld* (Amsterdam: Uitgeverij Prometheus, 1996); Jaap van Moolenbroek and Maaike Hogenhout-Mulder, eds., *Scolastica willic ontbinden: over de Rijmbijbel van Jacob van Maerlant* (Hilversum: Verloren, 1991). For the Alexander romances, see David John Athole Ross, *Alexander Historiatus: A Guide to Medieval Illustrated Alexander Literature* (London: Warburg Institute, University of London, 1963); see further bibliography of primary and secondary sources for the Alexander texts in Mark Cruse, *Illuminating the Roman d'Alexandre, Oxford, Bodleian Library, MS. Bodley 264: The Manuscript as Monument* (Cambridge: D. S. Brewer, 2011), 209–220.

For the history of the medieval *Romance of Alexander*, see George Cary, *The Medieval Alexander*, ed. D. J. A. Ross (Cambridge: Cambridge University Press, 1956, repr. 2009). Maurits Smeyers, *Flemish Miniatures from the 8th to the mid-16th Century: The Medieval World on Parchment*, trans. Karen Bowen and Dirk Imhof (Leuven: Uitgeverij Davidsfonds, 1999), 190–191, gives a brief overview of production of texts in fourteenth-century Flanders.

21 As also noted by Judith H. Oliver, "The Herkenrode Indulgence, Avignon, and Pre-Eyckian Painting of the Mid-Fourteenth-Century Low Countries," in *Flanders in a European Perspective: Manuscript Illumination Around 1400 in Flanders and Abroad*, Maurits Smeyers and Bert Cardon, eds. (Leuven: Peeters, 1995), 195. She cites the Rummen manuscripts as the chief products of the southern Netherlands in the mid-fourteenth century. From Ypres there was the now-destroyed Kuerboec of 1363; other now-unknown illuminated manuscripts may have perished in the fire. A breviary in two volumes, each volume bound in three parts, from the Abbey of St. Peter, Ghent, UGU, Ms. 3381, is dated 1373 in an inscription (1:2, fol. 215r). See "579. Breviar van de Sint-Pietersabdij te Gent," *Boekdrukkunst, boekbanden, borduurkunst, edelsmeedkunst, miniatuurkunst*, vol. 2 of *Gent: duizend jaar kunst en cultuur*, exhib. cat., Bijlokemuseum, Ghent, 1975 (Ghent: Stadt Gent, 1975), 352–353. A *Somme le Roi* from Bruges or Ghent (KBR, Ms. 10320) dates to *c*.1380. No doubt other illuminated manuscripts could be added to this short list, but even so, the decline from earlier decades, especially those of the era before 1335, is striking.

22 Henry Stephen Lucas, *The Low Countries and the Hundred Years War, 1326–1347* (Ann Arbor: University of Michigan Press, 1929), 5, 9.

INTRODUCTION

Maritime Flanders between 1323 and 1328 were only the beginning. During this century, Flanders was pummeled by continuous episodes of war and violent civil unrest.[23] The middle decades were particularly turbulent. These years were marked by the first phase of the Hundred Years' War, which began in 1338 upon the arrival in Antwerp of the English king Edward III with a fleet of several hundred English ships. In the ensuing years, Edward, his wife Queen Philippa of Hainault, and a number of his nobles spent much time in the Low Countries negotiating with and cajoling the cities, especially Ghent, where Edward and his queen wintered in 1340; Edward's son John of Gaunt (Ghent) was born there the following spring.[24]

The conflict brought widespread devastation, by the armies of both Philip VI of France and Edward III and his allies, to the countryside in southern Flanders and Hainault, and siege to the cities of Cambrai and Tournai in 1340.[25] The Flemish-speaking cities of Ghent, Bruges, and Ypres, dependent on England for wool and on France for grain, were pressed from both directions. The cities tended towards alliance with the English not only for economic reasons but also in order to counter the territorial aggressions of Philip VI and the Francophile leanings of the Flemish counts, against whom the cities struggled for rights and independence. Neither Philip VI nor Edward III was above using severely coercive measures on the Flemings. The English king imposed an embargo on wool between 1336 and 1340; the French king embargoed shipments of grain to Flanders in the early 1340s.[26] Troubles continued through the 1340s and 1350s. The Battle of Crécy in 1346 resulted in the death of Louis II, Count of Nevers (1322–1346—who was also Count of Flanders),[27] and the accession to the countship of his sixteen-year-old son Louis of Male, one of the most nefarious political figures of the century—a man both astute and maladroit—and the last of the essentially independent counts of Flanders.

Louis was the eventual owner of Arnold's Winter Missal, which passed at his death to his daughter Margaret, married to Duke Philip the Bold of Burgundy, and thence into the library of the Dukes of Burgundy.[28] To the disasters of war were added the devastations of the Black Death. Once thought to have virtually bypassed Flanders, the Plague has been shown to have killed as many there as elsewhere in Europe, around a third of the population; quicker recovery of the Low Countries' cities was keyed in part to a larger reserve of rural population that could replenish urban areas through immigration.[29] The Plague was equally or even more costly of life in subsequent decades, above all in the severe outbreak of 1368–1369.[30]

In Ghent, the most powerful, populous, and contentious of the Flemish cities, the politics of the war combined with those of the city and with economic troubles to create episodes of severe upheaval.[31] These episodes included in 1345 a pitched battle between weavers and fullers in the city square in which about a thousand men died and the murder during the same year of James of Artevelde, the ally of the weavers who had controlled Ghent since 1338. In 1349 the Count's troops stormed the city, in one of the repeated acts of bloody repression by Louis of Male in response to recurrent opposition to him in Ghent and elsewhere. Civil war and conflict between Ghent and Louis were endemic until the Count's death in 1384. Matters were not helped by extensive blood feuds and general lawlessness.

Political troubles were accompanied by economic troubles. In 1349, Louis imposed a heavy, continuing indemnity on the weavers, who consistently opposed him; many left the city, and the wool trade went into a severe decline. This decline was hastened by competition from England, which began to export not only wool but increasing quantities of finished cloth. Furthermore, small communities in Flanders began to challenge Ypres, Bruges, and Ghent with production in quantity of lower grades of cloth. Foreigners moved in as drapers, middlemen in the cloth

---

23 David Nicholas, *Medieval Flanders* (London: Longman, 1992), 209.

24 Lucas, *The Low Countries*, 220.

25 Lucas, *The Low Countries*, 330–331, 386–389; 408–421.

26 Nicholas, *Medieval Flanders*, 219–220, 222; Lucas, *The Low Countries*, 190, 362.

27 Count Louis II of Nevers was Count Louis I of Flanders. His father, Louis I of Nevers, predeceased his father Robert of Bethune, Count of Flanders (1305–1322), by a few months and so never inherited the title Count of Flanders. See Nicholas, *Medieval Flanders*, 442, for the genealogy of the Counts of Flanders. See also Claudine Lemaire and Dominique Vanwijnsberghe, "Cote-Signalement KBR 9217," *Textes liturgiques, ascétiques, théologiques, philosophiques et moraux*, vol. 1 of *La Librairie des ducs de Bourgogne: Manuscrits conservés à la Bibliothèque Royale de Belgique*, ed. Bernard Bousmanne and Céline Van Hoorebeeck (Turnhout: Brepols Publishers, 2000), 108–109.

28 Lemaire and Vanwijnsberghe, "Cote-Signalement KBR 9217," *Textes liturgiques*, 104.

29 Joris Roosen and Daniel R. Curtis, "The 'Light Touch' of the Black Death in the Southern Netherlands: an Urban Trick?" *The Economic History Review* 72:1 (February 2019): 32–56. https://onlinelibrary.wiley.com/doi/epdf/10.1111/ehr.12667. Accessed 29 July 2022.

30 Nicholas, *Medieval Flanders*, 266.

31 See Nicholas, *Medieval Flanders*, 222–224 for events in Ghent 1348–49. For the conflicts around James of Artevelde, see David Nicholas, *The Van Arteveldes of Ghent: The Varieties of Vendetta and the Hero in History* (Ithaca: Cornell University, 1988).

trade, competing with the established textile aristocracy in Ghent and elsewhere.[32]

This catalog of troubles sapped the vitality of the major cities of Flanders. One can only reason that these many difficulties likely contributed to the decline in production of illuminated books, especially in Ghent. After the death of Louis of Male in 1384, political discord subsided and the economy recovered under the less heavy-handed rule of Louis's son-in-law, Philip the Bold, Duke of Burgundy (Count of Flanders 1384–1410). Not coincidentally, around this time the production of illuminated manuscripts in Ghent revived.

9   The Historical Context of 10 A 14

Thus, Arnold's Winter Missal came out of a particularly eventful era in Flemish history. The general economic decline of the major Flemish cities in the mid-fourteenth century, the English presence in Flanders occasioned by the opening of the Hundred Years' War, and the Black Death of 1349 may have affected production of the missal in various ways. The manuscript had an indirect connection to the aforementioned James of Artevelde. His deputy Simon of Mirabello, a fabulously wealthy financier and *ruuward* (counselor) of Flanders, married in 1324 Elisabeth of Lierde, a natural daughter of Count Louis I of Nevers, half-sister of Count Louis II of Nevers, and aunt of Louis of Male.[33] Simon was murdered in 1346, not long after James; and his extensive holdings of property throughout Flanders and Brabant passed to his widow. Elisabeth was then free to marry Arnold of Rummen, which she did in 1350, or perhaps a little earlier.[34] The

three manuscripts with Rummen heraldry, KBR 9427, KBR 9217, and 10 A 14, could have been begun at the time of the marriage or in anticipation of it, the *terminus post quem* being the death of Simon.[35] Elisabeth may have been significantly older than Arnold, as she was married for over a quarter of a century to Simon before contracting the marriage with Arnold.[36]

Louis of Male instigated much of the decades-long conflict and civil unrest in Ghent and, ironically, may have contributed indirectly to a delay in completion of the manuscript he was eventually to own. Louis's relations with Elisabeth and Arnold were marked by conflict. Simon of Mirabello had sided with the city of Ghent and Edward III against the Count in the conflict with the French crown. On his accession to the countship in 1346, Louis took possession of Elisabeth's property and of the rights to her residence at the fine palace of ten Walle in Ghent, partly as retribution for her first husband's political disloyalty to

---

32   Nicholas, *Medieval Flanders*, 273–285.

33   For a short biography of Simon of Mirabello, see Napoléon de Pauw, "Mirabello (les)," in *Biographie nationale*, 14 (Brussels: Bruylant-Christophe and Cie, successeur Émile Bruylant, 1897), cols. 869–882, especially cols. 871–877. See also Paul H. Rogghé, "Simon de Mirabello in Vlaanderen," in *Appeltjes van het Meetjesland: jaarboek van het Heemkundig Genootschap van het Meetjesland*, 9 (1958): 5–54. For the genealogy of Elisabeth of Lierde, see Lieve Vandecapelle-Haagdorens, "Het zgn. missaal van Lodewijk van Male (Brussel, Koninklijke Bibliotheek, ms. 9217): Bijdrage tot de studie van de miniatuurkunst in het Maasland tijdens het derde kwart van de 14de eeuw" (thesis for licentiate, Catholic University of Leuven, 1983), 92.

34   Rogghé, 20. See F. Van der Haeghen, pub., *Het klooster ten Walle en de abdij van den Groenen Briel. Stukken en oorkonden* (Ghent, 1888), no. 52, dated 14 December 1350. This entry refers to Elisabeth as the wife of Rummen: "Arent van Huerle, heer van Rumene, bevestigt de giften en beloften door zijne gezelnede Lysbeth, vrouw van Rumene en van Somerghem, aan Simoens ser Domaes 'onsen cnape' gedaan." https://www

.dbnl.org/tekst/_klo002klo001_01/_klo002klo001_01_0003.php. Accessed 14 May 2022. J. Baerten, "Rummen, reenentan, pretendent graaf van Loon," in *Nationaal Biografisch Woordenboek*, 2 (Brussels: Koninklijke Vlaamse Academie van België, 1966), col. 772, notes the date of the marriage as after 9 May 1346 ("na 9 mei 1346"). An entry for 28 May 1349, in the Cartulary of Louis of Male refers to Elisabeth as the wife of van Halen, not the wife of Arnold. See Thierry de Limburg-Stirum, ed., *Cartulaire de Louis de Male, Comte de Flandre: Decreten van den grave Lodewyck van Vlaenderen 1348 à 1358*, 1 (Bruges: Imprimerie de Louis de Plancke, 1898), 212. However, the exact date of Arnold and Elisabeth's marriage is elusive. For a short biography of Arnold of Rummen, see Jules de Chestret de Haneffe, "Oreye, (Arnould d')," *Biographie nationale*, 16 (Brussels: Émile Bruylant, 1901), cols. 248–255; see also Mathias Joseph Wolters, *Notice historique sur la Commune de Rummen et sur les anciens fiefs de Grasen, Wilre, Bindervelt et Weyer, en Hesbaye* (Ghent: Imprimerie de Léonard Hebbelynck, 1846), 103–123.

35   For heraldry in KBR 9427, see Gaspar and Lyna, *Les principaux manuscrits à peintures*, 1:347 and Mary E. Wolinski, "Plainchant and the Aspirations of a Noble Couple: The Psalter of Arnold of Rummen and Elisabeth of Lierde" (paper delivered at the 43rd International Congress on Medieval Studies, 2008, Kalamazoo, MI, 9 May 2008, and at A Celebration of the Teaching Career of Edward Nowacki, College-Conservatory of Music, University of Cincinnati, 17 May 2008); heraldry in KBR 9217 is also identified and discussed in this paper. For heraldry related to the Rummen-group manuscripts, see Appendix 1.

36   Philippe de l'Espinoy, *Recherches des antiquitez et noblesse de Flandres* (Douai: Marc Wyon, 1631), 66, writes that Simon had two daughters with Elisabeth, one of whom married in 1350, around the time Elisabeth married Arnold. He also writes that Elisabeth's marriage to Arnold was recorded in the same register as that of her daughter, though he does not attach a date to Elisabeth's marriage. However, according to both Rogghé and de Pauw, the daughters were from Simon's earlier marriage, or at least from a prior liason. See Rogghé, "Simon de Mirabello," 9, and de Pauw, "Mirabello (les)," col. 872.

INTRODUCTION

Louis's father.[37] However, most of Elisabeth's property in Flanders and her right to live in ten Walle were remitted to her in 1357.[38] In addition, in Louis's skirmish with Brabant between 1355 and 1357, Arnold sided with his employer Wenceslas of Bohemia, Duke of Brabant (1355–1383), against his wife's nephew and refused to do Louis homage when the latter entered Brabant as victor.[39] Louis ordered the confiscation of Arnold's property in retaliation.[40]

The manuscript was almost certainly caught up in the catastrophic demise of the County of Loon, a fact of some historical interest. Arnold of Rummen was a man whose ambition to become Count of Loon outpaced his judgment.[41] He was the son of Johanna of Loon, Lady of Quaetbeecke (Quabeek, Kwabeek), and her second husband, William of Oreye and Rummen. On his mother's side Arnold was the grandson of Arnold V of Loon and Chiny (Count 1279–1323) and nephew of Louis IV of Loon and Chiny (Count 1323–1336).[42] As his descent with respect to Loon was through his mother, the younger of Arnold V's two daughters, Arnold of Rummen had only a dubious claim to the office of Count. In 1331 Arnold's father William, his mother Johanna, and Arnold were given Rummen in fief by Johanna's brother Count Louis IV.[43] Four years later, in 1335, Arnold and Johanna renounced any claim on Loon to Arnold's cousin Diederik of Heinsberg, the nephew and designated heir of Count Louis IV, in return for several properties.[44] Diederik became count in 1336. Having no male heir, he designated as successor his nephew Godfried of Dalenbroek, grandson of Johanna's sister Matilda and thus Arnold's first cousin once removed. But when Diederik died in 1361, the countship was contested by Engelbert of the

Marck, the prince-bishop of Liège, who took the title of Count to himself, citing an imperial decree of 1246 that provided reversion of the fief to the bishop if the vassal died without male issue.[45] Thus a crisis of succession was generated, as both Godfried of Dalenbroek and Bishop Engelbert claimed the countship.[46]

Arnold meanwhile served in the court of Duke Wenceslas of Brabant and his wife Johanna. He was prominent in the affairs of governance: He attended an assembly of the estates of Brabant at Cortenberghe in 1350; in 1355 he joined the declaration of the communes of Brabant and Limburg affirming desire for a common sovereign.[47] Around 1356 he became the Duke's seneschal, a high judicial official whose position was well compensated. Arnold's marriage to the wealthy Elisabeth of Lierde had greatly increased his means. Around the time of his marriage Arnold began building a magnificent, costly castle in Rummen. This endeavor was supposedly a cause of great ill will, as Arnold forced the peasants of his domain not only to work on the castle but to provide building materials at their own expense.[48]

Bishop Englebert was not willing to cede the County of Loon to Godfried. In April of 1361 Engelbert marched into the county with a municipal army and soon occupied much of its territory, handing Godfried a defeat at Stokkem. Shortly thereafter, Arnold purchased the countships of Loon and Chiny, or at least the right to pursue them, from the dispirited Godfried. His hold on Chiny was short-lived, however; financial difficulties forced him to sell his rights to the county to Duke in 1364.

The emperor Charles IV reprimanded Engelbert by investing Arnold with the fief of Loon in 1363.[49] Thinking he had the support of the Emperor and of the Duke of Brabant, Arnold marched with a military force into Loon

---

37   This surrender of rights to Louis was confirmed in 1351; see Wolters, *Notice historique*, 106 and 387–390.

38   Rogghé, "Simon de Mirabello," 21–22.

39   De Chestret de Haneffe, "Oreye," col. 249. Nicholas, *Medieval Flanders*, 226, briefly summarizes the Brabant campaign and some of its aftermath.

40   Wolters, *Notice historique*, 107, 392–393.

41   Arnold is cited for his magnificence and lavish spending in Jacques de Hemricourt, *Miroir des Nobles de Hesbaye* (Liège: Imprimerie de J. F. Bassompierre, 1791), 206.

42   J. Baerten, *Het graafschap Loon (11de–14de eeuw): ontstaan politiek-instellingen* (Assen: *Van Gorcum and Comp. N.V.*—Dr. H. J. Prakke and H. M. G. Prakke, 1969), 253, provides a genealogy of the Counts of Loon. Chiny, to the south, was linked with Loon beginning in the thirteenth century through the marriage of Arnold IV of Loon and Jeanne de Chiny (p. 87).

43   Wolters, *Notice historique*, 103; 231–234. Haagdorens, "Sint-Truidense handschriften," 262–264, provides a good summary of relevant events in Arnold's life.

44   Wolters, *Notice historique*, 104; 378–386; de Chestret de Haneffe, "Oreye," col. 248.

45   De Chestret de Haneffe, "Oreye," col. 250; Baerten, *Het graafschaap Loon*, 141, 148.

46   On the succession crisis in Loon, see Baerten, *Het graafschap Loon*, 141–150; J. Lyna, *Het graafschap Loon: politieke en sociale overzichtelijke geschiedenis* (Beringen: Drukkerij J. Peeters, 1956), 82–84.

47   Wolters, *Notice historique*, 106–107, 391.

48   The tone of historical commentary on Arnold is highly partisan. Wolters, *Notice historique* 114–115, presents him as a valiant defender of his family's ancient patrimony; de Chestret de Haneffe, "Oreye," cols. 249–250, paints him as a cruel taskmaster and a scurrilous oath-breaker.

49   Wolters, *Notice historique*, 110–111, 114; de Chestret de Haneffe, "Oreye," col. 251. Wolters states that this first act of investiture was confirmed by a second act later that year. However, de Chestret de Haneff states that, questions of adjudication having been raised by a tribunal of judges assembled in Bohemia in December of 1363 to hear the case, the emperor decided to postpone the decision of the dispute.

and soon came into conflict with John of Arkel, who had recently replaced Engelbert as the prince-bishop of Liège. Unfortunately, Arnold received no reinforcements from either the Emperor or the Duke.[50]

At this point the chronology has some uncertainties, but the most likely timeline of events is as follows: The bishop's forces from Liège joined villagers from Sint-Truiden and laid siege to Arnold's castle on 11 August 1365. After nine weeks the defenders surrendered; they were conducted to the fortress at Musal on 14 October.[51] The forces of Liège burned the castle, filled in the moats, and demolished every vestige of the structure. Arnold and Elisabeth fled to Ghent, where she died "of grief" in March of 1366.[52] On 21 September 1366, the humiliated Arnold renounced his claim on the County of Loon before the bishop and the chapter of St. Lambert in Liège.[53] He retired to Liège where, encumbered by debts, he died in 1373.[54] Arnold's renunciation occurred nine days after the manuscript's completion on 12 September 1366. Details are obscure, but Arnold faced financial ruin and may have been compelled to sell his manuscript to his nephew by marriage, Louis of Male, with whom Arnold's relations were not good, as has been seen.

The second colophon can be viewed in the light of these events. It titles Arnold Lord of Rummen and Baron of Quaetbeecke ("*arnoldus . dominus . de . rimmen . et . de . quaetbeecke . Baro.*"), two lesser properties that came to him through his mother.[55] The colophon does not mention Loon or Chiny, the two greater prizes. The fortunes of Arnold were greatly diminished by 1366; Loon was lost and Chiny, to which he had rights for only two or three years, had slipped away. He was formally to renounce his claim to Loon only a few days after the completion of the manuscript. Although "*Orate pro eo*" is a standard expression, it takes on added poignancy, where, as the final sentence of the second colophon, it may reflect the scribe's appeal to his readers on behalf of the blighted Arnold.

It is hardly surprising that a manuscript created proximate to a major European war, to regional conflicts over territory and succession, and to historic urban upheaval should bear the imprint of multiple disruptions. The illumination and penwork manifest significant differences in style that indicate a break in the first campaign of illumination and a change of artists when the endeavor was resumed ten to fifteen years later. Furthermore, these changes happen within quires and in some cases even upon the page. A disruptive change in ownership at a very early stage of the missal's existence is evidenced by the numerous overpaints. Multiple difficulties and complications are tightly woven into the fabric of the design and execution. Careful study can begin to address them, while also elucidating some extraordinary aspects of theological and conceptual content, producing some insights into the rich dynamics of the workshops that produced 10 A 14, and enhancing appreciation of the fertility manifested in its decoration.

Ms. 10 A 14 is mentioned in the inventory of the estate of Philip the Good, 1469, and in the inventory of the library of the Dukes of Burgundy, 1485–1487.[56] It is mentioned by the cleric and historian Antonius Sanderus in his *Bibliotheca Belgica Manuscripta*, 1641–1644, but not in the catalog of the librarian Philippe, made in 1731 after a fire in the palace at Brussels; thus the manuscript may have left the Duke's library in the interim.[57] This conjecture is given further credence by an inscription in a

---

50   For an account of events between 1361 and 1366 and speculation on the reasons for the inaction of Charles IV, see Fritz Quicke, *Les Pays-Bas à la veille de la période bourguignonne 1356–1384: Contribution à l'histoire politique et diplomatique de l'Europe occidentale dans la seconde moitié du XIVᵉ siècle* (Brussels: Presses de Belgique, 1947), 105–107, 125–130.

51   Nine weeks: Eugène Bacha, *La chroniquel liégeoise de 1402* (Brussels: Librairie Kiessling et Cᵉ, 1900), 354; and de Chestret de Haneffe, "Oreye," col. 253. Baerten's statement (*Het graafschap Loon*, 150) that the siege lasted nine months appears to be an error. This siege is cited by J. Lyna, *Het graafschap Loon*, 84, as the first instance of the use of the blunderbuss firearm in the Netherlands.

52   De Chestret de Haneffe, "Oreye," col. 254. De Pauw, "Mirabello," col. 877, gives the date of her death as 27 March 1365; Wolters, *Notice historique*, 122, places her death in 1367. She was buried in the Church of St. Pharailde in Ghent, next to Simon of Mirabello, her first husband.

53   S. Bormans and E. Schoolmeesters, eds., *Cartulaire de l'Église de Saint-Lambert de Liège* (Brussels: Librairie Kiessling et Cᵉ, 1900), 4:434–435; Baerten, *Het graafschap Loon*, 150. However, J. Lyna, *Het graafschap*, 84, gives the date of renunciation as 11 September 1366; G. I. Lieftinck, *Les manuscrits d'origine étrangère*, vol. 1 of *Manuscrits datés conservés dans les Pays-Bas: catalogue paléographique des manuscrits en écriture latine portant des indications de date* (Amsterdam: North-Holland Publishing Company, 1964), 50; and Boeren, *Catalogus van de handschriften*, 17, repeat this date of 11 September. Bacha, ed., *La chronique*, 354–355, and Wolters, *Notice historique*, 122, place the renunciation in 1367.

54   See Wolters, *Notice historique*, 344–347, for the text of Arnold's will, dated 1370.

55   De Chestret de Haneffe, "Oreye," col. 248.

56   Bousmanne and Hoorebeeck, *La librairie*, 1:104. Thomas Falmagne and Baudouin van den Abeele, *Dukes of Burgundy* (Leuven: Peeters, 2016), 211.

57   Bousmanne and Hoorebeeck, *La librairie*, 1:107; see also François Joseph Ferdinand Marchal, Viglius Zuichemus ab Aytta, and Philippe Gaudence Emmanuel de Francquen, *Catalog des manuscrits de la bibliothèque royale des ducs de Bourgogne*, 3 vols. (Brussels: C. Muquardt), 1842.

INTRODUCTION

seventeenth-century hand, pricing the volume at 2 guilders 8 stuivers, on the inside cover (fig. 2).[58] The missal's whereabouts are unknown until 1830, when it surfaced at an auction by J. W. van Leeuwen in Leiden and was purchased by Bartholomeus van Holten, an agent of Baron van Westreenen.[59] The manuscript is bound in an eighteenth-century brown leather cover (figs. 1, 1a). The spine is ridged with rectangular bosses and stamped with gold stippling and filigree designs in rectangular panels. The color of the leather, the pattern of ridges on the spine, and the color and patterning of the spine's stamped gold decoration suggest the work of an early eighteenth-century bindery in The Hague.[60] The spine bears a label inscribed with the number 46, lot number of the manuscript in the Leiden auction of 1830.

10   Overpaints and Heraldry

The overpainting of shields and helmets has precluded identification of some heraldry in 10 A 14. Hyperspectral imaging might yield further information about overpainted elements.[61] A reading of currently decipherable overpaints is compatible with the historical record of Arnold's losses and of his conflicts with, and marital connections to, Louis of Male.

The ineptly overpainted helmets and shields on fols. 7r, 22r, 27v (figs. 15, 33, 39), and the obliterated donor figure, almost certainly Arnold, on fol. 143v were noted by Byvanck and have been remarked upon ever since.[62] Folios 7r and 143v were decorated during the first campaign; folios 22r and 27v, during the second campaign. Heraldry from both

campaigns was subjected to overpaints, executed during a brief third campaign initiated solely for that purpose.

The first overpaints are on fol. 7r (fig. 15). Seven shields painted inside the medallions studding the border bar are overlaid with coarsely shaped gold rosettes detailed in black. In addition, one helmet and one shield, both similarly overpainted with gold rosettes, flank the buttresses supporting the architecture of the miniature. The helmet is certainly Arnold's. The helmet of Oreye, home of Arnold's father, featured a crest of white plumes issuing from a bowl, and a black mantle. (See Appendix 1 for identification of heraldry.) The spray of plumes escaped the overpainting and is clearly visible. The shields can be read from the stains on fol. 7v (fig. 16), stains indicative of silver paint.[63] Four of the seven shields beneath the medallions have fields entirely of silver. These are almost certainly the arms of Oreye, which feature a black lion on a silver field. Three shields are quartered and silvered in quadrants 2 and 3. These could be the arms of Brabant; Margaret of Brabant was the wife of Louis of Male; Margaret's arms featured Flanders's lion impaled with quartered arms of Brabant-Limburg. If this is indeed the case, a question arises: Why did the arms of Brabant appear along with those of Arnold, where arms connected to Arnold's wife Elisabeth would be expected? Any explanation must engage the tangle of complexities evidenced by this manuscript's illumination.

Wolinski proposed a pivotal moment in the six months that separated the death of Elisabeth in March of 1366 and the completion of the manuscript in September of that year: At Elisabeth's death, arms had not been painted in the manuscript and so the shields prepared for her devices were left blank, while Arnold's were added.[64] Shortly after this, but presumably before the manuscript was completed, it came into the possession of Louis. At this point the arms of Louis's wife Margaret of Brabant were painted on the blank shields. This simple task having been completed, the illuminator was now confronted with the greater difficulty of converting Arnold's shields and helmet to Louis's. Instead of repainting Louis's arms over Arnold's, possibly with poor results (as evidenced in the clumsy conversions by overpaint of Arnold's arms to those of Margaret of Brabant in 9427, fol. 14r, fig. 177), a decision was made to conceal all the arms by overpainting. Thus, all work on the manuscript, including overpaints, would have been completed by the date of the colophon, 12 September 1366, and the manuscript would have been delivered to Louis rather than to Arnold. This

---

58   Inscription: *pro ligatura 2–8*. Boeren, *Catalogus van de handschriften*, 18.

59   Boeren, *Catalogus van de handschriften*, 17; Haagdorens, "Sint-Truidense handschriften," 270. De Mare places the acquisition in 1829 and names a price of ninety-two guilders; see A. J. de Mare, "Afbeeldingen van muziekinstrumenten in het handschrift van Priester Laurentius voltooid in 1366," in *Gedenkboek aangeboden aan Dr. D. F. Scheurleer op zijn 70sten verjaardag: bijdragen van vrienden en vereerders op het gebied der muziek* (The Hague: Martinus Nijhoff, 1925), 201.

60   Compare to the bindings of CKB, Mss. Thott 517.4°, a *Livret de saintes*, and Thott 547.4°, the Bohun Hours. See Lucy Freeman Sandler, *Illuminators and Patrons in Fourteenth-Century England: The Psalter and Hours of Humphrey de Bohun and the Manuscripts of the Bohun Family* (London: British Library, 2014), 165–168 and figs. 124 and 125.

61   Preliminary examination of overpaints by hyperspectral imaging was conducted in July of 2019 by Mr. Lionel Fiske and Professor Maurice Aalders of the Academic Hospital, Amsterdam. Results were indeterminate.

62   Byvanck, *Les principaux manuscrits*, 99–100.

---

63   These stains are discussed by Mary Wolinski, "Plainchant."

64   Wolinski, "Plainchant."

is a possible explanation for the presence of the quartered shield on fols. 22r and 27v; these were illuminated in the second campaign, the campaign ending in 1366, the year Elisabeth died. Perhaps the shields were drawn but not painted before her death. However, this reasoning is less convincing for the shields on fol. 7r. The decoration of this page, exclusive of overpaints, is of the first campaign. Presumably all the shields were drawn and four were painted during this campaign as well. Why would the remaining shields have been left unpainted for over a decade?

Other scenarios, none without difficulties, can be proposed. Perhaps the manuscript, including the page in question, was begun before Arnold finalized his marriage to Elisabeth in 1350. Why would three shields be left unpainted for more than a decade after the marriage was contracted? Furthermore, why would traces of Elisabeth's device be visible beneath overpainted shields in 9427 and 9217, both of which stylistically slightly predate 10 A 14?[65] Yet another possibility, though unlikely, is that the arms of Brabant were intended by Arnold as a nod to his patron and employer, the Duke of Brabant. Hyperspectral examination of the overpaints might yield more information for consideration of these perplexing issues.

On fol. 22r (fig. 34), illuminated during the second campaign, the shapes of two overpainted shields are legible in the intercolumniation under pairs of feathery foliage (figs. 34b, 34c). Silver stains of the two shields, the lower one quartered, are visible on fol. 22v (fig. 35). The plumey leaves are similar to those in the border bars but are painted with heavier, more contrasting white highlights and are less organically connected to the main tendril than are the other foliate elements. A flying angel in each of the four corners of the page originally bore a helmet trailing a black mantle and crested with white ostrich or cock's feathers. (See fol. 22r, lower right corner, fig. 34d.) These were clumsily and incompletely overpainted with scrolled tendrils bearing small flowers; elements of the plume and mantle of Arnold's helmet are visible in each location.

On 27v, the overpaints are more complex and more difficult to decipher. Two lions flank and face the text below the miniature of the Adoration of the Magi (figs. 39, 39a). One is below each of the two kneeling patrons, who are

positioned in architectural niches adjacent to the main scene. Each lion holds a silver sword in its right paw; below the left paw of each is a shield. The lions' heads, presumably helmed, are now comically concealed by overpaints; a tall pink bag covers the head of Arnold's lion. Where the mouth of the bag meets the lion's mane, the trailing edge of the black mantle of Arnold's helmet remains visible. The shield on Arnold's side is overpainted with a white-and-pink tendril on a blue field. Stains on fol. 27r indicate that the shield on Arnold's side had a silver field, as did the arms of Oreye.[66] A pot sprouting twigs, or stag horns, covers the head of the lion beneath Elisabeth. A tall fan of black peacock feathers, liberally salted with white eyes, is easily visible behind the twigs. The shield below Elisabeth's lion is overpainted with a geometric pattern in blue. Stains on fol. 27r reveal that this shield had silver quadrants 2 and 3 (fig. 38). The crest of Arnold's patron, the Duke of Brabant, features a peacock's tail but in the reverse coloration—dark eyes on light feathers. Moreover, given the position of the motif directly below Elisabeth, Brabant is not an immediately convincing association. What, then, is the significance of these feathers?

On fol. 143v the kneeling female figure (fig. 106a) is an image from the first campaign, never reworked or overpainted. She can be identified as Elisabeth, deceased in 1366 just before the completion of the manuscript.[67] The blank space in front of her, from which Arnold was erased and replaced by squares of the diapered background, looks oddly empty. Byvanck observed that the erasure of the kneeling donor was incomplete; his shoes remain. Outlines of his hair and praying hands remain as well, visible near the hands of the kneeling Elisabeth, and a fold of blue fabric, probably a remnant of his cloak, is visible near the lower buttons of her *cote*.

The identity of Louis of Male as the new owner is whispered, rather than trumpeted, in the overpaints. In the illumination of the Presentation in the Temple, fol. 167r (fig. 121a) dating to the first campaign, black-on-gold lions, the emblem of the Counts of Flanders, decorate the two panels hanging in front of the altar cloth. The paint on the panels is heavier, darker, and coarser in grain than is the

---

65 Wolinski, "Plainchant." Wolinski notes that the shields in question appear to have been inscribed with the letters PES, for Perweis, Eeklo, Somerghem, three of Elisabeth's properties. Perweis came to her through her first husband Simon of Mirabello; Eeklo and Somerghem were part of her dowry at her marriage to Arnold. See Wolters, *Notice historique*, 104–105 and n.1; de Pauw, "Mirabello (les)," 871–875.

66 It is worth noting that neither the arms of Chiny, which featured two gold salmon, addorsed on a red field, nor those of Loon, barry red and gold, ten pieces, appear in penwork and none, at least discernibly, beneath overpaints. (See Appendix 1.) Throughout it is rather the arms of Oreye that are imaged.

67 Boeren, *Catalogus van de handschriften*, 18, and Wolinski, "Plainchant," identify this woman not as Elisabeth but as an unknown later owner. However, the style of her figure is that of the first campaign. Boeren speculates that the manuscript may have been delivered upon its completion to this unknown woman.

INTRODUCTION

paint elsewhere in the image. The black and gold match those of the palette used to paint the rosettes on fol. 7v. The lions were likely added during the campaign of overpaints, imprinting this image with the mark of Louis, the manuscript's new owner. Thus, the overpainter not only covered arms of Arnold in various places but also added a new touch that referenced the identity of the new owner.

If the second owner of the manuscript was Louis of Male, as seems likely, he is the obvious answer to the question, "Who was responsible for the overpaints?" But if so, why did Louis have Arnold erased and leave Elisabeth? His confiscation of his aunt's possessions in his early years of rule indicates that he bore some animus towards her at that point. However, he ultimately restored all her property in Ghent. Perhaps he regarded her, his blood relative, with more sympathy than he accorded Arnold, with whom his enmity was ongoing. The twin blows of the loss of the castle at Rummen and the loss her fortune were seen by contemporaries as tragic; she was said to have died of grief; after her death, great conflict ensued between Arnold and Louis over her property.[68]

If Louis took possession of the manuscript shortly after its completion, his aunt was not long dead. Perhaps the freshness of the loss, the poignancy of her suffering, and the solemn character of the devotional Crucifixion image prompted him to preserve the likeness of this close relative whose presence was already erased, so to speak, from the world, while sharp conflict with the widower over the disposal of her property fueled Louis's decision to erase Arnold, who was all too much a presence and an obstacle.

In sum, the overpaints in 10 A 14 suggest, though they do not prove, a change in ownership of the manuscript from Arnold to Louis just after the manuscript's completion in 1366. The overpaints were likely executed at Louis's behest—not as a part of the second campaign, which identifies Arnold and Elisabeth as commissioners, but shortly thereafter—in a brief third campaign. Some elements of the illumination remain unexplained; the overpainted quartered shields on fols. 7r, 22r, and 27v are chief among them. The third campaign was seemingly executed without the same careful finish or deliberation as the first two. Arnold's arms were incompletely concealed in numerous instances, as on fol. 22r, noted above; Arnold's very image was incompletely erased on the Crucifixion page, fol. 143v. In a penwork initial on fol. 147v, Arnold's helmet

(with white mantle) was ignored altogether (fig. 108). An element of haste is implied in these failures of complete coverage. The overpaint is often thick and clumsy and in tones inharmonious with the predominant palette. This third campaign was an ad hoc, perhaps half-hearted, endeavor.

11   Overpaints and Heraldry in KBR 9427 and KBR 9217

Both 9427 and 9217 provide evidence of a campaign of overpaints similar to that in 10 A 14. In 9427, the ownership of Louis of Male is emphatically asserted. As in 10 A 14, so also in 9427, shields received more attention from the overpainter than did Arnold's helmet. On fols. 43r, 81v, 100v, and 124r, several shields were covered over, while Arnold's helmet was bypassed. On each of these pages the helmet is visible adjacent to the historiated initial (figs. 180, 182). Arnold's helmet was overpainted with Louis's on fol. 14r, bas-de-page (fig. 177); Elisabeth's device was scraped off shields which were then repainted with Louis's black-on-gold lion on fols. 14r, 43r, 81v, and 100v, while Arnold's arms were clumsily overpainted with those of Margaret of Brabant, Louis's wife, on fols. 14r, 43r and 100v (figs. 177, 180).[69]

Similar overpaints occur in 9217, on fols. 11v, 33r, 115r, 116r, and 123r.[70] As in 10 A 14, some arms are covered over with heavy gold and black; the black-on-gold lion of Flanders and gold rosettes with black detailing are chief among the motifs imaged with this technique. Other overpaints are in opaque white and various other pigments, as is also the case in 10 A 14. Heretofore unremarked, the background on the Crucifixion page of 9217 includes numerous traces of helmets with white plumes and trailing mantles; these can only be Arnold's. (See discussions of 9217's Crucifixion in Chapter 5 and in Appendix 4, Pt. 3.) The smeared results from overpainting in 9427 are avoided in 9217, as also in 10 A 14.[71]

As is the case in 10 A 14, so also in 9427 and 9217, Arnold's helmet appears, untouched by overpainting, in the penwork decoration. In 9427 the helmet appears unaltered

---

68   "Tantamque tristiciam de destructione domus sue habuit quod parum supervixit. Ipsa mortua dominus de Rumynes maritus suus habuit magnam discordiam contra comitem Flandrie de bonis ejus." Bacha, *La chronique liégeoise*, 354. Also see de Chestret de Haneffe, "Oreye," 254.

69   Noted by Wolinski, "Plainchant." On fol. 20r of 9427, the three-line penwork initial *D(omine)* encloses a magnificent castle with twin cylindrical towers, a large arched doorway, battlements and a pitched or conical roof. This may well be a reference to Arnold's fine castle.

70   Overpaints in 9217 are enumerated and further described in Haagdorens, "Het zgn. missaal," 76–77.

71   As suggested by Wolinski, "Plainchant."

in initials, mostly three liners, on ten different pages.[72] In 9217, the helmet is found in two-line penwork initials on fols. 8v and 45v. Why was the heraldry in penwork left untouched? Perhaps the medium of ink did not lend itself to alteration.

---

72 Arnold's helmet appears in initials on fols. 20v, 40r, 82v, 103v, 111v, 159v, 185r, 193r, 203v, and 221v, as noted by Wolinski, "Plainchant."

In conclusion, the techniques of overpainting and the selection of elements both targeted and bypassed are similar in 9427, 9217, and 10 A 14. Overpainting in all three manuscripts likely occurred after Louis's acquisition of them and as part of the same campaign, initiated at his direction. In 10 A 14, there is considerable evidence of haste in the conduct of the alterations; perhaps it was the last of the three to be overpainted.

CHAPTER 2

Contents, Codicology, and Script

This chapter will review the content, physical construction, and script of the manuscript, and their significance for the circumstances of its creation and the chronology.

1   The Calendar

The calendar (fols. 1r–6v, figs. 3–14) has one page for each month. It is not graded. (See Appendix 2 and Chapter 6 for transcription and further discussion.) Among its red-letter feasts are several for Liège-honored saints, including Servatius, Lambert, and Hubert.[1] Leonard, venerated in Liège and Sint-Truiden, is given a red-letter feast.[2] A number of other saints associated with Liège, Cologne, and/or areas nearby are also in the calendar.[3] In addition, and perhaps of some significance for the origins of the manuscript, two feasts are specific to Ghent: the deposition of Macharius, entered simply as Macharius, and Amalberga.[4]

Following the calendar, the Temporale text begins with the First Sunday in Advent and continues through Good Friday. The Ordinary of the Mass begins with preparatory prayers and continues through the Postcommunion and concluding prayers. Then follow the Sanctorale, with Proper of Saints, the Common of Saints, and finally various Masses. A summary of contents by quire is provided below. A more complete inventory of contents is found in Appendix 7.

2   Quires and Contents

The missal's 204 parchment folios are gathered in quires, primarily quaternions, as indicated below.

Quires have catchwords; some catchwords occur within quires.[5] A few pages have signatures, but in most quires

TABLE 1   Quires and contents

Quire	Construction	Folios	Contents
1	Ternion	1–6	Calendar
2–17	Quaternions	7–134	Temporale: Advent through Good Friday
18	Duernion	135–138	Continuation of Good Friday through the Creed
19	Quaternion	139–146	Prefaces of the Canon of the Mass. Ordinary of the Mass, 139r–142v with musical notation. Canon of the Mass through Commemoration of the Dead, 144r–146v
20	Duernion	147–150	Continuation of the Canon. Musical notation, 147v, 148r. Postcommunion prayers
21–26	Quaternions	151–198	Sanctorale (Proper and Common), various Masses
27	Ternion	199–204	Various Masses, colophon

---

1   Respectively 13 May, 17 September, 3 November.

2   6 November.

3   These saints include Gudile 7 January, Aldegundis 30 January, Vedastus and Amandus 6 February, and Gertrude 17 March, as noted by Wolinski, "Plainchant." For saints particularly honored in Ghent, see Maurice Coens and Joseph van der Straeten, "Un Martyrologe du XIIe siècle à l'usage de Saint-Bavon de Gand (Brit. Mus., Egerton 2796)," *Analecta Bollandiana* 84, fasc. 1–2 (1966): 139–160. Gudile is not found in Liège calendars. See Judith H. Oliver, *Gothic Manuscript Illumination in the Diocese of Liège (c. 1250–c. 1330)*, (Leuven: Uitgeverij Peeters, 1988), 2:214.

4   Respectively 10 April and 10 July. Wolinski, "Plainchant": "Perhaps they were entered by a scribe in Ghent, who accidentally wrote them by force of habit." If the calendar, like the text, were written in Sint-Truiden, however, some other explanation for the two Ghent feasts would be needed.

---

5   Within Quire 6 (fols. 39–46), a catchword is written at the bottom of fol. 41v in a less formal script and in lighter ink than are the catchwords at the end of each gathering. The decoration of fols. 41–44 is by Artist 4 of the second campaign, while the decoration of fols. 39–40 and 45–46 is by Artist 2 of the first campaign. The unfinished state of the quire may have introduced potential confusion for Artist 4. In Quire 11 (fols. 79–86) at the bottom of fol. 79v a catchword precedes a folio that has no decoration on recto or verso; folios 81v–83r in this quire are also without decoration. The introduction of the catchword may have been necessitated somehow by these undecorated pages. In Quire 13 (fols. 95–102), a catchword at the bottom of fol. 97v cannot be explained by either of the scenarios above.

they are lacking.[6] Guide letters are visible beside most initials; on occasion, there are prompts in the margins for rubrics, as on fols. 199v and 200r.

3 Ruling

Pages measure about 37 × 26 cm; the text block is about 25 × 16 cm.[7] That the leaves have been trimmed (and at an oblique angle) is shown by the lateral prickings, which generally survive at the top of the page but at the bottom have been sliced off. Most text pages (those with the Canon of the Mass and following excepted) are ruled with a reddish-brown line in two columns of twenty-eight lines. Lines are spaced about 0.9 cm apart. Text columns measure 6.7 or 6.8 cm in width; the intercolumniation measures about 2.5 cm in width.[8]

Seven vertical lines and nine horizontal lines extend beyond the text block on most pages. The vertical lines extend to the top and bottom edge of each page; a single vertical line frames each side of the two text columns; another single vertical line marks the inside of each page's ruled area, near the stitching; double vertical lines mark the outer boundary of the page's ruled area. The horizontal lines end where they intersect the outermost vertical line on each side of the page. Double horizontal lines mark the top and bottom of each page's ruled area; on most pages, more than four-fifths of the page's area lies within the rectangle defined by the outermost vertical and horizontal ruled lines. Ruling does not organize or contain the penwork decoration; the disposition of the latter is independent of the former.

The space between the two lowermost horizontal lines is the usual locus of catchwords. The first, second, fourteenth, twenty-seventh, and twenty-eighth horizontal lines ruled for text extend beyond the text block to the outermost vertical ruled line. Three of these—the second, fourteenth, and twenty-seventh—do not cross the intercolumniation.

The text block is positioned on the page so that the inner margin, from seam to text block, is about half the width of the outer margin, from text block to the edge of the page. The lower margin, from text block to the bottom edge of the page, is about 2.5 times the corresponding height of the upper margin. The trimming of pages compromises precise assessment of original proportions of text block to page. Ruling is minimized on pages with major illumination in Quires 2–4; outside the text block, lines are absent or very lightly sketched. In subsequent quires this accommodation is absent, except on the Crucifixion page, fol. 143v, which has no ruling.

Quire 1 (fols. 1–6), the calendar, is ruled in one column of thirty-two lines, the text block measuring 29 × 15 cm. Single vertical lines frame the text block; four additional vertical lines create small compartments for the golden numbers, dominical letters, nones-ides-kalends, and countdown numbers. All vertical lines extend to the top and bottom of the page, whereas all horizontal lines stop at the edge of the text block. Text and decoration are placed differently on rectos and versos; outer margins are wider than inner on rectos; inner margins are wider than outer on versos. Quires 19 (fols. 139–146) and 20 (fols. 147–150), inscribed with chant for the Prefaces (fols. 139r–142v) and with prayers and chant for the Canon of the Mass and its sequelae (fols. 144r–149v), are ruled in two columns of the same dimensions and spacing as are the columns of the text folios.[9] Chant is notated in staves of four lines, with text below. The horizontal lines that frame the top and bottom of each column are single rather than double, and there is no middle-line extension. On pages with prayers of the Canon and those immediately following, lines are spaced about 1.5 cm apart, and the text block, comprising nineteen lines, is about 26.5 × 16 cm, a little taller than elsewhere; the lower margin is correspondingly reduced. On fol. 150r the text returns to twenty-eight lines per column. Three pages are blank: fols. 143r, 150v, and 204v.

Stitching that presumably attached protective flaps to cover miniatures appears at the top of the page on fols. 7r, 27v, and 192v. Trimming of pages is witnessed by sliced penwork loops and clipped foliage in the terminal complexes in some upper margins (e.g., 105v, 106r, 204r). Small

---

6 The following folios have signatures: 18r (Quire 3); 58r (Quire 8); 65r partial, and 66r (Quire 9); 79r (Quire 11); 147r partial, 148r and 149r, the latter two cognates in a quire of two bifolia (Quire 20); 192r (Quire 26).

7 Measurements to the nearest millimeter, which of course vary from page to page, are of little use for most purposes; Byvanck, *Les principaux manuscrits*, 99: 370mm × 267mm; P. J. H. Vermeeren and A. F. Dekker, *Inventaris van de handschriften van het Museum Meermanno-Westreenianum* (The Hague: Staatsdrukkerij en Uitgeverijbedrijf, 1960), 21; and Boeren, *Catalogus van de handschriften*, 17: 368mm × 260mm, text block 205 mm × 157 mm. The figure of 205mm for height of text block seems to be an error, perhaps a reversal of the last two digits, as the ratio of height to width of the text block is consistently just a little under 1.6. Haagdorens: 370 × 267mm, text block 249/250 × 160mm. Website of the Koninklijke Bibliotheek, The Hague: 368 × 265, text block 247 × 160 mm. http://manuscripts.kb.nl/show/manuscript/10+A+14. Accessed 21 June 2022.

8 In 10 A 14, the placement of the ruling on the page, the number and formatting of the ruled lines, and the spacing of the lines is similar, though not identical in every respect, to the corresponding features in 9217. See Haagdorens, "Het zgn. missaal," 16–19.

---

9 A few irregularities can be noted, as for example the extra horizontal line at the bottom of the text block, fol. 145v.

CONTENTS, CODICOLOGY, AND SCRIPT 19

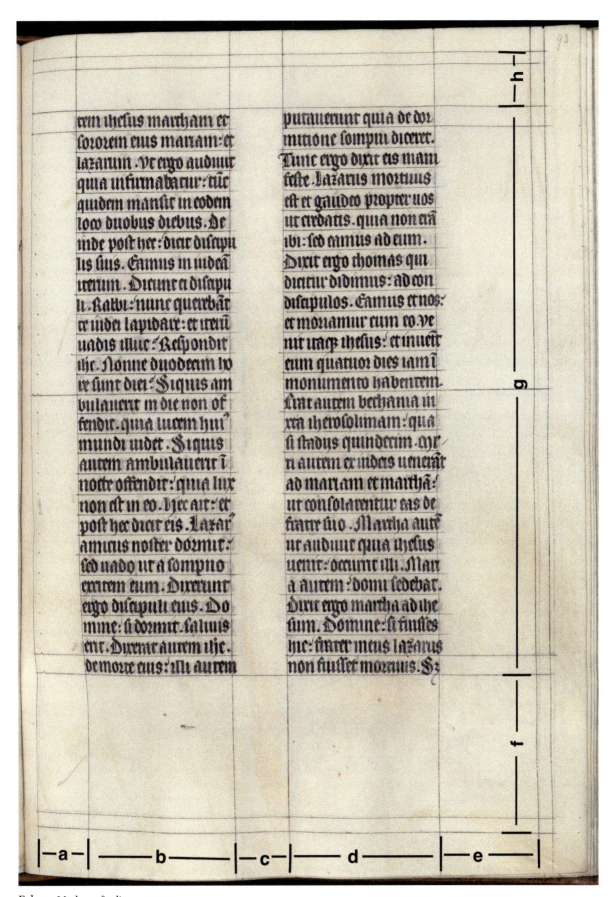

Fol. 93r: Markup of ruling
a. 2.1cm. b. 6.8cm. c. 2.5cm. d. 6.8cm. e. 5.1cm. f. 6.7cm. g. 25cm. h. 0.9cm. (Scale: approx. 1:3). Winter Missal of Arnold of Rummen, Sint-Truiden (text), Ghent (decoration and illumination), c.345–1366, fol. 8v, detail. The Hague, Huis van het boek, Ms. MMW 10 A 14
PHOTO: HUIS VAN HET BOEK, MARKUP: AUTHOR

rips in the parchment are sewn on a number of folios.[10] Other minor defects such as small holes (e.g., fol. 89) and patches (e.g., fols. 24, 83, 84) mark more than a few pages. Quires 8 (fols. 55–62) and 12 (fols. 87–94) have the most pages with imperfections. On the whole, pages of Artist 1's quires have fewer of these imperfections than do pages of Artist 2's quires.

4 Script

The script is a formal Gothic bookhand written in dense black ink, judged to be the work of a single scribe.[11] Text is inscribed a little above the ruled line. On text pages of twenty-eight lines, script is of two sizes, one slightly larger than the other. The size of the script changes at the beginning of each prayer, perhaps as a visual aid to the celebrant. On folio 154v, for example (fig. 113), the Offertory is written in the smaller script, the Secret in the larger, the Communion in the smaller, and the Postcommunion in the larger. The next prayer, the Introit for the Holy Innocents, is in the smaller script, followed by the Collect, in the larger. However, the reading from the Apocalypse, immediately after the Collect, is also in the larger script; it is generally the case that the two scripture readings, wherever they fall in the sequence of alternations, are in the larger script.

The script displays virtually all significant features of Northern Textualis formata; it can be classified more specifically as Textualis quadrata (the second most formal grade of the script), in consequence of the pointed serifs at the headline and baseline of minims.[12] Ascenders and descenders are short. The ascenders are never looped at the top. The use of the two-compartment *a* is ubiquitous; a scribal peculiarity is the closure of the lower compartment by a hairline whose direction—rising, falling, or horizontal—varies. Straight *s* is used at the beginning and in the middle of a word, round *s* as the last letter. Round *r* follows letters with bows: *b*, *d*, *p*, as well as *o*.[13] The top of ascender in *b*, *l*, *h* is bifurcated, generally by the addition of a short, angled hairline stroke to the left. Spurs appear

very rarely except on upright *s* at the headline, where they are a product of construction rather than embellishment. Decorative hairline flourishes are relatively few; *z* is the letter most often given hairline extensions. An occasional terminal *t* is thus flourished with a vertical downward line.[14] Fusions are used freely and flexibly throughout the text, often to justify the right margins. The letter pairs so treated include *ba, bo, da, de, do, og, oo, pe, po, pp*, and *vo*.[15]

Abbreviations, suspensions, contractions, superscript letters, and special characters for letters and combinations of letters are used multiple times on every text page; they are especially abundant in the rubrics.[16] Some marks have an ad hoc character; meaning is read by context as much as by form. The tilde-like, short convex arc and the apostrophe, used generously for both contractions and suspensions, function as generic tools of flexible application, used to produce efficiency and economy of communication and to conform lines of script to the standard length. Line fillers are rare. These are to be distinguished from line-endings, which are also rare, but are decorative as well as functional.[17]

The scribe employs the *punctus* and *punctus elevatus*, both followed by a minuscule, for short pauses. A *punctus* followed by a majuscule indicates a final pause. The question mark is used as well, as on fol. 8va, ll. 6, 15.

In spite of the quality and precision of the script, there are scribal mistakes of various sorts. In the calendar, the letters *ty* are entered on the line for 23 January (fol. 1r); the scribe must have quickly realized the mistake, for the inscription was abandoned. On the line below, 24 January, *tymothei apli*, is entered correctly. Likewise, on fol. 17vb, l. 14, the word *unigeniti*, mistakenly inscribed, is struck from the Collect. On fol. 7r, l. 12, the convex arc above the *o* in *comessationibus* is unnecessary. On fol. 11va the first reading for the Wednesday of Ember Week in Advent (*feria iiii in quattuor temporibus*) is labeled Jeremiah although it is from Isaiah.

---

10   Fols. 1, 6, 44, 49, 58, 59, 61, 68, 78, 87, 89, 91, 92, 94, 199.

11   The ruling, script, and some elements of decoration are similar to those of a group of manuscripts with a destination for the Abbey of Sint-Truiden. These are discussed in Chapter 7.

12   See the discussion of Northern Textualis in Albert Derolez, *The Palaeography of Gothic Manuscript Books: From the Twelfth to the Early Sixteenth Century* (Cambridge: Cambridge University Press, 2003), 72–101.

13   Examples from fol. 98ra: *Libri*, l. 16; *draconem*, l. 21; *protectione*, l. 4.

---

14   Fol. 8va, l.9.

15   Fusions: *ba*: fol. 98rb, l.24; *bo*: fol. 35ra, l.3; *da*: fol. 34ra, l.7; *de*: fol. 197rb, l.14; *do*: fol. 97va, l.13; *og*: fol. 28va, l.10; *oo*: fol. 149va, l.8; *pe*: fol. 97va, l.4; *po*: fol. 32vb. l.19; *pp*: fol. 16rb, l.4; *vo*: fol. 32vb, l.17.

16   For a discussion of abbreviations, contractions, special characters, and punctuation, see Bernhard Bischoff, *Latin Palaeography: Antiquity and the Middle Ages*, trans. Dáibhí Ó Cróinín and David Ganz (Cambridge: Cambridge University Press, 1990), 150–178.

17   Line filler in the form of a vertical zigzag, similar to the type described by Derolez, *Palaeography*, 186, is found on fol. 32vb. l. 15. Colophon 2, fol. 204r, has four line-endings.

CONTENTS, CODICOLOGY, AND SCRIPT

5 Rubrics and Directives

Ms. 10 A 14's rubrics label scripture readings and prayers: Preface, Introit, Collect, Psalm, Offertory, Secret, Communion, Postcommunion, etc. Designations for these prayers are highly and unsystematically abbreviated. Rubrics identify the day in the liturgical calendar (e.g., Vigil of the Nativity of the Lord, first Sunday after the Nativity of the Lord) at the Introit of each set of propers and for a few chants on the pages with musical notation. They also provide instructions for the priest's actions, especially during the liturgies of the Triduum, and prompt the priest, in turn, to direct the actions of the worshippers.[18] The Holy Week Passion narratives from the gospels, fols. 107v–133v, are marked within the text by small red superscript letters for the different speaking parts; placement of these letters, in turn, is keyed to the presence of guide letters in the adjacent margins.

In Quires 2–17, large asterisks, presumably cues for the illuminator, are very lightly sketched in plummet or graphite in the margins beside painted initials (e.g., fol. 11v, fig. 24, beside initial *R*[*orate*]). Asterisks are not found in Quires 21–26, all decorated by Artist 1. The asterisks may have been sketched by Artist 2 to mark his Introits for decoration. Artist 1, not planning so to mark the Introits, had no need for the asterisks. On fol. 40v, where Artist 2's painted initial seems erroneously placed, marking the Postcommunion rather than the Introit, there is no asterisk.

6 Decoration

Each page of the calendar has painted and illuminated borders on three sides, with extensions into the fourth side, and a pair of medallions depicting signs of the zodiac and labors of the months (figs. 3–14). Borders are constructed of gold bars and baguettes sprouting trilobes, grotesques, and feathery foliage. KL initials, on gold leaf, are hybrid constructions of decorated lettering and small grotesques.

At the opening of the Canon of the Mass, fols. 143v–144r (frontispiece; figs. 106, 107), a full-page Crucifixion miniature set within an architectural frame is paired with a *Te igitur* miniature and figural initial, accompanied by nearly full borders with bas-de-page vignettes. Ten additional pages with miniatures and/or initials of three to ten lines in conjunction with full or nearly full borders mark Introits of important feasts or liturgical events: fols. 7r, 22r, 26r, 27v, 106v, 139r, 151r, 167r, 176v, 192v. These are decorated with bars, baguettes, foliage, flowers, figures, animals, and grotesques in quite a variety of types and combinations. On four of these pages the border bar and attendant decoration extend through the intercolumnar space.

Numerous initials, penwork and painted, of two to four lines, most in blue or gold and accompanied by partial borders or extensions, mark the beginnings of prayers, versicles, and various divisions of the text. Every column of text with at least one two-line initial is accompanied by a border bar and penwork flourishing.

---

18 For discussion of the various functions of rubrics in late medieval manuscripts, see Kathryn M. Rudy, *Rubrics, Images and Indulgences in Late Medieval Netherlandish Manuscripts* (Leiden: Brill, 2017), 3–29.

CHAPTER 3

Penwork Initials and Borders

In this chapter, the various penwork initials and borders in 10 A 14 are described and characterized. The artists are referenced summarily, in order to facilitate discussion of these penwork elements, as stylistic differences are in no small part attributable to different hands. In Chapter 4, attention shifts from the decoration to its makers: There the identities and oeuvre of the artists will be considered.

Artists 1 and 2 worked during the first campaign; evidence of artistic style and depictions of clothing suggest a date of 1345–1355 for this campaign. Work was apportioned by liturgical sections. Artist 1 was responsible for the calendar (Quire 1) and the Sanctorale (Quires 21–26); Artist 2 did much of the work in the Temporale (Quires 2–18), though he did not complete these quires, and in Quire 27.[1] In Quires 19 and 20, the Ordinary, the two artists shared the work. In the second campaign of c.1365–1366, Artist 3, with the assistance of Artist 4, reprised unfinished work by Artist 2 in Quires 3–6, 9, and 14. Circumstances as well as artistic style and fashions in clothing testify to the date. The question as to whether Artists 2 and 3 were the same person, whose work was interrupted by a 15-year interval, will be considered.

1 One-Line Initials

Flourished one-line initials begin prayers written in the smaller script. These initials loosely alternate blue and gold. Blue initials are flourished red; gold initials, with blue or red. A variety of simple geometric and foliate motifs appear in counters and around the initials.[2] Unlike two-line initials, one-line initials are placed wherever they occur in the text. When one-line initials happen to find place at the start of a text line or in the lowest line of a column, embellishment may extend into the margin (fig. 115).[3]

2 Two-Line Initials

Two-line initials generally mark the beginnings of the scripture readings and of prayers written in script of the larger size. Penwork initials, which occur throughout the text quires of the manuscript, are distinguished from painted initials on the basis of medium and technique, though there is some overlap between the two types. In 10 A 14 the letterform of the two-line penwork initials is blue or gold. Two-line penwork initials, like their one-line counterparts, loosely alternate gold and blue in color, with many interruptions in strict pattern. Gold initials are most often flourished in purple or blue and blue initials in red, though this pattern has many variations, notably in Quire 2 and in the Quires 19 and 20, which have musical notation. Initials are drawn, colored and decorated with tinted, water-based wash; the gold wash is more nearly opaque than the blue. The tool is probably a pen, both for drawing the initial and applying the decorative penwork. The thickness of letterforms in the text testifies to the capability of the pen to create broad strips as well as fine lines. A fine brush could also be used for initials of this sort and for some elements of the border bar.

The ascenders or descenders of initials *F*, *H*, *L*, and *P*, and the tail of the *Q* add to the height of the initial but displace little text and do not add to the height or area of the counter, which is uniformly two lines in height and thus determines the designation as a two-line initial. The counter contains decorative motifs—geometric, foliate, animal, grotesque, and human. Technique is varied as well; among the techniques employed are hatching, cut-out effects, figure-ground reversals, grisaille, and dot patterns. The highly flourished, colorful penwork border bars that accompany penwork initials expand into the upper and lower margins in ensembles of herein named terminal complexes. These initials and borders will be considered later. Penwork around the letterforms is often shaped to suggest a squared frame, patterned and decorated with various elements.

---

1   See Inventory 1 for the distribution of flourishing by quire and artist. Apportioning work by liturgical divisions to illuminators of a missal occurs elsewhere in approximately contemporary manuscripts, as in the Temporale and Sanctorale of the Litlyington Missal of 1383–1384, London, Westminster Abbey, Ms. 37. For bibliography on the Litlyngton Missal, see Jayne Wackett, "The Litlyngton Missal: Its Patron, Iconography, and Messages" (PhD diss., University of Kent, 2014); see pp. 91–129 for a discussion of the missal's artists.

2   The term *counter*, in reference to a decorated or illuminated initial, is defined as "an area within the face of a letter wholly or partly enclosed by strokes" (*Merriam-Webster's Collegiate Dictionary*, 10th ed.).

3   Similarly embellished one-line initials occur on fols. 11v and 66r.

© KONINKLIJKE BRILL BV, LEIDEN, 2025 | DOI:10.1163/9789004427136_004

Two-line penwork initials are of particular interest for least four reasons. First, the flourishing attendant on them is one of the glories of this manuscript, competing with illumination in visual panache and outdoing illumination in variety, creativity, and abundance. Second, two-line penwork initials are the site at which the techniques and medium of pen and brush are in closest conversation, as noted in Chapter 1. Third, two-line initials are the site at which iconography of penwork and painting is shared: Faces, grotesques, and animals are depicted in two-line initials of both media. Fourth, penwork initials are the locus of the most playful and improvisational passages in the manuscript, as noted in Chapter 1 and as further explained in Chapter 4. Two-line initials challenge the notion of categorical distinctions in medium, technique and iconography. Two-liners function as a sort of growth node for change and exchange between media, fed by the interplay of imagination and convention. Thus, these initials are worthy of close attention. (See Tables 2–5.)

3 The Initial *I*

The initial *I* is singular, having no counter, by which other initials are sized, and no decoration internal to the letter, though often a penwork frame containing decoration surrounds it.[4] Nonetheless, in color, in connections to the penwork borders, and in use as the initial for a defined set of prayers and readings, *I*s are well integrated into the pattern established for two-line initials and can be considered with them. Positioned at the edge of the text column, mostly in the margin, *I* manifests a number of variations in form, the most obvious being convex and concave (figs. 30, 17. 5.). A few *I*-initials are figural (fig. 54). Both convex and concave forms of the letter are common in contemporary and earlier illumination. Except in Quire 2, in which all *I*-initials are concave three-liners, the former greatly outnumber the latter. In Quires 3–16 the *I* is five to eight lines in height and convex on the outside, flat for most of its length on the inside. The convex *I* is used with several variations, some seemingly playful. If it appears at the very bottom of the text block, it may be cracked open and placed in two sections at right angles to one another, so that the lower section runs horizontally, either flush with the text line or somewhat below it (fig. 84). Variations of this treatment are in contemporary and earlier manuscripts.[5] Decoration is inserted into the right-angled cleft. If the *I* occurs in the last few text lines from the bottom, it may project into the lower margin without cracking or angling; sometimes it carries with it the lower penwork border bar or a section thereof (fig. 75). Sometimes the *I* is upside down, its stem edging the text above the reading it introduces (fig. 68).[6] This configuration is in places a response to crowding from another two-line initial just below it and in others a device to avoid projection into the lower margin (fol. 156r, fig. 115). Although the form of both variants of the letter is standard, differences in the frequency with which they are used can be coordinated with differences in artists. Artist 1, discussed below, used variations of the *I* far more than did the other artists. This pair of characteristics—a standard formal vocabulary coupled with a personalized freedom of expression and variation—suggests a program of training which both respects artistic conventions and allows for innovation.

4 Initials in Musical Notation and Three- and Four-Line Penwork Initials

Pages with musical notation in the Prefaces and Canon (fols. 139r–142v, 147v–148r) are decorated with large penwork initials extending the full height of one set of musical lines. (See Inventory 7, Pt. B.) These initials are about equivalent in height to three lines of text in the Temporale and Sanctorale. Blue initials alternate with gold. Some initials are very laterally compressed. Flourishing is in green, mauve, and yellow as well as red and blue. In the Prefaces on fols. 139v–141r, the cross-inscribed letter *A* in *Aeterne*, first word of the Preface, is followed immediately by a tall, laterally compressed cadel initial *E* in brown ink (fig. 104). The inscribed *A* occurs elsewhere in the manuscript as the first letter of *Aeterne*, as on fol. 20v, but the cadel *E* is found only on the folios with music.

Three- and four-line initials mark several prayers in both the Temporale and the Sanctorale. (See Inventory 7, Pt. B, and Table 8.) In Quire 18 the Good Friday liturgy includes three-line penwork initials that begin the Gloria and the Creed (fol. 138r); the initial of the former is blue with red penwork and that of the latter is gold with green penwork. In Quire 21 the Feast of St. Stephen (fol. 152v) begins with a three-line initial. In Quire 24, the Introit of the Mass for the Vigil of an Apostle (fol. 178r, figs. 127, 127b) begins with an exceptionally decorative four-line initial, featuring the Apostle Andrew in front of his cross.

---

4 See Inventory 3 for types and frequency of *I*-initials in the work of each artist.
5 As in KBR 9217, fols. 16v, 80v, 95r.

6 The upside-down *I* is not found in KBR 9217; however it is found elsewhere in manuscripts of *c*.1340, as in the Missal of St. Vaast, MSV, Ms. 601, fols. 16r, 177r, 199v.

The Introit for the Mass of the Blessed Virgin Mary in Quire 26 (fol. 198v) is likewise marked by a four-line initial. It depicts an enthroned, crowned Virgin with the Child. Both initials are gold, with figures in grisaille and penwork in blue, brown, red, and yellow.

5 Penwork Borders and Their Flourishing

Study of border bars and their decorative attachments and extensions elucidates the creativity of the flourishing, reveals its potential and limitations for expression, and allows insight into the processes of development in decoration. I shall categorize and describe the four main types of border bars in order to show how they contribute to the beauty, variety, and abundance of flourishing. Penwork borders and their associated decorative flourishing occur as extensions of two-line initials, and thus are found on most pages in this manuscript. It is impossible to separate entirely discussion of the initials and borders as the two are connected physically, formally, and aesthetically. In Chapter 4 the personal, expressive use of border bars by each of 10 A 14's artists will be considered. (See also Inventory 2.)

Penwork borders have several parts, of which there are numerous variations. Borders have what may be termed an inner bar and an outer bar. The two strips are often separated by one or more very thin lines (figs. 43, 55). Additional lines may separate the inner bar from the text block (fig. 70a.). The inner bar is typically an extension of the letter form of a two-line initial. The inner bar generated by each initial ends above or below the next two-line initial in the text column and may extend into the upper or lower margin as an element of a terminal complex (figs. 24, 65) or end in a knob at the last ruled line (fig. 124, bottom of text column a).

The second major element of most borders is the outer bar of two or more colors, placed to the left of the inner bar and parallel to it. This bar is treated in various ways, categorizable as types. For the distribution of border bar types within quires, see Table 6.

Type 1, the most common, occurs in almost all quires of the manuscript and to the exclusion of all other types in Quires 21–26. It is composed of scalloped segments which alternate red and blue in color. Segments sprout nibs, often bifurcated and /or filamented, at regular intervals (figs. 32, 131). From the gaps between segments of the bar emerge filaments originating in the very thin lines between inner and outer bars. These bear foliate, floral or geometric motifs. In Quires 21–26, the motifs are almost exclusively ball-and-squiggle trilobes (figs. 115, 124).

Quire 2, by contrast, presents a plethora of motifs: Spirals of pearls or toothed pearls are accompanied by foliate sprigs of eight or nine varieties of ivy, maple, and prickle leaves (figs. 17, 21–23), in addition to buds, corkscrews, and both floating and anchored rosettes (figs. 26, 29). Thus, even so seemingly mundane an element as a border bar becomes a vehicle for creative variation.

Type 2, which appears less frequently in 10 A 14 than does Type 1, features blue and red segments articulated with a feathered, fringed, or comb-like motif (figs. 20, 45, 55). In Type 2, as Type 1, segments of a standard length are separated by filaments bearing various decorative motifs.

Type 3 bars have an inner strip but no continuous, solidly colored outer segments; for the latter is substituted a row of small motifs very closely spaced. This type occurs mostly in Quires 6–8. The effect is of a strip or band of openwork, of airy mesh, or of a net of many thin fibers (figs. 47, 53).

Type 4 differs markedly from the other three. It consists of a continuous, ribbon-like strip of uniform width, without scallops or feathering, colored in hatched or solid segments of red, green, and blue of various lengths. Embedded in the strips are pearls, buttons, or rosettes, some colored, and spaced at regular intervals (figs. 31, 82). The decorative motifs borne on stems spring from the bar at regular intervals. In Quires 10–13, in which Type 4 bars occur on almost every flourished page, the garnishing is of great variety and abundance. Oak leaves, acorns, and lilies (fig. 81) appear along with maple, ivy, and ball-and-squiggle trilobes (fig. 78). Some motifs are tiered: Blossoms open to support sprays of trilobes (figs. 70, 71). One finds spiraling strings of pearls, some beaded or spiked (fig. 79), in ever-changing combinations with rosettes, circle-complexes, and corkscrews (figs. 69, 76); with various foliate motifs; and even with small urns (figs. 70, 70a, 70b). On fol. 91v (fig. 82) a magnificent row of penwork butterflies lines the left margin.[7] The cumulative richness of effect in these quires is quite remarkable.

Common to all four types of border bars is the change of decoration at each two-line initial. The change may be in the color of some element of the bar or its flourished extension, in the direction of some element of flourishing, in the motif of some element of garnish—or some combination of these. Some changes are subtle; others, obvious.

Types 1 and 2 border bars are found in the Loppem-Bruges antiphonal and in 6426, 9427, 9217, and Douce 5–6 from

---

7 Compare with the upper margin of the Festal Missal of Johannes of Marchello, HKB, Ms. 78 D 40, Amiens, 1320s., fol. 1r; and with the right margin of the English Psalter of Queen Philippa, LBL, Ms. Harley 2899, 1328–c.1340, fol. 8r.

Ghent, as well as in fourteenth-century manuscripts of northern France and Cologne; Type 1 is more common than Type 2. Type 3 has a prototype of sorts in penwork from Sint-Truiden. (See Chapter 7.) Type 4 is known to me only in 10 A 14. Type 3 seems to be an experiment in lightening, aerating, the border bars. Type 4 is the rendering in penwork of a species of painted bar common in Flemish, French, Mosan, and Rhenish illumination. This bar consists of a thin colored strip decorated with geometric or simple foliate patterns and doubled by a baguette. Gold balls or gold studs are attached to the outside of the bar, as in the Ceremonial of St. Peter's Abbey, Ghent, of 1322 (fig. 164, hereinafter referred to as the Ghent Ceremonial), or are embedded within it at intervals, as in the psalter Ms. Douce 5 from Ghent of *c.*1330–1335 (fig. 150) and a missal from Cologne of *c.*1330 (fig. 158).[8] A similar bar often frames miniatures, as in the Bodley *Alexander*, Tournai, 1338–1344 (fig. 146).[9] The inner edge of the miniature's frame is a pink-and-blue strip with embedded gold balls. Transposition of the design from paint to ink may well have been Artist 2's idea, a transmedial innovation later employed by Artist 3, but not widely adopted by other flourishers.

6 Terminal Complexes

The border bars of almost all penwork pages spill into the upper and lower margins, where they produce elaborate terminal complexes (figs. 55, 112a), composed of segments of the border bar and/or its linear extensions, ornamented with leaves of many types in singles or multiples, rosettes, corkscrews, pearl strings. Artist 1's terminals include faces (fig. 112a) and fish (fig. 111, bottom).[10] Right-angle segments combine with ribbon-like forms and curves to create a rich decorative effect. The generous lower margins give more surface for expansion of the terminal complexes than do the upper margins. Likewise, on versos the left margin provides more space for development of complexes than does the right margin or the intercolumniation (fig. 55). In the quires of Artist 2, penwork loops and filaments often extend almost to the edge of the page. On rectos the right margin is not decorated, except where the terminal complex reaches the right side of the page. Terminal complexes of 9217 and 9427 resemble those of 10 A 14 in general design, and 6426 has very few penwork borders; their sparse extensions below the text block hardly qualify as complexes.

7 Conclusion

The border bars of 10 A 14 are extraordinary in their variety, far beyond what was usual in manuscripts of the era. They can hardly be dismissed as exercises in rote embellishment. Types 3 and 4 are novelties, one exploring the possibilities of dematerializing the border bar and the other of giving it weight, richness, and substance. Further, the translation of a painted border into the medium of penwork marks a creative venture. Chapter 4's reprise of the border bars analyzes each artist's treatment of these bars for patterns in occurrence, aesthetics, expression, and structural qualities.

Border decoration is an enterprise physically connected to the text through the origin of bars as extensions of two-line initials. Each two-line initial is marked by a change of some kind in the adjacent border bar, thus creating a pattern of decorative renewal. The borders, like their associated initials, are conceptually connected with the text: Each initial introduces a prayer or a scripture reading, which pulses into the border as a new and unique moment, decorative and spiritual, existential and eternal, in liturgical life. In a missal, which exists to

---

8   The Ghent Ceremonial is UGU, Ms. 233; see Albert Derolez, with assistance of Hendrik Defoort and Frank Vanlangenhove, *Medieval Manuscripts: Ghent University Library* (Ghent: Snoeck, 2017), 102, 105. The Ghent psalter, bound in two volumes, is OBL, Mss. Douce 5–6; see Elizabeth Solopova, "MS. Douce 5, MS Douce 6: SC nos. 21579, 21580; Portable Psalter," *Latin Liturgical Psalters in the Bodleian Library: A Select Catalogue* (Oxford: Bodleian Library, 2013), 379–387; Alison Stones, *Gothic Manuscripts 1260–1320* (London: Harvey Miller Publishers, 2013), pt. 1, vol. 2, cat. nr. III-74, pp. 344–354; Elizabeth B. Moore, "The Urban Fabric and Framework of Ghent in the Margins of Oxford, Bodleian Library, MSS Douce 5–6," in *Als Ich Can: Liber Amicorum in Memory of Professor Dr. Maurits Smeyers*, ed. Bert Cardon, Jan Van der Stock, and Dominique Vanwijnsberghe, Corpus of Illuminated Manuscripts 12 (Leuven: Uitgeverij Peeters, 2002), 983–1006, especially pp. 1004–1006. See also Mary Coker Joslin and Carolyn Coker Joslin Watson, *The Egerton Genesis* (London: British Library, 2001), 131, n. 5. The missal from Cologne is DUL, Ms. 876, Cologne, fol. 12r: See "Nr. 37: Missale, Köln, St. Kunibert, um 1330," Leo Eizenhöfer and Hermann Knaus, *Die liturgischen Handschriften der Hessischen Landes- und Hochschulbibliothek Darmstadt* (Wiesbaden: Otto Harrassowitz, 1968), pp. 127–132.

9   OBL, Ms. Bodley 264. For discussion of this manuscript and for further bibliography, see Cruse, *Illuminating the* Roman d'Alexandre; D. J. A. Ross, *Illustrated Medieval Alexander-Books in French Verse*, ed. Maud Pérez-Simon and Alison Stones with Martine Meuwese (Turnhout: Brepols, 2019), 74–94, 135–141, 149–150, 169–171; M. R. James, *The Romance of Alexander: A Collotype Facsimile of Ms. Bodley 264* (Oxford: Clarendon, 1933).

---

10   See Inventory 5 for the many faces in Artist 1's penwork.

facilitate confection of the Eucharist, this pulse can be termed *eucharisma*.

The pattern of decorative change at initials marks the work of both artists, but it is more pronounced in the work of Artist 2 than in that of Artist 1 (Cp. figs. 60, 112); perhaps Artist 2 was a priest, someone especially attuned to Eucharistic prayer. Additional evidence indicating a priestly identity for Artist 2 emerges from a study his iconography, both in penwork and in painting, as discussed in Chapters 4 and 5.

Penwork flourishing creates exuberant visual effects in this missal, rivaling and even outdoing illumination in the quality of design and execution. Arnold's patronage may have played some role in the visual pyrotechnics of decoration. By birth, by marriage, and by dint of effort, he was a man of wealth and social standing, with aspirations to rise considerably higher. For such a man, visual display for the proclamation of status may have been particularly important.

CHAPTER 4

The Flourisher-Illuminators of the Two Campaigns

This chapter will summarize the evidence for dating the campaigns of flourishing and illumination, review the scholarship relevant to the identification of 10 A 14's flourisher-illuminators, and specify the work and characterize the styles of the artists who executed these campaigns. The iconography of the illumination is considered in Chapter 5, along with style as it relates to the individual miniature or initial.

1 Two Campaigns and an Addendum

The decoration of 10 A 14 was produced in two campaigns, plus a third which hardly qualifies as more than an addendum. The first was the main campaign of illumination; the second was essentially a campaign to complete lacunae in the first; the third was the very limited enterprise of overpaints and a few other additions. The current study concludes that three or four artists were responsible for all decoration of the first two campaigns—the penwork initials, the penwork borders, the painted initials and borders, and the major illumination. One of the three artists probably worked in both campaigns. The third campaign, that of overpaints, though important for questions of commission and ownership, is given little attention here, as the overpaints are minimal in quantity in comparison with other types of decoration, are modest in quality, and were primarily conducted not to embellish but to conceal.

2 Scholarship on Illumination and Decoration

A century of scholarship slowly extracted from the manuscript's dense complexities the dates of 10 A 14 and the number of artists who worked on it. Scholars assigned various roles to Laurence, the priest-illuminator mentioned in the first colophon. The most significant contributions to the problem of artistic hands in 10 A 14 are those of Byvanck and Dennison. Byvanck's initial analysis of illumination served as the basis for later discussions and further distinctions in style.[1] He recognized two artists characterized by very different styles of illumination; one he identified as Laurence the Priest. In addition to the two artists, he proposed a fifteenth-century retoucher. He assumed

only one major campaign, dating to 1366, the year of the colophon, and named Ghent as the site of production.[2] For the next sixty years, art historians repeated his thesis of a single campaign, dated 1366 and localized in Ghent. His thesis of retouches was also adopted, though not the fifteenth-century date. Scholarly opinion differed on the number and role of illuminators.[3]

Observations of various sorts added breadth and context over time: Lieftinck noted that the two main artists shared the work in fols. 111–150, thus introducing the recognition of a close and complex collaboration between artists.[4] Boeren found the hand of the second artist, whom he identified as Laurence the Priest, in the final quire of the

---

1 Byvanck, *Les principaux manuscrits*, 99–101.

2 To the first artist Byvanck assigned the calendar and the initial letters and borders on fols. 139r, 151r, 167r, 176v, 192v, and the miniature on fol. 144r. The artist's somewhat old-fashioned style is characterized by competent modeling, strong color, and highly burnished gold leaf. A second artist did the miniatures and borders on fols. 7r, 22r, 26r, 27v, 106v, part of the border on fol. 144r, and the miniature on fol. 143v, though the full-page format did not suit his talent. He used softer color mixed with white and produced well-modeled, slender figures with ample, well-arranged draperies. The third artist, whom Byvanck associated with the second colophon, did the overpainting of arms and retouches on fols. 7r, 22r, 26r, 27v, and 143v, and repainted architecture on fols. 7r and 143v.

3 Panofsky cited three illuminators but discussed, briefly, only one miniature, the *Nativity* on fol. 22r, in which he saw a typically Flemish interest in establishing volume. See Erwin Panofsky, *Early Netherlandish Painting: Its Origins and Character* (New York: Harper and Row, 1953), 1:36 and 374, ns. 1 and 2. Like Panofsky, Vermeeren and Dekker, *Inventaris*, 21–22, saw three illuminators; one they identified as Laurence the Priest. Following the colophon, they cited 1366 as the date of completion. Lieftinck accepted Byvanck's division of the main work between two artists and assessed the second artist as the greater of the two. He did not detect more than one campaign and further consolidated the time of execution, suggesting that the original atelier may have done the overpaints. See Lieftinck, *Manuscrits datés*, 1:50. Boeren in the main followed Lieftinck; see *Catalogus van de handschriften*, 17. De Winter, *La bibliothèque de Philippe le Hardi*, 229–230, saw at least three illuminators and identified Laurence as the retoucher, an artist of lesser talent. In her thesis of 1983 Haagdorens reiterated Byvanck's identification of hands in 10 A 14—two main artists and one retoucher. After the appearance of Dennison's dissertation in 1986, Haagdorens recognized in fols. 22r, 26r, and 27v a third, more progressive hand, possibly Laurence the Priest, but she did not associate his work with a later campaign. See Vandecapelle-Haagdorens, "Het zgn. missaal," 180; Haagdorens, "Sint-Truidense handschriften," 271.

4 *Manuscrits datés*, 1:50.

© KONINKLIJKE BRILL BV, LEIDEN, 2025 | DOI:10.1163/9789004427136_005

manuscript.[5] De Winter saw Rhenish and Bohemian influence in the style of 10 A 14.[6] Vandecapelle-Haagdorens was the first to recognize that 10 A 14 and 9217 are two parts of the same missal.[7] She also argued for Sint-Truiden, rather than Ghent, as the site of production.[8]

The most comprehensive and astute consideration of artists in 10 A 14 was that of Dennison, who first clearly articulated two campaigns separated by some ten to fifteen years.[9] She convincingly dated the first campaign 1345–1355; the second, which was not limited to retouches and overpaints but rather was initiated to complete "an earlier abandoned project," she dated 1366.[10] She also defined characteristic features of artists' styles more fully than other scholars and made more specific connections between hands in 10 A 14 and hands in 6426, 9427, and 9217, the three Brussels manuscripts.

Dennison identified two hands, whom she termed Artist C2 and Artist B, in the first campaign of 10 A 14. Artist C2, the less problematic of the two artists, is essentially Byvanck's first artist and is for the most part the same as the herein designated Artist 1.[11] To Artist C2 she assigned the illumination of the calendar and six pages with major illumination.[12] Artist C2's style is linear and his palette cool. He outlines in black. His figures compare

to those of Pierart dou Tielt, who worked in Tournai during the 1330s and 1340s on French-influenced manuscripts such as in Bodley 264. Dennison correctly differentiated Artist C2 from the illuminator of 9217, whom she designated Artist C.[13] (See Appendix 4, Pt. 2, for discussion of the differences between these two artists.)

Dennison's Artist B is essentially identical to the artist herein designated Artist 2. This artist produced three pages of major illumination.[14] He exhibited considerable capacity for stylistic development. Dennison connected certain elements in his style with English illumination between 1345 and 1350, specifically with the heavy white modeling of the most progressive artist of the Luttrell Psalter and with the solidly constructed and vigorously modeled architecture and mannerisms of pose in the Fitzwarin Psalter.[15] Artist B's palette is hotter and his "dry, etched" technique is more painterly than the more mannered and linear style of his colleague, Artist C2. He outlines borders and foliage in red.

Artists of the first campaign had direct connections with the three aforementioned manuscripts in Brussels, all of which were produced shortly before 10 A 14. The antiphonal 6426 was first, followed by the liturgical psalter 9427, then a summer missal, 9217.[16] Artist B worked on initials and borders in both 6426 and 9427.[17] Very similar

---

5   *Catalogus van de handschriften*, 17. This observation must have been gleaned from penwork, as the final quire contains neither miniatures nor painted initials with extensions.

6   De Winter, *La bibliothèque de Philippe le Hardi*, 230.

7   Haagdorens, "Sint-Truidense handschriften," 267; Vandecapelle-Haagdorens, "Het zgn. missaal," 180. Ms. 10 A 14 ends with Good Friday; 9217 picks up with the Easter Vigil and continues through the twenty-fifth Sunday after Pentecost. Haagdorens's entry in "Sint-Truidense handschriften," 267, erroneously states that 9217 continues through the fifteenth Sunday after Pentecost. The twenty-fifth Sunday is correctly noted in "Het zgn. missaal," 26.

8   "Het zgn. missaal," 182–184; "Sint-Truidense handschriften," 270.

9   "Stylistic Sources," 115–119, and "Dating and Localisation," 509–514.

10   "Dating and Localisation," 510–511. In "Stylistic Sources," 124, she cited 1345–1350 as the most likely date for the first campaign of 10 A 14.

11   Nomenclature is one of the difficulties of tracking an artist across manuscripts, locations, and time, through research written by different scholars. An artist whose name is unknown is designated by a plethora of different criteria: by apparent degree of prominence in the production process, by a manuscript in which work is prominent, by striking features of style or motifs, or by order of appearance of work in the quires. However, often the frame of reference is reset for each manuscript; the same artist has a different designation in different contexts. Moreover, different scholars see the complex of relevant factors in different ways.

12   Pages, in addition to the calendar, with major illumination by Artist C2 (Artist 1 of 10 A 14): fols. 1–6 (figs. 3–14); fols. 139r, 144r, 151r, 167r, 176v, and 192v.

13   "Dating and Localisation," 509; Haagdorens, unlike Dennison, saw the same hand in the illumination of 9217 and in 10 A 14; see "Sint-Truidense handschriften," 271.

14   Fols. 7r, 106v, and 143v (figs. 15, 91, 106).

15   Luttrell Psalter, LBL, Ms. Add. 42130; Fitzwarin Psalter, BNF, Ms. lat. 765; Dennison, "Dating and Localisation," 511.

16   "Dating and Localisation," 508.

17   Artist B was responsible for five initials and borders in the second half of 6426: fols. 117v, 128r, 132v, 147v, and 195v. (However, text and decoration on fol. 195v are in fact later additions; see Gaspar and Lyna, *Les principaux manuscrits à peintures*, 1:342.) Dennison ascribes to a hand she designates as Artist A the initials and borders in the first half of 6426: fols. 2r, 9v, 14r, 17v, 19v, 26r, 28v, 36r, 42r. This artist's style derives from the circle of OBL, Ms. Bodley 264, the *Romance of Alexander*, and thus originates in Tournai. See Dennison, "Dating and Localisation," 507, 508 and n. 16; Lynda Dennison, "The Artistic Context of Fourteenth Century Flemish Brasses," *Transactions of the Monumental Brass Society* 14, pt. 1 (1986): 12, 16.

     In 9427, Artist B illuminated initials and borders in the first third of the manuscript on, fols. 14r, 43r, and 62v. Artist C illuminated initials and borders on fols. 81v, 100v, 124r, 145v, and 170r; see "Dating and Localisation," 508, n. 18, and "Stylistic Sources," 116, n. 6. Dennison also proposed that Artist A of the antiphonal worked subsequently on Bohun manuscripts in England. For the Bohun connection, see "Stylistic Sources," especially 115–156. Sandler holds a different view of the origins of the Bohun artists. See Lucy Freeman Sandler, *Gothic Manuscripts 1285–1385* (London: Harvey Miller, 1986), 1:19–22, and *Illuminators and Patrons*, 11, and 34, n. 46.

THE FLOURISHER-ILLUMINATORS OF THE TWO CAMPAIGNS

in drawing, shading, and arrangement of draperies are the figures of King David in the *Beatus* initial in 9427, fol. 14r (figs. 177, 177a) and in the initial *A* of *Ad te levavi* in 10 A 14, fol. 7r (fig. 15a). Monsters with confronted, conjoined mouths constitute initial stems in both initials. Red outlines borders and foliage in Artist B's illumination in both 6426 and 9427, as it does in Artist 2's work in 10 A 14. Artist C2 was also connected to the Brussels manuscripts; his style is closely related to that of the illuminator of 9217, whom Dennison termed Artist C.

Dennison's relative chronology, like her determination of hands, was based on style. She noted that in the course of his work on 6426, 9427, and, finally, 10 A 14, Artist B exhibited a remarkable capacity for stylistic development. His designs become more organized and more symmetrical and his brush more painterly. His compositions increased in monumentality; only in 10 A 14, the last manuscript of the series, did he employ architecture.[18] Dennison regarded Artist C2 of 10 A 14 as an imitator of Artist C;[19] it can be inferred that 10 A 14 is the later of the two manuscripts.

In the second campaign, characterized by a style distinct from, but "sympathetic" to, that of the first, Dennison saw the contributions of two artists she designated Artists D and D2. Artist D, the more skilled, she identified as Laurence the Priest. He completed two pages of major illumination, while Artist D2, his less-skilled assistant, completed one page.[20] To Laurence she also assigned work in manuscripts of later decades.[21] An unspecified number of overpainted minor initials and extensions on folios preceding 143v were probably the work of D2, perhaps executed over preliminary drawing from the first

campaign.[22] The style of the second campaign has relatively few comparanda among Flemish manuscripts.

Byvanck and Dennison were both partly correct in their identification of hands in 10 A 14. Byvanck rightly saw a single hand on fols. 7r, 22r, 27v, and 143v, but did not recognize a different hand on fol. 26r; nor did he recognize two campaigns. Dennison assigned a distinct identity to the hand on fol. 26r and recognized two campaigns but did not introduce the possibility that one artist, working in both campaigns, could have illuminated fols. 7r, 106v and 143v in the first campaign, and 22r and 27v in the second.

3   The First Campaign, *c.*1345–1355

The dating of the first campaign to 1345–1355 depends on the style of clothing, the role of line in defining form, and the treatment of volume and space. In the donor portrait on fol. 139r of the first campaign (figs. 103a., 106a), Elisabeth wears the *cote* with closed sides that was in vogue in the 1340s. Arnold's *chaperon* has the dagging which makes an early appearance in a few images of the Bodley *Alexander*, completed in 1344 (fig. 146, upper left). Arnold's *cote hardie* flairs into boxy pleats below the hip-belt; it is a bit more advanced—shorter and more fitted—than those in the Bodley *Alexander*. His shoes have pointed tips, or *pouleines*; these appear in the *Alexander* along with the traditional round-toed shoes.[23] The use of both streaky white modeling of faces and heavy outline are compatible with the decade following 1345, as are both the interest in spatial environments and the particular inconsistencies in realizing them.

Artists 1 and 2 worked in the first campaign. They completed about four-fifths of the decoration. The two divided the work between them, Artist 1 taking the calendar and the Sanctorale, Artist 2 taking the Temporale and the Ordinary of the Mass. However, there are significant deviations from a strict division of work, and these for more than one reason. Artists 3 and 4 completed the

---

Apologies to the reader for confusion entailed in differences between Dennison's the nomenclature and that employed in this book. Absent the names, the limitations and parameters of the field of research for each scholar must determine the nomenclature, else even greater confusion would result.

18   The proposed relative chronology of the manuscripts is corroborated by a parallel development in the style of Artist C, who worked on both 9427 and 9217; his figures in 9217 are more monumental than those in 9427, and the architecture is more complex; thus 9217 is probably later than 9427.

19   Dennison, "Dating and Localisation," 509.

20   Artist D illuminated fols. 22r and 27v (figs. 34, 39); Artist D2 illuminated fol. 26r (fig. 37).

21   Dennison assigns to Artist D a miniature of the Virgin Enthroned added around 1380 to a book of hours, OBL, Ms. lat. liturg. f. 3, fol. 118r, and a portion of a *Bible historiale*, BNF, Ms. fr. 152, dated a little earlier than the Bodleian hours. See Dennison, "Dating and Localisation," 513–514; and "The Artistic Context," 28–29.

22   Dennison, "Dating and Localisation," 510. She also assigned to either Laurence or D2 the completion of the border on fol. 144r. Delaissé and de Winter both associated Laurence the Priest with the repaints and with some completions. See L. M. J. Delaissé, "Enluminure et peinture dans les Pays-Bas," *Scriptorium* 11:1 (1957): 111; de Winter, *La bibliothèque de Phillippe le Hardi*, 228–229. Lemaire and Vanwijnsberghe, "Cote-Signalement KBR 9217," *Textes liturgiques*, 108, also assigned the overpaints to Laurence the Priest and suggested that he may have added little scenes evoking proverbs in the borders, but material evidence is lacking.

23   *Pouleines* with criss-crossed strapwork very like Arnold's appear in the Bodley *Alexander* on 57r.

illumination and penwork in 1366. Artist 3, who completed two-thirds of the major illumination in the second campaign, is here identified with Laurence the Priest, named in the colophon. These artists are discussed and differentiated below. The style of each is characterized, and the oeuvre of each is identified.

As noted at the beginning of Chapter 3, it is possible that Artists 2 and 3 were the same person, one artist who worked in two campaigns. Evidence from penwork for the identity of Artist 2 with Artist 3 is presented in this chapter; evidence from illumination is presented at the end of Chapter 5. This evidence is threefold. First, it involves identifying elements of likeness that connect the two bodies of work associated with these two artists: congruences in style, in the repertoire of motifs, and in aesthetic. Second, it involves placing the changes—principally in style, but also in the repertoire of motifs—within a coherent trajectory of development oriented towards a consistent way of organizing design, and within the framework of certain persistent interests and goals. This trajectory is in turn contextualized within overall artistic developments in illumination of the mid-fourteenth-century. Third, it involves discerning similar patterns in relations with fellow illuminators.

Although Artist 2 and Artist 3 are very likely aliases of the same person, different designations are retained, since the identity of the two artists cannot be proved. When a clear equivalence of certain elements is in view, the designation is sometimes collapsed as Artist 2/3.

4 The First Campaign: Artist 1

The core work of Artist 1 in 10 A 14 is well established; he illuminated the twelve pages of the calendar (figs. 3–14) and supplied six pages, all in the final third of the manuscript, with illuminated miniatures and/or initials accompanied with full or nearly full borders (figs. 103, 107, 110, 121, 125, 132).[24] To his oeuvre can be added illuminated initials and/or partial borders on five pages in Quires 15–18 (figs. 94, 99).[25] Prior to 10 A 14, Artist 1 worked on the Loppem-Bruges antiphonal and earlier still in the ateliers of Tournai. These connections are further considered in Chapters 5 and 7 and in Appendix 4, Pt. 1.

He was responsible for flourishing on 106 pages. He flourished four pages in Quires 15–17, half the pages in

Quire 18, and one page in Quire 19.[26] He completed all penwork initials and flourishing in Quires 21–26. He flourished most of the colophon page, fol. 204r, at the end of the manuscript (fig. 138). The first and last pages of the manuscript are his, and he completed most of the major illumination. He was likely in charge of the first campaign of the artistic enterprise.

Artist 1 was methodical and careful in his work. His repertoire of penwork motifs was limited. He had a penchant for the humorous and playful and for the visually suggestive, which manifests in subtle, subliminal correspondences. His aesthetic was for organic, fluttering, airy designs, animated but tidy and contained within an overall organizational grid.

Gold two-line initials are flourished predominantly in purple; blue two-line initials, in red. Minor touches of other colors occasionally appear. His outer border bars are all some variation of Type 1, composed of scalloped segments of red and blue, dotted regularly with buttons sprouting small filaments. Spiraling filaments from the inner bar support corkscrews that serve as the base for ball-and-squiggle trilobes (fig. 124, text column b). Corkscrews also decorate two-line penwork initials and five- to eight-line initials; terminal complexes include a few corkscrews (fig. 112a). The bodies of Artist 1's corkscrews are rendered impressionistically, as stacked, slightly dished, disconnected floating lines; except as the base for ball-and-squiggle trilobes, corkscrews are not numerous. They most often end in a fluent, but restrained, inward spiral or small hook (fig. 124a). His decorative repertoire and his style change little.

Artist 1's terminal complexes (figs 112, 127), most on an armature of multiple closely spaced straight lines, produce a decorative repertoire of curling, fluttering forms composed of the same elements as those in the border bars. Large, paired oak, fern, and maple leaves (figs. 111, 112) are common. Most complexes in the lower margin conform to a right-angle design; bundles of horizontal lines branch off at right angles to the main group. Trailing whiplash forms flourished by secondary curls and curves soften the angularity (figs. 115, 131). In the narrow top margin terminal complexes have a stronger element of radial design.

4.1 Two-Line Penwork Initials
Artist 1's work includes over 300 decorated and inhabited two-line penwork initials, blue and gold in color. Blue initials are framed in red penwork and gold initials in

---

24 See n.11 above for folio numbers of Artist 1's pages. See "Dating and Localisation," 509.

25 Fols. 112v, 114v, 119v, 126r, 128v.

---

26 Artist 1's flourished pages in Quires 15–17: fols. 112r&v, 121r, 130r; Quire 18: fols. 136r&v, 137r&v; Quire 19: fol. 144r. See Table 2.

purple penwork. Internal spaces of about four-fifths of the initials are decorated with beads or plant forms—buds, palmettes, leaves, or vines. (See Tables 3 and 4.) The remaining initials contain faces, birds, mammals, and grotesques, the latter in a style connected to penwork motifs in manuscripts from Sint-Truiden and, through Sint-Truiden, to work from Cologne and the Rhineland.[27] Motifs are in reserve, most on solid backgrounds, some on hatched grounds, with linear detailing. Backgrounds are red in blue initials, blue and cordovan in gold initials. Heads are mostly men's; a few are women's (figs. 129a, 130). Heads are three-quarters or profile and are types rather than portraits. One is full-view (fig. 123); his headgear is that of a Jew. Male heads are both beardless and bearded (figs. 117, 127a), bare-headed and hooded (figs. 117, 129). None is tonsured or mitred, but several are depicted with wings that hug the sides of the head (fig. 127c), perhaps in reference to a mythical being such as Hypnos. A circle or rosette may be suspended before an open mouth (fig. 127c). Many faces have exaggerated, expressive features.

Grotesques are mostly bipeds with various mammalian and avian features, often with human or humanoid faces; most have long, recurved necks that accommodate the curvature of the initial's counter (figs. 70a, 116). Among the many vegetal motifs, buds, palmettes, oak leaves, and trilobes are common; most of these motifs can be found in the initials on fol. 155v (fig. 114).

4.2   I-*Initials*

Artist 1 shows a penchant for use of the upside-down *I*-initials. Twenty-two of his seventy-nine *I*-initials are inverted, a far higher percentage than those of other artists. (See Table 5.) Some inversions seem chosen to avoid crowding the initial below; but others, placed above an ample length of unobstructed border (fig. 126), seem to be whimsical inversions, which easily harmonize with the other spirited elements in the penwork of Artist 1.

4.3   *Puns, Play, and Challenges to Boundaries*

Artist 1 teases the viewer with the many penwork faces in terminal complexes and beside and within initials. (See Inventory 5.) In terminal complexes, fish and humanoid fish are common (figs. 94a, 115). The mouth of a knobby profile head sprouts a tendril above a pair or trio of large oak, ivy, or maple leaves (figs. 112a, 118). Knobby profiles

attached to the lower terminal complex are visual puns on grouped pearls (figs. 113a, 128).

The artist creates playful and imaginative interactions between faces within the initial and the flourished decoration outside of the initial. The knobs of buds aligned in a pod inside an initial are reworked as protrusions of forehead, nose, lips, and chin of a gnome-like face, complete with floating rosette, in the initial's adjacent penwork (fig. 119). Similar knobby faces, some simian, and pearl-face puns are attached to left side of many two-line initials (figs. 96, 113a, 113b). Some of these pearl-derived faces are quirky refrains of the penwork face in the adjacent initial (figs. 122). In a bold pun on reception of the Eucharist, a rosette hovering before an open mouth repeats the motif of a wafer before an open mouth, a motif in a number of Artist 1's initials (fig. 120). Iconography slips over the physical boundary between the interior and exterior of the initial, as it does over the conceptual boundary between the suggested and the depicted. The allusive, the protean, are recurrent in Artist 1's designs.

4.4   *Style of Illumination*

Artist 1's style of illumination was characterized in scholarship as old-fashioned, linear, and technically skilled but stereotyped in expression. Noted were his treatment of gold—dense, carefully applied and highly burnished—and his typology of facial features, especially the long, pointed noses (figs. 110a, 121a). His style is relatively uniform. Hair is articulated with heavy curling or curving lines in contrasting strokes of black and white, often washed with beige or blue. Locks and curls are of different lengths, widths, and patterns of curvature, so that the look verges on unkempt; one feels the coiffures could profit from a comb. White highlights, dark outlines, and internal details are drawn with heavy line (fig. 175a). Skin tones have a pronounced grayish cast; small patches of orange or blue may add color to skin. Color is sometimes applied to drapery or architecture as a wash, over which the white or black hairline strokes are applied as modeling. Although orange and red appear, the latter mostly in backgrounds and initials, the overall tone of his palette is cooler and soberer than those of his confreres.

Architecture hovers among functions as frame, setting, and backdrop. Its elements—wall strips supported by arches or columns, scalloped underpinnings, hanging arches, pinnacles and conical turrets, domed towers on columns, ribbed vaulted ceilings viewed from beneath—can all be found in the illustrations of the Bodley *Alexander*. In 10 A 14, however, consistencies in scale, the predominance of monochromatic color, and bands of dot decoration tame and homogenize the riot of colors, dimensions,

---

27   See Beer, *Beiträge zur oberrheinischen Buchmalerei*; for example, descriptions and images of penwork initials in the thirteenth-century Engelberg "Bibly" and related manuscripts, pp. 9–17, 22–25. Haagdorens discusses initials similar to those in 10 A 14 in "Het zgn. missaal," 144–146, and in "Sint-Truidense handschriften," 260.

styles, and proportions that characterize the *Alexander*. Artist 1's taste in architecture is for the miniature and the delicate.

4.5 *Minor Illumination*

Artist 1's minor illumination consists of five painted two-line initials, with accompanying extensions or partial borders, all in Quires 15–17, quires in which he shared work with Artist 2.[28] These initials are executed and decorated primarily with a brush and with at least some opaque paint. Each marks an Introit for a Mass of Holy Week. Two of the painted initials are grotesques that function as the letter *I* (fig. 94a). The remaining three are two-line initials enclosed by square, burnished gold panels. The initials enclose a hare, a grotesque, and a face in the form of a bearded, cowled monk (figs. 99, 99a). Initial bodies are blue or pink. The heavy black outlines; heavy white line-and-circle detailing; and palette of blue, orange and pinkish-beige are characteristic of Artist 1's style. Tendril extensions from initials and grotesques are backed by Artist 1's highly polished, cusped gold strips and sprout trilobes, maple leaves, flowers, and large deeply scalloped cabbage leaves of the sort Haagdorens termed "the flame motif."[29] The possible reasons for the appearance of these few painted Introit initials in these particular quires are discussed below.

4.6 *Artist 1: Conclusion*

Artist 1's illumination and penwork are both consistent and predictable in overall design and display a limited repertoire of decorative elements, in which ball-and-squiggle trilobes predominate. The "flame motif" in his illuminated borders brings an element of organic movement that correlates with the aesthetic of the flourishing in his terminal complexes. The presence of many winged heads suggestive of mythical deities and the minimal presence of saints, clerics, and religious in the imagery of his two-line initials suggest that he was not himself a cleric, that his interests were primarily secular rather than religious.[30] The motif of a floating rosette before an open mouth certainly evokes the Eucharist, but not as a pious convention. There is rather a certain kinship in this motif to the parodies of religious figures and rituals in the marginalia

of Flemish manuscripts. His use of heavy line in illumination, the grayed palette, and the conventional iconography give a weightier feel to his illumination than to his light, curvilinear flourishing, almost rococo in feeling and spiced with humor and play. In sum, while flourishing and illumination share certain characteristics, there are differences in the two that give breadth to his artistic personality. The interests and aesthetic that surface in Artist 1's illumination are further considered in Chapter 5.

5 The First Campaign: Artist 2

Artist 2's oeuvre has been defined more gradually than Artist 1's. He illuminated the full-page Crucifixion, fol. 143v, and the miniature, initials, and borders on fols. 7r and 106v. These three folios were assigned to him by Byvanck, along with fols. 22r, 26r, and 27v.[31] Subsequent scholars separated these three latter folios from his oeuvre and assigned them to other artists. An unspecified number of painted borders and initials in quires antecedent to Quire 19 were assigned to him by Dennison, as noted above.

Artist 2's contributions can be clarified and expanded. He was responsible for thirty-nine painted initials, extensions, and partial borders in Quires 2–14. (See Inventory 4.) All penwork in Quires 2, 7, 8, 10–13, and 20 is his, and all but the colophon page in Quire 27. Except possibly for some preliminary sketches, he skipped Quires 4 and 9 entirely. Other quires he left incomplete. In Quires 3, 5, and 6 he completed all painted and penwork decoration on some sheets and pages but did no penwork and, at most, perhaps some preliminary drawing for the painted initials and borders on others. In Quire 14 he completed one page of major illumination, fol. 106v, but left the page's penwork untouched, to be executed in the second campaign along with most of the quire's remaining decoration. In Quires 15–19, he did most of the penwork and one page of major illumination, the Crucifixion page, but none of the minor illumination.[32] In all, Artist 2's flourishing appears on 168 pages. Irregularities in his patterns of work will be considered further below.

Judging from results, Artist 2 was very different in almost all respects from Artist 1. He was much less systematic than his colleague. His partially completed quires

---

28   Fols. 112v, 114v, 119v, 126r, 128v.

29   "Het zgn. missaal," 121, 123.

30   Clerics occur in Artist 1's major illumination where the iconography requires them, fols. 139r, 144r, and 192v, but very rarely where the artist might have a choice of subject matter, as in minor illumination and two-line penwork initials. In addition to the monk on fol. 128v, the only other "elective" image of a monk's or priest's head is in a two-line initial on fol. 137r.

31   *Les Principaux manuscrits*, 100. Byvanck also assigned this second artist an unspecified part of the border on fol. 144r.

32   Quires 15–17 contain lengthy scripture passages for Holy Week and thus relatively few two-line initials and many unflourished pages.

contrast with the highly finished condition of his colleague's quires. An interest in structure and framework, coupled with an impulse to expansive reaching, creates a tension that permeates his work. He was more creative than Artist 1 but less inclined to humor and less concerned with subtleties of pattern. His repertoire of decorative motifs was far larger than that of Artist 1, and it developed continually.

Artist 2 used color with a greater range of effects than did Artist 1. Border bars of Artist 1 are blue and red only; Artist 2 expanded the palette to incorporate green, beige, and yellow (figs. 73, 105). He used white to enhance and intensify hues: A creamy white pigment, applied as lines and feathery touches, enhances pastels in his painted initials (fig. 53). The margins of his pages exhibit a plethora of foliate and floral types: ivy leaves, various trilobes, oak leaves, prickle leaves, ball-and-filament leaves, lilies, composite flowers, asters, buds, rosettes—more than twenty varieties can be counted in all (figs. 32, 61, 70). The work of the other artists in 10 A 14 cannot rival this variety of foliage. An abundance of foliate and floral types occurs in East Anglian manuscripts of the 1320s and 1330s, manuscripts such as the Ormsby and St. Omer Psalters, but no direct connection with these can be discerned.[33] The penwork embellishments in the margins of Artist 2's pages are predominantly foliate but are spiced with occasional faces and animal motifs such as a bird (fig. 57) and an upside-down head (fig. 136), the latter seemingly referenced by Artist 3 in the second campaign (fig. 93).

Artist 2's abundant corkscrews have a characteristic form (figs. 19a, 83). Seemingly made of stiff wire, they are most often placed in right-angle alignment with respect to the border bar. His corkscrews are drawn in foreshortening as an unbroken spiral with well-aligned coils of about equal diameter. By contrast, the corkscrews of Artist 1 are drawn more impressionistically, as a series of disconnected dished elements, like a stack of plates (fig. 124a). Artist 1's corkscrews are less rigid, as though made of more flexible wire, and generally coil inward at the tip. The most characteristic terminal for Artist 2's corkscrews is a crisp circular arc, with a taut, barbed or recurved tip that points into the space beyond; variations of this tip-form occur in about one-fourth of the corkscrews: Some tips are barbless; others are accompanied by a pair of squiggles. Other variations occur infrequently.

Artist 2 exhibits a strong feeling for right-angle alignments and proper order. Only four upside-down *I*-initials occur in the 168 folios of Artist 2, many fewer than in the work of Artist 1. (See Table 5 for *I*-initials.) Nonetheless, Artist 2's aesthetic is not for containment but for moving out, using elements that expand into and interact with the surrounding space. He employs emphatic alternations in rhythm: mass-void, heavy-light. He makes more pronounced use than does Artist 1 of the play of sweeping curves and reverse curves, the latter created with sharp angular bends, in his penwork tendrils (figs. 46, 135a). The tense, wiry feel of his work contrasts with the softer, more fluttering, organic feel of Artist 1's work.

In narrow upper margins, the spine of Artist 2's terminal complex is typically a bundle of thin parallel lines (fig. 78), as was generally the case for the terminal complexes, both upper and lower, of Artist 1. However, in the lower margin, his terminal complexes usually include at least a partial extension of the inner and outer bar strips into the lower margin, where the bar produces one or two right-angle extensions that heighten the visual impact of the terminal complexes (fig. 78). Extensions may branch to one side, or to both sides, of the vertical arm (figs. 20, 74, 75). An extension may be positioned immediately below the lowest line of text or at a distance equivalent to the space of one to four text lines below the text. Motifs that ornament the text bar also appear around the extensions.

A striking and complex feature of his aesthetic is the simultaneous pairing of elements along multiple axes, macro and micro. The use of symmetries across the vertical and horizontal axes is a strategy of design used by many artists, but it is further developed in the work of Artist 2 than in the designs of his contemporaries. On fol. 12v (fig. 26), numerous paired elements in the penwork of the upper terminal complex are echoed in the pairings of the painted partial border at the bottom of the page; on fol. 51r (fig. 56) in the lower terminal complex, leaves paired on small stalks above the border bar are doubled by pairs below; likewise there is some pairing of elements across the vertical axis of the border bar—there are pairs of pairs of pairs, one might say.

5.1 Two-Line Penwork Initials

Artist 2 produced a remarkable body of penwork imagery in his 344 two-line penwork initials. (See Table 2 for distribution by quire.) Nearly three-fifths of this imagery is human or animal, as opposed to one-fifth of such imagery in the corresponding initials of Artist 1. (See Tables 3 and 4.) A correspondingly lower proportion of Artist 2's motifs are foliate forms, about one-third as opposed to four-fifths for Artist 1. Backgrounds in Artist 2's initials are red, blue,

---

33   Borders and initials of the Ormsby Psalter, OBL, Ms. Douce 366, dated *c.*1280–*c.*1325, and borders of the St. Omer Psalter, LBL, Ms. Yates Thompson 14, begun *c.*1330–1340, are decorated with a variety of leaves and flowers. For the Ormsby and St. Omer Psalters, see Sandler, *Gothic Manuscripts*, II:49–51 and 113–115.

green, or purple, are solid or hatched; white or colored circles are used as filler. Some hatching is bicolored. Motifs are in reserve, some with grisaille shading. Internal features and outlining may be in red, purple, and gray or black; and many combinations of color and technique in background and detailing occur. The use of grisaille is noteworthy as it connects this work to decoration in earlier work at Sint-Truiden; this connection is considered in Chapter 7. Artist 2's faces manifest a remarkable variety in types and in poses, within very tight compositional constraints. Profile, frontal, and three-quarters views are all common. Beardless young men with short, curly hair (fig. 27) and older men with long beards and hair (fig. 100) occur in many variations.[34] Doubled and tripled profiles also occur (figs. 50, 62). Secular types include a crowned king (fig. 79), the beardless face in a hood with liripipe (fig. 80), and a soldier in chain mail and helmet (fig. 86a). Several initials depict women in hoods edged with ruffles (figs. 58, 58a).[35] On the whole, these penwork heads do not seem to be portraits, though the variety of physical and expressive types is remarkable. Developed in the relative iconographical freedom afforded by the two-line initial, they foreshadow seventeenth-century Flemish and Dutch tronies.

A number of heads are clerical, either tonsured (figs. 102, 102a, 135b) or mitred (fig. 79).[36] Seven initials depict the head of Christ, presented frontally with shoulder-length hair and beard, both parted in the middle. Circles may be placed around the head of Christ to suggest a cruciform halo (figs. 74a, 135c). The face in the initial *D(eus)* on fol. 46r (fig. 51) is crowned with thorns, the face bruised and the beard bloody.[37] This interest in imagery of Christ's face suggests the possibility that Artist 2 may have been a priest. In a larger context, these initials may be seen as antecedent to the contemplative images of the face of Christ in Northern panel painting of later centuries.

Some subjects in two-line initials appear episodically in Artist 2's penwork. For example, Quires 8, 17, and 27 each have nine initials with birds. Quires 2–6, 11–16, and 18–20 each have none or few. Cyclical deposits of motifs

also characterize Artist 2's border bar decoration as discussed below.

Grotesques are similar to those of Artist 1—humpbacked bipeds, often with human or humanoid heads, recurved necks, and bodies with various avian and mammalian features (figs. 97, 98). Some have animal heads as well as animal bodies (fig. 56). Some have curling tufts of fur that lift off from the body and help conform its shape to the curvature of the initial's counter (figs. 16a, 56, 70b). White or colored circles are used as filler.

Mammals appear rarely in Artist 2's many initials.[38] Nineteen of his two-line initials are decorated with geometric elements, such as small, toothed blocks and *x*-inscribed squares, the former analogous to the toothed pearls that decorate some border bars (fig. 33, initials *M[unera]* and *A[ccipe]*).[39] These abstract motifs are not found in two-line initials by Artist 1.

5.2   *Five Cycles of Flourishing*

Although flourishing has been studied in terms of *Motivengeschichte*, generic motifs tracked over decades across geographical regions, the work of individual flourishers is rarely identified, even less often analyzed for cyclical development.[40] In the work of Artist 2, five cycles of flourishing can be identified, each defined by decorative elements which are absent or less common elsewhere and which are combined in various ways to explore, through a series of pages, the possibilities of a particular repertoire and aesthetic. The cycles are woven through quires in which the artist also worked in more generic ways; Artist 2 apparently worked simultaneously along multiple decorative tracks.

The use of technical nomenclature—Cycle 1, Cycle 2, etc.—has the unfortunate effect of terminologically desiccating the organic beauty and abundance of Artist 2's creative expressions. However, in order to define and track connections in this profusion of decoration, the terminology is helpful. The hope is that the reader finds technical language not an obstacle to the goal of understanding but a tool to facilitating it.

At least five internal cycles of development are encountered within the leviathan of Artist 2's penwork. All share

---

34   As, for example beardless with chin-length crimped hair; short, curly hair coupled with long, straight beard; a short cap of straight black hair with black beard, among others. (Fol. 47r, *C[elestis]*; fol. 199v, *D[eus qui]*; fol. 135r, *P[opule]*).

35   Women are also depicted in Artist 2's two-line penwork initials on fols. 9v, 11r, and 14v.

36   Additional tonsured heads in Artist 2's two-line penwork initials: fols. 75r, 95v, 97va.

37   Additional two-line penwork initials, by Artist 2, with head of Christ: fols. 11v, 21r, 56r, 57r, 78v. Faces of Christ in painted, or partly brushed, initials: fols. 22r, 26v, 107r.

---

38   Initials on fol. 9v display a dog and an ape (fig. 20); dogs also appear in initials on fols. 39r and 78r. Rabbits appears on fols. 157v (fig. 117) and 203r.

39   *X*-inscribed squares: fol. 61v, *A(b omnibus)* and fol. 114v, *A(duuia)*; toothed blocks: fol. 139r, *(E)t cum*, fig. 103.

40   See Patricia Stirnemann, "Fils de la vierge. L'initiale à filigranes parisiennes: 1140–1314," *Revue de l'art* 90 (1990): 58–73, for a study in the development of the filigree initial in Parisian illumination over nearly two centuries.

THE FLOURISHER-ILLUMINATORS OF THE TWO CAMPAIGNS

the general style and aesthetic of Artist 2 as described above: interest in structure, rigidity, an interest in symmetry, a certain compositional openness, greatly varied combinations of motifs, a rich and varied use of color. However, within this general framework, each cycle displays its own particular aesthetic. Though Artist 2 skipped over entire quires and within quires skipped sheets for reasons unknown, he nonetheless seems to have worked through in their present sequence the quires he completed. Thus, each cycle can be seen in part as a response to its predecessor in the sequence of quires.

Cycle 1, found in Quire 2, has a retrospective character. Decoration throughout the quire conveys a certain static heaviness through the proliferation of solid-colored leaves and rosettes and of small, tightly curved and neatly aligned forms. Cycle 1 comprises three different subsets of motifs, designated Cycles 1A, 1B, and 1C. Cycle 1A (figs. 19, 28) is of particular interest because it is the most closely connected with Artist 2's prior work in 6426 and 9427; this cycle is an initial statement of the flourisher's style at the beginning of a new endeavor. Rolls of pearls populate the reentrant angles in terminal complexes of Cycles 1B and 1C. Cycle 1B (figs. 20, 29) features compressed pearls, diagonal alignments and lines with hooked terminals. This sub-cycle references an artist herein identified as Artist 9217-2, who flourished much of 9217. Artist 2 may have considered him a friend or mentor; Cycle 1B might be read as Artist 2's tribute to him. Cycle 1C (fig. 25), featuring strings and spirals of toothed pearls, is not at present connected to any specific earlier work or other artist. Border bars are of Types 1 and 2 throughout. Further description and analysis of these three sub-cycles is in Appendix 3.

Elements of Cycle 2, characterized by a lighter touch and openwork designs, begin to appear in Quire 3 (figs. 32, 33), but this cycle is developed fully in Quires 6–8 (figs. 47, 53, 60).[41] Pearl rolls disappear from reentrant angles in terminal complexes and, on the whole, pearls play a less prominent role in design. The new trend as developed in Quires 6–8 is often accompanied by Type 3 border bars (figs. 47, 53, 60), which did not appear previously in the work of Artist 2, with exception of a single instance on fol. 7rb. The solidly painted outer border bars of Types 1 and 2 are replaced on these pages by the linear, lacelike forms. A band of toothed pearls and a line of tiny circles with

attached squiggles exemplifies this cycle's lighter touch (fig. 47). The number of weighty, solid-colored leaves and rosettes greatly diminishes in comparison to their numbers in Quire 2. Elongated bud- or acorn-like leaves appear frequently as do prickle leaves (figs. 53, 56). Oak leaves and several other varieties also appear.

Cycle 3 unfolds mainly in Quires 10–13 (figs. 68–89). Here the trend is towards richer, more energetic patterns and larger forms. Perhaps Artist 2 decided that the effect of Cycle 2's decoration was too disembodied, ethereal. Most characteristic of the third cycle is the combination of Type 4 ribbon-strip border bars and floral composites in several varieties.[42] The Type 4 ribbon-strip bar is derived, as noted in Chapter 3, from a type of painted bar used in Flemish illumination (figs. 150, 164). The composites may be flowers from whose open blooms emerge additional flowers or stalks, or stalks that produce a calyx-like platform from which rises a second tier of paired leafed or floral stems (figs. 70, 70a, 71). Pages with these flowers seem almost Middle Eastern in aesthetic. They affect like a Turkish carpet, dense with rich, intense colors of jewel-like, mid-range values, sweeping abstract lines, and many small, repetitive decorative embellishments. These effects are augmented by the ribbon bars, which create patterns of color richer and more intense than those of the border bars of other types, in part because they maintain a consistent width, unthinned by feathering or scalloping. Strips with segments of alternating colors, hatched or solid (figs. 80, 86), are studded with pearls, buttons, or rosettes of various types and sizes (figs. 72, 73). They may be outlined in a color contrasting to the main color of the strip, further enriching the design. All the above-enumerated elements occur in many different combinations.

Other noteworthy decorative elements of this third cycle include the pearl spirals that line the border bars (figs. 79, 85). Some are imbued with a sense of intrinsic potential energy: They strain at their attachments to the bar, as though ready to spin off and out (fig. 85). Large, animated, and varied leaf forms contribute to the character of this cycle as well (fig. 86, bottom). A spectacular row of penwork butterflies graces fol. 91v (fig. 82); the motif was reworked, and used on fol. 106v in the second campaign (fig. 91).

The transition to Cycle 4 begins in Quires 14–18. The liturgy for Holy Week commences in Quire 14. In Quires 14 and 15, all Artist 2's border bars are Type 4. The range of color in ribbon strips expands to include lavender-pink

---

41   Cycle 2 flourishing appears in Quire 3 on fols. 16r&v and 21r&v; in Quire 5 on fols. 34r–35v; in Quire 6 on fols. 39r–40v and 45r–46v; and throughout Quires 7 and 8. For the Type 3 border bars often, but not always, used in Cycle 2, see Inventory 2. Flourishing in Quire 4 and most of that in Quire 5 is the work of Artist 4, whose style can be likened to a sparse version of Cycle 1A.

42   The Type 4 bar appears in short segments in Quire 6, on fol. 40r, and in Quire 8, on fols. 60r&v.

(fig. 101), yellow and beige (fig. 105). The composite flowers disappear. Penwork in other respects is similar to that in Cycle 3 but is more subdued. In Quires 16–20, still in the liturgy for Holy Week, a technique used in Quire 2 reappears in a new variation. This technique is the loose, painterly application of tinted wash, mostly to foliage, though in some instances it is applied to pearl spirals as well as to leaves (fig. 95). In most instances the ink is green, though other colors are used also (fig. 105).[43] The almost impressionistic application, which overwashes outlines, is a counterpoint to the structure and control that generally characterize Artist 2's work. The technique was forecast by the solidly colored leaves in the penwork of Quire 2, but in the earlier iteration outlines contained the color. The aesthetic of reaching and expansion, always present in Artist 2's work and mostly articulated with tense, controlled lines, is echoed in a freer way in this wash technique.

Cycle 4 emerges fully in Quires 19 and 20 which are marked by the manuscript's most monumental effects in penwork. Quire 19 contains three pages of major illumination: the full-page Crucifixion by Artist 2 (fig. 106) and two pages with miniatures, initials and full borders by Artist 1 (figs. 103, 107). The texts of Quire 19, Prefaces for the Canon of the Mass, are presented with musical notation. The accompanying initials in Quires 19 and 20 are larger in size and more developed in iconography than are the initials in the twenty-eight-line quires. The monumentality of effect carries through almost to the end of Quire 20. In these two quires the range of color is greater and the color combinations more varied than anywhere else in the work of Artist 2. The freely washed foliage first seen on a few pages in Quire 16 appears throughout this cycle. The combination of magnificently illuminated pages, large initials, many foliate bands freely-washed with color, and range of color produces not the richest but the grandest penwork effects in the manuscript (figs. 108, 109). Perhaps not coincidentally, in this section of the manuscript appear depictions of a castle and fine helmet, both Arnold's (fol. 147v).

Cycle 5 is found in Quire 27 (fols. 199–204), the final quire of the manuscript, in which Artist 2 returns after six quires (Quires 21–26) decorated by Artist 1. Artist 2 synthesizes selected motifs from Cycles 1 and 2 with the animation, amplitude, and solidity of form from Cycles 3 and 4 (figs. 133–135, 137). Border bars are of Types 1 and 2 as in the early quires, but with new complexities and variations. Terminal complexes liberally endowed with pearls create an effect reminiscent of Quire 2. (Cp. fig. 135a with fig. 25.) Toothed pearls, abundant in Quire 2, also appear.[44] On the other hand, motifs from Cycles 3 and 4—composite flowers typical of the Cycle 3 and the loosely overwashed foliage of Cycle 4—feature not at all. Motifs that reference the Type 4 border bars typical of Cycle 3 appear, but only as short segments in the panels surrounding initials.[45]

If motifs mark a return to the early quires, the visual power of the penwork draws from developments in later quires, the quires of Cycles 3 and 4. Solid rather than hatched backgrounds intensify the impact of two-line initials. Hair and beards in grisaille are delineated with high contrasts in value. Spirals and pearls expand in size and reach, through their many crinkled extensions. The term *cycle* proves apt here, given the return to the starting point, the sense of completion and closure as well as of synthesis. A synthesis, or unity, of iconography also emerges on some pages in this quire, as on fol. 200r, where the heads in the two-line initials sprinkled over the page all gaze at the bishop in the initial at top right (fig. 134).

5.3 *Style of Illumination*

Scholars remark on Artist 2's use of reddish-brown outlining as opposed to Artist 1's use of black, Artist 2's painterly technique, featuring many small strokes of white and black in shading, hot colors, ample drapery carefully arranged, and heavy architectural frames. He is seen as skilled in modeling and arranging drapery but unsuited to handling the full-page format.[46] Mouths touched with red, hair that is red-brown or red-blonde, and/or that is neatly patterned with small, repetitive strokes also characterize his style.

In earlier scholarship Artist 2's work was generally conflated with that of Artists 3 and 4, muddying the definition of his style, but also suggesting that it was more advanced than that of Artist 1 and that it underwent change or development, as indeed it did. This strong developmental dynamic is absent in the work of Artist 1, as noted above. The style of Artist 2's painting in the miniature for the *Ad te levavi*, fol. 7r (fig. 15a), is close to that of his work on fol. 14r, the *Beatus* initial of 9427 (fig. 177a), as Dennison noted.[47] Facial type and hairstyle, fold types, background treatment, and initial type with pairs of confronted gorgon heads, are all similar. A move towards realism

---

43 Red, blue, and yellow-beige are used variously on fols. 129r&v and fol. 141v.

44 Fol. 199v, initial S(*umentes*).

45 Fol. 199v, initial H(*ostias*).

46 Byvanck, *Les principaux manuscrits*, 100.

47 "Dating and Localisation," 509. See the section entitled "Scholarship on Illumination and Decoration," at beginning of Chapter 4, above.

appears in 10 A 14 in the replacement of red outline with an understated brown and more consistent modeling. Development continues in 10 A 14; the application of line is lighter and more refined in the Crucifixion than in the *Ad te levavi* and *Domine ne longe* images. There does however remain a certain awkwardness to gestures and poses and an element of incongruity between treatment of figures and architecture.

The components of Artist 2's architecture are solid, cubic forms, roofed in blue and trimmed in gold. Linear decoration, conspicuous in the architecture of Artist 1, is subdued. Artist 2 employs the Italianate device, widely used in France and England by the mid-fourteenth century, of abruptly changing value or hue at architectural corners to create a sense of depth, solidity, and of directional light. Development of architecture is linked to the development of space. On fol. 7r, space is dependent on the layering of elements, and the view of vaults from beneath is rendered inconsistently. On fol. 106v (fig. 91a), space is deepened but confused; on fol. 143v the deeper space is retained and rationalized, and its organization is coordinated with planar aspects of the design. Bouquets of vault ribs converge to corbels, and a corresponding depth is developed at the bottom of the image with recession in the spatial platform.

5.4 Minor Illumination

Artist 2 was responsible for thirty-nine painted initials placed at Introits in Quires 2–18, which comprise the Temporale or Proper of Seasons. These painted initials, with extensions or partial borders, constitute emphatic visual bookmarks, surely welcomed by the celebrant as he paged through the volume in search of his starting text. If Artist 2 was himself a priest, he would have understood the value of such markers. Gold panels outlined in red or black, and some with pouncing, frame his painted initials. Most are accompanied by extensions or partial borders.[48] (See also Inventory 4 and Table 7.) Fourteen are decorated exclusively with leaves (fig. 59). A few initials are purely figural and so have no independent letterform (figs. 41, 54, 61). Others are hybrid, having elements of letterform supplemented by figural elements (fig. 53).

Ten of the initials are decorated with human heads, six tonsured (figs. 44, 60a, 80). Most heads are youthful and beardless, with reddish-blonde hair (figs. 18, 61). One, with a heavy chin, large ear, and stubble beard, suggests a portrait (fig. 77). Grotesques and gold trilobes in about equal numbers decorate the remaining painted initials. Extensions include sprays of gold-ball trilobes attached to the initial panel and tendrils with gold strips, cusping, trilobes, or lancets (fig. 60a). Some extensions take the form of grotesques whose bodies overflow the initial and extend into the border along the text (figs. 42, 47); this impulse to expansion also characterizes the penwork of Artist 2. In two instances the extension is not part of the body of a figural initial but is a discrete creature attached to the initial or its panel (fig. 77; fol. 51v). Two more initials are accompanied by detached partial borders and feature a head in the initial with a human-headed grotesque of very similar physiognomy floating in the border above or below the initial (figs. 22, 86b); visual repetition thus links elements that are not physically connected.

The palette is dominated by warm colors with creamy white highlights. In Quire 2 the letterforms alternate blue and pink, but thereafter the painted series does not establish a discernible pattern of alternation or repetition. A vivid orange-red is used with blues of both high and low value. In painted initials, as in penwork, a distinctive change of style occurs after Quire 2; technique becomes more fluent, especially in the application of white. Most initials in Quire 2 are decorated with old-fashioned *x*-motifs that almost disappear in later quires.

5.5 Incompletions

The study of Artist 2 is complicated by the compounded irregularities of his production. Unlike the style of Artist 1, Artist 2's style changed significantly in the course of his work on the manuscript. Moreover, the change is not regular or consistent: the rate and nature of change is itself variable. Irregularity can be predicated not only of his style but also of his work habits. As noted above, some of his quires are incomplete. Within these incomplete quires, the same compound of the regular and the irregular can be noted. Within the incomplete quires, he almost always completed penwork on some sheets and left others untouched. But there is no pattern to the selection of sheets, which are variable in number and in their position within the quires. In Quire 3 (fols. 15–22), he decorated only the second sheet (16/21); in Quire 5 (fols. 31–38), the middle sheet (34/35); in Quire 6 (fols. 39–46), the first and second sheets (39/46, 40/45). In a certain respect he was thorough: He rarely left any page with half-finished

---

48   There seem to be a few errors and deviations in placement of the decoration for Introits. On fol. 40v the painted initial and partial border mark the Postcommunion prayer for Sexagesima Sunday, which is followed by additional Scripture readings rather than by the Introit for the next Sunday, as is usual. On fol. 128v the painted initial *H* and accompanying border mark the first lesson for the Good Friday liturgy, for which there is no Introit prayer.

penwork. His flourished pages are fully flourished; they evidence an all-or-nothing approach.[49]

The pattern of incompletions in Artist 2's painted decoration is less tidy than the pattern in penwork. In view here is not the degree of finish of individual elements *per se* but the overall design. On some pages he sketched in graphite for illumination that he completed with deviations, usually minor, from the sketch (fols. 61vb, bottom of page and 85v, figs. 63, 76).[50] Other sketches were for work that he drew and colored to varying degrees and then left unfinished, to be completed in the second campaign, mostly by Artist 4, some with striking changes in design (fig. 37a) and others with less dramatic alterations (figs. 40, 40a). Close inspection is required to discern where Artist 2's work ends and where Artist 4's begins. Artist 2's incompletions were likely the major reason for the need of a second campaign of illumination.

Why did he complete all the decoration in some quires, including some that are contiguous and stylistically similar (Quires 7, 8 and 10–13), and in other quires decorate only selected sheets (Quires 5, 6)? Why did he skip some quires entirely (Quires 4, 9)?[51] Given the chaotic conditions in much of Flanders during the mid-fourteenth century, it is entirely possible that external events contributed to interruption of work on the manuscript. However, Artist 1 managed to complete all his quires; perhaps he had the habit of completing discrete units before moving on. If so, his habit parallels his aesthetic, his liking for contained, polished, repetitive designs. Artist 2 likewise may have had work habits congruent with his aesthetic, to wit,

a toleration of the incomplete that meshes with his feeling for open-endedness in many aspects of design.

For whatever reason, Artist 2 did not illuminate fols. 22r and 27v, two of the three pages with miniatures and borders in Quires 3 and 4. These pages were left for the second campaign. The third page, bearing the Introit to the Circumcision (fol. 26r), is very problematic. It may have been begun by Artist 2 but was completed by Artist 4 in the second campaign. In the left margin two figures lightly sketched in plummet or graphite in the style of the first campaign are faintly visible (fig. 37a). In the initial, however, figures are of the later style, which features softer shading, fuller volume, and less emphatic linear detailing than the earlier style. This initial is discussed in Chapter 5.

5.6   *Artist 2: Conclusion*

Artist 2 opened the possibilities of penwork as a medium for artistic life and thought. Development of aesthetic and expression flow in his penwork through every organizational unit, both physical and liturgical, in his quires of 10 A 14. The variety of motifs, their combinations and arrangements, and their cycles of development are encompassed within a metanarrative of reaching across boundaries between media, between the formal and the metaphysical, while simultaneously maintaining a strong structural framework, manifested in part through symmetry and nested pairs. Relentlessly expansive, his artistic expression is also wholistic, as proved by the recapitulation and synthesis of penwork in his final quire. In two-line initials the multiplicity of birds, faces, and grotesques, and the variants of each, speaks to the same interest in expansive exploration.

A strong interest in religion is manifested both in iconography and in aesthetic concepts. Monks, priests, bishops, and Christ himself are well represented in his penwork initials. The pervasive movement of reaching towards the beyond, the across, has the feeling of a religious impulse. This impulse is verbalized in the prayers of the missal and is imaged in its iconography, but in the aesthetic of design it is injected as an energy, an intuition. This latter mode of expression broadens understanding of Artist 2's personality. The deftness of touch and the pulsating, changing life of his buoyant flourishing are a counterbalance to the profound and weighty theological insights in his illumination. These well-articulated, complementary aspects of religion point to the possibility that Artist 2 was Laurence the Priest of the colophon.

Some factors that contributed to Artist 2's mastery as a flourisher are considered in Chapter 7. Whether Artist 2's penwork is an outlier, or whether penwork in

---

49   One exception is fol. 23rb, at the top (fig. 36). The one-line initial *D* is flourished in red in Artist 2's clean, sure manner, with elongated trilobes, ball-and-squiggle trilobes, and prickle leaves, accompanied by corkscrews. Directly across the page, at the top of fol. 23a, in the same dark red ink, is a corkscrew and a pair of ball-and-squiggle trilobes. Artist 2's aesthetic for reaching into space is manifested in the straining of elements towards each other across the page. By contrast, the purple wavy trilobes and corkscrew just above, by Artist 4, droop with an insouciance that ignores the tense dialogue below. (See further discussion of Artist 4's penwork in this chapter.) Where Artist 4 picks up the flourishing of fol. 23b below the initial *D*, the red ink changes to a more orange hue. Why the change of hand happened here is uncertain; the remaining penwork on the page is by Artist 4, as evidenced by the loose, sparse, and flaccid decoration. This page, 23r, marks the beginning of Quire 4, the minor and major illumination of which also bears the stylistic imprint of both Artists 2 and 4.

50   Fol. 85v, 3–4 lines below initial *D(eus)*. Also fol. 94v, 4 lines below initial *S(itientes)*.

51   Quire 4 with the very minimal exception explained above.

other manuscripts might be freighted, graced, with a multi-faceted conceptual and intuitive creativity akin to Artist 2's is perhaps worth considering, along with the question of whether and how to expand the study of penwork.

6 Collaboration between Artists 1 and 2

Collaboration can be distinguished from incompletion, the former being intentional and presuming relatively contemporaneous activity on the part of the participants and the latter more likely unintentional and more likely involving an interval of time separating the work executed by the parties involved. Here instances of collaboration between the two artists of the first campaign will be considered; incompletions which involve the second campaign are considered further on.

Artists 1 and 2 collaborated, in a general way, on 10 A 14, in that they apparently divided the work between them, largely by quire. The sections of text with particularly significant content, and the illumination that accompanied them, were considered separately with a special attention to equitable distribution—not of labor but of privilege. In these special sections the two artists shared work within quires. The artists were surely practical in their division of work largely by quire, but at certain points the sacred content of the text asserted priority and prompted deviations from the purely practical.

The first instances of likely collaboration within quires occurs in Quires 15–18. In these quires are five pages with minor illumination (figs. 94, 99).[52] On all five pages the illumination was executed by Artist 1. In addition, four pages in these quires were flourished by Artist 1 (fig. 94); twenty-two pages, by Artist 2 (fig. 99). The remaining twenty-five pages, all in Quires 15–17, are without two-line initials and consequently required no decoration. (See Inventory 1.)

The two artists may have decided to work together in these quires for devotional reasons. In the liturgy of the Winter Missal, lacking Easter, Good Friday is the holiest feast; it is preceded by Holy Week. The Holy Week liturgy begins with Palm Sunday on fol. 106v in Quire 14 and continues through the end of the Good Friday liturgy on fol. 136r in Quire 18; thus, all of the text in Quires 15–17 and some in Quire 18 is dedicated to Good Friday. For Palm Sunday and throughout Holy Week, the very lengthy scripture passages resulted in many pages without Introits and thus without two-line initials and attendant flourishing.

The Introits for Monday through Thursday of Holy Week and the first lesson of the Stations of the Cross, which is the *de facto* Introit for Good Friday, are each embellished with a painted initial and partial border by Artist 1, while Artist 2 did the penwork borders and two-line penwork initials on these Introit pages. Perhaps the two artists agreed that the quires with especially holy text should bear the personal imprint of each man and so divided the work between them—painted decoration and some penwork went to one and the greater share of penwork to the other.

One consideration in evaluating this explanation is that Artist 1 nowhere else provided partial borders and painted initials for Introits: His quires, Quires 21–26, lack these entirely, whereas Artist 2 decorated almost all Introits in his quires with painted borders and initials. Thus Artist 1's production of painted borders/initials in these quires is not in line with his usual practice. If the dual authorship of these Good Friday quires was the result of a joint decision to mark them with the work of both men, then one might see evidence of a spirit of collaboration rather than competition in the workshop. This collaboration was likely elicited not only by practical necessities but by an awareness on the part of both artists of the spiritual importance of Good Friday; their response to this higher holiness is akin to an act of offering, or even worship.

It is also possible that Artist 1 completed work in these quires that was left undone by his colleague. Again, the special character of the text might explain why, among the many pages left undone by Artist 2, these were selected by Artist 1.

A second instance of a likely planned collaboration occurs in Quire 19 at fol. 139r (fig. 103), the Preface for the Canon of the Mass, another particularly significant prayer, as it introduces the liturgy of consecration. On this page the painted decoration is by Artist 1, but the penwork is by Artist 2.

A third instance, also in Quire 19, is on fols. 143v–144r, the opening that pairs the Crucifixion and *Te igitur* at the Canon of the Mass, the most sacred prayers of the missal. This pair of pages, one the work of Artist 2 and the other of Artist 1, is the apex of the missal, both in quantity of illumination and in spirit. One may suppose that both artists wished to be represented at the Canon prayers; as the texts were read and as the miracle of transubstantiation occurred, they themselves were in a sense present, one in the image of the priest and the other in the image of the crucified Christ. In a continuum of offering, the artists present their image-gifts as the priest depicted offers his gift of bread and wine, which becomes the self-offered crucified Christ in the moment of consecration. Also

---

52   Fols. 112v, 114v, 119v, 126r, 128v.

present are the donors, originally both Arnold and Elisabeth. Their offering is their prayer at the Mass and their gift of the manuscript's commission. The opening then functions as a window into an eternal *now*, where the past and the present, the physical and the spiritual, the divine and the human, the temporal and the eternal, the laity, the clergy, and the artists, are all drawn into a unity of sacrificial offering. The viewer, reading the prayers and the images, is likewise invited into this union of offering.

Quire 18 has no undecorated pages; each artist decorated two sheets of the quire's four. Here one might reasonably, though not conclusively, infer a decision to split the work.

7 The Second Campaign, *c.*1366

During the second campaign of *c.*1366, three pages of major illumination—miniatures, painted initials and painted full borders—were produced (fols. 22r, 26r, and 27v; figs. 34, 37, 39), as well as twenty pages with minor illumination—painted two-line initials with extensions or partial borders.

The work of Artists 3 and 4 was conflated with that of Artist 2 in earlier scholarship, as noted above, until Dennison first clearly identified the second campaign. In their flourishing, the artists of the second campaign adopted, or continued, much of the vocabulary of the first campaign; this commonality of motifs can make the second campaign's penwork decoration difficult to differentiate from that of the first campaign. The date of the second campaign is more readily perceived in illumination, in which the figures are more three-dimensional and the architecture is more spatially coherent than are the respective elements of the first campaign. A comparison of the miniatures of the *Ad te levavi* of the first campaign (fol. 7r, fig. 15a) and the Adoration of the Magi of the second campaign (fol. 27v, fig. 39a) is instructive. The heavy, form-concealing folds of David's garments contrast with the more delicate and clinging folds of the three Magi's garments, and their crowns are smaller and lighter than David's. The undersides of the corbeled vaults above the Magi are articulated in more consistent patterns of converging ribs, which while not illusionistically accurate, at least exhibit a certain artistic self-confidence that suggests a greater familiarity with conventions of illusionism as compared to the earlier miniature. Architectural detail of the second campaign is more delicate and refined than that of the first. The Italianate foliage of the borders in the Magi scene, compared to the familiar trilobes around the image of David praying, is also telling. The absorption of

Italianate space and form coupled with the influence of French refinement indicates a date after the mid-century for the Adoration of the Magi and is a harbinger of the International Gothic Style, still two or three decades away.

The costumes of Arnold and Elisabeth (fig. 39a) are of the early-to-mid 1360s. He wears the tight-fitting *cote hardie* with padded chest and pleated skirt, small hood buttoned close to the neck, and shoes with long *pouleines*, all of which are characteristic of those years. His streamlined hairstyle has lost the central curl, or *dorlott*. Elisabeth wears the open *surcot* which first appeared around 1350–1352 and greatly increased in popularity during the decade following. By contrast, she wears the older close-sided *cote* in both images from the first campaign (figs. 103a, 106a).[53]

In flourished two-line initials, advances in style that are in agreement with the proposed interval between campaigns are also apparent, though the differences are more understated than in the miniatures. In two-line initials, those of the second campaign provide more instances of volumetric rendering of faces and bodies, achieved with the use of softer line and washed grisaille shading, perhaps in consultation with Italianate models, as compared with similar initials of the earlier campaign. (Cp. fig. 134a with fig. 90.)

8 The Second Campaign: Artist 3

Artist 3 decorated fewer pages and thus furnished considerably less material for stylistic analysis than did the other three artists. He produced fifteen pages of penwork and two pages of major illumination, fols. 22r, 27v (figs. 35, 39) but no pages with minor illumination; that is, no pages decorated only with painted initials and extensions or partial borders. All his work appears in Quires 3, 4, and 14. His identity was folded into the amalgam that Byvanck termed the second artist, until Dennison identified him as an illuminator and differentiated him from Artist 2 on the basis of style and from Artist 4 on the basis of quality.[54]

Most of his border bars are of Type 4; Types 1 and 2 appear not at all in his work. Trilobes with tremulous outline occur frequently (fig. 88). The effect of a general fizz

---

53 See Anne H. van Buren and Roger S. Wieck, *Illuminating Fashion: Dress in the Art of Medieval France and the Netherlands 1325–1515* (New York: Morgan Library and Museum in association with D. Giles Limited, London, 2011), 52–59, 62–67; Stella Mary Newton, *Fashion in the Age of the Black Prince: A Study of the Years 1340–1365* (Woodbridge, Suffolk: Boydell Press, 1980), 1–5, 29–39, 53–56.

54 Artist 3 is Dennison's D; Artist 4 is her D2.

or vibration in foliage results. Ball-and-squiggle trilobes grouped in pairs of two (pairs of pairs) are also common (fig. 31). Penwork on most pages feels clipped and contained. The compositions are denser than those of his colleague Artist 4 but comparable in density to those of Artist 2. Corkscrews are more varied, looser, and softer than Artist 2's; some are constructed like his as a continuous compressed spiraling line (figs. 87, 87a), others are more like the corkscrews of Artist 1. The terminals of many corkscrews are looser versions of Artist 2's recurved barbs.

Artist 3's borders are less exuberant, loops and extensions neater and more repetitive, than Artist 2's. Green frequently colors Artist 3's Type 4 bars (figs. 35, 87). Artist 3's pearls are a little softer than Artist 2's, more subject to deformation. (Cp. figs. 89a, 135a.) As a border motif, he employed, among others, a four-part foliate sprig organized as a pair of pairs—the nested symmetry that Artist 2 also used (figs. 31, 56, 89).[55]

Like Artist 2, Artist 3 chose the iconography of animals, grotesques and human faces for more than half of his two-line penwork initials. Artists 1 and 4, by comparison, used the animals, grotesques, and faces in only a small fraction of their initials. (See Tables 3 and 4.)

Certain features of Artist 3's style in painting were summarized above: His figures, architecture, and treatment of space are more three-dimensional, more rational, and more refined than are those of Artists 1 and 2; he unites Italianate space and French delicacy. He relies less on

heavy, linear modeling and on heavy white highlights than do the artists of the first campaign, and his shading employs subtle gradations in value. The eyes with small black irises do not greatly differ in form or color from those of Artist 2, but they are more noticeable because the face as a whole is treated with softer line and fewer contrasts in value. The drapery folds are smaller and more numerous than those of Artists 1 and 2; beneath the overlay of folds, the body's rounded surfaces are continuous and readable and are tracked between the folds rather than disappearing beneath wide heavy folds or expanses of drapery. Worth noting are his very fine, expressive heads of Christ in the two-line initials on fols. 22r, C(oncede, fig. 34c) and 107r, D(eus, fig. 92); the technique is halfway between penwork and more opaque painting.

The use of nested pairs of elements marks the borders of both his pages with major illumination: Pairs of paired trilobes populate the borders of the Nativity and Adoration pages (figs. 34, 39). In places the pairing is developed in mirror-image configurations across vertical and horizontal axes in the borders, creating a third level of pairs.

9   Were Artist 2 and Artist 3 the Same Person? Evidence from Penwork

The penwork styles of Artist 2 and Artist 3 have more in common than either shares with the styles of Artists 1 and 4. Artist 3's repertoire of motifs can be seen as a subset of Artist 2's. The iconography of decoration in two-line penwork initials of Artists 2 and 3 is comparable, as noted above. Neither artist indulges in the humor and playfulness that interests Artist 1, nor in the bursts of emotional expression occasionally produced by Artist 4. Designs of both Artist 2 and Artist 3 are structured by symmetry and the use of multiple nested pairs. The possibility presents itself that Artist 3 is in fact Artist 2 and that changes in style—a general loosening of line and a greater sense of uniformity and containment in overall design of the page—may reflect not a difference in hand but the difference of ten to fifteen years in the dates of execution and a shift in interest from penwork to illumination.

Comparisons between Artist 3 and Artist 2 should consider the relative quantities of their work. Artist 3's sixteen decorated pages are less than one-tenth of Artist 2's 168 pages; Artist 3's two-line penwork initials number forty-three; Artist 2's number 345. It is only in considering the entirety of Artist 2's output that both the great range of his motifs and the consistencies of his aesthetic become apparent. Were sixteen pages to be lifted

---

55   Several curiosities appear in the flourishing of Artist 3. On fol. 22va two sets of motifs in penwork are seemingly drawn one over the other (fig. 35). Seven pairs of wavy lancet-shaped leaves decorate the border bar. The third pair from the top is overlaid with an extension, at the very middle of the page, of lines, trilobes, and pearls. Such extensions occasionally occur in the flourishing of Artist 2, as on fol. 73v (fig. 69).

In each case, the extension is into the outer margin of a verso which has no two-line initial in the middle of the page. However, in Artist 2's work, a caesura in the sequence of border motifs makes a place for the extension; in Artist 3's work, extension and foliage are superimposed. Another idiosyncrasy is the discontinuity in coloring of the inner border strip. Typically in 10 A 14, inner border bar originates from a two-line initial, from which it extends either downward or upward to the neighboring two-line initial. The border bar is the same color as its initial of origin—either blue or gold. Normally initials alternate in color—a blue, then a gold, then a blue, etc.—and the inner border bar changes color at each initial to match the initial. However, in two instances in the work of Artist 3, the border strip changes color in the middle of a segment. On fol. 22va (fig. 35), the inner strip changes from gold to blue four lines below the middle of the text block. On fol. 106rb the same thing happens one line below the middle of the block. In both cases the penwork foliage also changes color at this point. Alternations of various sorts are prominent in the decoration of Artist 3.

from his oeuvre—say four from Quire 8 and twelve from Quire 13—one would hardly arrive at an understanding of his character as an artist. Evaluation of Artist 3 must be conducted with cognizance of the relatively small quantity of his output.

The question of whether Artists 2 and 3 might be one and the same will be reprised in Chapter 5, where evidence furnished by painted illumination will be considered in addition to that provided above by penwork.

10 The Second Campaign: Artist 4

Scholarship lodged Artist 4 under the broad roof of Byvanck's second artist until Dennison recognized him as a distinct entity. Artist 4 was responsible for the major illumination on fol. 26r, the Circumcision page (fig. 37); for penwork and minor illumination on twenty folios; and for penwork decoration on an additional thirty-four folios—a total of fifty-five pages of illumination and penwork. His work appears in Quires 3–6 and 9.

10.1 *Two-Line Penwork Initials and Border Bars*

Most of the 102 two-line initials by Artist 4 are flourished with buds, leaves, or other stylized foliate motifs; he uses very few faces, animals, or grotesques. (See Tables 2 and 3.) His corkscrews resemble those of Artist 3. They are variable in shape and length of terminal filament, in the shape and number of the coils (figs. 48, 49). Artist 4 used Type 1 borders almost exclusively. (See Table 6.) The foliate decoration of the bars displays a limited repertoire. Ball-and-squiggle trilobes and trilobes with frilly outline constitute almost the entirety of foliate garnish applied to his border bars. Both leaf types are also used by Artist 3, but as only two of a much larger inventory of foliate forms. Artist 4's penwork is more contained, less reaching, than Artist 2's, lacks the playful subtleties of Artist 1's, and is sparser than that of any of the other three artists. Though not without an interest in spatial complexities, Artist 4 is the least accomplished of the four who worked on 10 A 14.

10.2 *Minor Illumination*

Minor illumination on some folios in Quires 4, 5, and 9 may well have been begun by Artist 2 and completed by Artist 4. (See Inventory 4.) In the initials and extensions on these pages, the black outlines and reductionist touch of Artist 4 and the orange outlines and deft modeling of Artist 2 are found together. On fol. 29v (figs 40, 40a), the black outlines of the initial *E*(*cce*) and the heavy treatment of its trilobe decoration contrast with the

initial extensions—prickle leaves outlined and stemmed in orange. The change from orange to black outlining is quite abrupt. A similar change from the lighter and more nuanced style of Artist 2 to the heavier, flatter touch of Artist 4 can be seen in the bird-billed grotesque in the margin above the initial; the change occurs at about the distal tip of the grotesque's wing (fig. 40).

10.3 *Style of Illumination*

Artist 4's twenty painted initials mark Introits; for most of these an asterisk in the margin serves as a cue for painted initials, as is the case for Artist 2's Introits. This consistent appearance of the same marker throughout quires either entirely or partly decorated by Artist 2 as well as in Quire 9, which is bracketed by Artist 2's work in Quires 8 and 10, is further evidence that Artist 4 was tasked with completing work that had been assigned to Artist 2 and had been prepared by him in certain ways.

Artist 4's gold initial frames are heavily outlined in black; internal detail in the frames is also mostly black (fig. 43a). The initials are blue or pink with old-fashioned circle detailing. Human heads decorate fourteen of his twenty painted initials. (See Table 7.) One head, the only one in grisaille, is a woman's (fig. 64). A curious face in the initial on fol. 64r might be either a grotesque or a human with a harelip (fig. 65). Seven heads are tonsured (fig. 66); might Artist 4 have been a monk or priest, an assistant to Laurence the Priest? Several of his heads are depicted behind the crossbar of the letter *E*, almost as though somehow confined (fig. 67). The remaining initials contain grotesques or trilobes, the latter mostly orange with white shading.

Artist 4's figure style is very like that of Artist 3, but less accomplished. The hallmark of his work and aesthetic is a species of minimalism, perceptible in both his painted illumination and in his penwork. He also manifests a particular interest in the relative positions of figures in space and an interest in emotional expression.

Extensions of, and accompaniments to, the initials include sprays of gold trilobes outlined heavily in black and attached to the outer edge of some frames (fig. 43a), as well as tendrils variously combined with gold strips, cusping, trilobes, lancets and maple leaves, in orange, blue, pink, gold, and black (figs. 41, 66). Seven initials are accompanied by partial borders in the form of winged grotesques with human or bird heads (figs. 43, 65). These are free-floating, separated from the initial by a small interval; Artist 2's borders include similar free-floating partials (fig. 22, lower left). The study of Artist 4's initials and extensions is complicated by antecedent work of Artist 2.

Artist 4 looked closely at Artist 2's work, from which he adapted many of his motifs and patterns of design for initials and extensions.[56] His subjects, both grotesque and human, can be more strongly, though less subtly, emotional than those of Artist 2. Some grotesques boldly threaten the initial extensions (figs. 43, 65); the raw surprise on the open-mouthed face in initial *L*(*ex*, fol. 69v) contrasts with the more understated pathos in faces of Artist 2 (figs. 44, 51, 66). Coloring of the extensions is similar to that of the initials; the palette resembles that of Artist 2 but is less rich and exuberant. Sobriety of color is effected by the heavy black outlining and the heavier touch with line in general and by the reduction in use of creamy white and the expanded use of gray-green.

Artist 4's figure style is similar to that of Artist 3 but is executed with less refinement and less mastery of form. His faces' black pupils are larger and the noses more prominent than Artist 3's. He experiments with the positioning of bodies in space. The Circumcision initial (fig. 37b) is the only illumination in the manuscript that presents four different views of the face—three-quarter from left and right as well as full view and profile. Apart from the awkward configuration of Christ's legs, Artist 4 handles the spatial distribution of the composition's six figures fairly well, though he does not create a spatial platform for the feet.

The painted decoration of the Circumcision page by Artist 4 (fig. 37) has the same sparse feel as Artist 4's penwork pages. (Penwork in the intercolumniation of fol. 26r is by Artist 3, as noted above.) The border bars are not continuous but float in segments in the margins, with blank space between them. This abundance of empty space is used to advantage: It renders the sometimes-humorous activities of the grotesques more immediately legible than those of the figures buried in the border strips of Artists 2 and 3 (figs. 15, 39). The element of humor is largely lacking in the imagery of Artists 2 and 3.

11 Parallels between the First and Second Campaigns

The practice of dividing work on important pages was apparently carried over from the first campaign to the second. On fol. 26r, the Circumcision page (fig. 37), Artist 4 did the painting of initial and borders on top of some preliminary work by Artist 2 while Artist 3 did the penwork border between columns.

12 Conclusion

This chapter demonstrates the rich artistic character of the penwork of 10 A 14. The close relationship between two-line penwork initials and two-line painted initials is apparent. A common iconographical and decorative repertoire as well as instances of hybridization show that the two media were not rigidly separated.

The differences in style, aesthetic, artistic interests, and work habits of the Winter Missal's three or four flourisher-artists have been articulated and summarized above. (See especially the Conclusion sections for Artists 1 and 2.) Artist 2 manifests in many respects a viewpoint and set of interests that would be associated with a priest, while Artist 1 manifests more secular interests.

The medium of penwork has great potential for expressive and conceptual development, as demonstrated by Artist 2. The common features in the penwork of Artists 2 and 3 strongly suggest that these two were the same person. The dynamic developmental trajectory of Artist 2 reasonably could be extended to produce changes that would result, over a decade or more, in a style like that of Artist 3. As will be seen in Chapter 5, Artist 2's illumination also shows development in style and conceptual interests. However, the ownership by one artist of this entire trajectory is more immediately perceptible in penwork than in illumination, as penwork lacks the greatly complicating potential for spatial illusionism which is so insistently attractive to illuminators. By contrast with Artist 2/3, neither Artist 1 nor Artist 4 manifests any interest in change or development of penwork; their aesthetic and expression are essentially static.

Collaboration of Artists 1 and 2 in the quires of the Canon suggests a desire to leave on these most sacred pages the personal mark of both artists. Incompletions, one of the most mystifying aspects of this manuscript, also raise presently unanswerable questions about Artist 2's work habits and raise the possibility that external turmoil may have interrupted the project for a decade or more. Some incompletions in the quires of Artist 2 were later competently completed, it seems, by him; others were completed, some ineptly, by Artist 4.

---

56   Artist 4's figural initial *I* on fol. 30v is a variant of Artist 2's *I* on fol. 58v. (Cp. figs. 41, 61a.) The face with harelip on fol. 64r (fig. 65) is derived from Artist's 2' leonine grotesque in the initial on fol. 47r. (Cp. figs. 52, 65a.) The motif of a face behind the arm of *E* is likely adapted from the instance on fol. 38v (fig. 44), begun by Artist 2 but finished by Artist 4. (See Inventory 4.)

CHAPTER 5

The Miniatures: Style and Iconography

This chapter discusses the style and iconography of the full-page Crucifixion and the ten pages with major miniatures and initials in 10 A 14. The iconography is for the most part familiar, though some unusual elements also appear. Here each image is described, and its construction is analyzed. With variations depending on the particulars, each image is considered for its meaning; for clues to the identity, character, and interests of the artists; for evidence of artistic sources and artistic kinships in its technique, decorative vocabulary and iconography; and for clues to the circumstances and location of production. Miniatures will be considered in the order of their occurrence in the manuscript. The calendar images are considered separately, in Chapter 6.

1 Fol. 7r: the First Sunday in Advent, *Ad te levavi*. First Campaign, Artist 2

The first of Artist 2's illuminations is the 10-line initial *A*(*d te levavi*) which marks the Introit for the First Sunday in Advent (figs. 15, 15a). In the initial a kneeling David lifts up his soul to God; variants of this iconography are common for this Sunday in missals of the early fourteenth century in northern Europe.[1]

The page's border consists of a gold strip about 1cm in width studded with seven medallions containing the overpainted arms discussed in Chapter 1. The design of the border has some kinship with borders in the East Anglian St. Omer Psalter, *c.*1330–1340, as fols. 57v, 70v.[2]

Grotesques arranged in symmetrical pairs, with black linear detailing, occupy sections of the strip. Motifs very similar in design and coloring are found in border strips in illumination of the 1330s, both in Ghent, as in the psalter Douce 5 (fig. 148), and in Cologne, as in a missal for St. Cunibert, Cologne (fig. 158).[3] Similar confronted pairs of elongated grotesques are found in the initial stems of the Loppem-Bruges antiphonal, as on fol. 2r, initial *H*(*odie*, fig. 210).

The initial *A* takes the form of a pink, furry, winged gorgon with tubular neck and two confronted heads having conjoined, open mouths and sharing a tongue rendered as a chain motif.[4] The torso and wings are positioned at the left margin of the page, overlapped by one of the buttresses that support a superstructure of two arches crowned with battlements and a hipped-roofed building. A ribbed barrel vault is visible beneath each of the two arches. Spatial depth created by the recession of the vaults in the upper part of the miniature is not carried down to the floor, rendered as a planar strip. The background is patterned with blue and gold squares, each inscribed with a gold *x*.

The space beneath the vault is constructed of four layers of overlapping elements: the paired buttresses, a pair of columns directly behind them, a horizontal tendril that ends in a foliated curl at each side of the miniature, and finally the diapered background. In this defined space King David, wearing a large gold crown, a blue tunic, and a pink cloak trimmed in gold, kneels before an altar, holding up his soul in the form of a small nude figure. As in myriad versions of this iconography in manuscripts, he is here articulated as a human body-soul composite. Above

---

1 Variations of this iconography for the initial to the introit for the Mass on the First Sunday in Advent are found in missals from France, the Low Countries, Germany and England: 1. Missal, Princeton, PUL, Ms. Garrett 41, Paris, *c.*1300, fol. 5r (PUIMA 122005). 2. Missal of St. Vaast, MSV, Ms. 278 (933), Arras, *c.*1290–1300, fol. 1r (PUIMA 115330). 3. Missal of St. Vaast, MSV, Ms. 601, Arras, mid-fourteenth c., fol. 9r. 4. Missal, DUL, Ms. 876, Cologne, *c.*1330, fol. 12r. 5. A second missal, DUL, Ms. 837, also from Cologne and of about the same date, fol. 16r; see Eizenhöfer and Knaus, "Nr. 36: Hs 837 Missale, Köln, St. Cunibert, um 1330," *Die liturgischen Handschriften*, pp. 123–127. 6. Missal of Sankt Salvator, Prüm, SPK, Ms. theol. lat. fol. 271, Luxembourg, *c.*1300–1310, fol. 17r; see Stones, *Gothic Manuscripts*, pt. 1, vol. 2, cat. nr. III-71, pp. 337–339. 6. Sherbrooke Missal, NLW, Ms. 15536E, English, *c.*1310–1320, fol. 1r; see Sandler, *Gothic Manuscripts*, 2:73; PUIMA 45736.

2 LBL, Ms. Yates Thompson 14; see Sandler, *Gothic Manuscripts*, 1:113–115. The St. Omer Psalter is notable for its borders populated with small, agile figures, its Italianisms in pose and its rendering of space.

The borders of this psalter, like those of 10 A 14, are host to a great variety of foliate types; it is possible that English illumination influenced Artist 2 in this respect. However, the aesthetic for uniformity in scale and consistency in the placement of elements manifested in 10 A 14 is not shared by the East Anglian manuscript.

3 For DUL, Ms. 876, *c.*1330; see n.1, above. Similar confronted pairs of elongated grotesques are found in the initial stems of the Loppem-Bruges antiphonal, as on fol. 2r, initial *H*(odie).

4 Baltrusaitis used the word *gorgon* for creatures of ancient artistic lineage characterized by gaping single, double, or triple mouths. Jurgis Baltrusaitis, *Le Moyen âge fantastique: Antiquités et exotismes dans l'art gothique* (Paris: Armand Colin, 1955), 44–45. He traces this motif to English Apocalypses, one of which Carlvant posits was in Ghent in the thirteenth century; see *Manuscript Painting*, 109–111.

THE MINIATURES: STYLE AND ICONOGRAPHY

the altar hovers the face of Christ, nimbed and framed by a scalloped cloud.

The creature's double heads turn to meet and engage the gaze of the viewer, while its curiously human hands point toward the figures in the miniature. The gorgon thus performs the function of connecting the viewer to the composition and is therefore a precursor of the linking figures who gaze at the viewer but point to the subject in paintings of later centuries. The creature's three-dimensional body and individual members are rendered naturalistically. However, the parts are assembled in a fantastical anatomy. The gorgon's long, thin neck weaves through, over, behind, and under the spatial layers, traversing a three-dimensional pathway. Uncanny, impossible freedom of movement in the rigidly constructed space thus enhances both the element of realism and the element of the preternatural in the gorgon's persona. This dual ontology is already an expansion of its original mode of existence as a letter, a signifier which is inherently flat in form, and is abstract in both form and content. The signifier points to meaning as the gorgon's hands point to Christ, whose head the gorgon partially obscures. Empowered by the realism of its depiction, its presence and actions begin to intrude on and even threaten the other actors.

The initial becomes a metaphysical congress, the meeting place of ontological states: The scene is set in the physical world, the world of nature and illusion. In this space exists man, the ontological body-soul composite. Furthermore, like David's, Christ's being has a dual aspect: Christ manifests the divine, the Godhead, united preveniently (as this is an Old Testament image) with humanity. He is ontologically both God and man. He is thus, to paraphrase Barthes, a sort of second-order ontological statement.[5] Monstrous yet humanoid, the gorgon alludes to both the strange possibilities of composite being. The creature that cannot be—but somehow is—he points both literally and analogically to the God-man, the being in whom the impossible is accomplished, with the resulting redemption of humanity, body and soul. The artist addresses important philosophical and religious ideas, in a highly sophisticated way, in the visual essay of the image. He does not merely play with illusion and reality, two and three dimensions, nature and preternature; he does not merely vaunt his own prowess as a master of illusion, but collects these resources for the sake of pointing, like the gorgon, to mysteries that begin in our world but pass beyond human understanding.

2 Fol. 22r: the Nativity of Christ. Second Campaign, Artist 3

The miniature at the Introit for Christmas is conventional in iconography (figs. 34, 34a). It depicts Mary lying on a draped bed with the Christ child in a manger beside the bed, Joseph seated at the foot of the bed, and the heads of ox and ass stationed together behind the manger and gazing at the child. The background is of alternating gold and blue squares. Gold squares are pounced and blue squares have linear detailing in white and orange. Any number of Nativity images from northern Europe and Italy in the later thirteenth and fourteenth centuries employ this iconography or slight variations of it. However, the arched and pinnacled Gothic frame, familiar from Flemish and French examples, is here replaced by a stable depicted as a wooden shed with pitched thatched roof, rafters, gables, and a circular hole, inscribed with a rafter-cross, positioned to wash the child with the light of the Eastern Star.

The architecture has Italian sources, perhaps mediated through Parisian examples.[6] The figure style is significantly different from the two-dimensional style, heavily dependent on line for shapes and contours, of the first campaign. Line is refined rather than robust, and figures have the doll-like feel of the English Bohun illumination, the earliest products of which are contemporaneous with 10 A 14's Nativity. Scholars have suggested Bohemian influence on both figure style and borders of the second campaign.[7] A comparison of technique with respect to that of first campaign shows that the quality of line has shifted quite dramatically away from the robust towards the refined. In the first campaign surfaces often have a grainy or streaky appearance, resulting from the use of thick white-line highlighting and the application of dark-line internal detail and shading with unblended linear strokes (figs. 106b, 106c). The white highlighting

---

5 Roland Barthes, *Mythologies*, trans. Annette Lavers (New York: Noonday Press, 1972); see especially pp. 111–117.

6 For example, in the Bolognese Missal of Cardinal Bertrand de Deux of *c.*1338–1348, fol. 15r, the Nativity's shed is a simpler version of the shed in 10 A 14. Bolognese examples of this construction dating to the 1340s and later can be multiplied, as in BAV, Cod. cap. 63B. See Elly Cassee, *The Missal of Cardinal Bertrand de Deux: A Study in 14th-Century Bolognese Miniature Painting*, trans. Michael Hoyle (Florence: Istituto Universitario Olandese di Storia dell'Arte, 1980), 21–22 and figs. 29, 46. The architectural type of the shed in 10 A 14 proves remarkably persistent; some two or three decades after the completion of the Winter Missal, in the *Très Belles Heures of Notre Dame*, probably from Paris, BNF, Ms. n. acq. lat. 3093, fol. 41v, the shed that shelters the Holy Family in the Nativity image is very close to that in 10 A 14, though space is handled more adeptly, especially in the lower part of the miniature.

7 Dennison, "Dating and Localisation," 516–517; De Winter, *La bibliothèque de Philippe le Hardi*, 230.

may have sources in Italian manuscripts from the earlier fourteenth century, as in a Bible, probably from Palermo (fig. 154), or a Bolognese Decretals of Gregory IX (fig. 139), where thick white linear highlights mark the faces.[8] English intermediaries such as the Luttrell Psalter are certainly possible; Cologne is another possible source of such effects. (See Appendix 4, Pt. 5.)

This linear technique had in turn replaced the smooth, creamy modulation developed by Master Honoré and seen in Flemish manuscripts such as Douce 5 (fig. 147), a modulation that produced elegant, sophisticated surfaces but also introduced an element of the slickly artificial. The streaky, textured surfaces with heavy outlines and internal linear articulation are symptomatic, in both the Flemish and English illumination, of an interest in realism. In the case of England this interest is coupled with a penchant for expressionism. In Flanders, the perennial interest in realism carries into fifteenth-century illumination and panel painting.

The technique of the 1360s greatly reduces the abstraction of line while holding onto the tendency towards realism (fig. 34a). Individual strokes are refined, and internal detail is downplayed, used with less contrast. The role of line shifts away from defining forms with bold strokes to modeling and detailing. Many small strokes carry the potential of differentiating textures. Heavy line is retained in places, as in the black outline around the haloes of the Virgin and Christ child and at the neck and cuffs the Virgin's dress, but the fabrics of dress and bedclothes are treated as described above.

The bedclothes are of particular interest with respect to the repeated flat, narrow, triangular folds that simultaneously define the spatial planes of the bed and reveal the cylindrical forms of the Virgin's legs underneath the coverlet; in fact, the folds perform this function almost too well, as the mismatch of size and alignment between torso and legs is clearly revealed (fig. 34a). These folds forecast the faceted, triangular drapery of fifteenth-century Flemish panel painting. Both 10 A 14's illumination and the later panel painting demonstrate the Northern mastery of surface coupled with an Italian-derived element of interest in volume and anatomy. However, in Flemish painting, anatomical volume is generated in Northern fashion from the outside in, through surfaces of drapery folds overlaying an interior of uncertain structure. Shading in the illuminations of Artist 3 is applied to articulate form rather than to enhance expression. Italian anatomical volume, on the other hand, is generated from the inside out: a robustly solid and expressive, if not anatomically accurate, internal form is overlaid by fold patterns with a certain independence of the structural core. (Cp. figs. 139 and 154 with figs. 34a and 39a.)

The wrinkled brow of Joseph, straining to understand, is a note of emotion in an otherwise emotionally placid image.

The borders of 10 A 14's Nativity page synthesize a complex of Italian motifs with Northern European structure and Parisian delicacy. The thin, vertical, marginal tendril, the brightly colored feathery foliage, the urns, the Möbius-like knots that encircle the tendril at intervals, the proliferation of gold balls all have antecedents in Italian manuscripts, as in a Paduan Bible of the late thirteenth century (fig. 155).[9] In contrast with Italian manuscripts, in which borders are assembled of elements of various sizes and formats, and are rarely continuous around the entire text block, the borders on fol. 22r of 10 A 14 convey a much greater sense of structural sobriety, consistency, and continuity, although there is some difference in treatment between the vertical and horizontal segments of the border. Antecedents for straight, full borders, including an intercolumnar strip, are numerous in England, northern France, and Lorraine.[10] The light touch has the flavor of Parisian private devotional books from the era of Jean Pucelle and for decades thereafter.[11] Pucellian Parisian book decoration is more understated than that in manuscripts from the other regions.[12]

---

8 Palermo Bible: MLM, Ms. G.60, c.1325, fol. 293v; Bolognese Decretals: BAV, Ms. Vat. lat. 1389, 1330s or 1340s, fol. 3v. For Ms. G.60, see http://ica.themorgan.org/manuscript/description/76984. Accessed 21 April 2022. For Ms. Vat. lat. 1389, see Cassee, *The Missal of Cardinal Bertrand de Deux*, 26; also *Lexicon van Boekverluchters*, https://www.bookilluminators.nl/register-handschriften/bewaarplaatsen-v/vatican-city-biblioteca-apostolica-vaticana. Accessed 20 April 2022.

9 MLM, Ms. M. 436, c.1287–1300, fol. 4r.

10 As antecedents for the full borders in KBR 9217, Haagdorens cites the Alphonso (Tenison) Psalter, LBL, Ms. Add. 24686; the Psalter of Yolande of Soissons, MLM, Ms. M. 729; and the Prayerbook of Marguerite (or Renaud) of Bar, LBL Ms. Yates Thompson 8, but examples could be multiplied. See "Het zgn. missaal," 122.

11 As for example, the Belleville Breviary, BNF, Ms. lat. 10483.

12 On Jean Pucelle, see François Avril, *Manuscript Painting at the Court of France: The Fourteenth Century, 1310–1380*, trans. Ursule Molinaro and Bruce Benderson (New York: George Braziller, 1978), 12–22, 44–59; Kyunghee Pyun and Anna D. Russakoff, eds., *Jean Pucelle: Innovation and Collaboration in Manuscript Painting* (London: Harvey Miller, 2013). The latter has extensive bibliography on Pucelle. For a facsimile, with commentary volume, of the Hours of Jeanne d'Evreux, see Barbara Drake Boehm, Abigail Quandt, and William D. Wixom, *Das Stundenbuch der Jeanne d'Evreux / The Hours of Jeanne d'Evreux / Le Livre d'Heures de Jeanne d'Evreux*, 2 vols. (Lucerne: Faksimile Verlag, 2000).

3 Fol. 26r: the Circumcision of Christ. Second Campaign, Artist 4; Some Preliminary Drawing by Artist 2, First Campaign

The Circumcision of Christ is infrequently depicted in missals of the late thirteenth and early fourteenth centuries. Fol. 26r (fig. 37) is primarily the work of Artist 4 in the second campaign, though preliminary drawing seems to be by Artist 2 in the first campaign. The decoration presents some puzzling elements. In the left margin, pencil sketches of two figures, one just above, and the other just below, the initial *K(arissime*, fig. 37a), are in the style of the first campaign. They do not relate to the decoration of the border as it was later completed. Other problematic elements relating to the initial and the scene it encloses also manifest a disjunction between the first and second campaigns.

In the miniature partially enclosed by the initial *P(uer*, fig. 37b), the nude, nimbed Christ child sits on an altar table, draped with a cloth fringed and patterned on its vertical face. The Virgin supports him beneath his arms; her right hand is unfinished, paw-like. St. Joseph, viewed full face, stands immediately to her left, his hands together in prayer. The mohel with knife and two attendants, one holding the catch-bowl, complete the scene. Gold, orange, brown, and blue are used throughout, with detailing in white and black. The background is of inscribed squares in gold, orange and blue.

The altar cloth bears six roundels, each decorated with a black or red lion on a beige—not gold—field. The texture, tonality, and application of paint is similar in figures and roundels, indicating that the roundels were painted with the figures, not as a later emendation. The heraldic significance of the imagery is questionable, given the sketchy depiction.[13] The lion is a common motif in heraldry of the Low Countries; the arms of both Flanders and Oreye featured a black lion, but neither displayed it on a beige field.[14] A likely possibility is that the lions

are generic regional references along the lines of those in some of the fourteenth-century *Alexander* manuscripts.[15]

The scene is staged in the space created by the architecture of a pitched roof, tiled in blue and carried on two buttress-like pink piers. The underside of the vault is arched and ribbed, creating a sense of three-dimensional space, but the illusion is not carried through lower down; the floor is defined as a line rather than as a spatial platform and the overlapping of elements is ambiguous. This aspect of the treatment of space comports with that of Artist 2's *Ad te levavi* initial (fig. 15a) and contrasts with the more consistent spatial treatment in Artist 3's Adoration on fol. 27v, in which the space-defining perspective of the floor matches that of the ceiling, the overlapping is rationalized, and the angling of buttresses is more consistent. In other respects, however, the architecture of this Circumcision is close in style to that of Artist 3's Adoration, with which it shares slender moldings and piers, a refinement in gold architectural decoration, and a more adept positioning of doorways than Artist 2 displays in his miniature on fol. 106r. These features testify to a date in the 1360s. Perhaps the architecture was sketched during the first campaign by Artist 2 in such a way as to determine the basic disposition of elements, but the painting and detailing were left for Artist 4, who had the benefit of acquaintance with more advanced imaging.

A discordant element is introduced by the placement of the initial body of the *P* in relation to the scene of the Circumcision (fig. 37a). The *P* is not a true historiated initial; it is better described as an overlay *post factum*. Architecture and figures of the scene extend beyond its boundaries on all sides. The initial was clumsily completed or altered, resulting in a strikingly inept transition from frame to image. The very two-dimensional five-line initial is composed of two, winged, gorgon-esque grotesques with strangely conjoint anatomical parts: The maxillary jaw of one is joined to the mandible of the second; the mandible of the second connects to the tail of the first. The forms are harshly outlined and detailed in black and are flatly painted in pounced gold, in contrast to the very three-dimensional, lightly outlined, and softly colored figures of the scene within the initial. Below the counter of the *P* the architecture changes abruptly and

---

13 The arms of the Count of Flanders are marked by the black-on-gold lion, and those of Oreye by a black-on-silver lion, but telling details such as claws, tongue, and teeth are not here included, and the background is neither gold nor silver. The red-on-gold lion is in the arms of the Counts of Holland, but 10 A 14 appears to have no connection with Holland and the background color is, again, not gold. A naissant red lion on gold also appears in some versions of the arms of Bergen-op-Zoom in Zeeland. The first husband of Johanna of Loon, Arnold's mother, was Arnold of Wesemaele, Lord of Bergen-op-Zoom (de Chestret de Haneffe, "Oreye, [Arnould d']," 248). A reference in the miniature to a relative so far removed seems unlikely, however.

14 See Appendix 1for the heraldry. Likewise, a red lion appeared on the arms of Holland and Limburg, but neither used a beige field.

See *Gelre: B.R. Ms. 15652–56* (Leuven: Editions Jan van Helmont, 1992), fol. 83r (#1010, p. 337); fol. 72v (#805, p. 328), and 76r (#907, p. 333).

15 See Alison Stones, "Notes on Three Illuminated Alexander Manuscripts," in *The Medieval Alexander Legend and Romance Epic: Essays in Honour of David J. A. Ross*, ed. Peter Noble, Lucie Polak and Claire Isoz (Millwood, N.Y.: Kraus International Publications, 1982), 198–200.

incongruously to a heavily outlined, flat gold strip in the style of the initial.

The oddities in the design of the Circumcision initial suggest that originally the architecture enclosing the scene was to serve double duty as the letterform. Between the text block and the descender of the *P*, one can see two sketched architectural elements, a small, squared projection just below the counter of the *P* and, three text lines below, a triangular footing at the base of the *P*'s descender. These were drawn but not colored. Perhaps originally the piers framing the arched doorway were extended downward to the triangular footing. For some reason this design was deemed unsatisfactory, perhaps because this configuration introduced gross asymmetry into the architecture as such. The demands of the *mise en scène* thus clashed with those of the letterform. Artist 2 here may have attempted the integration of image and initial frame, as he did in a different way in the *Ad te levavi*. Here he was less successful and perhaps abandoned the attempt, leaving Artist 4 in the second campaign the thankless task of trying to disentangle letterform from archtiecture, an endeavor that eventuated in this infelicitous design.

In the borders of fol. 26r are six grotesques (fig. 37). Two at lower right engage in combat, one with sword and shield, the other with a bow which has released an arrow, still in transit. A grotesque at lower left holds to his mouth, as though playing a double flute, the handle of a broom and the stake on which the carcass of a roasted fowl is spitted. Motifs of these kinds are common in the borders of Flemish and northern French manuscripts of the first four decades of the fourteenth century.[16] At the top of the page a pair of grotesques wearing feathered caps display a wreath between them. This motif has its sources in Italian manuscripts, in which mirror-image paired flying angels, ultimately of Classical origin, support an emblem or device of some sort, as in a Bolognese Decretals, fol.

3v (fig. 139), upper margin, and fol. 4r, in both upper and lower margins.[17]

The tails of all the grotesques sprout gold ball trilobes and maple leaves of red, pink, brown, and blue, shaded heavily in white, the same foliate varieties that appear in Artist 4's painted two-line initials and partial borders (figs. 41, 66). The pounced gold strips that line the tendril-tails of the grotesques in the margins are likewise familiar from the borders and extensions of other pages decorated by Artist 4 in the manuscript. At left, feathery foliage of pink and blue, lined in orange, curls around segments of gold stripping, cusped at intervals. This foliage is of Italian origin; manuscripts from Florence and Bologna from the first half of the fourteenth century provide numerous examples (fig. 156).[18] The borders thus manifest a mix of Italian and Flemish elements.

4 Fol. 27v: the Epiphany. Second Campaign, Artist 3

The miniature, equivalent in height to about twelve lines of text, is framed by a pair of smoothly surfaced, slender, slab buttresses with projecting triangular moldings (figs. 39, 39a). Changes in light and shade are strongly marked at corners. The buttresses support four trefoil arches surmounted by crocketed gables and separated by corbeled pinnacles. Four ribbed vaults beneath the four arches are rendered in perspective, as if seen from the left and in shadow. To either side of the main scene is a small spatial compartment which houses a praying donor, Arnold on the left and Elisabeth on the right. Both are splendidly dressed in fashions of the 1360s.

The work of Artist 3, this scene conforms to 1360s style in all respects; it has none of the stylistic disjunctions apparent in the Circumcision scene. For the most part the iconography deviates little from convention. The Three Wise Men crowned as kings and representing three ages of man and three stages of understanding of the mystery of the Incarnation occur in many variations in medieval iconography.[19] The oldest, wisest, Magus has removed

---

16 Motifs with the double flute and the like occur in OBL, Ms.Douce 6: Grotesque line-endings play a double flute, fol. 123r, and attempt to play a large spoon as a wind instrument on fol. 134r. A line-ending holds a spitted fowl, fol. 169r. Randall indexes scores of examples of men and grotesques shooting with a bow; however, not all images show the arrow in transit. See Lillian M. C. Randall, *Images in the Margins of Gothic Manuscripts* (Berkeley: University of California P ress, 1966), p. 151, "hunting with bow and arrow." A few examples with arrow in transit from northern France and the Low Countries: The Aspremont Psalter-Hours, OBL, Ms. Douce 118, Metz or Verdun, *c.*1302–1305, fol. 95r; the Festal Missal of Johannes of Marchello, HKB, Ms. 78 D 40, Amiens, 1323, fols. 1r, 149v; a psalter, OBL, Ms. Douce 5, Ghent, *c.*1325–1335, fols. 77r, 159v, and Ms. Douce 6, fols. 26v, 117r, 190v; a psalter, OBL, Canon Lit. Ms. 126, Liège, 1320s, fol. 141v; a *Voeux du paon*, MLM, Ms. G.24, Tournai, *c.*1350, fol. 111v.

---

17 BAV, Ms. Vat. lat. 1389, 1330s or 1340s.

18 A Florentine example is the single leaf from a copy of the Laudario of Sant'Agnese, MLM, Ms. M. 742, *c.*1340 (fig. 156). The Missal of Cardinal Bertrand de Deux displays similar foliage, as on fols. 211r, 225v.

19 Variants of this iconography are in the Peterborough Psalter, KBR, Ms. 9961–9962, East Anglia, *c.*1300–1318, fol. 12r; a missal, Princeton, PUL, Ms. Garrett 41, Paris, *c.*1300, fol. 21v; the Hours of Jeanne d'Evreux, New York, Metropolitan Museum, Cloisters Ms. 54.1.2, Paris, 1325–1328, fol. 69v; a Gradual of Johannes von Valkenburg, Bonn, Universitäts- und Landesbibliothek, Ms. 384,

THE MINIATURES: STYLE AND ICONOGRAPHY

his crown and kneels before the Christ child, to whom he presents his gift. The middle-aged Magus stands behind the elder king. He removes his crown with his right hand and holds his gift with his left; he looks up, apparently at the star, positioned in the margin above the initial frame. The youngest king, still crowned, holds his gift and watches but makes no act of worship.

The positioning of the donors Arnold and Elisabeth is of considerable interest. Prayerful kneeling donors are a commonplace, housed either within an initial or miniature, or else outside and below; 10 A 14 and its Brussels cohort are richly supplied with such figures.[20] The donor pair appears twice in the illumination of 10 A 14's first campaign. In the Crucifixion miniature, fol. 143v, Elisabeth kneels at the base of the right side of the Cross behind the mostly-obliterated figure of Arnold. They appear again on fol. 139r (fig. 104).

As in the Crucifixion in 9217, fol. 115v (fig. 175), so in 10 A 14's Adoration of the Magi, Arnold and Elisabeth are positioned not in tandem but separated from and facing one another. They are crowded into small spaces on either side of the text column; perhaps they were not planned in the initial layout of the page.[21] Arnold's feet extend into the text area, where they are accommodated by the partial erasure of a ruled line. As on fol. 139r of 10 A 14, architecture partially, but not completely, separates the donors from the actors in the sacred story. The floor level for the adjunct spaces is lower than that of the main space; and the lateral compartments are roofed at half the height of the main space and with significant differences in articulation and color. The buttresses partially obstruct the

---

Cologne, 1299, fol. 28v. In an Italian gradual, MLM, Ms. M. 795, Florence, c.1300–1332, fol. 24r, the youngest Magus points out the star to his middle-aged companion. In a *Speculum Humanae Salvationis* from Cologne of c.1360–1370, DUL, Ms. 2505, fol. 18v, the middle Magus removes his crown, as he does in 10 A 14.

20 In KBR 6426, the antiphonal, a nun kneels in prayer just outside and below the historiated initials on fols. 2r, 117v, 128r, 132v, 142v. In KBR 9427, the liturgical psalter, Arnold and Elisabeth are depicted inside the initial *D(ominus)*, fol. 43r, kneeling in prayer behind the priest who stands before an altar with paten, or chalice, and Host (fig. 180). In KBR 9217, the Summer Missal, a man, surely Arnold, kneels outside and below the initial *V(iri)* on fol. 33r; the woman who kneels similarly outside and below the initial *V(enite)* on fol. 205r is surely Elisabeth. In the Crucifixion miniature on fol. 115v, the pair kneel in prayer at the foot of the Cross, one on the right side and the other on the left (fig. 175).

21 "Les deux personnages ont été ajoutés assez maladroitement de chaque côté d'une lettrine 'E'. Celle-ci n'étant plus guère lisible, un 'E' majuscule a été introduit dans la marge au début du texte," according to Lemaire and Vanwijnsberghe, "Cote-Signalement KBR 9217," *Textes liturgiques*, 107. The letter *E(cce)* beneath the miniature is also crowded. It is unclear what the original design was to have been.

donor's visual access to the main scene. Thus, the donors are at once linked to and separated from the Epiphany, which is both event and mystery. In location and in time they are separated from it, but spiritually they participate.

The technique used in the Nativity of applying paint with small strokes, understated but still separated to allow texturing, is used here as well. This technique points towards van Eyck's micro-technique, resulting for him in hyperrealism but even here used with similar intention, a Flemish drive towards realism.

Elements of two very different concepts of the body, also seen in the Nativity, conflict here; and the effect is somewhat jarring at first. The Italian conception of the body as a sculptural form with an intrinsic solidity articulated by drapery folds is quite unlike the Northern concept of the body as a construct of line and surface, with shaded and folded drapery as its primary expressive language; a sense of the body under this surface emerges but is secondary. In Flanders and the Mosan region—perhaps owing to the latter's access to the wealth of Roman art preserved in Cologne, Trier, and other former *civitates*—there is more interest in the volume of the body than in England or France, but this is nonetheless communicated with Northern means. The drapery of the Magi and the costume of Arnold are skillfully shaded to create a sense of three-dimensional form, but employing delicate, patternized, and repetitive drapery folds in a way that affirms the importance of surface. Where limbs protrude from the wrapping of drapery, they are flat and delicate. Precisely shaped, spaced, and flattened identical folds overlying the Virgin's left thigh present the leg as a three-dimensional solid, rendered in perspective foreshortening; but the effect of solid form is completely generated by the surfaces. The tiny foot that peeps out from beneath the inflated, drapery-defined leg could only be the terminal of a matchstick. The body does not have Italianate robust solidity; stripped of its Northern linear structural framework, it manifests an unnerving vulnerability. The little black dot pupils are too strong in an eye no longer defined with a correspondingly strong linear outline. Physiques are aptly termed "doll-like."

The bland emotional tenor of the scene voids a source of possible distraction from the enterprise of creating form. Drapery is assuming the faceted, angular appearance that characterizes it in fifteenth-century Flemish panel painting, as opposed to the soft, heavy folds of the International Gothic. The 1360s campaign in 10 A 14 may represent a development in parallel to that of the International Gothic. Both the shingling technique and the heavy fluency of International Gothic create volume through manipulating drapery rather than through the

Italianate means of developing and asserting the body's intrinsic internal structure. Flemish artists of the fifteenth century may have been aware of the shingling technique and might have tapped it, along with elements of earlier Rhenish *Zackenstil* drapery.

The study of fourteenth-century manuscripts' donor portraits has opened up a rich trove of possible associations and meaning for owners, for successor-owners, and for other viewers as well.[22] Arnold and Elisabeth are exemplars of this multi-dimensional signification. They are both wealthy donors and lowly beggars; participants and viewers; they both draw attention to themselves and direct it beyond themselves; they both read (each has a prayer book) and contemplate. The fact that Arnold's image survived the campaign of overpaints unaltered in appearance (though not in attributes) suggests that it offers a certain invitational, generic appeal to the viewer.

Iconographical elements of the Adoration's kneeling donors and those on other folios in the Winter Missal are antecedent to some that appear in panel painting of the early 1400s, such as the Mérode Altarpiece, in which the donors are positioned in an open courtyard, adjunct to, but separate from, the space of the main scene.[23] This is not to suggest direct dependence of the fifteenth-century panel on this miniature but to provide further material for consideration of the relationship between fifteenth-century Flemish panel painting and the iconography and spatial constructions in illumination of in the Low Countries during the fourteenth century.

The border employs many of the same elements that appeared in the Nativity, with the addition of Northern grotesques to Italianate feathery foliage. The border consists of a gold bar about a centimeter in width, framing the text and passing between the text columns, where its width is greater. Within the strip diminutive angels alternate with grotesques. The angels play a variety of wind, percussion, and stringed instruments.[24] Angels are framed by plumy foliage of two types: spreading pairs of fronds and tightly interlaced clusters rising from calyxes. Six of the angels are positioned in foliate frames symmetrical with respect to both horizontal and vertical axes, a restatement of the complex symmetry found in Artist's 2's penwork. Grotesques are mostly generic variations of those in the illumination of the first campaign. The long-tailed grotesque in the middle of the border left of the first column of text is very like that of the figural initial *I* on fol. 73v (fig. 69) and testifies to Artist 3's acquaintance with, and sympathy for, the earlier work. Throughout the border angels and grotesques are paired across the text block.

It is not immediately obvious that the music of the angels in the border strip is performed in praise of the Madonna and Christ child in the initial. The angels are much smaller than the adults in the miniature; their narrow, spaceless strip is radically separated from the space of the miniature; and they are interspersed with grotesques that have no connection to the music. Nonetheless, most of the angels turn toward the Adoration scene. The angels can be seen as an expansion of worship of the Christ child from the biblical past and historical present into the heavenly and eternal. The impulse to reach beyond and across, manifested in the penwork of Artist 2, is carried into subject matter by Artist 3.

The motif of musical angels is reflected in later illumination. Iconography in the borders of the English Bohun hours, *c*.1380–1384, a manuscript with connections to the Rummen Group, reprises the serenading angels of the Adoration of the Magi in 10 A 14.[25] The movement of

---

22   See Laurel Ann Wilson, "'De novo modo': The Birth of Fashion in the Middle Ages" (PhD dissertation, Fordham University, 2011), especially Chapter 4. ProQuest Dissertations and Theses A and I. https://www.proquest.com/pqdt/docview/1719260830/full textPDF/A02C31D1B3614F7CPQ/1?accountid=11012. Accessed 3 October 2022.

23   Floor level of the courtyard is considerably lower than that of the interior, and visual access of the donors to the interior is partly, but not entirely, blocked by the open door. Fenestration admitting strong illumination, tiled floors, corbeled brackets attached to the wall, a shelf below a window, and open books are other elements in the Mérode altarpiece for which the Adoration of the Magi in 10 A 14 supplies prototypes. For bibliography on the Mérode Altarpiece, see notes in Reindert Falkenburg, "The Household of the Soul: Conformity in the *Mérode Triptych*," in *Early Netherlandish Painting at the Crossroads: A Critical Look at Current Methodologies*, ed. Maryan W. Ainsworth (New York: The Metropolitan Museum of Art, 2010), 2–17. See also the entry on the Mérode Altarpiece, in Maryan W. Ainsworth and Keith Christensen, eds., *From Van Eyck to Bruegel: Early Netherlandish Painting in the Metropolitan Museum of Art*, exhib. cat., New York, Metropolitan Museum of Art, 1998–1999 (New York: The Metropolitan Museum of Art, 1998), 89–96.

24   The instruments played by angels in the strip at the left of the text column, from top to bottom: shawm, bagpipes, handbells, mandolin; in the strip between text blocks, from top to bottom: shawm or flute, drum, fiddle; at the right side of the miniature, above the oratory of Elisabeth, upper corner: bladder pipe (?); in the strip below, psaltery, portatief. See de Mare, "Afbeeldingen van muziekinstrumenten," 201–206.

25   Angels playing musical instruments serenade the Virgin from cusped quatrefoils in the border bars accompanying initials for Matins and Prime, fols. 1r and14v of the Bohun Hours, CKB, Ms. Thott 547,4°, and from loops in the bar accompanying the initial for Compline, fol. 28v. The Bohun Hours post-dates the second campaign of 10 A 14 by some fifteen years or more (Dennison, "Stylistic Sources," 342; Sandler, *Illuminators and Patrons*, 348). Dennison's Artist A of KBR 6426 emigrated to England around 1350 and worked on almost all the Bohun manuscripts, including the Hours. Dennison terms this artist the Flemish Bohun

THE MINIATURES: STYLE AND ICONOGRAPHY

the motif from Flanders to England is accompanied by modifications in design. As compared to 10 A 14, in the Bohun hours the disparity in scale between the angels and their audience diminishes and compositional integration of the two cohorts is stronger.

Music-making angels appear in fifteenth-century panel painting as well. The concert in 10 A 14 foreshadows the serenading angels of the Ghent Altarpiece (completed 1432). Like the angels of Artist 3's Adoration, the altarpiece's angels are smaller in scale than the figures of the main image field and are placed in spatial compartments discontinuous with the space inhabited by Christ and the Virgin. The manuscript may have remained for a time in Ghent after its completion there in 1366 and might have been seen by artists in that city. If the missal was in the possession of Margaret of Male, Duchess of Burgundy, after the death of her father Louis of Male in 1384, it may have been accessible to artists, including van Eyck (himself widely held to have been an illuminator as well as a panel painter), working for the Burgundian court at the end of the fourteenth century and later.[26] The common-

alities of subject matter and of treatment of drapery, and the common use of disjunctions in scale and space are relevant to the issue of illumination's connections to panel painting, connections perhaps appropriately characterized as a dialog between the two pictorial genres.

5   Fol. 106v: Palm Sunday: Christ Entering Jerusalem. First Campaign, Artist 2

This page with the Introit for Palm Sunday (figs. 91, 91a, 91b) is striking for its eclectic design, which reflects the gap between the commencement of the page in the first campaign and its completion in the second, and for its bold use of the columbine motif, which frames the text column that begins Holy Week.[27] By the hand of Artist 2 in the first campaign are the four-line miniature of the Entry into Jerusalem, the initial *D(omine)* below it, the bas-de-page frieze of stag and doe below text block b, and the vignette of cavorting rabbits, or hares, above text block a. To Artist 2 can also be ascribed the decoration along the right side of text block b and in the intercolumniation, both featuring imposing stalks of large, showy columbine, blue at right and red at left. The absence of Italianisms in the foliage and flora speak for production during the first campaign, and the red outlining of gold strips is typical of Artist 2. The border bar, penwork, and butterflies along

---

(as distinct from his co-worker the English Bohun artist) when discussing his work in England. His connections to Flanders may help explain the appearance of the concert iconography in English illumination. See Sandler, *Illuminators and Patrons*, 26 and 166, for illustration of fols. 14v and 1r.

26   See for example, the studies on van Eyck's likely contributions to the illumination of the ambitious and sumptuous *Très Belles Heures de Notre Dame*. As eventually constituted, it consisted of a book of hours, BNF, Ms. n. acq. lat. 3093; a prayer book, formerly Turin, Biblioteca Nazionale, Ms. K. IV.29 (destroyed in a fire in 1904); and a missal, Turin, Museo Civico d'Arte Antica, Manuscript Inv. No. 47. The prayer book, fortunately, was photographed, in black and white, in 1902. For a review of the history of this extraordinary manuscript and for a thorough description and analysis of its illumination, see *François Boespflug and Eberhard König, Les "Très Belles Heures" de Jean de France, duc de Berry: Un chef-d'oeuvre au sortir du Moyen Âge (Paris: Les Éditions du Cerf, 1998). Boespflug and König assign a number of miniatures in the destroyed Turin prayer book and in the Turin missal to van Eyck. See pp. 243–247 for the difficulties of relating the miniatures in the Très Belles group to panel painting. On the other hand,* Ludwig Baldass, *Jan van Eyck* (London: Phaidon Press, 1952), 30–33 and 90–96, does not see van Eyck's hand in the miniatures of either the prayer book or the missal. *For an account of the attempt to reconstruct the original color of the illuminations in the now-destroyed Turin Prayer Book, see* Albert Châtelet, "Les miniatures de Jan van Eyck revisitées," *Art de l'enluminure* 15 (Dec. 2005–Feb. 2006): 36–66. For the landscapes in the manuscript's miniatures and their relation to those in van Eyck's panels, see Katherine Crawford Luber, "Recognizing Van Eyck: Magical Realism in Landscape Painting," *Philadelphia Museum of Art Bulletin* 91 (Spring 1998): 14–15. For the intersection of painting and illumination in the fifteenth century, see Thomas Kren and Maryan W. Ainsworth, "Illuminators and Painters: Artistic Exchanges and Interrelationships," in *Illuminating*

---

the Renaissance: The Triumph of Flemish Manuscript Painting in Europe, ed. Thomas Kren and Scot McKendrick, exhib. cat., J. Paul Getty Museum, Los Angeles, and Royal Academy of Arts, London, 2003–2004, (Los Angeles: The J. Paul Getty Museum, 2003), 35–57; and Kren, "From Panel to Parchment and Back: Painters and Illuminators Before 1470," in *Illuminating the Renaissance*, 81–119.

27   See Elizabeth Moore's entry "63: Winter Missal of Arnold of Rummen," in Adelaide Louise Bennett et al., *Medieval Mastery: Book Illumination from Charlemagne to Charles the Bold 800–1475*, trans. Lee Preedy and Greta Arblaster-Holmer, exhib. cat., Leuven, Stedelijk Museum Vander Kelen-Mertens, 2002 (Leuven: Uitgeverij Davidsfond nv, and Brepols Publishers, 2002), 255 wo compositions that share the compacted composition, though not the placement of the donkey inside the arch, are the miniature of the Entry in the Ghent psalter Douce 5 (fig. 148), *c.*1335, and the Entry in a leaf from an antiphonal made in Cologne, *c.*1345, Ms. WRM, Inv.-Nr. M 6. Other examples of the subject are many, as are variations in the iconography. Two approximately contemporary French missals with the Entry into Jerusalem at *Domine ne longe* depict Christ outside the city, the disciples following him, and a man laying a coat in front of him: the St. Denis missal, London, V&A, MSL/1891–1346, Paris or possibly Tournai, *c.*1350, fol. 121v; a Franciscan missal, OBL, Ms. Douce 313, Paris (?), mid-fourteenth c., fol. 108r; The Franciscan missal includes heads in the doorway to the city.

the left side of text block are the work of Artist 3 in the second campaign.

The miniature of the Entry into Jerusalem is condensed. The artist depicts a moment in the procession in which Christ's mount is moving through the gate and into the city rather than approaching the gate of Jerusalem from outside the city, as is more usual for this episode. Christ's gentle expression, gesture of blessing, unadorned tunic, and large bare foot all communicate his humility. Both the inhabitants who spread their garments on the road in front of Christ and the disciples who follow him are missing. The crowds that acclaim him are represented by three figures in the architectural superstructure.

The city is depicted as two sturdy towers with conical roofs, connected by a pair of arches over ribbed vaults. A complex of ventilators, corbeled rooms, a chimney pot and additional openings complicate the architecture and contribute to the confusion of space, which is most striking in the awkward placement of the donkey. The attempt to impart depth throughout the space, from the vaults down to the floor—a project not undertaken in the *Ad te levavi* miniature—is ambitious but unsuccessful. Figures are colored and modeled with the grainy strokes of the first campaign. The palette consists of intense red, blue, and gold, offset by soft shades of pink, blue, and beige; the hues are those of the *Ad te levavi* (fig. 15a), but orange and blue are favored over gold in the Entry miniature.

Subjoined to the miniature is a three-line figural initial, a gorgon, shaped as the first letter in the Introit, *Domine ne longe*, for Palm Sunday (fig. 91a). The remaining letters of the word *Domine* are written in the top line next to the miniature. A woman in a red dress decorated with white stripes, standing in the counter of the initial, looks and points up toward Christ, the *Dominus*. The initial directs the reader to the continuation of the word, and to entry into the text, by way of the Lord who is the Word, himself depicted entering the city, where his Passion, symbolized by the columbines, awaits.[28]

The two stalks of large, abundant, and carefully rendered columbines are unusual; indeed they visually dominate the page. The columbine is associated in medieval art with Christ, for several reasons.[29] Its corona of projecting spurs suggests the Crown of Thorns, hence both his Passion and his kingship. The leaf divides into three leaflets, which in turn may subdivide into three lobes, thus

inviting Trinitarian associations. In Middle Netherlandic the word for columbine, *Aglei*, may have been connected with AGLA, a kabbalistic acronym for *Atah Gibor Leolam Adonai*, "Blessed be the Lord forever, amen."[30] Large columbines appear, usually as singles, in the borders and initials of fourteenth-century manuscripts.[31] Large columbines in the border of the *Te igitur* page, fol. 23v, of a missal for the use of Cologne, first quarter of the fifteenth century, clearly refer to the Passion, as the miniature and historiated initial on the page feature the Crucifixion and the Christ of Pity, respectively.[32] Columbines appear in several places in the Ghent Altarpiece: in the crown of Mary; in the grass beside the procession of virgin martyrs; and in the tilework beneath the feet of the serenading angels, alternating with tiles inscribed AGLA and tiles with images of the Lamb and the IHS monogram.[33]

In the top left margin and in the bas-de-page at right are two pastoral scenes. Above, rabbits frolic in a landscape with grassy hills, burrows, and small trees bearing gold balls. Below, a confronted stag and doe stand on opposite sides of a tree bearing gold-brown fruit. The beasts stand on a strip of grassy ground, from which at either end rise the stems of columbine that border the text. The seamless transition from grass strip to stems witnesses to the contemporaneity of borders and bas-de-page. The scene of rabbits at the top of the page is very similar in style and

---

30　In Latin, "Benedictus Dominus in aeternum, fiat, fiat," Löber, *Agaleia*, 20.

31　Columbines in borders and initials include the following: The lower border of fol. 14v, of the London Alphonso Psalter, LBL, Ms. 24686, *c.*1284–1302; see Sandler, *Gothic Manuscripts*, 2:13–14. Four columbines appear in the lower border of an East Anglian *Polychronicon*, of the 1390s, OBL, Ms. Bodley 316, 1390s, fol. 8r. (For additional English examples of the columbine and their possible significance, see Dennison, "Significance of Ornamental Penwork," 33 and n. 14, and p. 52, fig. 1.) The Breviary of Renaud of Bar, from Verdun, LBL, Ms. Yates Thompson 8, *c.*1302, fol. 1r, right border; see Stones, *Gothic Manuscripts*, pt. 2, vol. 1, cat. nrs. IV-16a and IV-16b, pp. 78–88, ill. 127. As decoration in a penwork initial, fol. 106r, in the St. Severin (later St. Cunibert) missal of *c.*1330 from Cologne; see DUL, Ms. 874; see Eizenhöfer and Knaus, *Die Liturgischen Handschriften*, 133–135. The later fifteenth century saw a dramatic increase in imagery of the columbine in manuscripts and in panel painting, the latter especially in Germanic-language lands.

32　LBL, Ms. Egerton 3018, Cologne (?). Illumination and flourishing of this manuscript have elements of Dutch, Rhenish, and Italianate style. See "Eg. 3018," British Museum, *Catalogue of Additions to the Manuscripts 1916–1920* (London: The Trustees, 1933), 333–334.

33　See Löber, *Agaleia*, Chapter 6, "Akelei in der Heilsgeschichte." Löber cites multitudinous examples of the columbine in iconography of all stages of the life of Christ, including the Entry into Jerusalem, p. 99.

28　My thanks to Richard Gameson for noting the dual reference of *Dominus*.

29　See Karl Löber, *Agaleia: Erscheinung und Bedeutung der Akelei in der mittelalterlichen Kunst* (Cologne: Böhlau Verlag, 1988), especially pp. 17–22, and 99–104.

THE MINIATURES: STYLE AND ICONOGRAPHY

concept to the bas-de-page scene and so is also likely of the first campaign.

Very different are the border bar along the outer column of text and the terminal complex below. Hues of the Type 4 border bar, garnished with motifs standard in the work of the second campaign, are similar to those used elsewhere on the page, but values and intensity are lower. The penwork bears Artist 3's signature nervous line, loose corkscrews, and his even, uniform spacing of elements. The butterflies, evenly spaced and along the border bar like a line of boats floating at the slips of a dock, are a response to the spectacular row of penwork butterflies in the border of the first campaign of 10 A 14, on fol. 91v (fig. 82), where they are likewise associated with a Type 4 border bar. Here again the intention of tying the later the work to that of the first campaign can be inferred.

In sum, this page's imagery is significant for its bold attempt at expanding space, for its emphasis on the humility of Christ, for the floral announcement of his impending Passion, and for its attempt to link the first campaign to the second through reuse of a striking motif. The page's design, however, exhibits discontinuities in scale, medium, and palette.

6   Fol. 139r: the Preface of the Canon for Easter. First Campaign, Artist 1

This miniature attached to the *Per omnia secula seculorum* of the Preface to the Canon for Easter (figs. 103, 103a) is the first of Artist 1's major illuminations after his work in the calendar. The miniature is placed at the beginning of the notated prayers of the Canon. It occupies the height of two staves plus accompanying text and extends into the margin to the very top of the page. The priest, robed in alb, chasuble and maniple, stands at the altar, hands raised. On the altar rests an open book; a paten, or chalice, with host balanced on its rim stands beside it. Immediately to the right of the architecture framing the altar is the tall, compacted *P* of the *Per omnia*. To the left of the priest and in a separate architectural compartment kneel Arnold and Elisabeth, hands folded in prayer. They wear the styles of the 1340s: his dagged capelet and hood and his *cote hardie* without padded chest, her *cote* with closed sides. The scene is enclosed by arches carried on piers and crowned with gables, pinnacles, and a conical roof. The palette is dominated by orange and blue, less intense and grayer than Artist 2's, and by dusty pink. The highly burnished gold of the background brightens the color.

The iconography of the priest at the altar is largely conventional: Many missals depict variations of the priest at

the altar at the Preface to the Canon, either, as here, at the *Per omnia*, or at the *Vere dignum*, immediately following.[34] Many also include praying donors separated in some way from the priest. In 10 A 14's *Per omnia* image, the details of this separation are of interest. The arch above Arnold and Elisabeth is adjacent to and slightly lower than the arch over the priest. The couple's compartment, roofed with its own conical tower, extends into the left margin. The two compartments are also distinguished by differences in the color of all analogous architectural elements. Arnold's raised hands overlap the pier between cells, and his head bends slightly forward, affording him a partial view around the obstructing support. Thus, the architecture at once separates the donors from, and unites them with, the priest and altar. The asymmetry of Artist 1's architecture contrasts with the symmetry employed by Artist 3 in the Adoration of the Magi on fol. 27v. The largely planar space avoids ambitious forays into depth.

The splendid border, loaded with polished gold bars, gold panels that back the passages of interlace, and gold trilobes, has only a few grotesques. An archer is positioned just below the miniature. At bottom left is a pair of winged, confronted male-female grotesques; at bottom right, a bird-headed grotesque hovers over a grotesque with a man's head. These are conventional in subject and anatomy.

Elements of the arrangement of figures and the use of architecture are derived from earlier compositions. They can be compared with those on fol. 13r of the reconstructed remnants of a Liège psalter of *c.*1300.[35] In this image of the Mass of St. Giles, Charlemagne and Gisela kneel at prayer before a priest celebrating at the altar. The two arched spatial compartments are vaulted at different levels. The tall, narrow space occupied by a Franciscan in this psalter is analogous to the space of the tall, narrow initial *P(er omnia)* in 10 A 14.

As in the Adoration miniature (fol. 27v), the disposition of the donors relates to later panel painting. In the

---

34   A very similar image of the priest at the altar is in KBR 9217, fol. 109r, at the *Per omnia*. A few other examples: Missal, Tournai, Bibliothèque du Chapitre cathédrale, Ms. A 11, Tournai, *c.*1267, fol. 81r; and a missal, TBM, Ms. 12 (9), Tournai, *c.*1275–1280, fol. 64r; Missal of Sankt Salvator, Prüm, SPK, Ms. theol. lat. fol. 271, Luxembourg, *c.*1300–1310, fol. 64r; Missal of Saint-Nicaise, Reims, Bibliothèque municipale, Ms. 230, *c.*1270, fol. 85r; the Festal Missal of Stephen Becquart of Panoul, Auxerre, Trésor de la Cathédrale, Ms. 8, Paris, *c.*1300. All the preceding are catalogued in Stones, *Gothic Manuscripts*, pt. 1, vol. 2.

35   LBL, Ms. Add. 28784B; see Judith Oliver, "Reconstruction of a Liège Psalter-Hours," *British Library Journal* 5, no. 2 (Autumn 1979): 108 and 127, n.12; Oliver, *Gothic Manuscript Illumination*, 1:179; 2:266; illustration, p. 399.

space of the Mérode Altarpiece, referenced above, the two donors kneel, woman behind man, in a space partly separated from that in which the sacred event takes place, an event of which they have only a partial view. In the altarpiece the separation is more developed; it is spiritual and psychological as well as physical, but the germ of the concept is already present in 10 A 14.

Unlike the donors in the Adoration or those in the later Mérode Altarpiece, Arnold and Elisabeth are physically present at the event depicted in 10 A 14's *Per omnia*. In the Adoration of the Magi, the architecture is a device for organizing the scene and articulating distinctions in hierarchy and in levels of both historical and mystical reality. In the *Per omnia* the hierarchical and mystical distinctions remain, but there is no disjunction between the historical moment of the event depicted and that of its witnesses. A similar motif is employed to significantly different effects in the two images.

7   Fol. 143v: the Crucifixion. First Campaign, Artist 2

The Crucifixion as depicted in the Winter Missal of Arnold of Rummen emphasizes both the humanity and divinity of Christ and also the theme of sacrificial offering (fig. 106). Thus, it is both Christological and soteriological. In conjunction with the facing *Te igitur* page (frontispiece and fig. 107), the Crucifixion images Eucharistic theology as well.[36] Both Artist 2's aesthetic and the details of the iconography serve the expression of these concepts.

The image is framed by a red strip of varying width, outlined in gold, to which are attached sprigs bearing large gold trilobes, outlined in red and attached to gold balls. A gold medallion containing a red Greek kissing cross is placed directly below the miniature and touches the architecture where it overlaps the frame. Originally a total of sixteen or seventeen figures were depicted on the page; one has certainly been erased or covered over, and a second may have been as well.

A disproportionately large Christ, eyes closed, head encircled by a black-and-gold cross nimbus, hangs on the Cross. His body, encircled by a voluminous wrap at the hips, is pocked with dozens of small, bloody, lancet-shaped wounds, each with a dark center, evenly spaced. A larger

wound of similar size and coloring marks his right side. The thorns of his crown are shaped and colored to look much like the wounds on his body, which sags and bends markedly. Three nailed spikes are visible, but his feet are positioned to require a fourth, perhaps hidden behind the third. The emphasis is on his suffering and hence on his humanity. Above the red-orange Tree-of-Life Cross are the personified sun and moon.

Below Christ, at his right, swoons the Virgin, in an expressive, hipshot pose, her left hand on her breast. Her eyes are open, and she looks out at the viewer, communicating her anguish in her glance and gesture, and inviting the viewer's participation. St. John stands behind her; his right hand supports her right elbow, a gesture that echoes that of John in the Crucifixion of the missal of St. Peter's Abbey, Ghent, fol. 7v (fig. 160).[37] The role of John as caretaker of the Virgin marks a change from the traditional Northern configuration, in which the Virgin and John are on opposite sides of the Cross. The change reflects the influence of Italian panel painting via Parisian intermediaries.[38] This new grouping occurs very early in Ghent; by about 1280, in the missal of St. Peter's the fainting Virgin is already supported by St. John (fig. 160), as noted above; in the Ghent Ceremonial of forty years later, a variation of this pairing is used (fol. 70v, fig. 163).[39] In 10 A 14, faces

---

36   A brief introduction to theology of the Eucharist is provided by Giles Dimock, *The Eucharist: Sacrament and Sacrifice* (New Haven: Catholic Information Service, n.d.). A broad introduction to the topic with references to additional articles are found in the *Catholic Encyclopedia* s.v., "Eucharist."

---

37   SMG, inv. A60.01, *c.*1275–1285. The Virgin and St. John are similarly posed in a Liège book of hours, *c.*1310–1320, LBL, Ms. Stowe 17, fol. 107v, where the Virgin's heart is pierced by a sword.

38   See Gerhard Schmidt, "Die Wehrdener Kreuzigung der Sammlung von Hirsch und die Kölner Malerei," in Gerhard Bott and Frank Günter Zehnder, eds., *Vor Stefan Lochner: Die Kölner Maler von 1300 bis 1430; Ergebnisse der Ausstellung und des Colloquiums, Köln 1974* (Cologne: Druckhaus Rudolf Müller, 1977), 11–27, especially 11–16, for a consideration of Italian influences in early fourteenth-century Northern panel painting. The Crucifixion in Pucelle's Hours of Jeanne d'Evreux, MMA, Cloisters Ms. 54.1.2, 1325–1328, fol. 68v, depicts St. John and a woman, perhaps Mary Magdalene, supporting a fainting, collapsed Virgin.

39   The artist of the Ghent Ceremonial, UGU, Ms. 233, must have known the Ghent missal. See Lori Walters, "Marian Devotion in the Tournai Rose: From the Monastery to the Household," in *De la Rose: texte, image, fortune*, ed. Herman Braet and Catherine Bel (Leuven: Peeters, 2006), 236–242, for discussion of the iconography of the Ghent Ceremonial's Crucifixion and the relationship of this image to the earlier missal of St. Peter's Abbey. St. John supporting the fainting Virgin is also depicted in a Brabatine psalter-hours of the 1270s, ex-Fürstlich-Fürstenbergische Hofbibliothek, Donaueschingen, Ms. 316, fol. 13v. (See Oliver, *Gothic Manuscript Illumination*, 2:464, pl. 169.) Oliver, 2:165, cites Flemish influence on this psalter. The whereabouts of this psalter are unknown.

The disposition of figures in the missal from St. Peter's Abbey invites comparison with the Crucifixion of *c.*1330 in the missal in DUL, Ms. 876, fol. 223v. Five Jews and soldiers stand on one

are touched with the strong white highlights common in much illumination in the 1340s in England and on the Continent.

Below the Cross, at Christ's left, kneels the small figure of a female donor who must be Elisabeth of Lierde, arms bent at the elbow, hands together in prayer. She wears a white veil with crimped lining, over hair styled in fashionable *cornettes*, and a white cloak, fastened by a gold broach, over a blue *cote* decorated with large gold buttons. On the ground just in front of her are the scraped remains of a pair of feet, almost certainly Arnold's. His figure, still visible as a silhouette in shadow, has been covered over in a pattern to match the background. Just above Elisabeth is another silhouette, of a shape that suggests a shield or helmet, probably Arnold's, and likely supported by an angel; if this is indeed the case, then the main image field originally held six figures.

Figures and the Cross are placed on a narrow strip of bare, dimpled ground within an architectural framework remarkable in its era for its solidity and balance, its orderly construction in both two and three dimensions, and its restraint in color and decoration. In front of the figures extends in tilted perspective a stage-like platform of unjointed masonry; its color can be read as either blue with white highlights, or white with blue shadows. The platform features a trapezoidal forward projection. Masonry piers, similar to the platform in articulation and coloring, frame the figural tableau. Sharp changes in color at angles create the illusion of light falling on three-dimensional forms. The general effect is of solid, strongly illuminated masses existing in an illusionistic space of sorts.

A superstructure of arches is crowned with battlements and roofed buildings, all grouped in threes. Each of the three arches covers a cell of fan-like ribbed vaulting. Triangular projections splayed in an ad hoc perspective divide each buttress into stories, each with an opening topped by a keyhole arch. All but the lowest opening on each side encloses a small praying angel, eight in total. Angels lodged in the left buttress all turn in toward Christ.

In the right buttress, angels face two toward Christ and two toward the page opposite.

The image accommodates a total of sixteen or seventeen figures and heads, yet even before the overpaints the space would not have been crowded. This result is achieved by the use of four different sizes of figures, Christ the largest and angels the smallest, and by generous use of the architecture to house both figures and heads.

In the superstructure, as in Heaven, Christ appears a second time, alive rather than dead; his is the middle head of the three that peer out from openings in the battlements of the central unit. Identified by his cross nimbus, he gazes directly and impassively at the viewer. Two nimbless heads with gray hair and beards, both positioned in three-quarters, look out and upward, in mirror-image arrangement. The number, physical types, and positioning of the three heads suggest the Trinity, imaged as three human persons, an unusual depiction but not unknown in English illumination of the Anglo-Saxon era and later.[40] The small praying angels in the niches of the supporting piers speak to further associations between the architecture and Heaven and also, in their tiered arrangement, to the reality of a connection between Heaven and earth. Clearly presented is a statement of the two natures of Christ. His humanity is emphasized in his image on the Cross, where his mortality is displayed and his suffering made visible in the scourge-marks and the bloody wounds and in the pathos of his posture. His eternal and impassible Divinity is communicated by the image in the superstructure.

The treatment of the miniature's background promotes the sense of orderly structure that the architecture also presents. The background is articulated as a grid of gold squares with line-and circle decoration, a near-perfect exercise in Panofskian scholastic subdivisions.[41] Within each gold-framed square are four smaller, black-framed squares, and the diagonals inscribed within each square

---

side, the fainting Virgin and St. John on the other. The figure of Christ and the depiction of the Cross are also very similar. These correspondances suggest another instance of the movement of influence from west to east, as Oliver has proposed in the case of the von Valkenburg style, which, she argues, shows significant influence from Liège, and as proposed by Haussherr for the choir screens of Cologne Cathedral, which exhibit connections to the style of stained glass from the choir of St. Ouen, Rouen. See Judith Oliver, "The Mosan Origins of Johannes von Valke," *Wallraf-Richartz-Jahrbuch* 40 (1978): 23–37; and Reiner Haussherr, "Die Chorschrankenmalereien des Kölner Doms," in Bott and Zehnder eds., *Vor Stefan Lochner* 1977, 28–59.

40 See Jane E. Rosenthal, "Three Drawings in an Anglo-Saxon Pontifical: An Anthropomorphic Trinity or Threefold Christ?" *Art Bulletin* 63, no. 4 (1981): 547–562. This iconography has an ancestry from Early Christian times in the typology of Abraham's three heavenly visitors, two or even all three of whom may be nimbless in fourteenth-century iconography. Usually one of the three visitors has a cross-nimbus and the other two have uninscribed nimbi, but in some English examples of the fourteenth century this is not the case. In the Queen Mary Psalter, LBL, Ms. Royal 2.B.VII, fol. 11r, the three visitors have wings but are all nimbless; in two scenes in the Egerton Genesis, LBL, Ms. Egerton 1894, fol. 11r (10r), the central figure has a cross-nimbus and the other two are nimbless.

41 See Erwin Panofsky, *Gothic Architecture and Scholasticism* (New York: Meridian Books, 1957).

are in turn sliced by smaller diagonals. This design exemplifies the concept of nested symmetries, identified above in the borders of Artist 3's Nativity, fol. 22r (fig. 34). The Crucifixion's squares-within-squares are either blue or beige, arranged in A-B alternation, and are inscribed with either white or red linear detailing, again in a regularly alternating pattern. In the shadow areas of erasure and/or overpaint, values are somewhat darker, but hues are the same. Color contrast is used in a sophisticated way to produce optical effects; there appears to be a greater range of hues and values than is actually employed. The disciplined patterning of design contributes to the solemnity of content. Emotion is contained by a framework of rational order created by treatment of architecture and background, just as the cosmic order frames and contains the human world.

Artist 2's feeling for structure is manifested in the solidity, symmetry, and consistent articulation of his architecture and in the systematic subdivisions of the background decoration. The architecture is substantial but not overpowering in effect. It occupies relatively little of the image field. (See Appendix 4, Pt. 4, for discussion of the sources of the architecture in this image.) Artist 2's economy of palette, limited to the three primary hues, much of the application highly saturated and emphasized with a wide range of values, contributes to the monumental feel of the image.[42] Figures and drapery are modeled with blue and beige of lower intensity, but the absence of pink that appeared in Artist 2's two previous images results in a severity of color.

7.1 The Sources for 10 A 14's Crucifixion: 9217

The Crucifixion relates to various Northern Crucifixion images, none completely determinative of its style or iconography; it manifests an ambitious, if not entirely successful, synthesis expressive of Artist 2's interests.

An immediate source might be sought in the full-page Crucifixion on fol. 115v in 10 A 14's slightly earlier complement 9217, the Summer Missal (fig. 175); this image was the work of Artist 9217-1, the manuscript's sole illuminator. Substantial differences between the two manuscripts in aesthetics, style, and content are apparent in spite of significant agreement in design. (See Appendix 4, Pt. 3, for further description and analysis of the Crucifixion in 9217.)

Resemblances of the Crucifixion in 9217 to 10 A 14's are numerous: the dimensions of the image; its surround of gold trilobes; the kissing cross; the posture of Christ; the inclusion of Mary, John, and donors; the tripartite architectural superstructure supported on multi-story piers; the placement of the cross in a strip of ground fronted by masonry; the gridded, colorfully patterned background; and even the use of overpaint to conceal arms.

Differences are also many: In 9217 the image is framed by two vertical strips patterned in squares, anchored top and bottom by quatrefoils with the evangelist symbols. The strips are overpaints concealing heraldry.[43] The crucified, dead Christ is affixed to the plain, brown cross with three nails. His body is unmarked by wounds of flagellation. The diminutive bones and skull at the base of the cross introduce typology absent from 10 A 14.

The Virgin and St. John stand on opposite sides of the Cross, in poses traditional and contemplative, less expressive than those of their counterparts in the Winter Missal. Neither figure looks out at the viewer. The small figures of Arnold and Elisabeth, both fashionably dressed, kneel in prayer, one on either side of the Cross, supporting inscribed banderoles that present a joint petition for salvation: His reads NUNC ARBOR NOS, and hers reads DEFENDE CRUCIS AMBOS.[44]

The grid in the background of 9217's Crucifixion is composed of rectangles in quadrants 1 and 4 and small squares in quadrants 2 and 3. Shifts in pattern and color between quadrants enhance the decorative effect of the background. In quadrants 1 and 4, every other rectangle was originally painted with Arnold's white-plumed, black-mantled helmet; the gold squares with red and white linear decoration are all overpaints, concealing these helmets.[45] Traces of the white plumes and black mantles are visible at the edges of numerous rectangles. Feathery tendrils overlap the pier beside the end of the cross at the left side of the image (fig. 175a) and the trailing edge of the black mantle is visible both at the bottom of the rectangle between Elisabeth's head and John's right elbow and again overlapping Elisabeth's banderole directly above the final *E* of *DEFENDE*. (fig. 175b. See Appendix 4, Pt. 3 for further discussion of the overpainted heraldry.) The mathematical discipline of nested symmetry worked so thoroughly into the background of 10 A 14's Crucifixion is not apparent in 9217; rather, emphasis was on the decorative display of heraldry.

The very slender piers, busy with angled setbacks and various attachments and openings, are oddly

---

42 Arms of Oreye, Chiny, Loon—those most likely to have been covered by overpaints—all employ various combinations of hues found in the image.

43 Haagdorens, "Het zgn.missaal," notes these overpainted shields.

44 "Tree of the Cross, protect us both now."

45 To my knowledge, these overpaints are noted here for the first time in published literature on 9217. Examination of this page under special conditions of light is certainly warranted to confirm these observations.

two-dimensional, as though they were strips peeled from the surface of more substantial structures. They can be likened to the spindly piers that frame some prefatory miniatures of the Ghent-produced psalter Douce 5 (fig. 147). The curvature of the barrel vault's lower edge overshoots the vertical and seems to collapse the space of the vault into two dimensions. The heads in the superstructure, four in number, are more ambiguous in meaning than those of 10 A 14; the secular (woman in ruffled hood) and the religious (prophet-like figure with a banderole) are both referenced.

The two Crucifixion images do not approach a close model-copy correspondence, though comparison reveals multiple parallels. One can conclude that Artist 2 carefully studied Artist 9217-1's Crucifixion in the Summer Missal and took pains to craft for the Winter Missal an image in harmony with it, while introducing in every respect his own aesthetic and theological emphasis. In the Winter Missal, the theme of sacrificial offering is developed as both God's gift and humanity's response: The bloody wounds of Christ bespeak his death as a sacrificial offering; the swooning, beseeching Virgin communicates her emotional participation in his sacrifice. The patrons at the foot of the Cross offer to the Crucified their sacrifice of prayer, and originally (as seems likely) their arms, emblematic of wealth and status. In the Summer Missal, the iconography is less tightly integrated. Wounds are understated; figures grieve introspectively; the death of the first Adam is a gloss on the death of Christ. Arnold and Elisabeth, who have the only "speaking" parts in the pictorial drama, present their joint petition, seeking to receive salvation rather than to offer themselves or their worldly status. Arms are dispersed as a decorative carpet rather than collected and presented. In sum, the Winter Missal's image is focused on the Christological and the sacrificial; the Summer Missal's, more discursive, is contemplative, petitionary, and decorative.

7.2 Connections to Cologne

A potpourri of connections has been made between Rummen-group manuscripts, especially 9217, and illumination in Cologne of the 1330s through the 1350s. In common are various features of style in figures and borders, of palette, and of animal iconography in initials and borders. In figure style, Haagdorens cites the use of soft color, form-concealing drapery featuring the "cone motif;" in border treatment, she points to C- and I-form border types, and the "flame motif."[46] De Winter identifies angular

forms, with heavy outline and an artificial vivacity generated by a large number of decorative elements and dissonant colors.[47] In the foregoing, Cologne was presumed antecedent. However, influence in the opposite direction, from the Rummen atelier to Cologne has been proposed as well. The Rummen Summer Missal has been suggested as a source for the Crucifixion, fol. 51v, in the Missal of Conrad of Rennenberg, made c.1350–1357 for a Clarissan convent in Cologne (fig. 157).[48] Whatever the direction of influence, there are indeed correspondances in the general disposition, attitudes and melancholy mood of the figures in the two manuscripts.

Assessment of possible connections to Cologne must also take into account the considerable differences. The architecture of flatly rendered arches, gables, and pinnacles in the Cologne manuscripts is a traditional ecclesiastical Northern Gothic, very different from the secularisms and Italianisms of 10 A 14 and 9217. The backgrounds of Cologne-produced Crucifixions, such as that of a missal for St. Cunibert of the 1330s, are mostly of gold with pounced or painted linear designs (fig. 159).[49] The Rennenberg missal's background is keyed to simple alternations and repetitions and to expansion; white diamonds in the overlay are larger than the underlying black squares (fig. 157). Thus, its mathematics is quite other than the rigorous severity of nested containment in 10 A 14's Crucifixion or the decorative multiplicities of 9217's. In the missals from Cologne both the secular and the theological elements of the Rummen manuscripts are absent, as are the intellectual complexities of pattern in the backgrounds. The Cologne Crucifixions are devotional images, painted in conservative style with conventional iconography. The differences in patronage can account in part for these differences.

No single artist who worked in Cologne has been identified with an artist in a Rummen-group manuscript; however, the style and arrangement of the figures in the large initials on several leaves from an antiphonal for the Clarissan convent in that city, dated c.1345 or earlier,

---

46   "Het zgn. missaal," 121–123, 161–163. She references in particular KBR, Ms. 212, a missal of Cologne of the mid-fourteenth century.

47   De Winter, *La bibliothèque de Philippe le Hardi*, 228.

48   CDD, Cod. 149. The artist of the Rennenberg missal has been identified as Loppo de Speculo, a Franciscan sister of the Convent of St. Claire in Cologne. See "77: Missale des Domdekans Konrad von Rennenberg," in Rolf Wallrath, ed., *Vor Stefan Lochner: Die Kölner Maler von 1300 bis 1430*, exhib. cat., Wallraf-Richartz Museum, Cologne, 1974 (Cologne: Wallraf-Richartz Museum, 1974), p. 134.

49   DUL, Ms. 876, fol. 223v. See Eizenhöfer and Knaus, "Nr. 37: Hs 876 Missale, Köln, St. Kunibert, um 1330," *Die Liturgischen Handschriften*, pp. 127–132.

resonate with some of the work of 9217-1 (fig. 173a).[50] The possibility that Artist 9217-1 might have worked in Cologne at an earlier stage in his career warrants further investigation. Artist 1 may have worked in Cologne sometime before his work with Artist 2, as will be considered in Chapter 7. For Artist 2, however, exposure to Cologne can be explained by intermediaries through Sint-Truiden and the other Rummen-group artists.

7.3   *The Scourge Wounds*

Unusual in 10 A 14's Crucifixion are the many bloody scourge wounds on the body of Christ (fig. 106c). Similar though not identical imagery is familiar from later German panels, such as the Isenheim Altarpiece, and from Vesperbilds, but comparanda from Crucifixion iconography of fourteenth-century date are few. Three scenes in the Holkham Bible Picture Book, an English-made manuscript of *c.*1320, are relevant.[51] The first two scenes are images of the Crucifixion, and the third is the Deposition. Christ's body is pocked with many small, circular black blemishes, suggesting scabbed scourge wounds, in contrast with the very bloody wounds on the hands, feet, and side of Christ in 10 A 14's Crucifixion.

Closer in appearance are the scourge wounds in two images in the Ghent psalter Douce 5, *c.*1330–1335. A half-length Man of Sorrows (fol. 60v, fig. 149) and Christ in the Flagellation (fol. 145v) both depict Christ's body covered with small, bloody wounds.[52] In the Man of Sorrows

image, the crown and its flame-like bloody thorns are similar to those in 10 A 14.[53] Similar also is the scourge-marked Christ on the page with the *Arma Christi*, fol. 10r, in the Passional of the Abbess Kunigunde, a Bohemian manuscript of *c.*1312–1321.[54] Christ is superimposed on an image of the Cross, to which he is not attached. His wounds are bright red circles, evenly spaced over his body as in 10 A 14, but they are fewer in number. A similar treatment of the Man of Sorrows, the body marked by many small, bloody wounds, can be found in a leaf from the Hungarian Anjou Legendary, made in Italy or Hungary, of *c.*1325–1340.[55] Thus, English, Italian, Bohemian, French, and Flemish illumination are all possible sources for 10 A 14's scourge-pocked, crucified Christ, though none is a prototype in all important respects.[56]

8   Fol. 144r: the Opening of the Canon of the Mass. First Campaign, Artist 1

The text of the Canon of the Mass begins with the *Te igitur* prayer, which in 10 A 14 faces the Crucifixion on fol. 143v. The miniature accompanying the prayer occupies six lines and continues into the upper margin for the equivalent of two additional lines (fig. 107a). The priest in liturgical vestments, hands together in prayer, stands at the altar. Behind him is a praying acolyte. Wafer and paten, or chalice, are prominently displayed on the forward edge of the altar; the wafer stands upright on the lip of the vessel. At the back edge of the altar is an open service book. The scene is framed by an architectural canopy of three arches crowned by fenestrated battlements in three sections

---

50   Compare to WRM, Inv.-Nrs. M 5, M 8, M 16, M 18, M 22, reproduced at www.kulturelles-erbe-koeln.de/documents/obj/0507 2645/. Accessed 4-29-22. See also "80: Vier Einzelbläter aus einem Antiphonar," in Wallrath, ed., *Vor Stefan Lochner* 1974, pp. 136, 139.

51   LBL, Ms. Add. 47682, fols. 32r, 32v, and 33r. See John Lowden, "The Holkham Bible Picture Book and the *Bible Moralisée*," in *The Medieval Book: Glosses from Friends and Colleagues of Christopher de Hamel*, ed. by James H. Marrow, Richard A. Linenthal, and William Noel (Houten, Netherlands: Hes and De Graaf, 2010), 75–83; Michelle P. Brown, *The Holkham Bible Picture Book: A Facsimile* (London: The British Library, 2007); Sandler, *Gothic Manuscripts*, 2:105–107; W. O. Hassall, *The Holkham Bible Picture Book* (London: Dropmore, Press, 1954).

52   In iconography of the Man of Sorrows, the scourge wounds are not typical, but they do occur in a handful of manuscripts and panels, from various places, of the mid-fourteenth century and a little earlier, including in the Hungarian-Anjou Lectionary, referenced three notes below, and in the Epitaph of Abbot Frederick of Nirzelach, Abbey Church, Heilsbronn, Germany. This is a panel painting of *c.*1350 depicting the standing Christ, arms crossed over abdomen, scourge wounds on torso.

In images of the Flagellation of Christ, bloody scourge wounds sprinkled evenly over all, or part, of the body of Christ are sometimes depicted, as in two Bruges psalters, Boston Public Library, Ms. fMed84, fol. 10v, *c.*1255 (Carlvant, *Manuscript*

Painting, 155–160 and fig. 3i) and OBL, Ms. Auct.D.4.2, fol. 13v (Carlvant, *Manuscript Painting*, 216–219); in the English M. R. James Memorial Psalter, LBL, Ms. Add. 44949, *c.*1350, fol. 4v, the scourge wounds are small black scabs, as in the Holkham Bible Picture Book, cited in note 51.

53   On the other hand, Christ's body has no bloody wounds in Douce 6's *Deposition*, fol. 37v.

54   Prague, National Library, Ms. XIV.A.17. For bibliography, see Kathryn Rudy, "Touching the Book Again: The Passional of Abbess Kunigunde of Bohemia," in *Codex und Material*, ed. Patrizia Carmassi and Gia Toussaint (Wiesbaden: Harrassowitz Verlag, 2018), 247–257.

55   MLM, Ms. M 360.13; see Stones, *Gothic Manuscripts*, pt. 1, vol. 2, p. 277. The largest single surviving portion of this manuscript is Vatican City, 8541, Vat. lat. 8541, with additional leaves in New York, Berkeley and St. Petersburg. Further bibliography and history of the manuscript can be found on the Morgan Library website.

56   Metz illumination of the early fourteenth century and later also features bloody Passion imagery of Christ. See Paris, Bibliothèque de l'Arsenal, Ms. 288, Stones, *Gothic Manuscripts*, pt. 2, vol. 1, cat. nr. IV-7, pp. 27–30.

THE MINIATURES: STYLE AND ICONOGRAPHY

and undergirded by ribbed vaults. Perspective of both superstructure and vaults is awkwardly handled in the lateral compartments. A pair of slender piers—pierced, storied, pinnacled, and lined on the inside with thin colonnettes—supports the superstructure. The floor is rendered as a two-dimensional strip to which is attached a forward-projecting trapezoidal platform. The background is a grid of cross-inscribed squares, in four different paired color combinations. The squares are not entirely regular in arrangement; they approximate, but do not entirely achieve, two different repeating patterns that alternate row by row.[57]

Although Artists 1's miniature on 144r is much smaller in scale than Artist 2's full-page work on 143v, correspondences in their treatment of architecture and background are striking. Both employ a primarily secular architecture of piers, battlements, and walls enclosing roofed structures. Both architectures have a three-part, ribbed-vaulted understory, a central projecting trapezoidal platform, and a pair of lateral piers articulated with projecting triangular buttresses. Both have a background of inscribed squares in alternating or semi-alternating arrangements. In addition, both miniatures are framed by a gold strip to which are attached sprigs of large gold trilobes. Evidently the two artists coordinated and harmonized their work, but without sacrificing their personal styles, which differ in feeling for and mastery of the figure and of line, mass, space, and color.

Below the miniature on 144r is the three-line initial *T* of the *Te igitur*. The initial is partly formed by a winged, bearded grotesque and contains a similar, smaller version of the same, a humorous commentary on container and contents. The border is an eclectic design, possibly reflecting a change in the plan of decoration in the course of the first campaign. A strip on each side of the text is composed of large feathery foliage, colored in the gold, orange-pink, blue, and white of the miniature. The baguette-like tendril on each side of the page connects to a double-bodied grotesque whose head is positioned below the text. The foliate forms, but not the color, owe something to both Bolognese foliate borders and English cabbage-leaf borders of preceding decades. Across the bottom of the page the border changes to penwork of Type 1 in a blue-red-gold palette which is bolder than the pastels of the lateral strips. The same penwork edges the inside of the right-hand column of text. In the bas-de-page (fig. 107b) the palette changes yet again, to grisaille, and the iconography sounds a quiet theological note. Two vignettes of trees and grass are inhabited by animals—a

pair of confronted wild pigs at left, one tusked, and at right three rabbits, or hares, outside their burrows. Two rabbits in semi-upright posture gaze upward at the crowns of trees above them, akin in stance and behavior to hares in the upper margin of fol. 106v (fig. 91b).[58] Unfinished clusters of leaves attached to stumpy branches are in various stages of incompletion, perhaps indicative of a change of design, as suggested above. Conflict between animals in these bas-de-page scenes is absent; the message is rather one of peaceful Nature, of Creation restored to its original state of harmony through Christ's sacrifice on the Cross, re-presented in the Eucharist.[59] Artist 1's signature fluttering, ribbon-like tendrils, ball-and-squiggle corkscrews, bubble-pearls, and bundled linear terminal extensions are visible in curiously faded ink in the intercolumniation to the right of the miniature and in the lower margin. Blue and red rosettes accompany some of this faded inkwork.

8.1 *The Crucifixion-*Te igitur *Pairing and the Feast of Corpus Christi*

The two pages viewed together expand the visual theology of the manuscript from Christology into yet another dimension—an exposition of the Eucharist as the body and blood of Christ, as celebrated in the Feast of Corpus Christi. Essential to the expression of this theology is the pairing of the Crucifixion with the image of the elevation of the Host on the page immediately facing.

The Crucifixion has been associated in illumination with the opening of the Canon of the Mass from Carolingian times. In Carolingian, Ottonian, and Romanesque sacramentaries and missals, the Crucifixion often replaces or historiates the *T* of the *Te igitur*.[60] The association, indeed

---

57   1,2,3,4/1,2,3,4, etc. and 2,3,4,3/2,3,4,3, etc.

58   Vignettes of hares and rabbits are very commonly depicted in the margins of Flemish, Franco-Flemish and English manuscripts; see Randall, *Images in the Margins of Gothic Manuscripts*, 103–110, 202. Most such scenes are either hunts or parodies involving anthropomorphic behavior. Hares gazing up at trees are rare. In 6426, fol. 117v, bas-de-page, Artist 2 depicts a similar scene with the hare in a posture of prayer. The imagery is suggestive of Psalm 104 (103):16–18.

59   Associations between the Eucharist and peace in nature are ancient, Early Christian, as seen in the chancel vault mosaics of San Vitale; animals and foliage surrounding the sacrificial lamb in the vault are part of a Eucharistic ensemble. The idea is repeated in the twelfth-century apse mosaic of San Clemente in Rome with scrolling foliage inhabited by animals surrounding the Crucifixion.

60   The history of decoration of the *Te igitur* is briefly reviewed in Otto Pächt, *Book Illumination in the Middle Ages*, trans. Kay Davenport (London: Harvey Miller, 1986), 36–44. See also Adalbert Ebner, *Quellen und Forschungen zur Geschichte und Kunstgeschichte des Missale Romanum im Mittelalter* (Freiburg im Breisgau: Herder'sche Verlagshandlung, 1896), 445–448. The subject is treated at somewhat greater length in Rudolf Suntrup,

identification, of the image of the crucified Christ with the letters of the Canon prayer, makes the statement that the Crucified is in not only the one to whom the prayer is addressed but is himself the substance of the sacrifice that the prayer accompanies. The twelfth- and thirteenth-century developments described below visually enrich and expand this fundamental intuition, which is not altered but rather deepened and refocused in the context of Corpus Christi, beginning in the later thirteenth century. In the later Middle Ages, art dedicated to expounding the theology of Corpus Christi and to promoting devotion to the Eucharist proliferated; the imagery of 10 A 14 is part of this widespread and multi-faceted devotional movement in art.[61]

In the twelfth century the Crucifixion is often extracted from the *Te igitur* initial and expanded into a full-page illustration, often with ancillary subjects—evangelist symbols, scenes from the life of Christ, typological and allegorical figures—in medallions attached to the frame. A different iconography is then selected for the *T* of *Te igitur*, or for its proximate miniature. The *Te igitur*, with historiated initial or associated miniature, may be placed on the recto page opposite the Crucifixion, to create an opening, as is the case in 10 A 14; frequently, however, the recto page of the opening is instead decorated with a full-page *Maiestas Domini*.[62] Crucifixion and *Maiestas Domini* together make a Christological statement about the two natures of Christ, human and divine. On the pages immediately following the Crucifixion-Maiestas Domini opening, the initials *P* of the *Per omnia*, *V* and *D* of the *Vere Dignum*, and *T* of the *Te igitur* may be historiated with various iconographies, typological, allegorical,

or liturgical. In the twelfth and thirteenth centuries, and into the fourteenth, Old Testament antetypes are frequently selected: Moses and the Brazen Serpent, and the Sacrifice of Isaac by Abraham.[63] In other cases, allegorical imagery of Ecclesia and Synagoga is extracted from its earlier location in either the Crucifixion image or its associated medallions and employed at the *Te igitur*.[64] Liturgical imagery of the priest at the altar for the Preface or the priest elevating the host at the Canon may also appear in prefatory or canon initials on pages following the Crucifixion-*Maiestas* opening, often in combination with typological imagery.[65]

Crucifixion-*Te igitur* openings in which the *T* is historiated with the image of the priest elevating the Host began to appear in illumination at least as early as the later 1260s. In the following decades, this iconography was widely adopted in illumination.[66] The immediacy of pairing, of proximity, shifted the theology from the Christological to the Eucharistic. The Consecration, heretofore employed

---

"Te Igitur-Initialen und Kanonbilder in Mittelalterlichen Sakramentarhandschriften," in *Text und Bild: Aspekte des Zusammenwirkens zweier Künste in Mittelalter und früher Neuzeit*, ed. Christel Meier and Uwe Ruberg (Wiesbaden: Dr. Ludwig Reichert Verlag, 1980), 278–382.

61   For an overview of the many forms of visual attention to the Eucharist in late medieval art, see Kristen Van Ausdall, "Art and the Eucharist in the Late Middle Ages," in *A Companion to the Eucharist in the Middle Ages*, ed. Ian Christopher Levy, Gary Macy, and Kristen Van Ausdall (Leiden: Brill, 2012), 541–597.

62   Instances of the pairing, at the Canon, of full-page Crucifixion with full-page Maiestas Domini in thirteenth- and early fourteenth-century missals are numerous. A few examples include MSV, Ms. 38, *c.*1238–1250, fols. 105v–106r; the Missal of St. Louis, Assisi, Museum of the Treasury of the Basilica; the Missal of St.-Denis, BNF, Ms. lat. 1107, Paris, 1254–1286, fols. 209v–210r; the Festal Missal of Johannes of Marchello, HKB, Ms. 78 D 40, Amiens, 1323, fols 62v–63r; a missal, BNF, Ms. lat. 830, Paris, *c.*1270–1290, fols. 123v–124r. There are many variations of these arrangements. See Suntrup, *Te igitur-Initialen*, 330–366, for more examples of Crucifixion imagery at the Canon in sacramentaries and missals.

63   Some examples of Moses and the Brazen Serpent at the *Te igitur*: The Ghent Ceremonial, UGU, Ms. 233, Ghent, 1322, fol. 71r; the Missal of St. Vaast, MSV, Ms. 278 (933), Arras, *c.*1290–1299, fol. 117r. Examples of the Sacrifice of Isaac at the *Te igitur*: a missal of St. Denis, London, Victoria & Albert Museum, Ms. MSL/1891/1346, Paris, *c.*1350, fol. 236r; the English Sherbrooke Missal, NLW Ms. 15536E, fol. 230r.

64   Again, there are many variations of this iconography. Ecclesia and Synagoga appear beside the Cross in the Crucifixion image at the *Te igitur* in a sacramentary, Museum August Kestner, Hanover, Ms. 3969, from Helmarshausen, 1150–1160, fol./page nr. 2. In the Missal of Henry of Chichester, Manchester, University of Manchester John Rylands Library, Lat. Ms. 24, Salisbury, *c.*1250, fol. 153r, the Crucifixion is the *T* of *Te igitur*, and Ecclesia and Synagoga stand beside the Cross. Ecclesia and Synagoga appear in a medallion on the Tau cross of the *Te igitur* in a missal of Notre-Dame, BNF, Ms. lat. 1112, Paris, 1212–1220, fol. 103v (PUIMA. 36893) and appear flanking the initial *T* in a missal, Rouen, Bibliothèque municipale, Ms. 299A.334, Normandy, 1250–1274, fol. 153r.

65   As in the Festal Missal of Johannes of Marchello, HKB, Ms. 78 D 40, fol. 64r; in a missal BNF, Ms. lat. 830, Paris, *c.*1270–1290, fol. 125; in the missal MSV, Ms. 38, fol. 107r. There are many variations of these arrangements.

66   Northern France: A missal of Tournai, Bibliothèque du Chapitre cathédral, Ms. A 11, Tournai, *c.*1267, fols. 136v–137r (Stones, *Gothic Manuscripts*, pt. 2, cat. nr. III-63, pp. 324–326) and another missal of Tournai (?), TBM, Ms. 12 (9), fols. 76r (Crucifixion) and 76v (*Te igitur* with priest at altar), in which the two subjects are on recto-verso of the same folio. England: The Tiptoft Missal, MLM, Ms. M.107, Cambridge (?), *c.*1320, may have paired the existing *Te igitur* Elevation (fol. 142r) with a now-missing Crucifixion (Sandler, *Gothic Manuscripts*, 2:84, ill. 199); in its present state it has a small three-figure Crucifixion overlapping the border directly above the *Te igitur* miniature. Cologne: A missal for St. Cunibert, Cologne, DUL, Ms. 837, fols. 145v–146r, and the Missal of Conrad of Rennenberg, CDD, Cod. 149, fols. 51v–52r.

THE MINIATURES: STYLE AND ICONOGRAPHY

on the periphery of the Christological diptych as one among several images, assumed a new importance.

Corpus Christi was proclaimed a universal feast of the Church in 1264 upon Pope Urban IV's issuing of the bull *Transiturus*. However, this act was preceded by decades of events that contributed to the creation of the feast, and it was succeeded by more decades before the feast was celebrated throughout Europe.

The Feast of Corpus Christi began with Juliana of Mont Cornillon (*c.*1192–1258), an orphan raised near Liège in a Premonstratensian house of which she eventually became prioress.[67] She understood her early visions of the full moon missing a slice as signifying the need for a feast dedicated to the Eucharist in order to complete the liturgical year. Through ecclesiastical connections in Liège, her idea won the approval of powerful churchmen, including Guiard of Laon, bishop of Cambrai; Hugh of St.-Cher, Prior Provincial of the Dominicans and later promoted to cardinal; and James of Troyes, the archdeacon of Liège who became Pope Urban IV. However, she was also opposed, forcefully, by local ecclesiastics who saw no need for the feast, including the canons of the Cathedral of St. Lambert and a prior of her own house in Mont Cornillon. Political conflicts between the papacy and the emperor contributed to Juliana's difficulties and to the delay of Corpus Christi's implementation.

Robert of Turotte, the bishop of Liège, established the feast for his diocese in 1246, but after his death the same year it was observed only sporadically. It was officially recognized in 1287–88 by John of Cambrai, son of Guy of Dampierre, Count of Flanders and bishop of Liège.[68] In 1312 at the Council of Vienne, *Transiturus* was included in the Clementines, a legal compendium that was finally circulated by Pope John XXII in 1317. After this second promulgation by papal bull, the Feast of Corpus Christi began to take hold, initially through adoption by Dominican houses. Corpus Christi texts were added in the fourteenth century to numerous missals and breviaries of thirteenth-century date.[69] In the early fourteenth century, the Feast also began to appear in the original text of missals, not as a later addition, with illumination reflective of the theology of the feast. In the Festal Missal of Johannes of Marchello for Amiens, 1323, at the Introit for the Feast

of Corpus Christi, the Priest elevates the Host, inscribed with a cross.[70] Juliana and her confessor John of Lausanne had composed an early version of the Office for Corpus Christi; Thomas Aquinas, an acquaintance of Hugh of St.-Cher, composed around 1264 two versions of the Office and a Mass.[71] Both Aquinas's versions drew heavily on biblical material, unlike Juliana and John's version which relied more on medieval commentaries.[72]

The first Thomistic version of the office, *Sapenciae aedificavit* (SAS) used the imagery of *Sapiencia*, Wisdom personified; the associated Mass begins *Ego sum*.[73] In Thomas's second version of the office, *Sacerdos in Aeternum*, the primary imagery is of the sacerdotal priesthood, replacing that of personified Wisdom; the associated Mass, which begins with *Cibavit eos*,[74] was the version officially adopted; it is found in 9217, beginning on fol. 54v. The pairing of the Crucifixion with the *Te igitur*-priest image reflects the emphasis on priestly function in Thomas's second office and Mass.

The general popularity of the paired Crucifixion-*Te igitur* images in missals, including 10 A 14, in the middle decades of the fourteenth century can be correlated to the spread of Corpus Christi throughout Europe after 1317. Furthermore, certain ideas in St. Thomas's theology of the Eucharist illuminate the design and iconography of 10 A 14's Crucifixion in particular. Three points are relevant.

First, for Thomas, the power of the Eucharist, as of all the sacraments, derives from the Passion of Christ. The Sacraments "obtain their effect through the power of Christ's Passion; and Christ's Passion is, so to say, applied to man through the sacraments" (*Summa Theologiae*, III, 61, 1, Reply to Objection 3).[75] In 10 A 14 the Passion is indeed very powerfully presented through the sagging, oversized body of Christ, the shocking proliferation of bloody scourge wounds and other bloody piercings, and

---

67   See Barbara R. Walters, Vincent Corrigan, and Peter T. Ricketts, *The Feast of Corpus Christi* (University Park: Pennsylvania State University Press, 2006), 3–36, and Rubin, *Corpus Christi*, 164–176, for a short biography of Juliana of Mont Cornillon and for the origins of Corpus Christi in Liège.

68   Rubin, *Corpus Christi*, 179; Walters et al., *Feast of Corpus Christi*, 41.

69   Rubin, *Corpus Christi*, 196–201.

70   HKB, Ms. 78 D 40, fol. 64r.

71   Walters et al., *Feast of Corpus Christi*, 34–36, summarizes the questions in scholarship of the authorship of the office by St. Thomas.

72   Walters et al., *Feast of Corpus Christi*, 61.

73   Rubin, *Corpus Christi*, 190; Walters et al., 51–53. This office is in MSV, Ms. 601, *c.*1340, beginning on fol. 142r.

74   Rubin, *Corpus Christi*, 190; Walters et al., 63.

75   St. Thomas Aquinas, *Summa Theologica: Complete English Edition in Five Volumes*, trans. Fathers of English Dominican Province (New York: Benziger Brothers, 1947–1948; repr., Notre Dame, Indiana: Christian Classics, 1981), 4:2347. "Quia operantur in virtute passionis Christi, et passio Christi quodammodo applicatur hominibus per sacramenta. ..." (Thomas Aquinas, *Sacraments*, trans. David Bourke, vol. 56 in *Summa Theologiae* [London: Blackfriars, 1965], 38).

the emotionalized expressions and postures of the Virgin and St. John.

Second, the Eucharist is not bound by time; it unites past, present, and future:

This sacrament has a threefold significance, one with regard to the past, inasmuch as it is commemorative of our Lord's Passion, which was a true sacrifice. ...

With regard to the present, it has another meaning, namely, that of Ecclesiastical unity, in which men are aggregated [i.e., drawn together] through this Sacrament; and in this respect it is called "Communion" or Synaxis. ...

With regard to the future it has a third meaning, inasmuch as this sacrament foreshadows the Divine fruition, which shall come to pass in heaven; and according to this it is called "Viaticum," because it supplies the way of winning thither.

Summa Theologiae, III, 73, 4, Answer.[76]

Thus, the Eucharist commemorates the Passion in the past, unites humanity in the present, and foreshadows the Heavenly future.

Details in the imagery of 10 A 14 make it a powerful statement of the past, present, and future significance of the Eucharist. The narrative, expressive aspects of this Crucifixion—the realism of the wounded body of the Savior and the pathos of expression and bodily posture of Mary and Christ—commemorate the past event; the priest at the altar models and images the man who reads the text and performs the liturgical actions in the present. The donors kneeling before the Cross live in the present yet pray before the dead Christ in a slippage of time, bringing the past event into their present. The serene and divine Christ in the heavenly superstructure points to the Beatific Vision, the hoped-for future for the donors and for all who believe in the Real Presence. The two heads flanking Christ's, as indicated above, may be a further pointer to the future hope of Heaven.

Third, St. Thomas asserts the character of the Eucharist as a sacrifice and the appropriateness of referring to the consecrated wafer as a Host, i.e., *hostia*, or victim: "This sacrament is called *Sacrifice* inasmuch as it represents the Passion of Christ; but it is termed a *Host* inasmuch as it contains Christ who is a *host* [i.e., victim] of sweetness" (*Summa Theologiae*, III, 73, 4, Reply to Objection 3).[77]

The oversized and blood-spotted body of Christ underscores the reality of his death as a sacrifice and of his body and blood as those of a victim, a Host. This becomes the Real Presence in the consecrated elements on the altar, where, in the *Te igitur* image, the wafer is mysteriously balanced on the rim of the vessel. The Thomistic combination of the realist and the sacramental, made visible in the imagery of 10 A 14, avoids the twin errors of the over-realism and the over-spiritualization.[78]

The paired images of Artists 1 and 2 reflect Thomistic explication of the Eucharist's connection to the sacerdotal priesthood. In addition, Artist 2's imagery of the Crucifixion moves deep into Thomistic theology of the Eucharist. Would this fine-tuning of the Crucifixion iconography be the product of a project director working at some remove from the artist's pen and brush, or the work of the artist himself, more directly present to the orchestration of details? The latter seems more likely. One can characterize the imagery of fols. 143v–144r as visual theology and the imagery's designer, probably Artist 2, as a theologian of the visual. The possibility that Artist 2 was a priest is further considered below.

The decades-long gap between the introduction of Corpus Christi into liturgical calendars and its appearance in Crucifixion-*Te igitur* iconography contrasts with the speedy appearance in iconography of other additions to the liturgical calendar, such as the Feast of St. Thomas Becket. Perhaps the abstraction of the festal subject, or its lack of potential for political exploitation, or even its

---

76 Dicendum quod hoc sacramentum habet triplicem significationem. Unam quidem respectu praeteriti: inquantum scilicet est commemorativum Dominicae passionis, quae fuit verum sacrificium, ut supra dictum est. Et secundum hoc nominatur 'sacrificium'.

Aliam autem significationem habet respectu rei praesentis, scilicet ecclesiasticae unitatis, cui homines congregantur per hoc sacramentum. Et secundum hoc nominatur 'communio' vel 'synaxis'. ...

Tertiam significationem habet respectu futuri: inquantum scilicet hoc sacramentum est preafigurativum fruitionis Dei, quae erit in patria. Et secundum hoc dicitur 'viaticum', quia hoc praebet nobis viam illuc perveniendi. (Thomas Aquinas, *Eucharistic Presence*, trans. William Barden, vol. 58 in *Summa Theologiae*, [London: Blackfriars, 1965], 14, 16).

---

77 Ad tertium dicendum quod hoc sacramentum dicitur 'sacrificium', inquantum repraesentat ipsam passionem Christi. Dicitur autem 'hostia', inquantum continent ipsum Christum, qui est hostia suavitatis. ... (*Eucharistic Presence*, trans. Barden, 16).

78 See Rubin, *Corpus Christi*, 17–35, for a review of the development of the theology of the Eucharist and the controversies corollary to the process. Over-realism was associated, among others, with the theology of Paschasius Radbertus; over-spiritualization with that of Ratramnus and Berengar of Tours.

origins in association with a woman's vision, contributed to the slow spread of its introduction into iconography.

9 Fol. 151r: the Feast of St. Lucy. First Campaign, Artist 1

The ten-line Introit initial *D(ilexisti)* for the Feast of St. Lucy, 13 December, is singled out for major illumination for unknown reasons (figs. 110, 110a.). Its location as the first entry in the manuscript's Sanctorale may perhaps account for the historiation. As told in the *Golden Legend*, St. Lucy of Syracuse prayed with her ailing mother Eutychia at the tomb of St. Agatha.[79] Lucy fell asleep, and Agatha appeared to her in splendor in a dream to tell Lucy that her mother was already cured.

The strapwork initial, decorated with foliate patterns in light blue and white, is framed by a gold panel with gold-on-red grotesques in two corners. The background is of red, blue, and gold squares inscribed in contrasting hues. The two women kneel at the foot of an open sarcophagus; from within it emerges, somewhat alarmingly, the arm of St. Agatha, hand configured in blessing. Two scrolls bear inscriptions written in the lettering of the second colophon (fig. 138a); the texts are uncertain.[80] Architecture typical of Artist 1 backs the scene. Piers and spindly columns support a complex of rounded arches crowned by battlements, louvered turrets, and domes. Four-part ribbed vaults float on hanging corbels. This architectural superstructure is related to the architecture depicted in Bodley 264, the *Romance of Alexander*. Battlements that project forward in space, spindly columns, vaults with converging ribs viewed from beneath, round turrets with conical roofs, louvered shades, domes supported by open arcades are found in many variations of color and detail in Bodley 264 (fig. 146).[81]

The hagiographical episode of Lucy and her mother at St. Agatha's tomb is unusual. When Lucy appears in manuscripts of the thirteenth and fourteenth centuries, she is usually rendered either as a standing figure, alone or in a group of saints, or in a scene of her trial or martyrdom.[82] Closer in iconography to 10 A 14 are images in Italian panel painting. Both the Polyptych of St. Lucy of about 1340, by Paolo Veneziano or his workshop, in the chancery of the bishopric on the island of Krk (Veglia), Croatia, and a polyptych by Jacobello del Fiore of about 1410 in the museum in Fermo include depictions of St. Lucy and her mother praying at the tomb of St. Agatha.[83] An Italian panel may inform the image in 10 A 14. Another possible source would be an image from an illustrated copy of the *Golden Legend*. De Voragine's Latin text, though widely copied, was rarely illustrated. However, it was translated into French by Jean de Vignay around 1333; at least twenty-four of the French copies are illustrated, though none has the combination of date and iconography such as to present a possible source for the image in 10 A 14.[84] The surprising, almost bizarre, image of St. Agatha, more akin to a resuscitating corpse than to a heavenly vision, is

---

79 For a modern English translation of the legend of St. Lucy, see Jacobus de Voragine, *The Golden Legend: Readings on the Saints*, 2 vols., trans. William Granger Ryan (Princeton: Princeton University Press, 1993), 1:27–29.

80 Daniel Sheerin proposed *Ecce sanata est* ('Behold, she is healed') or *sanata est*, a phrase from the text of the *Golden Legend*, as a possible reading for the upper scroll. De Voragine's life of St. Lucy in the *Legenda* (in Latin) is available at http://thelatinli brary.com/voragine/luc.shtml. Accessed 1 May 2022.

81 Fol. 101v (fig. 146); see also fols. 51v, 67v. Style on these folios agrees with that of Pierart dou Tielt as seen in Paris, Bibliothèque de l'Arsenal, Ms. 5218, *La queste du saint Graal*, signed by Pierart as scribe, illuminator, and binder and dated by him 1351. See François Avril, "301: La queste du saint Graal," in "Manuscrits," *Les fastes du gothique: Le siècle de Charles V*, exhib. cat., Galeries

---

nationales du Grand Palais, Paris, 1981–1982 (Paris: Éditions de la Réunion des musées nationaux, 1981), 348–349; Albert d'Haenens, "Pierart dou Tielt, enlumineur des oeuvres de Gilles Li Muisis: note sur son activité à Tournai vers 1350," *Scriptorium* 23:1 (1969), 88–93.

82 Single figure with a palm: Missal, DUL, Ms. 837, Cologne, *c.*1330, fol. 197v; Martyrdom by the sword: *Picture Book of Madame Marie*, BNF, Ms. n. acq. fr. 16251, Hainaut, Cambrai or Tournai, *c.*1285, fol. 99v; Queen Mary's Psalter, LBL, Ms. Royal 2.B.VII, London, *c.*1310–1320, fol. 287r; Breviary of Blanche of France, BAV, Ms. Urb. lat. 603, Paris, *c.*1320, fol. 352v. Trial of Lucy before the Consul, Queen Mary's Psalter, fol. 286v.

83 In Venziano's image St. Agatha stands beside her canopied tomb and speaks with the kneeling Lucy, while Eutychia sits with back turned to the other two. In del Fiore's image, a half-length Agatha, surrounded by a mandorla, rises out of her tomb and touches the halo of Lucy, asleep and leaning on the monument. A kneeling Eutychia watches in awe. See Enrica Cozzi, "Paolo Veneziano e bottega: il politico di Santa Lucia e gli *antependia* per l'isola di Veglia," *Arte in Friuli, Arte a Triest*, 35 (2016), 235–293; and Daniele Benati, "Jacobello del Fiore: A Crucifixion and a Reconstruction of his Early Career," trans. Frank Dabell, in Patrick Matthiesen, *Jacobello del Fiore: His Oeuvre and a Sumptuous Crucifixion* (London: Matthiesen Fine Art Ltd., 2007).

84 Most of the French copies do not include an image of St. Lucy and her mother at the tomb of St. Agatha; an exception is BNF, Ms. fr. 414, Paris, 1404, which includes, on fol. 16v, an image of this episode. See Hilary Elizabeth Maddocks, "The Illuminated Manuscripts of the *Légende Dorée*: Jean de Vignay's Translation of Jacobus de Voragine's *Legenda Aurea*" (Ph.D. diss., Univ. of Melbourne, 1989), especially p. 17, n. 66, and p. 120.

congruent with the dark humor that spices the work of Artist 1.

10 Fol. 167r: the Presentation in the Temple. First Campaign, Artist 1

The Feast of the Presentation is depicted in a few missals of the late thirteenth and early fourteenth centuries.[85] The eight-line figural initial *S*(*uscepimus*, figs. 121, 121a) depicts imagery familiar from illumination and sculpture: The Virgin places the small Christ child on an altar, and Simeon receives him with outstretched, veiled hands. Joseph, with a basket of doves and a candle, stands behind Mary. The scene is depicted in front of an arched and scalloped band of masonry on spindly columns, a simplified reworking of motifs related to those of Bodley 264.

Behind the figures the initial *S* is formed as an avian grotesque with a beaked head at each end of its body. Its abdomen, the spine of the initial, is a gorgon whose two maxillary jaws are partially obscured by the figures. The gorgon's maw is directly behind the Christ child, as though threatening to swallow him. A curl of the creature's lip overlaps the child's halo, and the contours of its nose, lips, and fangs echo those of the paired, outstretched, veiled hands of Simeon. However, eyes which might further animate the creature and confirm its role as an actor are occluded by the placement of the figures. The gorgon suggests menacing forces, perhaps echoing its origins as the apocalyptic Hellmouth, but the motif hovers just below the threshold of participation in the narrative. The iconography of Artist 1's gorgon-initials opens into a dimension of preternatural fantasy not apparent in his comparatively light-hearted flourishing.

Other instances of the play between the gorgon-initial and its narrative contents, complete with dark overtones of meaning, are found in Artist 1's initials of the Loppem-Bruges antiphonal. See Appendix 4, Pt. 1, for a discussion of these images in the antiphonal and Appendix 6 for broader consideration of the gorgon motif.

---

85 As for example, the Missal of Corbie, Amiens, Bibliothèque municipale, Ms. 157, Amiens, *c*.1295 and after *c*.1312, fol. 30v; the Missal of St. Denis, BNF, Ms. lat. 1107, Paris, 1254–1286, fol. 222v; a missal, BNF, Ms. lat. 830, Paris, 1270–1290, fol. 218v; and the Sherbrooke Missal, NLW, Ms. 15536E, fol. 246r, in which the Christ child is lifted by the Virgin and passed over the spine of the *S*, which separates her from Simeon, into the waiting veiled hands of the priest. Forty days after the birth of Christ, this feast is also Candlemas and the Feast of the Purification of the Virgin. It is illustrated less frequently in missals than in service and devotional books of other sorts.

The enigmatic relationship between initial and image can be contextualized within the broader array of such relationships in the many initials of 10 A 14. Initials with a horizontal element—*A*, *E*, M, and *S*—present a bisected image field. In two-line penwork initials, the two parts of a divided image field are usually treated as independent visual units, each containing its own motif, as in the four examples of such initials on fol. 149r (fig. 109). A step up in sophistication can be seen in painted initials, two-line and larger. The divided image field often contains a single motif; and an illusionistic spatial element, also present in the much larger Presentation initial, is introduced into the relationship between letter and image. A face or a figure may be treated as though placed behind, and partially obstructed by, a barrier (figs. 6, 127).

11 Fol. 176v: the Annunciation. First Campaign, Artist 1

The eight-line initial *R*(*orate*, figs. 125, 125a) is at the Introit of the Mass for the Feast of the Annunciation, 25 March. The diapered background, of lozenges in three colors inscribed in contrasting hues or values, is typical of Artist 1. The iconography is unexceptional; however, some clumsy drawing around the head of the angel confuses the design. Gabriel kneels at left; he holds a scroll, inscribed AVE GRATIA, in script of the first campaign. Beside the scroll stands the Virgin, her right hand at her breast. Her left, covered by a fold of drapery, supports a codex. A vase with a tripartite white stalk rests on the floor between Gabriel and the Virgin. The scene is framed by an architecture, all in gray, employing the vocabulary typical of Artist 1 and similar to that in the preceding miniature: delicate colonnettes supporting a thin strip of arched wall reinforced by four round towers with conical roofs.

The initial is constructed of gorgon heads in two variant views, frontal and profile. A pair of frontal faces with wide, squared cranial boxes and large ears constitute the initial's stem at left. Maxillary jaws are joined by tendril extensions. At right, a pair of confronted profile heads constitutes the bowl of the *R* and another pair the leg. Both upper and lower jaws of each pair are joined by tendril extensions. Each head has a very small, curved cranial box and a large, wide mouth. Gorgons do not interact with the figures inside the initial. The terminals of the initial are inward-scrolling tendrils bearing five-part leaves that curl in three dimensions.

Drapery is washed in blue and orange and overlaid with feathery shading in white and black. Folds are marked with heavy black lines.

12 Fol. 192v: the Dedication of a Church. First Campaign, Artist 1

This ten-line figural initial *T*(*erribilis*, figs. 132, 132a), immediately below the abbreviated rubric *In dedicatione ecclesie* features a mitred bishop, who grasps a crozier with his left hand and asperges a small basilica with his right. He is accompanied by an acolyte who holds a situla and a staff topped with a cross. The stunted basilica has a nave and choir, both fenestrated and aisled, and a façade with a round-arched doorway topped by a polygonal tower on tall, open arches. Architecture is colored blue and orange, with some detailing in white and shading in gray. A small plot of grass defines and gives some spatial depth to the foreground. The background is diapered with lozenges of three colors inscribed in two patterns of contrasting hues. The combined effect is very busy. The crosspiece of the *T* is a gaping-mouthed winged grotesque; the stem (or bowl) is a double gorgon of the profile type; mandibular and maxillary jaws are joined by angular interlace.

Gorgons do not intrude on the interior of the initial; however, the dragon's relationship to the scene is ambiguous. The glance of acolyte and bishop and the bishop's aspergillum seem directed not at the small basilica but at the dragon above, whose furry tufts graze the church's tower and whose hooves dangle over the roof. Is this a dedication or an exorcism? Perhaps Artist 1 intentionally introduced an element of visual *double entendre*. Humor verging on the irreverent is recurrent in his imagery, as in the Presentation initial, discussed just above, and also in his work in the Loppem-Bruges antiphonal. (See Appendix 4, Pt. 1.)

The Mass for the Dedication of a Church is occasionally illustrated in missals, more often in pontificals.[86] Perhaps, like other grand residences of the era, Arnold's magnificent castle was projected to have a chapel, for use in which this very missal might well have been commissioned.[87] The liturgy for the ceremony of dedication and the image accompanying would be explicable if that were indeed the case.

13 Were Artist 2 and Artist 3 the Same Person? Evidence from Illumination

Evidence from illumination supports the hypothesis, formulated from the study of penwork in Chapter 4, that Artist 2 and Artist 3 were the same person. Similarities in the use of border bars and in the density, symmetries, and aesthetic of penwork provide evidence that one artist produced both bodies of work, that from the first campaign and that from the second.

The study of illumination shows that three distinctive, related interests unite the work associated with Artists 2 and 3, but the means of realizing these interests differ. The first is the interest in three-dimensional form and three-dimensional space, more convincingly realized by Artist 3 than by Artist 2. Artist 2 achieves the effect of three-dimensional form through shading and modeling with multiple linear strokes; the effect can be streaky, grainy. Along with shading and modeling, Artist 2 uses line to define, strengthen, and frame forms. Spatial depth is created through spatial layers created by overlapping figures and architectural elements, as in the *Ad te levavi* initial, fol. 7r (fig. 15a). In the *Domine ne longe* miniature, fol. 106v (fig. 91a), the double attempt to deepen space and to situate in it a three-dimensional body in motion is less successful. Furthermore, the asymmetries of the architecture complicate the reading of the narrative. In the *Crucifixion*, fol. 143v (fig. 106), the spatial inconsistencies of the *Domine ne longe* are remedied by the symmetry of the architecture and by the construction of the projecting platform; a progressive mastery of the means for constructing illusionistic depth is apparent. At this point, however, figures stand on a narrow slab of ground behind, rather than on, the platform and do not profit from the expansion of space. A comparison of the praying David from the *Ad te levavi* and the praying Elisabeth in the Crucifixion reveals a progression in the three-dimensionalization of drapery. Heavy folds of David's cloak and its decorative gold edge are all pulled towards the frontal plane, whereas the folds of Elisabeth's cloak overlap in sequence as they recede from the viewer, enhancing the sense of three-dimensional form. From this treatment to the shingling of folds in the work of Artist 3 is a small step.

In the work of Artist 3, three-dimensional form is created by skillful modeling of figures with refined, small strokes of the brush and pen in the Nativity, fol. 22r (fig. 34a) and the Adoration of the Magi, fol. 27v (fig. 39a). The role of line in outlining and in producing internal detail is greatly diminished. This refinement—miniaturization—of line facilitates the shift from a two-dimensional to a three-dimensional conception of form; volumetric figures are

---

86   The Missal of St. Denis, BNF, Ms. lat. 1107, Paris, 1254–1286, fol. 228r; a missal of Saint-Corneille, Compiègne, BNF, Ms. lat. 17322, *c.*1280–1290, Paris and Amiens (?), fol. 155r; a pontifical of Cambrai, Toledo, Archivo de la Catedral, Ms. 56.19, fol. 108v. See Stones, *Gothic Manuscripts*, pt. 1, vol. 2, cat. nrs. I-14, pp. 27–29; I-22, p. 46; and III-49, pp. 278–285.

87   Pleshey Castle, Essex, residence of the Bohun family in the second half of the fourteenth century had such a chapel; see Sandler, *Illuminators and Patrons*, 5, 9.

produced, but in the absence of the Italian robust assertion of internal form, these have a certain limpness and fragility. Volume is gained, but the strength of line is lost. In addition to modeling, Northern manipulation of surfaces through shingling with faceted folds helps define volume. As previously noted, this technique, along with the Germanic *Zackenstil* of the mid-thirteenth century, may be a source for the treatment of drapery in fifteenth-century Flemish panel painting.

Artist 3's mastery of spatial depth at floor level has advanced beyond Artist 2's, and in conjunction with vaulting produces an integrated space in which placement of figures is rationalized. Architecture is used skillfully to define and develop space. The spatial box is afforded more integrity through greater skill and complexity in the depiction of the undersides of vaults and through expanded use of tilted and receding elements (the Virgin's bed, fig. 34a, and her leg, fig. 39a). The depth of the spatial box at floor-level matches the spatial depth of the vaults in the Adoration of the Magi.

The second significant interest found in both bodies of work, Artist 2's and Artist 3's, is the sophisticated use of symmetry, including complex nested symmetries, as a structural device. Where Artist 2 deviates from symmetry, an element of confusion results. Although symmetry is also a feature of design in the work of Artist 1, it is often glossed with decorative, asymmetrical, and non-structural elements. It is not prominent in Artist 4's designs, which in all respects are sparser and more limited in repertoire than those of the other artists.

A third common interest of Artists 2 and 3 is in the use of decorative motifs and designs that reach and expand across the blank areas that frame the text block. In the Adoration, Artist 3's angels translate a formal interest characteristic of Artist 2's penwork—the interest in connecting across areas of blank parchment—into the metaphysics of time and eternity, connecting heaven and earth.

If Artists 2 and 3 were the same person, the work likely proceeded along the following lines: Artist 2/3 worked with, and probably under, Artist 1 in the first campaign. Artist 1 completed his work, but Artist 2/3, for reasons unknown, did not complete his. Ten or fifteen years later, Artist 2/3 and Artist 4, an assistant, completed illumination and decoration on the manuscript. In the interval between the first and second campaigns, Artist 2/3 developed skill in the rendering of three-dimensional volumetric figures by refining and reducing line; by reducing the size of brushstrokes; and by overlaying surfaces with repetitive, flat, angular folds. He may have had contact with Italian, English, or Bohemian pictorial sources during this interval, but some elements of his development seem to be his own innovations. He advanced in the rendering

of three-dimensional architecture through refinement of architectural members, greater consistency in perspective of vaults, and development of perspective depth in ground planes. He wrote the first colophon, identifying himself as Laurence the Priest. Artist 4 may have written the second colophon at about the same time.

While Artist 3's style in painting is more refined in brushwork and his figures more delicate in physique than Artist 2's, his penwork is by contrast looser and freer in structure than Artist 2's. However, towards the end of his work in 10 A 14, Artist 2's penwork exhibits tendencies that point in the direction of Artist 3's style. The introduction of the loose, painterly application of ink to foliage beginning on fol. 119r, as noted, shows this tendency. Likewise, Artist 3's work exhibits structural tendencies and approaches to design that connect his work to that of Artist 2. He prefers Type 4 border bars, used extensively by Artist 2 in his later quires, but never by Artist 1 and only once, as a short segment, by Artist 4. (See Inventory 2.) Artist 3 also exhibits the feel for symmetry so marked in Artist 2's work of the first campaign.

However, there are significant differences in form and aesthetic between the work of Artists 2 and 3. As noted in Chapter 4, Artist 3 uses fewer corkscrews than does Artist 2, and his corkscrews are looser and less disciplined in shape than those of Artist 2 (figs. 87, 87a). In addition, Artist 2's aesthetic of reaching across spaces, of varied arcs of curvature and lengths of tendril, and his wealth of variety in decorative elements are not entirely absent but are less pronounced in Artist 3's more domesticated aesthetic. The tense, structural geometry of two-dimensional line, manifested in the penwork corkscrews of the first campaign, is sacrificed in the second campaign in order to develop structure in the third dimension. Thus, the structural impulse metamorphoses, reappears on a larger scale, in the firm geometry of page layout and overall design in illumination.

There is certainly iconographical evidence to support the proposal that Artist 2/3 was a priest. The sophisticated theology of the Eucharist presented in the Crucifixion-Consecration opening, fols. 143v–144r, speaks for a priestly designer. As explained above, both penwork and painted two-line initials of Artist 2 manifest the ecclesiastical and Christological iconography which might be of particular interest to priests. Artist 3's fine initials of the head of Christ on fols. 22r and 107r demonstrate the same interest.

Reasonable arguments can be made in support of the view that Artists 2 and 3, though possessed of similar abilities and sympathies, were not the same person. On balance, however, it seems more likely than not that Artist 2 and Artist 3 were indeed the same person. If this was the case, and if Artist 3 was Laurence the Priest, as proposed at the end of Chapter 3 above, then Artist 2 must also have been Laurence. The theological depth of his iconography and the prevalence of ecclesiastical and Christological subjects in his initials can be seen as manifestations of priestly interests and understanding.

14   Conclusion

Artists 1 and 2/3, the main artists of 10 A 14, were very different in outlook and interests and probably in their respective states of life. Artist 4, the third artist, stayed mainly, though not entirely, in the shadow of Artist 3.

Artist 2 used familiar iconographical motifs, which he developed in novel ways and used in unusual combinations to the end of strengthening and developing Christological and theological ideas. His style is marked by an interest in realism, manifested in his warm palette, by his somewhat grainy modeling, and by the quick assimilation of advanced developments in volume, space, and architecture. His sense of structure is very strong, as seen in the discipline of the background patterns in the Crucifixion and in its monumental, symmetrical, and balanced architectural frame; where he ventures into a complex narrative, with attendant asymmetry and multiple interactions, he falters. These characteristics of illumination have parallels in his penwork, which exhibits structural rigidity, symmetry, and a wealth of motifs. The narrative element suggested by corkscrews and foliate tips that reach and respond across space is more successfully articulated in the non-figural vocabulary of penwork than in illumination. Artist 2's illumination is not notable for humor; its solemnity and depth balance the joyous and pulsating vitality of his non-figural penwork flourishing.

Artist 1, like his colleague, used conventional iconography for the most part in his painted initials and miniatures; the St. Lucy image is unusual but not innovative; it seems to be modeled on Italian prototypes. However, in his illumination, he introduced quirky elements, some edging on subversive: the ominous monsters in initials, the odd gesture of St. Lucy from her tomb. This tendency is comparable to his penchant for subliminal references in penwork. His style of illumination is flatter, more miniaturist and conservative than Artist 2's; and his penwork, limited in its stock of motifs, is consistently light and fluttering. It is a counterpoise to his rather cool palette and staid figures. Neither penwork nor illumination exhibits significant development.

The study of iconography also shows that the gorgons of 10 A 14's first campaign, and those of the earlier Rummen

manuscripts, were used in different ways by Artists 1 and 2. Artist 1 used flatness of style and the separation of initial from its historiation as an aid to exploration of simple mathematical oppositions and pairings—internal versus external, configurations involving mirror images, vertical versus horizontal alignments, profile versus frontal views, merging and splitting, twinning and doubling. In some cases, Artist 1's juxtapositions of humans and gorgons produce an aura of the uncanny, intimated rather than developed. Artist 2 used three-dimensional and illusionistic effects, coupled with greater interaction between initial and historiation, to transmute the gorgon into an actor in a metaphysical theo-drama that integrates the initial and its narrative.

The style and iconography of the miniatures and their accompanying borders indicate that the Artists of 10 A 14 in both campaigns drew on a wide range of European sources: Tournai, Ghent, northern France, Paris, Liège, Cologne, England, Italy, and perhaps Bohemia. It seems that the manuscript was produced at a time and place marked by extraordinary conditions. The unusually large pool of possibilities at hand suggests production in a city of some size and cosmopolitan connections but also one in which this wealth of stylistic resources was coupled with the lack of a single pervasive influence. Parisian style does not dominate 10 A 14, nor does the stylistic keynote of some other center. This non-directionality, or multi-directionality, could be evidence of a significant cultural disruption, to which the break in the 1340s campaign of production also testifies. The two artists of the first campaign worked in styles that are easily distinguishable, yet the two artists endeavored to coordinate many elements of design. Unity of purpose does not translate into unity of aesthetic, such as might result from a well-established, highly structured, and stable workshop. The two artists seemed to function almost, if not quite, as equals in execution of this project. Again, this relationship suggests a moment in which organizational structure is compromised, flexible, or tentative, as it might be in a period of unrest or in a workshop assembled and functioning ad hoc, for the purpose of executing a particular commission. In any case, the organizational structure of the first campaign did not enable Artist 2 to complete his gatherings, in spite of help from Artist 1.

When the project was resumed in the 1360s, the passage of time is evident in the stylistic changes that separate the scenes of the Nativity, the Circumcision, and the Adoration from the other illuminations. The translation, within the medium of miniatures, of Italianate spatial ideas into a Northern idiom is underway in the second campaign. Whether these fourteenth-century miniatures stand as a prelude or a parallel to developments in four-teenth- and fifteenth-century panel painting remains to be investigated.

The sensitivity of the second campaign to the style of the first is also evidence of continuity, which might be construed logically as continuity in location. Ghent is not only mentioned in the colophon but was the locus of conditions enumerated above. It was large and cosmopolitan, at least in some respects, and had a long and vigorous tradition of manuscript production and illumination, one that drew on many different sources. It was subjected to multifarious, severe disruptions in the 1340s, as described in Chapter 1 above: the French grain embargo, the murder of Artevelde and the civil war between weavers and fullers, the Black Death, the punitive indemnities imposed by Louis of Male. Judging from the paucity of remains, relatively little illumination, excluding that of the Rummen manuscripts, was produced in Ghent for almost three decades between 1340 and 1370 in comparison with its prolific output of texts religious and secular between about 1310 and 1335, and prior to that, of private devotional books in the 1270s and 1280s.

Ghent was the home of Elisabeth of Lierde, who fled there in 1365 to die a few months later. Her first husband, a fabulously wealthy Italian, was a major actor in events in the city in the 1340s; Elisabeth's second husband Arnold, the patron of the manuscript named in the colophon, was from the region of Liège in the diocese of Cologne, to which city he traveled to be invested with a countship by the Holy Roman Emperor; and he spent years in the service of the Duke of Brabant. His property in Rummen, the site of his magnificent castle, was only ten kilometers from Sint-Truiden. Through Elisabeth and her two husbands, the artists might have had access to manuscripts and other works of art produced in Italy, Liège, and Cologne. The Count of Flanders, Elisabeth's nephew Louis of Male, was in Paris for considerable periods of time and was also in close contact with the King of England, whose daughter he was expected to marry during the early years of his tenure as count. Access to manuscripts from France and England, never difficult to explain in Flanders, is especially non-problematic under these circumstances. The question of place of production will be reprised in Chapter 8.

CHAPTER 6

The Calendar

In this chapter the entries in 10 A 14's calendar (transcribed in full in Appendix 2) will be considered first, then its illumination; the evidence that each offers for its origin and/or destination will be assessed.

Each month is given a single page. KL monograms in the upper left corner of each page are followed by the name of the month, the number of days, and the number of days in the lunar month, all written in red. There are no verses, nor are there notations for Egyptian days. Golden numbers, dominical letters, nones-ides-kalends, and countdown numbers are aligned in the customary four columns to the left of the of feasts. The main entries are not graded, and more than half of the days are without a designated feast. The script here is slightly less formal than that of the main text, though written in the same very dark, black ink.

The thirty-five rubricated entries include solemnities such as Christmas and Epiphany, feasts of apostles, and some saints, mostly of local or regional importance.[1]

Abbreviations beside the names of saints indicate ecclesiastical status, state in life, martyrdom, and inclusion of companions. Associations between the calendar of 10 A 14 and calendars of Liège and the Mosan region, including Sint-Truiden on the one hand and Ghent on the other, will be considered for what they might suggest about the origins of the Rummen Winter Missal.

Calendrical evidence for the origins of 10 A 14 is not decisive, as has been recognized.[2] Saints with cult centers in each of the three cities that have been proposed as sites of the manuscript's production are found in the calendar, but important saints for each city are omitted as well. Moreover, many saints in the missal's calendar were widely venerated in the Low Countries and hence are of little help in specifying the city of origin or destination. The cult of Aldegundis 30 January was centered in Maubeuge (Hainaut); Gertrude 17 March in Nivelles (Brabant); Medardus 8 June in Tournai and Soissons; Gaugericus 11 August in Cambrai; Gereon and

companions 10 October in Cologne.[3] Others whose cult centers were outside the Low Countries include Germanus 28 May in Paris; Germanus 31 July in Auxerre; Egidius (Gilles) 1 September in St.-Gilles-du-Gard but with a vast and far-flung following; Evortius 7 September in Orléans; Crispinus and Crispianus 25 October in Soissons; Boniface 5 June in Fulda; Leonard 6 November (in red) in St.-Léonard-de-Noblat. These connections can point in many directions, but it is possible that many came into 10 A 14's calendar via Liège and/or Sint-Truiden.

1   Liège and the Mosan Region

Saints in 10 A 14's calendar for whom Liège was a major cult center are Servatius, bishop of Tongres (in red) 13 May, Theodardus, bishop of Liège 9 September (10 September in Liège calendars), and Lambert, bishop of Liège and martyr (in red) 17 October.[4] On the other hand, in 10 A 14 none of these saints receives a second entry for translation or deposition; in Liège psalters, entries for translation, deposition and elevation of these saints are common. Hubert 3 November is also in calendars of Liège.[5] Amandus 6 February is entered in Liège calendars without Vedastus, with whom he shares the day in 10 A 14 and in most Ghent calendars. St. Martin (in red) 11 November has a particular prominence in 10 A 14, as he is accorded one of the seven octaves in the calendar; most others are for the major feasts (Christmas, Epiphany) and for apostles. He is certainly not a local saint, but he is important in calendars and litanies of Liège.[6] Perhaps the presence in Liège of a church dedicated to St. Martin had some bearing on this emphasis, though Martin's octave is in calendars of other Low Country destinations as well.

Ursmar of Lobbes, Domitian bishop of Tongres and Maestricht and patron of Huy, Monulphus and

---

1 Rubricated entries in 10 A 14's calendar of saints with varying degrees of local and regional connection are Servatius 13 May, Lambert 17 September, Dionysius (Denis) and companions 9 October, Hubert 3 November, Leonard (of Noblac, a convert of St. Remigius) 6 November, Martin 11 November.

2 Dennison, "Dating and Localisation," p. 517 and n. 71; Wolinski, "Plainchant," discusses the calendars of KBR 9217, 10 A 14, and KBR 9427 at length.

3 See the *Catholic Encyclopedia,* https://www.catholic.org/encyclopedia/, for origins and residences of saints. See Mary Wolinski, "Plainchant," for some discussion of the geographical associations of saints in the calendars of 9217 and 10 A 14. See also Oliver's inventories of Liège calendars, *Gothic Manuscript Illumination,* 2:212–228.

4 Oliver, *Gothic Manuscript Illumination,* 2:211–212.

5 Oliver, *Gothic Manuscript Illumination,* 2:226. Hubert is a later addition to the calendar of.

6 Oliver, *Gothic Manuscript Illumination,* 2:226, 230.

© KONINKLIJKE BRILL BV, LEIDEN, 2025 | DOI:10.1163/9789004427136_007

Gondulphus, bishops of Maestricht, are all common in Liège calendars but are not found in 10 A 14's.[7]

2　Sint-Truiden

The calendar of 10 A 14 has some indications for Sint-Truiden.[8] The abbey's name-saint, Trudo 23 November, is entered after Pope Clement.[9] Hubert 3 November is also associated with Sint-Truiden.[10] Omitted from the calendar of 10 A 14 are additional important saints of Sint-Truiden: Eucherius 20 February, bishop of Orléans who died at the abbey; Libertus 14 July, a monk of the abbey; Rumbold of Mechelen, whose biography was written by Abbot Theodoric of Sint-Truiden.[11]

3　Ghent

Remigius, archbishop of Reims 1 October, was widely venerated, but there may be a particular connection to Ghent. The entry "Remigius et al.," 1 October, in the calendar of 10 A 14 is often expanded in other calendars to "Remigius, Germanus, Vedastus, Bavo," as in the calendar of a psalter from Ghent, second quarter of the thirteenth century.[12] The date is that of the translation of relics of the four saints, though this is not noted in the calendar. Thus, the notation "et al." thus almost certainly includes a short-hand reference to St. Bavo, patron of Ghent, whose feast is also 1 October. However, if the calendar was written in and for Ghent, one wonders at the elision of the city's patron saint. By contrast, in the entry for 1 October in the calendar of the missal from St. Peter's Abbey of 1275–1285, Bavo is inscribed first in the list of five confessors.[13] By the

fourteenth century Ghent's two major abbeys had long since adopted many of each other's saints, so one would have to look beyond monastic partisanship to determine the reason for folding Bavo into an "et al."[14] Moreover, Remigius is also given an entry on 13 January, the Octave of the Epiphany, along with Hilary; Remigius's death was 13 January. Macharius 10 April, a bishop of Antioch, died in Ghent in the early eleventh century and was buried and venerated there.[15] The relics of Amalberga 7 October have been at St. Peter's since the fifteenth century. Ghent calendars, like that of 10 A 14, enter Amandus and Vedastus together on 6 February.[16] As Amandus was founder of both St. Peter's Abbey and St. Bavo's Abbey in Ghent, the city has hardly less claim to this ubiquitous apostle of Flanders than does St.-Amand-les-Eaux, the place of his namesake abbey in France, and more claim to him than does Liège. Of the fourteen saints Carlvant cites as associated with St. Bavo's Abbey, only three, Macharius, Brictius, and Amalberga, are in the calendar of 10 A 14. Of the thirteen she identifies as associated with St. Peter's, only Vedastus, Servatius, and Amalberga are in 10 A 14. Servatius is also a marker for Liège, as noted; Brictius is also in Liège calendars.

Carlvant assesses Elisabeth of Hungary 18 November (usually 19 November) in the calendars and/or litanies of thirteenth-century psalters as an indicator for Ghent.[17] However, comparing psalters with surviving calendars and/or litanies, the proportion of those with Elisabeth appears to be somewhat higher for Liège (sixteen of thirty-five) than for Ghent (three of twelve). Moreover, Elisabeth was also significant for Sint-Truiden; her *vita* is included in the second volume of a *Passionarium*

7　Oliver, *Gothic Manuscript Illumination*, 2:211–212.

8　Coens, "Les saints particulièrement honorés à l'Abbaye de Saint-Trudo," *Analecta Bollandiana* 73 (1955): 166–170, has a transcription of the calendar of BUL, Ms. 315, a customary for the liturgy of Sint-Truiden in the early fifteenth century.

9　Coens, "Les saints," 170. However, Trudo is not an exclusive marker for Sint-Truiden, as he also appears in calendars and litanies of many Liège psalters Oliver, *Gothic Manuscript Illumination*, 2:226, 230, and Saucier, 145. In Liège calendars his feast is often on 24 November.

10　Coens, "Les saints," 169. Hubert's is one of the red-letter feasts; see n. 1 above.

11　Coens, "Les saints," 142, 148.

12　BOB, Ms. 8; see Carlvant, *Manuscript Painting*, p. 233.

13　Bavo, Remigius, Vedastus, Germanus, Wasnulfus (?). In the calendar of the Breviary of Saint Peter's Abbey of 1373, UGU, Ms. 3381, 1:2, fol. 224v, Bavo precedes Remigius, Germanus, et al.; in the calendar of 2:2, fol. 124v, Bavo precedes Remigius and Vedastus.

14　Coens and van der Straeten, "Un Martyrologe du XIIᵉ siècle," 134.

15　Bishop Macharius 10 April is in the calendar of the missal of St. Peter's Abbey and in both calendars of the Breviary of Saint Peter's Abbey of 1373: 1:2, fol. 221v, and 2:2, fol. 124v, in which latter the feast is specified as deposition. The elevation of Bishop Macharius is entered on 9 May in both calendars of this breviary (1:2, fol. 222r, and 2:2, fol. 125r). In Bruges calendars, Bishop Macharius is also entered on 9 May, but the feast is that of his translation; see Carlvant, *Manuscript Painting*, 373. Bishop Macharius does not appear in Liège calendars; see Oliver, *Gothic Manuscript Illumination*, 2:217–218.

16　Coens and van der Straeten, "Un Martyrologe du XIIᵉ siècle," 134. Likewise, Amandus and Vedastus are entered 6 February in the calendar of missal of St. Peter's Abbey and in both calendars of the Breviary of Saint Peter's Abbey of 1373 (1:2, fol. 220v and 2:2, fol. 123v).

17　Ghent psalters with St. Elisabeth of Hungary in the calendar and/or litany are KBR, Ms. 5163–5164 and OBL, Ms. Buchanan g.2; Cambridge, Magdalene College, Ms. F-4-8. See *Manuscript Painting*, 236–237, 243, 265. Liège psalters with Elisabeth in calendar are tabulated in Oliver *Gothic Manuscript Illumination*, 2:226; in litanies on 2:231.

THE CALENDAR

from Sint-Truiden completed in 1352.[18] Perhaps she was included in the calendar of 10 A 14 in part because her cult united the connections of Elisabeth (Ghent) with those of Arnold (Liège, Sint-Truiden). Furthermore, Elisabeth of Hungary is the only saint in the calendar of 10 A 14 designated as *electa*; perhaps Elisabeth of Lierde had a special devotion to the saint with whom she shared a name.

4   Gallican Elements

A few elements in the Sanctorale of 10 A 14 are imports from the ancient Gelasian and Gellone Sacramentaries, whence they came from the even older Gallican rite. One such element is the entry of Zoticus, Irenaeus, and Iacinctus in the Sanctorale of 10 A 14, fol. 170r.[19] These saints appear in relatively few missals and psalters of the Low Countries.[20] Moreover, their occurrence in 10 A 14 may suggest a connection to Ghent, as they are also found in both the calendar and Sanctorale of the missal of St. Peter's Abbey, on 10 February and in the calendar and Sanctorale of the Breviary of 1373 for St. Peter's.[21] These three saints are not in the calendar of 10 A 14; saints in a missal's calendar are very often omitted from the Sanctorale, for obvious reasons, but the reverse requires some further explanation.

A second Gelasian element is Soteris.[22] She is in the Sanctorale of 10 A 14 immediately after Zoticus, Irenaeus, and Iacinctus and, like them, is omitted from the calendar.

A third element of Gelasian origin is the occurrence of Emerentiana and Macharius, Early Christian martyrs whose feast day is 23 January in the Gelasian Sacramentary.[23] They are not in the calendar of 10 A 14 but are in the Sanctorale (fol. 163r) immediately after Vincent, whose feast is 22 January in the calendar. Emerentiana and Macharius are in the calendars of the Rummen Summer Missal KBR 9217 and the Rummen liturgical psalter KBR 9427 but are in neither the missal nor breviary of St. Peter's.[24] A final Gelasian element of Gallican origin is the entry of Eufemia on 13 April instead of 16 September.[25] She is also entered on 13 April in the calendar of KBR 9427, the liturgical psalter of the Rummen group. However, Eufemia on this date is hardly a marker for city of origin, as she is entered on 16 September in some Ghent manuscripts such as the missal and the breviary from St. Peter's, and on 13 April in the calendars of many Liège psalters.[26]

Coens and van der Straeten noted a number of other saints who, though not properly Ghent saints, nonetheless received special attention in the twelfth-century martyrology of St. Bavo, Ghent.[27] Several of these also appear in the calendar of 10 A 14: Brigid 1 February, Blaise 3 February

---

18   Ms. 58; see Coens, "Les saints," 151. This *Passionarium* is discussed in Chapter 7.

19   Zoticus, Irenaeus, and Hyacinthus (Iacinctus) 10 February are in the Sanctorale of the Gelasian Remedius-Sacramentary, St. Gallen, Stiftsbibliothek, Cod. Sang. 348, *c.*800, p. 78. See V. Leroquais, *Les sacramentaires et les missels manuscrits des bibliothèques publiques de France* (Paris, 1924), 1:XLV, for Gelasian saints who entered the Roman Sanctorale beginning in the ninth century; see Leroquais, *Les sacramentaires*, 1:2, for entry of Zoticus, Irenaeus, and Hyacinthus in the Gellone Sacramentary, BNF, Ms. lat. 12048, fol. 18v, and also Richard W. Pfaff, *The Liturgy in Medieval England: A History* (Cambridge: Cambridge University Press, 2009), 58, 59.

20   Zoticus, Ireneus, and Iacinctus are in the calendars of only four of the twenty-three Liège-area psalters with calendars, according to Oliver's inventory. See Oliver, *Gothic Manuscript Illumination*, 2:215.

21   UGU, Ms. 3381, 2:2, fol. 404r. Zoticus and Iacinctus (Hyacinthus), with Amantius, are in the calendar of the missal of St. Peter's Abbey, fol. 1v. Zoticus, Ireneus, Iacinctus (and Amantius) are all in the Sanctorale on 10 February, following Scholastica. Ireneus and Zoticus are in one of the two calendars of the breviary of St. Peter's Abbey, UGU, Ms. 3381: They appear as entries for 10 February in 1:2, fol. 220v, but not as entries for this date in 2:2, fol. 123v. Zoticus, et al., are not in the calendar of Douce 5, which is also of Ghent origin.

22   Margaret Gibson, T. A. Heslop, and Richard W. Pfaff, eds., *Eadwine Psalter: Text, Image, and Monastic Culture in Twelfth-Century Canterbury* (London: Modern Humanities Research Association, 1992), 66. Pfaff refers to her as "the obscure (Gelasian) Soteris, a virgin martyr," and remarks on her occurrence in the calendar of the twelfth-century Eadwine Psalter. Soteris 10 February is entered in the Sanctorale of the Vatican copy of the Gelasian Sacramentary, BAV, Ms. Reg. lat. 316, late seventh or early eighth century, fol. 136r, and in the Sanctorale of the Gelasian Sacramentary in St. Gallen, p. 78, on 10 February, immediately before Iacinctus, Zoticus, and Ireneus. Soteris is in six of the twenty-three Liege-area psalters with calendars; see Oliver, *Gothic Manuscript Illumination*, 2:215.

23   H. A. Wilson, ed., *The Gelasian Sacramentary: Liber Sacramentorum Romanae Ecclesiae* (Oxford: Clarendon Press, 1894), xlvii, 322.

24   The martyr Macharius is not to be confused with the eleventh-century Antiochene bishop Macharius 10 April, already noted as a saint venerated in Ghent. Emerentiana and Macharius martyrs appear in a number of Liège calendars; see Oliver 2:214.

25   Eufemia is entered on 13 (ides) April in the Sanctorale of the Gelasian Sacramentary, BAV, Ms. Reg. lat. 316, fol. 138v. In the Sanctorale of the breviary from St. Peter's, UGU, Ms. 3381, hers is among the September feasts (1:3, fol. 244r).

26   Oliver, *Gothic Manuscript Illumination*, 2:217. Eufemia 16 September is in the calendar of the Breviary of St. Peter's Abbey, 1:2, fol. 224r, and 2:2, fol. 127v.

27   LBL, Ms. Egerton 2796. The attention takes the form of "soit une mise en relief spéciale, soit une mention qui ne se rencontre pas

(2 February in the martyrology), Gertrude (of Nivelles) 17 March,[28] Bernard of Clairvaux 20 August, Leonard (in red) 6 November, Martin (in red) 11 November, Octave of Martin 17 November (entered on 18 November in 10 A 14), and Thomas of Canterbury 29 December. Leonard and Thomas of Canterbury, however, are also commonly found in calendars of Liège.

5   England

Bede 27 May is in 10 A 14 but not in 9217, nor in psalters of Liège or Bruges, the Sint-Truiden martyrology of 1429, the St. Peter's missal, nor the St. Peter's breviary of 1373. He is obviously not of Gallican origin, nor were the Gelasian manuscripts a vehicle of his transmission to 10 A 14. Certainly, English saints are no strangers to Low Country calendars, but further research might help explain the inclusion of Bede in 10 A 14.

6   Brussels

Gudile 7 January, Geneviève 3 January, and Gertrude 17 March were particularly venerated in Brussels and Brabant; all three are in the calendar of 10 A 14. However, Gertrude is universal in calendars of Liège; both Gertrude and Geneviève are entered in a fifteenth-century customary from Sint-Truiden.[29]

7   Cologne and Münster

Gereon and his companions 10 October were venerated in a number of locations in Flanders and the Mosan region as well as in Cologne, the center of their cult. The 11,000 virgins 21 October, companions of St. Ursula, were reputedly martyred in Cologne, a center of their cult.[30]

Ludger 26 March, bishop of Münster, is in the calendar of 10 A 14 and in that of one Liège psalter-hours.[31]

8   The Illustration of the Calendar

Artist 1 decorated the calendar (fols. 1r–6v, figs. 3–14). The KL letters, in the upper left corner of each page of the calendar, are hybrid designs, partly painted of blue or pink decorated with geometric decoration in white, and partly constructed of grotesques, which also inhabit the internal spaces. Each page has full or nearly full borders, consisting of two thin tendrils that emanate from the baguette that borders the KL initial and accompanied either continuously or at intervals by a strip, gold or colored, and decorated in white. Stems bearing colored trilobed feathery leaves, or large grotesques with various human, animal, bird, and fish morphologies branch off at intervals; and they terminate in paired opposed elements in the lower or right margin. Both feathery leaves and grotesques are large and showy.

Labors of the month and signs of the zodiac are in medallions on the right side of each page. The diameter of the medallions is the equivalent of about four text lines. Each medallion has an inner rim consisting of a colored strip and an outer rim of gold studded with filamented gold balls. The upper disc on each page, extending from the eighth to the twelfth lines from the top, is decorated with the appropriate labor of the month and the lower, spanning the fourth to eighth lines from the bottom, with the corresponding sign of the zodiac.

Appendix 5 presents the iconography of the labors of the month for 10 A 14, 9217, and Douce 5, and collectively for calendars from thirteenth-century Ghent, Bruges, and Liège.[32] In terms of the selection of subjects, 10 A 14 shares the most months with 9217 (nine), then with Ghent (eight). Calendars of manuscripts from Bruges and Liège share fewer subjects with 10 A 14 (five and four, respectively).[33] However, two subjects 10 A 14 shares with Liège—the viol-player for May and the flower-picker for June—are especially significant because they do not appear elsewhere in calendrical iconography, neither in that of Ghent nor in that of calendars from other cities in the Low Countries. Another telling connection with Liège

---

dans ses textes de base, Usuard ou le Pseudo-Florus" (Coens and van der Straeten, 146).

28   The sister of St. Bavo, she is universal in calendars of Liège (Oliver, *Gothic Manuscript Illumination*, 2:211).

29   Coens, "Les saints," 167.

30   The Abbey of Sint-Truiden was richly endowed with ursuline relics (Coens, "Les saints," 150).

31   BUL, Ms. 431; see Oliver *Gothic Manuscript Illumination*, 2:216.

32   Iconography for labors of the month in Ghent and Bruges calendars of the thirteenth century is compiled and discussed in Carlvant, *Manuscript Painting*, 295–313. Iconography for the labors in calendars of Liège for this period is compiled and discussed in Oliver, *Gothic Manuscript Illumination*, 1:29–32. My data is taken primarily from these two sources.

33   The numbers are for double correspondence—identical subjects that appear in identical months. Some subjects are the same but appear in different months; for example, the subject of slaughtering a cow appears in November in 10 A 14, but in December in calendars of Liège.

is the inclusion of the medallions with signs of the zodiac, in addition to the medallions with the labors;[34] signs of the zodiac do not appear on the calendars from Ghent. Ghent calendars are distinguished by the iconography of candle-bearing (one candle) in February and baking in December.[35] The Winter Missal displays these subjects for these two months; Liège, on the other hand, displays pruning for February and butchering for December.

Iconography for the months of May, July, and August—respectively, the bearing of flowering stalks, mowing, and reaping—is of lesser value for purposes of determining origins, as these subjects are the same in all these manuscripts and groups, excepting Douce 5, which is missing the pages for those months. The warming, drinking, and feasting iconography for January and the various harvesting and slaughtering activities for summer and autumn are common in many variants in the iconography of thirteenth-century European calendars.

The calendar of the 9217 gives one page to each month, as does that of 10 A 14.[36] Labors of the month, in stream-lined quatrefoil frames, are about three or four text-lines in height. In the Summer Missal these are insets within the lower border bar of each page rather than discrete units floating on the text lines as in 10 A 14.

Bruges is included in Appendix 5 not because it has been proposed as either a site of production or destination of 10 A 14 but as a foil to place comparisons into a broader regional perspective and, by its differences with 10 A 14, to throw into relief some of the specific connections of 10 A 14 to Ghent and Liège. The Bruges iconography shows that Bruges was not the source of two candles for February, the viol-playing for May, or the baking for December. Nor was it the source for the zodiac images.

Douce 5, a product of Ghent in the years immediately antecedent to the creation of the Rummen manuscripts, is included because it is temporally proximate, although it is missing one-third of its calendrical pages. Six of its extant eight months, including February and December, are illustrated with iconography connected to that of 10 A 14, albeit with narrative embellishments.[37] Thus Ghent calendars of both thirteenth- and fourteenth-century manuscripts share key iconographical elements with 10 A 14. Few other manuscripts with illustrated calendars from relevant areas are as close in time to 10 A 14 as is Douce 5.[38]

In sum, the comparanda show that the iconography of the labors of the month in 10 A 14, considering the number, placement and significance of subjects, is closest, first, to that of 9217, and then to that of late thirteenth-century psalters from Ghent, with carryover into the fourteenth century. If the additional factor of signs of the zodiac is included in the calculation of connections, Liège, sharing this feature with 10 A 14, is equal to Ghent in linkages with the Winter Missal. It seems likely that the iconography was selected with the goal giving equal consideration to Ghent and to Liège.

9 Conclusion

Neither the calendar nor its illumination points decisively to one destination; Liège and Ghent are both favored. Arnold of Rummen had connections to Liège, where he died in 1373; Sint-Truiden was only about 10 km from Rummen. Active and influential in the service of the Duke of Brabant, Arnold most likely spent considerable time in Brussels, to which 10 A 14 pays homage with the inclusion of three of its saints. Elisabeth of Lierde, on the other hand, was securely tied to Ghent, where she had lived with her first husband Simon of Mirabello, where she fled after the destruction of the castle at Rummen, and where she died and was buried in 1366. Perhaps the planner of the manuscript, or the scribe, was instructed to produce a calendar with saints familiar to both Arnold and Elisabeth. If the

---

34   Layout of images of labors of the months and signs of the zodiac on the calendar pages in 10 A 14 comports with Liège. A psalter of *c*.1261 now in MLM, Ms. M. 440, is typical of Liège psalters and psalter-hours in depicting both labors and signs. As in 10 A 14, these occupy medallions on the right side of the page, the labor above and the sign below. Given that the pages of 10 A 14 are twice the height and width of M. 440 (37 × 26cm vs 18 × 13cm) and therefore offer four times the surface area, the medallions, which are of approximately the same diameter in M. 440 as in 10 A 14, visually punctuate the pages differently in the two manuscripts. For Ms. M. 440, see Oliver, *Gothic Manuscript Illumination*, 2:280–283. For calendar pages of Ms. M. 440, see http://ica.themorgan.org/manuscript/page/1/77322. Accessed 19 August 2022.

35   Of the many Liège manuscripts examined by Oliver, baking for December occurs only in LBL, Ms. Stowe 17, *c*.1310–1320. See *Gothic Manuscript Illumination*, 1:32 and 2:269.

36   See Vandecapelle-Haagdorens, "Het zgn. missaal," 94–99.

---

37   See Stones, *Gothic Manuscripts*, pt. 1, vol. 2, p. 344 for discussion of the iconography of the calendar in Douce 5 and p. 353 for provenance.

38   The Ghent Ceremonial of 1322 has no calendar and that of the Ghent missal of *c*.1275–1285 is not illustrated. Three important Ghent psalters and psalter-hours of the early fourteenth century, produced approximately contemporaneously with Douce 5–6, are either without calendars or are without illustration for the labors of the months: HKB, Ms. 135 E 15; CKB, Ms. G.K.S. 3384,8°, WAG, Ms. 82.

manuscript were begun around or a few years before 1350, as the clothing in illumination of the first campaign suggests, its production would have coincided with, or shortly preceded, the marriage of Elisabeth and Arnold. Perhaps the manuscript was commissioned to celebrate their marriage and bring together their different connections. The calendar's dearth of translations and elevations, and its relatively few octaves and inventions accord with secular ownership. The book may well have been made for use in a private chapel, and, as its splendid decoration suggests, with a secondary purpose as a show book.

CHAPTER 7

The Origins and Formation of the Flourisher-Illuminators

This chapter addresses the question of the formation of the flourisher-artists of 10 A 14 and their work prior to the Winter Missal. Chapter 8 will consider the location of the workshop that produced 10 A 14.

What influences, from other artists, manuscripts, or locations, contributed to shaping the style and aesthetic of each artist before he worked on 10 A 14? Pre-existent to the process of formation is the artist's particular feeling for design, expressed in his personal style—in particular forms, patterns, motifs, and details. A number of factors contribute to shaping the expression of this feeling as a style. One is foundational training, conducted in a particular workshop, located in a particular city, monastery, or elite residence. A second is subsequent exposure to material from different locations, whether through the movement of manuscripts or of the artist. A third is the type of commission and the tastes and means of the patron. I assume that the resulting amalgam of factors imprints the artist's personal style with evidence of his artistic journey. The flourisher-artists of 10 A 14 are likely to have known and worked on manuscripts associated with Tournai, Sint-Truiden, and Ghent prior to their work on the Winter Missal; concerning possible involvement in manuscripts from Cologne, there is less evidence; for connection to books from Brussels, no evidence can currently be identified.

The larger visual culture of a location—its sculpture, wall paintings, and architecture in particular—are possible sources of additional influences on the artist. The monumental brasses of Tournai and Flanders are relevant to the understanding of style of Flemish illuminators. (See Appendix 4, Pt. 4.)[1] Some Rummen-group artists may have worked on brasses before they illuminated the Rummen manuscripts. Both French-influenced sculpture and local funerary reliefs may have influenced Ghent's manuscript painters in the thirteenth century.[2] The style

of illumination of the Rummen-group manuscripts exhibits general parallels to that of monumental wall painting in mid-fourteenth-century Ghent.[3] More could be done to contextualize the manuscript illumination of Ghent within its contemporary visual environment.[4] However the scarcity of the surviving sculpture and wall painting and the poor condition of many remnants greatly hamper the investigation of connections to both media. This endeavor must wait until remains are better known and studied.

1 Artist 1: the Loppem-Bruges Antiphonal, Tournai, Perhaps Cologne

Artist 1's style was formed in part in the ateliers of Tournai, though he cannot be identified in a particular manuscript. The evidence of penwork, considered in Chapter 4, and the double gorgon iconography, discussed in Chapter 5, identify the hand of Artist 1 in the Loppem-Bruges antiphonal. Further evidence, provided here, from faces, heads, drapery, and borders, supports this attribution. Important elements in style and iconography point to Ghent as the site of production for the antiphonal, whose destination is unknown.

The characteristic long, pointed noses of Artist 1 in 10 A 14 are also found in the antiphonal. (Cp. figs. 121a, 210.) Hair is rendered in both manuscripts with locks of varied widths, lengths, and degrees of curvature. The effect is somewhat unkempt; one feels the coiffures could benefit from a comb. Drapery is rendered as sometimes blotchy

---

l'écluse des Braemgaten (Ghent: Imprimerie Eug. Vanderhaeghen, 1892).

3   See Carina Fryklund, *Flemish Wall Painting* (Turnhout: Brepols Publishers, 2011), especially Chapters 3 and 4. She connects the style of mid-century wall painting at the Castle of Laarne, near Ghent, with that of KBR 9217, KBR 9427, and Ms. 10 A 14 (pp. 174–175). More broadly, she places the styles of a number of much-damaged wall-painting cycles in Flanders in the context of styles of illumination, stained glass, and contemporary wall painting in France, Flanders, Cologne, and England. Though Flemish wall painting of this era is scarce in quantity, some appears to be of high quality.

4   The three volumes of *Gent: duizend jaar kunst en cultuur*, published in conjunction with the exhibition of 1975, survey artifacts in many media, including ceramics, metalwork, and tapestry, in addition to architecture, wall painting, sculpture, and manuscript illumination. This publication is a good start for a broad view of the visual culture in Ghent in the fourteenth century.

---

1   See Lynda Dennison, "Flemish Influence on English Manuscript Painting in East Anglia in the Fourteenth Century," in *East Anglia and its North Sea World in the Middle Ages*, ed. David Bates and Robert Liddiard (Woodbridge, Suffolk: Boydell Press, 2013), 330–335.

2   Carlvant, *Manuscript Painting*, 92, 106, 112. Carlvant remarks on the smooth, bland quality of the wooden statue of St. Autbertus from the Poortakker Chapel in Ghent. "Smooth and bland" could be said of the effect generated by Artist 1's figures in the Rummen manuscripts: Staid human expression often contrasts with emotionalized, dramatic gorgons. For the funerary relief slabs, see Jean Béthune-de Villers, *Catalogue des dalles funéraires retrouvées à*

washes of color; an overlay of black lines, many of them short and choppy, defines folds in the antiphonal; in 10 A 14 this same scheme is present, enriched by modeling with feathery black and white lines. Painted border bars on all relevant pages of the antiphonal, as well as on four of the six relevant pages of 10 A 14, are a variation of the slender strip-baguette-tendril derived from Parisian illumination. Segments of alternating colors, mostly red and blue, are decorated in geometric or foliate patterns of white, some with added contrasting hues. In the antiphonal, the bar segments are generally outlined on three sides with a thin gold strip; in 10 A 14 this outlining extends to all four sides. Segments are separated by loops, squared knots, or circles in the accompanying baguette. Foliage includes gold trilobes, blue and red maple leaves, and passages of the "flame motif." In 10 A 14, though not in the antiphonal, the maple leaves begin to curl in the third dimension. This development of a more illusionistic idiom, also manifested in 10 A 14's enhanced techniques in modeling, as well as the complexities of design introduced by the architecture in 10 A 14, indicate that it is the later of the two manuscripts.

Artist 1's illumination in the Loppem-Bruges antiphonal is similar in style to that in 10 A 14 but more spirited. The antiphonal has more bas-de-page vignettes and more grotesques, many that project into the margins as terminals to segments of the border bar. Similar grotesques are found on the calendar pages of 10 A 14. (Cp. figs. 12, 201.)

Tracking back in time, evidence indicates that before the antiphonal, Artist 1 worked in Tournai as a member of the wide and prolific circle that included, among others, Pierart dou Tielt, Jehan de Grise, and the artist of the Ghent Ceremonial. These artists produced work over a period of about two decades. Among the manuscripts decorated by their group were a *Roman de la rose* of *c*.1330, now in Tournai; a breviary of Sainte-Aldegonde de Maubeuge, now in Cambrai, also of about 1330; the Bodley *Alexander* of 1338–1344; a copy of the *Lancelot du lac*, now in Paris, of 1344; and the Morgan Library's copy of the *Voeux du paon*, *c*.1348–50.[5]

Broadly speaking, the style of Tournai is an amalgam of the Parisian and the Flemish, to which are added elements from Cologne and Artois. The elegant and the earthy, the realistic and the fantastical, the French Gothic and the Italianate, the highly finished and the slipshod, all have a place in this rich output.

Characteristics of Artist 1's figure style can be related to Tournaisian style, especially to that of the Peacock Master, as Leo terms the more Parisian of the two artists of the Morgan *Voeux du paon*, to whom he also ascribes the frontispiece of the *Lancelot*.[6] Artist 1's faces in the Loppem-Bruges antiphonal and 10 A 14 on the one hand, and those of the Peacock Master in the *Voeux du paon* on the other, employ heavy black line to define facial features. The head of the Wildman, *Voeux du paon* (fig. 153), compares with those of Sts. Peter and John, Loppem-Bruges antiphonal (fig. 203) ,[7] and Arnold of Rummen, 10 A 14 (fig. 103a). No line defines the lower eyelid. In the *Voeux*, as in the other two manuscripts, expression of the elegant characters in the miniatures is conveyed primarily by sidelong glances and tilted heads that tend towards

---

Leo, *Images, Texts, and Marginalia*. The text of the *Voeux* contains two poems, both incomplete: a copy of the *Voeux du paon*, the poem by Jacques de Longuyon, written for Thibaut de Bar, bishop of Liège, in 1312, and a copy of the *Restor du paon* written by Jehan le Court in or before 1338.

The Morgan *Voeux* is generally dated 1348–1351 on the evidence of the flagellant iconography in its margins, fols. 95r and 140v. Flagellants are associated with the years of the Black Death. The flagellant costume in the *Voeux*'s images comports with that of flagellants in the image of the procession of flagellants in the *Antiquitates Flandriae* of Gilles Li Muisis of *c*.1349, KBR, Ms. 13076–13077, fol. 16v. However, flagellants were not exclusively a phenomenon of the Plague. Self-flagellation as a form of penitence was practiced from the time of the Apostle Paul (1 Corinthians 9:27) and both individual and communal self-flagellation were pious practices in the thirteenth century. See John Henderson, "The Flagellant Movement and the Flagellant Confraternities in Central Italy, 1260–1400," *Studies in Church History* 15 (1978): 147–160. Imagery of lone figures (as opposed to processional groups) engaging in self-flagellation appears in earlier manuscripts, as on a leaf of the Hungarian Anjou Legendary of 1325–1340, MLM, Ms. M. 360.26. The image depicts a nude St. Dominic of Bologna scourging himself. See the Morgan's website at http://ica.themorgan.org/manuscript/page/28/158381.

5   The *Roman de la rose* is TBM, Ms. 101; for bibliography, see the notes in Walters, "Marian Devotion," 207–270. The breviary is CMM, Ms. 133; see Avril, "250: Bréviare de Sainte-Aldegonde de Maubeuge (partie d'été)," *Les fastes du gothique*, 303. For the Alexander, see Mark Cruse, *Illuminating the* Roman d'Alexandre, 187; for illuminators of this manuscript, see also Ross, *Illustrated Medieval Alexander*, 70–73; Domenic Leo, *Images, Texts, and Marginalia in a "Vows of the Peacock" Manuscript* (*New York, Pierpont Morgan Library MS G24*) (Leiden: Brill, 2013), 264–266. The *Lancelot* is BNF, Ms. fr. 122; See the "About" text in the entry for this manuscript on the website of the BNF: https://gallica.bnf.fr/ark:/12148/btv1b10533299h/f1.item. For the *Voeux du paon*, MLM, Ms. G.24, see

6   Leo identifies two artists. The Peacock Master was responsible for all twenty-two miniatures and for the abundant marginalia on about half the manuscript's folios. The Scat Master was responsible marginalia on the remaining folios. See *Images, Texts, and Marginalia*, 45–60. A *Queste du saint Graal* of 1351, Paris, Bibliothèque de l'Arsenal, Ms. 5218, is signed by Pierart dou Tielt as scribe, illuminator, and binder of the manuscript. See Walters, "Marian Devotion," 265–270, for a list of manuscripts with illumination by the Master of the Ghent Ceremonial and Pierart dou Tielt.

7   The initial *D* here is a mistake. It should be *C*, as the chant begins, "*Cum complerentur dies pentecostes.*" *C*, the correct letter, is written in red after the historiated *D*.

THE ORIGINS AND FORMATION OF THE FLOURISHER-ILLUMINATORS

the mannered. More emotionalized faces with eyebrows shaped as inverted V's and pronounced arches are found in the penwork heads in the margins of Artist 1 and likewise in the marginalia of the Peacock Master. While these similarities are significant, they fall short of identifying Artist 1 as the Peacock Master. A larger selection of common features is lacking. More could be done to clarify the relationships.

Artist 1's architecture relates not to that of the *Voeux* but rather to that of Bodley 264, in which the spectacular and varied castles and superstructures almost become participants in the pagentry. The architecture of Artist 1's illuminations in the Winter Missal could be read as a selection of Bodley 264's architectural elements. Battlemented wall strips reinforced by turrets with conical roofs, spindly columns, louvered windows, stepped gables, and rib-vaulted ceilings viewed from beneath are common to both Bodley 264 and Artist 1's work in 10 A 14. In the latter, the diversity and profusion of Bodley 264 is tamed, subjected to consistency in scale and color and to a miniaturization and dessication that return it to more conventional functions as backdrop, setting and frame. Unlike 10 A 14, the antiphonal furnishes little architecture for comparison with Tournai. In the antiphonal, architecture does not frame miniatures, and the church on fol. [4r] (fig. 201a) is the only building within any miniature.

The basic elements of Artist 1's painted border bars in 10 A 14 and the Loppem-Bruges antiphonal, enumerated above, are found in Tournaisian manuscripts: The strips of different colored segments, paralleled by a thin baguette; the cusping; the cabbage leaves; the tendrils bearing foliage are all similar to those in the *Voeux*, the *Roman de la rose*, and Bodley 264, among others. Border bars in Bodley 264 exhibit the "flame motif" (fols. 58r, fig. 143), which Haagdorens cited in connection with Cologne, but which could be from Tournai.[8]

As noted in Chapter 4, Artist 1's work in the Winter Missal shares with the antiphonal a vocabulary of penwork motifs and an aesthetic (figs. 202, 204), though the quantity of flourishing is less in the antiphonal. Artist 1's flourishing in these two manuscripts was not a legacy of flourishing in Tournai; the aforementioned Tournaisian manuscripts either lack flourishing altogether or are very minimally flourished.[9]

Some iconographical motifs that appear in Artist 1's flourishing and painting may have origins in imagery from Tournai. The human heads with grotesquely rippled profiles found in initials and in terminal complexes of 10 A 14 (figs. 113, 128) bear comparison with those in Flemish brasses from Tournai. The shovel-mouth grotesques in some of his painted initials (fig. 132a) can be compared with those in Tournaisian brasses and in the marginalia in the *Voeux*.[10] These beasts with gaping mouths may furnish one component of the origin of the gorgon motif. However, Ghent is more promising than Tournai as the origin of the gorgon motif in its characteristic version. The gorgons are considered further in Chapter 8 and in Appendix 6. Ghent is also the most likely source for Artist 1's style of penwork flourishing.

There remains the difficult question of Artist 1 and workshops in Cologne. Two observations are of significance, both of which connect Artist 1 indirectly to Cologne. First, Artist 9217-1's style is connected to Cologne in numerous ways. Artist 1's style, in turn, is close to that of 9217-1. Second, Artist 1's style is close to that of the *Voeux du paon*. Marginalia and grape leaf foliage of types in illumination from Cologne are found on the pages of the *Voeux*.[11] These two circumstances hint that Artist 1 may have worked in Cologne, perhaps along with Artist 9217-1, before working in Tournai and Ghent.

2 Artist 2: Sint-Truiden

The picture is clearer for Artist 2 than for Artist 1. Artist 2 worked in Sint-Truiden before he worked on 10 A 14. Comparisons between the script, the penwork initials, and the borders of Sint-Truiden manuscripts with those in Rummen books suggest that the former were a source for the latter.[12] Though illumination in the Sint-Truiden manuscripts is not abundant, it manifests some significant similarities with illumination of Artist 2. Artist 2 probably flourished much and illuminated some in Sint-Truiden prior to his work on 10 A 14.

The manuscripts with penwork initials and flourishing of relevance were made for two holders of ecclesiastical office in the Abbey of Sint-Truiden, Johannes van Myrle (d. 1355), dean or provost 1338–1353, and Robert

---

8 Haagdorens, "Het zgn. missaal," 121–123.

9 Unflourished or minimally flourished are the Bodley *Alexander*, the *Lancelot*, the *Voeux*, and the *Queste du saint Graal*. I have not been able to examine the *Roman de la rose* or the Breviary of Sainte-Aldegonde de Maubeuge for flourishing. The pages available to me in reproductions are unflourished.

10 See Dennison, "The Artistic Context," p. 8 and pl. VI(D) and the *Voeux*, fols. 27v, 28v, 65v, 80v.

11 See Leo, *Images, Texts, and Marginalia*, 241, 244.

12 Haagdorens, *Het zgn. missaal*, 145, notes that connections between initials of Sint-Truiden and Rummen manuscripts were made as early as 1951.

van Craenwyck (d. 1366), abbot 1350–1366.[13] Van Myrle's manuscripts are intellectual in content; van Craenwyck's are devotional and pastoral.

Van Myrle commissioned a copy of the *Catholicon*, by Johannes of Balbua, dated 1348; a *Rationale divinorum officiorum* by Guillelmus Durandus, completed around 1350–1352; and a two-volume *Speculum historiale* by Vincent of Beauvais, the first volume completed in 1350 and the second in 1352.[14] Among the manuscripts made for van Craenwyck are a copy of the *Dialogues* of Gregory the Great; a copy of Gregory's *Homilies on the Gospels*, 1350–1366; and a two-part *Passionarium*—an account of lives of saints honored at the Abbey of Sint-Truiden—hereinafter referenced as *Passionarium 1* and *Passionarium 2*.[15] *Passionarium 1* was completed in 1366 according to an inscription on fol. 1v, and the other van Craenwyck manuscripts have been assigned *c.*1361–1366 as a likely date of completion.[16]

The dates of completion of these Sint-Truiden manuscripts make them close contemporaries of the Rummen group—the van Myrle manuscripts with 6426, 9427, 9217, and 10 A 14's first campaign, and the van Craenwyck manuscripts with the second campaign of 10 A 14. However, the dates of commencement are not known. Van Myrle was resident in the abbey and moved up in ecclesiastical rank for many years before he became provost in 1338. If van Craenwyck, like van Myrle, had been in residence at the abbey, or closely connected to it, prior to his appointment to office, the associated manuscripts could have been begun before the commencement of his tenure as abbot. Completion of the manuscripts may have been delayed by civil unrest; conflict between the abbey and the town of Sint-Truiden was such that van Craenwyck spent much of his abbacy in Liège, Zoutleeuw, and Cologne.[17]

The script of 9217 and 10 A 14 is closely comparable to the formal script of Martinus de Venne, scribe of the van Craenwyck manuscripts. The script of Willem de Dycka, chief scribe of the van Myrle manuscripts, is somewhat less formal. The ruling of the page and the script of 10 A 14, 9217, and 9427 are very similar to some in the Sint-Truiden group.[18] Haagdorens, Smeyers, and Dennison place the production of the texts of the Rummen group in Sint-Truiden, either at the monastery or in the town close by; further, Haagdorens and Smeyers point to Sint-Truiden as the locus of illumination as well, whereas Dennison argues for Ghent as its location.[19]

The Sint-Truiden atelier emphasized penwork over illumination. All Sint-Truiden manuscripts feature beautifully decorated penwork initials of two to ten lines or more, with counters containing palmette, leaf, and vine motifs in reserve against hatched or solid backgrounds. In addition, counters and initial bodies in Mss. 57 and 138 are decorated with animals, birds, faces, and grotesques, some elongated and some with humped backs. White and gold balls are used as fillers. Sint-Truiden codices display various combinations of penwork pearls, corkscrews, ball-and-squiggle trilobes, and floating rosettes. All these are features that the Sint-Truiden manuscripts share with 10 A 14 and other Rummen-group manuscripts, though details of style and design differ.

Other features of the Sint-Truiden group differ from those in 10 A 14: Large *littera duplex* or puzzle initials that abound in northern Netherlandish and German manuscripts and are not uncommon in Flemish and French illumination are in the penwork of Sint-Truiden (fig. 194) but not in that of 10 A 14, 9217, 9427, or 6426. In the Sint-Truiden group, border bars of Types 1 and 2 are used far less frequently than in 10 A 14. Type 4 bars appear not at all, and Type 3 only as what, at most, could be termed a prototype (*Passionarium 2*, fol. 16v).

2.1 The Evidence from Penwork

The most telling connections with 10 A 14 are in the treatment of counters in penwork initials, both those with hatching and foliate motifs in reserve and those

---

13 Smeyers, *Flemish Miniatures*, 168–171, and "Die verluchting in handschriften uit de abdij van Sint-Truiden," in *Handschriften uit de abdij van Sint-Truiden*, 59–60.

14 BUL, Ms. 223 (*Catholicon*), Ms. 150 (*Rationale divinorum officiorum*), Mss. 60–61 (*Speculum historiale*). Description, discussion, and catalog entries with bibliography for the van Myrle manuscripts are provided by B. Cardon, "Het mecenaat van Johannes van Myrle," in *Handschriften uit de abdij van Sint-Truiden*," 220–230.

15 BUL, Ms. 43 (*Dialogues* of Gregory the Great), Ms. 138 (*Homilies on the Gospels*), Mss. 57, 58 (*Passionarium 1, 2*). Description, discussion, and catalog entries with bibliography for the van Craenwyck manuscripts are provided by P. Valvekens, "De handschriftenproduktie onder Abt Robert van Craenwyck (1350–1366)," in *Handschriften uit de abdij van Sint-Truiden*," 231–245.

16 Transcribed in Valvekens, "De handschriftenproduktie," 234. An inscription in yet another van Craenwyck manuscript, BUL, Ms. 326, a Rule of St. Benedict and necrologium, is inscribed with 1361 as its date of completion; see Valvekens, "De handschriftenproduktie," 243–245. Valvekens therefore dates all the van Craenwyck group to 1361–1366.

17 Valvekens, "De handschriftenproduktie," 231.

18 Dennison, "Dating and Localisation," 516.

19 Dennison, "Dating and Localisation," 518–519; Haagdorens, "Sint-Truidense handschriften," 265–266; "Het zgn missaal," 183. Smeyers, *Flemish Miniatures*, 171; and Smeyers, "Die verluchting in handschriften uit de abdij van Sint-Truiden," in *Handschriften uit de abdij van Sint-Truiden*, 62.

with animals, grotesques, and faces.[20] Penwork in the *Homilies, Dialogues*, and especially *Passionarium 1*, shares the most with that of 10 A 14 in aesthetic. The two volumes of the *Speculum historiale*, hereinafter referenced as *Speculum 1* and *Speculum 2*, offer some comparative material for Artist 2's illumination in 10 A 14 and in 6426 and 9427. Inquiry here is limited to clarifying the connection between the work of Artist 2 and the most salient decoration in the Sint-Truiden group.

Evidence for the presence of Artist 2 of the Rummen manuscripts in Sint-Truiden is strongest in the penwork of the *Passionarium 1* (figs. 185–192). The trimming of pages of this manuscript compromises the evaluation of some penwork designs. Initials of five or more lines, placed at *Incipits* in the text, are accompanied by Type 1 border bars and are embellished with pearls, corkscrews, floating rosettes, ball-and-squiggle trilobes, and wavy ivy leaves. Penwork extensions from these initials expand in the upper and lower margins into rectilinear terminal complexes, often truncated by trimming (fig. 186). All the penwork elements in *Passionarium 1*, and many more, can be found in 10 A 14, the latter discussed in Chapters 3 and 4. Profile and three-quarters heads in reserve decorate the bodies of penwork initials in *Passionarium 1* (fig. 189); faces in profile and three-quarters occur often in the counters of Artist 2's painted and penwork initials in 10 A 14 (fig. 80).

Rather stiffly posed humpbacked grotesques, often cited as originating in Cologne and the Rhineland, inhabit a number of the large initials in *Passionarium 1* (figs. 187, 188).[21] These grotesques are surrounded by curling tendrils; circles of contrasting color are sprinkled among abundant foliage. Closely comparable in pose and foliage in 10 A 14 is Artist 2's grotesque in musical notation (fig. 109a). Grotesques inhabit the counters of scores of Artist's 2's two-line initials (figs. 70b, 97, 98; Table 3). In spite of the relatively small size of these two-line initials in 10 A 14, the feeling for form is larger and simpler; the grotesque fills the initial. Heads are turned back, and *S*-curved necks echo the curvature of the surrounding initial, streamlining the fit of form to form. No longer needed to mediate between the curve of the initial and the upright posture of the figure, foliage disappears; instead, a few circles suffice as filler. The stiff, busy initials of *Passionarium 1* precede in development and time these more fluent penwork initials in 10 A 14. The richer color and more varied motifs in 10 A 14 not only testify to its status as a luxury commission but also reinforce the attribution of a date later than that of the Sint-Truiden manuscript.

The commonality of aesthetic manifested by line in 10 A 14 and in *Passionarium 1*, despite the trimmed margins of the latter, is striking. Similarities include tautly stretched curves and recurves in terminal complexes (figs. 190, 192. Cp. fig. 19), a tendency to the complex symmetrical pairing of extensions, not merely in simple planar alignments but in more complex spatial configurations. (Cp. figs. 192 and 191 with fig. 24.) The almost magnetic alignment of forms across spaces, as between trilobe tips and rosettes, is suggestive of both yearning and confrontation. Finally, the great variety of combinations in elements of border bars is common to 10 A 14 and *Passionarium 1*—this in spite of the limited decorative repertoire of the latter. (See Inventory 6.)

On the whole, the penwork style in *Passionarium 1* strongly suggests that Artist 2 worked in the Sint-Truiden atelier, probably shortly before beginning work on the Rummen manuscripts.[22] This atelier's specialization in flourishing, rather than in figural and narrative miniatures, helps to explain the magnificent flourishing, which rivals illumination, in 10 A 14. The aesthetic and motifs of penwork in the *Homilies* is very close to that of the *Passionarium 1* and to that of 10 A 14 (figs. 184, 199). It is possible that Artist 2 did penwork for the *Homilies*. The

---

20 Haagdorens, "Het zgn. missaal," 149–150, raised the possibility that one and the same artist might have been responsible for the penwork initials in 9217, BUL, Ms. 43, and BUL, Ms. 57, and made a similar, but less specific, connection in "Sint Truidense handschriften," 260, 268.

21 Haagdorens, "Het zgn. missaale," 141, 143, 145–151, discussed scholarship on the origins of these humpbacked grotesques in illumination of Cologne and environs. See also Delaissé, "Enluminure et peinture dans les Pays-Bas," 111–112, and Beer, *Beiträge zur oberrheinischen Buchmalerei*, 9–31.

22 The dating of Ms. 57 to 1366 rests on the inscription on the verso of the first ruled sheet in the manuscript, (Valvekens, "De handschriftenproduktie," 234). As van Craenwyck is tagged "of pious memory (*pie memorie*)," the inscription must postdate his death in May of 1366—by how much we cannot know. The inscription characterizes the manuscript as completed and bound in 1366 but does not address the year in which it was begun. Van Craenwyck's tenure as abbot was marked by significant disruptions in the life of the monastery. The abbot built a tower and wall around the abbey in response to repeated invasions by the townspeople; he left Sint-Truiden several times, living for extended periods in Liège, Zoutleeuw, and Cologne. The turmoil may have interfered with work on his manuscripts; thus, circumstances by no means preclude a commencement for the commission toward the beginning of his tenure as abbot, well before 1366. Moreover, given the simpler style of the flourishing of Ms. 57 relative to that of 10 A 14, a date antecedent to that of 10 A 14 can be considered. Marked differences in medium, figure style, and borders in the introductory images of the two volumes of the *Passionarium* greatly complicate assessments of the chronology of execution.

Dialogues, Passionarium 2, and both parts of the *Speculum historiale* were flourished by other artists.[23]

In the penwork decoration of the Sint-Truiden manuscripts some elements relate to Cologne, especially the humpbacked grotesques in initials, mentioned just above and discussed in Chapter 4. Other elements found in penwork from Cologne and that of northern France and the Low Countries are absent from, or infrequent in, the Rummen manuscripts, among them the puzzle initials and the elongated animals, hybrids, and grotesques that populate the stems of bi-colored initials in the Sint-Truiden manuscripts.[24]

2.2 *The Evidence from Illumination*

Relatively few in number, diverse in style, and uneven in quality, the illuminations in the Sint-Truiden manuscripts pose a challenge to the search for connections with illumination at other centers. Consideration here is directed to elements of style and iconography relevant to the question of origins of the Rummen group's decorators. Viewed through this filter, Artist 2, already connected by his penwork, is the most likely of the Rummen artists to have illuminated in Sint-Truiden. Artist 3's style has some similarities to the illumination of *Passionarium 2*, but not of such kind as to suggest an identity of hand. Artists 1 and 4 exhibit no significant connections to Sint-Truiden.

The two-part *Speculum historiale* has three pages with large historiated initials and partial borders: fols. 1r and 17r in *Speculum 1* (figs. 196, 196a; 197, 197a), and fol. 1r in *Speculum 2* (figs. 198, 198a). The initials in question are eight, twelve, and twelve lines, respectively. The decoration of all three pages is very probably by Artist 2, but early in his career, as an inexperienced illuminator.[25] The three pages were likely illuminated in the order in which they occur in the text. Each page's illuminated letter is enclosed in a squared panel with gold piping, patterned with either white filigree on blue, or with red squares with linear overlay in contrasting hues.

Backgrounds within the initials are gold. The letter forms on fol. 17r of *Speculum 1* and fol. 1r of *Speculum 2* have passages of knotwork, and the latter has a double gorgon, to be considered below. The counter of the initial *Q(uoniam)* on fol. 1r of *Speculum 1* (fig. 196a), is imaged with a "green man" from whose mouth and head emerge vines bearing colored trilobes. In *Speculum 1*, the initial *D(eus)* on fol. 17r (fig. 197a), and in *Speculum 2*, the initial *A(b anno)* on fol. 1r (fig. 198a), contain images of van Myrle kneeling before St. Trudo. In *Speculum 1*, van Myrle and St. Trudo are enclosed within a hexagon inscribed in gold ink as a seal: "*Signum Johannis de Myrle propositi sancti trudonis.*"[26]

A border bar consisting of a thin strip piped in gold extends downward from each initial, lining the left side and bottom of the text.[27] The bar of *Speculum 1*, fol. 1r, is inhabited by a small dragon whose tendril-like tail becomes a running, foliate vine. On fol. 17r the bar contains a vine bearing red and blue trilobes against a background of white filigree on blue and red. The bar of *Speculum 2*, fol. 1r, is patterned with white filigree on blue and red segments. Bars are variously articulated with knotwork, quatrefoils, and sprigs of additional vegetation that invade the borders.

Each page has illumination in the lower margin and/or bas-de-page, with vignettes of cavorting apes who engage in their typical activities, such as dancing, music-making, jousting, and obscene games. Each image includes an extra, larger, figure in the right margin. Fol. 1r in each volume has heraldry: a shield in both left and right lower corners of the bar in the first volume and a shield in the lower left corner of the bar in the second volume.

The uniformity of the initial panels and border bars speaks for the same artist, as does the uniformity of palette, keyed to dark tones and blue-gray. Elements in figure style shared with illumination in the Rummen group point to the hand of Artist 2. Adjustments in scale and

---

23   Penwork in the *Dialogues* has filler motifs like those of 10 A 14 but is, on the whole, aesthetically unlike the penwork of Artist 2. In *Passionarium 2* and both parts of the *Speculum historiale*, a different flourisher, or flourishers worked in a style featuring long, oblique, diagonal tendrils below the initial, shorter diagonals above, and ovoid loops that may enclose floating stellate rosettes (fig. 195). Parisian influence is possible.

24   In 10 A 14, the initial stem of the four-line initial *V(ultum)*, fol. 198v, by Artist 1, provides the closest analog to the Sint-Truiden manuscripts' initial stems decorated with elongated animals and grotesques. Occasionally in 10 A 14 elongated creatures are pressed not into the stem but into penwork decoration adjacent to the initial (fig. 21).

25   These pages are discussed more fully by Cardon, "Het mecenaat van Johannes van Myrle," 225–230. Cardon sees two artists; Ms. 61's illuminator was less gifted than the illuminator of Ms. 60. De Winter, *La librairie des ducs de Bourgogne*, 228, considers the illumination in Mss. 60–61 to be a feeble copy of the style of 6426, 9427, and 9217 and thus later than these three.

26   Cardon, "Het mecenaat van Johannes van Myrle," 225. For the involvement of fourteenth-century illuminators in the making of seals, see Marc Gil, "Jean Pucelle and the Parisian Seal-Engravers and Goldsmiths," trans. Raeleen Chai-Elsholz, in Pyun and Russakoff, eds., *Jean Pucelle*, 27–52.

27   The border bars on these illuminated pages of Mss. 60 and 61 resemble those in manuscripts of Verdun, such as the winter part of the Breviary of Renaud de Bar, LBL, Ms. Yates Thompson 8, 1302–1303. See Stones, *Gothic Manuscripts*, 2:1, 78–82, and ills. 117, 118, 121, 125, 126.

progressive changes in design, towards fuller integration and greater complexity, suggest that the order of execution follows the sequence of the text.

Adjustments in scale involve foliage and figures. On fol. 1r of *Speculum 1*, the border bars sprout at intervals wispy vines with tiny heart-shaped leaves that do not harmonize with the more largely conceived and robust border elements. The delicate, calligraphic line of these vines suggests a flourisher transitioning to an illuminator. The large falconer in the lower right corner is out of scale with the apes.

In the initial *D*, fol. 17r of *Speculum 1*, (fig. 197a), an oversized van Myrle kneels before St. Trudo, whom he would dwarf should he stand. Along most of the bar sturdy single leaves of larger size replace the wispy vines with tiny leaves, here appearing only as filler in the ape-scene. The figure at the right lower corner of the page is an ape only slightly taller than his companions. Unity of design is strengthened by the introduction of square knotwork at the corners and center of the lower border bar, echoing the knotwork extensions of the initial's panel.

Evaluation of the initial in the third illumination, *Speculum 2*, fol. 1r (fig. 198a), is vitiated by damage to both painting and gilding. Color is smudged and the gilding is cracked and rubbed. The kneeling van Myrle has shrunk to the scale of St. Trudo, and the wispy sprigs have disappeared altogether, replaced by robust paired vine stocks with gold cusping and multi-colored trilobes that are fewer in number and more largely conceived than the wispy vines. The tall stork atop the vine in the lower right margin has neck and legs of dimensions that harmonize with the vine's. Knotwork interludes in lateral and lower border bars echo the squared corners of the initial. Color is brightened by the addition of red segments in the border bar. In sum, the design is better integrated and unified than those of the other two pages and is enlivened in various ways.

The style relates to that of Artist 2. Modeling in the *Speculum's* illuminations is mostly in the style of Artist 2's work in 6426 and 9427, in which modeling is more fluent and uses less white-line highlighting than is the case in 10 A 14. Both heads of St. Trudo in the just-cited initials of *Speculum 1* and *2* compare in facial shape and rendering of features and expression with the faces of David in 9427 (fol. 14r, fig. 177a) and 10 A 14 (fol. 7r, fig. 15a). The drapery folds in all four of these figures are rendered with a largeness of conception, a fluency and slight plasticity, that are harnessed to expression of posture and movement, as opposed to the more brittle, numerous, and patternized folds of Artist 1.

The double gorgons that abound in the initial bodies of the Rummen manuscripts have one analog in the Sint-Truiden group, in *Speculum 2*, fol. 1r (figs. 198, 198a). The stem of the initial *A*, outlined in black, houses a double gorgon, the jaws of whose two heads are joined by tendril-like extensions in familiar angular knotwork, which is simpler in construction than the conjunctive knotwork in 10 A 14 (fig. 125a). Each head in the initial in Ms. 61 has a fiery red tongue with white-line detailing. The technique is not as deft as in 10 A 14. There is little visual distinction between the initial and its enclosing panel, as they are colored the same blue and both are decorated with a white linear tendril motif. This design suggests an early attempt to incorporate a complex motif into an initial stem.

As noted in Chapter 5, the source of the gorgon initial is yet to be satisfactorily identified. English Apocalypses mentioned above may have been contributory as might Flemish brasses.[28] If Artist 2 worked on the Sint-Truiden manuscripts at about the time Artist 1 was illuminating the Loppem-Bruges antiphonal, then the double gorgon made its appearance at approximately the same time in two different locations, albeit in far greater quantity and with greater panache in the Loppem-Bruges manuscript than in Sint-Truiden. It seems that the double gorgon motif in its developed, relevant form was primarily

---

28 In England the double gorgon occurs in a psalter, LBL, Ms. Egerton 3277, *c.*1360, in initials illuminated by Dennison's Artist A of KBR 6426. Dennison argues, convincingly, that this artist emigrated to England and worked on a number of the Bohun manuscripts after he completed work on the Rummen-group antiphonal 6426; see "Dating and Localisation," 505–507, 512. This appearance of the double gorgon in Ms. 3277 is not relevant for the question of sources for the gorgon motif in the Rummen manuscripts. For manuscripts commissioned by the Bohun family—the most important patrons of illumination in England during the second half of the fourteenth century—see Sandler's *Illuminators and Patrons*. A list of extant Bohun manuscripts is on pp. 346–349.

To return to the vexing question of the naming of artists (Chapter 4, n. 10), the decorator whom Dennison terms Artist A with respect to the Rummen group, Artist D in the Vienna Bohun Psalter, VON, Cod. 1826*, and the Flemish Bohun Hand in the overall context of Bohun illumination—this decorator is the same artist Sandler designates as the Egerton Master, from his work in the LBL, Ms. Egerton 3277 (*Illuminators and Patrons*, 11). Tracking identities, sequences, shifting roles, influences, locations, etc., quickly becomes an unmanageable labyrinth, as exemplified, for example in Alison Stones's monumental *Gothic Manuscripts*. Perhaps at some point in the future a comprehensive, consistent system for designating and tracking artists might be possible, though this would require a mountain-moving effort, mined with difficulties.

a phenomenon of illumination in Ghent; this matter is further addressed in Chapter 8. Whether it originated in Ghent or was imported is unresolved.

In *Passionarium 1* a ten-line penwork initial, C(*unctorum*), fol. 4r, is a variant of the *littera duplex* type, decorated with a monster and vine motif in reserve (fig. 185). Within the initial the Baptist, in a moderately hipshot stance, holds a lamb in one hand and points to it with the other. He stands on a patch of green grass, one of the relatively few occurrences of green in the penwork of these manuscripts. The figure is modeled with soft, almost melting, grisaille penstrokes. The technique of the figure contrasts strongly with the much harder, more linear style of the enclosing initial and vine filler.

The juxtaposition of the flat, linear style of the initial with the softly modeled figure it encloses has parallels; among them are the treatment by Artist 2 of the figure and its enclosing initial in 10 A 14's musical notation (fig. 105a) and in his two-line penwork initials of the manuscript's final quire. In the letter *D(eus)* on fol. 200r (fig. 134a), the head is in grisaille; the letter form and the panel around it are flatly colored. The style of the figure in *Passionarium 1* is softer and more three-dimensional than that of the heads in 10 A 14, while the penwork style of the rest of the *Passionarium's* page seems earlier; further study is required to explain the relationships. The Abbey's contacts with Cologne may have played a role in the softness of rendering.

The pointing gesture and hipshot stance of St. John have been linked to the International Gothic Style, but are just as likely to reflect Parisian influence, specifically that of Jean Pucelle whose work in the second quarter of the fourteenth century includes hipshot figures in grisaille, some with pointing gestures (fig. 152).[29] Parisian influence of the first half of the fourteenth century is thus represented in the illumination of the Sint-Truiden manuscripts, which may or may not have received all figural imagery where the text was produced. The date of the figure of John the Baptist is not necessarily pushed by its style into the 1360s; the manuscript's text and its illumination could date 1345–1350; the decoration of the initial stem is certainly compatible with those years.

In conclusion, Artist 2 was likely a flourisher who became a painter; before he worked as a flourisher and painter in 10 A 14, he worked as a flourisher on manuscripts of the Sint-Truiden atelier and did a limited amount of

painting. However, his work in the Sint-Truiden manuscripts does not entirely explain his later style, which developed an unparalleled richness of repertoire and of effects in penwork, and in illumination absorbed Flemish and English influences. He moved from Sint-Truiden to a more cosmopolitan environment, with enhanced opportunities for work, interaction with fellow artists, and visual stimuli.

3 Artist 3

Artist 3 is probably identical to Artist 2, from whose style his work evolves, as explained above. His penwork borders and the motifs that characterize his flourishing are almost all those of Artist 2, or closely related thereto. The interest in structure and the concern with three-dimensional figures and space that characterize the work of Artist 2 likewise characterize the work of Artist 3. Changes are observed in the means of articulating structural concerns and in a transposition of concerns from detail to the broader scheme of design. Where this artist is above all an innovative and prolific flourisher in the first campaign, his innovative contributions in the second are transposed to illumination, which offers a broader field of expression.

Influences from Italian illumination likely contributed to the changes in his style. Bolognese solid, rounded figures and borders with feathery foliage may have drawn his attention. Bohemian illumination, sometimes offered as a possible influence, tends to a delicacy of form, fluency of paint, and intensity of color that have less to offer the interests of Artist 3. A question remains as to the sources for the music-making angels in the borders of Artist 3's Adoration. The Winter Missal, the Bohun hours, and the Ghent Altarpiece, all feature variants of this iconography and all have connections to Ghent; perhaps the motif existed in earlier art of the city.

The illumination in the Sint-Truidan manuscripts most comparable in the style to that of Artist 3 in the Rummen Winter Missal is in *Passionarium 2*, though it is not likely that the same hand appears in the two manuscripts. Two initials on fol. 2r (figs. 193, 193a) are accompanied by full borders, in a style of *c.*1360–1370, related to the incipient International Gothic Style; some scholars have suggested the influence of Bohemian painting as well.[30] The style of

---

29 Another example in the *Hours of Jeanne d'Evreux* is the Angel in the Annunciation to the Shepherds, fol. 62r. Valvakens, "De handschriften produktie," 234, connects the image of St. John in Ms. 57 to International Gothic Style.

---

30 Valvekens, "De handschriften produktie," 237; Dennison, "Dating and Localisation," 516, 517, notes the connections of this illumination to Artists 3 and 4 (her D and D2) in 10 A 14. She does not see an identity of hands or of workshop but a common Bohemian influence in figure style and border construction.

Passionarium 2's initials is not found elsewhere in the illumination of the Sint-Truiden manuscripts. The counter of the ten-line initial *G(loriose)* tells the story of the miraculous communion of St. Denis, in a space crowded with figures and architecture. The artist of the *Gloriose* initial (fig. 193a) inserted a packed composition into the counter of the encircling initial *G*, set against a square panel patterned with alternating gold and blue squares, the former pounced and the latter inscribed, that resembles the background of the Winter Missal's Nativity (fig. 34a). A total of four animal hybrid and two human-headed grotesques are integrated into the initial's letter form. The left side of the initial is occupied by a prophet whose head is in one of the mouths of a two-headed grotesque and from whose lower body emerges a bird-mammal hybrid. Another large human-headed grotesque, from whose lower body emerges yet another mammalian head, is positioned on the right side of the initial. The initial largely encloses an asymmetrical, two-storied, busy architecture of three arches through which is visible a ceiling partly vaulted and partly tiled and a small room with a door and a window. A section of rocky ground, fitted to the curvature of the initial, supports two slumbering soldiers, guards of St. Denis, whose head is visible through a small window in the lower storey. Christ brings the Eucharist to St. Denis; the initial partially slices the lower part of Christ's body. The second storey has battlements, a room and a porch enclosing a small structure with pitched roof. Two female heads peer from a small, gridded window below the battlements;[31] and to the right a soldier's head peers through an arch in the subsidiary structure.

Compared to the deliberate, spatially regulated, and symmetrical designs of Artist 3, the composition is a crammed conglomeration of elements, vignettes assembled with little regard for symmetry, continuity, or spatial consistency. In spite of resemblances in shading and in the shared tendency to minimize use of black outlining and detailing in drapery, the *G(loriose)* initial is very unlike the work of Artist 3 in the Winter Missal.

Both the Adoration of the Magi in the Winter Missal and the *Gloriose* page in *Passionarium 2* are framed by a thin gold strip bordered by black lines and small black circles and enclosing human heads and figures, grotesques, and Italianate foliage. In the Adoration, the strip extends into the intercolumniation, and the composition is developed around and unified by the theme of music-making angels, whose figures are interspersed at regular intervals with grotesques and foliate elements. On the *Gloriose* page, the strip at the bottom is replaced by a bas-de-page. The palette is more intense than that of the Adoration page. In the former, the strip's decoration is not iconographically unified. On the left side, heads are interspersed in the intensely colored Italianate feathery fronds, and at the center of the strip is positioned a woman gathering flowers. On the right side, pairs of birds and climbing figures of men are interspersed with foliage, which is intensely colored in green, red, pink and blue. A human-fish monster tops off this strip. In the bas-de page is a vignette of hunters and dogs in a landscape of grass, flowers, and trees much influenced by the style and iconography of Parisian illumination of the 1350s and 1360s.

A seven-line initial *P(ost)* toward the bottom of the right column of text contains the single, monumental figure of the decapitated St. Denis, in frontal stance, presenting his head. He is depicted against a pounced gold background, without ancillary elements inside the initial. The drapery folds of his pink cope have the heavy, curved form of the International Gothic Style.[32]

The similarities in style between this illuminated page in *Passionarium 2* and the work of Artist 3 on fols. 22r and 27v of 10 A 14 are significant, but differences are very telling. The style of 10 A 14 is more measured and more liberal in spacing. The architecture of 10 A 14 is more monumental and symmetrical. Figures are less contorted, and themes are better developed. Drapery is used more intentionally to articulate the body The palette is less intense and is keyed to blue and orange rather than to pink and gold. Some passages of color on *Passionarium 2*'s page seem poorly executed. Artist 3 may have been acquainted with the St. Denis-page in *Passionarium 2* and the two illuminations must be close in date, but the sensibilities of the St. Denis artist and those manifested in the work of Artist 3 of 10 A 14 were different.

Artist 2/3 was most likely Laurence the Priest, named in the first colophon. He was from Antwerp, but residing in Ghent in 1366, by his own testimony; however, no evidence has surfaced that shows him working in Antwerp as an artist. He was first a flourisher in Sint-Truiden; in Ghent he developed into an illuminator whose style anticipates important developments, both international and Flemish, in the late fourteenth and fifteenth centuries.

---

31   These women could hardly be Saints Rusticus and Eleutherius, deacon and subdeacon, though identified as such by Valvakens, "De handschriften produktie," 235.

32   Noteworthy is the bust of woman, holding an inscribed scroll at the upper corner of the initial. Valvakens, "De handschriften produktie," 237, suggests that she may be Laërtia, mentioned in the *Golden Legend*, chapter 153.

4 Artist 4: a Follower of Artist 3

Artist 4 hardly ventures out from under the shadow of Artist 2/3. Both his border bars and his repertoire of motifs in flourishing and decoration are subsets of those of Artist 3. His figure style is very close to that of Artist 3. No indication of his origin apart from these connections appears in his work. He may well have been a priest, as priests feature in the decoration of his painted initials. The second colophon may have been written by him.

5 Conclusion

Artist 1's work prior to 10 A 14 is connected most immediately to Ghent, and before that to Tournai; Cologne, if he worked there, was at some remove. Artist 2's prior work was in Sint-Truiden, in the Diocese of Liège. The selection of artists for 10 A 14 echoes the calendar and the attachments of the two patrons. Arnold and Elisabeth thus placed the imprint of both Liège and Ghent on their manuscript, as much in the artistry as in the register of saints. This implies some awareness on their part of the identities and careers of artists and of correlations between style and location of production. Assuming such was the case, it encourages one to wonder more generally whether patrons might have made statements of regional identity via the selection of artists and, reciprocally, whether the regional connections of artists might suggest the loyalties of patrons. Many questions and qualifications immediately present themselves around this possibility, but it could be a useful tool in some cases. Here it appears that patrons had a level of awareness of art as identity that went beyond the depiction of their heraldry.[33]

---

33 Dennison has suggested that in fourteenth-century England, Benedictine monasteries and Augustinian establishments provided a framework within which manuscripts were written and decorated by itinerant or semi-itinerant artists and that a similar dynamic may have been at play in the case of the Rummen group. However, this model does not seem to explain the core Rummen enterprise, realized at the initiative of wealthy and powerful secular patrons, likely on the occasion of their marriage, which was both a celebratory commemoration and an expression of identity. Lynda Dennison, "Monastic or Secular? The Artist of the Ramsey Psalter, now at Holkham Hall, Norfolk," in *Monasteries and Society in Medieval Britain: Proceedings of the 1994 Harlaxton Symposium*, ed. Benjamin Thompson (Stamford: Paul Watkins, 1999), 223–261; Dennison, "Dating and Localisation," 519–520.

CHAPTER 8

The Place of Production

Brussels/Brabant, Sint-Truiden, and Ghent have all been proposed as locations for the illumination of 10 A 14. Liège, to which the calendar of 9217 is primarily directed and which is important for 10 A 14 as well, is unlikely to have been the site of production; manuscript illumination there seems to have ceased shortly after 1300. Tournai, although associated with the formation of Artist A of 6426 and Artist 1 of 10 A 14, has not been suggested as a possible site of production. One can equally exclude Cologne and the Rhineland, since connections with them were indirect, mediated primarily by way of Mosan sites.

1   Brabant/Brussels

Assessment of Brabant as a location for the making of illuminated books through much of the fourteenth century is hampered by the scarcity of surviving manuscripts that can be ascribed with certainty to Brussels and other Brabantine cities. A diverse group of manuscripts dating from the mid-thirteenth century into the first third of the fourteenth century incorporate French, Flemish, and Liègeois influences and have connections of various kinds to Brabant. Most cannot be assigned to one location with certainty, and the latest of them predates the Rummen manuscripts by a decade or more.[1] Some are comparable

to 10 A 14 in quality, but none in style. English influence, very marked in 10 A 14 and its cohort, is much less pronounced in the illumination of these manuscripts; the same can be said of Italianisms.

Manuscripts known to have been made in Brussels in the 1340s and 1350s—the decades most relevant for most illumination in the Rummen books—seem to be virtually nonexistent. Records do not provide evidence to connect any specific book of these decades with Brussels; no style comparable in definition to that of the Tournaisian style of Pierart dou Tielt and Jean de Grise, or to the style of Cologne's illumination and wall painting of the 1330s and 1340s, has emerged in connection with Brussels/Brabant.[2]

Delaissé assigned to Brussels the scriptorium that illuminated 6426, based on thin iconographical evidence; and based on its resemblances to 9217 and 10 A 14, assigned these latter to that city as well.[3] Brussels under the rule of Duke Wenceslas of Bohemia (Duke of Brabant 1355–1383), has also been tagged by De Winter and Oliver as the location of the scriptorium that produced the Rummen manuscripts.[4] However, very little stylistic or iconographical evidence is cited linking the Rummen manuscripts to those produced in Brussels. Oliver and De Winter rely

---

1   Among the later manuscripts of this group are the following: A copy of the *Histoire ancienne jusqu'à César* and *Li fais des Romains*, KBR, Ms. 9104–9105; a volume of saints' lives and two volumes of miracles of the Virgin, KBR, Mss. 9225 and 9229–9230; a copy of *Les grandes chroniques de France*, KBR, Ms. 5; and a copy of *Li livres des sept sages de Romme*, Marques le seneschal, etc., KBR, Ms. 9245. For Ms. 9104–9105: "110. Waulchier de Denain. *Histoire ancienne: Li fais des Romains*. Ms. 9104–9105," Gaspar and Lyna, *Les principaux manuscrits à peintures*, 1: 266–270; "Wauchier de Denain. *Histoire ancienne*. MS 9104–05," Georges Dogaer and Marguerite Debae, *La librairie de Philippe le Bon: Exposition organisée à l'occasion du 500e anniversaire de la mort du duc* (Brussels: Bibliothèque Albert 1er, 1967), pp. 266–270.

For Mss. 9225 and 9229–9230: "109. *Recueil de légendes pieuses.* Mss. 9225 et 9229–30," Gaspar and Lyna, *Les principaux manuscrits à peintures*, 1:259–264; "71. *Légendes de saints*, vol. 1. MS 9225," Dogaer and Debae, *La librairie*, 55–56. For Ms. 5: "111. *Les grandes chroniques de France* jusqu'en 1321. Ms. 5," Gaspar and Lyna, *Les principaux manuscrits à peintures*, 1:270–275; "179. *Grandes chroniques de France*. MS 5," Dogaer and Debae, *La librairie*, 120–121; Anne D. Hedeman, *The Royal Image: Illustrations of the Grandes Chroniques de France, 1274–1422* (Berkeley: University of California Press, 1991), 200–203.

For Ms. 9245: "*Li livres des sept sages de Romme, Marques le Seneschal*, etc. Ms. 9245," Gaspar and Lyna, *Les principaux manuscrits à peintures*, 1:275–282; "140. *Les sept sages de Rome*. MS 9245," Dogaer and Debae, *La librairie*, 97–98. For the earlier Brabantine manuscripts, see Smeyers, *Flemish Miniatures*, 154–156, and 172, notes 95–104; Oliver; *Gothic Manuscript Illumination*, 1:164–172.

2   This dearth of material for Brussels in the mid-fourteenth century is referenced, by implication, by Oliver, "The Herkenrode Indulgence," 195, and is further discussed by Dennison, "Dating and Localisation," 515. The Brabantine workshop that illuminated KBR Mss. 9225, 9229–9230 and others, and worked in a style marked by large figures with large heads, massive architecture, and expressive play of lines, had apparently ceased production by the era in question. See Gaspar and Lyna, 1:259–282, for this group of manuscripts.

3   Evidence consists of several images of a praying Benedictine nun in the margins of 6426 and the inscription *Aspiciens abatisse* on the inside front cover. Delaissé suggested the Abbey of van Vorst, southwest of Brussels. See L. M. J. Delaissé, *Middeleeuwse miniaturen van de librije van Boergondië tot het handschriftenkabinet van de Koninklijke Bibliotheek van België* (Brussels: J. M. Meulenhoff, 1958), 69. Delaissé follows Gaspar and Lyna, *Les principaux manuscrits*, 1:341–342, who assign 6426 to Brussels based on the calendar's entries for Geneviève, Gertrude and Gudule, all honored in Brussels. Delaissé, "Enluminure et peinture," 111–112.

4   De Winter, *La bibliothèque de Philippe le Hardi*, 229–230. Oliver, "Herkenrode Indulgence," 196, and n. 37.

instead on the known interests of the Duke Wenceslas, who was a patron of artists and a connoisseur of the visual arts; records indicate that the production, decoration, and sale of books flourished during the 1360s, 1370s and 1380s, after he became duke.[5] The manuscripts connected to Brabant in the later decades of the century include some creative elements and some influence by Flemish realism, but, like the earlier Brabantine manuscripts, show little English influence and are not close to the Rummen group in style. De Winter's assignment of manuscripts to Brussels rests primarily on connections between patrons and a certain interpretation of the personal and political dynamics among Louis of Male, Arnold, and Duke Wenceslas, who was both the employer of Arnold and an in-law of Louis, as Wenceslas married Johanna of Brabant, the sister of Louis's wife Margaret. In De Winter's view, hostilities between Arnold and Louis, whose home territory was Ghent, would have made that city an unlikely locus for illumination commissioned by Arnold. Brussels would have been much friendlier to him. The Rhenish character of the earlier manuscripts in the group, especially 9217, became softer after 1365, under the influence of Bohemian art, associated with the accession of Wenceslas as Duke of Brabant.[6] It is in the context of this later style that he primarily considers 10 A 14. Oliver likewise argues for production in Brussels primarily on the circumstances of patronage.

In sum, there seem to be no surviving manuscripts comparable to 10 A 14 in style and quality that can be assigned to Brussels or its environs in the middle decades of the century. The stylistic evidence for Brussels as the site of production for the Rummen manuscripts is minimal.

2 Cologne

Cologne has not been proposed directly as the site of production for 10 A 14; however, it has been suggested as such for 9217 by Lemaire and Vanwijnsberghe.[7] As the question of 10 A 14's origins is closely connected with that of its complement's, Cologne merits brief consideration here. Lemaire and Vanwijnsberghe referenced generic

resemblances in architectural frames, initials, baguettes, and grotesques between 9217 and liturgical codices from Cologne. Cologne's influence on the Rummen group artists is cited in a variety of connections, primarily with the Summer Missal. Connections between color and figure style in the Crucifixion imagery in 9217 and that of the Rennenberg Missal and other Cologne manuscripts of the era are discussed in Chapter 5 and in Appendix 4, Pt. 5, of this study. Resemblances, by way of Sint-Truiden, between two-line penwork initials of 9217 and those in manuscripts from Cologne and the Rhineland have been noted.[8]

A promising substantive connection between Cologne and Tournai has been articulated by Gerhard Schmidt.[9] Specific common elements of style between some peripheral scenes in the Cologne choir screens and some imagery on the pages of the *Voeux du paon* are evident. In addition, connections in both style and iconography have been noted between the *Voeux* and certain manuscripts from Cologne dating *c.*1340–1360.[10] Further investigation of the possibility that the same artist or artists worked in both Cologne and Tournai is warranted. It is possible, as noted in Chapter 5 above, that Artist 9217-1 worked on an antiphonal in Cologne before he illuminated 9217. Whether or not that is the case, imagery from Cologne, much of it of very high quality and accomplished in its synthesis of a diversity of elements, may have influenced the Rummen-group artists, but the path of transmission has yet to be determined. Certainly 10 A 14 was not made in Cologne.

3 Sint-Truiden

Haagdorens and Smeyers propose Sint-Truiden as the location of production for the Rummen manuscripts. Manuscripts were made at Sint-Truiden in the thirteenth century, but economic decline quelled the output in the early fourteenth century. The abbey and town had recovered somewhat by the middle of the century; Haagdorens argues that the recovery made possible in the town of Sint-Truiden the creation of illuminated manuscripts of high quality, commissioned by wealthy patrons.[11] Indeed, texts with script of high quality, decorated with penwork of equally high quality, were apparently written there,

---

5 Smeyers, *Flemish Miniatures*, 223–227.

6 Rhenish elements in 9217, according to De Winter, were mediated via the Abbey of Sint-Truiden, one of the many connections with the Benedictines among these manuscripts; he includes BUL, Mss. 60–61 (*Speculum 1 and 2*), in which he sees a pale reflection of the predominant style of the Rummen-related group; see *La bibliothèque de Philippe le Hardi*, 230.

7 Lemaire and Vanwijnsberghe, "Cote-Signalement KBR 9217," *Textes liturgiques*, 107–108.

8 Delaissé, "Enluminure et peinture," 111–112; Hagdorens, "Het zgn. missaal," 143–150.

9 Gerhard Schmidt, "Die Chorschrankenmalereien des Kölner Domes und die europäische Malerei," *Kölner Domblatt: Jahrbuch des Zentral-Dombauvereins*, 44–45 (1979–1980): 300–310.

10 Leo, *Images, Texts, and Marginalia*," 244.

11 "Sint-Truidense handschriften," 265–267.

THE PLACE OF PRODUCTION

as noted in Chapter 7, but evidence of a corresponding output in illumination is lacking. In the manuscripts produced for Johannes van Myrle and Robert van Craenwyck, illuminations are so few in number and differ so greatly in style, technique, and quality that they do not suggest a settled workshop of illumination with artistic resources necessary to create the abundant, stylistically integrated, and sophisticated illumination of the Rummen manuscripts. However, it is possible that the Rummen manuscripts were indeed written in Sint-Truiden. It is also possible that the scribe, likely Willem de Dycka, traveled from Sint-Truiden to Ghent to execute commissions.

4   Ghent

Ghent is the most likely site of illumination for 10 A 14, and for 9217 and 9427, as also for 6426 and the Loppem-Bruges antiphonal (though the evidence for these two is less, as both patronage and destination are unknown for them). Ghent had a history of making illuminated manuscripts; it offered possibilities of patronage and access to a rich range of superior artistic resources. In addition, many specific features of style and iconography connect 10 A 14 with products of earlier illumination in Ghent.

High-quality illuminated manuscripts were demonstrably made at Ghent during two periods in the century prior to the creation of 10 A 14. During the first of these periods, which extended from *c.*1270–1295, Ghent replaced Bruges as the center of the book industry in Germanic Flanders. Psalters, a missal, a Bible, and a life of St. Lutgardis, this last written in Middle Netherlandic, were produced in a workshop led by a highly skilled illuminator who had thoroughly assimilated French High Gothic influences and some English elements while retaining a Flemish sensibility.[12] Some of this influence may have come through French or French-influenced sculpture; in Ghent, influences crossed the boundaries of medium, as both Carlvant and Dennison have argued.[13] Members of this Ghent workshop traveled to other parts of Flanders to work on additional manuscripts. Although the best illumination was highly accomplished, the scripts in which texts were written varied in quality. In addition to the books with first-rate illumination, at least ten psalters with illumination of lesser quality have been localized

to Ghent during these years; interest in books evidently spread beyond the merchant elite.[14] Political conflicts in Ghent that pitted the wealthy burghers and the Count against the merchant oligarchy and the French crown may have been responsible for the marked decline in production at the end of the thirteenth century.

During a second period of manuscript production, *c.*1310–1335, gifted painters based in Ghent and working in a vigorous Flemish style illuminated a number of liturgical and devotional manuscripts, as well as at least one didactic work, a copy of Jacob van Maerlant's Middle Dutch *Spiegel Historiael*.[15] Ghent's artists also may have illuminated Arthurian manuscripts during this second period.[16] More refined and Parisian in style, but equally important, is the Ghent Ceremonial of 1322. Civil unrest and the Black Death may have contributed to the decline of illumination of the second period.

The first colophon of 10 A 14 furnishes evidence for Ghent as the location of production. It is certain that the manuscript was in Ghent in September of 1366, and that the artist who completed it was "*commoranti gandavi*"—residing in Ghent. Additional evidence is furnished by the penwork, iconography, figure style, and treatment of borders and frames in manuscripts from both antecedent eras of production, especially the missal of St. Peter's, the Ceremonial of St. Peter's, and the psalter Douce 5–6. The missal is a product of the first period of Ghent illumination; the Ceremonial and the psalter are products of the second era. Further evidence of 10 A 14's connection with Ghent comes from the decades subsequent to its production, from a breviary of St. Peter's dated 1373.[17] Some iconographical elements common to 10 A 14 and the Ghent Altarpiece also suggest the manuscript's origins in Ghent, as discussed in Chapter 5.

The penwork of Artist 1 in 10 A 14 relates to that of Douce 6, from fol. 48r to the manuscript's end. (Cp. figs. 151, 124). Both bodies of penwork are characterized by sweeping whiplash curves with a downward diagonal slant, floating rosettes, fernlike feathery tendrils, and

---

12   See Carlvant, *Manuscript Painting*, 95–115, for definition and discussion of this workshop.

13   See Carlvant, *Manuscript Painting*, 106, 112, for the influence of wood and stone sculpture and monumental painting; see Dennison, "The Artistic Context," 28–29, for influence of brasses.

14   Carlvant, *Manuscript Painting*, 241–248.

15   Among these are CKB, Mss. GKS 3384,8° and Ny kgl. saml. 41,8°; WAG, Ms. 82; LBL, Ms. Add. 29253; and Cambridge, Trinity College, Ms. B.11.22. HKB, Ms. 135 E 15, could be added; and Stones, "Another Short Note," 186–189, associates, in one way or another, a number of other manuscripts with this group. The *Spiegel Historiael* is HKB, Ms. KA XX.

16   Smeyers, *Flemish Miniatures*, 143. Stones, "Another Short Note," 188, sees an artist of the Amsterdam/Douce/Rylands Arthurian manuscript, *c.*1320, also working in Ghent. She sees St. Omer or Thérouanne as the most likely sites of the manuscript's production but mentions Ghent as a possibility also.

17   UGU, Ms. 3381.

corkscrews constructed of a tight spiral or stack of zig-zags with sweeping, recurved tips. The touch of the artist in Douce 6 is consistently freer and more exuberant than that of Artist 1 in 10 A 14, but the decorative repertoire and general aesthetic are common to both. This style contrasts with the tight, dense Parisian penwork in the filiation of Jaquet Maci.[18] The prominence of penwork in Douce 6 suggests the influence of the northern Netherlands, to which one of its artists had connections.[19] Ghent was a hub of influences converging from all directions.

The flowery, fluttering, rosette-sprinkled style continued to characterize penwork in Ghent, as seen in the breviary of 1373 from St. Peter's. This breviary in two volumes, each comprising three individually bound parts, is decorated throughout with two-line penwork initials having palmette, bud, and foliate motifs in the counters and is flourished in two distinct styles, one like that of Artist 1 in 10 A 14 and the other Parisian. Volumes 2:1 and 2:3 (respectively, the fourth and sixth of the six bound sections of the breviary) display penwork closely related to that of Artist 1, as demonstrated by a comparison between the flourishing in the breviary, 2:1, fol. 4v (fig. 166), and that of Artist 1 in 10 A 14, as just cited above. Both examples feature soft, fluttering ribbon-like forms, floating rosettes, ball-and-squiggle trilobes, and pearls in twos and threes. A similar style of flourishing is found throughout volume 2:3 of the breviary. Corkscrews in the breviary are fewer and less regular than those in 10 A 14; line is slightly tighter, and the quality of work is less fine; but resemblances are clear.[20]

However, the penwork of Ghent's manuscripts was not dominated by one style but manifested a remarkable freedom, variety, and vitality which may have spurred development of Artist 2's penwork. First-period penwork from Ghent includes that of the missal of St. Peter's, with a decoration of short curlicues, rather like shavings in appearance, punctuated by a few long dangling tendrils with curled ends (fig. 161), akin in colors, motifs, and layout to a species of penwork found in late thirteenth-century Parisian manuscripts.[21] Very different is the dense, frizzy, electrified irregularity of the second-period Ghent Ceremonial (fig. 162), inspired by fourteenth-century Parisian penwork, and the spare, nervous tentacles of a second ceremonial made in Ghent for St. Peter's Abbey, from the first half of the fourteenth century (fig. 165).[22] The penwork style of Artist 2 originated not in Ghent but in the van Craenwyck and van Myrle manuscripts from Sint-Truiden, as discussed in Chapter 7. His penwork in 10 A 14, however, far outdoes the combined repertoire of the Sint-Truiden and Ghent manuscripts in abundance of motifs. Some of his motifs may have been transmedial adoptions, from the iconography of painted border decoration in French and English manuscripts or from brasses; others may have been invented by the Artist 2. The production of text in Sint-Truiden with transferal of the manuscript to Ghent for decoration and illumination is explicable as the decision of a regionally well-connected patron and patroness who were familiar with the strengths and weaknesses of various local centers of book production and who wanted the highest quality of both script and illumination for their commission. A double origin—the writing of the text in Sint-Truiden and illumination in Ghent—would reflect the respective regional identities of patron and patroness and ensure representation of the interests of each.

Significant iconographical elements, as noted in Chapter 5, connect the Crucifixion image in 10 A 14 with Ghent. The many small, red scourge wounds on the body of the crucified Christ in 10 A 14 have a precedent in Douce 5's Man of Sorrows, of *c*.1330–1335, one of the earliest occurrences of this iconography in Northern art. The pose of the Virgin (fig. 106b)—gazing intently at the viewer, swooning, her right elbow supported by St. John—is found in the Crucifixion of the missal from St. Peter's of 1275–1285, an exceptionally early appearance of this motif; a similar arrangement of figures is also in the Ghent Ceremonial's Crucifixion. Unusual motifs that mark 10 A 14 reappear—reworked and recontextualized—in art

---

18   See Avril, "Un enlumineur ornemaniste," 249–264.

19   See Korteweg, *Kriezels, aubergines en takkenbossen*, 9, on the distinctive character of Northern Netherlandish penwork in the fifteenth century. One of the artists of Douce 5–6 has been assigned the illumination of HKB, Ms. 135 E 15, a psalter of *c*.1333 with a calendar of the Diocese of Utrecht. See Kerstin B. E. Carlvant, "Collaboration in a Fourteenth-Century Psalter: The Franciscan Iconographer and the Two Flemish Illuminators of MS 3384,8° in the Copenhagen Royal Library," *Sacris Erudiri*, 25 (1982): 162, n. 52; Joslin and Watson, *Egerton Genesis*, 204–206.

20   This Parisian style of flourishing is found vol. 1:2 of the St. Peter's Abbey breviary, where the aesthetic is for denser composition and for kinks, angles, contrasts, and reversals—a cultivated irregularity of line that yields a frizzy, electrified effect, typical of Parisian penwork such as that associated with Jacobus Mathey (Jaquet Maci) and his circle in the second quarter of the fourteenth century. A comparison between the flourishing on fol. 416v (vol. 1:3) of the St. Peter's breviary and (for example) that of fols. 42v–43r of the Parisian *Hours of Jeanne d'Evreux*, MMA, Cloisters Ms. 54.1.2, shows, without suggesting any direct connection between the two manuscripts, a commonality of linear forms. Maci worked with Pucelle on decoration of the Billyng Bible, BNF, Ms. lat. 11935; see Avril, *Manuscript Painting at the Court of France*, 14.

21   As, for example, the missal BNF, Ms. lat. 830.

22   UGU, Ms. 114. See Derolez, *Medieval Manuscripts*, 126.

THE PLACE OF PRODUCTION

with connections to Ghent in later decades: Columbines, fol. 106v, and serenading angels, fol. 26r, both appear in the Ghent Altarpiece, connected to Ghent by patronage if not by manufacture. By van Eyck's time, 10 A 14 was in the library of his patron Philip the Good, who was the great-grandson of Louis of Male. It is not out of the question that van Eyck may have seen Arnold's splendid missal and, not inappropriately, may have referenced it in a major commission for the city named in the missal's colophon. Alternatively, the columbines and serenading angels may have had sources, as yet unidentified, in Ghent from which both the manuscript and the altarpiece drew. Further research might elucidate the connections.

The figure style of Ghent's illumination in the thirteenth and fourteenth centuries drew on Germanic, Parisian, and Franco-Flemish sources, enriched in the later decades by English influence. In illumination of the first period, c.1270–1295, Mosan and Parisian components inform the figures of Flemish artists such as the Dampierre and Bruges Masters: Sturdy figures were rendered with Parisian treatment of hair and posture.[23] The elegance and delicacy of Parisian style, enlivened by English expression, was particularly assimilated by the Ghent Master of the first period. In the second period, c.1310–1335, the Mosan element, perhaps in conjunction with influence from the northern Netherlands, can be discerned in figures with a heavy, robust physicality, as in Douce 5–6 and in a psalter-hours WAG, Ms. 82. The Parisian current, with some admixture of Tournai, was represented by the Master of the Ghent Ceremonial—himself likely a Parisian with experience in Tournai.[24]

The work of the first campaign of 10 A 14 and of the other manuscripts of the Rummen group manifests the legacy of all the above threads: Parisian, Flemish and Franco-Flemish, English, Northern Netherlandish, and Mosan; work of the second campaign of 10 A 14 adds an element of Italianism, already present in a limited way in the earlier work, and perhaps some Bohemian flavor. Artist 1's figures relate to the style of Tournai. Artist 2's style in the earlier manuscripts of the Rummen group is marked by heavy, robust Mosan-influenced figures, carried into 10 A 14 in the Christ of the *Domine ne longe* fol. 106v (fig. 91a) and the heavy, powerful Christ in the Crucifixion, fol. 143v (fig. 106c); a Parisian element appears with the slender angels and donor figure; the swaying Virgin's pose and gesture (fig. 106b) infuse elegance in the tradition of

the Ghent Master into Anglo/Italian expression. The modeling of figures and some elements of iconography have English sources. These various elements are not fully synthesized into a consistent style but they are tapped for a common expressive purpose.

The painted elements in miniature frames and borders of Douce 5–6 furnished material for 10 A 14. The lower strip of the frame around the miniature of the Entry into Jerusalem on fol. 16v of Douce 5 is inscribed with confronted, horizontally aligned grotesques, in gold outlined in black (fig. 148); one grotesque is partly covered by a cloak. This same motif fills the frame of Artist 2's border on fol. 7r (fig. 15).[25]

The particularly rich mix of artistic influences that converge in 10 A 14 is more comprehensible in Ghent than in Brussels or Sint-Truiden. Cologne certainly equaled Ghent as a receptor and synthesizer of diverse artistic influences and may have surpassed Ghent, in the mid-fourteenth century, in the integration and polish of these elements and in the quantity and range of artistic output. However, Cologne has not been proposed as a possible site of production for 10 A 14.

A further pointer towards Ghent as the origin of the Rummen manuscripts is provided by the double gorgon, found in the initials of the Rummen manuscripts and in *Speculum 2* (ULB, Ms. 61) from Sint-Truiden. One of the English Apocalypses, which feature a version of this imagery in the context of depictions of Hell, is posited to have been in Ghent, and accessible to artists, in the thirteenth century and if so, then perhaps in the fourteenth century as well.[26] In addition, a variant of the double gorgon appears in an initial in a Parisian Bible of c.1350 now in Stockholm (fig. 208).[27] This Bible's primary illuminator was the artist of the Ghent Ceremonial. He apparently originated in Paris in the orbit of Pucelle, then worked in the Low

---

23   Carlvant, *Manuscript Painting*, 107–108, 125–128.

24   Avril discusses the very early work of this artist in Paris; see "248: Cérémonial de l'abbaye Saint-Pierre au Mont Blandin," *Les fastes du gothique*, 300.

---

25   A similar motif is in Cologne illumination of c.1330, as in the frame of the Crucifixion in DUL, Ms. 876, fol. 223v (fig. 159), but at further remove from 10 A 14 in place and time than the Ghent psalter.

26   Carlvant, *Manuscript Painting*, 109–112.

27   National Library of Sweden, Ms. A 165. Information on this manuscript is in Eva Lindqvist Sandgren, "National Library of Sweden, A 165," (2003, rev. 2011), unpublished description from database of illuminated manuscripts in Sweden. Document was provided by the National Library of Sweden. See also "93. Biblia Latina," in Kåre Olsen and Carl Nordenfalk, eds., *Gyllene böcker: illuminerade medeltida handskrifter i dansk och svensk ägo*, exhib. cat., Nationalmuseum, Stockholm, 1952 (Stockholm: Caslon Press Boktryckeri, 1952), 55, pl. XIV. The Bible is dated to the third quarter of the fourteenth century; 1350 or even a few years earlier is likely on stylistic grounds. The Bible's illuminations show little influence from Italianate spatial developments that began to appear in the Northern illumination around 1340.

Countries—first on the Ceremonial and then with Pierart dou Tielt in Tournai—and finally returned to Paris.[28] A comparison of historiated initials in the Ceremonial and the Stockholm Bible (figs. 164a, 206a), reveals similarities in the shape of human heads with wide cranial box and squared face and nose, similar drawing of hands, similar folds in the habits' sleeves and hoods. The backgrounds in both initials are patterned with squares of three colors organized with corresponding schemes of alternating diagonal alignments. The Stockholm Bible displays more pronounced modeling of the figures and more extensive and subtle use of color than does the Ceremonial.

The flourishing of the Stockholm Bible and that of the Ceremonial are also quite similar; both are in the Parisian style of Maquet/Maci with dense, electrified treatment of tendrils—short, kinked and curled in arrangements that suggest deliberate and sophisticated rejection of easy pattern (figs. 162, 206, 206a). Slim, elegant, border bars likewise appear in both manuscripts.

In the stems and bowls of the Bible's initials, interlaced tendril extensions connect identical grotesque heads, as in initials of the Rummen manuscripts. A number of these heads are modified versions of the double gorgons (fig. 207). Heads are not joined jaw to jaw, creating a possibly inelegant maw, but rather are joined by pairs of intertwined tendrils looping up or down from the top and bottom of the profile heads, as though extensions of hair and beard. Shaping of the heads and their features and

modeling with white penstrokes recall the gorgons of the Rummen manuscripts. None of the Bible's gorgons interacts with figures inside the initial. Upon his return to Paris, the Ceremonial's artist appears to have produced a version of the gorgon motif packaged for Parisian consumption.

The Ghent Ceremonial has no gorgons; their absence suggests that the motif was not in the artist's repertoire when he arrived from Paris in the Low Countries.[29] The appearance of this striking motif in a modified, toned-down form subsequent to the Parisian artist's work on the Ghent Ceremonial strengthens the case for Ghent as the center of the gorgon-initial fad. Its status as an outlier in Parisian illumination suggests that it was not to Parisian tastes.

Arnold of Rummen had ties to Liège and Sint-Truiden. Elisabeth, after 1350 his wife, was firmly grounded in Ghent and its environs. Perhaps Arnold and Elisabeth decided to celebrate their marriage in 1350 by commissioning manuscripts destined for their fabulous castle under construction at Rummen from 1357 on, and probably envisioned and planned well before that, as Arnold had been reaching for the Countship of Loon since the 1330s. Imagery in the manuscripts—the stout castle and fine helmet in the initials on fol. 147v in 10 A 14 (fig. 108) and a very similar castle in a three-line penwork initial on fol. 20r of 9427—testify to Arnold's preoccupation with his social position and his aspiration for a magnificent residence. The backgrounds and interests of the patrons, along with the nuptial occasion for the commission, would encourage visual motifs and textual elements that celebrated the loyalties and tastes of both parties: Liège and Sint-Truiden for Arnold, Ghent for Elisabeth. Calendars exemplify the interests and connections of the spouses: 9427's is of Ghent use; 9217's is of Liège use; 10 A 14's is primarily of Liège but with significant concessions to Ghent as well. Brabantine saints are not ignored, perhaps in acknowledgment of Arnold's position at the Brabantine court. The calendar of 10 A 14 is at once a spiritual, geographical, personal, and diplomatic statement.

Ghent was well established as a center of the book business, one that ebbed and flowed for decades in the late thirteenth and early fourteenth centuries. Political difficulties, detailed in Chapter 1, of the late 1330s and 1340s

---

28 For a discussion of the artist, his relationship to Pucelle and his Parisian contemporaries, and his work in Flanders, see Kathleen Morand, *Jean Pucelle* (Oxford: Clarendon Press, 1962), 43–44; see also n. 23 above. Cruse, *Illuminating the Roman d'Alexandre*, 91, remarks that Pierart dou Tielt worked on the Ghent Ceremonial, but this does not seem to be the case, as the illumination of the Ceremonial is consistently in the style of the Master of the Ghent Ceremonial. Avril, *Les fastes du gothique*, 300–301, assigns production of the Ceremonial to Paris, Ghent, or Tournai. For discussion of the work of the Master of the Ghent Ceremonial in Tournai, alone and in conjunction with Pierart dou Tielt, see Walters, "Marian Devotion," 236–242 and 265–266. For the suggestion that the artist may have originated in Ghent, see Nigel Morgan and Stella Panayatova, eds., 161: Fitzwilliam Museum, MS 20: Literary Miscellany (verse and prose), *The Meuse Region. Southern Netherlands* (London: Harvey Miller Publishers, 2009), 53–56, pt. 1, vol. 2 of *A Catalogue of Western Book Illumination in the Fitzwilliam Museum and the Cambridge Colleges*. Paul Trio suggests this artist may have been from Ypres and that the Ceremonial may have been produced there; see Paul Trio, "L'enlumineur à Bruges, Gand et Ypres (1300–1450): Son milieu socio-économique et corporatif," in *Flanders in a European Perspective: Manuscript Illumination Around 1400 in Flanders and Abroad*, edited by Maurits Smeyers and Bert Cardon, 721–729 (Leuven: Peeters, 1995).

29 The Ceremonial predates the earliest of the Rummen manuscripts, the Loppem-Bruges antiphonal and the antiphonal, Ms, 6426, by twenty to twenty-five years. The gorgon motif may have circulated in Ghent prior to its appearance in the 1340s; alternatively, the artist of the Ghent Ceremonial may have kept in touch with illumination in that city after he completed the Ceremonial.

had slowed the economy and the book trade. However, prior to 1350 Ghent was still fresh in the aftermath of the second lively era of book production; many newly written and illuminated manuscripts of the preceding decades must have been easily available.

The connections of 10 A 14 to Ghent extend not only back in time but also forward, not only in penwork but also in techniques of rendering. The shingled and faceted drapery folds in the Nativity, fol. 22r (fig. 34a), and Adoration, fol. 27v (fig. 39a), are one precursor of the angular drapery in fifteenth-century Flemish panel painting, a medium to which Ghent made important contributions. In 10 A 14, this approach to drapery happens in conjunction with a miniaturization of brushstrokes, the latter opening the door to another aspect of Eyckian technique. The emergence of these features in the second campaign of 10 A 14 suggests a stylistic will to spatial and textural realism that was parallel to, but distinct from, the emerging International Gothic Style.

In spite of political turbulence, money and patronage were at hand; key players in Ghent's lively internal politics were a fabulously wealthy Italian, English nobility and royalty, a Francophile Count who lived at times in the city, and the native moneyed burghers, all of whom had the capacity to manifest their tastes and interests in commissioning and displaying art and artifacts, even if their time and attention were primarily directed to commerce and politics. In this city with a rich heritage of manuscript production, still within recent memory in the late 1340s, with easy connections to any number of regions and a plethora of wealthy booklovers, would it be difficult to constitute a workshop to produce high-quality illumination?

Why was the first campaign of work on Arnold and Elisabeth's Winter Missal interrupted? If this stage occurred in Ghent around 1350, as was likely the case, it was pursued in a place and time of extraordinary political and economic turmoil, as has been explained. The question of the Black Death of 1348–1349 as a possible cause of the break in campaign has been referenced above but merits further consideration. The possible role of the Plague is difficult to assess in the case of 10 A 14 because it was only one of a whole complex of disruptive forces that came to a head in Ghent during the late 1340s. In Flanders relatively few manuscripts were in production during the years of the Plague and immediately antecedent to it. We must look elsewhere for comparanda; England affords such.

In England, where economics and politics in this era were not radically unsettled, the Plague is easier to identify as a source of disruption in manuscript production. The Egerton Genesis was left unfinished around 1350 and was never completed.[30] The Vienna Bohun Psalter was decorated by a succession of artists, three of whom apparently died, one after the other, during the months of the Plague.[31] Nonetheless, commissioned under the artistic protectorate of the Bohuns, a family well established and stable in their location, means, and dynastic continuity, the manuscript was essentially completed between 1350 and 1360, by two artists who took up the project with little delay. Apparently, the Bohun family had at hand the resources, connections, and mechanisms—whatever it took—to push their project onward through the obstacles presented by the Plague. On the other hand, the Egerton Genesis, a manuscript modest in materials and conception compared to the Vienna Psalter, was perhaps inherently a more precarious enterprise. The Egerton manuscript's risqué imagery and the buffoonery in its iconography virtually certify that it was not commissioned by a wealthy monastery or ecclesiastic. Noble patronage is also unlikely, given the absence of overt evidence such as heraldry. The patron may have been a merchant of some means involved in the Norwich cloth trade. The Plague or its disastrous short-term economic aftermath may have killed the artist or patron or may have economically crippled the latter. Such ill fortune might well have constituted the deathblow to completion of a project lacking the layers of protection afforded to manuscripts commissioned by the Bohuns.

In terms of the resources required for its production, 10 A 14 might be judged to fall somewhere between the Bohun and Egerton projects. Arnold had means—very considerable means after his marriage to Elisabeth—and he did not spare expense on his manuscript. However, his position in the nobility was precarious, and his aspirations to higher position were never realized. He had no legitimate heir and probably no possibility of begetting one with Elisabeth, who was likely approaching the end of her child-bearing years at the time of their marriage. Nor did they enjoy a secure place of residence: Ten Walle, Elisabeth's residence in Ghent, lacked the insulation from civic disturbances afforded by a castle such as the Bohun family's Pleshey, situated some fifty miles from London. Her right to live at ten Walle was at the mercy of Louis's whims, and Arnold's quarters at Rummen or Liège were apparently unsatisfactory, given his dedication to building a castle. Whatever interrupted the first campaign

---

30   See Joslin and Watson, *Egerton Genesis*, 252–253.

31   VON, Cod. 1826*. See Dennison, "Stylistic Sources," 91, 250–251. Sandler, *Illuminators and Patrons*, 356, extends the possible date of the psalter's completion to 1373.

of illumination—possibly the Plague, but also possibly an episode of unrest in Ghent or the urgent demands of Arnold's dramatic initiatives in pursuit of lands, title, and castle—it would seem that the will to complete the manuscript was compromised; perhaps the Winter Missal was half-forgotten in the interval between first and second campaigns. In the 1360s, the spiral of events towards their disastrous climax for Arnold and Elisabeth may have sparked a new impetus to complete the illumination of 10 A 14, a reactive rather than a proactive move.

Though the execution of the manuscript was interrupted, the two campaigns manifest a fulfilment and continuity of intention on the part of both patrons and artists: If the patrons initially envisioned a luxurious, high-status manuscript, the second campaign fulfilled the promise of the first. Artist 2/3 carried over into the second campaign the lively, pulsating penwork, the variety of motifs, and the conceptual acuity of design that characterized the first.

Nonetheless, in the interval between the first and second campaigns, the artists, especially Artist 2/3, pivoted from a predominantly medieval conception of space and the figure towards one that came to characterize the fifteenth-century Northern Renaissance. In the end, the interruption in the illumination of 10 A 14 produced an even richer and more complex work of art than would have been the case otherwise.

5 Conclusion

A convergence of evidence from style, iconography, penwork, history of past production, political history, and social history indicates Ghent as the location of production of 10 A 14.

CHAPTER 9

Conclusions

Below are summarized the substance of this study's nine contributions, enumerated in Chapter 1.

The role and possibilities of penwork flourishing: The art of flourishing has a range of possibilities. It is primarily decorative but also hosts a potential for expressive vitality and for conceptual and theological depth. As a medium without painting's custodianship of traditional iconic meanings, it allows for humor and suggestion. Its quickness of execution and translucency facilitate expression of the associative and subliminal, without discarding structure. It has the capacity for assimilating and transforming elements from other media and for integrating these into a vigorous development. This study shows that in 10 A 14, among the loci of flourishing, the two-line initial and the terminal complex are of particular interest; the first is a node of convergence of flourishing and painting, of the suggested and the explicit, of decoration and iconography; the second uses the expanses of open margin for spectacular display.

The flourisher-illuminators: (This subject was discussed in Chapter 1 at length in the section entitled "Why study flourishing?" after the other eight subjects.) Three men likely executed all the flourishing and illumination in 10 A 14, with the exception of later overpaints. The flourishing and illumination of Artists 1 and 2 reveal much about their artistic interests, gifts, motivations, and limitations. Artist 1's flourishing develops little. Artist 2's flourishing undergoes an astounding journey of development. In some respects, each flourisher-artist manifests in his penwork the same personality as in his painting. Artist 1's fluttering pen-flourishes and his insubstantial architecture are both marked by a certain delicacy of touch. His penchant towards the bizarre is seen in both media. Artist 2's interest in imparting structure through the use of symmetry and nested forms permeates painting and penwork.

In other respects, the two media reveal different facets of personality, as enabled by the particular possibilities of each medium. The secular orientation of Artist 1 is expressed in his choice of subjects for the counters of initials. Artist 2 expresses freely through his penwork the theological cast of mind that also informs his illumination. The overwhelming abundance and variety of his flourishing and its pulse of continual change, manifesting *eucharisma*, are possible in this technique unburdened by the *gravitas* and limitations of subject matter traditionally in the domain of painted imagery.

Artist 1 was probably a layman; where he has choices, his iconography tends to the secular; Artist 2 was almost certainly a priest; his iconography has theological depth in prescribed subjects and tends to the religious where he has choices. In his quires, the treatment of Introits shows awareness and understanding of the needs of the manuscript's user, the priest. The study of flourishing and illumination leads to the conclusion that Artist 2 and Artist 3 were likely the same person, probably Laurence the Priest. Artist 4, possibly also a priest, worked largely under the direction of Artist 3.

Artists 1 and 2 were probably regional artists; Artist 1's work on the Loppem-Bruges antiphonal is reflective of Tournai and Ghent, with Cologne a shadow in the background. Though he designated himself as *de antwerpi,* Laurence worked in Sint-Truiden, primarily as a flourisher, before coming to Ghent.

Ghent as the site of flourishing and illumination: The Winter Missal is most fully explicable in the context of Ghent, given the city's traditions in manuscript illumination and its habituation to the reception of influences from many directions, its tumultuous history, and its status as the primary domicile of one of the patrons of 10 A 14.

Iconography: The iconography of the major illumination in 10 A 14 introduces some new elements and modifies others but is not radically innovative per se. Artist 1 includes elements of commentary that are humorous, even startling or distracting, within imagery that is otherwise conventional. Artist 2 drills deeply into the theological meaning of his subjects, not challenging them but explicating their profundity. His visual development of the theology of Corpus Christi is one of the many and varied ways this feast impacted fourteenth-century European art.

Collaborations, discontinuities, disruptions, and overpaints: Collaboration likely was directed towards a higher end, the desire of both artists to leave a mark on important pages of the manuscript. Disruptions and discontinuities probably stemmed from two sources, one internal to production and the other external: On the one hand, Artist 2 seemed to proceed in random fashion in the decoration of his quires; even the degree to which work was left unfinished varied from page to page. This work was completed in the second campaign, some by himself (as Artist 3) in a reprised endeavor and some by his associate Artist 4; in

© KONINKLIJKE BRILL BV, LEIDEN, 2025 | DOI:10.1163/9789004427136_010

some cases, the discontinuities are obvious and intrusive. On the other hand, the recurrent civic turmoil in Ghent during the mid-fourteenth century and the Black Death, immediately antecedent to or concurrent with the commencement of 10 A 14's production, may have created conditions inimical to the completion of the initial campaign.

Overpaints were conducted, rather clumsily and less than thoroughly, after the manuscript passed from Arnold's hands into Louis's, probably in 1366. Though Arnold was erased (incompletely) from the Crucifixion scene, the manuscript's centerpiece, his image was untouched in two other illuminations. A showy penwork helmet of Arnold was untouched also, and even painted arms were incompletely concealed. Furthermore, the only reference to Louis's Lion of Flanders was in a subordinate position, on the altar linens of fol. 167r. Did the artist responsible for the overpaints deliberately downplay references to Louis and retain hints of Arnold's initial ownership? This possibility gains some traction from the second colophon, which sympathetically references Arnold.

Patronage: Evidence from donor portraits and from the calendar testify that Elisabeth played an important role in patronage of the manuscript, that she was much interested in the project. She is imaged in three places as Arnold's companion in pious prayer and contemplation. The calendar points almost as much to her city of Ghent as to his of Liège. She shared a name with Elisabeth of Hungary, the only saint designated as *electa* in the calendar. Unfortunately, the overpainting of arms has made it impossible to determine whether her heraldry was imaged with Arnold's. The two patrons maintained their regional loyalties to the end: Elisabeth died and was buried in Ghent; Arnold, in Liège. Perhaps the childlessness of their marriage incentivized Elisabeth to keep a tight grip on her ancestral identity.

The social status of the patrons is analogous to the artistic position of the manuscript. Elisabeth, a natural daughter of Count Louis I of Nevers and widow of the foreigner Simon of Mirabello, was wealthy but on the fringe of high social position. Arnold had connections to nobility and even to royalty through his position with the Duke of Brabant, but the position that would have sealed his place in that company, the Countship of Loon, was just beyond his grasp. Likewise, Arnold's Winter Missal is a work whose painted decoration falls just short of the highest artistry. It offers a variety of artistic riches, decorative and conceptual. Its style is prescient of future developments. But its figure style, as practiced by Artist 1, is sometimes dry and uninspired. Artist 2's figures are informed by highly developed ideas that outrun his integration of expressive means,

and he does not excel in narrative compositions. On the other hand, in its penwork decoration, the manuscript has few equals for variety, abundance, and vitality; 10 A 14's penwork, quite remarkably, makes of the non-figural, non-verbal medium of penwork decoration a vehicle of expression for theological content. Furthermore, 10 A 14's very shortcomings humanize the patrons and invest the manuscript with a poignant appeal. The fact that completion of the manuscript required two campaigns and that, in the end, it slipped away from Arnold and Elisabeth speaks to the limitations of the patrons' ability to buffer their project from disruptive forces.

The Eucharistic principle, or eucharisma: I propose that Artist 2, Laurence the Priest, was powered as a decorator by a belief in the divine life inherent in the Eucharist as a vital, self-renewing, creative agent in the world. This belief is evidenced by the pulsating changes in decoration from prayer to prayer and in the vigorous, rich developmental cycles of his penwork. In illumination *eucharisma* manifests, first, in the theology of Corpus Christi and of sacrifice and, second, in the development and application of the means of illusionism, of visual realism, in order to manifest the supernatural and preternatural. Style here can be read as a metaphor for the Eucharist, in which the transcendent is present under the appearance of ordinary food and drink.

The shift from the planar to the spatial in pictorialism: The changes in style between the first and second campaigns, catalyzed by Italian or Italianate painting, develop around a drive towards realism, both in the rendering of surfaces and in spatial effects. Whether or not there is a direct connection to panel painting in Ghent in the following century, these changes can be seen as preliminary to its development, as explained in discussion of 10 A 14's Nativity and Adoration miniatures (Chapter 5).

The missal and broader art historical questions: Study of the Winter Missal contributes to an array of issues in medieval art, religion, politics, and social relations. It opens a portal through which to perceive exchanges between penwork and painting, and hints of relationships with other media, such as metalwork. The two-line initial offered an iconographical field for development of expressive types that contributed to a long history in Northern art, as in the development of contemplative images of the Christ-face in the fifteenth century and of the tronie in the sixteenth and seventeenth centuries. The missal reveals collegiality and unity of purpose, rather than competition, as the underpinning for relationships among artists of different temperaments and motivations. It presents a case study in the impact of liturgical development on art.

CONCLUSIONS

The overpaints are alterations to a seal of possession; but in addition, both in what they erase and in what they leave visible, they demonstrate an instance of dysfunction in social and personal relations: They manifest the rivalries and resentments of two powerful men—but complicated, mitigated, and humanized through familial loyalties. The calendar indicates that a woman, a wife, could have considerable influence on a manuscript whose colophon names only her husband as commissioner. The identities of the artists and, consequently, of the manuscript's different artistic styles affirm her power to influence. Finally, the impetus to render space and structure in a particularly Northern idiom, along with many other factors, contributes to the understanding of fourteenth-century illumination as a fertile seedbed for the growth and development of fifteenth-century Flemish panel painting.

APPENDIX 1

Heraldry of Oreye, Loon, Chiny, Somerghem, Perweis, Flanders, and Brabant

Heraldry relevant to Arnold of Rummen and his wife Elisabeth of Lierde, of Louis of Male and his wife Margaret of Brabant, is presented here. The arms directly relevant to 10 A 14 are those of Oreye, the Count of Flanders, the Countess of Flanders, and Brabant. Arms of Loon and Chiny, associated with Arnold, and those of Somerghem, and Perweis, associated with Elisabeth, are not depicted in 10 A 14 but are described below in view of their connections to the patronage of the manuscript.

Arms and helmet of Oreye: Arms: "D'arg. au lion de sa., arm. et lamp. de gu."[1] (On a silver field a black lion with red claws and tongue.) Helmet, as depicted on his seal: "Ernoul, signeur de Ruminez et de Quatbeke, feal et bien ame du duc de Brabant, 1361: dans le champ du sceau, un casque, cimé d'un grand plumail, issant d'une cuve, terminée en volet."[2] (In the field of the seal, a helmet, topped with a large feathery plume, issuing from a bowl, trailing a mantle.)

Arms and crest of Loon: "Looz (Anciens comtes de)—*P. de Liége.* Burelé d'or et de gu. C.: deux plumes de faisan d'or."[3] (Loon, ancient counts of—Region of Liège. Barry gold and red. Crest: Two gold pheasant plumes.)

Arms of Chiny: "De gu. à deux saumons adossés d'or, acc. de neuf croisettes du même.—*Ou*: Ec.: aux 1 et 4 de gu. au lion d'arg., arm., lamp. et cour. d'or (Heinsberg); aux 2 et 3 de Chiny."[4] (Two gold salmon, back-to-back, on a red field, accompanied by nine small gold crosses. *Or*: Quartered: On 1 and 4 a red field with a silver lion with gold claws, tongue, and crown [Heinsberg]; on 2 and 3 the arms of Chiny.)

Arms of Somerghem: "d'az. au chef d'arg. à 3 pals de gu."[5] (Blue field with silver chief with three red pales.)

Arms of Perweis: "*Brab.* De gu. à trois huchets d'or. C. [(Cimier)]: un bonnet d'herm., bordé d'or."[6] (Three gold hunting horns on a red field.)

Arms and crest of Count of Flanders: "d'or au lion de sa. lamp. de gu. armé de gu. et d'arg.; denté d'arg. *C.*: la tête du lion entre un vol banneret d'or; couronne de même."[7] (On a gold field, a black lion with red tongue, red and silver claws, silver teeth. Crest: The head of a lion between conjoined, closed gold wings, crown of the same.)

Arms and crest of Old Flanders: "gironné (12 p) d'or et d'az. en coeur écu. de gu. *C.*: un vol d'herm. coupé de sa."[8] (gyronny, 12 parts, gold and blue; red shield at center. Crest: a pair of ermine wings with black chief.)

Arms of the Countess of Flanders, 1361: "Flandre—(La comtesse de), 1361: parti; A, un lion; B, écartelé; aux 1er et 4e, un lion, aux 2e et 3e, un lion cour. . à la queue fourchée (Brabant-Limbourg). Sans légende (B.)."[9] (Countess of Flanders, 1361: divided; *A*, a lion; *B*, quartered; 1 and 4, a lion, 2 and 3, a lion, crowned . with forked tail [Brabant-Limbourg]. No caption [B].)

Arms of Duke of Brabant: "Die Hertoge v. Brabant—éc. 1/4 de sa. au lion d'or arm. lamp. de gu. (Brabant) 2/3 d'arg. au lion à queue fourchue de gu. lamp. d'az. armé cour. d'or (Limbourg). *C.*: une queue de paon iss. d'un vol coupé d'herm. et de plumes de paon; capeline d'hermines."[10] (The Duke of Brabant—shield 1/4 gold lion on black field, with red claws and tongue [Brabant]. 2/3 on a silver field, red lion with forked tail, blue tongue, gold claws and crown [Limbourg]. Crest: A peacock fan issuing from a pair of wings, ermine above peacock feathers; mantle of ermine.)

---

1 J. B. Rietstap, "Orey ou Urie," *Armorial général: précédé d'un dictionnaire des termes du blatton*, 2nd ed. (Gouda: G. B. van Goor zonen, 1884–1887), 2:354.

2 Jean-Théodore de Raadt, *Sceaux armories des Pays-Bas et des pays avoisinants (Belgique—Royaume des Pays-Bas—Luxembourg—Allemagne—France): recueil historique et héraldique* (Brussels: Société Belge de Librairie, 1898–1901) 3:73.

3 Rietstap, *Armorial général*, 2:96.

4 Rietstap, *Armorial général*, 1:418.

5 Gelre (Claes Heinenzoon), *B.R. Ms. 15652–56* (Leuven: Uitgeverij-Editions Jan van Helmont, 1992), nr. 1008, p. 337; illustrated p. 193, bottom row, second from right.

6 Rietstap, *Armorial general*, 2:418.

7 Gelre, *B.R. Ms. 15652–56*, nr. 923, p. 334; illustrated p. 188, top left. Rietstap, *Armorial general*, 1:678, describes the arms and crest as follows: "Flandre (Anciens comtes de). D'or au lion de sa., arm. et lamp. de gules. Casque couronné. Cimier: le lion assis, posé de front, entre un vol d'or."

8 Gelre, *B.R. Ms. 15652–56*, nr. 928, p. 334; illustrated p. 188, middle row, second from right. The helmet in 9427, fol. 14r, bas-de-page, has the ermine wings of Old Flanders, but without the sable tips. This helmet is an overpaint over partly concealed white plumes; the latter are elements of Arnold's overpainted plumed helmet, as Wolinski indicated in "Plainchant."

9 De Raadt, *Sceaux armories*, 1:455.

10 Gelre, *B.R. Ms. 15652–56*, nr. 805, p. 328; illustrated p. 173, top row, first from left.

© KONINKLIJKE BRILL BV, LEIDEN, 2025 | DOI:10.1163/9789004427136_011

Arms of Ancient Duke of Brabant: "Brabant (Anciens ducs de). De sa. au lion d'or, arm. et lamp. de gu. Cq. cour. C: le lion, iss., cour. d'or, sommé d'une queue de paon au nat.; entre un vol de sa."[11] (Ancient Dukes of Brabant: gold lion on black field, red claws and tongue. Helmet with crown. Crest: issant lion with gold crown topped with a peacock tail in natural color, between a pair or black wings.)

---

11   Rietstap, *Armorial general*, 1:280.

APPENDIX 2

Transcription of Calendar of 10 A 14

January

1	Circumcision
2	Octave of Stephen
3	Octave of St. John (?). Genovese virgin
4	Octave of Holy Innocents
5	
6	Epiphany
8	
9	
10	
11	
12	
13	Octave of Epiphany. Hilary and Remigius confessors
14	
15	
16	Marcellus pope and martyr
17	Anthony abbot
18	Prisca virgin
19	Mary and Martha martyrs
20	Fabianius and Sebastian
21	Agnes virgin
22	Vincent martyr
23	ty *a mistake*
24	Timothy apostle
25	Conversion of St. Paul
26	
27	John Chrysostom
28	
29	
30	Aldegundis virgin
31	

February

1	Brigid virgin
2	Purification of St. Mary
3	Blaise bishop
4	
5	Agatha virgin
6	Vedastus and Amandus confessors
7	
8	
9	
10	Scholastica virgin
11	
12	
13	
14	Valentinus and companions

15	
16	Juliana virgin
17	
18	
19	
20	
21	
22	Chair of Peter
23	vigil
24	Matthias apostle
25	
26	
27	
28	Romanus martyr

March

1	Alban bishop
2	
3	
4	
5	
6	
7	Perpetua and Felicity
8	
9	
10	
11	
12	Gregory
13	
14	
15	
16	
17	Gertrude virgin
18	
19	
20	
21	Benedict abbot
22	
23	
24	
25	Annunciation to Saint Mary
26	Ludger bishop
27	Resurrection of the Lord
28	
29	
30	Quirinus martyr

April

1 Quintianus martyr
2
3
4
5
6
7
8
9
10 Macharius
11 Leo pope
12
13 Eufemia virgin
14 Tiburtius and Valerianus
15
16
17
18
19
20
21 Marcellus pope
22
23 George martyr
24
25 Mark evangelist
26
27
28 Vitalis martyr
29
30 Eutropius bishop

May

1 Philip and James apostles
2
3 Invention of the Cross
4
5
6 John Before the Latin Gate
7
8
9
10 Gordianus and Epymachus
11
12 Nereus and Achilleus
13 Servatius bishop
14
15
16
17
18
19 Pudenziana virgin
20
21
22
23
24
25 Urban pope
26
27 Bede priest
28 Germanus bishop
29
30
31 Petronilla virgin

June

1 Nicomedis martyr
2 Marcellinus and Peter martyrs
3
4
5 Boniface bishop and martyr
6
7
8 Medardus and Gildardus
9
10
11 Barnabas apostle
12
13
14 Basil bishop
15 Vitus and Modestus
16
17
18 Marcellus and Marcellinus
19 Gervasius and Protasius
20
21
22
23   vigil
24 John the Baptist
25 Eligius bishop
26 John and Paul
27
28 Leo pope.   vigil
29 Peter and Paul
30 Commemoration of St. Paul the apostle

July

1
2 Processus and Martianus
3
4

TRANSCRIPTION OF CALENDAR OF 10 A 14

5		21		
6	Octave of Peter and Paul	22	Timothy and Symphorien	
7		23	Timothy and Apollinaris. vigil	
8		24	Bartholomew apostle	
9		25		
10	Amalberga virgin	26	Irenaeus and Abundius	
11	Benedict abbot*	27	Rufus martyr	
12		28	Augustine bishop	
13	Margaret virgin	29	Beheading of John the Baptist	
14		30	Felix and Audactus *	
15	Dispersal of the apostles	31		
16				
17				
18				

*Audactus is misspelling of *Adauctus*.

September

19		1	Egidius (Gilles) abbot	
20		2		
21	Prassede virgin	3		
22	Mary Magdalene	4		
23		5		
24	vigil	6		
25	James the apostle	7	Evortius bishop	
26		8	Nativity of St. Mary	
27		9	Theodardus bishop	
28		10	Protus and Hyacinth	
29		11		
30	Abdon and Sennen	12		
31	Germanus bishop	13		
		14	Exaltation of the Holy Cross	

*This feast is not designated as the saint's translation.

August

		15		
		16		
1	Saint Peter in chains	17	Lambert martyr	
2		18		
3	Invention of Stephen	19	Eustachius and companions	
4		20	vigil	
5		21	Matthew apostle and evangelist	
6	Sixtus and Agapitus	22		
7		23		
8		24		
9	vigil	25		
10	Lawrence martyr	26		
11	Gaugericus bishop	27	Cosmas and Damian	
12		28		
13	Hippolytus	29	Michael the Archangel	
14	vigil	30	Jerome priest	
15	Assumption of St. Mary			
16				

October

17		1	Remigius and companions	
18	Agapitus martyr	3		
19	Magnus martyr	4	Francis	
20	Bernard abbot	5		

6	
7	Mark pope and companions
8	
9	Dionysius and companions
10	Gereon and companions
11	
12	
13	
14	Calixtus pope and companions
15	
16	
17	
18	Luke evangelist
19	
20	
21	11,000 virgins
22	
23	Severinus bishop
24	
25	Crispinus and Crispian
26	
27	vigil
28	Simon and Jude apostles
2	
30	
31	vigil

November

1	Feast of All Saints
2	Commemoration of all Souls. Eustasius
3	Hubert bishop
4	
5	
6	Leonard
7	
8	Four Crowned Martyrs
9	Theodore
10	
11	Martin bishop
12	
13	Brictius bishop
14	
15	
16	
17	Octave of Saint Martin
18	Elisabeth of Hungary chosen (*electe*)*
19	
20	

21	~~Cecilia virgin~~
22	Cecilia virgin
23	Clement pope. Trudo
24	Chrysogonus
25	Katherine virgin
26	
27	
28	Theodore martyr
29	vigil
30	Andrew apostle

*For resolving and translating this unusual abbreviation, I thank Barbara Haagh-Huglo. Elisabeth of Hungary, a widow of royal blood with children, may have been special to Elisabeth of Lierde,

December

1	Eligius bishop
2	
3	
4	Barbara virgin
5	
6	Nicholas bishop
7	Octave of Andrew
8	Conception of Saint Mary
9	
10	
11	Damasus pope
12	
13	Lucy virgin
14	Nicasius bishop
15	
16	
17	
18	
19	
20	vigil
21	Thomas apostle
22	
23	
24	vigil
25	Nativity of the Lord
26	Stephen
27	John the Evangelist
28	Holy Innocents
29	Thomas martyr
30	
31	Silvester pope

APPENDIX 3

Artist 2's Penwork Flourishing in Cycle 1 of 10 A 14 and Its Relation to Other Rummen-Group Manuscripts

What follows is a development of material on sub-cycles of Artist 2's penwork introduced in Chapter 4. The three sub-cycles of flourishing in Quire 2 (fols. 7–14) of 10 A 14 are described and analyzed. I have labeled these Cycles 1A, 1B, and 1C. An appendix was necessary in order to avoid congealing the text with excessive detail and an overflow of references to folios and figures. Cycle 1A is important because it reveals Artist 2's self-awareness of and reflection on his prior work as a flourisher in KBR 6426 and 9427, right as he began the project of flourishing in 10 A 14. Cycle 1B demonstrates that Artist 2 was aware of the style of flourishing in the Summer Missal, 9217, even though neither he nor his colleague Artist 1 participated in that manuscript's decoration. Cycle 1C presents material that is not easily connected to specific contemporary or prior sources and thus stands as a reminder of the very substantial gaps in our knowledge and understanding of flourishing in the Low Countries during this era.

Cycle 1A

Flourishing in Cycle 1A occurs on five of Quire 2's sixteen pages (fols. 9r, 14r; figs. 19, 28).[1] These pages might be seen as an initial statement by Artist 2, an introductory state-of-the-question assessment at the beginning of the new endeavor. Characteristic are Type 1 border bars accompanied by stiff, barbed corkscrews. The predominant foliate types are trilobes with wavy leaflets, ball-and-squiggle trilobes, and rosettes both floating and attached to stalks. Pearls are fewer than in other sub-cycles. Pearl spirals are attached to the corners of some two-line initials. Linear sequences of pearls are short, usually numbering only three or four pearls in a row.

A comparison of penwork on the relevant folios of 6426 and 9427 and the penwork of Cycle 1A in 10 A 14 reveals a commonality of decorative motifs and aesthetic. In 6426 Artist 2 executed illumination and flourishing on fols. 106r–153v, and in 9427 he illuminated and flourished fols.

14–77.[2] The vocabulary of penwork is quite restricted in comparison with 10 A 14, but all motifs and many of their groupings and configurations, as well as the pervasive aesthetic of design, are recognizably those used in 10 A 14.

a. Type 1 scalloped border bars accompanied by stiff, barbed corkscrews are found throughout Artist 2's work in 6426 (figs. 168, 169) and 9427 (figs. 181, 181a), as also on all folios of Cycle 1A in 10 A 14 and on additional pages of Quire 2 as well.[3] The number of Type 1 bars diminishes in subsequent quires of Artist 2's work in 10 A 14. After Quire 8, Type 1 border bars virtually disappear from his work. Thus Artist 2's earliest work in 10 A 14 is closely linked to his antecedent work in 6426 and 9427.

b. Additional common decorative motifs include the use of stellate, spiky rosettes, some threaded, in 9427 and 10 A 14, and the use of pearls of similar shape, grouping, and positioning in 6426, 9427 and in Cycle 1A of 10 A 14. (Cp. fig. 19 with figs. 168, 179.) Abundant ivy leaves with a curved or crooked middle lobe characterize the relevant work in all three manuscripts as well.

c. A shared aesthetic, manifested in both penwork and painted decoration, can be noted: The taut quality of line in Cycle 1A—and indeed throughout Artist 2's work in 10 A 14—is also evident in his quires of 6426 and 9427. Stiff arcs, slightly flattened and arranged in pairs or threes to emphasize tension and opposition, are characteristic. (Cp. fig. 19 with figs. 168, 169, 179.) Diagonal alignments are employed in 9427, as in 10 A 14, along the horizontal element of a terminal bar. Sprays of foliage are aligned in a row in which each element projects slightly further into the lower margin than does the preceding element, creating a rising or falling diagonal. (Cp. figs. 24, 181a.) The complex symmetries in Artist 2's penwork in 10 A 14 (fig. 56), noted above, can also be observed in the borders of his work in 6426 and 9427. Paired elements above the border bar are reflected in similar pairings below the border bar (figs. 170, 180).

---

1 Measurements to the nearest centimeter are given because dimensions vary somewhat; some pages are quite worn. Cycle 1A flourishing also appears on fols. 7v, 12v top, and 13ra below initial *H(ec)*.

2 Dennison assigned illumination in these folios to her Artist B (my Artist 2) in "Dating and Localisation," 509; and in "Stylistic Sources," 118. Artistic hands in flourishing were not considered.

3 Additional pages: fols. 8r, 10r, 11r, 11v, 14v.

© KONINKLIJKE BRILL BV, LEIDEN, 2025 | DOI:10.1163/9789004427136_013

d. *I*-initials throughout 9427 are of the concave type (figs. 180, 183).[4] In Quire 2 of 10 A 14 all *I*-initials are concave. In Quire 3 and thereafter, the concave *I* is largely replaced by the convex I. Once again, the closest connection with the KBR manuscripts is with the earliest of Artist 2's work in 10 A 14.

In sum, these connections are evidence that Artist 2 worked as flourisher as well as illuminator in both 6426 and 9427 before he worked on 10 A 14 and that his work in Quire 2, his first quire of 10 A 14, is especially close in style to his work in 9427; Cycle 1A in particular recalls his earlier work in the KBR Rummen manuscripts.

Cycle 1B

Flourishing of Cycle 1B (figs. 20, 29) appears on four folios of Quire 2.[5] In this subset of Cycle 1, Artist 2 references the work of another flourisher, here designated as 9217-2, a decorator whose penwork appears in 9217, on a number of folios in Quires 9 and 11 and on most folios in Quires 13–28 (figs. 174, 176). The work of 9217-2 is mostly in red ink, which is the primary color of penwork ink in Cycle 1B of 10 A 14. Artist 9217-2's work is characterized by long strings of flattened pearls that line bars and edge initials, almost dripping off projections with a pronounced diagonal emphasis. Many tendrils hook upward and terminate in a small human or grotesque face, as seen in the flourishing of both upper and lower terminal complexes

(figs. 174, 176). Corkscrews have a long, showy serpentine whiplash ending.

In Cycle 1B of 10 A 14 these elements are present, including a terminal head on an upward hook and the serpentine-tipped corkscrew (fig. 20). The packed, multiplied pearls give a heavier feel to Cycle 1B than is the case for 1A. However, the references to the style of Artist 9217-2 are somewhat diluted, as it were, with Artist's 2's own sensibility for the right-angle over the diagonal, for the stiff over the fluent; and for the rounded in corkscrews. Corkscrews of his primary type occur on the same page as the sinusoidal type that relates to Artist 9217-2. Artist 2's reference is something between a paraphrase and a direct quotation. One can hardly avoid the conclusion that Artist 2 intended to acknowledge Artist 9217-2 as a fellow decorator on these pages. Such a gesture suggests collegial, familiar, relationships among flourishers rather than antagonistic or competitive ones.

Cycle 1C

Cycle 1C, not presently known to reference other material, is found on eight pages of Quire 2 (figs. 21, 25).[6] Densely packed strings of toothed pearls predominate in the terminal complexes and fill their reentrant right angles. Pearl chains do not drip downward from the corners of initials as in Cycle 1B but rather project out at right angles. Corkscrews are of Artist 2's typical stiff form. Foliage consists primarily of trilobes, outlined but without infill of color, and slender, wavy leaflets. Rolls of toothed pearls fill reentrant right angles in terminal complexes.

---

4   Concave *Is* are found on all pages without full or partial borders also, as on fols. 23rb, 42rb.

5   Cycle 1B appears on fols. 8ra, upper left, and 8rb; 9v; 13vb, initial *I*(*n diebus*) and below; and 14v.

6   Fol. 8ra below initial *I*(*n ille*), 8v, 10r–12r, and 13va.

APPENDIX 4

Rummen-Group Manuscripts: Flourishing, Illumination, Artistic Hands, and Sources, Pts. 1–5

Pt. 1: the Loppem-Bruges Antiphonal and KBR Mss. 6426, 9427, and 9217

Flourishing and illumination of the three manuscripts in Brussels were discussed in Chapters 4 and 5. These manuscripts are further described and analyzed here. All three were illuminated and flourished before 10 A 14, and in the order they are discussed below.

Loppem-Bruges Antiphonal: This manuscript, 40 × 30 cm, consists of twelve leaves removed from an antiphonal and assembled without regard to their sequence in the liturgical year.[1] Style dates the illumination to around 1345. Each recto has a large historiated initial and borders on two or three sides of the page. No evidence suggests that this manuscript was commissioned by Arnold of Rummen, but stylistically its eleven fourteenth-century folios belong to the Rummen group. Artist 1 of 10 A 14 was responsible for all illumination and flourishing on fols. [1r] and [2r]–[11v]. The organic style buoyant with bubble-like pearls and fluttering ribbon-like tendrils; the corkscrew bodies drawn impressionistically as stacked plates, often with incurved tips (fig. 204); the slightly bulbous pearls, often grouped in threes, with tiny seeds between them; the use of paired ball-and-squiggle trilobes along with singles (figs. 202, 205)—all these motifs link penwork designs on these pages with those of Artist 1 in 10 A 14.[2] The vocabulary of motifs and forms is somewhat more limited than that of 10 A 14. Border bars, terminal complexes, faces, and fish are lacking in the Loppem-Bruges antiphonal. A second flourisher working in a 14th century style did the flourishing on fol. 1v; the style is tenser, more compact—more Parisian—than that of Artist 1; forms are smaller and more prolifically multiplied. A variant of the *littera duplex* is on this page, the initial *C(ustodit)*; this is also the only page with a penwork border bar. Fol. 12r, a leaf from a fifteenth-century antiphonal, is illuminated and flourished by a third hand.

In the Loppem-Bruges antiphonal, Artist 1's design in *S*-initials is similar to that of his *S*-initial in the Presentation in 10 A 14. (Cp. figs. 200, 200a; 201, 201a with

121a.)[3] The antiphonal's Corpus Christi initial, fol. [3r], *S(acerdos*, fig. 200a), depicts a priest elevating the Host before an altar; he is accompanied by an acolyte holding a candle and by three nuns, all kneeling. The body of the initial *S* is a double-mouthed gorgon whose open maw, containing a large rosette, is directly behind the priest and the Eucharistic wafer; the priest seems to be feeding the wafer to the gorgon. On fol. [4r], *S(i oblitus*, fig. 201a), a cleric in a conical hat stands on the porch of a church. He grasps the hand of a bishop to draw him into the building. The letterform *S* is treated as a two-headed avian grotesque whose abdomen opens into a large, double-mouthed gorgon. In this initial, as in the initial on fol. [3r], the monster is related both spatially and iconographically to the historiation. On fol. [4r] the monster's body is positioned in front of the architecture, obscuring part of the roof (fig. 201a). Inside the gorgon's open maw are two more grotesques, with intertwined necks—a humorous parody of the human pair below.[4] In this illumination the mathematics of pairs is quite complex, and in fact dominates the iconography. There are five pairs of forms—avians, gorgon heads, grotesques, clerics, and architectural projections (gable and tower)—and nested forms within forms—grotesques within gorgon within avian. The gable and tower are shaped to echo the two shapes of ecclesiastical headwear. Viewed in the light of these antecedent images, the Presentation initial in 10 A 14 (fig. is more subtle in the juxtaposition of gorgon and figures; in 10 A 14, the connection is an implied threat rather than an overt commentary. It should be noted that, unlike this painted initial, Artist 1's penwork does not typically exhibit the nesting and pairing of elements, both of which, however, appear quite often in the penwork of his coworker Artist 2.

KBR 6426: This antiphonal is a large volume of 196 folios with pages measuring 495 × 354 mm.[5] Musical notation is on eleven staves of four lines with text inscribed below

---

1 Smeyers, "64. Fragmenten van een antifonarium," in *Handschriften uit de abdij van Sint-Truiden*, 275–278.

2 Fol. [5v], initial *N[otam]*; fol. [11v], initial *I[ustus]*.

3 Fol. [3r], Corpus Christi, vespers, *S(acerdos)*; fol. [4r], Fourth Sunday after Easter, matins, first nocturn, *S(i oblitus)*. See Smeyers, "Fragmenten van een antifonarium," 276.

4 This striking motif has a predecessor in the two grotesques, face-to-face with intertwined long necks in Bodley 264, fol. 69r, in the initial *D(eus)* at the top of the page.

5 See Gaspar and Lyna, *Les principaux manuscrits à peintures*, 1:341–343; Smeyers, "Fragmenten van een antifonarium," 274–275.

© KONINKLIJKE BRILL BV, LEIDEN, 2025 | DOI:10.1163/9789004427136_014

each staff. Many large red and blue penwork initials, the height of a staff plus the text space, are decorated with tendrils, foliage, and pearls; flourishing is mostly in blue, red, and purple. Some initials of twice this height have figural imagery in reserve in the counter and initial stem. There are no terminal complexes, though the flourishing of initials often expands into margins.

Artist 2 worked in 6426 as both illuminator and flourisher, prior to working on 9427 and 10 A 14. He flourished fols. 100r, 106–153, and 188r. Dennison's Artist A flourished most of the first half of the manuscript as well as fols. 101r–105v and 154–187.[6] The repertoire of motifs in the work of Artist 2 is very limited in this manuscript compared to 10 A 14. Type 1 border bars, decorated with corkscrews, pearls and trilobes, are found on his pages. (See Chapter 3.) On Artist 2's pages corkscrews are the same compressed, wiry spirals with stiff, recurved, barbed tips that characterize his work in 10 A 14 (figs. 168, 169). Tendrils are drawn with tense curves; tendrils curling in opposite directions are often juxtaposed, as is also the case in 10 A 14. The penwork around initials is often squared, injecting an element of feeling for structure that typifies the work of Artist 2. The style of grotesques in large initials comports with Artist 2's in 10 A 14. (Cp. 6426's initial *D(um)* on fol. 100r with 10 A 14's initial *P(laceat)*, fol. 149v.)

KBR 9427: This liturgical psalter consists of 228 folios measuring 367 × 250 mm.[7] The calendar of this psalter is of Ghent.[8] Artist 2 flourished fols. 14–77; Artist 9217-1 flourished fols. 1–13 and 78 to the end. Each artist illuminated pages within his quires. The manuscript's large margins provide ample room for flourishing, which nonetheless is less developed than in 10 A 14. Initials are of various sizes, from one-line to the equivalent of six or more lines, these latter illuminated. The many line-endings are rectangular bars with painted decoration in a variety of foliate and geometric patterns. Three- or four-line gold psalm initials are framed in penwork; foliate and figural designs, the latter predominantly grotesques, decorate the counters and interiors of these initials. Penwork is in reserve.

Artist 2 uses Type 1 border bars in blue, red, and gold throughout his folios. These bars are decorated predominantly with paired trilobes, corkscrews, and rosettes, both floating and threaded. Floating rosettes are common in Artist 2's work in 10 A 14, but in this missal, he depicts only one threaded rosette—on fol. 9r, lower terminal complex (fig. 19). Corkscrews are the stiff, compressed spirals with barbed recurved tips familiar in 10 A 14. Pearl spirals in proximity to framed initials are common in 9427 and in 10 A 14. Taut filaments arranged in oppositional pairs are everywhere in the penwork of 9427, as in 10 A 14. (Cp. figs. 75, 179.) Pearls, also, in 9427 are stiff like those of Artist 2 in 10 A 14, rather than soft and bubble-like as are the pearls of Artist 4 (fig. 65) or protuberant as are those of Artist 1. (Cp. figs. 65, 75, 127, 175.)

Relationships between the double-headed grotesques that constitute figural initials and the narratives they enclose are imbued with comic-malevolent overtones by Artist 1. (See Chapter 5, discussion of the Presentation, fol. 167r.) Artist 1's treatment can be compared with the more subdued, less threatening and less humorous approach of Artist 9217-1. The latter's *S(alvum me fac)* initial in 9427 (figs. 182, 182a) is a double-headed human-bird monster. Its body effectively separates Christ, in the upper half of the image field, from David, submerged in the waters of the lower half. Christ curiously seems to address—perhaps to rebuke—not David, but the monster's human head, to which David's glance and querying gesture are likewise directed. The initial-monster's head turns away from his interlocutors and hides in a funnel-shaped hood; he seems defensive rather than threatening.

Artist 2's penchant in 10 A 14 for an overall symmetry in design marks border bars in 9427 as well, as seen in a comparison of the lower border on fol. 43v of 9427 (fig. 180) and the foliate terminal extension on fol. 49v of 10 A 14 (fig. 54). Similar slight deviations from symmetry can be noted, as well as the use of similar colors.

KBR 9217: The Summer Missal of Arnold of Rummen, 9217, consisting of 220 leaves measuring 367 × 277 mm, was flourished by two artists, herein termed 9217-1 and 9217-2.[9] The first is Dennison's Artist C;[10] the second is identified here, to my knowledge, for the first time. Neither of these two artists flourished or illuminated in 10 A 14. My study to this point indicates that Quires 2–8 and 12 (fols. 7–38, 87–94) were decorated by 9217-1. Quires 9 and 11 (fols. 63–70 and 79–86) contain penwork by both decorators.

---

6   For Dennison's discussion of Artist A's work in 6426, see "Dating and Localisation," 507.

7   Gaspar and Lyna, *Les principaux manuscrits à peintures,* 1:346–349; Haagdorens, "Sint-Truidense handschriften," 272–274; De Winter, *La bibliothèque de Philippe le Hardi,* 227–232; De Winter gives folio dimensions as 360 × 245 mm.

8   Coens and van der Straeten, "Un Martyrologe du XIIᵉ siècle," 158–159. Furthermore, Wolinski, "Ferial Office Chants," has linked the ferial antiphons of 9427 to those of the Diocese of Tournai, which included Ghent.

9   Measurements are from Haagdorens, "Sint-Truidense handschriften," 267.

10   See Dennison, "Dating and Localisation," 508–509.

In Quires 13–28 the sheets with illumination by 9217-1 mostly have his penwork as well.[11] However, most folios in Quires 13–28 lack illumination and have the penwork of 9217-2. In Quire 10, the curious painted borders on fols. 72r, 75r, 76r, and 78v and the penwork on these pages, need further study, as does all the penwork in this manuscript.

Ms. 9217's blue and gold two-line initials, decorated with red and purple penwork (figs. 172, 176), are typologically similar to those in 10 A 14.[12] Two-line initials in 9217 have an inventory of decorations in the counters similar to that of 10 A 14: palmettes, buds, leaves and leafy tendrils, grotesques, human heads. As in 10 A 14, so also in 9217 folios with musical notation and larger script have larger initials and a more developed repertoire of associated imagery.[13] (Cp. figs. 108, 174.) Penwork border bars in 9217 are variants of Types 1 and 2 throughout. Initials and borders are decorated with trilobes of various sorts. Artist 9217-1's corkscrews have long whiplash terminals, looser than those of his colleague Artist 9217-2 and unlike the tidier, more contained inward spirals of Artist 1. (Cp. figs. 172 and 94.) The great circular penwork loops enclosing corkscrews in a "starfish" pattern (fig. 172; fols. 22r, 24v, 34r) and large tendrils that spiral inward, making almost two complete revolutions (fols. 23r, 37v) are distinctive.

Most folios in Quires 13–28 feature the compacted pearls and sinuous corkscrews of Artist 9217-2 (figs. 174, 176), whose work is directly referenced by Artist 2 in 10 A 14, as noted in the discussion of Cycle 1B. (See Appendix 3.) Terminal complexes in 9217 are similar in motifs and structure to those in 10 A 14 but in general are less elaborate. Likewise, the inventory of foliate motifs in 9217 is similar to that of 10 A 14 but less varied. On the other hand, the repertoire of penwork human heads, animals, birds, fish, and monsters in the margins of 9217 is rich (figs. 172–174, 176), surpassing in fantasy the very limited varieties of penwork fish and human heads in the margins of 10 A 14.

Pt. 2: Stylistic Comparison of Illumination of Artist 1 in 10 A 14 and Artist 9217-1 in 9217

The discussion below is offered because Artist 1's style has similarities to that of Artist 9217-1; the two artists are sometimes conflated.[14] Artist 9217-1 produced all the major illumination in 9217.

Artist 1's style of illumination differs from that of Artist 9217-1. Artist 1 primarily colors both drapery and architecture with a wash of color, over which line is applied to add definition, decoration, modeling, and highlights (figs. 107a, 110a, 125a). Artist 9217-1, on the other hand, generally begins the modeling process in the initial application of paint, with broader, stronger strokes of different hues and values that contribute to a modeling with less reliance on line (figs. 171a, 173, 173a, 175). This technique, a legacy of the Parisian Master Honoré, is typical of much illumination of the early 1300s in Cologne.

The architecture of 9217-1 employs some motifs not used by Artist 1, such as notched buttress bases (fig. 171a) and the large acanthus corbel (fig. 175, center at top). Artist 9217-1's sturdy architectural supports impart a sense of stability to the architecture that frames initials; this sense is lacking in Artist 1's frames in 10 A 14, in which spindly supports are overweighted by their heavier superstructures. (Cp. figs. 171, 173, 173a with figs. 110a and 121a.)

Faces of Artist 9217-1 also differ from those of Artist 1. Artist 9217-1's noses are shorter, more rounded and more upturned at the tip, than those of Artist 1. On three-quarters faces, Artist 1's noses are often drawn as though viewed from a sharper angle than the rest of the face, whereas the angle of view is more nearly uniform in Artist 9217-1's faces. Locks of hair drawn by Artist 9217-1 are more uniform in size and more regular in shape and arrangement than the less orderly locks of Artist 1.

Artist 1's rendering of faces and his method of coloring architecture have corollaries on fol. 20v of Bodley 264. Artist 9217-1's palette is related to that of Cologne, characterized by soft colors and fluent modeling. Likewise, his figures in the Crucifixion of 9217 (fig. 175) have a certain emotional kinship with those in certain Crucifixions from Cologne (figs. 157, 159), a controlled emotion both contemplative and melancholy. The architecture of 9217-1's Crucifixion, on the other hand, points to Ghent and Tournai rather than to Cologne.

---

11   As for example, fols. 109r&v, 110r&v, 116v in Quire 15, which has illumination on fols 109r, 115v, and 116r; fol. 116 is cognate with fol. 110.

12   See Haagdorens, "Het zgn. missaal," 141–144, for a discussion of the penwork initials in 9217.

13   Musical notation in 9217 is found on fols. 109–113, 116–122.

14   "Sint-Truidense handschriften," 271. Haagdorens, "Sint-Truidense handschriften," 271, did not differentiate between Artist 9217-1 and Artist 1 but regarded them as one and the same; Dennison, "Dating and Localisation," 509, correctly saw two hands. (See the section entitled "Scholarship on illumination and decoration" in Chapter 4 above.)

Pt. 3: The Superstructure, Background, and Overpainted Heraldry of the Crucifixion in 9217, Fol. 115v (Figs. 175, 175a, 175b)

What follows expands the discussion in Chapter 5 of the Crucifixion page in 10 A 14 with further analysis of its closest comparable image, the Crucifixion in 9217.

Four miniscule heads appear in the superstructure of the Crucifixion, two at windows of a small cylindrical central tower and one at either end of the battlements.[15] The figures face each other in pairs. One figure is a woman; two are beardless men, one in a cap. The fourth, at the far right, also in a cap, is bearded and displays an uninscribed banderole. The banderole and beard suggest a prophet, but the lack of inscription introduces uncertainty; the other three figures appear secular. In sum, the relationship of superstructure and its denizens to the sacred scene is less determinate than in 10 A 14.

The background is more varied in pattern, less methodical in subdivisions, and more decorative in effect than that of 10 A 14. Tooled gold fills the space between the two blue strip-frames and the architecture they enclose. Within the architectural frame, the field is divided into rectangular quadrants that could be likened to heraldic quartering. Quadrants 1 and 4 are similarly patterned, as are 2 and 3.[16]

Quadrants 1 and 4 are subdivided by gold strips into sets of large rectangles, each internally articulated with a pattern of small squares. Rectangles with predominantly blue squares, set 1, alternate with rectangles having predominantly orange squares, set 2. The blue-square rectangles are not all identical, however; they are subdivided

into two subsets, 1a and 1b, based on internal decoration with white lines and dots. The rectangles repeat in sequence: 1a, 2, 1b, 2, 1a, 2, etc. Patterns are staggered in the six horizontal rows of quadrant 1 and, apparently, in the more occluded seven rows of quadrant 4. The painting of rectangles in set 2 is smudged; examination from the reverse, on fol. 115r, reveals overpaints in these rectangles.

Quadrants 2 and 3 contain small squares that repeat in a 1-2-3- pattern of decoration, but these squares are not grouped into larger rectangular units. Thus, the organizational pattern of the background in 9217, employing both rectangles and squares, and triples as well as pairs, is more decorative, more complex, and less consistent in overall concept than that of the background of 10 A 14 (fig. 106), in which divisions based on squares and their corollary, the number 4, permeate and unify the design.

As in the Winter Missal, arms have been covered over on 9217's Crucifixion page. Examination of the page's recto reveals the silhouettes of seven shields beneath the blue strip border, four beside St. John and three beside the Virgin (fig. 175).[17] Furthermore, all the orange-colored rectangles comprising set 2 in quadrants 1 and 4 are overpaints; silhouettes of oblong shapes are seen beneath these rectangles on fol. 115r; in quadrant 1, where figures do not obscure the ground, the staggered alignment of these oblongs is readily apparent. A close look at this quadrant of the miniature reveals feathery tendrils that overlap the architecture just beyond the end of the left Cross arm and at the top of the second full rectangle below Christ's right elbow (fig. 175a). In both cases the tendrils are white, like the plumes in Arnold's helmet. Traces of a domed outline can be seen at the top of a number of the orange rectangles in quadrants 1 and 4; traces of diagonal lines can be seen at the lower right corners of rectangles in these same quadrants (figs. 175a&b). The domed lines are likely remnants of Arnold's plumed crest; the diagonal lines are elements of the trailing mantle attached to the helmet. The oblongs, which number over two dozen, are the shapes of his helmet, depicted repeatedly in the background and later covered over incompletely.

Pt. 4: Sources of the Architecture of the Crucifixion, 10 A 14, Fol. 143v (Fig. 106)

Examination of the architecture in the illumination of 10 A 14 and of the possible sources of this architecture in

---

15   Figures and heads in the superstructure are especially common in English illumination of the 1340s. Some examples: a psalter, OBL, Ms. Douce 131, c.1325–1335, fol. 96v; a psalter, Brescia, Biblioteca Queriniana, Ms. A.V. 17, c.1330, fol. 7r; a psalter, OBL, Ms. Liturg. 198, c.1330, fol. 60r. These figures may have been inspired in part by slightly earlier Bolognese illumination in which figures in architectural superstructures are connected to the narrative in various ways. Examples include Decretals of Gregory the Great, MLM, Ms. M. 716, 1330–1335, fols. 1v and 2r; *Accursius*, BAV, Ms. Vat. lat. 1430, mid 1330s, fol. 179r.

16   Subdivision of the background grid into sections with different patterns or colors is cited as evidence of English influence, as in the Psalter of Robert de Lisle, LBL, Ms. Arundel 83, Westminster or London, c.1308–c.1339, fol. 132r, the Crucifixion. Continental manuscripts could also be a source for this feature, as they also employ backgrounds with sectioning of different colors and patterns: Two full-page Crucifixions in the Psalter-Hours of Yolande of Soissons, MLM, Ms. 729, Amiens, 1280–1299, fols. 4v and 337v; an earlier example of a Crucifixion with this treatment is in the Missal of St. Denis, BNF, Ms. lat. 1107, Paris, c.1254–1286, fol. 209v. Examples could be multiplied.

17   Haagdorens, "Het zgn. missaal," 77, notes these overpainted shields but does not make note of the overpainted helmets discussed in the text following this note.

slightly earlier manuscript illumination quickly leads to the realization that many elements are common to imagery in Europe of the era. One might conceive of a common pool of structural and decorative features from which artists selected and which they proceeded to combine in various ways, according to personal and regional aesthetic tastes, according to the requirements of patrons and of the genre of the manuscript. However, the idea of a common pool of visual resources does not quite work. Significant variations in the character of motifs and in aesthetic and conceptual ends which they served, are distinguishable in the architectural inventory. A survey of architectural comparanda illuminates both likenesses and differences.

Illumination of northern France and Flanders in the late thirteenth and early fourteenth centuries, it goes without saying, is replete with imposing architectural frames in ecclesiastical Gothic style. Arches carried on piers and crowned with gables and crocketed pinnacles, often overpassing the upper frame, are characteristic, as are niches, tracery and colonnettes. Perhaps the burgeoning production of illuminated romances and other secular texts in northern France and Flanders, as well as Italian influence, leads to more motifs associated with secular architecture: Battlements, round towers, rooftop ensembles, make an appearance in illuminated liturgical and devotional texts after about 1330.

With respect to the other manuscripts in 10 A 14's cohort, the architecture of the Winter Missal's Crucifixion has a close relationship to a structure in one miniature in 9427, the throne of David in the initial E(xultate) on fol. 124r (figs. 183, 183a). Similarities are evident, though the throne, as furniture, is not fully comparable to architecture. Simple, planar forms; controlled, stepped recession; and marked changes in shading at corners are common to both structures. Dennison saw these features as manifestations of a transient interest in Italianisms that pulsed through both Flemish and English illumination just before the mid-fourteenth century.[18] These Italianate features contrast with the more delicate, more ornamental,

and less rational constructions elsewhere in 9427, in 9217 and 6426, and in several miniatures of 10 A 14.

Connections of the architecture to monumental sculpture in Ghent are possible. The funerary relief for the children of Olivier van der Most, part of a cache of thirteenth- and early fourteenth-century reliefs excavated from a lock in the Scheldt near Ghent in the late nineteenth century, depicts a superstructure of pinnacles connected by balustrades, with a three-part, hipped-roof structure behind. However, the pointed arches and flat, layered construction without converging rib lines date the construction to an era earlier than 10 A 14.[19]

Beyond its immediate cohort, 10 A 14's Crucifixion architecture relates to a wide variety of Italian and northern sources.[20] Variants of many individual motifs in the architecture of 10 A 14's illuminations occur in generations of northern French and Flemish manuscripts. The single greatest concentration of relevant motifs is in the almost-contemporary Bodley 264, made in Tournai.[21] Battlements carried on corbeled arches backed by fenestrated roofed structures (fol. 43v);[22] lateral buttresses with

---

18   "Dating and Localisation," 512; "Stylistic Sources," 125. Foundational to this recognition of Italian influence is Otto Pächt, "A Giottesque Episode in English Medieval Art," *Journal of the Warburg and Courtauld Institutes*, 6 (1943):51–70. The Italian influence on the architecture of the throne is also seen in art of Cologne, as in the diptych of *c.*1330 from St. George in Cologne, now in Berlin, Staatliche Museen, Gemäldegalerie; the enthroned Virgin, with the Child, is seated on a throne with stepped, slab-like sides, and shading indicated by strong changes in value at angles. Architecture has none of the arches, tracery, crockets or pinnacles typical of northern Gothic. See Wallrath, ed., *Vor Stefan Lochner*, 1974, "4: Diptychon," 69.

19   A number of tomb reliefs from the thirteenth and early fourteenth centuries were excavated from a water lock on the Scheldt just outside of Ghent in the 1880s. Thought to have come from the Church of Saint John (now the Cathedral of Saint Bavo), these were published in a series of articles by Jean Béthune-de Villers, "Musée lapidaire des ruines de Saint-Bavon: Dalles funéraires retrouvées à l'écluse des Braemgaten," *Messager des sciences historiques ou archives des arts et de la bibliographie de Belgique* 65 (1891): 89–107, 257–269, 385–401; and 66 (1892): 1–16, 129–145, 261–273. The articles were later collected and published as *Catalogue des dalles funéraires*. The few illustrated reliefs feature standing frontal figures, usually single, under architectural canopies. Drapery is articulated in a few repetitive, vertical or triangular folds. A reproduction in Pl. II, p. 136, 1892, of the funeral slab for the children of Olivier van der Most, *c.*1300, shows six figures standing side by side in almost identical poses, hands together in prayer.

20   The uses of architecture in fourteenth-century manuscript imagery are varied and complex. Architecture can function as a purely formal frame for the scene it encloses; as a physical, geographical location for events that take place either outdoors or indoors; as a conceptual setting that offers some sort of interpretive commentary on the events, or, even as something approaching an actor in the narrative. Often elements of multiple functions are present. Architecture is incorporated in the sophisticated illusionism of fifteenth century illumination. See James H. Marrow, "History, Historiography, and Pictorial Invention in the Turin-Milan Hours," in *In Detail: New Studies of Northern Renaissance Art in Honor of Walter S. Gibson*, ed. Laurinda Dixon (Turnhout: Brepols, 1998), 1–14.

21   Dennison, "Dating and Localisation," 512, and "Stylistic Sources," 125, notes this connection.

22   Image available on the Bodleian website at https://digital.bodleian.ox.ac.uk/objects/ae9f6cca-ae5c-4149-8fe4-95e6eca1f73c

paired strip elements (fol. 51v);[23] pinnacles and ribbed vaults converging to a central boss and viewed from below (fig. 146);[24] faces peering from the superstructure, keyhole arches (fig. 143); colored masonry that changes in value at corners and angles in the masonry (figs. 143, 145). These elements are shuffled and combined with many others that do not appear in the Crucifixion of 10 A 14, such as oversized foliate capitals (fig. 146), twisted columns, projecting gabled windows, and flags (fol. 67v).[25] Nonetheless, the architecture of Bodley 264 is more miniaturist, complex, and decorative than that of the Crucifixion in 10 A 14. It is closer in feeling to the architecture of 9217, as is its figure style. Bodley 264, or something very like it, was likely known to the artists of 10 A 14 and 9217, but the elements that appealed to Artist 2 were not the same as those that interested the illuminator of the Summer Missal.

Less compelling but still worth remarking in the context of possible sources for 10 A 14 is Parisian illumination. The Hours of Jeanne d'Evreux (fig. 152), furnishes some architectural analogs to 10 A 14.[26] Pucellian architecture's solidity and simplicity forecasts similar qualities in 10 A 14, though the development of illusionistic interior space is not furthered in imagery of the first campaign in 10 A 14 and the spaces and structures of the Parisian hours are less unified in conception than are those on 10 A 14's Crucifixion page. The architecture of the Crucifixion miniature is considerably more massive, starker in lighting, and plainer in decoration and in design than that of the Hours of Jeanne d'Evreux. It is also less eclectic, more symmetrical and consistent—in brief, more structural—than the Parisian architecture. This character is congruent with Artist 2's theological depth and solemnity of purpose.

Some elements in 10 A 14's Crucifixion architecture—emphatic changes of lighting at angles, simplicity of decoration and articulation, sense of mass and solidity—suggest familiarity with architecture in Bolognese

manuscripts such as that in a copy of the Decretals of Pope Gregory IX, of 1330–1335.[27]

In English illumination, some manuscripts offer striking parallels to elements in 10 A 14, but these are coupled with equally striking elements of difference. It is as though the Low Country artist had a thoroughgoing understanding of that which in English illumination was congenial to, and that which was incompatible with, his sensibilities and aims. The Queen Mary Psalter of c.1310–1320, offers certain compositional correspondences, though virtually none in style and technique.[28] The architectural frame of the Psalter's Crucifixion, fol. 256v, has storied lateral piers containing niches that house small standing figures and support a triplet of arches in the architecture, in which, however, perspective elements are almost entirely lacking. Figures are graded in four sizes—Christ the largest and the pier figures smallest, as in 10 A 14. Connections between the architecture in 10 A 14 and that of its approximate contemporary, the Fitzwarin Psalter, have been noted.[29] The Fitzwarin Psalter's sixteen full-page prefatory miniatures of the life of the Virgin and the Passion employ massive architectural canopies rendered in a steely gray that makes for more foreboding contrasts than those of 10 A 14, and the blocky shapes of its structures are more ponderous than those of 10 A 14. However, the heavy superstructures in most Fitzwarin miniatures are supported, anti-tectonically, by spindly columns that hardly appear equal to the task and contrast with the solid piers of 10 A 14. In most miniatures of the Psalter the converging ribs beneath are projected as two-dimensional patterns (fig. 140), without the suggestion of three-dimensional depth found in 10 A 14. Closer to the architecture of 10 A 14's Crucifixion is that of the Fitzwarin's added bifolium of Christ in Majesty and the Crucifixion, fols. 21v–22r (figs. 141, 142), by a different artist than the creator of the other prefatory miniatures.[30] A feeling for weight and support

---

/surfaces/e70fd535-b81b-413b-bfc1-0baf516020f2/#, as of 19 April, 2023.

23 Image available on the Bodleian website at https://digital.bodle ian.ox.ac.uk/objects/ae9f6cca-ae5c-4149-8fe4-95e6eca1f73c/sur faces/f107f2ed-c1fd-42ab-9e21-35e4dff0b91b/, as of 19 April 2023.

24 Another example of pinnacled structures with converging ribbed vaults seen from below can be seen at the web address cited in the preceding note.

25 Image available on the Bodleian website, at https://digital.bodle ian.ox.ac.uk/objects/ae9f6cca-ae5c-4149-8fe4-95e6eca1f73c /surfaces/beebca02-6ca2-4051-9c1e-46fce190e3aa/, as of 19 April 2023.

26 MMA, Cloisters Ms. 54.1.2.

27 MLM, Ms. M. 716, fol. 4r. Image available at http://ica.themor gan.org/manuscript/page/5/158742 as of 19 April 2023.

28 LBL, Royal Ms. 2.B.vii. Image available at https://www.bl.uk /manuscripts/Viewer.aspx?ref=royal_ms_2_b_vii_f084r as of 19 April 2023.

29 BNF, Ms. lat. 765. Dennison, "Stylistic Sources," 124–125; "Dating and Localisation," 511. Dennison, "Dating and Localisation," 511, dates the Fitzwarin Psalter 1345–1350. Sandler, Gothic Manuscripts 2:134, dates it 1350–1370; she dates the added bifolium to the later years. Dennison's date is the more convincing. For commentary on the architecture of the Fitzwarin Psalter, see also Frances Wormald, "The Fitzwarin Psalter and its Allies," Journal of the Warburg and Courtauld Institutes 6 (1943): 71–72.

30 I proposed that this artist was also artist of the drawings and paintings in the Egerton Genesis, Ms. Egerton 1894. This thesis needs reevaluation; the possibility of the artist's connections to wall painting should be considered, given the monumental

and for symmetry, and a consistency in storey divisions and coloration, link these designs to those of 10 A 14, with which, however, substantial differences in proportions, articulation, and in number and placement of figures can be noted. The taste for wide, heavy frames in illumination, a perennial current in English illumination from Anglo-Saxon times, is not shared by Artist 2.

One cannot neglect to include as possible sources and certainly as parallels for the architecture of 10 A 14, Flemish brasses, produced mostly in Tournai but also in Ghent and Bruges and exported to both English and Continental destinations. These provide some striking parallels for structural elements of the architecture of 10 A 14's Crucifixion.[31] The closest surviving exemplars are of the 1360s at earliest and so post-date the Crucifixion in 10 A 14, but the paucity of survival of brasses and of documentation relative to their production precludes determination as to which medium has priority of appearance for the elements in question.[32] The Alan Fleming brass, at Newark, Nottinghamshire, depicts the deceased beneath a canopy framed by four stories of buttressed niches. These enclose small figures, not unlike the angels in the niches of the lateral piers in 10 A 14's Crucifixion. The architecture is developed in three dimensions; a projecting polygonal pedestal like that in 10 A 14 is beneath the feet of Fleming, and the tripartite superstructure above his head lifts to display a ribbed vault.

Faces and figures populate the architectural superstructures of illuminations in a number of Flemish and English manuscripts of the 1330s and 1340s, including Bodley 264 and the Fitzwarin Psalter. In Bodley 264 figures in the superstructure engage in secular activities, as is appropriate for the text they accompany: Fashionably coiffed and dressed, they play musical instruments (fol. 51v), engage in conversation and flirtation (fol. 67v), or dance (fol. 88v). Their activities are not always directly connected with the events imaged in the scenes below them, but the atmosphere of courtly life pervades both. The structures in which they act and perform can be presumed secular. Where heads rather than figures appear, they seem to be those of spectators of events depicted below (fig. 143).

In the Fitzwarin Psalter, the Passion miniatures are narrative rather than doctrinal and are colored with references to medieval drama which are lacking in 10 A 14. Four of the sixteen scenes in the psalter have inhabited superstructures, in which activity references a curious amalgam of stage, church, Heaven and Hell.[33]

The angels (as opposed to prophets, in the Queen Mary Psalter) in 10 A 14's Crucifixion-page architectural niches have antecedents in full-page Crucifixion images of

---

feel of design in miniatures such as those on fols. 4r and 5v. See Joslin and Watson, *The Egerton Genesis*, especially Chapter 6. The style of this Crucifixion is related to the style of illumination in MSV, Ms. 601, Missal of St. Vaast, Arras, c.1335–1340, especially the Crucifixion, fol. 153v. For discussion of style of this illumination, see Avril, "303: Missel de Saint-Vaast d'Arras," *Les fastes du gothique*, 350.

31 See Dennison, "The Artistic Context," especially pp. 1–3, Plate I(B), and pp. 28–33. Dennison presents stylistic evidence of close connections between the Tournai brass engravers and the artists of Bodley 264 and of 10 A 14 and its cohort. For Ghent as a probable location for the production of monumental brasses in the fourteenth century, see Malcolm Norris, *Monumental Brasses: The Memorials* (London: Phillips & Page, 1977) 1: 27, 42. For Tournai as a center for monumental brass production as early as the 1340s, see H. K. Cameron, "The 14th-century School of Flemish Brasses: Evidence for a Tournai Workshop," *Transactions of the Monumental Brass Society* 12, pt. 3 (1979): 199–203. Cameron also refers in these pages to the evidence for brass production in Ghent in the fourteenth century.

32 Much documentation relevant to brasses from Tournai was destroyed during World War II. In May 1940 more than 300,000 manuscripts, including over 100,000 chirographs, in the city's archives burned in a night of bombing (Cameron, "The 14th-century School," 203).

---

33 On fol. 20r, for example, The Descent of the Holy Spirit, Christ's head and upper body appear parallel to the picture plane through an arched opening in a tower of the superstructure. Christ holds a ribbon attached to the dove of the Holy Spirit, which he lowers to the group seated beneath. The superstructure thus represents both Heaven and the staged space of the liturgical drama, whence the Christ-actor dispatches the promised Holy Spirit. Other miniatures with inhabited superstructures reference the staging of Hell and the actions of stagehands. On fol. 15r, the Harrowing of Hell, demons occupy a terrace-like area above the figure of Christ leading the Old Testament worthies from the Hellmouth. Here again the drama may be an influence; both Heaven and Hell were sometimes staged with multiple stories and lifting devices connecting upper and lower levels. Furthermore, the pronounced asymmetries of its design are suggestive of chaos, irrespective of associations with drama. On fol. 9r, the Arrest of Christ, two bearded men with nude chests and arms lend assistance to the soldiers seizing Christ. Leaning down through openings in a central tower, one holds a lantern by a chain and the other hands an enormous spiked axe to a helmeted soldier below. This curious image recalls the staging of drama. If its source is in the liturgical drama, the superstructure in this image would represent the upper levels of a church, a physical location on earth.

Liturgical dramas of the fourteenth century and later were staged with the raising and lowering of objects, and perhaps even persons, between floor and ceiling. See M. D. Anderson, *Drama and Imagery in English Medieval Churches* (Cambridge, UK: Cambridge University Press, 1963), 150–152; Rosemary Woolf, The *English Mystery Plays* (Berkeley: University of California Press, 1972), 283–284; Hildburgh, *English Alabaster Carvings*, 63–65. Rubin, *Corpus Christi*, 62, notes the will of Thomas Goisman of Hull, who in 1502 left money for a machine that would lower angels at the elevation of the Host and raise them after the Our Father.

manuscripts from northern France, such as the two-part Cambrai Missal of *c.*1295.[34] The lateral piers contain arched niches that house two tiers of standing male and female figures, analogs of 10 A 14's angels.

Noteworthy also is the connection of this architectural-figural surround with Flemish panel painting of the fifteenth century. The small figural groups in grisaille, framed by canopies that double as platforms, in van der Weyden's *Miraflores Altarpiece* are rightly connected with the portal sculpture of Gothic Cathedrals; but the painted versions in manuscripts may be sources as well.

Pt. 5: Illumination of Cologne Relative to That of the Rummen-Group Manuscripts

What follows is an addition to the discussion of 10 A 14's Crucifixion miniature, fol. 143v (fig. 106) in Chapter 5. I expand observations on illumination in Cologne of the 1330s to 1350s as it is relevant to the question of sources for the Rummen manuscripts.

The use of heavy line, a sense of artificiality, and dissonant color are cited as common to the Missal of Conrad of Rennenberg and 9217.[35] The figure styles of both have a certain fragility, in spite of the heavy line. By contrast, the modeling and three-dimensionalized pose of the Christ in 10 A 14 impart a Flemish sense of robustness lacking in the other two figures.

Although both the Rennenberg missal and 9217 employ primarily mid-to-high values, color in the Rennenberg missal is of higher intensity than that of 9217. The Winter Missal's Crucifixion shares with Rennenberg's the palette of strong blue and red, tempered by beige and white. However, the distribution of color in the two images is very different, and Rennenberg exhibits a stronger and more consolidated use of gold. The complex patterns in the backgrounds of both Rummen missals are replaced by a simple, unified pattern of diapering in Rennenberg. The overall effect of these differences is an enhancement of the devotional character of the Rennenberg image.

The architecture of Rennenberg is unmarked by Italian influence or by the secular elements and ancillary rooftop figures of Bodley 264. The gables and pointed arches that define the articulation in Rennenberg are conventionally Northern. The spatial platform and vaulted undercarriage—attempted in 9217 and more successfully executed in 10 A 14—which contribute to creation of a

third dimension, are also lacking in the Rennenberg miniature. Some second-hand Italian naturalism is apparent in Rennenberg's bare, scored rock of Calvary, rendered in a patternized formula, and in the perspective treatment of the Cross.

The Rennenberg missal's Crucifixion is very similar to the now badly rubbed, full-page Crucifixions in two additional missals now in Brussels, both from Cologne in the mid-fourteenth century.[36] These two have been assigned to Loppa de Speculo, the Franciscan nun who illuminated the Rennenberg missal.[37] They are stylistically a little closer to 9217 than is Rennenberg in the handling of space and line. However, in all three Loppa de Speculo missals these secular architectural elements are absent, as are the Rummen manuscripts' intellectual and decorative complexities of pattern. The Cologne artist produced, instead, more purely devotional images.

Earlier Cologne manuscripts have little to offer as possible models for the Rummen Crucifixion images. The Crucifixion in a missal for St. Cunibert in Cologne, *c.*1330 (fig. 211), and that in the contemporaneous and stylistically similar Missal for St. Severin, Cologne, depict the Virgin and St. John on opposite sides of the Cross.[38] Their figures are in drapery heavier than that of the Rummen group, with fluent, satiny, white highlights that reflect the legacy of Master Honoré, perhaps by way of English models such as the Psalter of Robert de Lisle, made in London, *c.*1310.[39] The heavy drapery is not found in the Rummen manuscripts, and highlights have a matte, rather than a satiny, finish. The faces of the Virgin and the face of Christ in the Missal for St. Cunibert have streaky white highlights (fig. 211), ultimately of Italian origin, but mediated through English illumination, like those of the Virgin and St. John in 10 A 14, but given the wide diffusion of this technique, there is little reason to postulate a direct connection between 10 A 14 and illumination from Cologne.

In a second, slightly later, missal for St. Cunibert, drapery in the Crucifixion, fol. 223v (fig. 159), hangs in more and thinner folds; the satiny highlights have disappeared; and St. John has moved across the image to stand behind and support the Virgin, though not in the same

---

34   CMM, Ms. 153, fol. 112v, and Ms. 154, fol. 98v.

35   Rennenberg missal is CDD, Cod. 149. See De Winter, *La bibliothèque de Philippe le Hardi*, 228.

36   KBR, Mss. 209 and 212; see Gaspar and Lyna, 1:316–319.

37   "77: Missale des Domdekans Konrad von Rennenberg," in Wallrath, ed., *Vor Stefan Lochner*, 1974, pp. 134.

38   DUL, Ms. 837, fol. 145v, and DUL, Ms. 874, fol. 68v; see Eizenhöfer and Knaus, *Die Liturgischen Handschriften*, "Nr. 36: Hs 837," pp. 123–127, and "Nr. 38: Hs 874 Festmissale, Köln, St. Severin, später St. Kunibert, um 1330, erweitert um 1485," pp. 133–136.

39   Psalter of Robert de Lisle: LBL, Arundel Ms. 83 II.

position or with the same gesture as in 10 A 14.[40] His erstwhile place on the right side of the image is filled by the centurion and a closely-packed group of four bystanders. These changes are reflective of Italian influence, as noted above. The backgrounds of the Cologne missals' Crucifixions are unlike those of the Rummen group. The background of the Crucifixion in the first Missal for St.

Cunibert is of gold tooled with oak leaf and acorn patterns (fig. 211); in the second missal, the background of the Crucifixion is of gold with tooled diapering and imperial eagles (fig. 159).

In sum, it is possible that elements of the Rummen missals may have influenced some Cologne illumination, and vice versa. Nevertheless, differences in the iconography and in the treatment of architecture, color, and space testify to different artistic intentions, possibly linked to ecclesiastical patronage in the case of Cologne and secular, aristocratic patronage in the case of the Rummen books.

---

40   DUL, Ms. 876. See Eizenhöfer and Knaus, "Nr. 37: Hs 876 Missale, Köln, St. Kunibert, um 1330," *Die Liturgischen Handschriften*, pp. 127–132.

APPENDIX 5

Comparative Iconography of Labors of the Months

	10 A 14	*9217*	*Ghent*
January	Man warming	same	Man feasting
February	Woman w/2 candles	same	same
March	Man pruning tree w/ ax	same	Man digging
April	Man w/two flowering stalks	same	same
May	Man playing a viol	same	Man hawking
June	Woman gathering flowers	same	Man carries/chops tree/wood
July	Man mowing hay w/scythe	same	same
August	Man reaping grain w/sickle	same	same
September	Man gathering grapes	Man threshing w/ flail	same as 10 A 14
October	Man treading grapes	Nude man treading grapes	same as 10 A 14 or sowing
November	Man slaughtering a cow	Man slaughtering pig	same as 10 A 14
December	Man baking loaves in oven	same	same

	Bruges	*Liège*	*Douce 5*
January	Man warms, drinks	Feasting, warming	Same as 10 A 14
February	Woman w/1 candle	Pruning	Priest blessing men and women w/candles
March	Man digging	Digging	Men fell tree
April	Man w/two flowering stalks	same	Man kneeling.before woman.
May	Man hawking	same	*missing*
June	Man carries wood	Man gathering flowers	*missing*
July	Man mowing hay w/scythe	same	*missing*
August	Man reaping grain w/sickle	same	*missing*
September	Man gathering grapes or sowing	Man treading grapes	Men gathering, children trampling grapes
October	Gathering grapes or sowing	Man sowing	Man beating oak acorns to feed pigs
November	Beating oak for pigs	Man carrying pig	Man cleaning entrails, roasting pig, slaughtering pig
December	Butchering pig	Man slaughtering cow	Women kneading, man baking bread

© KONINKLIJKE BRILL BV, LEIDEN, 2025 | DOI:10.1163/9789004427136_015

APPENDIX 6

Gorgons

The gorgons in the Rummen-group manuscripts are a subset of the large and varied population of monsters, grotesques, and dragons that construct and enliven initials and borders in northern European manuscripts over many centuries, beginning well before the Romanesque era. Compared to its relative the dragon, the gorgon is uncommon in illumination of the later thirteenth and fourteenth centuries. Specimens in quantity occur chiefly in 10 A 14 and its circle.

The term *gorgon* as used in this study refers to motifs with a pair of confronted, identical grotesque heads with open mouths, generally conjoined. The heads share one or more anatomical extensions. Variations in design are numerous. Heads may be full-view, profile, or three-quarters. Extensions may be from the maxillary jaw, the mandibular jaw, or from both, or from the snout or chin. The heads may have fangs, teeth, and/or a more or less stylized tongue. The conjoined mouths often enclose a human figure, grotesque, or bird. Gorgons are generally placed into, or function as, a segment of an initial frame.

The gorgon appears in six initials in 10 A 14, five of which are of the first campaign; two are Artist 2's (figs. 15a, 91a [initial *D* [*omine*]]); three are Artist 1's (figs. 121a, 125a, 132a). The sixth gorgon initial, which might be termed more aptly gorgonesque (fig. 37) appears to be an inept reworking during the second campaign of a motif begun in the first. The absence of gorgons as integral elements of design in the second campaign suggests that the motif may have gone out of fashion during the interval between campaigns.

Gorgons appear in the initials of all illuminators of all Rummen-group manuscripts: in the initials of Artist 1 in the Loppem-Bruges antiphonal, in those of Artists A and Artist 2 in 6426, in those of Artist 2 and Artist 9217-1 in 9427, in those of Artist 9217-1 in 9217. They are not found, to my knowledge, in prior illumination from Tournai or Cologne, both of which have connections to 10 A 14. The sole example from Sint-Truiden is in *Speculum 2*, fol. 1r (figs. 198, 198a), discussed in Chapter 7, in the section entitled "Artist 2: Sint-Truiden." The Stockholm Bible, probably illuminated in Paris after the completion of the first campaign of 10 A 14, furnishes close comparanda to the Rummen-group gorgons. (See the section entitled "Ghent" in Chapter 8.)

Sources for the gorgon are elusive. Initial stems in painted initials of Bodley 264, the *Romance of Alexander*,

are decorated with painterly grotesque heads that bear some resemblance to the gorgon heads (figs. 144, 145), but in the *Romance* these heads are singles; none are pairs conjoined by the hallmark extension of the jaw. They are painted with a feathery touch that imparts a ghostly appearance. Another preliminary to the gorgons could be the grotesques with long undershot lower jaws and gaping mouths that are engraved as background decoration on some brasses of Tournai and also in the margins of some manuscripts from that city.[1] The gorgon owes something to a related group of creatures, the very lively, expressive, and fantastic dragons that constitute and interact with initials in northern French and Flemish manuscripts of the second half of the thirteenth century and early fourteenth century, including those of the circle of the Philomena manuscripts and the Marquette Bible of *c.*1270.[2] Some

---

1   See Dennison, "The Artistic Context," p. 8 and pl. VI (D) and the *Voeux*, fols. 27v, 28v, 65v, 80v.

2   Los Angeles, Getty Museum, Ms. Ludwig I 8, v.3 (83.MA.57.3), Lille, Tournai, or Cambrai. See, among many examples of these dragons, those in an Evangeliary, CMM, Ms. 189, of 1266; the Cambrai Pontifical, Toledo, Archivo de la Catedral, Ms. 56.19, of *c.*1275. See Stones, *Gothic Manuscripts*, pt. 1, vol. 2, cat. nr. III-43, pp. 254–257, and pt. 1, vol. 1, figs. 464, 467–471; pt. 1, vol. 2, cat. nr. III-49, pp. 278–285; and pt. 1, vol. 1, figs. 503–505, 507–509. The Cambrai/Arras dragons grow evermore realistic with time. In most manuscripts of the Philomena group the dragons in initials do not intrude dramatically upon the figures or action of the interior. Their lively aggressions are confined to the peripheries of compositions—to initial frames, stems, and tendril extensions; to fellow dragons in initial frames and margins—thus observing a physical and conceptual boundary between initial and contents. The boundary is sometimes breached, as in the Psalter of Guy of Dampierre, KBR Ms. 10607, Flanders, *c.*1278, fol. 189r, in which the dragon, whose body is the tail of the *Q*(*uo*), uses the exigencies of construction to enter the initial and bite the beard of the man whose head is enclosed therein. However, this breach is required by the structure of the *Q*. Expression is subordinate to structure; the dragon obeys a higher authority. Realism of the creatures is enhanced by the sidelong glance of eyes, the skillful modeling of cylindrical torsos with repeated curved lines, and the furry ears, legs and paws, which impart an element of mammalian warmth to the reptilian torsos. The dragon sometimes seems eager to invade the interior and comes within a hairsbreadth of doing so. The interplay of twin and single elements prepares the way for the double-mouthed gorgon. A dragon may have two heads and one body, as in the Marquette Bible, v. 3, fols. 248v, 256v; or it may have two bodies and one head, as in a Bible, MSV, Ms. 561, *c.*1260, fol. 95r. For images, see Ellen J. Beer, "Liller Bibelcodices, Tournai und die Scriptorien der Stadt Arras," *Aachener Kunstblätter* 43 (1972):219, Abb. 19; 213, Abb. 12. See also Getty Museum website for images of the Marquette Bible.

possibilities for use of gorgons were pioneered by the iconography of these dragons. The various interactions of the dragon/gorgon with the elements of the initial frame, and with the figures inside the initial contribute to the broad and deep foundation laid in the thirteenth and fourteenth centuries for the spectacular manipulations of levels of illusion and reality that challenge and broaden meaning in manuscripts of the later fifteenth and early sixteenth centuries in northern Europe.[3] A study of these interactions begs to be written.

In tracing the ancestry of the gorgon motif, Baltrusaitis pointed to English Apocalypses of the thirteenth century in which the Hellmouths were depicted with two or more conjoined mouths.[4] Intra-ostial inhabitants of the gorgons' maws call to mind the damned enclosed in the Hellmouths of English Apocalypses, but the horror of damnation is transmuted in the Rummen manuscripts into a range of less gripping responses: combat in KBR 6426 (fig. 167); mimickry in the Loppem-Bruges antiphonal (fig. 201a), obliviousness in KBR 9217 (fig. 173a). Carlvant speculated that an English Apocalypse of mid-thirteenth-century date may have been available in Ghent during the second half of the century and studied by the artist of the missal for St. Peter's Abbey, of 1275–1285.[5] An illuminated Apocalypse in the heart of Flanders might have been one source for the gorgon motif in the Rummen manuscripts.

The closest parallels to the gorgons in the Rummen-group manuscripts are not predecessors but sequels. These occur in initials of a Parisian Bible of *c.*1350, now in Stockholm, one of the artists of which had connections to Ghent.[6] The gorgon iconography of the Stockholm Bible and its relationship to Ghent is considered in Chapter 8.

---

3   Pictorial innovations that use levels of illusion to challenge boundaries, generate meaning, and prod viewer's awareness are explicated by James H. Marrow in *Pictorial Invention in Netherlandish Manuscript Illumination of the Late Middle Ages: The Play of Illusion and Meaning* (Paris: Uitgeverij Peeters, 2005).

4   *Le Moyen âge fantastique*, 44–45.

5   Carlvant, *Manuscript Painting*, 109–112.

6   National Library of Sweden, Ms. A 165, of *c.*1350. Information provided by Eva Lindqvist Sandgren, "National Library of Sweden, A 165: Preliminary Description," Kungliga Biblioteket, Stockholm, n.d.

APPENDIX 7

The Contents of 10 A 14 and Summary Description of Illumination, by Quire

Quire 1: Ternion
Folios: 1–6
Text: Calendar
Illumination: KL initials, medallions with signs of zodiac and labors of the months; full or nearly full borders.

Quire 2: Quaternion
Folios: 7–14
Text: Proper of Seasons (Temporale):

7ra–8vb:	1st Sunday of Advent: *Ad te levavi animam meam.*
8vb–10va:	2nd Sunday of Advent: *Populus syon ecce dominus veniet ad salvandas gentes.*
10va–11va:	3rd Sunday of Advent: *Gaudete in domino semper.*
11va–12vb:	Wednesday in 3rd week of Advent: *Rorate celi de super.*
12vb–13vb:	Friday in 3rd week of Advent: *Prope esto domine*
13vb–14vb:	Saturday in 3rd week of Advent (through 4th lesson, Isaiah 45:1–8, v. 6): *Veni et ostende nobis faciem tuam domine.*

Artists: Artist 2 responsible for all illumination and penwork.
Major Illumination: Miniatures and/or historiated initials, full or nearly full borders:
Fol. 7ra: Introit for 1st Sunday in Advent: Historiated ten-line initial *A(d te levavi)*: King David, under a double-arched canopy on piers, kneels before altar and lifts his soul to God, framed by gold nimbus. Background is of gold and blue squares with dot-and-line decoration. Letter form is a double-mouth grotesque (gorgon). Gold strip border bar, enclosing confronted grotesques, on four sides, with cusping and paired gold leaves. Gold medallions concealing overpainted heraldry. Birds and butterflies in right margin. Mounted, nude figures in combat below text columns.
Minor illumination: Two-line initials with partial borders on fols. 8v, 10v, 11v, 12v, 13v.

Quire 3: Quaternion
Folios: 15–22
Text: Continuation of Proper of Seasons (Temporale)

15ra–16vb:	Continuation of Saturday in 3rd week of Advent
16vb–17vb:	Sunday, Fourth Week in Advent: *M(emento) nostri domine in beneplacito populi tui*
17vb–19rb:	Christmas Eve: *Hodie scietis quia veniet dominus et salvabit nos.*
19rb–20vb:	First Mass of Christmas Day: *Dominus dixit ad me filius meus es tu.*
20vb–22rb:	Second Mass of Christmas Day: *Lux fulgebit hodie super nos.*
22rb–22vb:	Third Mass of Christmas Day: *Puer natus est nobis* through Epistle, Hebrews 1:1–12, v. 7

Major Illumination. Miniatures and/or historiated initials, full or nearly full borders:
Fol. 22r: Introit for Third Mass of Christmas Day (Nativity): Nine-line miniature of the Nativity with reclining Virgin, seated Joseph, ox and ass, and nude child in manger in an open stable with thatched roof. Background is patterned similarly to that of the *A(d te levavi)*, fol. 7r. Zoomorphic initial *P(uer)* and full borders consisting of gold strips flanking and between text columns. Urns held by angels sprout baguettes from which grow lancet leaves and Italianate feathery foliage. Overpainted heraldry in corners and on intercolumnial border strip.
Minor illumination: Two-line initial with extensions or partial borders on fols. 16v, 17v, 19r, 20v.

Quire 4: Quaternion
Folios: 23–30
Text: Continuation of Proper of Seasons (Temporale). Quire 4 begins with continuation of the Epistle for Third Mass of Christmas Day and ends with the Epistle of the First Sunday after the Octave of Epiphany.

23ra–23vb:	Continuation of Third Mass of Christmas Day
23vb–24vb:	Sunday within the Octave of Christmas: *Dum medium silentium tenerit omnia.*
24vb–25vb:	Last Ferial Day within the Octave of Christmas: *Dominus dixit ad me.*
26ra–26vb:	Circumcision (Octave of Christmas): *Puer natus est nobis.*
26vb–27vb:	Vigil of Epiphany: *Lux fulgebit hodie super nos.*
27vb–29va:	Epiphany: *Ecce advenit dominator dominus.*

29va–30va: Octave of Epiphany: *Ecce advenit dominator dominus.*

30va,b: First Sunday after Octave of Epiphany: *In excellso* (sic) *throno vidi sedere virum* through Epistle, Romans 12:1–5, v. 5

Major illumination: Miniatures and/or historiated initials, full or nearly full borders:

Fol. 26r: Introit for the Circumcision of Christ: Historiated eight-line zoomorphic initial *P(uer)*, in gold. Under a vaulted architectural canopy, nude Christ child, Mary, mohel and attendants. Background of gold and colored squares. Pronounced break in the work at the junction of bowl and descender of the initial *P*. Borders on four sides in short, curved segments consisting of gold strips with cusping, feathery foliage, and trilobes. Pairs of grotesques, with human heads and upper bodies in various activities. Gold, orange, pink, and blue predominate throughout. Two graphite sketches of partial figures in style of 1340s in the left margin. Hairstyle, lines of garments, and stance of drawn figures suggest the 1340s.

Fol. 27v: Introit for Epiphany: Miniature of Adoration of the Magi, ten lines. Subjoined initial *E(cce)* at left. Borders on four sides and in intercolumniation. Seated virgin holds nude Christ child on her lap. The three Magi present their gifts. Background of blue squares outlined in red, with gold detailing. Scene is framed by a vaulted architectural canopy with gables, piers, pinnacles. Donors in garments in style of the 1350s and 1360s kneel in small, open chapels flanking the main scene. Subjoined zoomorphic initial in form of winged grotesque in pink and blue, with foliate vine filler. Diapered background of gold squares, inscribed. Below initial two lions face each other across the text block. Both carry swords, wear helmets that are now overpainted, and support shields, also now overpainted.

A slender gold border bar frames much of the text and intercolumniation. Bar is populated with anthropomorphic and animal grotesques and music-making angels framed by feathery foliage, painted in pink, orange and blue. Angels are framed by pairs of symmetrical foliate plumes. Palette is dominated by pink, blue and gold, with some orange, white, and gray.

Minor illumination: Two-line initials with extensions and/or partial borders on fols. 23v, 24v, 26v, 29v, 30.

Quire 5: Quaternion
Folios: 31–38
Text: Continuation of Proper of Seasons (Temporale). Quire begins with the continuation of the Epistle for the First Sunday after Octave of the Epiphany and ends with the Epistle for Sexagesima Sunday.

31ra–32ra: Continuation of First Sunday after the Octave of Epiphany

32rb–34rb: Second Sunday after Epiphany: *Omnis terra adoret te deus*

34rb–36rb: Third Sunday after Epiphany: *Adorate deum omnes angeli eius.*

36rb–38va: Septuagesima Sunday: *Circumdederunt me gemitus mortis.*

38va, b: Sexagesima Sunday: *Exurge ob dormis domine.*

Major illumination: Miniatures and/or historiated initials, full or nearly full borders: None.

Minor illumination: Two-line initials with extensions and/or partial borders on fols. 32r, 34v. 36r, 38v.

Quire 6: Quaternion
Folios: 39–46
Text: Continuation of Proper of Seasons (Temporale). Quire begins with continuation of the Epistle for Sexagesima Sunday and ends with Communion prayer for Ash Wednesday.

39ra–40va: Continuation of for Sexagesima Sunday

40va–41vb: Epistle and Gospel for Wednesday, Sexagesima: Epistle: Hebrews 12:3–9, v. 3: *Recogitate dominum ihesum christum qualem sustinuit.*

41rb–41vb: Gospel for Friday of Sexagesima: Luke 17:20–37, v. 7: *Interrogatus ihesus a phariseis.*

41vb–43rb: Quinquagesima Sunday: *Esto michi in deum protectorem.*

43rb–44vb: Blessing and Imposition of Ashes on Ash Wednesday: *Exaudi quesumus domine supplicum preces*

44vb–46ra: Ash Wednesday: *Misereris omnium domine*

46ra–46vb: Thursday after Ash Wednesday: *Dum clamarem ad dominum.*

Major illumination: Miniatures and/or historiated initials, full or nearly full borders: None.

Minor illumination: Two-line initials with extensions and/or partial borders on fols. 40v, 41v, 43r, 44v

Quire 7: Quaternion
Folios: 47–54
Text: Continuation of Proper of Seasons (Temporale). Quire begins with continuation of Gospel for Thursday after Ash Wednesday and ends with the Versicle to the Tract for Wednesday in the First Week of Lent.

47ra,b: Continuation of Thursday after Ash Wednesday.

THE CONTENTS OF 10 A 14 AND SUMMARY DESCRIPTION OF ILLUMINATION, BY QUIRE 121

47rb–48va: Friday after Ash Wednesday: *Audivit dominus et misertus est michi.*

48vb–49vb: Saturday after Ash Wenesday: *Audivit dominus et misertus est michi.*

49vb–51va: First Sunday of Lent: *Invocavit* [sic] *me et ego exaudiam eum.*

51va–53ra: Monday, First Week of Lent: *Sicut oculi servorum in manibus dominorum suorum.*

53ra–54ra: Tuesday, First Week of Lent: *Domine refugium factus es nobis a generatione et progenie.*

54ra–54vb: Wednesday, First Week of Lent: *Reminiscere miserationum tuarum domine.*

Major illumination: Miniatures and/or historiated initials, full or nearly full borders: None.

Minor illumination: Two-line initials with extensions and/or partial borders on fols. 47r, 48v, 49v, 51v, 53r, 54r.

Quire 8: Quaternion

Folios: 55–62

Text: Continuation of Proper of Seasons (Temporale) from Versicle to the Tract for Wednesday, First Week of Lent to the end of the Offertory for the Second Sunday of Lent.

55vra: Continuation of Wednesday, First Week of Lent.

55va–57rb: Thursday, First Week of Lent: *Confessio et pulchritudo in conspectu eius.*

57b–58v: Friday, First Week of Lent: *De necessitatibus meis eripe me, domine.*

58vb–61vb: Saturday, Second Week of Lent: *Intret oratio mea in conspectus tuo.*

61vb–62vb: Third Sunday of Lent: *Reminiscere miserationum tuarum domine.*

Major illumination: Miniatures and/or historiated initials, full or nearly full borders: None.

Minor illumination: Two-line initials with extensions and/or partial borders on fols. 55v, 57r, 58v, 61v.

Quire 9: Quaternion

Folios: 63–70

Text: Continuation of Proper of Seasons (Temporale) from the Secret for the Second Sunday of Lent to the Lesson for Third Sunday of Lent.

63ra: Continuation of Second Sunday of Lent.

63ra–64rb: Monday, Second Week of Lent: *Redime me domine.*

64rb–65va: Tuesday, Second Week of Lent: *Tibi dixit cor meum quaesivi vultum tuum.*

65va–66va: Wednesday, Second Week of Lent: *Ne delinquas me domine deus meus.*

66va–68ra: Thursday, Second Week of Lent: *Deus in adiutorium meum intende.*

68ra–69vb: Friday, Second Week of Lent: *Ego autem cum iusticia apparebo*

69vb–70vb: Saturday, Second Week of Lent: *Lex domini irreprehensibilis convertens animas.*

Major illumination: Miniatures and/or historiated initials, full or nearly full borders: None.

Minor illumination: Two-line initials of Types 1, 2, or 3, with extensions and/or partial borders on fols. 63r, 64r, 65v, 66v, 68r, 69v.

Quire 10: Quaternion

Folios: 71–78

Text: Continuation of Proper of Seasons (Temporale) from Lesson for Saturday, Second Week in Lent to Postcommunion for Friday, Third Week of Lent.

72va: Introit for Third Sunday of Lent: *Oculi mei semper ad dominum.*

73vb: Introit for Monday, Third Week of Lent. *In deo laudabo verbum.*

75rb: Introit for Tuesday, Third Week of Lent. *Ego clamavi quoniam exaudisti me Deus.*

76va: Introit for Wednesday, Third Week of Lent. *Ego autem in domino speravi.*

78ra: Introit for Thursday, Third Week of Lent. *Salus populi ego sum dicit dominus.*

Major illumination: Miniatures and/or historiated initials, full or nearly full borders: None.

Minor illumination: Two-line initials with extensions and/or partial borders on fols. 72v, 73v, 75r, 76v, 78r.

Quire 11: Quaternion

Folios: 79–86

Text: Continuation of Proper of Seasons (Temporale) from Postcommunion for Thursday, Third Week of Lent to second Postcommunion for Monday, Fourth Week of Lent.

79ra: Introit for Friday, Third Week of Lent: *Fac mecum domine signum in bono.*

81rb: Introit for Saturday, Third Week of Lent: *Verba mea auribus percipe domine.*

84ra: Introit for Fourth Sunday of Lent: *Laetare iherusalem.*

85va: Introit for Monday, Fourth Week of Lent: *Deus in nomine tuo salvum me fac.*

Major illumination: Miniatures and/or historiated initials, full or nearly full borders: None.

Minor illumination: Two-line initials with extensions and/or partial borders on fols 79r, 81r.

Appendix 7

Quire 12: Quaternion
Folios: 87–94
Text: Continuation of Proper of Seasons (Temporale) from second Postcommunion for Monday, Fourth Week of Lent, to Lesson for Saturday, Fourth Week of Lent.

87ra:	Tuesday, Fourth Week of Lent: *Exaudi deus orationem meam.*
88rb:	Wednesday, Fourth Week of Lent: *Dum sanctificatus fuero in vobis.*
90vb:	Thursday, Fourth Week of Lent: *Letetur cor querentium dominum.*
92rb:	Friday, Fourth Week of Lent: *Meditatio cordis mei in conspectu tuo.*
94va:	Saturday, Fourth Week of Lent: *Sitientes venite ad aquas dicit dominus.*

Major illumination: Miniatures and/or historiated initials, full or nearly full borders: None.
Minor illumination: Two-line initials with extensions and/or partial borders on fols. 87r, 88r, 90v, 92r, 94v.

Quire 13: Quaternion
Folios: 95–102
Text: Continuation of Proper of Seasons (Temporale) from Saturday, Fourth Week of Lent, to Friday, Fifth Week of Lent.

95va:	Fifth Sunday of Lent: *Iudica me deus.*
96vb:	Monday, Fifth Week of Lent: *Miserere michi domine.*
98ra:	Tuesday, Fifth Week of Lent: *Expecta dominum viriliter age.*
99va:	Wednesday, Fifth Week of Lent: *Liberator meus de gentibus iracundis.*
100vb:	Thursday, Fifth Week of Lent: *Omnia que fecisti nobis domine.*
102ra:	Friday, Fifth Week of Lent: *Miserere michi domine.*

Major illumination: Miniatures and/or historiated initials, full or nearly full borders: None.
Minor illumination: Two-line initials with extensions and/or partial borders on fols. 95v, 96v, 98r, 99v, 100v, 102r.

Quire 14: Quaternion
Folios: 103–110
Text: Continuation of Proper of Seasons, from Friday, Fifth Week of Lent to Palm Sunday.

103ra:	Saturday, Fifth Week of Lent. *Miserere michi domine quoniam tribulor.*
106ra:	Palm Sunday. *Domine ne longe facias auxilium tuum a me.*

Major illumination: Miniatures and/or historiated initials, full or nearly full borders:
Fol. 106v: Introit for Palm Sunday. Miniature, historiated initial, and full borders. Four-line miniature that extends into the top border, with subjoined three-line initial *D(omine)*. Nearly full borders and animal vignettes in bas-de-page and upper margin. Intercolumniation and right border consist of stalks of giant columbines in style of 1340s–1350s. Left border and border below left text block consist of a strip with colored segments, gold balls, and attached penwork trilobes in the style of the 1360s.
Minor illumination: Two-line initials with extensions and/or partial borders on fol. 103r.

Quire 15: Quaternion
Folios: 111–118
Text: Continuation of Proper of Seasons from Palm Sunday to Tuesday in Holy Week.

112vb:	Monday in Holy Week. *Iudica domine nocentes me.*
114vb:	Tuesday in Holy Week. *Nos autem gloriari oportet in cruce domini nostri Jesu Christi.*

Major illumination: Miniatures and/or historiated initials, full or nearly full borders: None.
Minor illumination: Two-line initials with extensions and/or partial borders on fols. 112v, 114v.

Quire 16: Quaternion
Folios: 119–126
Text: Continuation of Proper of Seasons, from Tuesday in Holy Week to Maundy Thursday.

119vb:	Wednesday in Holy Week
126ra:	Maundy Thursday

Major illumination: Miniatures and/or historiated initials, full or nearly full borders: None.
Minor illumination: Two-line initials with extensions and/or partial borders on fols. 119v, 126r.

Quire 17: Quaternion
Folios: 127–134
Text: Continuation of Proper of Seasons from Maundy Thursday to Good Friday.

128vb:	First Lesson for Good Friday. *Hec dicit dominus deus.*

Major illumination: Miniatures and/or historiated initials, full or nearly full borders: None.
Minor illumination: Two-line initials with extensions and/or partial borders on fol. 128v.

THE CONTENTS OF 10 A 14 AND SUMMARY DESCRIPTION OF ILLUMINATION, BY QUIRE 123

Quire 18: Two bifolia
Folios: 135–138
Text: Continuation of Proper of Seasons: Liturgy for Good Friday. Preparatory prayers. Ordinary of the Mass: Gloria, Creed.

135r:	Collect for Jews, Collect for pagans, Reproaches.
135v:	Reproaches, Veneration of the Cross, *Pange lingua.*
136r:	Devotion of the Cross. Preparatory prayers and psalms.
136v:	Priest's prayer for himself, prayer as he washes his hands, prayers over the liturgical vestments.
137r:	Prayers at the altar, Blessing of the incense before the Gospel.
137v:	Continuation of Blessing of incense (?), blessing over the Lector (*Benedictio super dixitur*), Prayer during the burning of incense.
138r:	Continuation of the prayer during burning of incense, Blessing of the Deacon, the Gloria, the Creed.
138v:	Conclusion of the Creed.

Major illumination: Miniatures and/or historiated initials, full or nearly full borders: None.
Minor illumination: Two-line initials with extensions and/or partial borders: None.

Quire 19: Quaternion
Folios: 139–146
Text: Ordinary of the Mass: Prefaces, prayers

139r:	Preface for Easter Sunday
139v:	Continuation of Preface for Easter Sunday, Preface for the Nativity
140r:	Continuation of Preface for the Nativity, Preface for Epiphany, Preface for Lent
140v:	Continuation of Preface for Lent, Preface of the Holy Cross, Preface of the Apostles
141r:	Continuation of Preface of the Apostles, Preface of the Blessed Virgin Mary
141v:	Continuation of Preface of the Blessed Virgin Mary, Preface of the Holy Trinity
142r:	Continuation of Preface of the Holy Trinity, Preface for weekdays
142v:	Continuation of Preface for weekdays
143r:	Blank
143v:	Full-page miniature of the Crucifixion
144r:	Canon of the Mass begins: *Te igitur,* Commemoration of the Living

144v:	Continuation of Commemoration of the Living, *Communicantes*
145r:	Continuation of *Communicantes, Hanc igitur, Quam oblationem, Qui pridie*
145v:	Continuation of *Qui pridie,* Consecration of bread, Consecration of wine
146r:	Continuation of Consecration of wine, *Unde et memores, Supra quae*
146v:	Continuation of *Supra quae,* Commemoration of the Dead, *Nobis quoque*

Major illumination: Miniatures and/or historiated initials, full or nearly full borders:

Fol. 139r: Preface for Easter Sunday. Miniature, initial, and full border. Miniature the height of two staves of music, plus text line below. Miniature extends into the top margin. Adjoined to the miniature along its right edge is a decorated initial the height of two staves, text line for each staff, plus one additional line of music. Miniature depicts priest standing at the altar with service book, chalice, and host. Donor and wife kneel behind priest. The priest stands under a vaulted, arched architectural canopy on piers crowned with gables and pinnacles. Donors kneel in a smaller arched compartment. Background is gold incised with diapering. Palette is dominated by blue, orange, and dusty pink.

Fol. 143v: Crucifixion. Full-page illumination, paired with the facing *Te igitur* miniature and initial. The oversized dead, crucified Christ, is pocked with bright red scourge wounds. Beneath the cross, Mary, swooning in a hipshot pose, is supported by John. A small female donor figure in dress of *c*.1350 kneels at the foot of the Cross on the side opposite. Traces of a second figure, originally kneeling in front of her, and of overpainted arms above her, are discernible. Background is patterned with multicolored squares framed in a grid of gold lines. The scene is staged on a platform with a central projection. Sturdy, storied piers with arched niches occupied by angels support a vaulted, arched superstructure fronted by a parapet behind which three heads are visible. Sun and moon are beneath the vault. An orange panel decorated with gold trilobes frames the scene. Palette of red, blue, white, beige.

Fol. 144r: Canon of the Mass: *Te igitur.* Miniature, zoomorphic initial, border on three sides, animal vignettes in lower margin. Six-line miniature extends into the upper margin, depicts a priest and acolyte praying at an altar with service book, chalice, and host. Framing architecture is a less substantial version of that on the page facing. The background is patterned with inscribed multicolored squares. The format and decoration of the panel framing the miniature resemble those of the page facing.

The text is framed by a combination of penwork and painted borders, the latter with large fronds of feathery foliage which enclose crowned heads at their lower terminuses. In the bas-de-page, grisaille vignettes with trees, boars, and hares. Orange, blue, beige and gray dominate the palette; penwork borders are red and blue. Decoration is not unified in design but is all of the first campaign, 1340s–1350s.

Minor illumination: Two-line initials with extensions and/or partial borders: None.

Quire 20: Two bifolia
Folios: 147–150
Text: Continuation of Canon and Postcommunion prayers

147r:	*Nobis quoque* continues; *Per quem*
147v:	*Pater noster* (with musical notation)
148r:	*Libera nos, Agnus dei*
148v:	Kiss of peace, *Perceptio corporis* (priest's prayer before his Communion)
149r:	Priest's prayers at his Communion; Prayers at the Communion of the Faithful
149v:	Continuation of prayers at the Communion of the Faithful; Postcommunion prayers
150r:	Postcommunion prayers, Psalm verses

Major illumination: Miniatures and/or historiated initials, full or nearly full borders: None.

Minor illumination: Two-line initials with extensions and/or partial borders: None.

Quire 21: Quaternion
Folios: 151–158
Text: Proper of Saints (Sanctorale): St. Lucy (fol. 151ra), St. Thomas the Apostle (fol. 152ra), St. Stephen (fol. 152vb), St. John the Evangelist (153vb), Holy Innocents (154vb), Pope St. Sylvester (fol. 155vb), St. Genovese (fol. 156va), St. Felix (fol. 156vb), St. Marcellus (fol. 157vb), St. Prisca (fol. 158vb).

Major illumination: Miniatures and/or historiated initials, full or nearly full borders:
Fol. 151ra: Beginning of Proper of Saints (Sanctorale). Introit for St. Lucy. Ten-line historiated initial and borders on three sides of page. Ten-line initial *D(ilexisti)*, in the form of a tendril with strapwork passages, filigree decoration, and maple leaves depicts the unusual subject of St. Lucy and Eutychia at prayer before the tomb of St. Agatha, who is partially visible in a sarcophagus, resting on grass. Two scrolls have inscriptions difficult to read. An architecture of delicate vaults and arches on spindly piers and columns, crowned by turrets and domes, serves as a backdrop to the scene. Initial is framed in gold with

gold-on-red grotesques in two corners. Border bar consists of tendril paired with short, variously colored segments with filigree decoration, knotwork between segments, all outlined in gold. Various foliate elements including trilobes, maple leaves, and the "flame motif." (See index.) Orange, blue, beige, gray and gold dominate the palette. A vignette of apes is in the bas-de-page.

Minor illumination: Two-line initials with extensions and/or partial borders: None.

Quire 22: Quaternion
Folios: 159–166
Text: Continuation of Proper of Saints (Sanctorale): Continuation of St. Prisca (fol. 158v), Sts. Mary and Martha (fol. 159vb), Sts. Fabian and Sebastian (fol. 160ra), St. Agnes (fol. 161r), St. Vincent (fol. 162v), Sts. Emerentiana and Macharius (fol. 163r), Conversion of St. Paul (fol. 163r), Octave of St. Agnes (, fol. 165ra), Blessing of Candles for Feast of the Purification of the Virgin (fol. 166r).

Major illumination: Miniatures and/or historiated initials, full or nearly full borders: None.

Minor illumination: Two-line initials with extensions and/or partial borders: None.

Quire 23: Quaternion
Folios: 167–174
Text: Continuation of Proper of Saints (Sanctorale): Continuation of Blessing of Candles for the Feast of the Purification of the Virgin (fol. 167ra), Feast of the Purification of the Virgin (fol. 167rb), St. Agatha (fol. 168vb), Sts. Zoticus, Irenaeus, and Iacinctus (fol. 170ra), St. Soteris (fol. 170ra), St. Scholastica (fol. 170ra), Sts. Valentinus, Vitalis, Felicula, and Zenonis (fol. 170va,b), St. Juliana (fol. 171va), Chair of St. Peter (fol. 171vb), St. Mathias (fol. 173ra), Sts. Perpetua and Felicity (174rb), Pope St. Gregory (174va).

Major illumination: Miniatures and/or historiated initials, full or nearly full borders:
Fol. 167rb: Introit for Feast of the Purification of the Virgin. Initial, border bar on three sides and in the intracolumnar margin, tendril extensions across most of the top margin. Eight-line pink zoomorphic initial *S(uscepimus)* on rectangular gold and blue panel. Zoomorph has a long beak, a fringed crest; abdomen widens into a double-headed, open-mouthed gorgon with tusks. Mary presents the standing Christ child on the altar to Simeon, at the right of the altar. His draped arms are extended to receive the child. Joseph, behind Mary, holds a candle and a basket with two doves. The lion of Flanders decorates two panels that hang from the altar. A delicate, scalloped architectural canopy supported on spindly columns surmounts

the scene. The background is gold scored with diapering. A border framing three sides and the intercolumniation resembles that on fol. 151r. A vignette of an ape and a goose is in the bas-de-page. Palette is blue, orange, gray, and gold, with some red.

Minor illumination: Two-line initials with extensions and/or partial borders: None.

Quire 24: Quaternion
Folios: 175–182
Text: Continuation of Proper of Saints (Sanctorale); Common of Saints (Temporale). Continuation of Pope St. Gregory (fol. 175ra), St. Benedict (fol. 175va), Annunciation to the Virgin Mary (fol. 176va), Pope St. Leo (fol. 177vb), St. Euphemia (fol. 178ra). Common of Saints: Vigil of an Apostle (fol. 178rb), Feast of an Apostle (fol. 179ra), Vigil of a Martyr (fol. 180ra), Feast (*natale*) of a Martyr Pope (fol. 180vb), Feast (*natale*) of a Martyr (fol. 181vb), Vigil of two or more Martyrs (fol. 182vb).

Major illumination: Miniatures and/or historiated initials, full or nearly full borders: None.

Minor illumination: Two-line initials with extensions and/or partial borders: None.

Quire 25: Quaternion
Folios: 183–190
Text: Continuation of Common of Saints (Temporale). Common of two or more Martyrs (fol. 183vb), Vigil of a Confessor-Pope (fol. 185ra), Common of a Confessor (fol. 186ra), Vigil of two or more Confessors (fol. 187rb), Vigil of a Virgin (fol. 189rb).

Major illumination: Miniatures and/or historiated initials, full or nearly full borders:

Fol. 176va: Eight-line historiated initial *R(orate)* depicting the Annunciation, enclosed in square panel; borders on three sides of page. Initial features three gorgons, each with a pair of confronted, open-mouthed heads and jaws connected by strapwork or loops. Inside the initial, Mary stands, one hand over her heart, the other holding a book, and turns toward, Gabriel, kneeling at left. He holds a scroll inscribed "*AVE .GRATIA.*" Drawing and coloring are confused around his upper body and head. On the grass between the two figures is a vase from which spring three white shoots. The background within the initial is mostly diapered, colored in red, blue, and gold, and inscribed with a geometric pattern. In the panel enclosing the initial, the background is a variation on this pattern. An architectural canopy similar to that on fol. 167r rises over

the two figures; the treatment of the border bar is like that on fols. 151r and 167r. In the bas-de-page is a vignette of a seagull and a squirrel. The palette is the same as that in the two preceding miniatures.

Minor illumination: Two-line initials with extensions and/or partial borders: None.

Quire 26: Quaternion
Folios: 191–198
Text: Continuation of Common of Saints; Various Masses. Common of two or more Virgins (fol. 191rb); Dedication of a Church (fol. 192va); Dedication of an Altar (fol. 193bv); Saint buried in the Church (fol. 194ra); Feria ii: Vigil of Angels (fol. 195ra), Feria iii: For the Remission of Sins (*Missa de pecc[at]is*, fol. 195vb), Feria iv: For Wisdom (fol. 196va), Feria v: For Charity (*Missa de carite*, fol. 197rb); Feria vi: The Holy Cross (fol. 198ra); The Blessed Virgin Mary (fol. 198vb).

Major illumination: Miniatures and/or historiated initials, full or nearly full borders:

Fol. 192va: Introit for Dedication of a Church. Historiated ten-line initial and nearly full border, framed by a rectangular panel. Initial consists of a winged, gaping-mouth dragon and a double-mouth gorgon with baguette-like body that widens to jaws joined by knotwork. The scene enclosed by the initial depicts a mitred bishop with crozier, asperging a small church. He is accompanied by an acolyte with situla and cross. Both stand on the grass. The background is similar to that in the Annunciation, fol. 176v. Borders are constructed and decorated much as in the illuminations on fols. 151r, 167r, and 176v.

Minor illumination: Two-line initials with extensions and/or partial borders: None.

Quire 27: Ternion
Folios: 199–204
Text: Continuation of Various Masses. Colophons: For all Ecclesiastical Ranks (fol. 199va), for the Catholic People (fol. 200ra), for Brothers and Sisters (fol. 200rb), for Benefactors (fol. 200va), for the Dead(?) (*Missa generalis*, fol. 200va), for Parents (fol. 202ra), for a Woman (fol. 202rb), for a Servant (fol. 202va), On the Anniversary (of a death, fol. 202va), for Brothers and Sisters (fol. 202vb), for the Dead(?) (*Generalis*, fol. 203ra). Colophons (fol. 204r).

Major illumination: Miniatures and/or historiated initials, full or nearly full borders: None.

Minor illumination: Two-line initials with extensions and/or partial borders: None.

Inventories

Inventory 1: Flourishing by Quire and Artist

Quire 1, fols. 1–6   illuminated calendar, no flourishing

Quire 2, fols. 7–14   Artist 2

Quire 3, fols. 15–22

15r&v:	Artist 3
16r&v:	Artist 2
17r&v	Artist 4
18r&v	Artist 4
19r&v	Artist 4
20r&v:	Artist 4
21r&v:	Artist 2
22r:	very little flourishing, major illumination by Artist 3
22v:	Artist 3

Quire 4, fols. 23–30

23r&v	Artist 4; flourishing in dark red in top margin by Artist 2
24r&v	Artist 4
25r&v:	Artist 4
26r&v	Artist 3
27r:	Artist 3
27v	no flourishing, major illumination by Artist 3
28r&v	Artist 4
29r&v	Artist 4
30r&v:	Artist 4

Quire 5, fols. 31–38

31r&v	Artist 4
32r&v	Artist 4
33r&33v	Artist 4
34r&v	Artist 2
35r&v	Artist 2
36r&v	Artist 4
37r	no flourishing
37v	Artist 4
38r&38v	Artist 4

Quire 6, fols. 39–46

39r&v	Artist 2
40r&v	Artist 2
41r	Artist 4
41v	no flourishing, minor illumination by Artist 4
42r&v	Artist 4
43r&v	Artist 4
44r&v	Artist 4
45r&v	Artist 2
46r&v	Artist 2

INVENTORIES

Quire 7, fols. 47–54

	47r	Artist 2
	47v	no flourishing
	48r&v	Artist 2
	49r&v	Artist 2
	50r&v	Artist 2
	51r&v	Artist 2
	52r&v	Artist 2
	53r&v	Artist 2
	54r&v	Artist 2

Quire 8, fols. 55–62

	55r&v	Artist 2
	56v	no flourishing
	57r&v	Artist 2
	58r&v	Artist 2
	59r&v	Artist 2
	60r&v	Artist 2
	61r&v	Artist 2
	61r&62v	Artist 2

Quire 9, fols. 63–70

	63r&v	Artist 4
	64r&v	Artist 4
	65r&v	Artist 4
	66r&v	Artist 4
	67r&v	Artist 4
	68r	Artist 4
	68v	no flourishing
	69r&v	Artist 4
	70r	Artist 4
	70v	no flourishing

Quire 10, fols. 71–78

	71r	Artist 2
	71v	no flourishing
	72r&v	Artist 2
	73r&v	Artist 2
	74r&v	Artist 2
	75r&v	Artist 2
	76r&v	Artist 2
	77r&v	Artist 2
	78r&v	Artist 2

Quire 11, fols. 79–86

	79r&v	Artist 2
	80r&v	no flourishing
	81r	Artist 2
	81v–83r	no flourishing
	83v	Artist 2
	84r&v	Artist 2

85r&v	Artist 2
86r&v	Artist 2

Quire 12, fols. 87–94

87r&v	Artist 2
88r&v	Artist 2
89r	Artist 2
89v–90r	no flourishing
90v	Artist 2
91r	no Flourishing
91v–92v	Artist 2
93r&v	no flourishing
94r&v	Artist 2

Quire 13, fols. 95–102

95r&v	Artist 2
96r&v	Artist 2
97r&v	Artist 2
98r&v	Artist 2
99r&v	Artist 2
100r&v	Artist 2
101r&v	Artist 2
102r&v	Artist 2

Quire 14, fols. 103–110

103r&v	Artist 2
104r&v	Artist 3
105r&v	Artist 3
106r	Artist 3
106v	Artist 3, major illumination by Artist 2
107r&v	Artist 3
108r–110v	no flourishing

Quire 15, fols. 111–118

111r&v	no flourishing
112r&v	Artist 1
113r	Artist 2
113v, 114r	no flourishing
114v	Artist 2, minor illumination by Artist 1
115r	Artist 2
115v–118v	no flourishing

Quire 16, fols. 119–126

119r	Artist 2
119v	Artist 2, minor illumination by Artist 1
120r	Artist 2
120v	no flourishing
121r	Artist 1
121v–125r	no flourishing
125v	Artist 2
126r	Artist 2, minor illumination by Artist 1
126v	Artist 2

INVENTORIES

Quire 17, fols. 127–134

127r&v	Artist 2
128r	Artist 2
128v	Artist 2, minor illumination by Artist 1
129r&v	Artist 2
130r	Artist 1
130v–132v	no flourishing
133r&v	Artist 2
134r&v	Artist 2

Quire 18, fols. 135–138

135r&v	Artist 2
136r&v	Artist 1
137r&v	Artist 1
138r	Artist 2
138v	no flourishing

Quire 19, fols. 139–146

139r	Artist 2; major illumination by Artist 1
139v	Artist 2
140r&v	Artist 2
141r&v	Artist 2
142r	Artist 2
142v	no flourishing
143r	blank
143v	full-page Crucifixion, no flourishing
144r	Artist 1; major illumination by Artist 1
144v	Artist 2
145r&v	Artist 2
146r&v	Artist 2

Quire 20, fols. 147–150

147r&v	Artist 2
148r&v	Artist 2
149r&v	Artist 2
150r	Artist 2
150v	blank

Quire 21, fols. 151–158

151r–158v	Artist 1

Quire 22, fols. 159–166

159r–163v	Artist 1
164r	no flourishing
164v–166v	Artist 1

Quire 23, fols. 167–174

167r	no flourishing, major illumination by Artist 1
167v–174v	Artist 1

Quire 24, fols. 175–182

175r–176r	Artist 1
176v	Artist 1, major illumination by Artist 1

Quire 25, fols. 183–190   Artist 1

Quire 26, fols. 191–198   Artist 1

Quire 27, fols. 199–204

199r&v	Artist 2
200r&v	Artist 2
201r&v	Artist 2
202r&v	Artist 2
203r&v	Artist 2
204r	Artist 1, Artist 4?
204v	blank

Inventory 2: Penwork Border Bars of Types 1–4 by Quire and Artist

Type 1:	scalloped segments
Type 2:	feathered segments
Type 3:	sequence of small, identical elements defined by line, producing openwork effect
Type 4:	solid ribbon strip

Type 1 border bars by Artist 4 often change, for a width of about two to four lines at the top of the text column, to pearl strings which are categorizable as Type 3. These are not in the inventory if they do not constitute a substantial proportion of the overall length of the bar.

	Folio	Type of Bar	Artist	Notes
Quire 1	1–6	none		Illuminated calendar, no flourishing
Quire 2	7r	3	2	
	7v, 8r	1	2	
	8v	none		Type 2 bar by Artist 2 in terminal complex only
	9r	1	2	
	9v	2	2	
	10r	1	2	
	10v	2	2	
	11r	1, 2	2	
	11v	1	2	
	12r	2, 3	2	
	12v	1	2	
	13r	1, 2	2	
	13v	2	2	
	14r	1	2	
	14v	1, 2	2	

Quire 3	15r&v	4	3	
	16r&v	1	2	
	17r–18v	1	4	
	19r	none		Type 3 bar by Artist 4 in terminal complex only
	19v–20v	1	4	
	21r	1	2	
	21v	1, 2	2	
	22r	none		
	22v	4	3	
Quire 4	23r–24r	1	4	
	24v	1, 3	4	
	25r&v	1	4	
	26r	3	3	
	26v, 27r	3, 4	3	Ribbon strip decorated with zigzag line and circles.
	27v	none		
	28r–29v	1	4	
	30r	1, 3	4	
	30v	1	4	
Quire 5	31r–33v	1	4	
	34r–35v	1	2	
	36r&v	1	4	
	37r	none		
	37v	1, 3	4	
	38r&v	1	4	
Quire 6	39r	2	2	
	39v	1	2	
	40r&v	3, 4	2	
	41r	1	4	
	41v	none		
	42r–44v	1	4	
	45r&v	3	2	
	46r&v	1	2	
Quire 7	47r	3	2	
	47v	none		
	48r&v	3	2	
	49r	2	2	
	49v, 50r	1	2	
	50v	1, 2	2	
	51r&v	1	2	
	52r	2	2	
	52v	1	2	
	53r–54v	3	2	
Quire 8	55r	2	2	
	55v	1	2	
	56r	1, 2	2	

	56v	none		
	57r	3	2	
	57v–59r	3	2	
	59v	?	2	
	60r	3, 4	2	
	60v	3	2	
	61r–62r	1	2	
	62v	2	2	
Quire 9	63r	1, 2, 4	4	Only use of Type 4 by Artist 4 in 10 A 14 is here.
	63v–68r	1	4	
	68v	none		
	69r–70r	1	4	
	70v	none		
Quire 10	71r	4	2	
	71v	none		
	72r–78v	4	2	
Quire 11	79r&v	4	2	
	80r&v	none		
	81r	4	2	
	81v–83r	none		
	83v, 84r	4	2	
	84v	1	2	
	85r–86v	4	2	
Quire 12	87r	4	2	
	87v	1, 4	2	
	88r–89r	4	2	
	89v, 90r	none		
	90v	4	2	
	91r	none		
	91v–92v	4	2	
	93r&v	none		
	94r&v	1, 4	2	
Quire 13	95r	4	2	
	95v	1	2	
	96r	4	2	
	96v	1	2	
	97r–99r	4	2	
	99v	1, 4	2	
	100r–102v	4	2	
Quire 14	103r&v	4	2	
	104r–107v	4	3	
	108r–110v	none		

INVENTORIES

Quire 15	111r&v	none		
	112r&v	1	1	
	113r	4	2	
	113v, 114r	none		
	114v, 115r	4	2	114v: Painted initial, partial border by Artist 1
	115v–118v	none		
Quire 16	119r–120r	4	2	119v: Painted initial, extension by Artist 1
	120v	none		
	121r	1	1	
	121v–125r	none		
	125v–126v	4	2	126r: Painted initial, extension by Artist 1
Quire 17	127r–129v	4	2	128v: Painted initial, partial border by Artist 1
	130r	1	1	
	130v–132v	none		
	133r–134v	4	2	
Quire 18	135r&v	4	2	
	136r–137v	1	1	
	138r	4	2	
	138v	none		
Quire 19	139r–142r	4	2	139r: Miniature, painted initial, full border by Artist 1
	142v–143v	none		
	144r	1	1	
	144v–146v	4	2	
Quire 20	147r–150r	4	2	
	150v	none		
Quire 21	151r–158v	1	1	
Quire 22	159r–163v	1	1	
	164r	none		
	164v–166v	1	1	
Quire 23	167r	none		
	167v–174v	1	1	
Quire 24	175r–182v	1	1	
Quire 25	183r–190v	1	1	
Quire 26	191r–198v	1	1	
Quire 27	199r	1	2	
	199v, 200r	1, 2	2	
	200v	2	2	
	201r&v	1	2	
	202r	1, 2	2	

202v	1	2
203r	1, 2	2
203v	1	2
204r	1	1

Inventory 3: *I*-Initials by Quire and Artist

Quire 1: No two-line *I*-initials

Quire 2: fols. 7–14

Artist 2: all fols.		15
Convex *I*	0	
Concave *I*	15	
Upside down *I*	0	
Broken *I*	0	
		Total: 15

Quire 3: fols. 15–22

Artist 2: fols. 16r&v, 21r&v.		1
Convex *I*	1	
Concave *I*	0	
Upside down *I*	0	
Broken *I*	0	
Artist 3: fols. 15r&v, 22r&v		1
Convex *I*	1	
Concave *I*	0	
Upside down *I*	0	
Broken *I*	0	
Artist 4: fols. 17r–20v.		3
Convex *I*	3	
Concave *I*	0	
Upside down *I*	0	
Broken *I*	0	
		Total: 5

Quire 4: fols. 23–30

Artist 4: fols. 23r–25v, 28r–30v		6
Convex *I*	6	
Upside down *I*	0	
Concave *I*	0	
Broken *I*	0	
Artist 3: fols. 26r–27v		2
Convex *I*	2	
Concave I	0	
Upside down *I*	0	
Broken *I*	0	
		Total: 8

INVENTORIES

Quire 5: fols. 31–38
    Artist 2: fols. 34r–35v   5
        Convex *I*   5
        Concave *I*   0
        Upside down *I*   0
        Broken *I*   0

    Artist 4: fols. 31r–33v, 36v–38v; 37r
        no flourishing   9
        Convex *I*   8
        Concave *I*   0
        Upside down *I*   0
        Broken *I*   1
                Total: 14

Quire 6: fols. 39–46
    Artist 2: fols. 39r–40v, 45r–46v   7
        Convex *I*   7
        Concave *I*   0
        Upside down *I*   0
        Broken *I*   0

    Artist 4: fols. 41r–44v   5
        Convex *I*   5
        Concave *I*   0
        Upside down *I*   0
        Broken *I*   0
                Total: 12

Quire 7: fols. 47–54; 47v no flourishing
    Artist 2: all fols except 47v   10
        Convex. *I*   9
        Concave *I*   0
        Upside down *I*   1
        Broken *I*   0
                Total: 10

Quire 8: fols. 55–62; 56v no flourishing
    Artist 2: all fols.   12
        Convex *I*   11
        Concave *I*   1
        Upside down *I*   0
        Broken *I*:   0
                Total: 12

Quire 9: fols. 63–70; 68v; 70v no flourishing
    Artist 4: all fols.   12
        Convex *I*   11
        Concave *I*   1
        Upside down *I*   0
        Broken *I*   0
                Total: 13

Quire 10: fols. 71–78; 72 v no flourishing

Artist 2: all fols.	10	
Convex *I*	8	
Concave *I*	0	
Upside down *I*	1	
Broken *I*	1	
		Total: 10

Quire 11: 79–86; 80r&v, 81v–83r, no flourishing

Artist 2: all fols.	11	
Convex *I*	10	
Concave *I*	0	
Upside down *I*	1	
Broken *I*	0	
		Total: 11

Quire 12: fols. 87–94; 89v, 90r, 91r, 93r, 93v, no flourishing

Artist 2: all fols.	7	
Convex *I*	7	
Concave *I*	0	
Upside down I	0	
Broken *I*	0	
		Total: 7

Quire 13: fols. 95–102

Artist 2: all fols.	12	
Convex *I*	10	
Concave *I*	0	
Upside down I	0	
Broken *I*	2	
		Total: 12

Quire 14: fols. 103–110; no flourishing on 108r–110r&v

Artist 2: fols. 103r&v		2
Convex *I*	2	
Concave *I*	0	
Upside down *I*	0	
Broken *I*	0	
Artist 3: fols. 104r–106r; 106v, left column; 107r&v		3
Convex *I*	3	
Concave *I*	0	
Upside down *I*	0	
Broken *I*	0	
		Total: 5

Quire 15: fols. 111–118; no flourishing on 111r&v, 113v, 114r, 115v–118v

Artist 1: fols. 112r&v; 114v		1
Convex *I*	1	
Concave *I*	0	

INVENTORIES

Upside down *I*	0		
Broken *I*	0		
Artist 2: fols. 113r, 114v, 115r		4	
Convex *I*	4		
Concave *I*	0		
Upside down *I*	0		
Broken *I*	0		
		Total: 5	

Quire 16: fols. 119r–126v

Artist 1: fols. 121r		1	
Convex *I*	1		
Concave *I*	0		
Upside down *I*	0		
Broken *I*	0		
Artist 2: fols. 119r&v, 120r, 125v, 126r&v		2	
Convex *I*	2		
Concave *I*	0		
Upside down *I*	0		
Broken *I*	0		
		Total: 3	

Quire 17: fols. 127–134; no flourishing on 130v–132v

Artist 1: fol. 130r		4	
Convex *I*	4		
Concave *I*	0		
Upside down *I*	0		
Broken *I*	0		
Artist 2: fols. 127r–129v, 133r–134v		5	
Convex *I*	4		
Concave *I*	0		
Upside down *I*	1		
Broken *I*	0		
		Total: 9	

Quire 18, fols. 135–138; no flourishing on 138v

Artist 1: fols. 136r–137v	4		
Convex *I*	1		
Concave *I*	1		
Upside down *I*	1		
Broken *I*	1		
Artist 2: fols. 135r&v, 138r		0	
Convex *I*	0		
Concave *I*	0		
Upside down *I*	0		
Broken *I*	0		
		Total: 4	

Quire 19, fols. 139–146: No two-line *I*-initials

Quire 20, fols. 147–150: No two-line *I*-initials

Quire 21, fols. 151–158
    Artist 1: all fols.

Convex *I*	8	
Concave *I*	3	
Upside down *I*	4	
Broken *I*	1	
		Total: 16

Quire 22: fols. 159–166; no flourishing on 164r
    Artist 1: all fols. 10

Convex *I*	6	
Concave *I*	1	
Upside down *I*	3	
Broken *I*	0	
		Total: 10

Quire 23: fols. 167–174
    Artist 1: all fols. 10

Convex *I*	9	
Concave *I*	0	
Upside down *I*	1	
Broken *I*	0	
		Total: 10

Quire 24: fols. 175–182
    Artist 1: all fols. 7

Convex *I*	7	
Concave *I*	0	
Upside down *I*	0	
Broken *I*	0	
		Total: 7

Quire 25: fols. 183–190
    Artist 1: all fols. 15

Convex *I*	7	
Concave *I*	1	
Upside down *I*	7	
Broken *I*	0	
		Total: 15

Quire 26: fols. 191–198
    Artist 1: all fols. 10

Convex *I*	4	
Concave *I*	1	
Upside down *I*	5	
Broken *I*	0	
		Total: 10

INVENTORIES   139

Quire 27: fols. 199–204r
      Artist 2: fols. 199–203   9
            Convex *I*   9
            Concave *I*   0
            Upside down *I*   0
            Broken *I*   0

Artist 1: fol. 204r
      No two-line *I*-initials   0

                              Total: 9
                    Total for manuscript: 225

Inventory 4: Minor Illumination: Painted Initials, Partial Borders

Artist 1:
    Quire 15: 112v (flourishing by Artist 1), 114v (flourishing by Artist 2)
    Quire 16: 119v (flourishing by Artist 2), 126r
    Quire 17: 128v (flourishing by Artist 2)

Artist 2: (All pages flourished by Artist 2)
    Quire 2: 8v, 10v, 11v, 12v, 13v
    Quire 3: 16v
    Quire 5: 34r
    Quire 6: 40v
    Quire 7: 47r, 48v, 49v, 51v, 53r, 54r
    Quire 8: 55v, 57r, 58v, 61v
    Quire 10: 72v, 73v, 75r, 76v, 78r
    Quire 11: 79r, 81r, 84r, 85v
    Quire 12: 87r, 88r, 90v, 92r, 94v
    Quire 13: 95v, 96v, 98r, 99v, 100v, 102r
    Quire 14: 103r

Artist 3:
None

Artist 4:
    Quire 3: 17v, 19r, 20v
    Quire 4: 23v*, 24v*, 26v, 29v*, 30v
    Quire 5: 32r, 36r, 38v*
    Quire 6: 41v, 43r, 44v
    Quire 9: 63r, 64r*, 65v*, 66v*, 68r, 69v

*Some elements of the minor illumination on these pages may have been begun by Artist 2 and completed by Artist 4.

Inventory 5: Faces in the Penwork of Artist 1

Fish, mostly human-faced, in terminal complexes, upper margin: 130r, 151v, 155r, aw156r, 158v, 183r, 193r. In terminal complexes, lower margin: 112v, 153r, 153v, 160v, 173r, 181v, 182r, 186r, 189r, 189v

140   INVENTORIES

Face, many with tendril coming out of mouth: Fols. 154r; 155r, 156r, 158v, 166r, left and right; 167v, 168r, 168v, 171r, 174r top and bottom, 174v, 178v, 179r top and bottom, 179v, 180r, 181r, 185r, 193v, 197r, 204r

Simian or human faces next to initials:

   simian: 121r, initial *D*(*omine*); fig. 155v, *D*(*a quesumus*); 182r, *D*(*omini*); *B*(*enedicta*); 196v, *D*(*eus*)

   human: 112v, initial *D*(*a quesumus*); 154v, initial *R*(*efecti*); 158v, initial *D*(*a quesumus*); 160r, *D*(*eus*); 174v, initials *S*(*acerdotes*) and *D*(*eus*); 175r, initial *B*(*eatus*); 178v, *B*(*eatus*); 179r, *N*(*imis*); 180v, *V*(*otivus*); 182v, *B*(*eatorum*); 189r, *R*(*epleti*); 189v, *C*(*rescat*); *D*(*omine*); *D*(*ilexisti*); 195r, *A*(*eterne*); 198r, *N*(*os*)

Inventory 6: Combinations of Penwork Elements in the *Passionarium 1*, BUL, Ms. 57

Below is a sample of motifs, placements, and colors in the penwork borders of BUL Ms. 57, volume 1 of the *Passionarium* made in Sint-Truiden, *c.*1340. Elements are listed as they occur in the border, reading from left to right. This inventory shows the rich and varied treatment of border elements in this manuscript. Decoration is by Artists 2 of 10 A 14, prior to his work on the Rummen manuscripts.

1. 4r: red thin line, blue inner bar, red thin line with corkscrews at upper end, Type 1 outer bar with bisected segments, two button-halves between segments and single or double filamented button at lower end. One gold-red-blue floating rosette above lower end of each segment.

2. 28r: red inner bar, black (purple?) thin line, Type 1 outer bar with corkscrew at bottom of each segment, with slightly bifurcated button at top of each segment

3. 33v: black thin line, red inner bar, purple/black thin line, Type 1 outer bar with corkscrew at top of each segment, filamented button at bottom. Also employed on fol. 74r.

4. 34v: red thin line, blue inner bar, red thin line, Type 1 outer bar with red corkscrew at bottom of segment, lobed button at top of each red segment and filamented button at top of each blue segment.

5. 35v: red thin line, blue inner bar, red thin line, Type 1 outer bar with red corkscrew at bottom of each segment, lobed button at top of each blue segment and filamented (?) button at top of each red segment.

6   42v: red thin line, blue inner bar, two red thin lines, Type 1 outer bar with lobed button at top and red corkscrew at bottom of each segment.

7. 45v: red inner bar, purple (?) thin line, Type 1 outer bar with purple (?) corkscrew at bottom of each segment, lobed button at top of each segment.

8. 46r: red thin line, blue inner bar, red thin line, Type 1 outer bar with bisected segments, button at subdivision of each segment. Hooked filament at top and corkscrew at bottom of each segment.

9. 47r: black thin line, red inner bar, two black thin lines, Type 1 outer bar with filamented button at top and corkscrew at bottom of each segment.

10. 48r: purple (black?) thin line, red inner bar, two (?) black thin lines, Type 1 outer bar with double-filamented red or blue button at top and black corkscrew at bottom of each segment. Also employed on fol. 76r.

11. 51r: red thin line, blue inner bar, two red thin lines, Type 1 outer bar with red corkscrew at bottom, lobed button at top of each segment.

INVENTORIES

12. 53v: black (purple?) thin line, red inner bar, two purple (black?) thin lines, Type 1 outer bar with black (purple?) corkscrew at bottom of each segment and lobed button at top.

13. 63v: Above initial: purple (black?) thin line, red inner bar, purple (black?) thin line, Type 1 outer bar with bisected segments, a filamented button at subdivision of each blue segment and an unfilamented button at subdivision of each red segment; filamented button at bottom of each segment and corkscrew at top.

14. 63v: Below initial: red thin line, blue inner bar, red thin line, Type 1 outer bar with bisected segments, filamented button at subdivision of each segment, corkscrew at top and scroll at bottom of each segment.

15. 71r: black thin line, red inner bar, two black thin lines, Type 1 outer bar with filamented button at top and corkscrew at bottom of each segment. Left column: red thin line, blue inner bar, red thin line, Type 1 outer bar, red corkscrew at top, filamented button at bottom of each segment. Right column: purple (black?) thin line, red inner bar, two purple (black?) thin lines, Type 1 outer bar with black corkscrew below, filamented button above each segment.

Inventory 7: Miscellaneous Penwork Initials

A. Three- and Four-Line Penwork Initials within 28-Line Text

138r, G(*loria*):	Gloria	half-length prophet?	3 lines
138r, C(*redo*):	Creed	half-length apostle?	3 lines
152v, E(*t*):	St. Stephen	Hare and dog	3 lines
178r, E(*go*):	St. Andrew	Andrew with his cross	4 lines
198v, V(*ultum*):	Mary	Virgin and child	4 lines

B. Penwork Initials in Musical Notation, One Staff in Height (Fols. 139–148, Quires 19 and 20)

139ra, O(*men*)	*Omen Dominus*	foliate vine/oak leaves
139ra, D(*ominus*)	*Dominus vobiscum*	circles
139ra, E(*t*)	*Et cum spiritu*	toothed pearls/buds
139ra, S(*ursum*)	*Sursum corda*	circles, toothed pearls,/buds
139ra, H(*abemus*)	*Habemus ad*	circles
139ra, G(*ratias*)	*Gratias agamus*	circles
139vrb D(*ignum*)	*Dignum et iustum*	toothed pearls/buds
139rb, V(*ere*)	*Vere dignum*	full-length praying man
139rb, T(*e*)	*Te quidem domine*	toothed pearls/buds
139va, E(*t*)	*Et ideo cum*	trilobes
139vb,	Q(*uia*)	*Quia per incarna*
1440ra, E(t)	*Et ideo cum*	toothed pearls
140rb, Q(*ui*)	*Qui cum unigenitus*	grotesque
140rb, E(*t*)	*Et ideo, in excelsis*	toothed pearls
140rb, Q(*ui*)	*Qui corporali*	grotesque

140va, *Q(ui)*	*Qui salute humani*	grotesque
140vb, *T(e)*	*Te domine suppliciter*	trilobes
140ra, *E(t)*	*Et ideo de sancta*	buds
141rb, *(t)*	*Et te in veneratione*	nude, bald man
141va, *Q(ui)*	*Qui cum unigenito*	woman w/sprig
142va, P(er)	*Per omnia secula*	buds
142va, *D(ominus)*	*Dominus vobiscum*	toothed pearls
142vb, *S(ursum)*	*Sursum corda*	buds
142vb, *G(ratias)*	*Gratias agamus*	circles
142vb, *V(ere)*	*Vere dignum*	buds
144va, *C(ommunicantes)*	man holding rocks (?)	
147va, *P(er)*	*Per omnia*	castle
147va, *O(remus)*	*Oremus preceptis*	circles
147va,	*P(ater)*	*Pater noster*
147vb,	*A(d)*	*Adveniat regnum*
147vb, *F(iat)*	*Fiat voluntas*	toothed buds
147vb, *P(anem)*	*Panem nostrum*	circles
147vb, *E(t)*	*Et dimitte nobis*	circles
147vb, *E(t)*	*Et ne nos inducas*	toothed pearls
148rb *P(er)*	*Per omnia secula*	trilobes; trilobes

C. Two-Line Penwork Initials within 19-Line Text (*Fols. 144–149, Quires 19, 20*)

144rb *M(emento)*	*Memento domine*	oak leaves
145ra, *H(anc)*	*Hanc igitur*	grotesque
145rb *Q(uam)*	*Quam oblationem*	man praying
145rb *Q(ui)*	*Qui pridie*	grotesque
145va *H(oc)*	*Hoc est enim*	grotesque
145va *S(imili)*	*Simili modo postea*	palmettes, buds
145vb *H(ic)*	*Hic est enim*	grotesque
146ra *U(nde)*	*Unde et memores*	bird
146rb *S(upra)*	*Supra que*	foliate vine/oak leaf
146va *S(upplices)*	*Supplices te rogamus*	two birds
146vb *M(emento)*	*Memento etiam*	trilobes
146vb *N(obis)*	*Nobis quoque*	back view of woman (?), foliage
147rb *O(remus)*	*Oremus per quem*	grotesque
148ra *L(ibera)*	*Libera nos domine*	foliate vine; trilobes
148rb *F(iat)*	*Fiat hec sacrosancta*	foliage vine
149ra *A(ve)*	*Ave in eternum*	vine, bird

INVENTORIES

149ra *P(anem)*	*Panem celeste*	grotesque
149ra *E(cce)*	*Ecce ihesus*	vine
149rb *C(orpus)*	*Corpus domini*	grotesque
149rb *A(ve)*	*Ave in eternum*	vine, rosette
149rb *C(alicem)*	*Calicem salutaris*	grotesque
149rb *S(anguis)*	*Sanguis domini*	two grotesques
149va *D(omine)*	*Domine ihesu*	grotesque
149vb *P(laceat)*	*Placeat tibi sancta*	grotesque
150ra *T(rium)*	*Trium puerorum*	buds
150ra *D(eus)*	*Deus qui tribus*	trilobes
150ra *A(ffit)*	*Assit nobis domine*	geometric, circle
150rb *R(egi)*	*Regi seculorum*	buds
150rb *D(*omine)	*Domine ihesu*	palmette, buds

D. Initial A(eterne) *Inscribed with Sign of the Cross; Cadel* E *after the* A (*Fols. 139–142, Quire 19*)

(All Sign-of-Cross prompts have toothed pearl or bud decoration within the initial form, trilobes and rosette fillers outside the initial form.)

139vb	sc, cadel
140ra	sc, cadel
140rb	sc, cadel
140va	sc, cadel
140vb	sc, cadel
141rb	sc, cadel
141va	sc
142rb	sc

Tables

For Table 1, see, Chapter 2, above.

TABLE 2 Number of two-line penwork initials by each artist in each quire

	Number of two-line initials			
Quire	Artist 1	Artist 2	Artist 3	Artist 4
1	0	0	0	0
2	0	27	0	0
3	0	10	11	18
4	0	0	12	22
5	0	5	0	17
6	0	13	0	17
7	0	33	0	0
8	0	35	0	0
9	0	0	0	28
10	0	29	0	0
11	0	20	0	0
12	0	24	0	0
13	0	32	0	0
14	0	4	20	0
15	5	6	0	0
16	1	14	0	0
17	0	31	0	0
18	20	11	0	0
19	0	0	0	0
20	0	5	0	0
21	44	0	0	0
22	46	0	0	0
23	54	0	0	0
24	46	0	0	0
25	36	0	0	0
26	56	0	0	0
27	1	45	0	0
Total	309	341	43	102

TABLE 3 Iconography of two-line penwork initials by subject, in the work of each artist

	Abstract, serrated, geometric	Plant forms		Birds	Mammals	Faces	Grotesques	Other	Totals
		Beads, buds, palmettes	Leaves, vines						
Artist 1	0	105	141	3	3	38	19	0	309
Artist 2	19	65	56	37	5	80	79	4	345

© KONINKLIJKE BRILL BV, LEIDEN, 2025 | DOI:10.1163/9789004427136_019

TABLES   145

TABLE 3   Iconography of two-line penwork initials by subject, in the work of each artist (*cont.*)

	Abstract, serrated, geometric	Plant forms		Birds	Mammals	Faces	Grotesques	Other	Totals
		Beads, buds, palmettes	Leaves, vines						
Artist 3	0	6	11	1	1	5	16	3	43
Artist 4	2	56	39	0	0	2	3	0	102
Total	21	232	247	41	8	123	116	7	795

TABLE 4   Percent of two-line penwork initials by subject in the work of each artist

	Abstract, serrated, geometric	Plant forms			Birds	Mammals	Faces	Grotesques	Other
		Beads, buds, palmettes	Leaves, vines	All plant forms					
Artist 1	0	34%	46%	80%	1%	1%	12%	6%	0
Artist 2	6%	19%	16%	35%	11%	1%	23%	23%	1%
Artist 3	0	14%	26%	40%	2%	2%	12%	37%	7%
Artist 4	2%	55%	38%	93%	0	0	2%	3%	0

TABLE 5   *I*-initials by artist and type

Artist	Total *I*-initials	Convex *I*	Percent Convex	Concave *I*	Percent Concave	Upside down *I*	Percent U.-d.	Broken *I*	Percent Broken
Artist 1	79	48	60.5%	7	9%	22	28%	2	2.5%
Artist 2	112	89	79%	16	14%	4	4%	3	3%
Artist 3	6	6	100%	0	0%	0	0	0	0
Artist 4	36	34	94%	1	3%	0	3%	1	0
Total for manuscript	233	177	76%	24	10%	25	11%	6	3%

TABLE 6   Frequency of each type of border bar in the quires of Artists 1, 2, 3, and 4 (*Type abbreviated* T)

Artist 1

	T 1
Quires 15–27	104
Percent	100%

TABLE 6   Frequency of each type of border bar in the quires of Artists 1, 2, 3, and 4 (*Type abbreviated* T) (*cont.*)

Artist 2

	T 1	T 2	T 3	T 4	T 1&2	T 1&3	T 1&4	T 3&4	Totals
Quire 2	8	4	1	0	3	0	0	0	16
Quire 3	3	0	0	0	1	0	0	0	4
Quire 5	4	0	0	0	0	0	0	0	4
Quire 6	3	1	4	0	0	0	0	0	8
Quire 7	5	2	7	0	1	0	0	0	15
Quire 8	4	2	6	0	1	0	1	2	16
Quire 10	0	0	0	15	0	0	0	0	15
Quire 11	1	0	0	9	0	0	0	0	10
Quire 12	0	0	0	8	0	0	3	0	11
Quire 13	2	0	0	13	0	0	1	0	16
Quire 14	0	0	0	2	0	0	0	0	2
Quire 15	0	0	0	3	0	0	0	0	3
Quire 16	0	0	0	6	0	0	0	0	6
Quire 17	0	0	0	10	0	0	0	0	10
Quire 18	0	0	0	3	0	0	0	0	3
Quire 19	0	0	0	12	0	0	0	0	12
Quire 20	0	0	0	7	0	0	0	0	7
Quire 27	5	1	0	0	4	0	0	0	10
Totals	35	10	18	88	10	0	5	2	168
Percent	21%	6%	11%	52%	6%	0%	3%	1%	–

Artist 3

	T 3	T4	T 3&4	Totals
Quire 3	0	3	0	3
Quire 4	1	0	2	3
Quire 14	0	8	0	8
Totals	1	11	2	14
Percent	7%	79%	14%	--

Artist 4

	T 1	T 1&3	T 1&4	T 3&4	T 1,2&4	Totals
Quire 3	7	0	0	0	0	7
Quire 4	9	1	1	2	1	14
Quire 5	10	1	0	0	0	11
Quire 6	7	0	0	0	0	7
Quire 9	13	0	0	0	1	14
Totals	46	2	1	2	2	53
Percent	86.7%	3.8%	1.9%	3.8%	3.8%	--

TABLES 147

TABLE 7   Iconography of minor illumination

I   initial
E   extension (connected to initial)
PB   partial border (not connected to initial)

Artist 1

	Folio	Type of Decoration	Subject of Decoration
Quire 15	112v	I, E	grotesque, trilobes, maple leaves
	114v*	I, PB	rabbit, maple leaves, trilobes
Quire 16	119v	E	grotesque, composite flower
	126r	E	grotesque, maple leaves, trilobes, composite flower

Artist 2

	Folio	Type of Decoration	Subject of Decoration
Quire 2	8v	I, E	tonsured head, trilobes, maple leaf
	10v	I, PB	head, grotesque, trilobes
	11v	I, E	large trilobes
	12v	I, E	tonsured head, trilobes
	13v	I, E	head, trilobes, gold balls
Quire 3	16v	I, PB	grotesques, trilobes, prickles, lancets
Quire 5	34r	I, E	grotesque, prickle leaves, trilobes, lancet
Quire 6	40v	I, E	grotesque, lancets, elongated trilobes
Quire 7	47r	I, E	grotesque, lancets, lily
	48v	I, E	grotesque, lancets, lily, gold-ball trilobes
	49v	I, E	grotesque, lancets, lily, gold-ball trilobes
	51v	I, E	prickle leaves, lily, gold ball trilobes
	53r	I, E	head, grotesque, lancets, trilobes
	54r	I, E	trilobes, elongated trilobes, gold balls
Quire 8	55v	I, E	trilobes, large gold trilobes
	57r	I, E	tonsured head, trilobes, lancets, gold balls
	58v	I, E	grotesque, prickle leaves, gold ball trilobes
	61v	I, E	grotesque, trilobes, lily (?)
Quire 10	72v	I, E	head, wavy lancets, gold-ball trilobes
	73v	I, E	grotesque, trilobes
	75r	I, E	trilobes, gold-ball trilobes
	76v	I, E	trilobes, lancets, wavy lancets
	78r	I, E	grotesque, trilobes, wavy lancets
Quire 11	79r	I, E	trilobes, maple leaves, gold balls
	81r	I, E	trilobes, wavy lancets
	84r	I, E	maple leaves
	85v	I, E	tonsured head, maple leaves, gold ball trilobes
Quire 12	87r	I, E	trilobes, wavy lancets
	88r	I, E	tonsured head, maple leaves
	90v	I, E	maple leaves
	92r	I, E	grotesque, wavy lancets
	94v	I, E	grotesque, feathery leaves, wavy lancets

TABLE 7   Iconography of minor illumination (*cont.*)

Quire 13	95v	I, E	grotesque, lancets, gold-ball trilobes
	96v	I, E	trilobes, lancets
	98r	I, E	maple leaves, trilobes, gold-ball trilobes, gold balls
	99v	I, E	trilobes, gold-ball trilobes
	100v	I, E, PB	head, grotesque, gold-ball trilobes, lancets, 7composite flower
Quire 14	103r	I, E	grotesque, lilies, gold-ball trilobes

Artist 4

	Folio	*Type of Decoration*	*Subject of Decoration*
Quire 3	17v	I, E	tonsured head, trilobes, elongated trilobes
	19r	I, E	trilobes, gold strips, piscine grotesques
	20v	I, E	trilobes, gold balls
Quire 4	23v	I, E	head, wavy lancets, gold strips, trilobes
	24v	I, E	head, lancets
	26v	I, E	head of Christ, gold strips, grotesque, trilobes
	29v	I, PB	grotesques, prickle leaves, lancets, gold-ball trilobes
	30v	I, E	grotesque, lancets, gold balls
Quire 5	32r	I, E	tonsured head, gold trilobes
	36r	I, PB	head, grotesques, gold trilobes
	38v	I, PB	tonsured head, gold strips, grotesques, gold and orange trilobes, maple leaves
Quire 6	41v	I, PB	tonsured head, gold strips and balls, grotesques, black, gold, and orange trilobes
	43r	I, PB	trilobes, gold strip, grotesque, gold balls, gold trilobes
	44v	I, E	grotesques, gold and orange trilobes
Quire 9	63r	I, PB	woman's head in grisaille, gold strips and ball, trilobes, lancet
	64r	I, PB	harelip/grotesque, gold trilobes, dragon-like grotesque
	65v	I, E	tonsured head, gold strips, gold trilobes, maple leaves, black-ball trilobes
	66v	I, E	tonsured head, gold strips, trilobes, ivy leaves, gold balls
	68r	I, E	head, gold balls, gold trilobes
	69v	I, E	tonsured head, gold strip, trilobes, gold balls

TABLE 8   Iconography of large penwork initials

Penwork Initials in Musical Notation, fols. 139r–142v, 147v–148r (from Inventory 7, pt. A)

Type	Abstract (toothed pearls, circles, geometric)	Plant forms (buds, leaves, palmettes, vines)	Abstract/plant indeterminate	Human figures	Grotesques	Other	Totals
Number	12	9	4	3	4	2	34
Percent	35	26	12	9	12	6	100

TABLES 149

TABLE 8   Iconography of large penwork initials (*cont.*)

Penwork Initials in 19-line Text, fols. 144–149 (from Inventory 7, pt. B)

Type	Abstract (circles)	Plant forms (buds, leaves, palmettes, vines)	Birds	Human figures	Grotesques	Totals
Number	1	11	4	3	11	30
Percent	3	37	13	10	37	100

Bibliography

Académie royale des Sciences, des Lettres et des Beaux-Arts de Belgique. *Biographie nationale*. 44 vols., 16 supplements. Brussels: H. Thiry-van Buggenhoudt; Bruylant-Christophe; Émile Bruylant, 1866–1986.

Ainsworth, Maryan W. and Keith Christensen, eds. *From Van Eyck to Bruegel: Early Netherlandish Painting in the Metropolitan Museum of Art*. Exhibition catalogue, New York, Metropolitan Museum of Art, 1998–1999. New York: The Metropolitan Museum of Art, 1998.

Anderson, M. D. *Drama and Imagery in English Medieval Churches*. Cambridge, UK: Cambridge University Press, 1963.

Aquinas, Thomas. *Summa Theologiae of St. Thomas Aquinas: Part 1*. Translated by the Fathers of the English Dominican Province. 2nd rev. ed., 1920. 10 vols. London: Burns, Oates & Washbourne, Ltd. Also at https://www.newadvent.org/summa.

Aquinas, Thomas. *Summa Theologica: Complete English Edition in Five Volumes*. Translated by the Fathers of English Dominican Province. New York: Benziger Brothers, 1947–1948; repr., Notre Dame, Indiana: Christian Classics, 1981.

Aquinas, Thomas. *Summa Theologiae: Latin Text and English Translation, Introductions, Notes, Appendices and Glossaries*. Edited by Thomas Gilby and T. C. O'Brien. Translated by the Fathers of the English Dominican Province. 61 vols. London: Blackfriars in conjunction with Eyre & Spottiswoode, 1964–1980.

Arnould, Alain, et. al. *Textes liturgiques, ascétiques, théologiques, philosophiques et moraux*. Vol. 1 of *La librarie des ducs de Bourgogne: Manuscrits conservés à la Bibliothèque Royale de Belgique*. Bernard Bousmanne, Céline Van Hoorebeeck, and Tania van Hemelryck, eds. 5 vols. Turnhout: Brepols Publishers, 2000–2015.

A.s.b.l. le grand Liège. *Art mosan et arts anciens du pays de Liège*. Exhibition catalog, Musée des Beaux Arts, Liège, 1951. Liège: Éditions de l'a.s.b.l., 1951.

Avril, François. *Manuscript Painting at the Court of France: The Fourteenth Century, 1310–1380*. Translated by Ursule Molinaro and Bruce Benderson. New York: George Braziller, 1978.

Avril, François. "Un enlumineur ornemaniste parisien de la première moitié du XIVe siècle: Jacobus Mathey (Jaquet Maci?)." *Bulletin monumentale* 129 (1971): 249–264.

Avril, François. "Manuscrits." In *Les fastes du gothique: Le siècle de Charles V*. Exhibition catalog, Galeries nationales du Grand Palais. Paris, 1981–1982, 276–362. Paris: Éditions de la Réunion des musées nationaux, 1981.

Bacha, Eugène. *La chronique liègeoise de 1402*. Brussels: Librarie Kiessling et Cie. 1900.

Baerten, J. *Het graafschap Loon (11de–14de eeuw): Ontstaan-politiek-instellingen*. Assen: Van Gorcum & Comp. B.V.—Dr. H. J. Prakke and H. M. G. Prakke, 1969.

Baldass, Ludwig. *Jan van Eyck*. London: Phaidon Press, 1952.

Baltrusaitis, Jurgis. *Le moyen âge fantastique: Antiquités et exotismes dans l'art gothique*. Paris: Armand Colin, 1955.

Barasch, Mosche. *Theories of Art: From Plato to Winckelmann*. New York: New York University Press, 1985.

Barron, Caroline. "Introduction: England and the Low Countries 1327–1477." In *England and the Low Countries in the Late Middle Ages*, edited by Caroline Barron and Nigel Saul, 1–28.

Barthes, Roland. *Mythologies*. Translated by Annette Lavers. New York: Noonday Press, 1972.

Beer, Ellen J. *Beiträge zur oberrheinischen Buchmalerei*. Basel: Birkhäuser Verlag, 1959.

Beer, Ellen J. "Liller Bibelcodices, Tournai und die Scriptorien der Stadt Arras." *Aachener Kunstblätter* 43 (1972): 190–226.

Beer, Ellen J. "Das Scriptorium des Johannes Philomena und seine Illuminatoren." *Scriptorium* 23, no. 1 (1969): 24–38.

Benati, Daniele. "Jacobello del Fiore: A Crucifixion and a Reconstruction of his Early Career." Translated by Frank Dabell. In Patrick Matthiesen, *Jacobello del Fiore: His Oeuvre and a Sumptuous Crucifixion*. London: Matthiesen Fine Art Ltd., 2007.

Bennett, Adelaide Louise et al. *Medieval Mastery: Book Illumination from Charlemagne to Charles the Bold, 800–1475*. Translated by Lee Preedy and Greta Arblaster-Holmer. Exhibition catalog, Leuven, Stedelijk Museum Vander Kelen-Mertens, 2002. Leuven: Uitgeverij Davidsfond nv, and Brepols Publishers, 2002.

Béthune-de Villers, Jean. "Musée lapidaire des ruines de Saint-Bavon: Dalles funéraires retrouvées à l'écluse des Braemgaten." *Messager des sciences historiques ou archives des arts et de la bibliographie de Belgique* 65–66 (1891–1892).

Béthune-de Villers, Jean. *Catalogue des dalles funéraires retrouvées à l'écluse des Braemgaten*. Ghent: Imprimerie Eug. Vanderhaeghen, 1892.

Bischoff, Bernhard. *Latin Palaeography: Antiquity and the Middle Ages*. Translated by Dáibhí Ó Cróinín and David Ganz. Cambridge: Cambridge University Press, 1990.

Bober, Harry. "Flemish Miniatures from the Atelier of Jean de Grise: Ms. 11142 of the Bibliothèque Royale de Belgique." *Revue belge d'archéologie et d'histoire de l'art* 17 (1947–48): 15–21.

Boehm, Barbara Drake, Abigail Quandt and William D. Wixom. *Das Stundenbuch der Jeanne d'Evreux/The Hours of Jeanne d'Evreux/Le Livre d'Heures de Jeanne d'Evreux.* 2 vols. Lucerne: Faksimile Verlag, 2000.

Boeren, P. C. *Catalogus van de handschriften van het Rijksmuseum Meermanno-Westreenianum.* The Hague: Rijksmuseum Meermanno-Westreenianum/Staatsuitgeverij, 1979.

Boespflug, François and Eberhard König. *Les "Très Belles Heures" de Jean de France, duc de Berry: Un chef-d'oeuvre au sortir du moyen âge.* Paris: Les Éditions du Cerf, 1998.

Borman, C. de, ed. *Chronique de l'Abbaye de Saint-Trond.* 2 vols. Société des bibliophiles liégeois 10. Liège: Grandmont-Donders, 1877.

Bormans, S. and E. Schoolmeesters, eds. *Cartulaire de l'Église de Saint-Lambert de Liège.* Vol. 4.

Bott, Gerhard and Frank Günter Zehnder, eds. *Vor Stefan Lochner: Die Kölner Maler von 1300 bis 1430; Ergebnisse der Ausstellung und des Colloquiums, Köln 1974.* Cologne: Druckhaus Rudolf Müller, 1977.

British Museum. *Catalogue of Additions to the Manuscripts 1916–1920.* London: The Trustees, 1933.

Brown, Michelle P. *The Holkham Bible Picture Book: A Facsimile.* London: The British Library, 2007.

Byvanck, A. W. *Les principaux manuscrits à peintures de la Bibliothèque Royale des Pays-Bas et du Musée Meermanno-Westreenianum à La Haye.* Paris: La Société Française de Reproductions de Manuscrits à Peintures, 1924.

Byvanck, A. W. *La miniature dans les Pays-Bas septentrionaux.* Paris: Les Éditions d'Art et d'Histoire, 1937.

Cameron. H. K. "The 14th-century School of Flemish Brasses: Evidence for a Tournai Workshop." *Transactions of the Monumental Brass Society* 12, pt. 3 (1979).

Cardon, Bert. "Het mecenaat van Johannes van Myrle." In *Handschriften uit de abdij van Sint-Truiden*, Exhibition catalog, Sint-Truiden, Provinciaal Museum voor Religieuze Kunst, Begijnhofkerk, 1986, 220–230. Leuven: Uitgeverij Peeters, 1986.

Carlvant, Kerstin Birgitta Elisabet. "Thirteenth-Century Illumination in Bruges and Ghent." PhD diss., Columbia University, 1978.

Carlvant, Kerstin B. E. "Collaboration in a Fourteenth-Century Psalter: The Franciscan Iconographer and the Two Flemish Illuminators of MS 3384,8O in the Copenhagen Royal Library." *Sacris Erudiri*, 25 (1982), 135–166.

Carlvant, Kerstin. *Manuscript Painting in Thirteenth-Century Flanders: Bruges, Ghent and the Circle of the Counts.* Turnhout: Brepols, 2012.

Cary, George. *The Medieval Alexander.* Edited by D. J. A. Ross. Cambridge: Cambridge University, 1956. Digital reprint, 2009.

Cassee, Elly. *The Missal of Cardinal Bertrand de Deux: A Study in 14th-Century Bolognese Miniature Painting.* Translated by Michael Hoyle. Florence: Istituto Universitario Olandese di Storia dell'Arte, 1980.

Châtelet, Albert. "Les miniatures de Jan van Eyck revisitées." *Art de l'enluminure* 15 (Dec. 2005–Feb. 2006): 36–66.

Christie's. "Antiphonaire à l'usage franciscain, en latin, manuscrit enluminé sur vélin." Sale 1047, lot 13. 16 November 2011. https://www.christies.com/en/lot/lot-5495948. Accessed 27 September 2022.

Clemen, Paul. "Von den Wandmalereien suf den Chorschranken des Kölner Domes." *Wallraf-Richartz Jahrbuch* 1 (1924): 29–61.

Coens, Maurice. "Les saints particulièrement honorés à l'Abbaye de Saint-Trudo." *Analecta Bollandiana* 73 (1955): 166–170.

Coens, Maurice and Joseph van der Straeten. "Un Martyrologe du XIIe siècle à l'usage de Saint-Bavon de Gand, Brit. Mus., Egerton 2796." *Analecta Bollandiana* 84, fasc. 1–2 (1966): 129–160.

Conti, Alsessandro. *La miniatura bolognese: Scuole e botteghe.* Bologna: Alfa, 1981.

Corley, Brigitte. *Painting and Patronage in Cologne 1300–1500.* Turnhout: Harvey Miller Publishers, imprint of Brepols Publishers, 2000.

Cozzi, Enrica. "Paolo Veneziano e bottega: Il politico di Santa Lucia e gli antependia per l'isola di Veglia." *Arte in Friuli, Arte a Triest* 35 (2016): 235–293.

Cruse, Mark. *Illuminating the* Roman d'Alexandre *Oxford, Bodleian Library, Ms. Bodley 264: The Manuscript as Monument.* Cambridge, UK: D. S. Brewer, 2011.

D'Haenens, Albert. "Pierart dou Tielt, enlumineur des oeuvres de Gilles Li Muisis: Note sur son activité à Tournai vers 1350." *Scriptorium* 23:1 (1969): 88–93.

De Hemricourt, Jacques. *Miroir des nobles de Hesbaye.* Enlarged ed. Liège: Imprimerie de J. F. Bassompierre, 1791.

Delaissé, L. M. J. "Enluminure et peinture dans les Pays-Bas." *Scriptorium* 11:1 (1957): 109–118.

Delaissé, L. M. J. *Middeleeuwse miniaturen van de librije van Boergondië tot het handschriftenkabinet van de Koninklijke Bibliotheek van België.* Brussels: J. M. Meulenhoff, 1958.

De l'Espinoy, Philippe. *Recherche des antiquitez et noblesse de Flandres contenant l'histoire généalogique des Comtes de Flandres, avec une description curieuse dudit pays.* Douai: Marc Wyon, 1631.

De Limburg-Stirum, Thierry ed. *Cartulaire de Louis de Male, Comte de Flandre: Decreten van den grave Lodewyck van Vlaenderen 1348 à 1358.* 2 vols. Bruges: Imprimerie de Louis de Plancke, 1898–1901.

De Mare, A. J. "Afbeeldingen van muziekinstrumenten in het handschrift van Priester Laurentius voltooid in 1366." In *Gedenkboek aangeboden aan Dr. D. F. Scheurleer op zijn 70sten verjaardag: bijdragen van vrienden en vereerders op het gebied der muziek*, 201–206. The Hague: Martinus Nijhoff, 1925.

Dennison, Lynda. "The Artistic Context of Fourteenth Century Flemish Brasses." *Transactions of the Monumental Brass Society* 14, pt. 1 (1986): 1–38.

BIBLIOGRAPHY

Dennison, Lynda. "Monastic or Secular? The Artist of the Ramsey Psalter, now at Holkham Hall, Norfolk." In *Monasteries and Society in Medieval Britain: Proceedings of the 1994 Harlaxton Symposium.* Edited by Benjamin Thompson, 223–261. Stamford: Paul Watkins, 1999.

Dennison, Lynda. "Dating and Localisation of the Hague Missal (Meermanno-Westreenianum Ms. 10 A 14) and the Connection between English and Flemish Miniature Painting in the Mid Fourteenth Century." In *Als ich kan: Liber Amicorum in Memory of Professor Dr. Maurits Smeyers,* edited by Bert Cardon, Jan Van der Stock, and Dominique Vanwijnsberghe, 505–536. Leuven: Uitgeveri Peeters, 2002.

Dennison, Lynda. "The Technical Mastery of the Macclesfield Psalter: A Preliminary Stylistic Appraisal of the Illuminators and Their Suggested Origin." *Transactions of the Cambridge Bibliographical Society* 13, no. 3 (2006): 253–288.

Dennison, Lynda. "The Significance of Ornamental Penwork in Illuminated and Decorated Manuscripts of the Second Half of the Fourteenth Century." In *Tributes to Kathleen L. Scott: English Medieval Manuscripts; Readers, Makers and Illuminators,* edited by Marlene Villalobos-Hennessey, 31–64. London: Harvey Miller, 2009.

Dennison, Lynda and Nicholas Rogers. "The Elsing Brass and its East Anglian Connections." In *Fourteenth Century England,* edited by Nigel Saul, 167–193. Woodbridge, Suffolk: Boydell Press, 2000.

Dennison, Lynda Eileen. "Stylistic Sources, Dating and Development of the Bohun Workshop, ca 1340–1400." PhD diss., Westfield College, University of London, 1988.

De Raadt, J.-Th. *Sceaux armories des Pays-Bas et des pays avoisinants (Belgique—Royaume des Pays-Bas—Luxembourg—Allemagne—France): Recueil historique et héraldique.* Brussels: Société Belge de Librairie, 4 vols. Brussels: Société Belge de Librairie, 1898–1903.

Derolez, Albert. *The Palaeography of Gothic Manuscript Books: From the Twelfth to the Early Sixteenth Century.* Cambridge: Cambridge University Press, 2003.

Derolez, Albert, with assistance of Hendrik Defoort and Frank Vanlangenhove. *Medieval Manuscripts: Ghent University Library.* Ghent: Snoeck, 2017.

De Voragine, Jacobus. *The Golden Legend: Readings on the Saints.* 2 vols. Translated by William Granger Ryan. Princeton: Princeton University Press, 1993.

De Winter, Patrick M. *La bibliothèque de Philippe le Hardi, duc de Bourgogne 1364–1404: Étude sur les manuscrits à peintures d'une collection princière à l'époque du "style gothique international."* Paris: Éditions du Centre National de la Recherche Scientifique, 1985.

Dogaer, Georges et Marguerite Debae. *La librairie de Philippe le Bon: Exposition organisée à l'occasion du 500e anniversaire de la mort du duc.* Exhibition Catalog, Brussels, Bibliothèque Albert 1e, 1967. Brussels: Bibliothèque Albert, 1967.

Doyle, Maeve. "The Portrait Potential: Gender, Identity, and Devotion in Manuscript Owner Portraits, 1230–1320." PhD Diss., Bryn Mawr College, 2015.

Ebner, Adalbert. *Quellen und Forschungen zur Geschichte und Kunstgeschichte des Missale Romanum im Mittelalter.* Freiburg im Breisgau: Herder'sche Verlagshandlung, 1896.

Eizenhöfer, Leo and Hermann Knaus. *Die liturgischen Handschriften der Hessischen Landes- und Hochschulbibliothek Darmstadt.* Wiesbaden: Otto Harrassowitz, 1968.

Falkenburg, Reindert. "The Household of the Soul: Conformity in the Mérode Triptych." In *Early Netherlandish Painting at the Crossroads: A Critical Look at Current Methodologies,* edited by Maryan W. Ainsworth, 2–17. New York: The Metropolitan Museum of Art, 2010.

Falmagne, Thomas and Baudouin van den Abeele. *Dukes of Burgundy.* Vol. 5 of *The Medieval Booklists of the Southern Low Countries.* Leuven: Peeters, 1994–2016.

Fryklund, Carina. *Flemish Wall Painting: Late Gothic Wall Painting in the Southern Netherlands.* Turnhout: Brepols, 2011.

Galley, Eberhard. "Eine Kölner Buchmalerwerkstatt aus der ersten Hälfte des 14. Jahrhunderts." *Düsseldorfer Jahrbuch: Beiträge zur Geschichte des Niederrheins* 46 (1954): 121–136.

Gaspar, Camille and Frédéric Lyna. *Les principaux manuscrits à peintures de la Bibliothèque Royale de Belgique.* 2 vols. Paris: La Société française de reproductions de manuscrits à peintures. Reprint Brussels: Bibliothèque Royale Albert 1er, 1984.

Gelre. *Gelre: B.R. Ms. 15652–56.* Edited by F. Lyna. Leuven: Uitgeverij-Editions Jan van Helmont, 1992.

Gibson, Margaret, T. A. Heslop, and Richard W. Pfaff, eds. *Eadwine Psalter: Text, Image, and Monastic Culture in Twelfth-Century Canterbury.* London: Modern Humanities Research Association, 1992.

Gil, Marc. "Jean Pucelle and the Parisian Seal-Engravers and Goldsmiths." Translated by Raeleen Chai-Elsholz. In *Jean Pucelle: Innovation and Collaboration in Manuscript Painting,* edited by Kyunghee Pyun and Anna D. Russakoff, 27–52. London: Harvey Miller, 2013.

Greenhill, Eleanor S. "A Fourteenth-Century Workshop of Manuscript Illuminators and Its Localization." *Zeitschrift für Kunstgeschichte* 40, Bd., H. 1 (1977): 1–25.

Haagdorens, Lieve. "Sint-Truidense handschriften rond Arnold van Rummen." In *Handschriften uit de abdij van Sint-Truiden.* Exhibition catalog, Sint-Truiden, Provinciaal Museum voor Religieuze Kunst, Begijnhofkerk, 1986, 257–275. Leuven: Uitgeverij Peeters, 1986.

Haggh, Barbara. "Music, Liturgy, and Ceremony in Brussels, 1350–1500." 2 vols. PhD diss., University of Illinois at Urbana-Champaign, 1988.

Hassall, W. O. *The Holkham Bible Picture Book.* London: Dropmore Press, 1954.

Haussherr, Reiner. "Die Chorschrankenmalereien des Kölner Doms." In *Vor Stefan Lochner: Die Kölner Maler von 1300 bis 1430; Ergebnisse der Ausstellung und des Colloquiums, Köln 1974*, edited by Gerhard Bott and Frank Günter Zehnder, 28–59. Cologne: Druckhaus Rudolf Müller, 1977.

Hedeman, Anne D. *The Royal Image: Illustrations of the Grandes Chroniques de France, 1274–1422*. Berkeley: University of California Press, 1991. https://publishing.cdlib.org/ucpressebooks/view?docId=ft8k4008jd&chunk.id=d0e6866&toc.depth=1&toc.id=&brand=ucpress. Accessed 24 August 2022.

Henderson, John. "The Flagellant Movement and the Flagellant Confraternities in Central Italy, 1260–1400." *Studies in Church History* 15 (1978): 147–160.

Hildburgh, W. L. *English Alabaster Carvings as Records of the Medieval Religious Drama*. Oxford: Society of Antiquities of London, 1949.

James, M. R. *The Romance of Alexander: A Collotype Facsimile of Ms. Bodley 264*. Oxford: Clarendon, 1933.

Joslin, Mary Coker and Carolyn Coker Joslin Watson. *The Egerton Genesis*. London: British Library, 2001.

Koninklijke Vlaamse Academie van België. *Nationaal Biografisch Woordenboek*. 23 vols. Brussels: Paleis der Academiën. 1964–.

Korteweg, Anne S., ed. *Kriezels, aubergines en takkenbossen: Randversiering in Noordnederlandse handschriften uit de vijftiende eeuw*. Exhibition catalog, The Hague, Rijksmuseum Meermanno-Westreenianum/Museum van het Boek, Koninklijke Bibliotheek, 1992–1993. Zutphen: Walburg Pers, 1992.

Korteweg, Anne S. "Framing the Issues: A Codicological Approach to Dutch Border Decoration." Translated by Kathryn M. Rudy. In *Tributes in Honor of James H. Marrow: Studies in Painting and Manuscript Illumination of the Late Middle Ages and Northern Renaissance*, edited by Jeffrey Hamburger and Anne S. Korteweg. London: Harvey Miller Publishers, 2006.

Kren, Thomas. "From Panel to Parchment and Back: Painters and Illuminators Before 1470." In *Illuminating the Renaissance: The Triumph of Flemish Manuscript Painting in Europe*, edited by Thomas Kren and Scot McKendrick, Exhibition catalog, J. Paul Getty Museum, Los Angeles, and Royal Academy of Arts, London, 2003–2004. Los Angeles: The J. Paul Getty Museum, 2003, 81–119.

Kren, Thomas and Maryan W. Ainsworth. "Illuminators and Painters: Artistic Exchanges and Interrelationships." In *Illuminating the Renaissance: The Triumph of Flemish Manuscript Painting in Europe*, edited by Thomas Kren and Scot McKendrick, 35–57. Exhibition catalog, J. Paul Getty Museum, Los Angeles, and Royal Academy of Arts, London, 2003–2004. Los Angeles: The J. Paul Getty Museum, 2003.

Lacy, Norris J. et al., eds. *The New Arthurian Encyclopedia*. 3rd ed. New York: Garland, 1991.

Le Glay, Edward. *Histoire des Comtes de Flandre jusqu'à l'avènement de la maison de Bourgogne*. 2 vols. Brussels: La librairie ancienne et moderne de A. Vandale, 1843.

Lemaire, Claudine and Dominique Vanwijnsberghe. *Textes liturgiques, ascétiques, théologiques, philosophiques et moraux*. Vol. 1 of *La librairie des ducs de Bourgogne: Manuscrits conservés à la Bibliothèque Royale de Belgique*. Edited by Bernard Bousmanne and Céline Van Hoorebeeck. Turnhout: Brepols Publishers, 2000.

Leo, Domenic. *Images, Texts, and Marginalia in a "Vows of the Peacock" Manuscript: New York, Pierpont Morgan Library* MS *G24*. Leiden: Brill, 2013.

Leroquais, V. *Les sacramentaires et les missels manuscrits des bibliothèques publiques de France*. 3 vols. Paris, 1924.

Les Fastes du gothique: Le siècle de Charles V. Exhibition catalog, Galeries nationales du Grand Palais. Paris, 1981–1982. Paris: Éditions de la Réunion des musées nationaux, 1981.

Levy, Ian Christopher, Gary Macy, and Kristen Van Ausdall, eds. *A Companion to the Eucharist in the Middle Ages*. Leiden: Brill, 2012.

Lieftinck, G. I. *Manuscrits datés conserves dans les Pays-Bas: Catalogue paléographique des manuscrits en écriture latine portant des indications de date*. 2 vols. Amsterdam: North-Holland Publishing Company, 1964.

Löber, Karl. *Agaleia: Erscheinung und Bedeutung der Akelei in der mittelalterlichen Kunst*. Cologne: Böhlau Verlag, 1988.

Lowden, John. "The Holkham Bible Picture Book and the Bible Moralisée." In *The Medieval Book: Glosses from Friends and Colleagues of Christopher de Hamel*, edited by James H. Marrow, Richard A. Linenthal, and William Noel, 75–83. Houten, Netherlands: Hes & De Graaf, 2010.

Luber, Katherine Crawford. "Recognizing Van Eyck: Magical Realism in Landscape Painting." *Philadelphia Museum of Art Bulletin* 91 (Spring 1998): 7–23.

Lucas, Henry Stephen. *The Low Countries and the Hundred Years War, 1326–1347*. Ann Arbor: University of Michigan Press, 1929.

Luker, Emma. "Some Observations on the Artists of the Leiden Psalter (Leiden, University Library MS B.P.L. 76A) and Their Working Practices." In *Illuminating the Middle Ages: Tributes to Prof. John Lowden from his Students, Friends and Colleagues*, edited by Laura Cleaver, Alixe Bovey, and Lucy Donkin, 139–156. Leiden: Brill, 2020.

Lyna, Frederik. *De Vlaamsche miniatuur van 1300 tot 1530*. Brussels: N. V. Standaard-Boekhandel, 1933.

Lyna, J. *Het graafschap Loon: Politieke en sociale overzichtelijke geschiedenis*. Beringen: Drukkerij J. Peeters, 1956.

Macklin, Herbert W. *The Brasses of Medieval England*. New York: E. P. Dutton and Company, 1907.

Maddocks, Hilary Elizabeth. "The Illuminated Manuscripts of the *Légende Dorée*: Jean de Vignay's Translation of Jacobus de Voragine's *Legenda Aurea*." PhD diss., Univ. of Melbourne, 1989.

Maeterlinck, L. *La pénétration française en Flandre: Une école préeyckienne inconnue*. Paris: G. van Oest, 1925.

BIBLIOGRAPHY

Marchal, François Joseph Ferdinand, Viglius Zuichemus ab Aytta, and Philippe Gaudence Emmanuel de Francquen. *Catalog des manuscrits de la bibliothèque royale des ducs de Bourgogne*. 3 vols. Brussels: C. Muquardt, 1842.

Marrow, James H. "History, Historiography, and Pictorial Invention in the Turin-Milan Hours." In *In Detail: New Studies of Northern Renaissance Art in Honor of Walter S. Gibson*, edited by Laurinda Dixon, 1–14. Turnhout: Brepols, 1988.

Marrow, James H. *Pictorial Invention in Netherlandish Manuscript Illumination of the Late Middle Ages: The Play of Illusion and Meaning*. Edited by Brigitte Dekeyser and Jan van der Stock. Paris: Peeters, 2005.

Marrow, James H. "Scholarship on Flemish Manuscript Illumination of the Renaissance: Remarks on Past, Present, and Future." In *Flemish Manuscript Painting in Context: Recent Research*, edited by Elizabeth Morrison and Thomas Kren. Los Angeles: The J. Paul Getty Museum, 2006, 163–176.

McKendrick, Scot. "Between Flanders and Normandy: Collaboration Among Miniaturists or a Case of Influence?" In *Under the Influence: The Concept of Influence and the Study of Illuminated* Manuscripts, edited by John Lowden and Alixe Bovey, 139–149. Turnhout: Brepols Publishers, 2007.

Meuwese, Martine. "Jacob van Maerlant's Spiegel historiael: Iconography and Workshop." In *Flanders in a European Perspective: Manuscript Illumination around 1400 in Flanders and abroad; Proceedings of the International Colloquium Leuven, 7–9 September 1993*, edited by Maurits Smeyers and Bert Cardon, 445–456. Leuven: Uitgeverij Peeters, 1995.

Moolenbroek, Jaap van and Maaike Hogenhout-Mulder. *Scolastica willic ontbinden: Over de Rijmbijbel van Jacob van Maerlant*. Hilversum: Verloren, 1991.

Moore, Elizabeth B. "The Urban Fabric and Framework of Ghent in the Margins of Oxford, Bodleian Library, MSS Douce 5–6." In *Als ich can: Liber Amicorum in Memory of Professor Dr. Maurits Smeyers*, edited by Bert Cardon, Jan Van der Stock and Dominique Vanwijnsberghe, 983–1006. Leuven: Uitgeverij Peeters, 2002.

Morand, Kathleen. *Jean Pucelle*. Oxford: Clarendon Press, 1962.

Morgan, Nigel and Stella Panayotova, eds., with assistance of Martine Meuwese et al. *The Meuse Region. Southern Netherlands*. Pt. 1, vol. 2 of *A Catalogue of Western Book Illumination in the Fitzwilliam Museum and the Cambridge Colleges: Illuminated Manuscripts in Cambridge; A Catalogue of Western Book Illumination in the Fitzwilliam Museum and the Cambridge Colleges*. 5 pts. London: Harvey Miller Publishers, 2009–2017.

Museum voor Schone Kunsten. *Boekdrukkunst, boekbanden, borduurkunst, edelsmeedkunst, Miniatuurkunst*. Vol. 2 of *Gent: Duizend jaar kunst en cultuur*. 3 vols. Exhibition Catalogue, Ghent, Museum voor Schone Kunst, Bijlokemuseum, Centrum voor Kunst en Cultuur, 1975. Ghent: Snoeck-Ducaju et Zoon, 1975.

Newton, Stella Mary. *Fashion in the Age of the Black Prince: A Study of the Years 1340–1365*. Woodbridge, Suffolk: Boydell Press, 1980.

Nicholas, David. *The Van Arteveldes of Ghent: The Varieties of Vendetta and the Hero in History*. Ithaca: Cornell University, 1988.

Nicholas, David. *Medieval Flanders*. London: Longman, 1992.

Norris, Malcolm. *Monumental Brasses: The Memorials*. 2 vols. London: Phillips & Page, 1977.

Oliver, Judith. "The Mosan Origins of Johannes von Valke." *Wallraf-Richartz-Jahrbuch* 40 (1978): 23–37.

Oliver, Judith. "Reconstruction of a Liège Psalter-Hours." *British Library Journal* 5, no. 2 (Autumn 1979): 107–128.

Oliver, Judith H. *Gothic Manuscript Illumination in the Diocese of Liège (c. 1250–c. 1330)*. 2 vols. Leuven: Uitgeverij Peeters, 1988.

Oliver, Judith H. "The Herkenrode Indulgence, Avignon, and Pre-Eyckian Painting of the Mid-Fourteenth-Century Low Countries." In *Flanders in a European Perspective: Manuscript Illumination Around 1400 in Flanders and Abroad*, edited by Maurits Smeyers and Bert Cardon, 187–206. Leuven: Peeters, 1995.

Olsen, Kåre and Carl Nordenfalk, eds. *Gyllene böcker: illuminerade medeltida handskrifter i dansk och svensk ägo*. Exhibition catalog, Nationalmuseum, Stockholm, 1952. Stockholm: Caslon Press Boktryckeri, 1952.

Pächt, Otto. "A Giottesque Episode in English Medieval Art." *Journal of the Warburg and Courtauld Institutes* 6 (1943): 51–70.

Pächt, Otto. *Book Illumination in the Middle Ages*. Translated by Kay Davenport. London: Harvey Miller, 1986.

Palazzo, Éric. *Le souffle de Dieu: L'énergie de la liturgie et l'art au moyen âge*. Paris: Éditions du Cerf, 2020.

Panofsky, Erwin. *Gothic Architecture and Scholasticism*. New York: Meridian Books, 1957.

Panofsky, Erwin. *Early Netherlandish Painting: Its Origins and Character*. 2 vols. Cambridge: Harvard University, 1953. Reprint, New York: Harper and Row, 1971.

Patterson, Sonia. "Comparison of Minor Initial Decoration: A Possible Method of Showing the Place of Origin of 13th-Century Manuscripts." *The Library*, 5th ser., 27 (1972): 23–30.

Pfaff, Richard W. *The Liturgy in Medieval England: A History*. Cambridge: Cambridge University Press, 2009.

Platelle, Henri and Clauzel, Denis. *Des principautés à l'empire de Charles-Quint (900–1519)*. Vol. 2 in *Histoire des provinces françaises du Nord*, directed by Alain Lottin. 6 vols. Arras: Artois Presses Université, 1988–2016.

Provinciaal Museum voor Religieuze Kunst, Sint-Truiden. *Handschriften uit de abdij van Sint-Truiden*. Exhibition catalog, Sint-Truiden, Provinciaal Museum voor Religieuze Kunst, Begijnhofkerk, 1986. Leuven: Uitgeverij Peeters, 1986.

Provinciaal Museum voor Religieuze Kunst, Sint-Truiden. *In beeld geprezen: Miniaturen uit Maaslandse devotieboeken*

1250–1350. Exhibition catalog, Sint-Truiden, Provinciaal Museum voor Religieuze Kunst, Begijnhofkerk, 1989. Leuven: Uitgeverij Peeters, 1989.

Pyun, Kyunghee and Anna D. Russakoff, eds. *Jean Pucelle: Innovation and Collaboration in Manuscript Painting*. London: Harvey Miller, 2013.

Quednau, Rolf. Zum Programm der Chorschrankenmalereien im Kölner Dom. *Zeitschrift für Kunstgeschichte* 43, Bd., H. 3 (1980): 244–279.

Quicke, Fritz. *Les Pays-Bas à la veille de la période bourguignonne 1356–1384: Contribution à l'histoire politique et diplomatique de l'Europe occidentale dans la seconde moitié du XIVe siècle*. Brussels: Presses de Belgique, 1947.

Randall, Lillian M. C. *Images in the Margins of Gothic Manuscripts*. Berkeley: University of California Press, 1966.

Rietstap, J. B. *Armorial général: Précédé d'un dictionnaire des termes du blason*. 2nd ed. Gouda: G. B. van Goor Zonen, 1884–1887.

Rogghé, Paul. "Simon de Mirabello in Vlaanderen: Schatrijke Lombard—Grafelijk Ambtenaar Ruwaard van Vlaanderen—Vlaams Politicus." *Appeltjes van het Meetjesland: Jaarboek van het Heemkundig genootschap van het Meetjesland* 9 (1958): 5–54.

Roosen, Joris and Daniel R. Curtis. "The 'Light Touch' of the Black Death in the Southern Netherlands: An Urban Trick?" *The Economic History Review* 72:1 (February 2019): 32–56. https://onlinelibrary.wiley.com/doi/epdf/10.1111/ehr.12667. Accessed 29 July 2022.

Rosenthal, Jane E. "Three Drawings in an Anglo-Saxon Pontifical: Anthropomorphic Trinity or Threefold Christ?" *The Art Bulletin* 63, no. 4 (December 1981): 547–562.

Ross, David John Athole. *Alexander Historiatus: A Guide to Medieval Illustrated Alexander Literature*. London: Warburg Institute, University of London, 1963.

Ross, D. J. A. *Illustrated Medieval Alexander-Books in French Verse*. Edited by Maud Pérez-Simon and Alison Stones with Martine Meuwese. Turnhout: Brepols, 2019.

Rubin, Miri. *Corpus Christi: The Eucharist in Late Medieval Culture*. Cambridge: Cambridge University Press, 1991. Reprint, 1994.

Rudy, Kathryn M. *Rubrics, Images and Indulgences in Late Medieval Netherlandish Manuscripts*. Leiden: Brill, 2017.

Rudy, Kathryn M. "Touching the Book Again: The Passional of Abbess Kunigunde of Bohemia." In *Codex und Material*, edited by Patrizia Carmassi and Gia Toussaint, 247–257. Wiesbaden: Harrassowitz Verlag, 2018.

Sandler, Lucy Freeman. *Gothic Manuscripts 1285–1385*. 2 vols. London: Harvey Miller, 1986.

Sandler, Lucy Freeman. *Illuminators and Patrons in Fourteenth-Century England: The Psalter and Hours of Humphrey de Bohun and the Manuscripts of the Bohun Family*. London: British Library, 2014.

Schmidt, Gerhard. "Die Wehrdener Kreuzigung der Sammlung von Hirsch und die Kölner Malerei." In *Vor Stefan Lochner: Die Kölner Maler von 1300 bis 1430; Ergebnisse der Ausstellung und des Colloquiums, Köln 1974*, edited by Gerhard Bott and Frank Günter Zehnder, 11–27. Cologne: Druckhaus Rudolf Müller, 1977.

Schmidt, Gerhard. "Die Chorschrankenmalereien des Kölner Domes und die Europäische Malerei." *Kölner Domblatt: Jahrbuch des Zentral-Dombauvereins* 44–45 (1979–1980): 293–340.

Schnütgen-Museums der Stadt Köln and belgischen Ministerien für französische und niederländische Kultur. *Rhein und Maas: Kunst und Kultur 800–1400*. 2 vols. Exhibition catalog, Cologne, Kunsthalle and Brussels, Koninklijke Musea voor Kunst en Geschiedenis, 1972.

Scott-Fleming Sonia. *The Analysis of Pen Flourishing in Thirteenth-Century Manuscripts*. Leiden: E. J. Brill, 1989.

Smeyers, Maurits. "64. Fragmenten van een antifonarium." In *Handschriften uit de abdij van Sint-Truiden*. Exhibition catalog, Sint-Truiden, Provinciaal Museum voor Religieuze Kunst, Begijnhofkerk, 1986, 275–278. Leuven: Uitgeverij Peeters, 1986.

Smeyers, Maurits. "Die verluchting in handschriften uit de abdij van Sint-Truiden." In *Handschriften uit de abdij van Sint-Truiden*. Exhibition catalog, Sint-Truiden, Provinciaal Museum voor Religieuze Kunst, Begijnhofkerk, 1986. Leuven: Uitgeverij Peeters, 1986, 48–64.

Smeyers, Maurits. *Flemish Miniatures from the 8th to the mid-16th Century: The Medieval World on Parchment*. Translated by Karen Bowen and Dirk Imhof. Leuven: Davidsfonds, 1999.

Sotheby and Co. *The Hornby Manuscripts, Part 1: Thirty-four Manuscripts of the 11th to the 15th Century*. Illustrated Catalogue. Sale, Tuesday, 4 June 1974, London.

Stanford Encyclopedia of Philosophy. Summer 2022 ed. Edited by Edward N. Zalta. URL. Also at https://plato.stanford.edu/archives/sum2022/entries/beauty.

Stirnemann, Patricia. "Dating, Placement, and Illumination." *Journal of the Early Book Society for the Study of Manuscripts and Printing History* 11 (2008): 155–166.

Stirnemann, Patricia. "Fils de la vierge. L'initiale à filigranes parisiennes: 1140–1314." *Revue de l'art* 90 (1990): 58–73.

Stirnemann, Patricia and Anne-Ritz-Guilbert. "Cultural Confrontations." In *Under the Influence: The Concept of Influence and the Study of Illuminated* Manuscripts, edited by John Lowden and Alixe Bovey, 65–73. Turnhout: Brepols Publishers, 2007.

Stones, Alison, "Notes on Three Illuminated Alexander Manuscripts." In *The Medieval Alexander Legend and Romance Epic: Essays in Honour of David J. A. Ross*, edited by Peter Noble, Lucie Polak and Claire Isoz, 193–241. Millwood, N.Y.: Kraus International Publications, 1982.

BIBLIOGRAPHY

Stones, Alison. "Another Short Note on Rylands French 1." *Romanesque and Gothic: Essays for George Zarnecki*, edited by Neil Stratford. 2 vols. 1:185–199. Woodbridge, Suffolk: Boydell Press, 1987.

Stones, Alison. "'Mise en page' in the French Lancelot-Grail: The First Hundred and Fifty Years of the Illustrative Tradition." In *Companion to the Lancelot-Grail Cycle*, edited by Carol R. Dover, 125–144. Cambridge: D. S. Brewer, 2003.

Stones, Alison. *Gothic Manuscripts 1260–1320*. 2 vols. London: Harvey Miller Publishers, 2013.

Suntrup, Rudolf. "Te Igitur-Initialen und Kanonbilder in Mittelalterlichen Sakramentarhandschriften." In *Text und Bild: Aspekte des Zusammenwirkens zweier Künste in Mittelalter und früher Neuzeit*, edited by Christel Meier and Uwe Ruberg, 278–382. Wiesbaden: Dr. Ludwig Reichert Verlag, 1980.

Trio, Paul. "L'enlumineur à Bruges, Gand et Ypres (1300–1450): Son milieu socio-économique et corporatif." In *Flanders in a European Perspective: Manuscript Illumination Around 1400 in Flanders and Abroad*, edited by Maurits Smeyers and Bert Cardon, 721–729. Leuven: Peeters, 1995.

Van Buren, Anne H. and Roger S. Wieck. *Illuminating Fashion: Dress in the Art of Medieval France and the Netherlands 1325–1515*. New York: Morgan Library and Museum in association with D. Giles Limited, London, 2011.

Valvekens, Patrick. "De handschriftenproduktie onder Abt Robert van Craenwyck (1350–1366)." In *Handschriften uit de abdij van Sint-Truiden*. Exhibition catalog, Sint-Truiden, Provinciaal Museum voor Religieuze Kunst, Begijnhofkerk, 1986, 231–245. Leuven: Uitgeverij Peeters, 1986.

Vandecapelle-Haagdorens, Lieve. "Het zgn. missaal van Lodewijk van Male, Brussel, Koninklijke Bibliotheek, ms. 9217: Bijdrage tot de studie van de miniatuurkunst in het Maasland tijdens het derde kwart van de 14de eeuw." Thesis for licentiate, Catholic University of Leuven, 1983.

Van der Haeghen, Victor., pub. *Het klooster ten Walle en de abdij van den Groenen Briel: Stukken en oorkonden*. Ghent: G. Annoot-Braeckman, 1888.

Van der Hoerst, Koert. *Illuminated and Decorated Medieval Manuscripts in the University Library, Utrecht: An Illustrated Catalogue*. Cambridge: Cambridge University Press, 1989.

Van Oostrom, F. P. *Maerlant's Wereld*. Amsterdam: Uitgeverij Prometheus, 1996.

Vanwijnsberghe, Dominique. *"De fin or et d'azur": Les commanditaires de livres et le métier de l'enluminure à Tournai à la fin du moyen âge (XIVe–XVe siècles)*. Leuven: Uitgeverij Peeters, 2001.

Vermeeren, P. J. H. and A. F. Dekker. *Inventaris van de handschriften van het Museum Meermanno-Westreenianum*. The Hague: Staatsdrukkerij en Uitgeverijbedrijf, 1960.

Vitzthum, Georg Graf. *Die Pariser Miniaturmalerei von der Zeit des hl. Ludwig bis zu Philipp von Valois und ihr Verhältnis zur Malerei in Nordwesteuropa*. Leipzig: Verlag von Quelle und Meyer, 1907.

Vitzthum, Georg Graf. "Eine Minaturhandschrift aus Weigelschem Besitz." In H. Weizsäcker et al. *Kunstwissenschaftliche Beiträge August Schmarsow gewidmet zum fünfstigsten Semester seiner akademischen Lehrtätigkeit*, 61–72. Leipzig: Verlag von Karl W. Hiersemann, 1907.

Wackett, Jayne. "The Litlyngton Missal: Its Patron, Iconography, and Messages." PhD diss., University of Kent, 2014.

Wallraf-Richartz Museum. *Vor Stefan Lochner: die Kölner Maler von 1300 bis 1430*. Exhibition catalog, Cologne, Wallraf-Richartz Museum, 1974. Cologne: Wallraf-Richartz Museum, 1974.

Walters, Barbara R., Vincent Corrigan, and Peter T. Ricketts. *The Feast of Corpus Christi*. University Park, PA: Pennsylvania State University Press, 2006.

Walters, Lori. "Illuminating the Rose: Gui de Mori and the Illustrations of MS 101 of the Municipal Library, Tournai." In *Rethinking the Romance of the Rose: Text, Image, Reception*, edited by Kevin Brownlee and Sylvia Huot, 167–200. Philadelphia: University of Pennsylvania Press, 1992.

Walters, Lori. "Marian Devotion in the Tournai Rose: From the Monastery to the Household." In *De la Rose: Texte, image, fortune*, edited by Herman Braet and Catherine Bel, 207–270. Leuven: Peeters, 2006.

Weigelt, Curt H. "Rheinische Miniaturen." *Wallraf-Richartz Jahrbuch* 1 (1924): 5–28.

Wilson, H. A., ed. *The Gelasian Sacramentary: Liber Sacramentorum Romanae Ecclesiae*. Oxford: Clarendon Press, 1894.

Wilson, Laurel Ann. "'De novo modo': The Birth of Fashion in the Middle Ages." PhD diss., Fordham University, 2011.

Wolinski, Mary E. "Ferial Office Chants in Flanders, Paris, and Liège: A Study in Local Tastes." Paper presented at the 46th International Congress on Medieval Studies, 2011, Kalamazoo, MI, May 12, 2011.

Wolinski, Mary E. "Plainchant and the Aspirations of a Noble Couple: The Psalter of Arnold of Rummen and Elisabeth of Lierde." Paper delivered at the 43rd International Congress on Medieval Studies, 2008, Kalamazoo, MI, 9 May 2008, and at A Celebration of the Teaching Career of Edward Nowacki, College-Conservatory of Music, University of Cincinnati, 17 May 2008.

Wolters, Mathias Joseph. *Notice historique sur la Commune de Rummen et sur les anciens fiefs de Grasen, Wilre, Bindervelt et Weyer, en Hesbaye*. Ghent: Imprimerie de Léonard Hebbelynck, 1846.

Woolf, Rosemary. *The English Mystery Plays*. Berkeley: University of California Press, 1972. Reprint, 1980.

Wormald, Frances. "The Fitzwarin Psalter and its Allies." *Journal of the Warburg and Courtauld Institutes* 6 (1943): 71–79.

Index

Antonius Sanderus   12
Antwerp   7, 9, 83
Apocalypse, English   44n4, 81, 89, 118
Arnold of Rummen/Oreye
    biography   10n34, 11 and n43
    castle at Rummen   11, 12, 90, 91
    commissioner of manuscripts   2, 94, 107
    connections to Sint-Truiden and
        Liège   12, 68, 71, 73, 84, 90, 94
    financial difficulties   11, 12
    genealogy   11
    heraldry   10n35, 13–15, 90. *See also*
        Appendix 1.
    loss of County of Loon   12, 94
    loss of the Winter Missal   12–15, 91, 94
    marriage   10 and ns34, 36; 11; 14; 74
    political aspirations   1, 8, 11, 12, 90
    portraits   13, 14, 40, 48, 49 and n20, 50,
        53–57, 94
    relations with Louis of Male   9–13, 15
    social position   94
Arnold V of Loon and Chiny, Count   11
Artist 1
    collaboration between Artists 1 and
        2   27, 39, 43, 93
    decoration of borders
        ball-and-squiggle corkscrews   59
        fish faces. *See* Inventory 5.
        flame motif   32, 57, 76, 124
        fluttering, curviliear forms   30, 32, 67
        human faces. *See* Inventory 5.
        loose corkscrews   33, 41, 53
        rosettes   31, 59, 87
    humor   30, 32, 33, 59, 64, 65, 67
    iconography of two-line initials   31, 32.
        See also Tables 3 and 4.
    oeuvre in 10 A14   30
    stylistic sources in Tournai and
        Ghent   30, 84, 89, 94
    visual puns   31
Artist 2/3
    aesthetic of reaching   33, 36, 38 and n49,
        66, 67
    cycles of flourishing   34, 35 and n41, 36.
        See also Appendix 3.
    decoration of borders   33
        Artist 2's compared to Artist 3's   41
        loose corkscrews (Artist 3)   41, 53, 66
        nested pairs   38, 41
        foliate and floral types   33, 35
        tense, wiry corkscrews (Artist 2)   33,
            35, 66, 88
    humor, lack of   33, 41, 43, 67, 68
    iconography of two-line initials   34, 38,
        41. *See also* Tables 3 and 4.
    incompletion of work   38
    palette   33
    rosettes   33, 79, 108
    stylistic sources in Sint-Truiden   77, 94

symmetry   35, 38, 66, 67, 93
tension   38
See also Appendix 3.
Artist 4
    aesthetic of reaching, absence of   42
    completes Artist 2's incomplettions   38,
        42, 43, 47
    corkscrews   42
    emotionalism   42, 43
    follows and assists Artist 3   38, 42, 43, 84
    humor   43
    iconography of two-line initials   42. *See
        also* Tables 3 and 4.
    sparse style   35n41, 38n49, 41, 43, 66
    stylistic kinship to Artist 3   43 and n56
    tension, lack of   38n49

Baldwin IX, Count of Flanders   8
Baron van Westreenen   13
Barthes, Roland   45
Bartholomeus van Holten   13
bas-de-page   15, 21, 51–53, 59 and n58, 76,
    80, 83
Battle of Crécy   9
beauty
    Aquinas's definition of   3
    Classical vs. political notions of   3
Black Death/Plague   1, 9, 10, 68, 76n5, 87,
    91, 92, 94
Bohemia(n)   11n49, 28, 45, 58, 66, 67, 82 and
    n30, 86, 89
Bohun, Bohun family   13n60, 28n17, 45, 50
    and n25, 51 and n25, 65n87, 81n28, 82,
    91
Brabant, Brabantine   10; 11 and n39; 85 and
    ns1, 2; 86; 11 and n39; 13–15; 68; 69; 72;
    73; 85; 86; 90; 94
brass(es)   75, 77, 81, 87n13, 88, 113. *See also*
    Appendix 4.
Bruges   1n1, 6, 8 and n21, 9, 58, 70n15, 73
Bruges Master   89
Brussels   2; 12; 28; 29; 49; 73; 75; 85 and ns2,
    3; 86; 89

Cathedral of St. Lambert   61
Charles IV, Emperor   11, 12n50
Chiny, County of   11 and n42, 12, 14n66,
    56n42. *See also* Appendix 1.
Clementines   61
Cologne
    choir screens   55n39, 86
    site of production   85, 86, 89
    style/iconography   25, 31, 44, 46, 49, 52,
        57, 67, 75 and n3, 76, 79 and n21, 80,
        89n25
    relations to Rummen-group artists,
        manuscripts, patrons   17, 57 and n48,
        58, 68, 75, 77, 80, 82, 84, 85, 89, 93
    other   78, 79n22

colophon(s)
    date of   7
    demise of County of Loon and   1
    description of   6
    first colophon   7, 8, 27 and n3, 30
        indicates Ghent as place of
            production   68, 87, 89
        written by Laurence the Priest   7, 30,
            38, 66, 83
    flourishing of   7 and ns16 and 17; 8, 30
    second colophon   7, 8, 12, 20n17, 63
        written perhaps by Artist 4   66, 84
        mentions Arnold of Rummen   2, 68,
            94, 95
    transcription and translation of
        colophons   6 and n12, 7
columbines   1, 2, 51, 52 and n31, 89
connoisseurship of Morelli, Roger de
    Piles   5
Corpus Christi   1, 2, 59, 60, 61 and n67, 62,
    93, 94
Cortenberghe   11
costume and hairstyle
    chaperon   29
    cornettes   55
    cote   14, 29, 40, 53, 55
    cote hardie   29, 40, 53
    dorlott   40
    pouleines   29 and n23, 40
    surcot   40

Dampierre Master   6n11
Diederik of Heinsberg   11
Dominican/Dominicans   61
duplex/puzzle initial   78, 80, 82

Edward III, King of England   9
Eeklo   14n65
Elisabeth of Hungary   70 and n17, 71, 94, 104
Elisabeth of Lierde
    connections to Elisabeth of Hungary   71,
        94
    connections to Ghent   2, 68, 73, 90, 94
    death of   12–14, 68
    family   10 and n36
    genealogy   10n33
    heraldry   13, 14 and n65, 15. See
        Appendix 1.
    importance to patronage   94
    marriages   10 and ns34, 36, 11, 74, 84, 90,
        91, 94
    portraits of   29, 40, 48, 49 and n20, 50,
        53–57, 65
    properties   10, 11, 91
    relations with Louis of Male   2, 10, 11, 15
    social position   94
Engelbert of the Marck, Bishop of Liège   11,
    12
eucharisma   2, 26, 93, 94

INDEX 159

Eutychia 63 and n83

flagellants 76n5

Gallican elements 71, 72
Gelasian elements 71 and ns19, 22; 72
Ghent illumination
first period, c. 1270–1295 87–89
second period, c. 1310–1335 87–89
Ghent Master 5n8, 6n11, 89
Gilles Li Muisis 76n5
Godfried of Dalenbroek 11
Golden Legend 63 and n 80, 83n32
gorgon(s)
as metaphysical/theological
statement 45, 64, 67
English Apocalypses and Flemish brasses
as possible sources 77, 81
in initials of 10 A 14 1, 36, 44, 45, 47, 52,
64, 65, 67, 75
in Ms Egerton 3277 81n28
in *Speculum* 2 80, 81
in Stockholm Bible 89, 90
linking figures 45
markers for Ghent 2, 77, 81, 89, 90 and
n29
term coined by Baltrusaitis 44n4. *See
also* Appendix 6.
used by Artist of Loppem-Bruges
Antiphonal 75, 81
grisaille 22, 24, 34, 36, 40, 42, 59, 82
Guiard of Laon, Bishop of Cambrai 61

hatching 22, 34, 78
Hugh of St.-Cher, Prior Provincial of the
Dominicans 61
Hundred Years' War 1, 9, 10
hyperspectral imaging/examination 13 and
n61, 14
Hypnos 31

initials
one-line 22 and n3
three or more lines 23, 24, 59, 80 and
n24
two-line 4, 5, 16, 21, 22–25, 30, 31, 32 and
ns30, 32, 33, 34, 36, 38–40, 41 and n55,
42, 43, 48, 66, 79, 82, 86, 88, 93, 94. *See
also* Appendix 3.
International Gothic Style 40, 49, 82 and
n29, 83, 91
Italianate, Italianism(s) 2, 3, 37, 40, 41,
44n2, 49, 50, 51, 52n32, 57, 67, 76, 83, 85,
89 and n27, 94

Jacobus de Voragine 63ns79, 80
Jaquet Maci/Jacobus Mathey 3n3, 88 and
n20, 90
James of Artevelde 1, 9 and n31, 10
James of Troyes 61

Jan van Eyck 49, 51 and n26, 89
Jean de Vignay 63
Jean Pucelle 46 and n12, 54, 82, 88n20, 89,
90n28
Jehan de Grise 8, 76
Johanna of Brabant 11, 86
Johanna of Loon 11, 47n13
Johannes van Myrle, Provost 77, 78 and n14,
80 and n25, 81, 87, 88
John of Arkel, Bishop of Liège 8, 12
John of Cambrai 61
John of Gaunt 9
John of Lausanne 61
John XXII, Pope 61
Juliana of Mont Cornillon 61 and n67

Laurence the Priest 7, 27 and n3, 29 and
n22, 30, 38, 42, 66, 67, 83, 93, 94
Limburg 11, 13, 47n14
Loon, County/Countship of 1, 8, 11 and
ns42, 46, 12, 14n66, 56n42, 90, 94. *See
also* Appendix 1.
Louis I of Nevers, Count 9n27, 10, 94
Louis II of Nevers, Count 9 and n27, 10
Louis IV of Loon and Chiny, Count 11
Louis of Male, Count of Flanders
Cartulary of 10n34
character of 1, 9
genealogy, marriage, and kinship 10, 12,
13, 15, 68, 89
heraldry 2, 10, 13, 15
ownership of the Winter Missal and other
Rummen-group manuscripts 1, 9, 10,
12–15, 94
relations with Arnold of Rummen and
Elisabeth of Lierde 10, 11 and n37, 12,
13, 15, 86
relations with Ghent 9, 10, 68
See also Appendix 1

manuscripts, East Anglian 33, 44 and n2,
52n31
Margaret of Brabant 13, 15, 86. *See also*
Appendix 1.
Margaret of Male 9, 51
marginalia 6, 32, 38, 47, 76ns 5, 6, 77, 80,
81, 85n3
Martinus de Venne 78
Master of the Ghent Ceremonial 76n6, 89,
90 and n28
methods, inductive and deductive 6
Mérode Altarpiece 50 and n23, 54
Mosan 25, 49, 69, 72, 85, 89
Motivengeschichte 34
Musal 12
musical instruments 50 and ns24, 25

nomenclature of artists, difficulties
with 28n11, 29n17

Oreye, arms of 13, 14 and n66, 47 and n13,
56n42. *See also* Appendix 1.

panel painting
Flemish 3, 34, 46, 49, 50, 51 and n26,
52n31, 53, 54 and n38, 58n52, 66, 68
Italian 54 and n38, 63
Paolo Veneziano 63
penwork flourishers and flourishing
regional styles
Ghent 77, 88
northern Netherlands 3 and n3, 88
Paris 3 and n3, 88
Sint-Truiden 77–80
criteria for identifying artists 5 and n8
possibilities of flourishing 1, 3, 4, 24, 38,
93, 94
relationship to brush painting 4, 5
significance of in the study of
manuscripts 3, 4
Perweis 14n65. *See also* Appendix 1.
Philippe Gaudence Emmanuel de
Francquen 12
Philip of Alsace, Count of Flanders 8
Philip the Bold, Duke of Burgundy 9, 10
Philip the Good, Duke of Burgundy 12, 89
Philip VI, King of France 9
Philippa of Hainault, Queen 9
Pierart dou Tielt 8, 28, 63n81, 76 and n6, 85,
90 and n28
Pleshey Castle, Essex 65n87, 91
production, models of 5, 6

Quaetbeecke 7, 11, 12

Rhine/Rhineland/Rhenish 3 and n3, 25, 28,
31, 50, 52n32, 79, 85, 86 and n6
Robert of Bethune, Count of Flanders 9n27
Robert of Turotte, Bishop of Liège 61
Robert van Craenwyck, Abbot of Abbey of
Sint-Truiden 78 and ns15, 16, 79n22, 87,
88
Rummen-group manuscripts and artists 1
and n1, 5n8, 6, 10n35, 50, 57, 58, 71,
75, 78, 80, 81n28, 84, 86, 89. *See also*
Appendix 3.

shingling technique 49, 50, 65, 66
Simon of Mirabello 1, 10 and n33, 12n52,
14n65, 73, 94
Sint-Truiden, Abbey of 20 n11, 72n30, 77,
78, 86n6
Somerghem 10n34, 14n65. *See also*
Appendix 1.
St. Agatha 63 and ns83, 84
St. Lucy 63 and ns79, 80
St. Thomas Aquinas 3 and n5, 61 and n71, 62
stained glass 55n39, 75n3
Stokkem 11

160 INDEX

ten Walle, palace of   10, 11, 91
terminal complex(es)
  Artist 1's   7*n*17, 30–33, 77
  Artist 2's   33
    extensions   33
    in Cycles 1–5   35, 36. *See also*
      Appendix 3.
    in his manuscripts from
      Sint-Truiden   79
    symmetries   33
  definition and description of   22, 25, 35
  lower margin   24, 25, 31, 33, 53
  site of flourishing   25, 93

  site of visual puns on heads, faces   31,
    32, 77
  trimming of   18
  upper margin   7*n*17, 24, 30, 33
  with corkscrews   30
  See also Appendix 3.
Textualis formata   20
Textualis quadrata   20
Tournai   8, 9, 25, 28 and n17, 30, 67, 75–77,
  84
transmedial migration/adoption   5, 25, 88
Trier   49

tronie(s)   34, 94

Urban IV, Pope   2, 61

wall painting   75 and ns3, 4; 85
Wenceslas of Bohemia, Duke of Brabant   11,
  14, 68, 73, 85, 86, 94
Willem de Dycka   78, 87
William of Oreye   11
wool trade   9

Ypres   8 and n21, 9, 90

Index of Manuscripts Cited

Aberystwyth, National Library of Wales
Ms. 15536E (Sherbrooke Missal)
44n1, 60n63, 64n85

Amiens, Bibliothèque municipale
Ms. 157 (Missal of Corbie) 64n85

Arras, Médiathèque de l'abbaye Saint-Vaast
Ms. 38 60n62, 60n65
Ms. 278 (933) (Missal of St. Vaast)
44n1, 60n63
Ms. 561 117n2
Ms. 601 23n6, 44n1, 61n73, 113n30

Baltimore, Walters Art Gallery
Ms. 82 73n38, 87n15, 89

Bruges, Openbare Bibliotheek
Ms. SVC 10a/b (Loppem-Bruges antiphonal) 1 and n1, 24, 30, 44 and n3, 64, 65, 75, 76, 77, 81, 87, 90n29, 93, 107, 117, 118

Brussels, Koninklijke Bibliotheek/ Bibliothèque royale de Belgique
Ms. 5 (Les grandes chroniques de France) 85n1
Ms. 212 57n46
Ms. 5163–5164 70n17
Ms. 6426 1 and n1, 24, 25, 28 and n17, 29, 35, 49n20, 50n25, 59n58, 78, 79, 80n25, 81 and n28, 85 and n3, 87, 90n29, 105–108 and n6, 111, 117, 118
Ms. 9104–9105 85n1
Ms. 9217 1; 10 and n35; 14; 15 and n70; 16; 18n8; 23ns5, 6; 24; 25; 28 and ns7, 13; 29 and n18; 35; 46n10; 49 and n20; 53n34; 56 and n45; 57; 58; 61; 69ns 2, 3; 71; 72; 73; 75n3; 77; 78; 79n20; 80n25; 85; 86 and n6; 87; 90; 105–109 and ns12–14; 110; 112; 114; 116–118
Ms. 9225 85ns1, 2
Ms. 9229–9230 85ns1, 2
Ms. 9245 85n1
Ms. 9427 1 and n1, 10 and n35, 13, 14, 15 and n69, 16, 24, 25, 28 and n17, 29 and n18, 35, 36,
49n20, 69n2, 71, 75n3, 78–80n25, 81, 87, 90, 100n8, 105, 106, 107, 108 and n8, 111, 117
Ms. 9961–9962 (Peterborough Psalter) 48n19
Ms. 10320 8n21
Ms. 13076–13077 76n5

Cambrai, Médiathèque municipale
Ms. 133 (Breviary of Sainte-Aldegonde de Maubeuge) 76n5
Ms. 153 114n34
Ms. 154 114n34
Ms. 189 117n2

Cambridge, Magdalene College
Ms. F-4–8 70n17

Cambridge, Trinity College
Ms. B.11.22 87n15

Cologne, Dioezesan- und Dombibliothek
Cod. 149 (Missal of Conrad of Rennenberg) 57 and n48, 60n66, 114 and n35

Cologne, Wallraf-Richartz-Museum & Fondation Corboud, Graphische Sammlung
Inv.-Nr. M 5 58n50
Inv.-Nr. M 6 51n27
Inv.-Nr. M 8 58n50
Inv.-Nr. M 16 58n50
Inv.-Nr. M 18 558n50
Inv.-Nr. M 22 58n50

Copenhagen, Kongelige Bibliotek
Ms. G.K.S. 3384,8° 73n38, 87n15
Ms. Thott 517.4° 13n60
Ms. Thott 547.4° 13n60, 50n25
Ny kgl. saml. 41,8° 87n15

Darmstadt, Universitäts- und Landesbibliothek
Ms. 837 44n1, 60n66, 63n82, 114n38
Ms. 874 52n31, 114n38
Ms. 876 25n8; 44ns1, 3; 54n39; 57n49; 89n25; 115n40
Ms. 2505 49n19

The Hague, Koninklijke Bibliotheek
Ms. 78 D 40 (Festal Missal of Johannes of Marchello) 24n7; 48n16; 60ns 62, 65; 61 and n70
Ms. 135 E 15 73n38, 87n15, 88n19
Ms. KA XX (Spiegel Historiael) 87 and n15

Liège, Bibliothèque de l'Université de Liège
Ms. 43 (Dialogues of Gregory the Great) 78 and n15, 79 and n20, 80 and n23
Ms. 57 (Passionarium I) 78 and n15; 79 and ns20, 22; 82 and n29; 133
Ms. 58 (Passionarium 2) 71n18, 78 and n15, 79n22, 80 and n23, 82, 83
Ms. 60 (Speculum 1) 79; 80 and ns25, 27
Ms. 61 (Speculum 2) 79; 80 and ns25, 27; 81; 89; 117
Ms. 138 (Homilies on the Gospels) 78 and n15, 79
Ms. 150 (Rationale divinorum officiorum) 78 and n14
Ms. 223 (Catholicon) 78 and n14
Ms. 326 78n16
Ms. 431 72n31

London, British Library
Ms. Add. 24686 (Alphonso or Tenison Psalter) 46n10, 52n31
Ms. Add. 42130 (Luttrell Psalter Psalter) 28 and n15, 46
Ms. Add. 44949 58n52
Ms. Add. 29253 87n15
Ms. Egerton 1894 (Egerton Genesis) 55n40, 91, 112n30, 113n30
Ms. Egerton 3018 52n32
Ms. Egerton 3277 81n28
Ms. Harley 2899 24n7
Ms. Royal 2.B.VII (Queen Mary's Psalter) 55n40, 63n82, 112n28
Ms. Stowe 17 54n37, 73n35
Ms. Yates Thompson 14 (St. Omer Psalter) 33 and n33, 44 and n2
Ms. Yates Thompson 8 (Breviary of Renaud [or Marguerite] of Bar) 46n8, 52n31, 80n27

London, Victoria & Albert Museum
Ms. MSL/1891/1346 60n63

National Library of Sweden, Ms. A 165 (Stockholm Bible) 89 and n27, 90, 117, 118 and n6

New York, Metropolitan Museum of Art
Cloisters Ms. 54.1.2 (Hours of Jeanne d'Evreux) 46n12, 48n19, 54n38, 82n29, 88n20, 112

New York, The Morgan Library & Museum
Ms. G. 24 (*Voeux du paon*)
  48*n*16, 76 and n5, 77
  and n10, 86
Ms. G. 60 (Palermo Bible)
  46*n*8
Ms. M. 107 (Tiptoft Missal)
  60*n*66
Ms. M. 360.13 (Hungarian Anjou
  Legendary) 58*n*55
Ms. M. 360.26 (Hungarian Anjou
  Legendary) 76*n*5
Ms. M. 436 46 and n9
Ms. M. 440 73*n*34
Ms. M. 72 6*n*11
Ms. M. 729 (Psalter of Yolande of
  Soissons) 46*n*10, 110*n*16
Ms. M. 742 (Laudario of Sant'Agnese)
  48*n*18
Ms. M. 795 49*n*19

Oxford, Bodleian Library
Ms. Auct.D.4.2 58*n*52
Ms. Bodley 264 (*Romance of Alexander*)
  8 n20, 25 and n9, 28
  and n17, 29 and n23,
  31, 63 and n81, 64 and
  n9, 77*n*9. *See also*
  refs. to this ms. in
  Appendix 4.
Ms. Bodley 316 (*Polychronicon*)
  52*n*31
Ms. Buchanan g.2 70*n*17
Ms. Douce 313 51*n*27
Ms. Douce 366 (Ormsby Psalter)
  33 and n33
Ms. Douce 5 24; 25 and n8; 44; 46;
  48*n*16; 51*n*27; 57; 58;
  71*n*21; 72; 73 and ns37,
  38; 87; 88 and n19; 89.
  See also Appendix 5.

Ms. Douce 6 24, 25*n*8, 48*n*16, 58*n*53,
  73*n*38, 87, 88 and n19,
  89
Ms. Lat. liturg. f. 3 29*n*21

Paris, Bibliothèque nationale de France
Ms. fr. 122 (*Lancelot du lac*) 76 and n5,
  77*n*9 Ms. fr. 152 (*Bible historiale*)
  29*n*21
Ms. fr. 414 (*Golden Legend*)
  63*n*84
Ms. lat. 1107 (St. Denis Missal)
  60*n*62, 64*n*85, 65*n*86
Ms. lat. 1112 60*n*64
Ms. lat. 11935 (Billyng Bible)
  88*n*20
Ms. lat. 12048 (Gellone Sacramentary)
  71*n*19
Ms. lat. 17322 65*n*86
Ms. lat. 765 (Fitzwarin Psalter)
  28 and n15
Ms. lat. 830 60*n*62
Ms. n. acq. fr. 16251 63*n*82
Ms. n. acq. lat. 3093 (*Très Belles Heures de
  Notre Dame*) 45*n*6, 51*n*26

Reims, Bibliothèque municipale
Ms. 230 53*n*34

Rouen, Bibliothèque municipale
Ms. 299A.334 60*n*64

Staatsbibliothek Berlin Preussischer
  Kulturbesitz
Ms. theol. lat. fol. 271 (Missal of Sankt
  Salvator, Prüm) 44*n*1, 53*n*34

Stadsmuseum Gent
Inv. A60.01 (Missal of St. Peter's Abbey)
  5*n*8; 54 and n37, 39;
  70ns 15, 16; 71 and n21,
  87, 88

Toledo, Archivo de la Catedral
Ms. 56.19 65*n*86

Tournai, Bibliothèque du Chapitre cathédrale
Ms. A 11 53*n*34, 60*n*66

Tournai, Bibliothèque municipale
Ms. 12 (9) 53*n*34, 60*n*66
Ms. 101 (*Roman de la rose*)
  76 and n5, 77 and n9

Universiteit Gent Universiteitsbibliotheek
Ms. 114 (Ghent Ceremonial)
  88 and n22
Ms. 233 (Ghent Ceremonial of 1322)
  25*n*8; 54 and n39;
  60*n*63; 73*n*38; 76 and
  n6; 87–89; 90 and
  ns28, 29
Ms. 3381 (Breviary of St. Peter's Abbey)
  8*n*21; 70*n*13; 71ns 21
  and 25; 87*n*17

Vatican City, Biblioteca Apostolica Vaticana
Ms. Cod. cap. 63B 45*n*6
Ms. Reg. lat. 316 (Gelasian Sacramentary)
  71 and ns22, 25
Ms. Urb. lat. 603 (Breviary of Blanche of
  France) 63*n*82
Ms. Vat. lat. 1389 (Bolognese Decretals)
  46 and n8, 48 and n17

Vienna, Österreichische Nationalbibliothek
Cod. 1826* (Vienna Bohun Psalter)
  81*n*28, 91 and n31

Walters Art Gallery
Ms. 82 73*n*38, 87*n*15, 89

Figures

∵

Full Pages

∵

FIGURES 167

FIGURE 1 Front cover, calfskin. 18th c. Winter Missal of Arnold of Rummen, Sint-Truiden (text), Ghent (decoration and illumination), c.1345–1366. The Hague, Huis van het boek, Ms. MMW 10 A 14
PHOTO: HUIS VAN HET BOEK

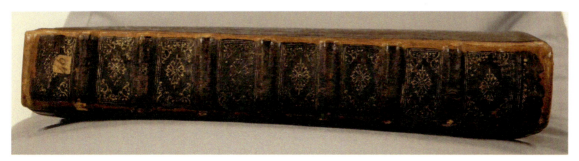

FIGURE 1A Spine of calfskin cover with gold stippling and filigree, 18th c. Winter Missal of Arnold of Rummen, Sint-Truiden (text), Ghent (decoration and illumination), c.1345–1366. The Hague, Huis van het boek, Ms. MMW 10 A 14
PHOTO: AUTHOR, BY PERMISSION

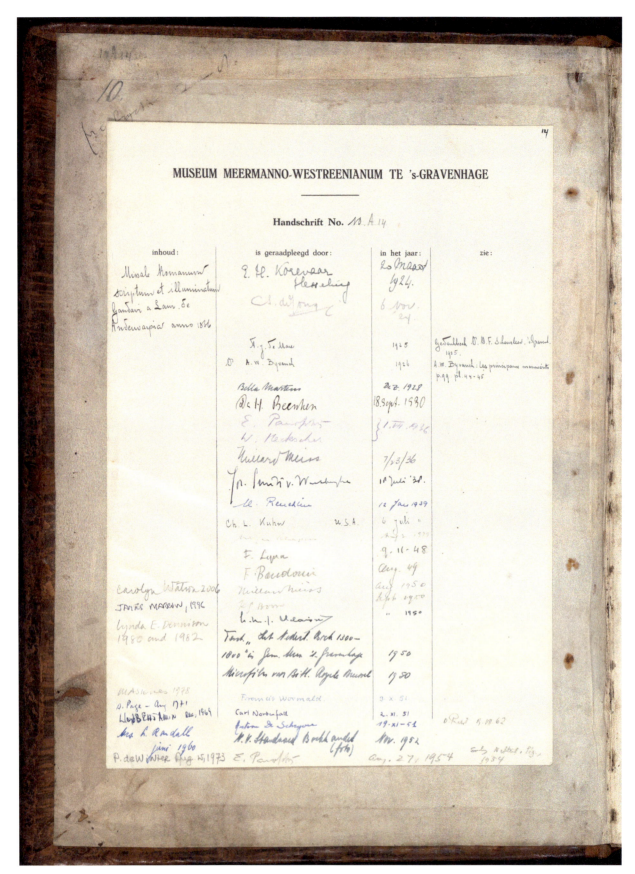

FIGURE 2 Inside of front cover. Winter Missal of Arnold of Rummen, Sint-Truiden (text), Ghent (decoration and illumination), c.1345–1366. The Hague, Huis van het boek, Ms. MMW 10 A 14

PHOTO: HUIS VAN HET BOEK

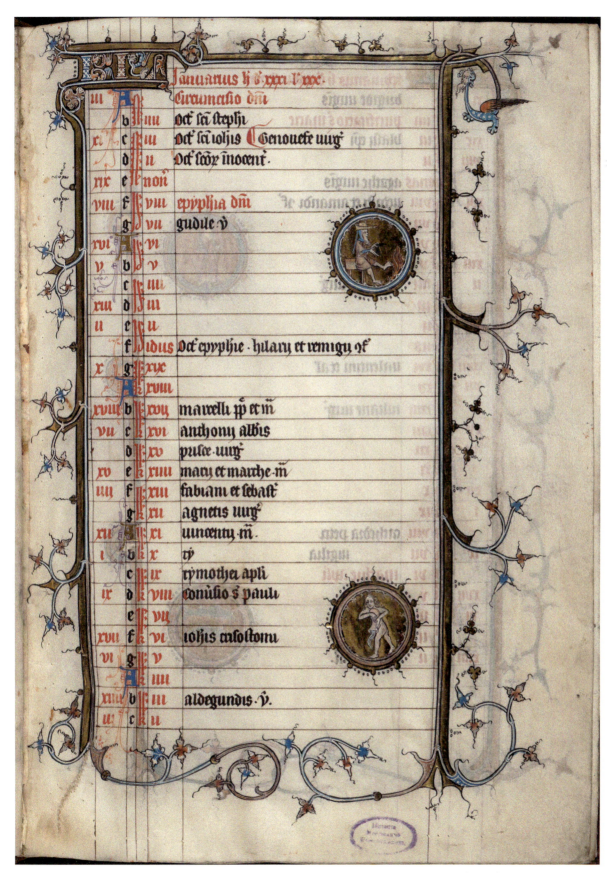

FIGURE 3 Calendar for January. Artist 1. Winter Missal of Arnold of Rummen, Sint-Truiden (text), Ghent (decoration and illumination), c.1345–1366. The Hague, Huis van het boek, Ms. MMW 10 A 14, fol. 1r
PHOTO: HUIS VAN HET BOEK

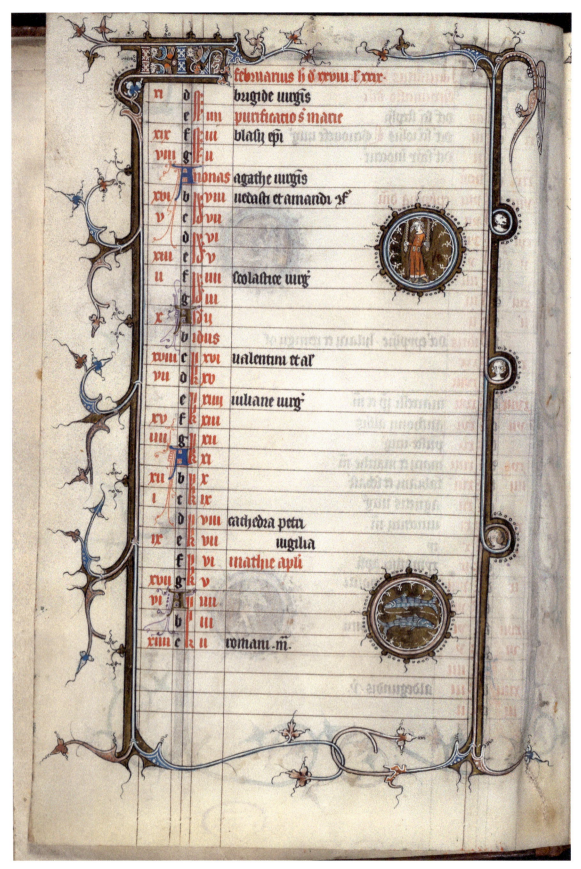

FIGURE 4   Calendar for February. Artist 1. Winter Missal of Arnold of Rummen, Sint-Truiden (text), Ghent (decoration and illumination), c.1345–1366. The Hague, Huis van het boek, Ms. MMW 10 A 14, fol. 1v
PHOTO: HUIS VAN HET BOEK

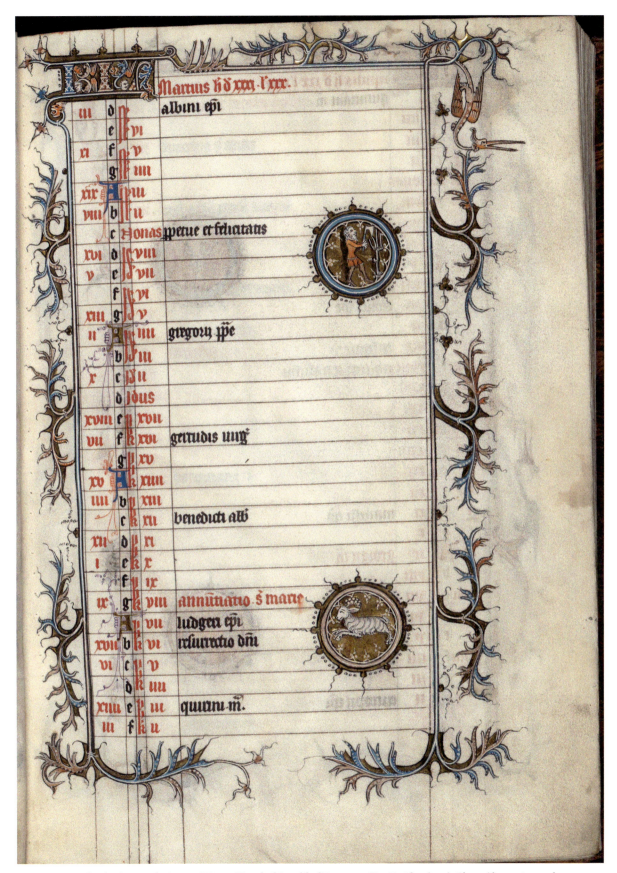

FIGURE 5   Calendar for March. Artist 1. Winter Missal of Arnold of Rummen, Sint-Truiden (text), Ghent (decoration and illumination), c.1345–1366. The Hague, Huis van het boek, Ms. MMW 10 A 14, fol. 2r
PHOTO: HUIS VAN HET BOEK

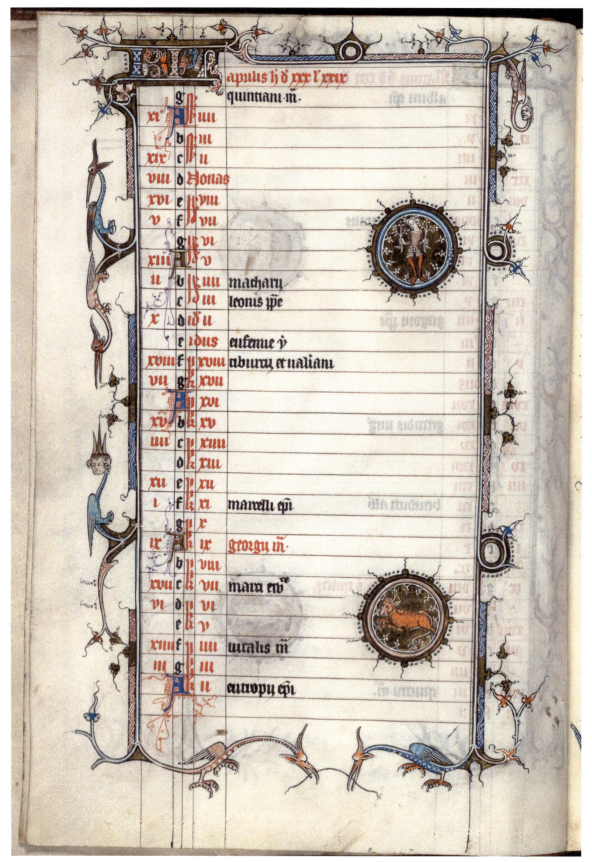

FIGURE 6 Calendar for April. Artist 1. Winter Missal of Arnold of Rummen, Sint-Truiden (text), Ghent (decoration and illumination), c.1345–1366. The Hague, Huis van het boek, Ms. MMW 10 A 14, fol. 2v
PHOTO: HUIS VAN HET BOEK

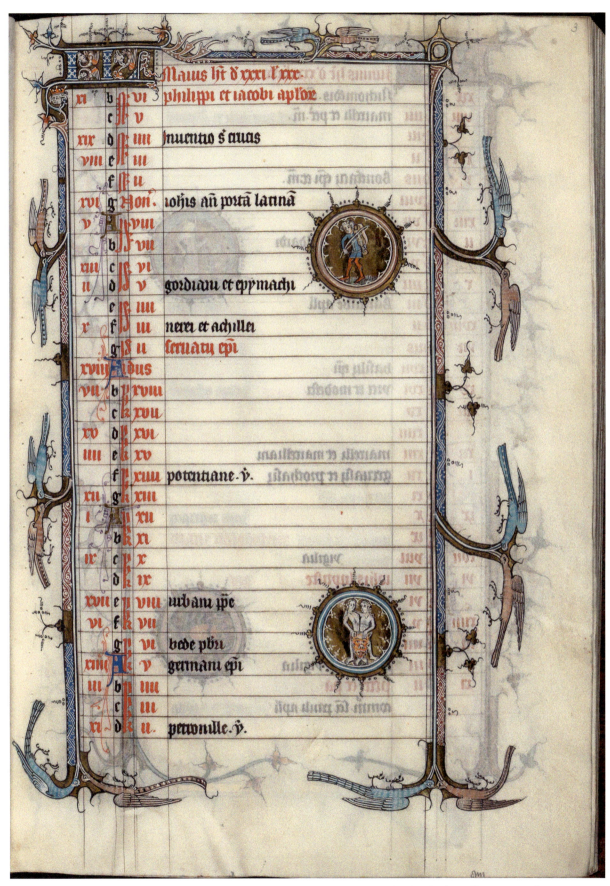

FIGURE 7   Calendar for May. Artist 1. Winter Missal of Arnold of Rummen, Sint-Truiden (text), Ghent (decoration and illumination), *c.*1345–1366. The Hague, Huis van het boek, Ms. MMW 10 A 14, fol. 3r
PHOTO: HUIS VAN HET BOEK

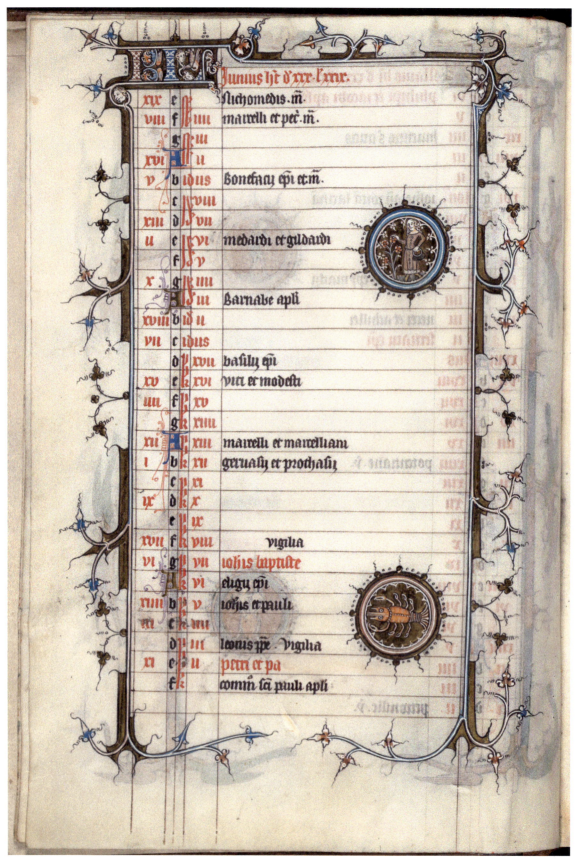

FIGURE 8 Calendar for June. Artist 1. Winter Missal of Arnold of Rummen, Sint-Truiden (text), Ghent (decoration and illumination), c.1345–1366. The Hague, Huis van het boek, Ms. MMW 10 A 14, fol. 3v
PHOTO: HUIS VAN HET BOEK

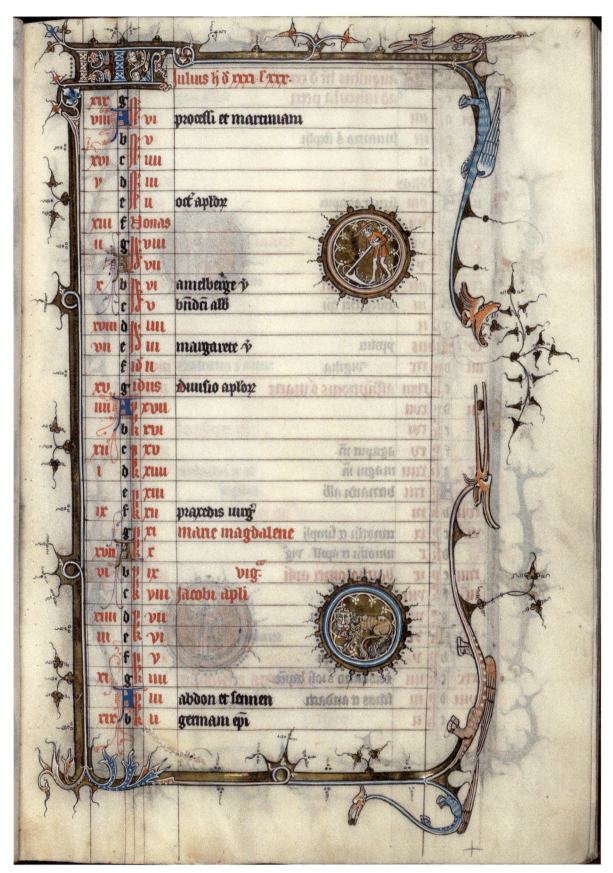

FIGURE 9   Calendar for July. Artist 1. Winter Missal of Arnold of Rummen, Sint-Truiden (text), Ghent (decoration and illumination), c.1345–1366. The Hague, Huis van het boek, Ms. MMW 10 A 14, fol. 4r
PHOTO: HUIS VAN HET BOEK

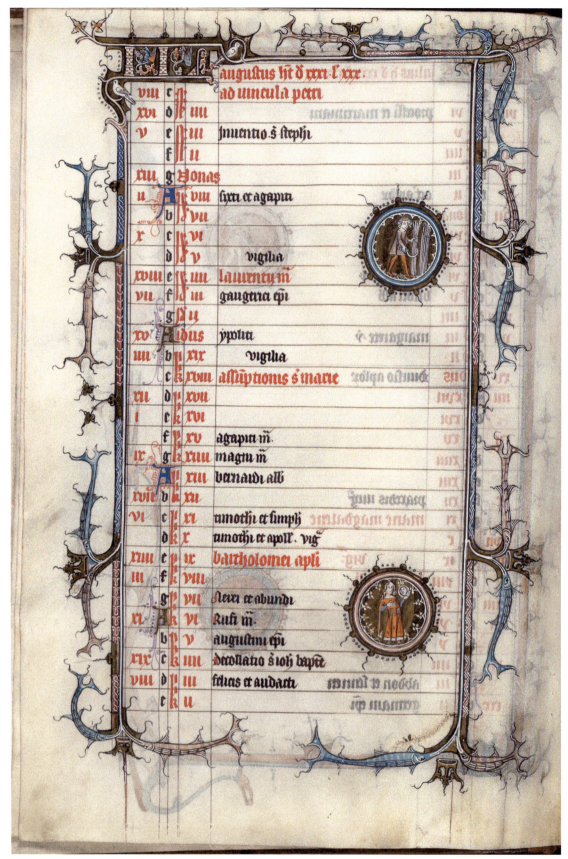

FIGURE 10 Calendar for August. Artist 1. Winter Missal of Arnold of Rummen, Sint-Truiden (text), Ghent (decoration and illumination), c.1345–1366. The Hague, Huis van het boek, Ms. MMW 10 A 14, fol. 4v
PHOTO: HUIS VAN HET BOEK

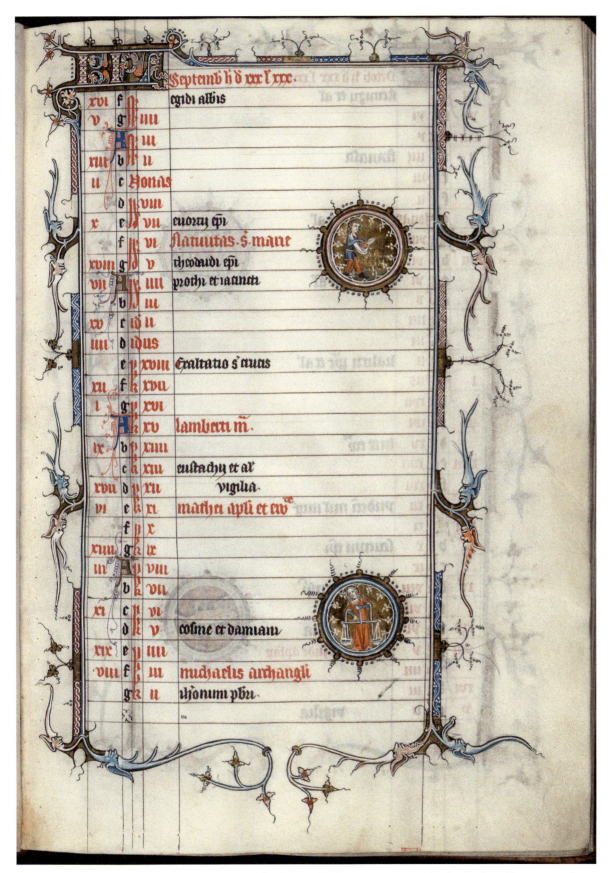

FIGURE 11 Calendar for September. Artist 1. Winter Missal of Arnold of Rummen, Sint-Truiden (text), Ghent (decoration and illumination), c.1345–1366. The Hague, Huis van het boek, Ms. MMW 10 A 14, fol. 5r
PHOTO: HUIS VAN HET BOEK

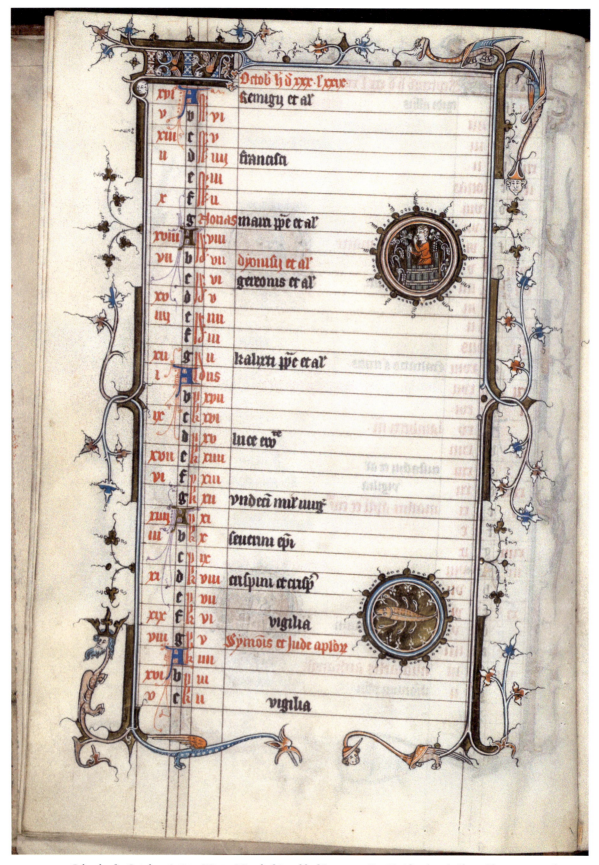

FIGURE 12 Calendar for October. Artist 1. Winter Missal of Arnold of Rummen, Sint-Truiden (text), Ghent (decoration and illumination), c.1345–1366. The Hague, Huis van het boek, Ms. MMW 10 A 14, fol. 5v
PHOTO: HUIS VAN HET BOEK

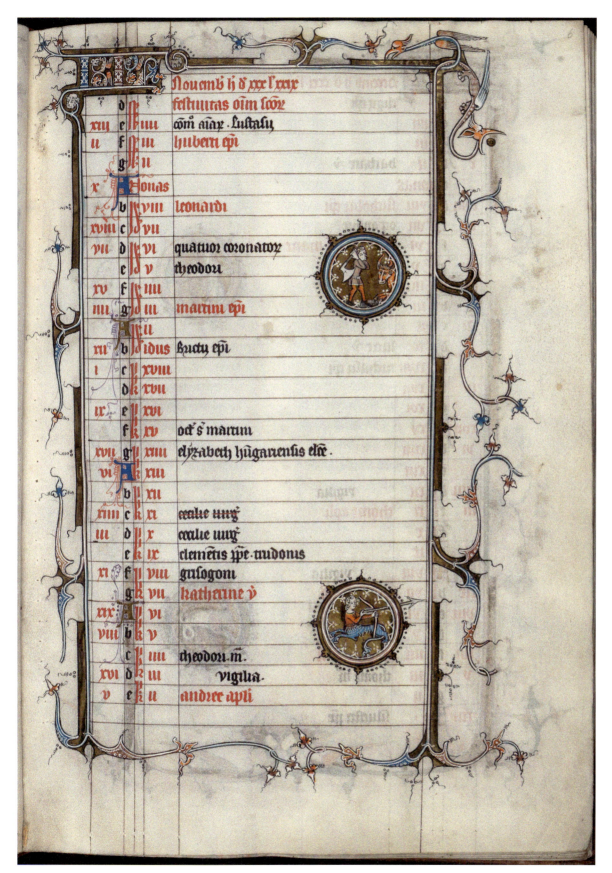

FIGURE 13   Calendar for November. Artist 1. Winter Missal of Arnold of Rummen, Sint-Truiden (text), Ghent (decoration and illumination), c.1345–1366. The Hague, Huis van het boek, Ms. MMW 10 A 14, fol. 6r
PHOTO: HUIS VAN HET BOEK

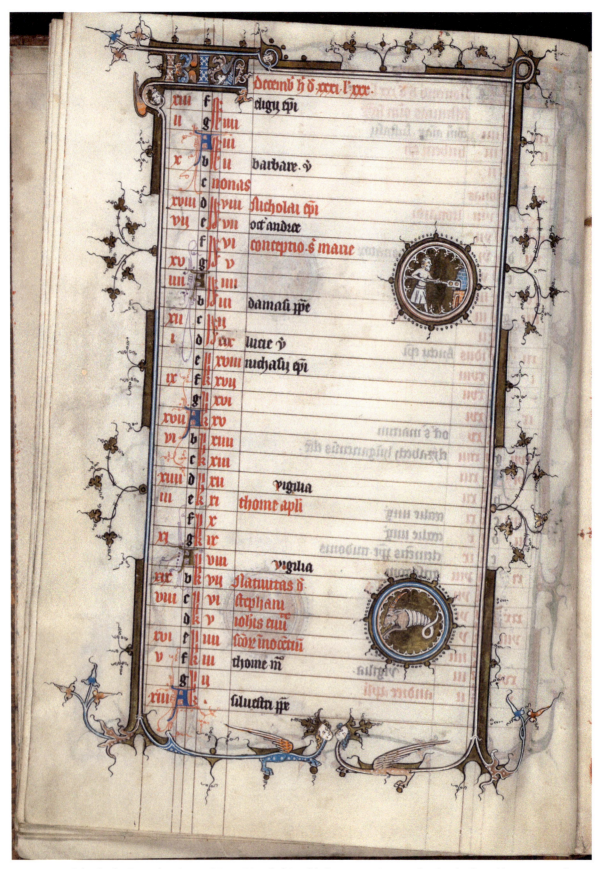

FIGURE 14 Calendar for December. Artist 1. Winter Missal of Arnold of Rummen, Sint-Truiden (text), Ghent (decoration and illumination), *c.*1345–1366. The Hague, Huis van het boek, Ms. MMW 10 A 14, fol. 6v
PHOTO: HUIS VAN HET BOEK

FIGURE 15 *Ad te levavi*, First Sunday of Advent. Artist 2. Winter Missal of Arnold of Rummen, Sint-Truiden (text), Ghent (decoration and illumination), *c*.1345–1366. The Hague, Huis van het boek, Ms. MMW 10 A 14, fol. 7r
PHOTO: HUIS VAN HET BOEK

FIGURE 16 Silver stains from overpainted shields. Winter Missal of Arnold of Rummen, Sint-Truiden (text), Ghent (decoration and illumination), c.1345–1366. The Hague, Huis van het boek, Ms. MMW 10 A 14, fol. 7v
PHOTO: HUIS VAN HET BOEK

FIGURE 17 Penwork with a variety of foliate types. Artist 2. Winter Missal of Arnold of Rummen, Sint-Truiden (text), Ghent (decoration and illumination), c.1345–1366. The Hague, Huis van het boek, Ms. MMW 10 A 14, fol. 8r
PHOTO: HUIS VAN HET BOEK

FIGURE 19 Penwork of Cycle 1A. Artist 2. Winter Missal of Arnold of Rummen, Sint-Truiden (text), Ghent (decoration and illumination), c.1345–1366. The Hague, Huis van het boek, Ms. MMW 10 A 14, fol. 9r
PHOTO: HUIS VAN HET BOEK

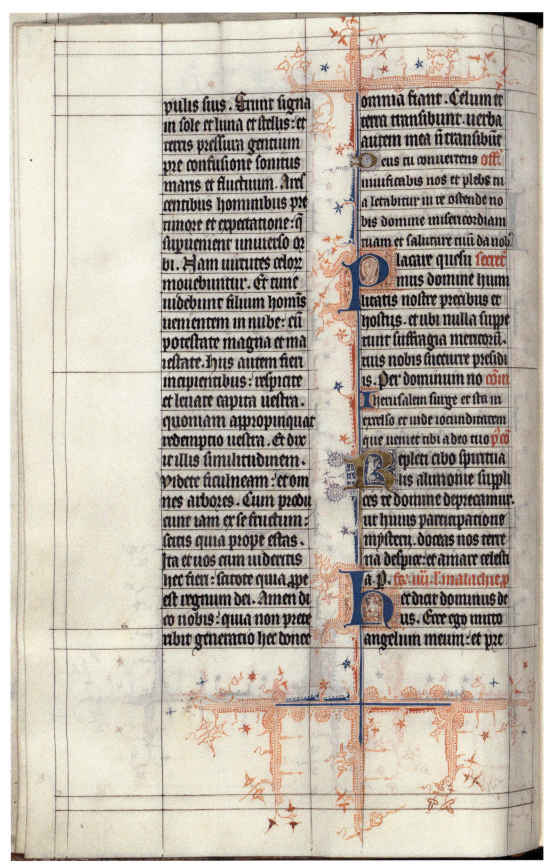

FIGURE 20 Lower terminal complex; hooked penwork tendril supporting a head; lateral extensions of lower terminal complex. Artist 2. Winter Missal of Arnold of Rummen, Sint-Truiden (text), Ghent (decoration and illumination), *c.*1345–1366. The Hague, Huis van het boek, Ms. MMW 10 A 14, fol. 9v
PHOTO: HUIS VAN HET BOEK

FIGURE 21 Initial *I(hesus)* with elongated grotesque pressed into panel beside initial. Artist 2. Winter Missal of Arnold of Rummen, Sint-Truiden (text), Ghent (decoration and illumination) *c*.1345–1366. The Hague, Huis van het boek, Ms. MMW 10 A 14, fol. 10r
PHOTO: HUIS VAN HET BOEK

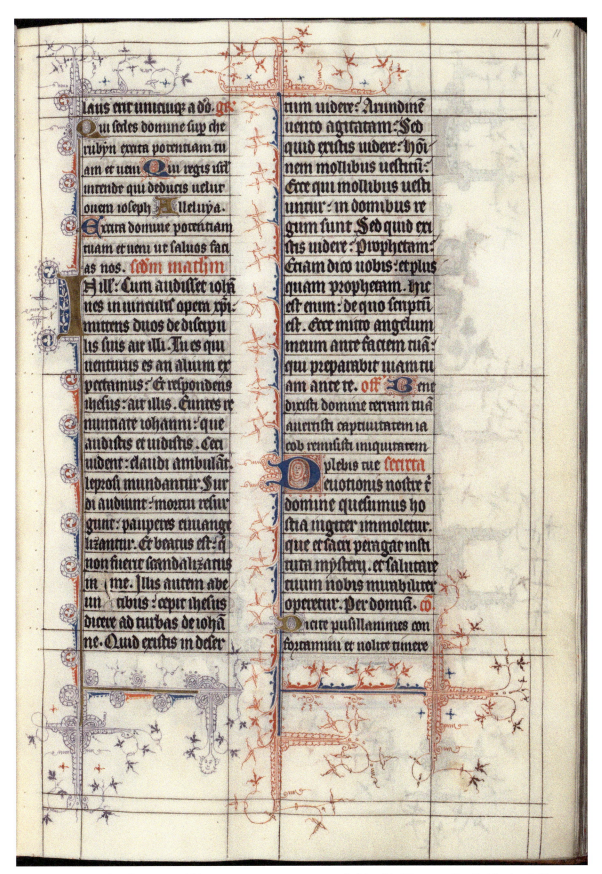

FIGURE 23 Penwork with a variety of foliate types. Artist 2. Winter Missal of Arnold of Rummen, Sint-Truiden (text), Ghent (decoration and illumination), c.1345–1366. The Hague, Huis van het boek, Ms. MMW 10 A 14, fol. 11r
PHOTO: HUIS VAN HET BOEK

FIGURE 24 Diagonal alignment of elements in lower terminal complex; extension of border bar into terminal complex. Artist 2. Winter Missal of Arnold of Rummen, Sint-Truiden (text), Ghent (decoration and illumination), c.1345–1366. The Hague, Huis van het boek, Ms. MMW 10 A 14, fol. 11v
PHOTO: HUIS VAN HET BOEK

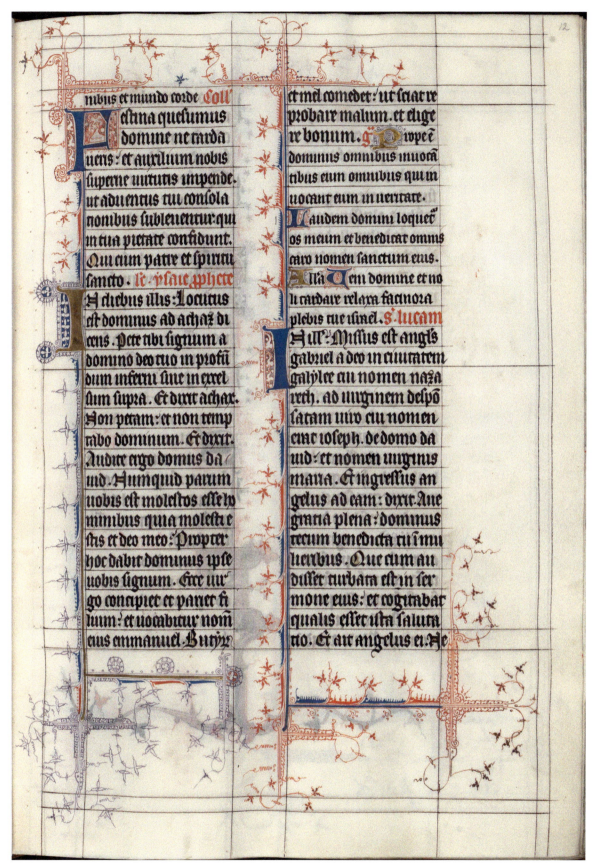

FIGURE 25   Penwork Cycle 1C. Artist 2. Winter Missal of Arnold of Rummen, Sint-Truiden (text), Ghent (decoration and illumination), c.1345–1366. The Hague, Huis van het boek, Ms. MMW 10 A 14, fol. 12r
PHOTO: HUIS VAN HET BOEK

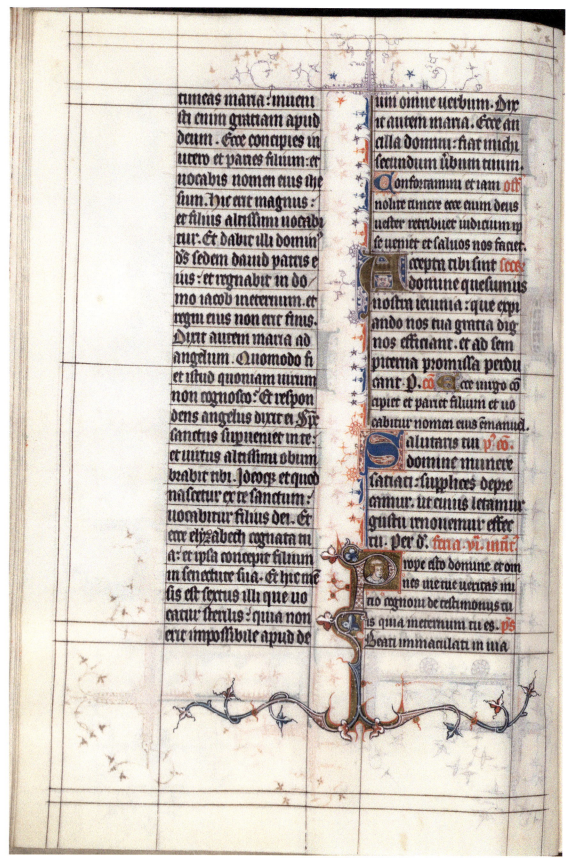

FIGURE 26 Anchored and floating rosettes; symmetries in penwork of upper terminal complex echoed in lower partial border. Artist 2. Winter Missal of Arnold of Rummen, Sint-Truiden (text), Ghent (decoration and illumination), c.1345–1366. The Hague, Huis van het boek, Ms. MMW 10 A 14, fol. 12v
PHOTO: HUIS VAN HET BOEK

FIGURE 27   Initial *D(eus)* with beardless man. Artist 2. Winter Missal of Arnold of Rummen, Sint-Truiden (text), Ghent (decoration and illumination), c.1345–1366. The Hague, Huis van het boek, Ms. MMW 10 A 14, fol. 13v
PHOTO: HUIS VAN HET BOEK

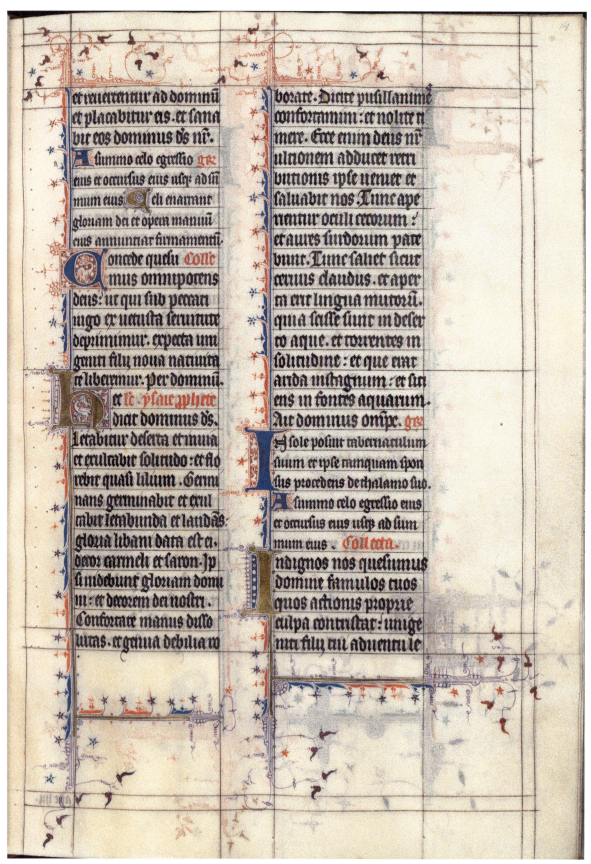

FIGURE 28　Penwork of Cycle 1A. Artist 2. Winter Missal of Arnold of Rummen, Sint-Truiden (text), Ghent (decoration and illumination), c.1345–1366. The Hague, Huis van het boek, Ms. MMW 10 A 14, fol. 14r
PHOTO: HUIS VAN HET BOEK

FIGURE 29 Floating and anchored rosettes. Artist 2. Winter Missal of Arnold of Rummen, Sint-Truiden (text), Ghent (decoration and illumination), *c.*1345–1366. The Hague, Huis van het boek, Ms. MMW 10 A 14, fol. 14v
PHOTO: HUIS VAN HET BOEK

FIGURE 30   Convex *I*. Artist 3. Winter Missal of Arnold of Rummen, Sint-Truiden (text), Ghent (decoration and illumination), c.1345–1366. The Hague, Huis van het boek, Ms. MMW 10 A 14, fol. 15r
PHOTO: HUIS VAN HET BOEK

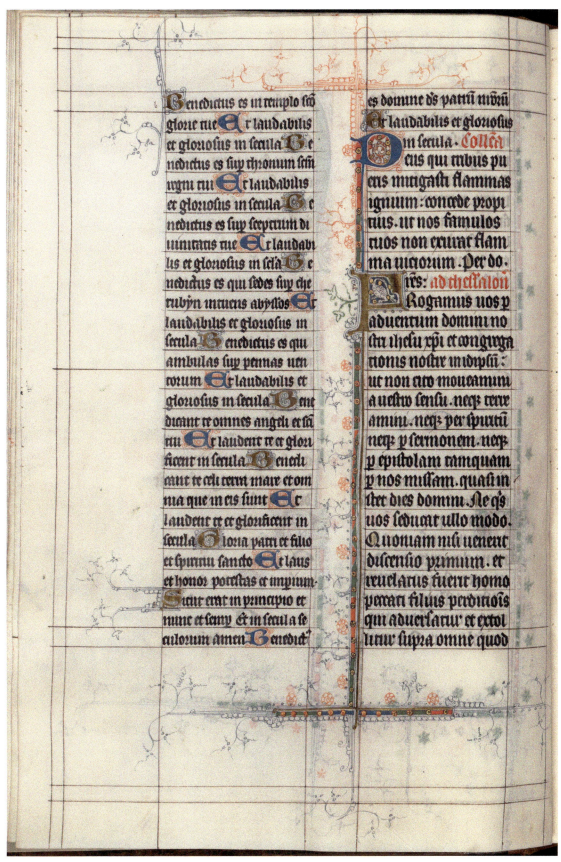

FIGURE 31 Penwork trilobes grouped as pairs of pairs; bubble-like pearls. Artist 3. Winter Missal of Arnold of Rummen, Sint-Truiden (text), Ghent (decoration and illumination), *c*.1345–1366. The Hague, Huis van het boek, Ms. MMW 10 A 14, fol. 15v
PHOTO: HUIS VAN HET HET BOEK

FIGURE 32 Type 1 border bar; beginning of penwork Cycle 2. Artist 2. Winter Missal of Arnold of Rummen, Sint-Truiden (text), Ghent (decoration and illumination), c.1345–1366. The Hague, Huis van het boek, Ms. MMW 10 A 14, fol. 21r
PHOTO: HUIS VAN HET BOEK

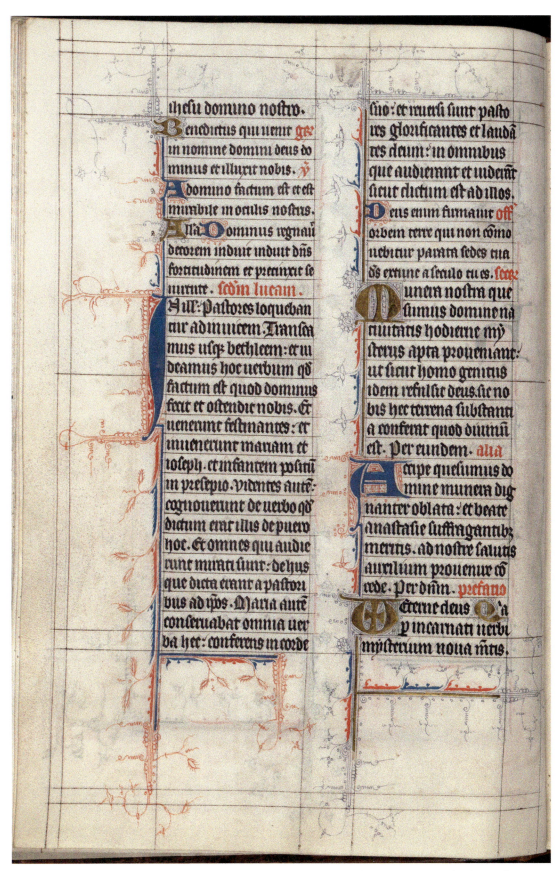

FIGURE 33 Beginning of penwork Cycle 2. Artist 2. Winter Missal of Arnold of Rummen, Sint-Truiden (text), Ghent (decoration and illumination), c.1345–1366. The Hague, Huis van het boek, Ms. MMW 10 A 14, fol. 21v
PHOTO: HUIS VAN HET BOEK

FIGURE 34 Introit for Christmas. Artist 3. Winter Missal of Arnold of Rummen, Sint-Truiden (text), Ghent (decoration and illumination), c.1345–1366. The Hague, Huis van het boek, Ms. MMW 10 A 14, fol. 22r
PHOTO: HUIS VAN HET BOEK

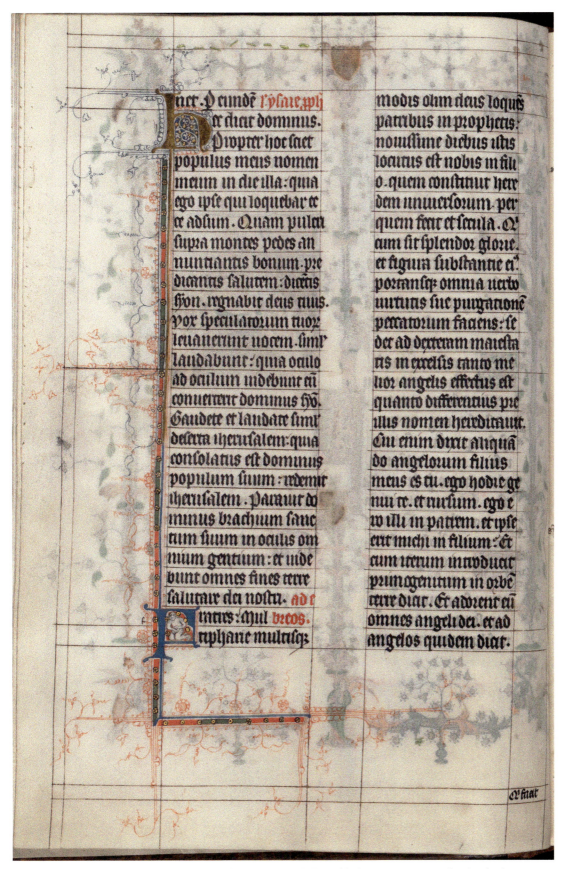

FIGURE 35   Silver stains from overpainted shields. Winter Missal of Arnold of Rummen, Sint-Truiden (text), Ghent (decoration and illumination), c.1345–1366. The Hague, Huis van het boek, Ms. MMW 10 A 14, fol. 22v
PHOTO: HUIS VAN HET BOEK

FIGURE 36 Page with flourishing begun by Artist 2 (red ink in upper margin) and completed by Artist 4. Winter Missal of Arnold of Rummen, Sint-Truiden (text), Ghent (decoration and illumination), c.1345–1366. The Hague, Huis van het boek, Ms. MMW 10 A 14, fol. 23r
PHOTO: HUIS VAN HET BOEK

FIGURE 37   Introit for the Circumcision of Christ. Artist 4, painting; Artist 3, flourishing. Winter Missal of Arnold of Rummen, Sint-Truiden (text), Ghent (decoration and illumination), c.1345–1366. The Hague, Huis van het boek, Ms. MMW 10 A 14, fol. 26r
PHOTO: HUIS VAN HET BOEK

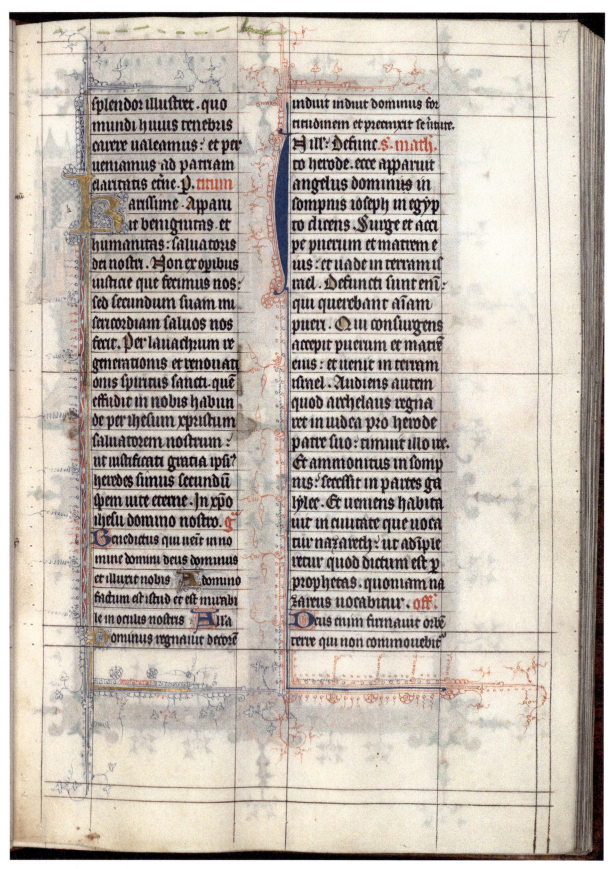

FIGURE 38 Silver stains from overpainted shields. Winter Missal of Arnold of Rummen, Sint-Truiden (text), Ghent (decoration and illumination), c.1345–1366. The Hague, Huis van het boek, Ms. MMW 10 A 14, fol. 27r
PHOTO: HUIS VAN HET BOEK

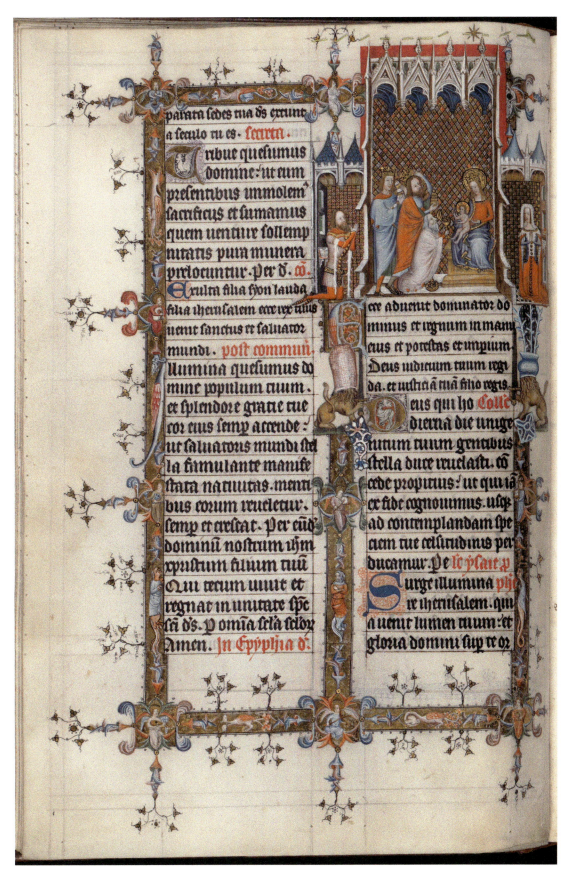

FIGURE 39 Introit for Epiphany. Artist 3. Winter Missal of Arnold of Rummen, Sint-Truiden (text), Ghent (decoration and illumination), c.1345–1366. The Hague, Huis van het boek, Ms. MMW 10 A 14, fol. 27v
PHOTO: HUIS VAN HET BOEK

FIGURE 40   Minor illumination begun by Artist 2, completed by Artist 4. Winter Missal of Arnold of Rummen, Sint-Truiden (text), Ghent (decoration and illumination), c.1345–1366. The Hague, Huis van het boek, Ms. MMW 10 A 14, fol. 29v
PHOTO: HUIS VAN HET BOEK

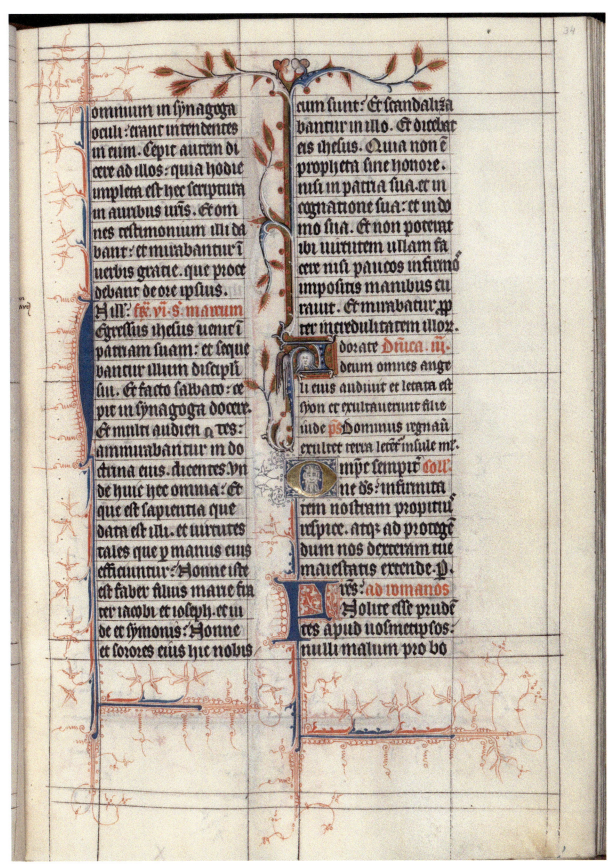

FIGURE 42 Grotesque overflows initial *A(dorate)*. Artist 2. Winter Missal of Arnold of Rummen, Sint-Truiden (text), Ghent (decoration and illumination), c.1345–1366. The Hague, Huis van het boek, Ms. MMW 10 A 14, fol. 34r
PHOTO: HUIS VAN HET BOEK

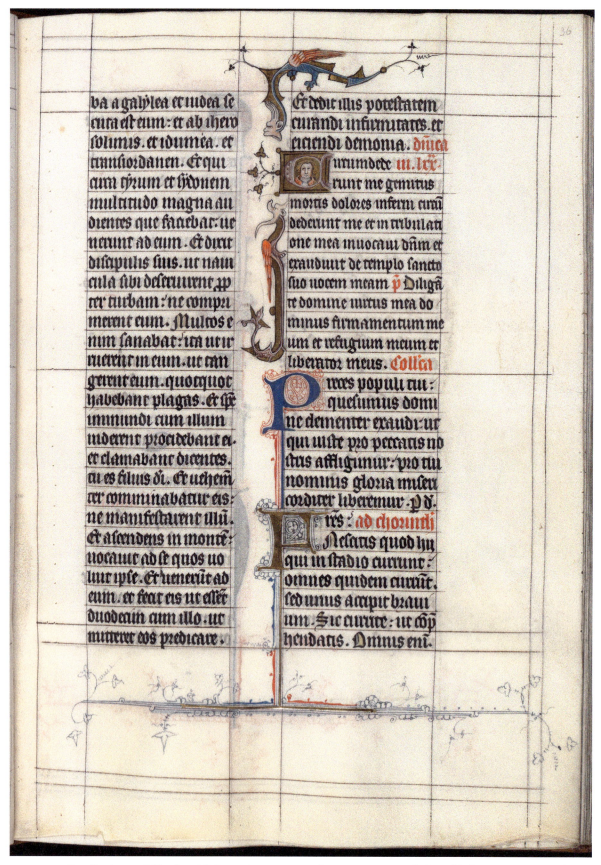

FIGURE 43 Free-floating partial border with threatening grotesques. Artist 4. Winter Missal of Arnold of Rummen, Sint-Truiden (text), Ghent (decoration and illumination), c.1345–1366. The Hague, Huis van het boek, Ms. MMW 10 A 14, fol. 36r
PHOTO: HUIS VAN HET BOEK

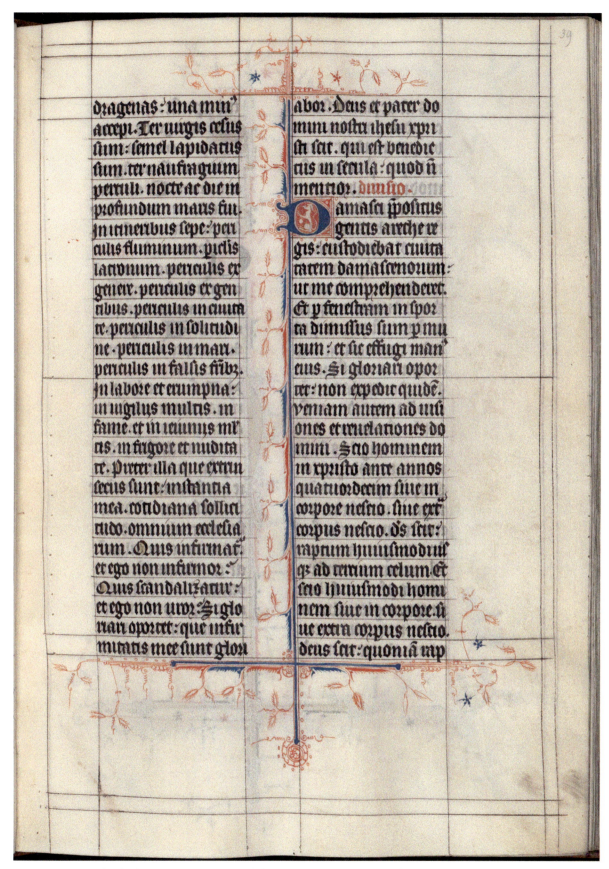

FIGURE 45 Type 2 border bar. Artist 2. Winter Missal of Arnold of Rummen, Sint-Truiden (text), Ghent (decoration and illumination), c.1345–1366. The Hague, Huis van het boek, Ms. MMW 10 A 14, fol. 39r
PHOTO: HUIS VAN HET BOEK

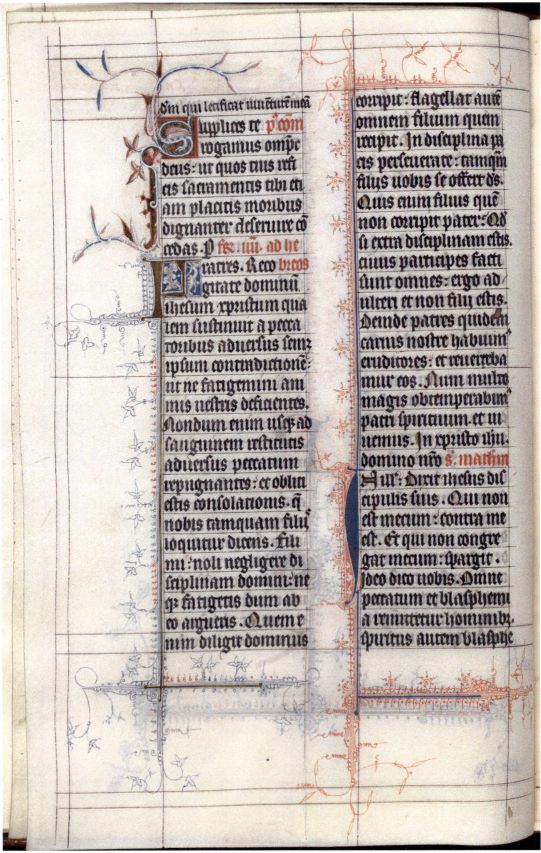

FIGURE 47 Type 3 border bar. Artist 2. Winter Missal of Arnold of Rummen, Sint-Truiden (text), Ghent (decoration and illumination), c.1345–1366. The Hague, Huis van het boek, Ms. MMW 10 A 14, fol. 40v
PHOTO: HUIS VAN HET BOEK

FIGURE 53　Type 3 border bar. Artist 3. Winter Missal of Arnold of Rummen, Sint-Truiden (text), Ghent (decoration and illumination), c.1345–1366. The Hague, Huis van het boek, Ms. MMW 10 A 14, fol. 48v
PHOTO: HUIS VAN HET BOEK

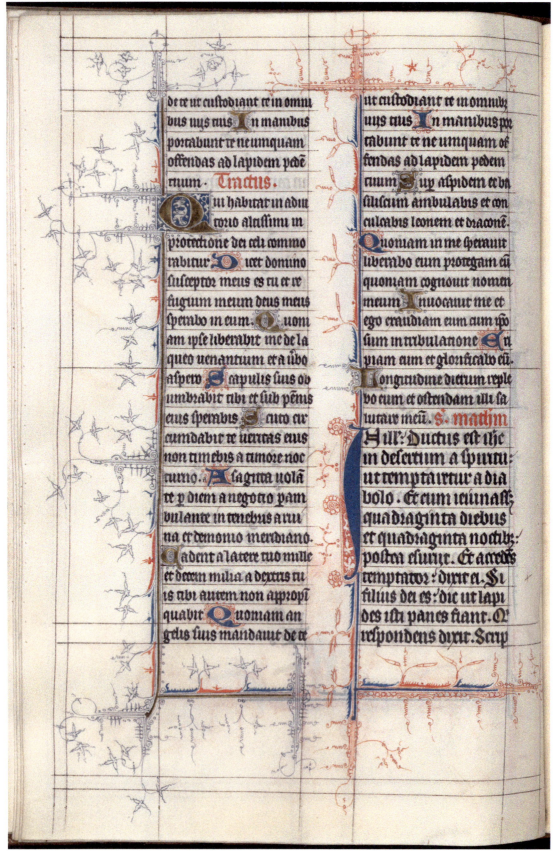

FIGURE 55 Type 2 border bar along column b. Artist 2. Winter Missal of Arnold of Rummen, Sint-Truiden (text), Ghent (decoration and illumination), c.1345–1366. The Hague, Huis van het boek, Ms. MMW 10 A 14, fol. 50v
PHOTO: HUIS VAN HET BOEK

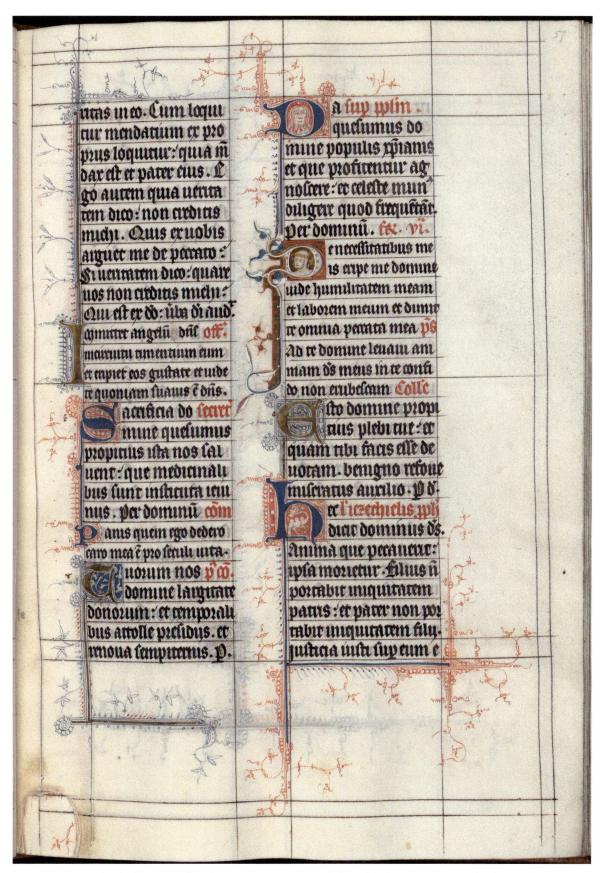

FIGURE 60 Type 3 border bar; penwork Cycle 2. Artist 2. Winter Missal of Arnold of Rummen, Sint-Truiden (text), Ghent (decoration and illumination), c.1345–1366. The Hague, Huis van het boek, Ms. MMW 10 A 14, fol. 57r
PHOTO: HUIS VAN HET BOEK

FIGURE 61 Artist 2's plethora of foliate types; penwork Cycle 2. Winter Missal of Arnold of Rummen, Sint-Truiden (text), Ghent (decoration and illumination), c.1345–1366. The Hague, Huis van het boek, Ms. MMW 10 A 14, fol. 58v
PHOTO: HUIS VAN HET BOEK

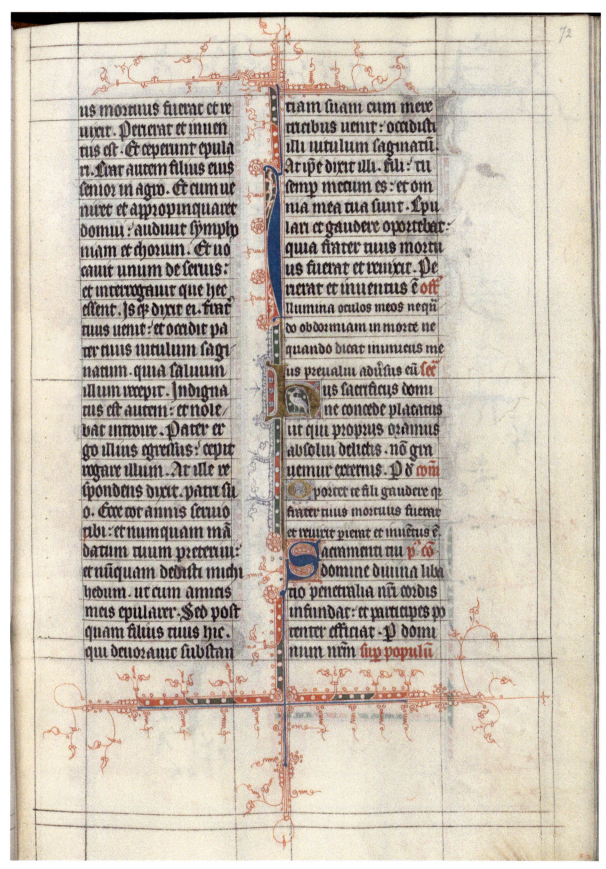

FIGURE 68 Upside down initial *I(llumina)*. Artist 2. Winter Missal of Arnold of Rummen, Sint-Truiden (text), Ghent (decoration and illumination), c.1345–1366. The Hague, Huis van het boek, Ms. MMW 10 A 14, fol. 72r
PHOTO: HUIS VAN HET BOEK

FIGURE 69 Mid-page extension into the left margin. Artist 2. Winter Missal of Arnold of Rummen, Sint-Truiden (text), Ghent (decoration and illumination), c.1345–1366. The Hague, Huis van het boek, Ms. MMW 10 A 14, fol. 73v
PHOTO: HUIS VAN HET BOEK

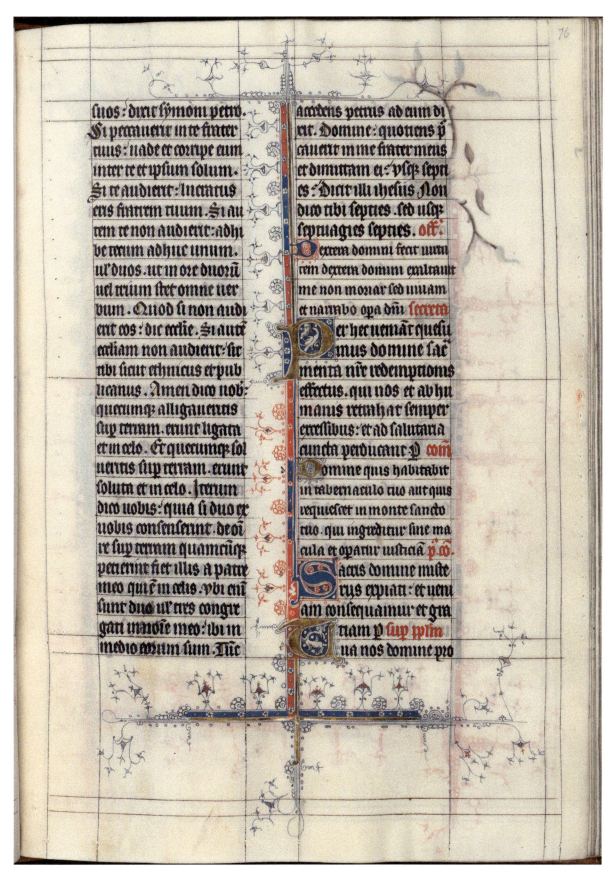

FIGURE 70 Tiered blossoms. Artist 2. Winter Missal of Arnold of Rummen, Sint-Truiden (text), Ghent (decoration and Illumination), c.1345–1366. The Hague, Huis van het boek, Ms. MMW 10 A 14, fol. 76r
PHOTO: HUIS VAN HET BOEK

FIGURE 71 Tiered blossoms. Artist 2. Winter Missal of Arnold of Rummen, Sint-Truiden (text), Ghent (decoration and Illumination), c.1345–1366. The Hague, Huis van het boek, Ms. MMW 10 A 14, fol. 76v
PHOTO: HUIS VAN HET BOEK

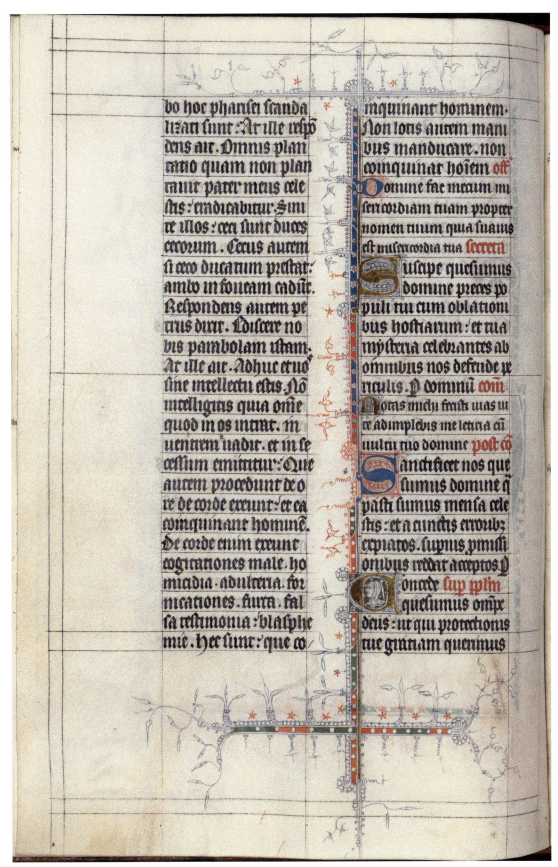

FIGURE 72 Type 4 border bars with varied buttons, pearls, rosettes. Artist 2. Winter Missal of Arnold of Rummen, Sint-Truiden (text), Ghent (decoration and Illumination), c.1345–1366. The Hague, Huis van het boek, Ms. MMW 10 A 14, fol. 77v
PHOTO: HUIS VAN HET BOEK

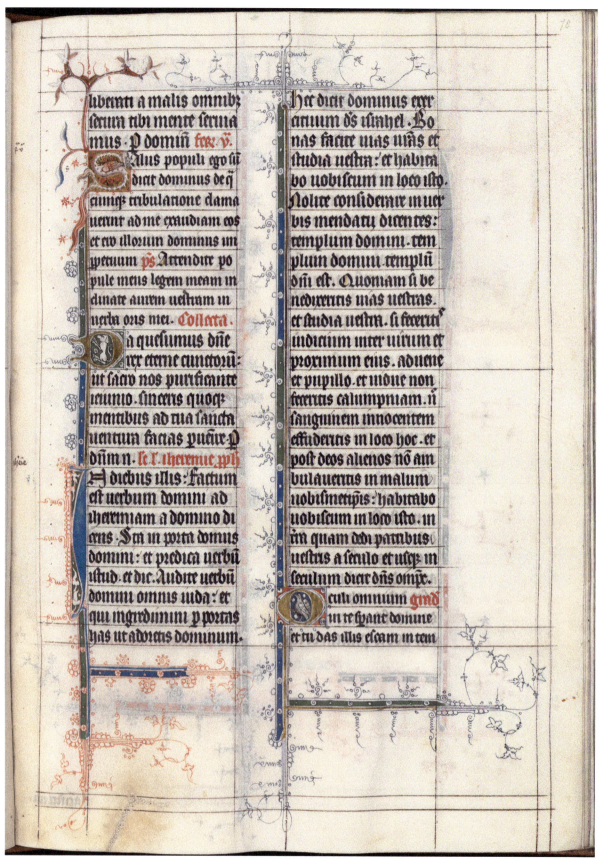

FIGURE 73 Green and blue border bar. Artist 2. Winter Missal of Arnold of Rummen, Sint-Truiden (text), Ghent (decoration and illumination), c.1345–1366. The Hague, Huis van het boek, Ms. MMW 10 A 14, fol. 78r
PHOTO: HUIS VAN HET BOEK

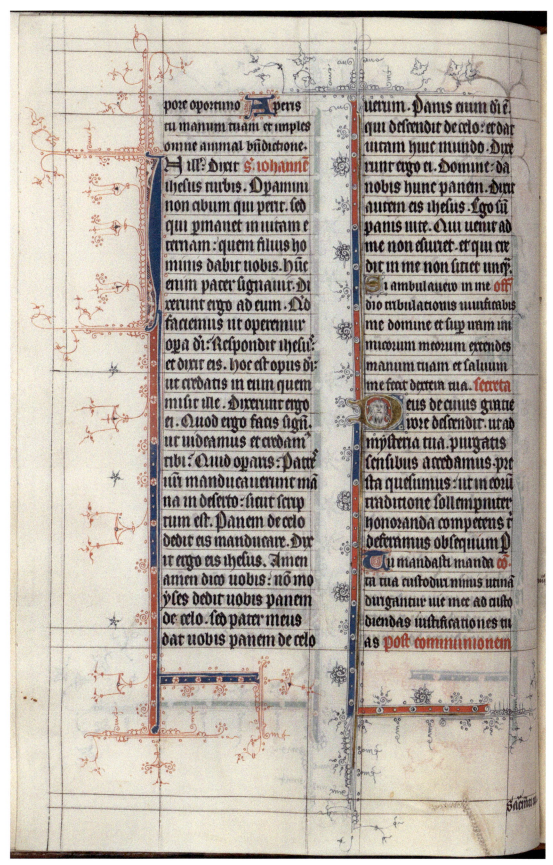

FIGURE 74 Border bars with extension into the lower margin. Artist 2. Winter Missal of Arnold of Rummen, Sint-Truiden (text), Ghent (decoration and illumination), c.1345–1366. The Hague, Huis van het boek, Ms. MMW 10 A 14, fol. 78v
PHOTO: HUIS VAN HET BOEK

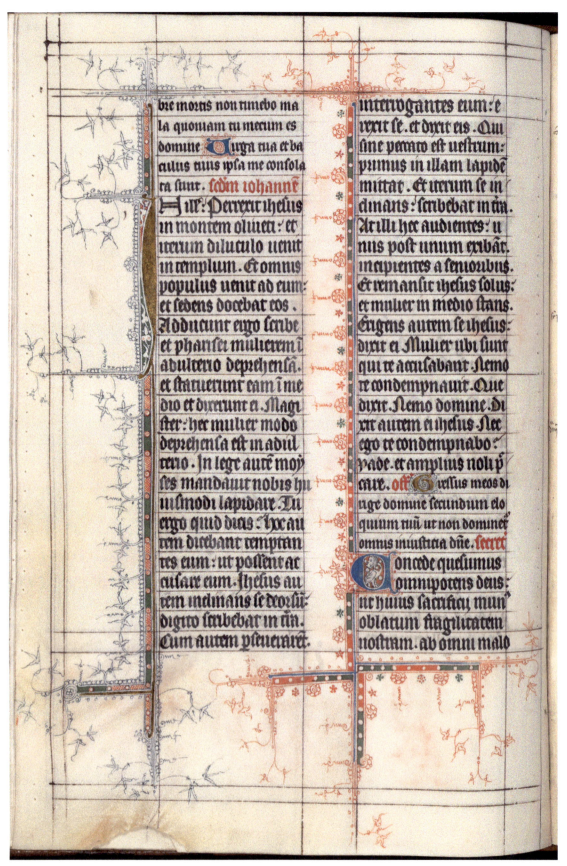

FIGURE 76 Rosettes, circle-complexes, corkscrews. Artist 2. Winter Missal of Arnold of Rummen, Sint-Truiden (text), Ghent (decoration and illumination), c.1345–1366. The Hague, Huis van het boek, Ms. MMW 10 A 14, fol. 83v
PHOTO: HUIS VAN HET BOEK

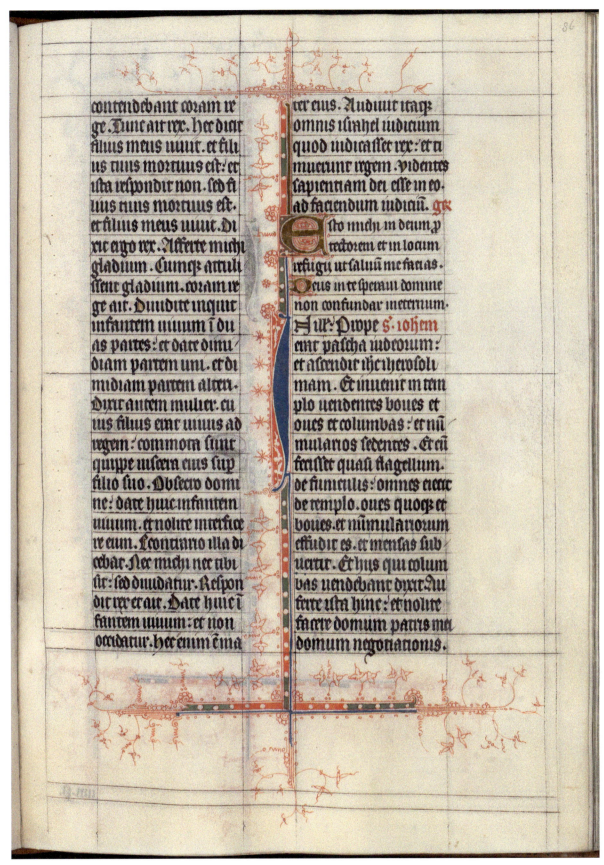

FIGURE 78 Penwork with ball-and-squiggle trilobes, maple leaves, ivy leaves. Artist 2. Winter Missal of Arnold of Rummen, Sint-Truiden (text), Ghent (decoration and illumination), c.1345–1366. The Hague, Huis van het boek, Ms. MMW 10 A 14, fol. 86r
PHOTO: HUIS VAN HET BOEK

FIGURE 81   Oak leaves, acorns, and lilies. Artist 2. Winter Missal of Arnold of Rummen, Sint-Truiden (text), Ghent (decoration and illumination), c.1345–1366. The Hague, Huis van het boek, Ms. MMW 10 A 14, fol. 90v
PHOTO: HUIS VAN HET BOEK

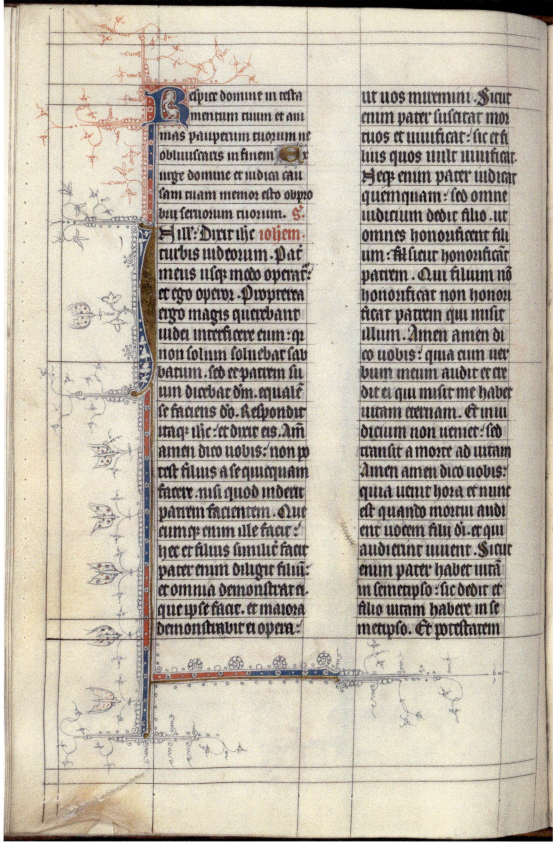

FIGURE 82 Penwork butterflies in left margin. Artist 2. Winter Missal of Arnold of Rummen, Sint-Truiden (text), Ghent (decoration and illumination), c.1345–1366. The Hague, Huis van het boek, Ms. MMW 10 A 14, fol. 91v
PHOTO: HUIS VAN HET BOEK

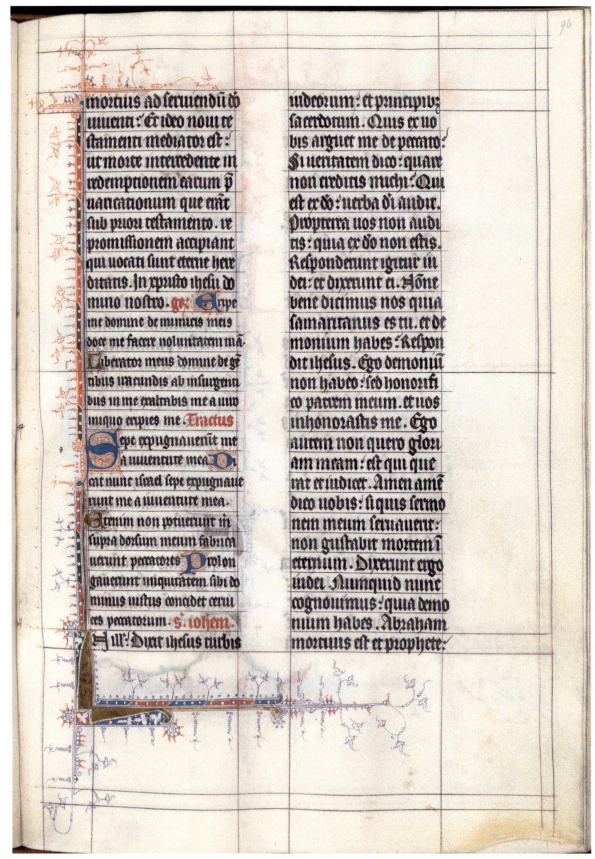

FIGURE 84   Cracked *I* in lower terminal complex. Artist 2. Winter Missal of Arnold of Rummen, Sint-Truiden (text), Ghent (decoration and illumination), *c.*1345–1366. The Hague, Huis van het boek, Ms. MMW 10 A 14, fol. 96r
PHOTO: HUIS VAN HET BOEK

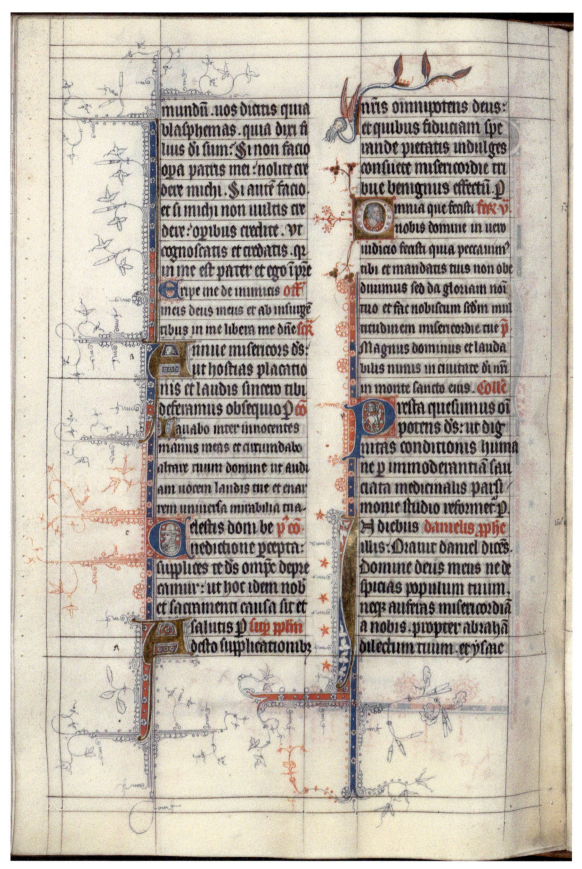

FIGURE 86 Type 4 border bar; large and varied leaves. Artist 2. Winter Missal of Arnold of Rummen, Sint-Truiden (text), Ghent (decoration and illumination), c.1345–1366. The Hague, Huis van het boek, Ms. MMW 10 A 14, fol. 100v
PHOTO: HUIS VAN HET BOEK

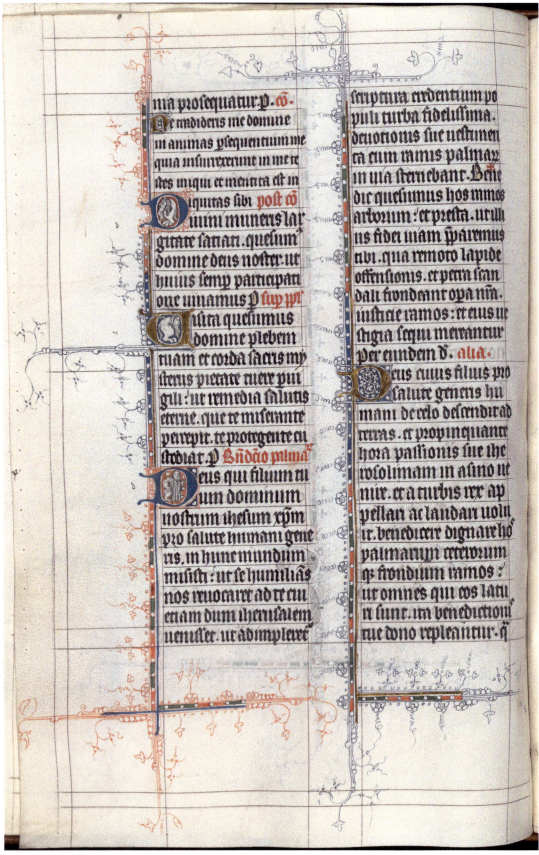

FIGURE 87 Artist 3's corkscrews. Winter Missal of Arnold of Rummen, Sint-Truiden (text), Ghent (decoration and illumination), *c.*1345–1366. The Hague, Huis van het boek, Ms. MMW 10 A 14, fol. 104v
PHOTO: HUIS VAN HET BOEK

FIGURE 89 Type 4 border bar. Artist 3. Winter Missal of Arnold of Rummen, Sint-Truiden (text), Ghent (decoration and illumination), c.1345–1366. The Hague, Huis van het boek, Ms. MMW 10 A 14, fol. 105v
PHOTO: HUIS VAN HET BOEK

FIGURE 91   Introit for Palm Sunday. Artist 2. Winter Missal of Arnold of Rummen, Sint-Truiden (text), Ghent (decoration and illumination), c.1345–1366. The Hague, Huis van het boek, Ms. MMW 10 A 14, fol. 106v
PHOTO: HUIS VAN HET BOEK

FIGURE 94 Page with all painting and penwork by Artist 1. Winter Missal of Arnold of Rummen, Sint-Truiden (text), Ghent (decoration and illumination), c.1345–1366. The Hague, Huis van het boek, Ms. MMW 10 A 14, fol. 112v
PHOTO: HUIS VAN HET BOEK

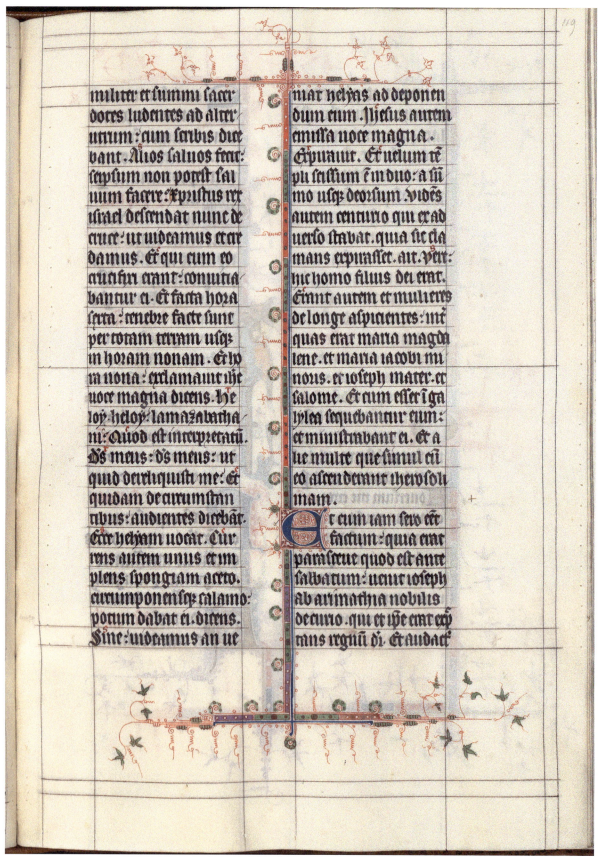

FIGURE 95 Painterly application of green inkwash. Artist 2. Winter Missal of Arnold of Rummen, Sint-Truiden (text), Ghent (decoration and illumination), *c.*1345–1366. The Hague, Huis van het boek, Ms. MMW 10 A 14, fol. 119r
PHOTO: HUIS VAN HET BOEK

FIGURE 99 Painted initial *H(ec)* and extensions by Artist 1; penwork by Artist 2. Winter Missal of Arnold of Rummen, Sint-Truiden (text), Ghent (decoration and illumination), *c.*1345–1366. The Hague, Huis van het boek, Ms. MMW 10 A 14, fol. 128v
PHOTO: HUIS VAN HET BOEK

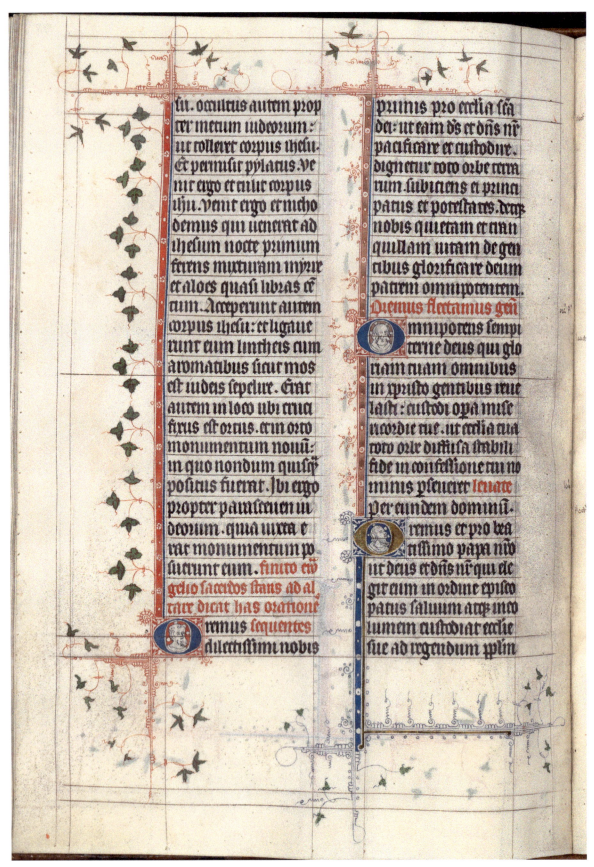

FIGURE 100   Three initials with bearded men. Artist 2. Winter Missal of Arnold of Rummen, Sint-Truiden (text), Ghent (decoration and illumination), c.1345–1366. The Hague, Huis van het boek, Ms. MMW 10 A 14, fol. 133v
PHOTO: HUIS VAN HET BOEK

FIGURE 101   Border bar with lavender-pink sections. Artist 2. Winter Missal of Arnold of Rummen, Sint-Truiden (text), Ghent (decoration and illumination), c.1345–1366. The Hague, Huis van het boek, Ms. MMW 10 A 14, fol. 134v
PHOTO: HUIS VAN HET BOEK

FIGURE 103   Preface for the Ordinary of the Mass. Initial and borders, Artist 1; penwork, Artist 2. Winter Missal of Arnold of Rummen, Sint-Truiden (text), Ghent (decoration and illumination), *c*.1345–1366. The Hague, Huis van het boek, Ms. MMW 10 A 14, fol. 139r
PHOTO: HUIS VAN HET BOEK

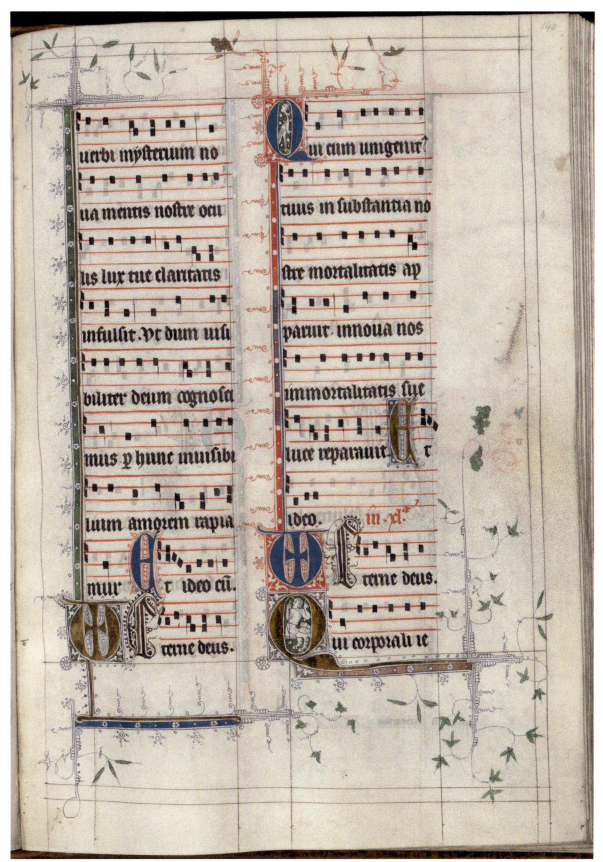

FIGURE 104   *AE*(*terne*) with cross-inscribed *A* and cadel *E*. Winter Missal of Arnold of Rummen, Sint-Truiden (text), Ghent (decoration and illumination), *c*.1345–1366. The Hague, Huis van het boek, Ms. MMW 10 A 14, fol. 140r
PHOTO: HUIS VAN HET BOEK

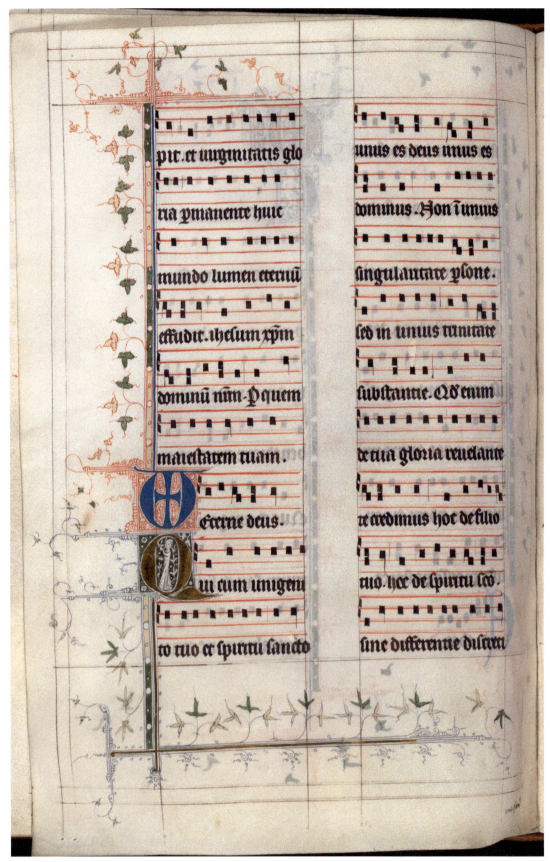

FIGURE 105 Leaves with yellow-beige inkwash. Artist 2. Winter Missal of Arnold of Rummen, Sint-Truiden (text), Ghent (decoration and illumination), c.1345–1366. The Hague, Huis van het boek, Ms. MMW 10 A 14, fol. 141v
PHOTO: HUIS VAN HET BOEK

FIGURE 106   The Crucifixion. Artist 2. Winter Missal of Arnold of Rummen, Sint-Truiden (text), Ghent (decoration and illumination), c.1345–1366. The Hague, Huis van het boek, Ms. MMW 10 A 14, fol. 143v
PHOTO: HUIS VAN HET BOEK

FIGURE 107   *Te igitur*, opening of the Canon of the Mass. Artist 1. Winter Missal of Arnold of Rummen, Sint-Truiden (text), Ghent (decoration and illumination), c.1345–1366. The Hague, Huis van het boek, Ms. MMW 10 A 14, fol. 144r
PHOTO: HUIS VAN HET BOEK

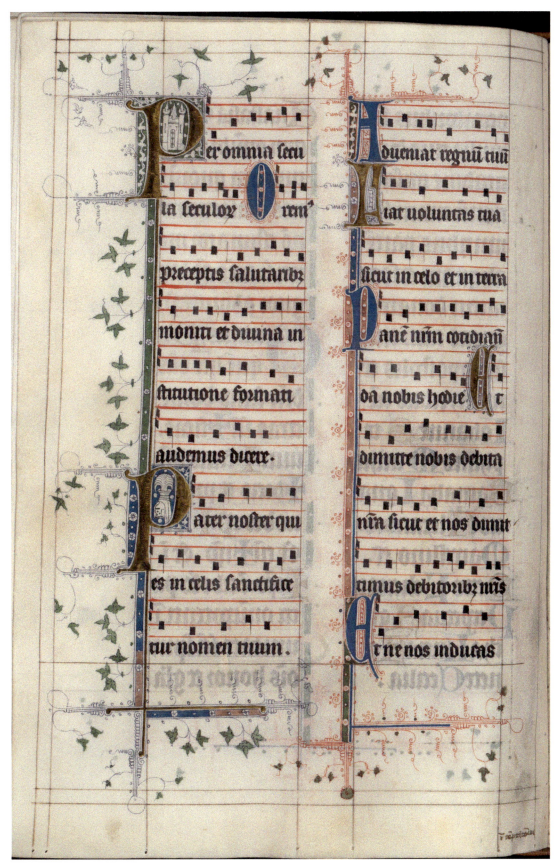

FIGURE 108 Grandest effects in decoration; initials *P(er)* with Arnold's castle and *P(ater)* with his helmet. Artist 2.
Winter Missal of Arnold of Rummen, Sint-Truiden (text), Ghent (decoration and illumination),
c.1345–1366. The Hague, Huis van het boek, Ms. MMW 10 A 14, fol. 147v
PHOTO: HUIS VAN HET BOEK

FIGURE 109   Grandest effects in decoration. Artist 2. Winter Missal of Arnold of Rummen, Sint-Truiden (text), Ghent (decoration and illumination), c.1345–1366. The Hague, Huis van het boek, Ms. MMW 10 A 14, fol. 149r
PHOTO: HUIS VAN HET BOEK

FIGURE 110   Introit for the Feast of St. Lucy. Artist 1. Winter Missal of Arnold of Rummen, Sint-Truiden (text), Ghent (decoration and illumination), c.1345–1366. The Hague, Huis van het boek, Ms. MMW 10 A 14, fol. 151r., detail
PHOTO: HUIS VAN HET BOEK

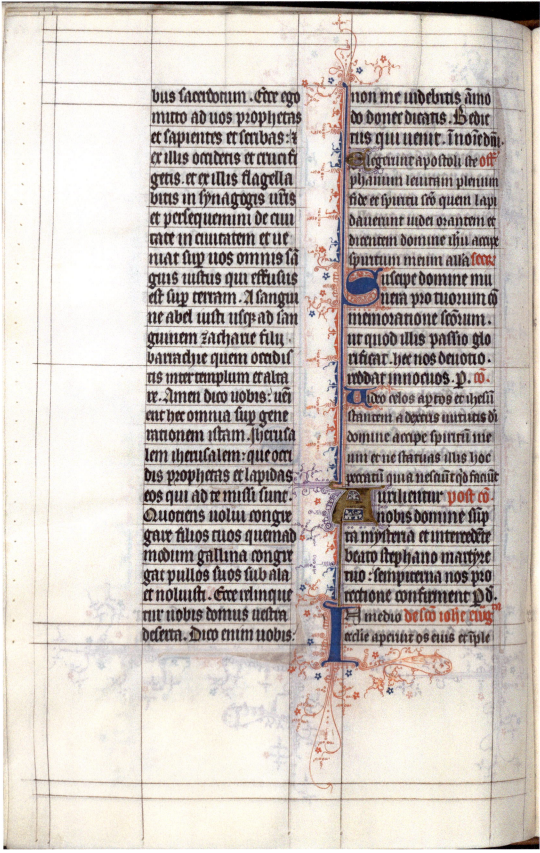

FIGURE 111   Penwork with fish face and ruffled maple leaves. Artist 1. Winter Missal of Arnold of Rummen,
Sint-Truiden (text), Ghent (decoration and illumination), c.1345–1366. The Hague, Huis van het boek,
Ms. MMW 10 A 14, fol. 153v
PHOTO: HUIS VAN HET BOEK

FIGURE 112 Terminal complexes and corkscrews. Artist 1. Winter Missal of Arnold of Rummen, Sint-Truiden (text), Ghent (decoration and illumination), c.1345–1366. The Hague, Huis van het boek, Ms. MMW 10 A 14, fol. 154r
PHOTO: HUIS VAN HET BOEK

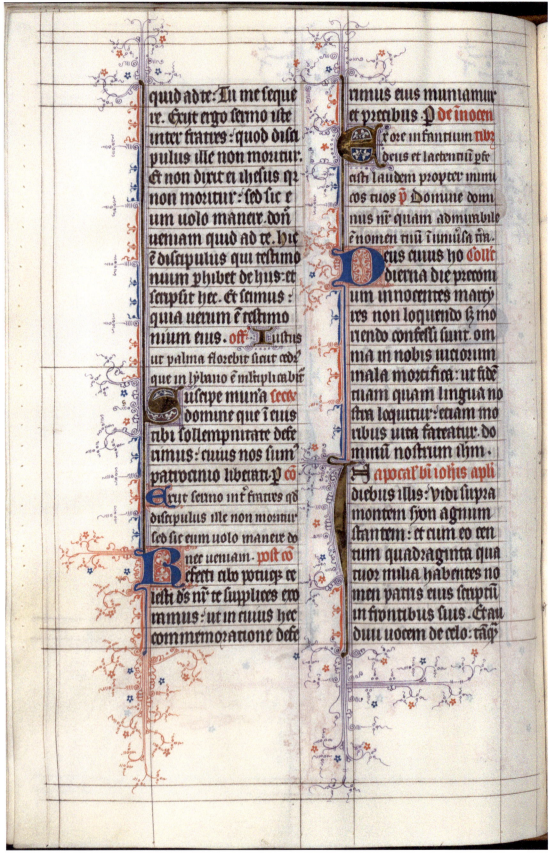

FIGURE 113   The sequence of prayers written in scripts of alternating sizes. Decoration by Artist 1. Winter Missal of Arnold of Rummen, Sint-Truiden (text), Ghent (decoration and illumination), c.1345–1366. The Hague, Huis van het boek, Ms. MMW 10 A 14, fol. 154v
PHOTO: HUIS VAN HET BOEK

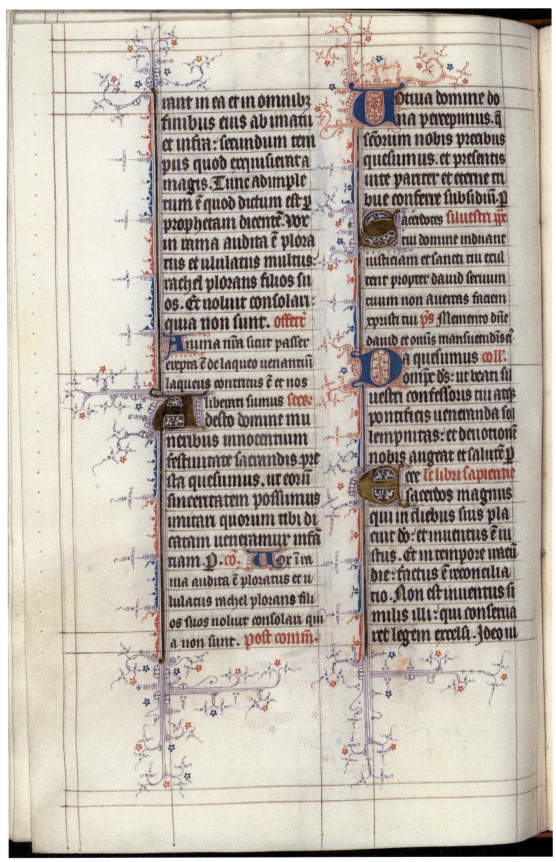

FIGURE 114 Four types of foliate initial decoration. Artist 1. Winter Missal of Arnold of Rummen, Sint-Truiden (text), Ghent (decoration and illumination), c.1345–1366. The Hague, Huis van het boek, Ms. MMW 10 A 14, fol. 155v
PHOTO: HUIS VAN HET BOEK

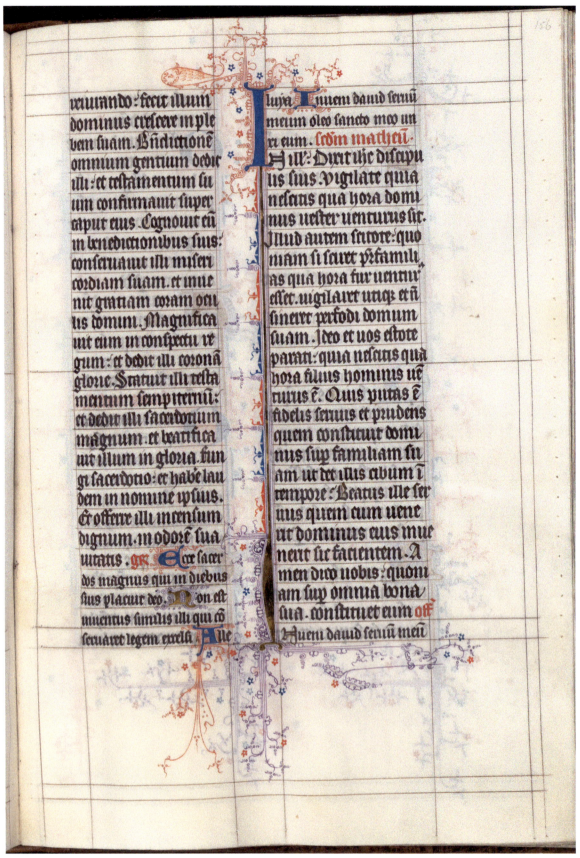

FIGURE 115　One-line initial and human face in penwork of lower margin; fish face in penwork of upper margin. Artist 1. Winter Missal of Arnold of Rummen, Sint-Truiden (text), Ghent (decoration and illumination), c.1345–1366. The Hague, Huis van het boek, Ms. MMW 10 A 14, fol. 156r

PHOTO: HUIS VAN HET BOEK

FIGURE 121   Introit for the Presentation of Christ. Artist 1. Winter Missal of Arnold of Rummen, Sint-Truiden (text), Ghent (decoration and illumination), c.1345–1366. The Hague, Huis van het boek, Ms. MMW 10 A 14, fol. 167r
PHOTO: HUIS VAN HET BOEK

FIGURE 124 Penwork border bars, corkscrews, and ball-and-squiggle trilobes. Artist 1. Winter Missal of Arnold of Rummen, Sint-Ttruiden (text), Ghent (decoration and illumination), c.1345–1366.
The Hague, Huis van het boek, Ms. MMW 10 A 14, fol. 175r
PHOTO: HUIS VAN HET BOEK

FIGURE 125   Introit for the Annunciation. Artist 1. Winter Missal of Arnold of Rummen, Sint-Truiden (text), Ghent (decoration and illumination), c.1345–1366. The Hague, Huis van het boek, Ms. MMW 10 A 14, fol. 176v
PHOTO: HUIS VAN HET BOEK

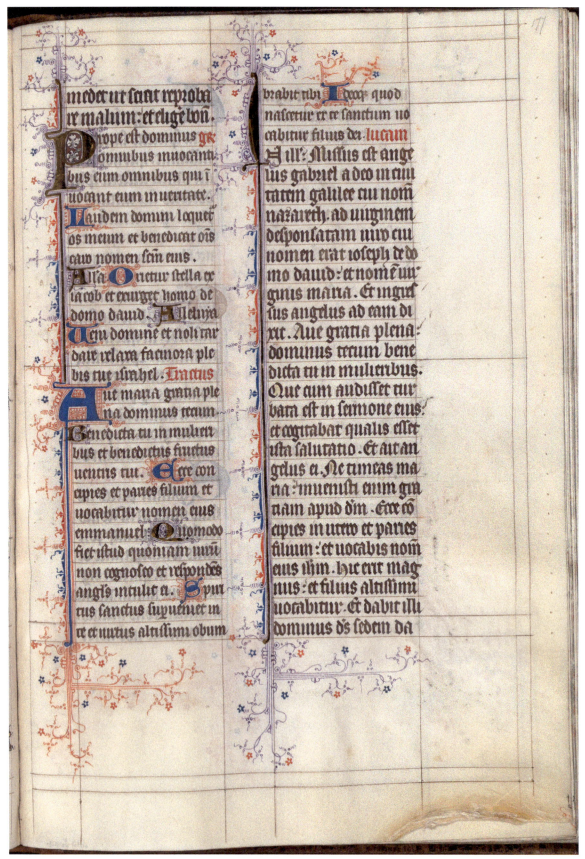

FIGURE 126 Upside-down *I*. Artist 1. Winter Missal of Arnold of Rummen, Sint-Truiden (text), Ghent (decoration and illumination), Sint-Truiden (text), Ghent (decoration and illumination), c.1345–1366. The Hague, Huis van het boek, Ms. MMW 10 A 14, fol. 177r
PHOTO: HUIS VAN HET BOEK

FIGURE 127 Introit for Vigil of an Apostle. Artist 1. Winter Missal of Arnold of Rummen, Sint-Truiden (text), Ghent (decoration and illumination), c.1345–1366. The Hague, Huis van het boek, Ms. MMW 10 A 14, fol. 178r
PHOTO: HUIS VAN HET BOEK

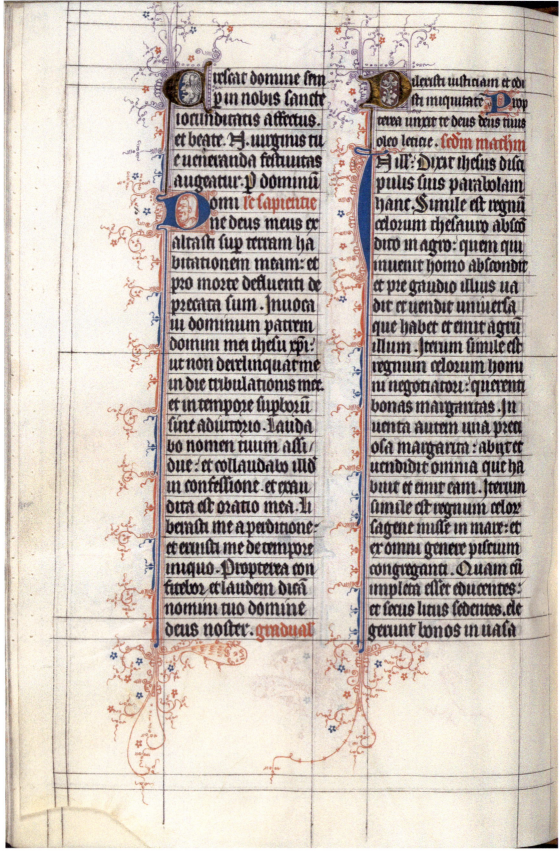

FIGURE 131 Whiplash penwork in lower terminal complex. Artist 1. Winter Missal of Arnold of of Rummen, Sint-Truiden (text), Ghent (decoration and illumination), c.1345–1366. The Hague, Huis van het boek, Ms. MMW 10 A 14, fol. 189v
PHOTO: HUIS VAN HET BOEK

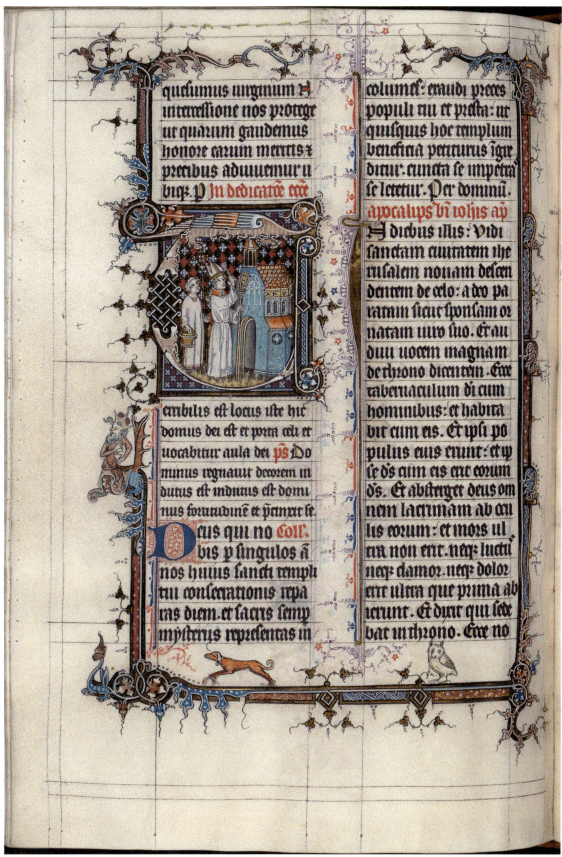

FIGURE 132   Introit for dedication of a church. Artist 1. Winter Missal of Arnold of Rummen, Sint-Truiden (text), Ghent (decoration and illumination), c.1345–1366. The Hague, Huis van het boek, Ms. MMW 10 A 14, fol. 192v
PHOTO: HUIS VAN HET BOEK

FIGURE 133 Decoration in Quire 27. Artist 2. Winter Missal of Arnold of Rummen, Sint-Truiden (text), Ghent (decoration and illumination), c.1345–1366. The Hague, Huis van het boek, Ms. MMW 10 A 14, fol. 199v
PHOTO: HUIS VAN HET BOEK

FIGURE 134　　Decoration in Quire 27: Synthesis of features from earlier quires. Artist 2. Winter Missal of Arnold of Rummen, Sint-Truiden (text), Ghent (decoration and illumination), c.1345–1366. The Hague, Huis van het boek, Ms. MMW 10 A 14, fol. 200r
PHOTO: HUIS VAN HET BOEK

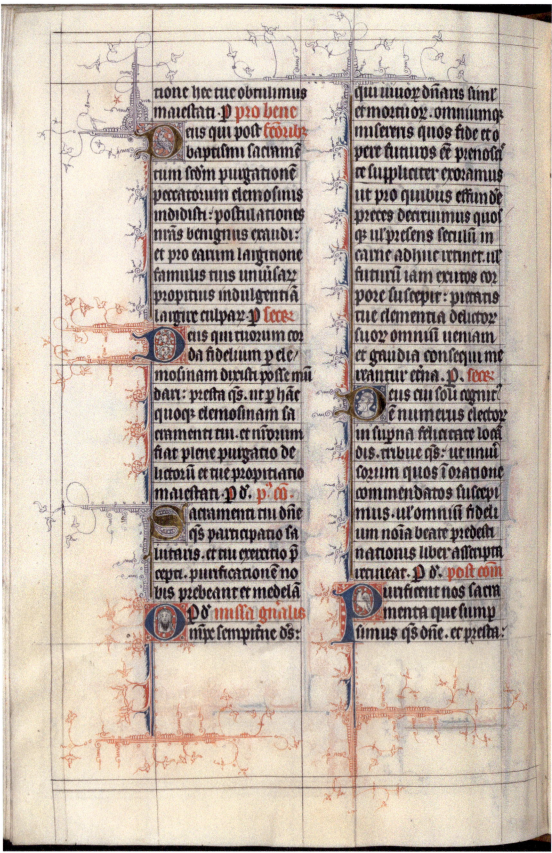

FIGURE 135 Decoration in Quire 27. Synthesis of features from earlier quires. Artist 2. Winter Missal of Arnold of Rummen, Sint-Truiden (text), Ghent (decoration and illumination), c.1345–1366. The Hague, Huis van het boek, Ms. MMW 10 A 14, fol. 200v
PHOTO: HUIS VAN HET BOEK

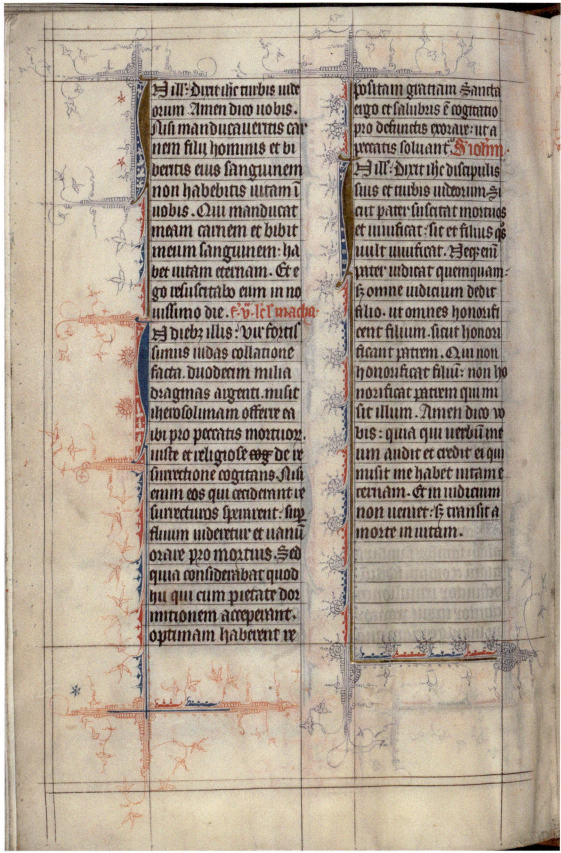

FIGURE 137 Decoration in Quire 27: Synthesis of features from earlier quires. Artist 2. Winter Missal of Arnold of Rummen, Sint-Truiden (text), Ghent (decoration and illumination), *c.*1345–1366. The Hague, Huis van het boek, Ms. MMW 10 A 14, fol. 203v
PHOTO: HUIS VAN HET BOEK

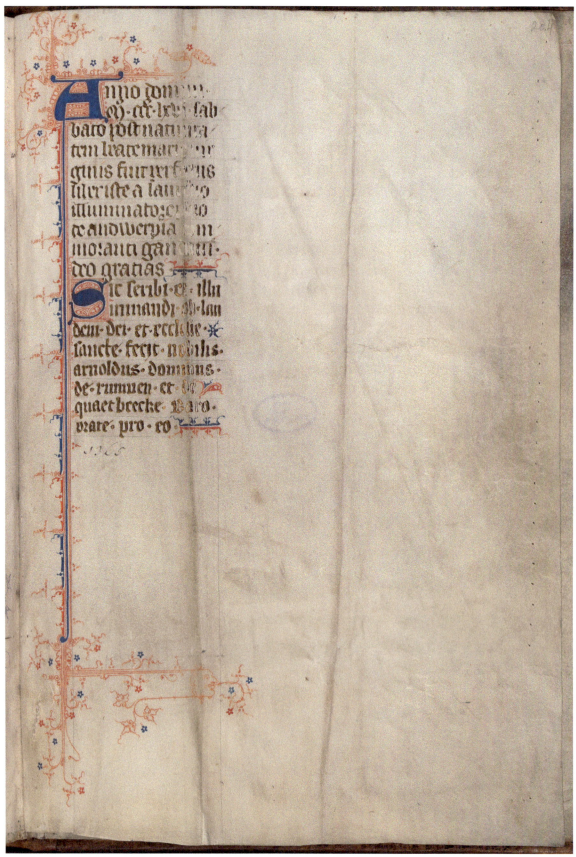

FIGURE 138   Colophon decoration. Artists 1 and 4. Winter Missal of Arnold of Rummen, Sint-Truiden (text), Ghent (decoration and illumination), *c.*1345–1366. The Hague, Huis van het boek, Ms. MMW 10 A 14, fol. 204r
PHOTO: HUIS VAN HET BOEK

FIGURE 139 Faces with thick white highlights. Decretals of Gregory IX, Bologna, 1330s or 1340s. Vatican City, Biblioteca Apostolica Vaticana, Ms. Vat. lat. 1389, fol. 3v
© BIBLIOTECA APOSTOLICA VATICANA. PHOTO: REPRODUCED BY PERMISSION OF BIBLIOTECA APOSTOLICA VATICANA, WITH ALL RIGHTS RESERVED

FIGURE 140 The Crucifixion: flattened converging ribs; proportion of figures to space compared to 10 A 14's Crucifixion. Fitzwarin Psalter, East Anglia or Diocese of Ely (?), c.1345–1350. Paris, Bibliothèque nationale de France, Ms. lat. 765, fol. 14r
PHOTO: BIBLIOTHÈQUE NATIONALE DE FRANCE

FIGURE 141 Christ in Majesty: weight, support, symmetry. Leaf of added bifolium. Fitzwarin Psalter, East Anglia or Diocese of Ely (?), c.1345–1350. Paris, Bibliothèque nationale de France, Ms. lat. 765, fol. 21v
PHOTO: BIBLIOTHÈQUE NATIONALE DE FRANCE

FIGURE 142 The Crucifixion: weight, support, symmetry. Leaf of added bifolium. Fitzwarin Psalter, East Anglia or Diocese of Ely (?), c.1345–1350. Paris, Bibliothèque nationale de France, Ms. lat. 765, fol. 22r
PHOTO: BIBLIOTHÈQUE NATIONALE DE FRANCE

FIGURE 143 Second battle of Alexander and Porus: colored masonry; spectators. *The Romance of Alexander*, Tournai, 1338–1344. Oxford, Bodleian Library, Ms. Bodley 264, fol. 58r

PHOTO: BODLEIAN LIBRARIES, UNIVERSITY OF OXFORD. HTTPS://DIGITAL.BODLEIAN.OX.AC.UK/. CREATIVE COMMONS LICENCE CC-BY-NC 4.0

FIGURE 145   Alexander's aerial adventure: colored masonry, initial *E(n viele)* with gorgonesque head in initial body. *The Romance of Alexander*, Tournai, 1338–1344. Oxford, Bodleian Library, Ms. Bodley 264, fol. 80v
PHOTO: BODLEIAN LIBRARIES, UNIVERSITY OF OXFORD. HTTPS://DIGITAL.BODLEIAN.OX.AC.UK/. CREATIVE COMMONS LICENCE CC-BY-NC 4.0

FIGURE 146   Scenes from the *La prise de Defur*: border strip with gold balls; music in superstructure; oversized foliate capitals. *The Romance of Alexander*, Tournai, 1338–1344. Oxford, Bodleian Library, Ms. Bodley 264, fol. 101v
PHOTO: BODLEIAN LIBRARIES, UNIVERSITY OF OXFORD. HTTPS://DIGITAL.BODLEIAN.OX.AC.UK/. CREATIVE COMMONS LICENCE CC-BY-NC 4.0

FIGURE 147 The Nativity: modeling with creamy white; spindly architectural supports. Psalter, Ghent, c.1330–1335. Oxford, Bodleian Library, Ms. Douce 5, fol. 14v

PHOTO: BODLEIAN LIBRARIES, UNIVERSITY OF OXFORD. HTTPS://DIGITAL.BODLEIAN.OX.AC.UK/. CREATIVE COMMONS LICENCE CC-BY-NC 4.0

FIGURE 148 Christ's Entry into Jerusalem: lower border with confronted grotesques. Psalter, Ghent, *c.*1330–1335. Oxford, Bodleian Library, Ms. Douce 5, fol. 16v
PHOTO: BODLEIAN LIBRARIES, UNIVERSITY OF OXFORD. HTTPS://DIGITAL.BODLEIAN.OX.AC.UK/. CREATIVE COMMONS LICENCE CC-BY-NC 4.0

FIGURE 149 Man of Sorrows. Psalter, Ghent, c.1330–1335. Oxford, Bodleian Library, Ms. Douce 5, fol. 60v
PHOTO: BODLEIAN LIBRARIES, UNIVERSITY OF OXFORD. HTTPS://DIGITAL.BODLEIAN.OX.AC.UK/. CREATIVE COMMONS LICENCE CC-BY-NC 4.0

FIGURES 269

FIGURE 150 Incipit for Psalm 51 (52): border strip with gold balls. Psalter, Ghent, *c.*1330–1335. Oxford, Bodleian Library, Ms. Douce 6, fol. 143r

PHOTO: BODLEIAN LIBRARIES, UNIVERSITY OF OXFORD. HTTPS://DIGITAL BODLEIAN.OX.AC.UK/. CREATIVE COMMONS LICENCE CC-BY-NC 4.0

FIGURE 151   Penwork flourishing. Psalter, Ghent, *c*.1330–1335. Oxford, Bodleian Library, Ms. Douce 6, fol. 59v
PHOTO: BODLEIAN LIBRARIES, UNIVERSITY OF OXFORD. HTTPS://DIGITAL.BODLEIAN.OX.AC.UK/. CREATIVE COMMONS LICENCE CC-BY-NC 4.0

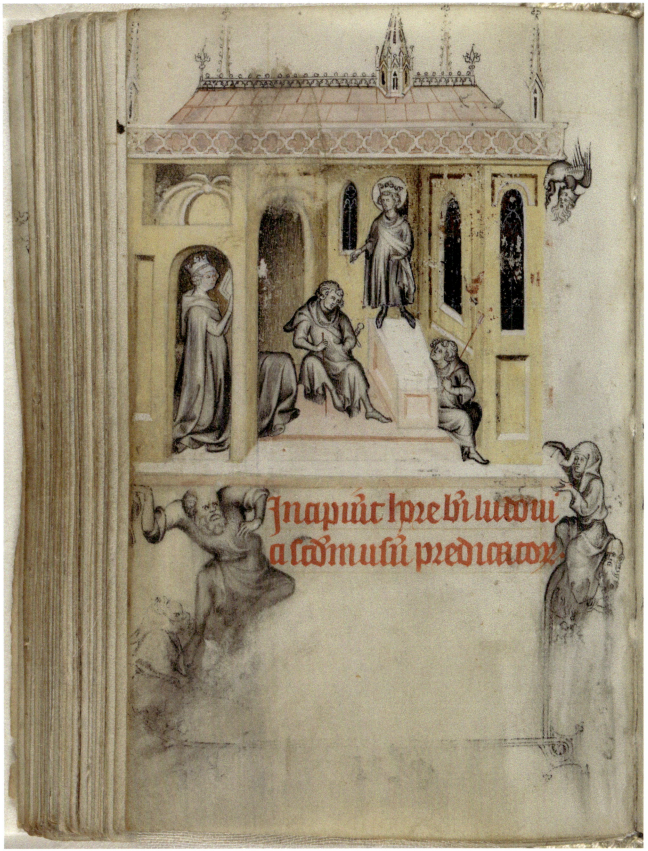

FIGURE 152 Jeanne d'Evreux at the Tomb of St. Louis. Hours of Jeanne d'Evreux, Paris, 1325–1328. New York, Cloisters Collection, Metropolitan Museum of Art, Ms. 54.1.2, fol. 102v
PHOTO: IMAGE COPYRIGHT © METROPOLITAN MUSEUM OF ART. IMAGE SOURCE: ART RESOURCE, NY

FIGURE 155   Page with border at far left comparable to those of Ms. 10 A 14. Bible, Padua, c.1287–1300. New York, The Morgan Library & Museum, Ms. M. 436, fol. 4r. Purchased by J. Pierpont Morgan (1837–1913), 1910
PHOTO: THE MORGAN LIBRARY & MUSEUM

FIGURES 273

FIGURE 157   The Crucifixion. Missal of Conrad of Rennenberg, Cologne, c.1350–1357. Cologne, Diözesan- und Dombibliothek, Cod. 149, fol. 51v
PHOTO: DIÖZESAN- UND DOMBIBLIOTHEK

FIGURE 158 *Ad te levavi*, First Sunday of Advent: stem of initial *A(d te)* with confronted grotesques. Missal for St. Cunibert, Cologne, c.1330. Darmstadt, Universitäts- und Landesbibliothek, Ms. 876, fol. 12r
PHOTO: UNIVERSITÄTS- UND LANDESBIBLIOTHEK

FIGURE 159   The Crucifixion: Compare to Rummen-group Crucifixions. Missal for St. Cunibert, Cologne, c.1330. Darmstadt, Universitäts- und Landesbibliothek, Ms. 876, fol. 223v
PHOTO: UNIVERSITÄTS- UND LANDESBIBLIOTHEK

FIGURE 160 The Crucifixion: St. John supports the Virgin. Missal of St. Peter's Abbey, Ghent, *c.*1275–1285. Ghent, STAM—Ghent City Museum, Inv. A60.01, fol. 7v
PHOTO: UNIVERSITEIT GENT UNIVERSITEITSBIBLIOTHEEK. CREATIVE COMMONS LICENCE CC-BY-NC 4.0

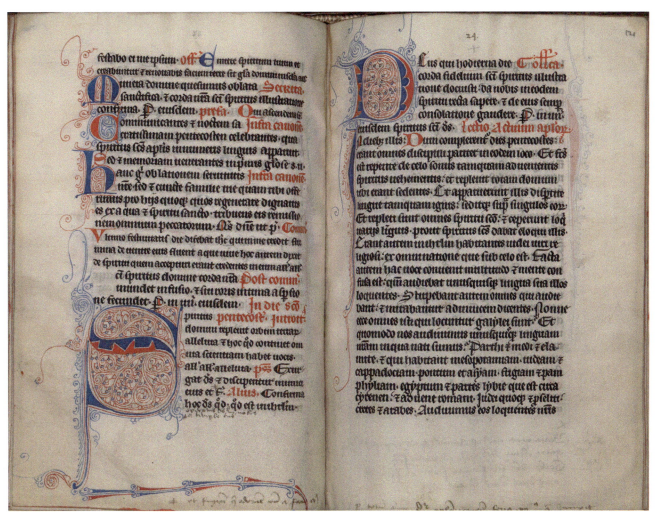

FIGURE 161　Penwork resembling curled shavings. Missal of St. Peter's Abbey, Ghent, *c.*1275–1285. Ghent, STAM—Ghent City Museum, Inv. A60.01, fols. 120v–121r
PHOTO: UNIVERSITEIT GENT UNIVERSITEITSBIBLIOTHEEK. CREATIVE COMMONS LICENCE CC-BY-NC 4.0

FIGURE 162　Frizzy penwork. Ghent Ceremonial, Ghent or Tournai, 1322. Ghent, Universiteit Gent Universiteitsbibliotheek, Ms. 233, fol. 66v
PHOTO: UNIVERSITEIT GENT UNIVERSITEITSBIBLIOTHEEK. CREATIVE COMMONS LICENCE CC-BY-NC 4.0

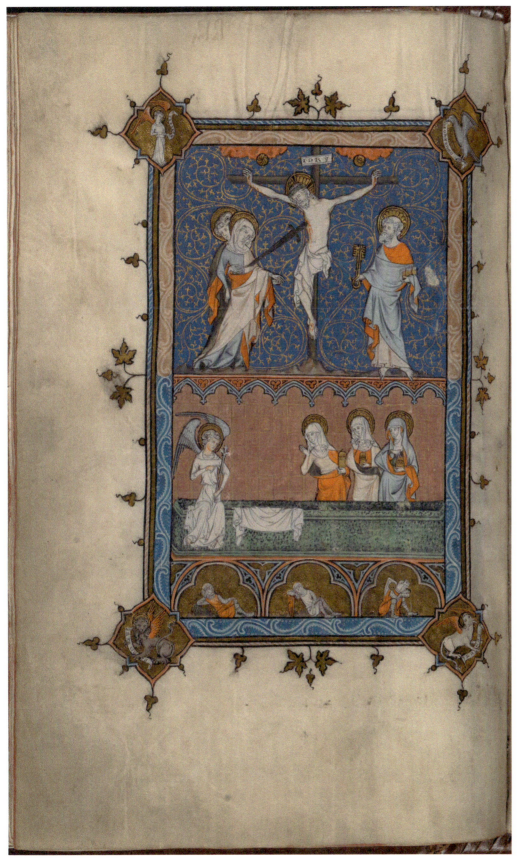

FIGURE 163 The Crucifixion: St. John supports the Virgin. Ghent Ceremonial, Ghent or Tournai, 1322. Ghent, Universiteit Gent Universiteitsbibliotheek, Ms. 233, fol. 70v
PHOTO: UNIVERSITEIT GENT UNIVERSITEITSBIBLIOTHEEK. CREATIVE COMMONS LICENCE CC-BY-NC 4.0

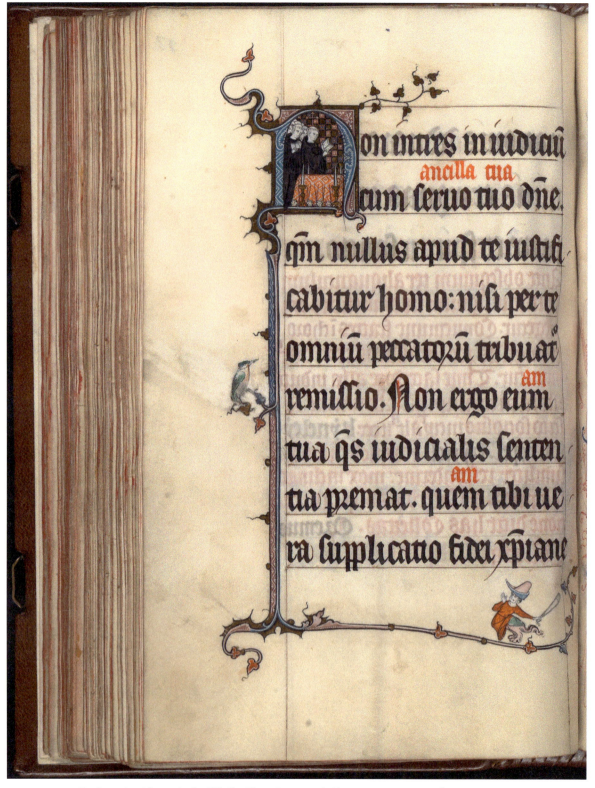

FIGURE 164 Border strip with attached gold balls. Ghent Ceremonial, Ghent or Tournai, 1322. Ghent, Universiteit Gent Universiteitsbibliotheek, Ms. 233, fol. 93v
PHOTO: UNIVERSITEIT GENT UNIVERSITEITSBIBLIOTHEEK. CREATIVE COMMONS LICENCE CC-BY-NC 4.0

FIGURE 165 Spare, nervous penwork flourishing. Ceremonial, Ghent, 1st half of the 14th c. Ghent, Universiteit Gent Universiteitsbibliotheek, Ms. 114, fols. 30v–31r
PHOTO: UNIVERSITEIT GENT UNIVERSITEITSBIBLIOTHEEK. CREATIVE COMMONS LICENCE CC-BY-NC 4.0

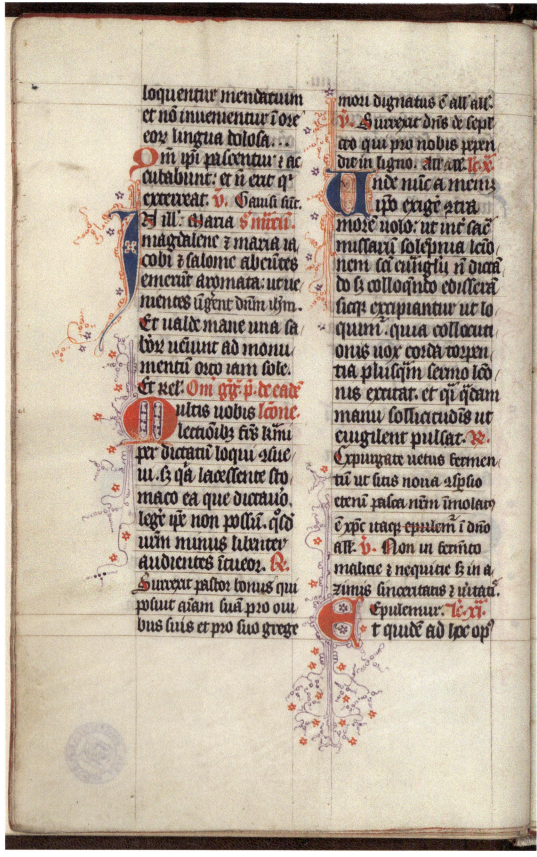

FIGURE 166 Penwork flourishing like that of Artist 1 in the Winter Missal of Arnold of Rummen. Breviary from St. Peter's Abbey, Ghent, 1373. Ghent, Universiteit Gent Universiteitsbibliotheek, Ms. 3381, fol. 4v
PHOTO: UNIVERSITEIT GENT UNIVERSITEITSBIBLIOTHEEK. CREATIVE COMMONS LICENCE CC-BY-NC 4.0

FIGURE 169 Penwork flourishing with stiff arcs and recurves, barbed corkscrews. Artist 2. Antiphonal, Ghent (?), c.1345. Brussels, Koninklijke Bibliotheek/Bibliothèque royale de Belgique, Ms. 6426, fol. 119v
PHOTO: KONINKLIJKE BIBLIOTHEEK/BIBLIOTHÈQUE ROYALE DE BELGIQUE

FIGURE 170   Complex symmetry in design of lower border. Artist 2. Antiphonal, Ghent (?), c.1345. Brussels, Koninklijke Bibliotheek/Bibliothèque royale de Belgique, Ms. 6426, fol. 147v
PHOTO: KONINKLIJKE BIBLIOTHEEK/BIBLIOTHÈQUE ROYALE DE BELGIQUE

FIGURE 171 Introit to Easter Sunday: bas-de-page vignettes with human figures. Summer Missal of Arnold of Rummen, Sint-Truiden (text), Ghent (decoration and illumination), c.1345–1350. Brussels, Koninklijke Bibliotheek/Bibliothèque royale de Belgique, Ms. 9217, fol. 11v
PHOTO: KONINKLIJKE BIBLIOTHEEK/BIBLIOTHÈQUE ROYALE DE BELGIQUE

FIGURE 172 Penwork flourishing. Summer Missal of Arnold of Rummen, Sint-Truiden (text), Ghent (decoration and illumination), c.1345–1350. Brussels, Koninklijke Bibliotheek/Bibliothèque royale de Belgique, Ms. 9217, fol. 22v
PHOTO: KONINKLIJKE BIBLIOTHEEK/BIBLIOTHÈQUE ROYALE DE BELGIQUE

FIGURE 173   Introit for the Ascension. Summer Missal of Arnold of Rummen, Sint-Truiden (text), Ghent (decoration and illumination), c.1345–1350. Brussels, Koninklijke Bibliotheek/Bibliothèque royale de Belgique, Ms. 9217, fol. 33r
PHOTO: KONINKLIJKE BIBLIOTHEEK/BIBLIOTHÈQUE ROYALE DE BELGIQUE

FIGURE 174   Musical notation with penwork flourishing. Summer Missal of Arnold of Rummen, Sint-Truiden (text), Ghent (decoration and illumination), c.1345–1350. Brussels, Koninklijke Bibliotheek/Bibliothèque royale de Belgique, Ms. 9217, fol. 112r
PHOTO: KONINKLIJKE BIBLIOTHEEK/BIBLIOTHÈQUE ROYALE DE BELGIQUE

FIGURE 175   The Crucifixion. Summer Missal of Arnold of Rummen, Sint-Truiden (text), Ghent (decoration and illumination), c.1345–1350. Brussels, Koninklijke Bibliotheek/Bibliothèque royale de Belgique, Ms. 9217, fol. 115v
PHOTO: KONINKLIJKE.BIBLIOTHEEK/BIBLIOTHÈQUE ROYALE DE BELGIQUE

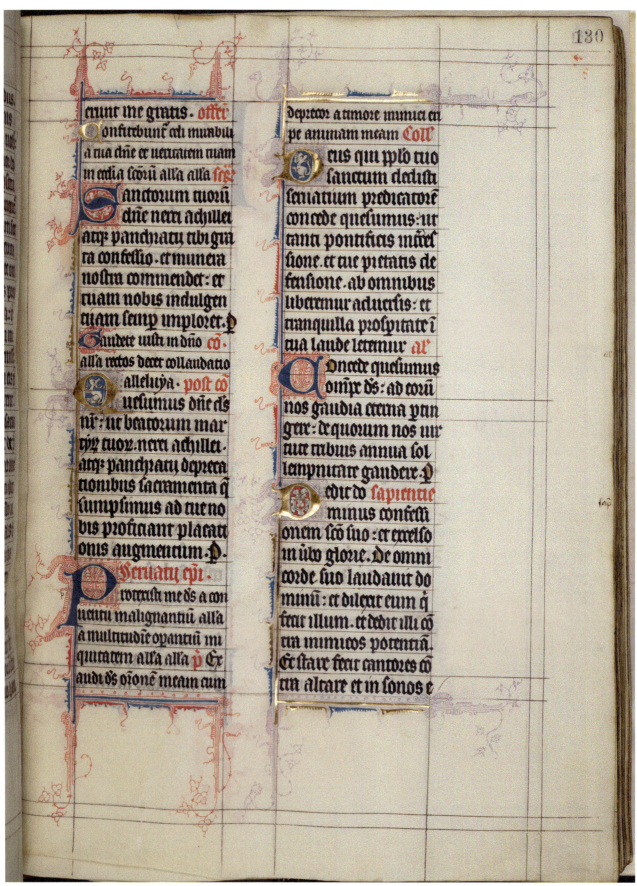

FIGURE 176 Penwork flourshing of Artist 9217–2. Summer Missal of Arnold of Rummen, Sint-Truiden (text), Ghent (decoration and illumination), c.1345–1350. Brussels, Koninklijke Bibliotheek/Bibliothèque royale de Belgique, Ms. 9217, fol. 130r
PHOTO: KONINKLIJKE BIBLIOTHEEK/BIBLIOTHÈQUE ROYALE DE BELGIQUE

FIGURE 177　　Overpainted arms. Liturgical psalter, Sint-Truiden (text), Ghent (decoration and illumination), c.1345–1350. Brussels, Koninklijke Bibliotheek/Bibliothèque royale de Belgique, Ms. 9427, fol. 14r
PHOTO: KONINKLIJKE BIBLIOTHEEK/BIBLIOTHÈQUE ROYALE DE BELGIQUE

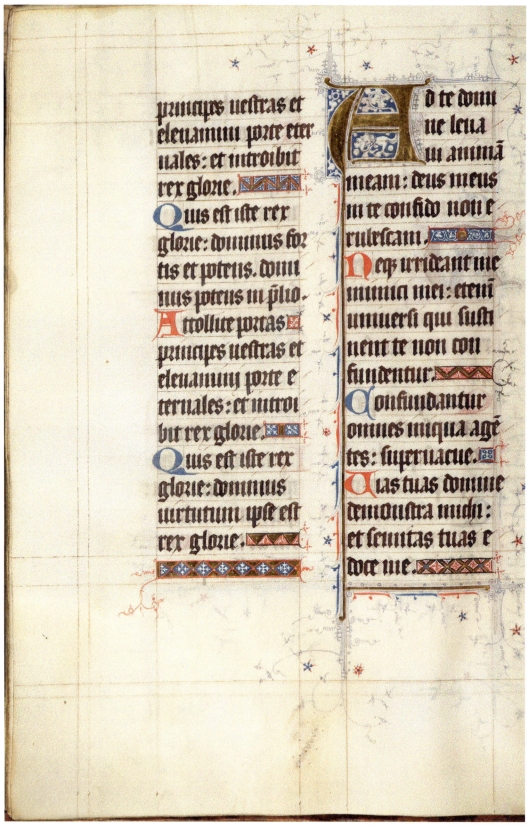

FIGURE 179   Flourishing with tension and opposition. Artist 2. Liturgical psalter, Sint-Truiden (text), Ghent (decoration and illumination), *c.*1345–1350. Brussels, Koninklijke Bibliotheek/Bibliothèque royale de Belgique, Ms. 9427, fol. 40v
PHOTO: KONINKLIJKE BIBLIOTHEEK/BIBLIOTHÈQUE ROYALE DE BELGIQUE

FIGURE 180　Overpainted arms; paired elements above and below border bar. Liturgical psalter, Sint-Truiden (text), Ghent (decoration and illumination), *c.*1345–1350. Brussels, Koninklijke Bibliotheek/Bibliothèque royale de Belgique, Ms. 9427, fol. 43r
PHOTO: KONINKLIJKE BIBLIOTHEEK/BIBLIOTHÈQUE ROYALE DE BELGIQUE

FIGURE 181 Type 1 border bars and corkscrews; diagonal alignment of penwork elements. Artist 2. Liturgical psalter, Sint-Truiden (text), Ghent (decoration and illumination), *c*.1345–1350. Brussels, Koninklijke Bibliotheek/Bibliothèque de Belgique, Ms. 9427, fol. 45r

PHOTO: KONINKLIJKE BIBLIOTHEEK/BIBLIOTHÈQUE ROYALE DE BELGIQUE

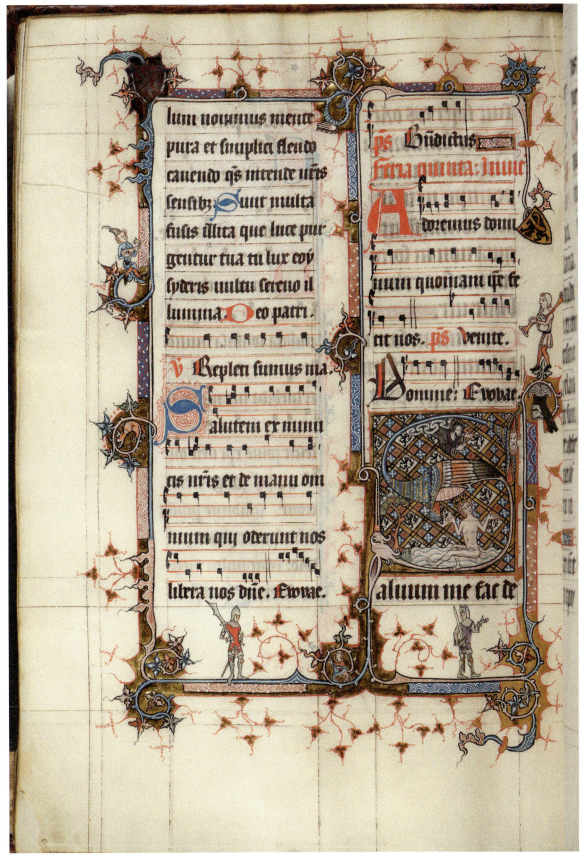

FIGURE 182   Overpainted arms. Liturgical psalter, Sint-Truiden (text), Ghent (decoration and illumination), c.1345–1350.
Brussels, Koninklijke Bibliotheek/Bibliothèque royale de Belgique, Ms. 9427, fol. 100v
PHOTO: KONINKLIJKE BIBLIOTHEEK/BIBLIOTHÈQUE ROYALE DE BELGIQUE

FIGURE 183 Incipit of Psalm 80 (81). Liturgical psalter, Sint-Truiden (text), Ghent (decoration and illumination), c.1345–1350. Brussels, Koninklijke Bibliotheek/Bibliothèque royale de Belgique, Ms. 9427, fol. 124r
PHOTO: KONINKLIJKE BIBLIOTHEEK/BIBLIOTHÈQUE ROYALE DE BELGIQUE

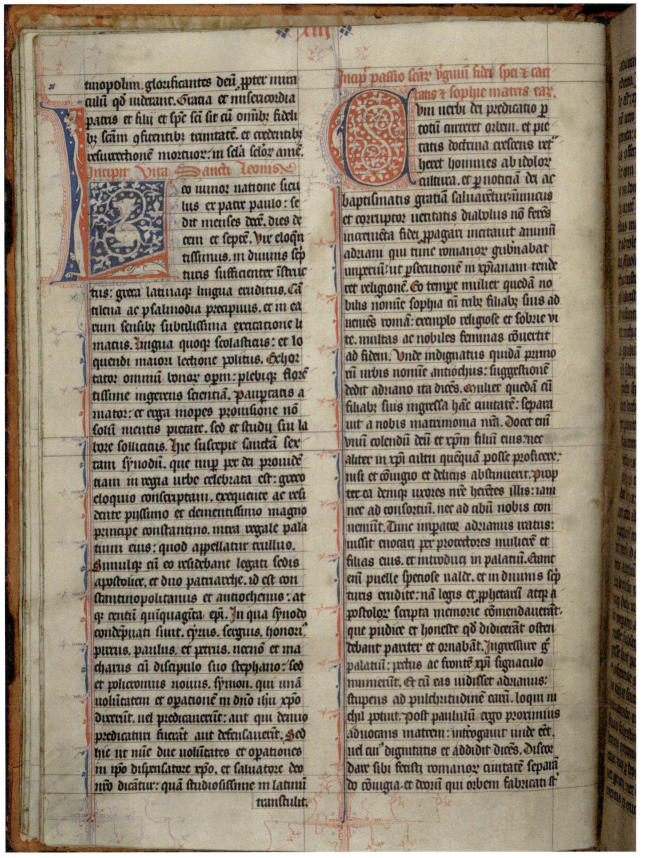

FIGURE 186   Truncated penwork extensions in lower margin. *Passionarium 1*, Sint-Truiden, completed 1366. Liège, Bibliothèque de l'Université de Liège, Ms. 57, fol. 14v
PHOTO: BIBLIOTHÈQUE DE L'UNIVERSITÉ DE LIÈGE

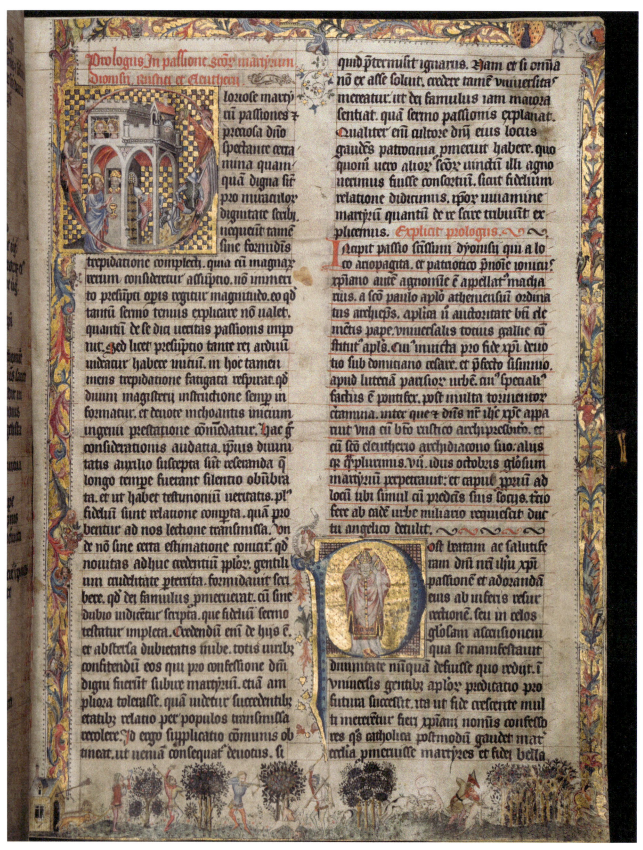

FIGURE 193 Prologue to passion of St. Dionysius, historiated initials *G(loriose)* and *P(ost)* and full borders. *Passionarium 2*, Sint-Truiden, completed *c.*1366. Liège, Bibliothèque de l'Université de Liège, Ms. 58, fol. 2r
PHOTO: BIBLIOTHÈQUE DE L'UNIVERSITÉ DE LIÈGE

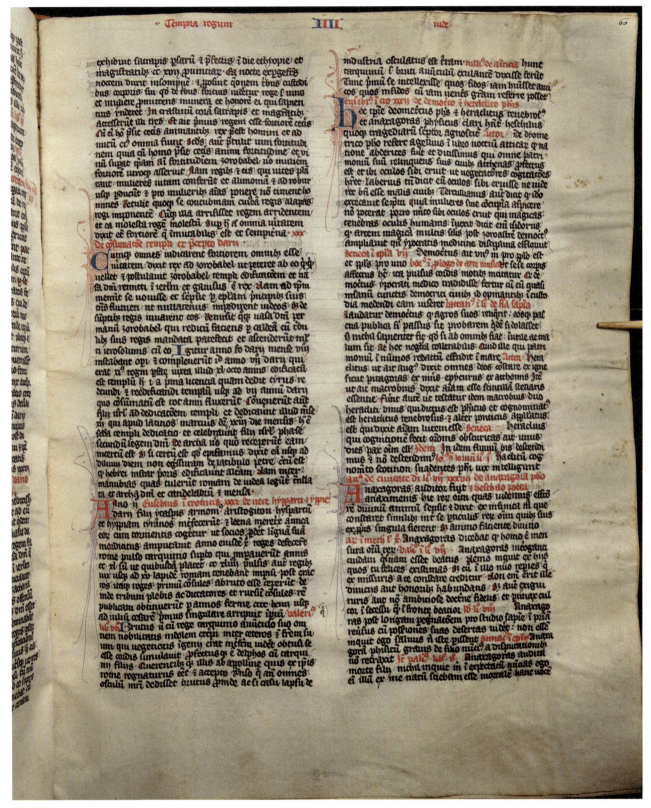

FIGURE 195   Parisian-influenced penwork flourishing. *Speculum historiale 1*, Sint-Truiden, completed 1350. Liège, Bibliothèque de l'Université de Liège, Ms. 60, fol. 60r
PHOTO: BIBLIOTHÈQUE DE L'UNIVERSITÉ DE LIÈGE

FIGURE 196   Decorated initial and partial borders. *Speculum historiale 1*, Sint-Truiden, completed 1350. Liège, Bibliothèque de l'Université de Liège, Ms. 60, fol. 1r
PHOTO: BIBLIOTHÈQUE DE L'UNIVERSITÉ DE LIÈGE

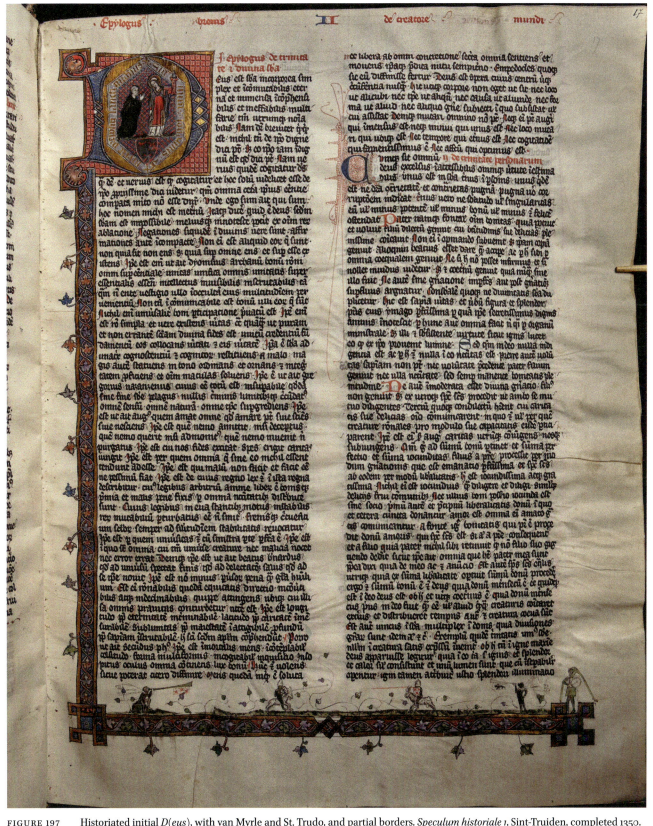

FIGURE 197   Historiated initial *D(eus)*, with van Myrle and St. Trudo, and partial borders. *Speculum historiale 1*, Sint-Truiden, completed 1350. Liège, Bibliothèque de l'Université de Liège, Ms. 60, fol. 17r
PHOTO: BIBLIOTHÈQUE DE L'UNIVERSITÉ DE LIÈGE

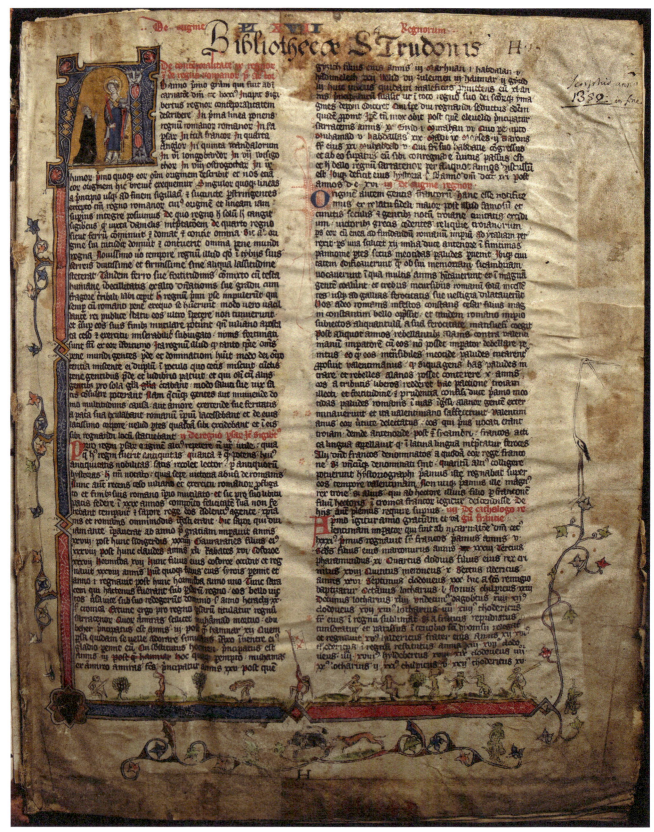

FIGURE 198 Initial *A(b anno)*, with van Myrle and St. Trudo, and partial border. *Speculum historiale 2*, Sint-Truiden, completed 1352. Liège, Bibliothèque de l'Université de Liège, Ms. 61, fol. 1r

PHOTO: BIBLIOTHÈQUE DE L'UNIVERSITÉ DE LIÈGE

FIGURE 200 End of Trinity and beginning of Corpus Christi, with historiated initial and partial borders. Loppem/Bruges Antiphonal, Ghent (?), c.1345. Bruges, Openbare Bibliotheek, Ms. svc 10a, fol. [3r]. On loan from Stichting Jean van Caloen
PHOTO: OPENBARE BIBLIOTHEEK

FIGURE 201 Continuation of Third Sunday after the Octave of Easter, with historiated initial and partial borders. Loppem/Bruges Antiphonal, Ghent (?), c.1345. Bruges, Openbare Bibliotheek, Ms. SVC 10a, fol. [4r]. On loan from Stichting Jean van Caloen
PHOTO: OPENBARE BIBLIOTHEEK

FIGURE 206　Incipit of letter of St. Jerome to Paulinus, with historiated initial, pen-flourished lettering, and borders. *Biblia*, Latin text with *Epistole* and *Prologi Hieronymi* and *Interpretationes*, Paris, c.1350. Stockholm, National Library of Sweden, Ms. A 165, fol. 2r

PHOTO: NATIONAL LIBRARY OF SWEDEN

FIGURE 209 Alexander's siege tower before Tyre; architecture comparable to some in KBR 9217. *The Romance of Alexander*, Tournai, 1338–1344. Oxford, Bodleian Library, Ms. Bodley 264, fol. 20v
PHOTO: BODLEIAN LIBRARIES, UNIVERSITY OF OXFORD. HTTPS://DIGITAL.BODLEIAN.OX.AC.UK/. CREATIVE COMMONS LICENCE CC-BY-NC 4.0

FIGURES

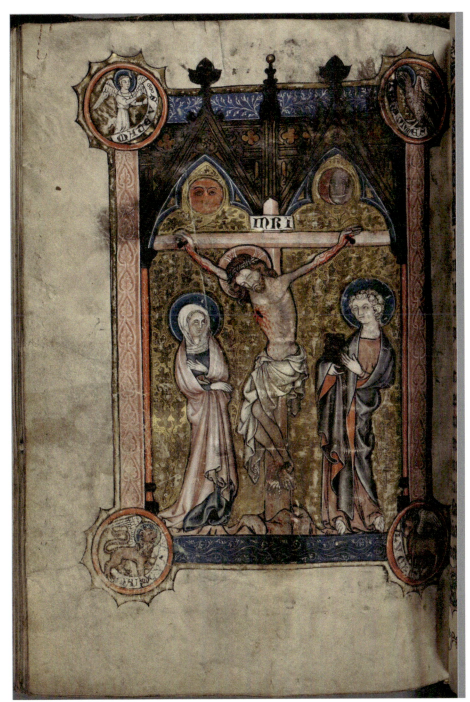

FIGURE 211　　The Crucifixion: Compare to Rummen-group Crucifixions. Missal for St. Cunibert,
　　　　　　　Cologne, *c.*1330. Darmstadt, Universitäts- und Landesbibliothek, Ms. 837, fol. 145v
　　　　　　　PHOTO: UNIVERSITÄTS- UND LANDESBIBLIOTHEK

Details

∴

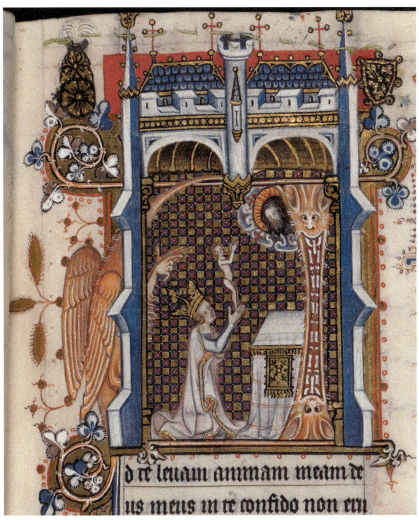

FIGURE 15A   Initial *A(d te)*. Artist 2. Winter Missal of Arnold of Rummen, Sint-Truiden (text), Ghent (decoration and illumination), *c*.1345–1366. The Hague, Huis van het boek, Ms. MMW 10 A 14, fol. 7r, detail
PHOTO: HUIS VAN HET BOEK

FIGURE 16A
Initial *H(ec)* with tufted grotesque. Artist 2. Winter Missal of Arnold of Rummen, Sint-Truiden (text), Ghent (decoration and illumination), *c*.1345–1366. The Hague, Huis van het boek, Ms. MMW 10 A 14, fol. 7v, detail
PHOTO: HUIS VAN HET BOEK

FIGURE 18
Initial *P(opulus)* with tonsured head. Artist 2. Winter Missal of Arnold of Rummen, Sint-Truiden (text), Ghent (decoration and illumination), *c.*1345–1366. The Hague, Huis van het boek, Ms. MMW 10 A 14, fol. 8v, detail
PHOTO: HUIS VAN HET BOEK

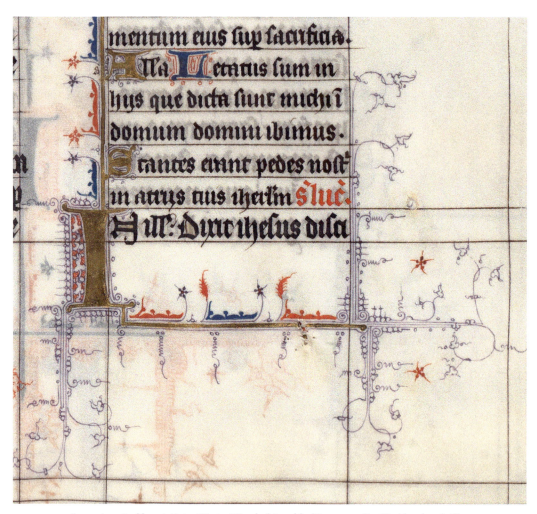

FIGURE 19A Lower terminal bar. Artist 2. Winter Missal of Arnold of Rummen, Sint-Truiden (text), Ghent (decoration and illumination), *c.*1345–1366. The Hague, Huis van het boek, Ms. MMW 10 A 14, fol. 9r detail
PHOTO: HUIS VAN HET BOEK

FIGURE 22 Penwork with a variety of foliate types. Artist 2. Winter Missal of Arnold of Rummen, Sint-Truiden (text), Ghent (decoration and illumination), *c.*1345–1366. The Hague, Huis van het boek, Ms. MMW 10 A 14, fol. 10v, detail
PHOTO: HUIS VAN HET BOEK

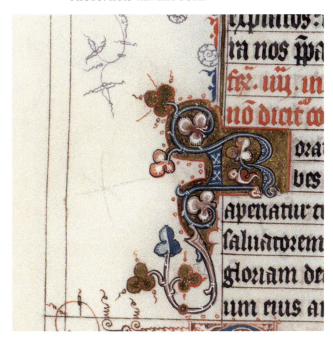

FIGURE 24A
Graphite asterisk in margin beside initial *R(orate)*. Winter Missal of Arnold of Rummen, Sint-Truiden (text), Ghent (decoration and illumination), *c.*1345–1366. The Hague, Huis van het boek, Ms. MMW 10 A 14, fol. 11v, detail
PHOTO: HUIS VAN HET BOEK

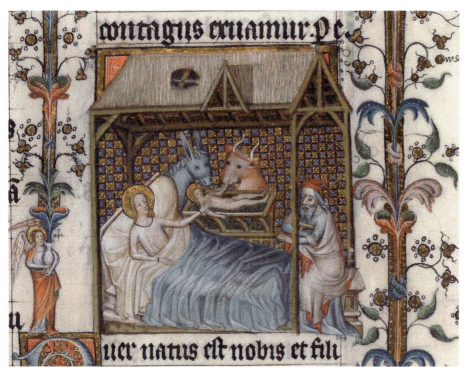

FIGURE 34A Miniature with the Nativity of Christ. Artist 3. Winter Missal of Arnold of Rummen, Sint-Truiden (text), Ghent (decoration and illumination), *c*.1345–1366. The Hague, Huis van het boek, Ms. MMW 10 A 14, fol. 22r, detail
PHOTO: HUIS VAN HET BOEK

FIGURE 34B Overpainted shield in upper section of intercolumniation. Winter Missal of Arnold of Rummen, Sint-Truiden (text), Ghent (decoration and illumination), *c*.1345–1366. The Hague, Huis van het boek, Ms. MMW 10 A 14, fol. 22r, detail
PHOTO: HUIS VAN HET BOEK

FIGURE 34C
Initial *P(uer)*, Artist 3; overpainted shield in lower section of intercolumniation; initial *C(oncede)* with head of Christ, Artist 3. Winter Missal of Arnold of Rummen, Sint-Truiden (text), Ghent (decoration and illumination), *c*.1345–1366. The Hague, Huis van het boek, Ms. MMW 10 A 14, fol. 22r, detail
PHOTO: HUIS VAN HET BOEK

FIGURE 34D
Overpainted helmet in lower right corner. Winter Missal of Arnold of Rummen, Sint-Truiden (text), Ghent (decoration and illumination), *c*.1345–1366. The Hague, Huis van het boek, Ms. MMW 10 A 14, fol. 22r, detail
PHOTO: HUIS VAN HET BOEK

FIGURE 37A
Graphite sketches of figures in margin. Artist 2. Winter Missal of Arnold of Rummen, Sint-Truiden (text), Ghent (decoration and illumination), c.1345–1366. The Hague, Huis van het boek, Ms. MMW 10 A 14, fol. 26r, detail
PHOTO: HUIS VAN HET BOEK

FIGURE 37B
Initial *P*(*uer*) with Circumcision of Christ. Artist 4. Winter Missal of Arnold of Rummen, Sint-Truiden (text), Ghent (decoration and illumination), c.1345–1366. The Hague, Huis van het boek, Ms. MMW 10 A 14, fol. 26r, detail
PHOTO: HUIS VAN HET BOEK

FIGURE 39A Miniature with Adoration of the Magi and donors; initial *E*(*cce*). Artist 3. Heraldic lions with overpaints. Winter Missal of Arnold of Rummen, Sint-Truiden (text), Ghent (decoration and illumination), *c*.1345–1366. The Hague, Huis van het boek, Ms. MMW 10 A 14, fol. 27v, detail
PHOTO: HUIS VAN HET BOEK

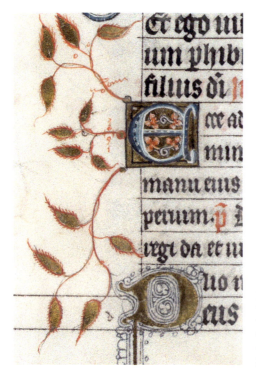

FIGURE 40A
Initials *E(cce)* with trilobe decoration, Artist 2; initial *D(eus)* with trilobe decoration, Artist 4. Winter Missal of Arnold of Rummen, Sint-Truiden (text), Ghent (decoration and illumination), *c.*1345–1366. The Hague, Huis van het boek, Ms. MMW 10 A 14, fol. 29v, detail
PHOTO: HUIS VAN HET BOEK

FIGURE 41
Figural initial *I(n excell'o)* as human-headed grotesque. Artist 4. Winter Missal of Arnold of Rummen, Sint-Truiden (text), Ghent (decoration and illumination), *c.*1345–1366. The Hague, Huis van het boek, Ms. MMW 10 A 14, fol. 30v, detail
PHOTO: HUIS VAN HET BOEK

FIGURE 43A Initial *C*(*ircumdederunt*) in gold frame with black internal detail. Artist 4. Winter Missal of Arnold of Rummen, Sint-Truiden (text), Ghent (decoration and illumination), *c*.1345–1366. The Hague, Huis van het boek, Ms. MMW 10 A 14, fol. 36r, detail
PHOTO: HUIS VAN HET BOEK

FIGURE 44
Initial *E*(*xurge*) with tonsured head behind initial arm. Artist 2. Winter Missal of Arnold of Rummen, Sint-Truiden (text), Ghent (decoration and illumination), *c*.1345–1366. The Hague, Huis van het boek, Ms. MMW 10 A 14, fol. 38v, detail
PHOTO: HUIS VAN HET BOEK

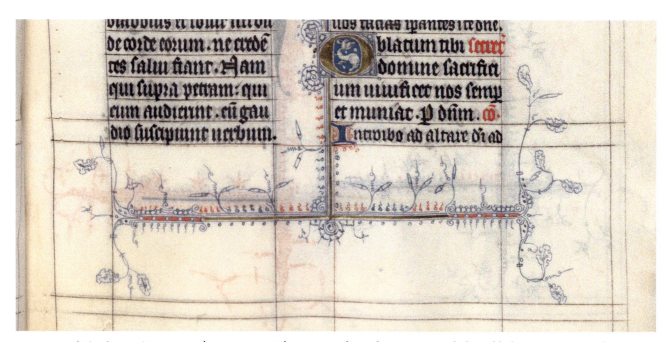

FIGURE 46 Artist 2's sweeping curves and reverse curves in lower terminal complex. Winter Missal of Arnold of Rummen, Sint-Truiden (text), Ghent (decoration and illumination), c.1345–1366. The Hague, Huis van het boek, Ms. MMW 10 A 14, fol. 39v, detail
PHOTO: HUIS VAN HET BOEK

FIGURE 48 Artist 4's corkscrews. Winter Missal of Arnold of Rummen, Sint-Truiden (text), Ghent (decoration and illumination), c.1345–1366. The Hague, Huis van het boek, Ms. MMW 10 A 14, fol. 42v, detail
PHOTO: HUIS VAN HET BOEK

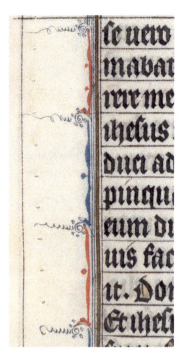

FIGURE 49
Artist 4's corkscrews. Winter Missal of Arnold of Rummen, Sint-Truiden (text), Ghent (decoration and illumination), *c.*1345–1366. The Hague, Huis van het boek, Ms. MMW 10 A 14, fol. 43r, detail
PHOTO: HUIS VAN HET BOEK

FIGURE 50
Initial *D*(*omine*) with double profile. Artist 2. Winter Missal of Arnold of Rummen, Sint-Truiden (text), Ghent (decoration and illumination), *c.*1345–1366. The Hague, Huis van het boek, Ms. MMW 10 A 14, fol. 45r, detail
PHOTO: HUIS VAN HET BOEK

FIGURE 51
Initial *D*(*eus*) with Christ bruised and crowned with thorns. Artist 2. Winter Missal of Arnold of Rummen, Sint-Truiden (text), Ghent (decoration and illumination), *c.*1345–1366. The Hague, Huis van het boek, Ms. MMW 10 A 14, fol. 46r, detail
PHOTO: HUIS VAN HET BOEK

FIGURE 52
Initial *A*(*udiunt*) with leonine grotesque. Artist 2. Winter Missal of Arnold of Rummen, *c.*1345–1366. Sint-Truiden (text), Ghent (decoration and illumination), The Hague, Huis van het boek, Ms. MMW 10 A 14, fol. 47r, detail
PHOTO: HUIS VAN HET BOEK

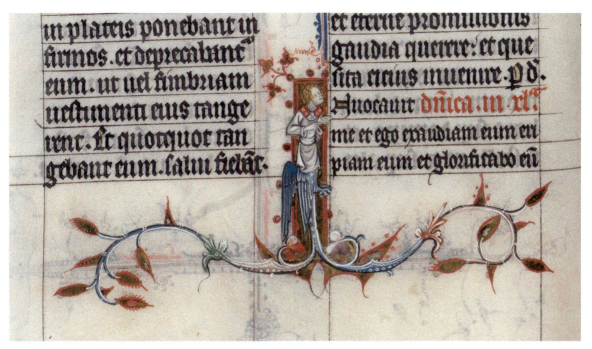

FIGURE 54 Grotesque as figural initial *I(nvocavit)*. Artist 2. Winter Missal of Arnold of Rummen, Sint-Truiden (text), Ghent (decoration and illumination), c.1345–1366. The Hague, Huis van het boek, Ms. MMW 10 A 14, fol. 49v, detail
PHOTO: HUIS VAN HET BOEK

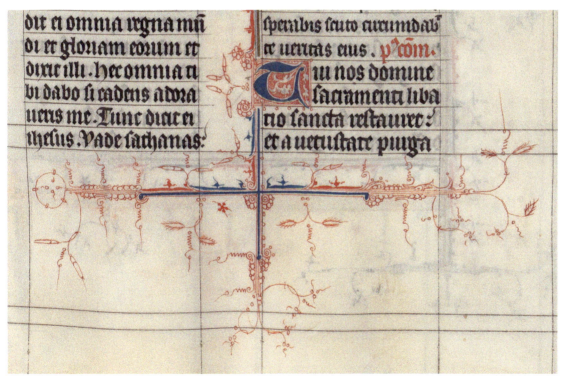

FIGURE 56 Lower terminal complex with pairs of pairs, complex symmetry. Artist 2. Winter Missal of Arnold of Rummen, Sint-Truiden (text), Ghent (decoration and illumination), c.1345–1366. The Hague, Huis van het boek, Ms. MMW 10 A 14, fol. 51r, detail
PHOTO: HUIS VAN HET BOEK

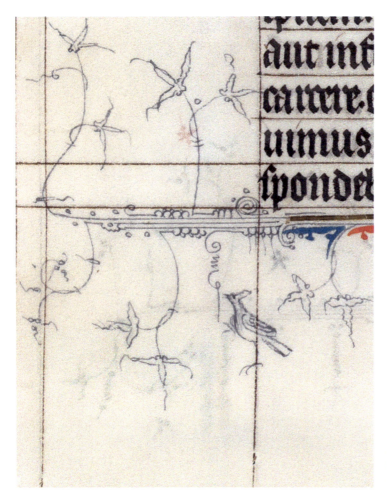

FIGURE 57
Penwork bird in lower margin. Artist 2. Winter Missal of Arnold of Rummen, Sint-Truiden (text), Ghent (decoration and illumination), *c*.1345–1366. The Hague, Huis van het boek, Ms. MMW 10 A 14, fol. 52v, detail
PHOTO: HUIS VAN HET BOEK

FIGURE 58
Initial *D*(*evotionem*) with woman in ruffled hood. Artist 2. Winter Missal of Arnold of Rummen, Sint-Truiden (text), Ghent (decoration and illumination), *c*.1345–1366. The Hague, Huis van het boek, Ms. MMW 10 A 14, fol. 54va, detail
PHOTO: HUIS VAN HET BOEK

FIGURE 58A
Initial *D*(*e necessitatibus*) with woman in ruffled hood. Artist 2. Winter Missal of Arnold of Rummen, Sint-Truiden (text), Ghent (decoration and illumination), *c*.1345–1366. The Hague, Huis van het boek, Ms. MMW 10 A 14, fol. 54vb, detail
PHOTO: HUIS VAN HET BOEK

FIGURE 59
Initial *C(onfessio)* with trilobes as decoration and extensions. Artist 2. Winter Missal of Arnold of Rummen, Sint-Truiden (text), Ghent (decoration and illumination), *c*.1345–1366. The Hague, Huis van het boek, Ms. MMW 10 A 14, fol. 55v, detail
PHOTO: HUIS VAN HET BOEK

FIGURE 60A
Initial *D(e necessitatibus)* with tonsured head. Artist 2. Winter Missal of Arnold of Rummen, Sint-Truiden (text), Ghent (decoration and illumination), *c*.1345–1366. The Hague, Huis van het boek, Ms. MMW 10 A 14, fol. 57r, detail
PHOTO: HUIS VAN HET BOEK

FIGURE 61A
Figural initial *I(ntret)* with human-headed grotesques. Artist 2. Winter Missal of Arnold of Rummen, Sint-Truiden (text), Ghent (decoration and illumination), *c*.1345–1366. The Hague, Huis van het boek, Ms. MMW 10 A 14, fol. 58v, detail
PHOTO: HUIS VAN HET BOEK

FIGURE 62
Initial *P(reces)* with triple profile. Artist 2. Winter Missal of Arnold of Rummen, Sint-Truiden (text), Ghent (decoration and illumination), *c*.1345–1366. The Hague, Huis van het boek, Ms. MMW 10 A 14, fol. 60r, detail
PHOTO: HUIS VAN HET BOEK

FIGURE 63   Initial *R(eminiscere)* and extension with graphite sk etch lines for cusping and tendrils. Artist 2. Winter Missal of Arnold of Rummen, Sint-Truiden (text), Ghent (decoration and illumination), *c*.1345–1366. The Hague, Huis van het boek, Ms. MMW 10 A 14, fol. 61v, detail
PHOTO: HUIS VAN HET BOEK

FIGURE 64
Initial *R(edime)* with woman's head in grisaille. Artist 4. Winter Missal of Arnold of Rummen, Sint-Truiden (text), Ghent (decoration and illumination), c.1345–1366. The Hague, Huis van het boek, Ms. MMW 10 A 14, fol. 63r, detail
PHOTO: HUIS VAN HET BOEK

FIGURE 65
Free-floating partial border with threatening grotesque. Artist 4. Winter Missal of Arnold of Rummen, Sint-Truiden (text), Ghent (decoration and illumination), c.1345–1366. The Hague, Huis van het boek, Ms. MMW 10 A 14, fol. 64r, detail
PHOTO: HUIS VAN HET BOEK

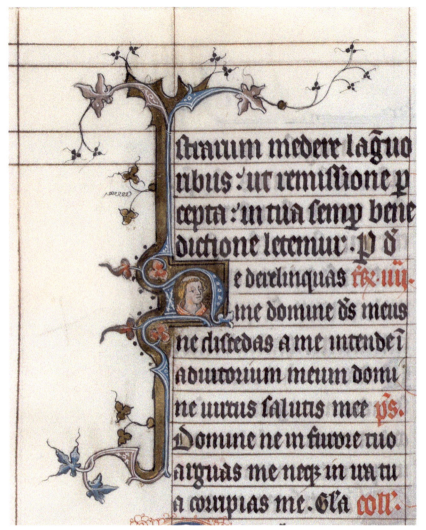

FIGURE 66   Initial *N*(*e derelinquas*) with tonsured head; foliage comparable to that on fol. 26r. Artist 4. Winter Missal of Arnold of Rummen, Sint-Truiden (text), Ghent (decoration and illumination), *c*.1345–1366. The Hague, Huis van het boek, Ms. MMW 10 A 14, fol. 65v, detail
PHOTO: HUIS VAN HET BOEK

FIGURE 67
Face behind arm of initial *E*(*go*). Artist 4. Winter Missal of Arnold of Rummen, Sint-Truiden (text), Ghent (decoration and illumination), *c*.1345–1366. The Hague, Huis van het boek, Ms. MMW 10 A 14, fol. 68r, detail
PHOTO: HUIS VAN HET BOEK

FIGURE 70A
Type 4 border bar with small urns; initial *P(er)* with humanoid grotesque having recurved neck. Artist 2. Winter Missal of Arnold of Rummen, Sint-Truiden (text), Ghent (decoration and Illumination), *c*.1345–1366. The Hague, Huis het boek, Ms. MMW 10 A 14, fol. 76r, detail
PHOTO: HUIS VAN HET BOEK

FIGURE 70B   Initial *T(ua)* with tufted grotesque and lower terminal complex. Artist 2. Winter Missal of Arnold of Rummen, Sint-Truiden (text), Ghent (decoration and Illumination), *c*.1345–1366. The Hague, Huis van het boek, Ms. MMW 10 A 14, fol. 76r, detail
PHOTO: HUIS VAN HET BOEK

FIGURE 74A
Initial *D(eus)* with head of Christ. Artist 2. Winter Missal of Arnold of Rummen, Sint-Truiden (text), Ghent (decoration and illumination), c.1345–1366. The Hague, Huis van het boek, Ms. MMW 10 A 14, fol. 78v, detail
PHOTO: HUIS VAN HET BOEK

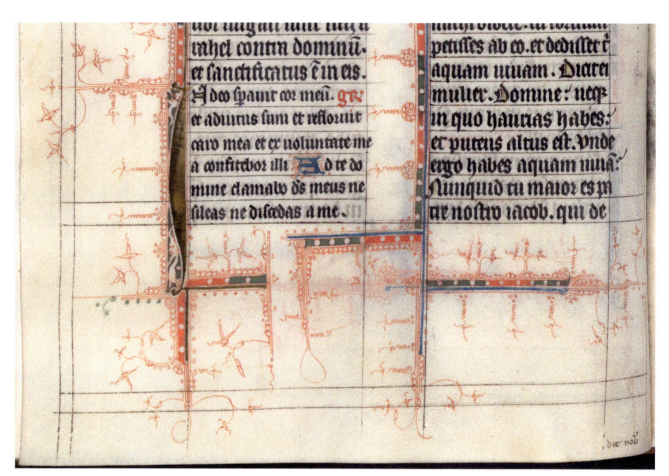

FIGURE 75 Initial *I(deo)* projects into lower margin and pushes terminal bar downward. Artist 2. Winter Missal of Arnold of Rummen, Sint-Truiden (text), Ghent (decoration and illumination), c.1345–1366. The Hague, Huis van het boek, Ms. MMW 10 A 14, fol. 79v, detail
PHOTO: HUIS VAN HET BOEK

FIGURES 331

FIGURE 77
Plummet asterisk in margin marks location of initial; portrait-like head in initial *D(eus)*. Winter Missal of Arnold of Rummen, Sint-Truiden (text), Ghent (decoration and illumination), *c.*1345–1366. The Hague, Huis van het boek, Ms. MMW 10 A 14, fol. 85v, detail
PHOTO: HUIS VAN HET BOEK

FIGURE 79   Initial *S(umptis)* with connection to border bar; spiked pearls; initials *O(blatum)* with mitred head and *D(eprecationem)* with crowned head. Artist 2. Winter Missal of Arnold of Rummen, Sint-Truiden (text), Ghent (decoration and illumination), *c.*1345–1366. The Hague, Huis van het boek, Ms. MMW 10 A 14, fol. 86v, detail
PHOTO: HUIS VAN HET BOEK

FIGURE 80   Hatched border bar. Initials *H*(*uius*) with profile hooded head and *D*(*um*) with three-quarters head. Artist 2. Winter Missal of Arnold of Rummen, Sint-Truiden (text), Ghent (decoration and illumination), *c*.1345–1366. The Hague, Huis van het boek, Ms. MMW 10 A 14, fol. 88r, detail

PHOTO: HUIS VAN HET BOEK

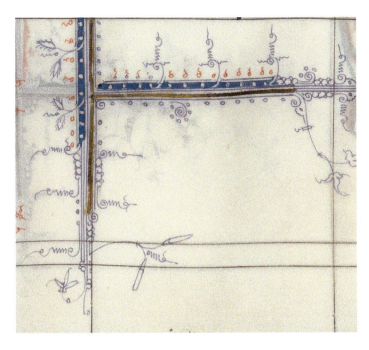

FIGURE 83
Lower terminal complex with corkscrews. Artist 2. Winter Missal of Arnold of Rummen, Sint-Truiden (text), Ghent (decoration and illumination), *c.*1345–1366. The Hague, Huis van het boek, Ms. MMW 10 A 14, fol. 95r, detail
PHOTO: HUIS VAN HET BOEK

FIGURE 85 Pearl spirals. Artist 2. Winter Missal of Arnold of Rummen, Sint-Truiden (text), Ghent (decoration and illumination), *c.*1345–1366. The Hague, Huis van het boek, Ms. MMW 10 A 14, fol. 100r, detail
PHOTO: HUIS VAN HET BOEK

FIGURE 86A
Initial C(*elestis*) with soldier in helmet and chain mail. Artist 2. Winter Missal of Arnold of Rummen, Sint-Truiden (text), Ghent (decoration and illumination), *c.*1345–1366. The Hague, Huis van het boek, Ms. MMW 10 A 14, fol. 100v, detail
PHOTO: HUIS VAN HET BOEK

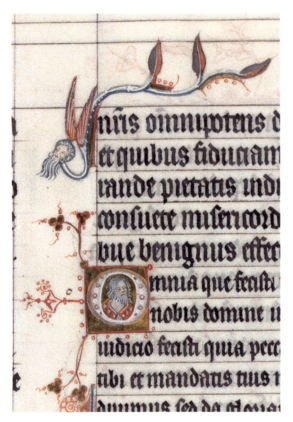

FIGURE 86B
Grotesque echoes appearance of head in initial O(*mnia*). Artist 2. Winter Missal of Arnold of Rummen, Sint-Truiden (text), Ghent (decoration and illumination), *c.*1345–1366. The Hague, Huis van het boek, Ms. MMW 10 A 14, fol. 100v, detail
PHOTO: HUIS VAN HET BOEK

FIGURE 87A
Artist 3's corkscrews. Winter Missal of Arnold of Rummen, Sint-Truiden (text), Ghent (decoration and illumination), c.1345–1366. The Hague, Huis van het boek, Ms. MMW 10 A 14, fol. 104v, detail
PHOTO: HUIS VAN HET BOEK

FIGURE 88
Penwork trilobes with tremulous outline. Artist 3. Winter Missal of Arnold of Rummen, Sint-Truiden (text), Ghent (decoration and illumination), c.1345–1366. The Hague, Huis van het boek, Ms. MMW 10 A 14, fol. 105r, detail
PHOTO: HUIS VAN HET BOEK

FIGURE 89A
Pearls. Artist 3. Winter Missal of Arnold of Rummen, Sint-Truiden (text), Ghent (decoration and illumination), *c.*1345–1366. The Hague, Huis van het boek, 10 A 14, fol. 105v, detail
PHOTO: HUIS VAN HET BOEK

FIGURE 90
Initial *C*(*um*) with face washed in grisaille. Artist 3. Winter Missal of Arnold of Rummen, Sint-Truiden (text), Ghent (decoration and illumination), *c.*1345–1366. The Hague, Huis van het boek, Ms. MMW 10 A 14, fol. 106r, detail
PHOTO: HUIS VAN HET BOEK

FIGURE 91A   Miniature and initial *D(omine)* with woman pointing to Christ. Artist 2. Winter Missal of Arnold of Rummen, Sint-Truiden (text), Ghent (decoration and illumination), *c*.1345–1366. The Hague, Huis van het boek, Ms. MMW 10 A 14, fol. 106v, detail
PHOTO: HUIS VAN HET BOEK

FIGURE 91B
Vignette of rabbits, burrows, and trees. Artist 2. Winter Missal of Arnold of Rummen, Sint-Truiden (text), Ghent (decoration and illumination), c.1345–1366. The Hague, Huis van het boek, Ms. MMW 10 A 14, fol. 106v, detail
PHOTO: HUIS VAN HET BOEK

FIGURE 92
Initial *D(eus)* with head of Christ. Artist 3. Winter Missal of Arnold of Rummen, Sint-Truiden (text), Ghent (decoration and illumination), 1345–1366. The Hague, Huis van het boek, Ms. MMW 10 A 14, fol. 107r, detail
PHOTO: HUIS VAN HET BOEK

FIGURE 93
Penwork head at upper left. Artist 3. Winter Missal of Arnold of Rummen, Sint-Truiden (text), Ghent (decoration and illumination), c.1345–1366. The Hague, Huis van het boek, Ms. MMW 10 A 14, fol. 107v, detail
PHOTO: HUIS VAN HET BOEK

FIGURE 94A Penwork face beside initial *D*(*a quesumus*). Artist 1. Winter Missal of Arnold of Rummen, Sint-Truiden (text), Ghent (decoration and illumination), *c*.1345–1366. The Hague, Huis van het boek, Ms. MMW 10 A 14, fol. 112v, detail
PHOTO: HUIS VAN HET BOEK

FIGURE 96
Simian face in penwork beside initial *D(omine)*. Artist 2. Winter Missal of Arnold of Rummen, Sint-Truiden (text), Ghent (decoration and illumination), *c.*1345–1366. The Hague, Huis van het boek, Ms. MMW 10 A 14, fol. 121r, detail
PHOTO: HUIS VAN HET BOEK

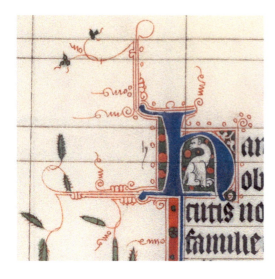

FIGURE 97
Initial *H(anc)* with grotesque. Artist 2. Winter Missal of Arnold of Rummen, Sint-Truiden (text), Ghent (decoration and illumination), *c.*1345–1366. The Hague, Huis van het boek, Ms. MMW 10 A 14, fol. 127v, detail
PHOTO: HUIS VAN HET BOEK

FIGURE 98
Initial *P(ostquam)* with humanoid-avian-mammalian grotesque. Artist 2. Winter Missal of Arnold of Rummen, Sint-Truiden (text), Ghent (decoration and illumination), *c.*1345–1366. The Hague, Huis van het boek, Ms. MMW 10 A 14, fol. 128r, detail
PHOTO: HUIS VAN HET BOEK

FIGURE 99A
Initial *H(ec)* with bearded, cowled monk. Artist 1. Winter Missal of Arnold of Rummen, Sint-Truiden (text), Ghent (decoration and illumination), *c.*1345–1366. The Hague, Huis van het boek, Ms. MMW 10 A 14, fol. 128v, detail
PHOTO: HUIS VAN HET BOEK

FIGURE 102
Initial O(*mnipotens*) with tonsured head. Artist 2. Winter Missal of Arnold of Rummen, Sint-Truiden (text), Ghent (decoration and illumination), c.1345–1366. The Hague, Huis van het boek, Ms. MMW 10 A 14, fol. 135r, detail
PHOTO: HUIS VAN HET BOEK

FIGURE 102A
Initial O(*mnipotens*) with tonsured head. Artist 2. Winter Missal of Arnold of Rummen, Sint-Truiden (text), Ghent (decoration and illumination), c.1345–1366. The Hague, Huis van het boek, Ms. MMW 10 A 14, fol. 135r, detail
PHOTO: HUIS VAN HET BOEK

FIGURE 103A
Miniature and initial for the Preface of the Ordinary of the Mass; donor portraits. Artist 1. Winter Missal of Arnold of Rummen, Sint-Truiden (text), Ghent (decoration and illumination), c.1345–1366. The Hague, Huis van het boek, Ms. MMW 10 A 14, fol. 139r, detail
PHOTO: HUIS VAN HET BOEK

FIGURE 105A
Initial Q(*ui*) with softly modeled, grisaille figure. Artist 2. Winter Missal of Arnold of Rummen, Sint-Truiden (text), Ghent (decoration and illumination), c.1345–1366. The Hague, Huis van het boek, Ms. MMW 10 A 14, fol. 141v, detail
PHOTO: HUIS VAN HET BOEK

FIGURE 106A
Donor portrait of Elisabeth of Lierde. Artist 2. Overpaint of Arnold of Rummen. Winter Missal of Arnold of Rummen, Sint-Truiden (text), Ghent (decoration and illumination), c.1345–1366. The Hague, Huis van het boek, Ms. MMW 10 A 14, fol. 143v, detail
PHOTO: HUIS VAN HET BOEK

FIGURE 106B
St. John supporting the Virgin; streaky modeling. Artist 2. Winter Missal of Arnold of Rummen, Sint-Truiden (text), Ghent (decoration and illumination), c.1345–1366. The Hague, Huis van het boek, Ms. MMW 10 A 14, fol. 143v, detail
PHOTO: HUIS VAN HET BOEK

FIGURES 343

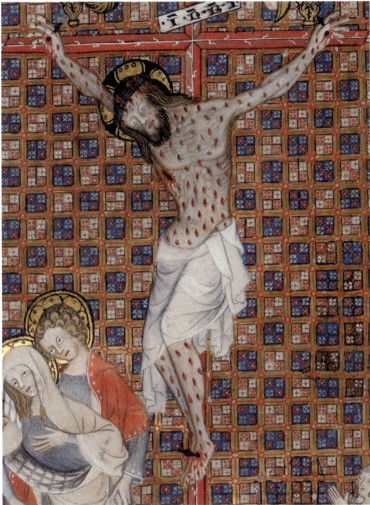

FIGURE 106C Crucified Christ; use of line in modeling the body of Christ.
Artist 2. Winter Missal of Arnold of Rummen, Sint-Truiden (text),
Ghent (decoration and illumination), *c.*1345–1366. The Hague,
Huis van het boek, Ms. MMW 10 A 14, fol. 143v, detail
PHOTO: HUIS VAN HET BOEK

FIGURE 107A   Miniature with priest and acolyte at the altar, and initial *T*(*e igitur*) with grotesques. Artist 1. Winter Missal of Arnold of Rummen, Sint-Truiden (text), Ghent (decoration and illumination), *c*.1345–1366. The Hague, Huis van het boek, Ms. MMW 10 A 14, fol. 144r, detail
PHOTO: HUIS VAN HET BOEK

FIGURE 107B Bas-de-page with wild pigs and hares. Artist 1. Winter Missal of Arnold of Rummen, Sint-Truiden (text), Ghent (decoration and illumination), *c.*1345–1366. The Hague, Huis van het boek, Ms. MMW 10 A 14, fol. 144r, detail
PHOTO: HUIS VAN HET BOEK

FIGURE 109A
Grotesque, curling tendrils to compare with those in *Passionarium 1*, BUL, Ms. 57. Artist 2. Winter Missal of Arnold of Rummen, Sint-Truiden (text), Ghent (decoration and illumination), *c.*1345–1366. The Hague, Huis van het boek, Ms. MMW 10 A 14, fol. 149r, detail
PHOTO: HUIS VAN HET BOEK

FIGURE 110A   Initial *D(ilexisti)* with St. Lucy and Eutychia at the tomb of St. Agatha. Artist 1. Winter Missal of Arnold of Rummen, Sint-Truiden (text), Ghent (decoration and illumination), *c.*1345–1366. The Hague, Huis van het boek, Ms. MMW 10 A 14, fol. 151r, detail
PHOTO: HUIS VAN HET BOEK PHOTO: AUTHOR, BY PERMISSION.

FIGURES 347

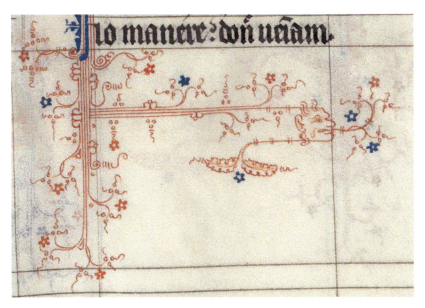

FIGURE 112A
Human face and oak leaves in lower terminal complex. Artist 1. Winter Missal of Arnold of Rummen, Sint-Truiden (text), Ghent (decoration and illumination), c.1345–1366. The Hague, Huis van het boek, Ms. MMW 10 A 14, fol. 154r, detail
PHOTO: HUIS VAN HET BOEK

FIGURE 113A
Knobby faces beside initial *R*(*efecti*) and in lower terminal complex. Artist 1. Winter Missal of Arnold of Rummen, Sint-Truiden (text), Ghent (decoration and illumination), c.1345–1366. The Hague, Huis van het boek, Ms. MMW 10 A 14, fol. 154v, detail
PHOTO: HUIS VAN HET BOEK

FIGURE 113B

Initial *I*(*n diebus*) with knobby face and pearl clusters. Artist 1. Winter Missal of Arnold of Rummen, Sint-Truiden (text), Ghent (decoration and illumination), *c.*1345–1366. The Hague, Huis van het boek, Ms. MMW 10 A 14, fol. 154v, detail

PHOTO: HUIS VAN HET BOEK

FIGURE 116

Initial *B*(*eate*) with humanoid grotesque. Artist 1. Winter Missal of Arnold of Rummen, Sint-Truiden (text), Ghent (decoration and illumination), *c.*1345–1366. The Hague, Huis van het boek, Ms. MMW 10 A 14, fol. 156v, detail

PHOTO: HUIS VAN HET BOEK

FIGURES 349

FIGURE 117   Two-line penwork initial *H(ostias)* with bearded male head. Artist 1. Winter Missal of Arnold of Rummen, Sint-Truiden (text), Ghent (decoration and illumination), *c.*1345–1366. The Hague, Huis van het boek, Ms. MMW 10 A 14, fol. 157v, detail
PHOTO: HUIS VAN HET BOEK

FIGURE 118   Penwork face above ivy leaves, lower terminal complex. Artist 1. Winter Missal of Arnold of Rummen, Sint-Truiden (text), Ghent (decoration and illumination), c.1345–1366. The Hague, Huis van het boek, Ms. MMW 10 A 14, fol. 158r, detail
PHOTO: HUIS VAN HET BOEK

FIGURE 119
Initial *D(eus)* with face-like form in adjacent penwork. Artist 1. Winter Missal of Arnold of Rummen, Sint-Truiden (text), Ghent (decoration and illumination), c.1345–1366. The Hague, Huis van het boek, Ms. MMW 10 A 14, fol. 160r, detail
PHOTO: HUIS VAN HET BOEK

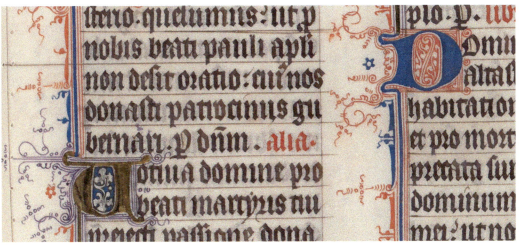

FIGURE 120 Penwork rosettes hovering before faces adjacent to initials *V(otiva)* and *D(omine)*. Artist 1. Winter Missal of Arnold of Rummen, Sint-Truiden (text), Ghent (decoration and illumination), c.1345–1366. The Hague, Huis van het boek, Ms. MMW 10 A 14, fol. 165r, detail
PHOTO: HUIS VAN HET BOEK

FIGURE 121A
Introit for the Presentation of Christ: initial *S(uscepimus)* with the Presentation. Artist 1. Winter Missal of Arnold of Rummen, Sint-Truiden (text), Ghent (decoration and illumination), c.1345–1366. The Hague, Huis van het boek, Ms. MMW 10 A 14, fol. 167r, detail
PHOTO: HUIS VAN HET BOEK

FIGURE 122

Initial *D*(*iffusa*): Penwork face beside the initial echoes face in the initial. Artist 1. Winter Missal of Arnold of Rummen, Sint-Truiden (text), Ghent (decoration and illumination), *c.*1345–1366. The Hague, Huis van het boek, Ms. MMW 10 A 14, fol. 167v, detail

PHOTO: HUIS VAN HET BOEK

FIGURE 123

Penwork initial *P*(*reces*) with Jew. Artist 1. Winter Missal of Arnold of Rummen, Sint-Truiden (text), Ghent (decoration and illumination), *c.*1345–1366. The Hague, Huis van het boek, Ms. MMW 10 A 14, fol. 170r, detail

PHOTO: HUIS VAN HET BOEK

FIGURES

353

FIGURE 124A
Corkscrews. Artist 1. Winter Missal of Arnold of Rummen, Sint-Truiden (text), Ghent (decoration and illumination), c.1345–1366. The Hague, Huis van het boek, Ms. MMW 10 A 14, fol. 175r, detail
PHOTO: HUIS VAN HET BOEK

FIGURE 125A
Introit for the Annunciation: initial *R(orate)* with the Annunciation. Artist 1. Winter Missal of Arnold of Rummen, Sint-Truiden (text), Ghent (decoration and illumination), c.1345–1366. The Hague, Huis van het boek, Ms. MMW 10 A 14, fol. 176v, detail
PHOTO: HUIS VAN HET BOEK

FIGURE 127A
Initial *C*(*oncede*) with beardless male head. Artist 1. Winter Missal of Arnold of Rummen, Sint-Truiden (text), Ghent (decoration and illumination), c.1345–1366. The Hague, Huis van het boek, Ms. MMW 10 A 14, fol. 178r, detail
PHOTO: HUIS VAN HET BOEK

FIGURE 127B
Initial *E*(*go*) with St. Andrew. Artist 1. Winter Missal of Arnold of Rummen, Sint-Truiden (text), Ghent (decoration and illumination), c.1345–1366. The Hague, Huis van het boek, Ms. MMW 10 A 14, fol. 178r, detail
PHOTO: HUIS VAN HET BOEK

FIGURE 127C
Initial *D*(*a nobis*) with winged profile head. Artist 1. Winter Missal of Arnold of Rummen, Sint-Truiden (text), Ghent (decoration and illumination), c.1345–1366. The Hague, Huis van het boek, Ms. MMW 10 A 14, fol. 178r, detail
PHOTO: HUIS VAN HET BOEK

FIGURE 128 Profile heads in penwork of lower terminal complex. Artist 1. Winter Missal of Arnold of Rummen, Sint-Truiden (text), Ghent (decoration and illumination), *c*.1345–1366. The Hague, Huis van het boek, Ms. MMW 10 A 14, fol. 178v, detail
PHOTO: HUIS VAN HET BOEK

FIGURE 129
Penwork face adjacent to initial *N*(*imis*) with profile head. Artist 1. Winter Missal of Arnold of Rummen, Sint-Truiden (text), Ghent (decoration and illumination), *c*.1345–1366. The Hague, Huis van het boek, Ms. MMW 10 A 14, fol. 179r, detail
PHOTO: HUIS VAN HET BOEK

FIGURE 129A
Initial *P*(*resta*) with head of woman wearing a hood. Artist 1. Winter Missal of Arnold of Rummen, Sint-Truiden (text), Ghent (decoration and illumination), *c*.1345–1366. The Hague, Huis van het boek, Ms. MMW 10 A 14, fol. 179r, detail
PHOTO: HUIS VAN HET BOEK

FIGURE 130
Initial *O(mnipotens)* with woman's head. Artist 1. Winter Missal of Arnold of Rummen, Sint-Truiden (text), Ghent (decoration and illumination), *c.*1345–1366. The Hague, Huis van het boek, Ms. MMW 10 A 14, fol. 186r, detail
PHOTO: HUIS VAN HET BOEK

FIGURE 132A
Initial *T(erribilis)* with bishop asperging church and acolyte with situla. Artist 1. Winter Missal of Arnold of Rummen, Sint-Truiden (text), Ghent (decoration and illumination), *c.*1345–1366. The Hague, Huis van het boek, Ms. MMW 10 A 14, fol. 192v, detail
PHOTO: HUIS VAN HET BOEK

FIGURE 134A
Initial *D(eus)* with head in grisaille. Artist 2. Winter Missal of Arnold of Rummen, Sint-Truiden (text), Ghent (decoration and illumination), *c.*1345–1366. The Hague, Huis van het boek, Ms. MMW 10 A 14, fol. 200r, detail
PHOTO: HUIS VAN HET BOEK

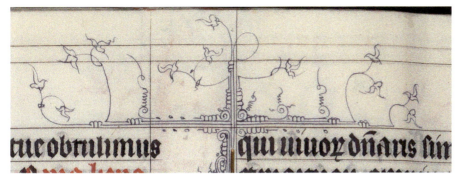

FIGURE 135A
Upper terminal complex; pearls. Artist 2. Winter Missal of Arnold of Rummen, Sint-Truiden (text), Ghent (decoration and illumination), *c.*1345–1366. The Hague, Huis van het boek, Ms. MMW 10 A 14, fol. 200v, detail
PHOTO: HUIS VAN HET BOEK

FIGURE 135B
Initial *D*(*eus*) with tonsured head. Artist 2. Winter Missal of Arnold of Rummen, Sint-Truiden (text), Ghent (decoration and illumination), *c.*1345–1366. The Hague, Huis van het boek, Ms. MMW 10 A 14, fol. 200v, detail
PHOTO: HUIS VAN HET BOEK

FIGURE 135C
Initial *O*(*mnipotens*) with head of Christ. Artist 2. Winter Missal of Arnold of Rummen, Sint-Truiden (text), Ghent (decoration and illumination), *c.*1345–1366. The Hague, Huis van het boek, Ms. MMW 10 A 14, fol. 200v, detail
PHOTO: HUIS VAN HET BOEK

FIGURE 136
Penwork head in upper margin. Artist 2. Winter Missal of Arnold of Rummen, Sint-Truiden (text), Ghent (decoration and illumination), *c.*1345–1366. The Hague, Huis van het boek, Ms. MMW 10 A 14, fol. 201r, detail
PHOTO: HUIS VAN HET BOEK

FIGURE 138A   First and second colophons. Winter Missal of Arnold of Rummen, Sint-Truiden (text), Ghent (decoration and illumination), c.1345–1366. The Hague, Huis van het boek, Ms. MMW 10 A 14, fol. 204r, detail
PHOTO: HUIS VAN HET BOEK

FIGURE 144
Initial *U(ns)* with gorgonesque head in initial body. *The Romance of Alexander*, Tournai, 1338–1344. Oxford, Bodleian Library, Ms. Bodley 264, fol. 79v
PHOTO: BODLEIAN LIBRARIES, UNIVERSITY OF OXFORD. HTTPS://DIGITAL.BODLEIAN.OX.AC.UK/. CREATIVE COMMONS LICENCE CC-BY-NC 4.0

FIGURE 153
Wildman. *Les voeux du paon*, Tournai, c.1348–1350. New York, The Morgan Library & Museum, Ms. G. 24, fol. 81r, detail. Gift of the Trustees of the William S. Glazier Collection, 1984
PHOTO: THE MORGAN LIBRARY & MUSEUM

FIGURE 154
Initial *P(arabolae)*, with streaky, white modeling. Bible, Palermo (?), *c*.1325. New York, The Morgan Library & Museum, Ms. G. 60, fol. 293v, detail. Gift of the Trustees of the William S. Glazier Collection, 1984
PHOTO: THE MORGAN LIBRARY & MUSEUM

FIGURE 156   Single leaf with borders comparable to those of Ms. 10 A 14. The Laudario of the Compagnia di Sant' Agnese, Florence, *c*.1340. New York, The Morgan Library & Museum, Ms. M. 742. Purchased in 1929
PHOTO: THE MORGAN LIBRARY & MUSEUM

FIGURES

FIGURE 164A
Initial *N(on)* with monks praying at a draped coffin. Ghent Ceremonial, Ghent or Tournai, 1322. Ghent, Universiteit Gent Universiteitsbibliotheek, Ms. 233, fol. 93v, detail
PHOTO: UNIVERSITEIT GENT UNIVERSITEITSBIBLIOTHEEK.
CREATIVE COMMONS LICENCE CC-BY-NC 4.0

FIGURE 167 Initial *A*(*spiciens*) with gorgon mouth enclosing man in combat. Antiphonal, Ghent (?), *c.*1345. Brussels, Koninklijke Bibliotheek/Bibliothèque royale de Belgique, Ms. 6426, fol. 2r, detail
PHOTO: KONINKLIJKE BIBLIOTHEEK/BIBLIOTHÈQUE ROYALE DE BELGIQUE

FIGURES 363

FIGURE 168   Penwork flourishing with stiff arcs and recurves, barbed corkscrews, and other motifs. Artist 2. Antiphonal, Ghent (?), c.1345.
Brussels, Koninklijke Bibliotheek/Bibliothèque royale de Belgique, Ms. 6426, fol. 106v, detail
PHOTO: KONINKLIJKE BIBLIOTHEEK/BIBLIOTHÈQUE ROYALE DE BELGIQUE

FIGURE 171A
Initial *R(esurrexi)* with sturdy architecture. Summer Missal of Arnold of Rummen, Sint-Truiden (text), Ghent (decoration and illumination), c.1345–1350. Brussels, Koninklijke Bibliotheek/Bibliothèque royale de Belgique, Ms. 9217, fol. 11v, detail
PHOTO: KONINKLIJKE BIBLIOTHEEK/BIBLIOTHÈQUE ROYALE DE BELGIQUE

FIGURE 173A
Initial *V(iri)* with sturdy architecture; fluent application of paint; oblivious man in gorgon's mouth. Summer Missal of Arnold of Rummen, Sint-Truiden (text), Ghent (decoration and illumination), c.1345–1350. Brussels, Koninklijke Bibliotheek/Bibliothèque royale de Belgique, Ms. 9217, fol. 33r, detail
PHOTO: KONINKLIJKE BIBLIOTHEEK/BIBLIOTHÈQUE ROYALE DE BELGIQUE

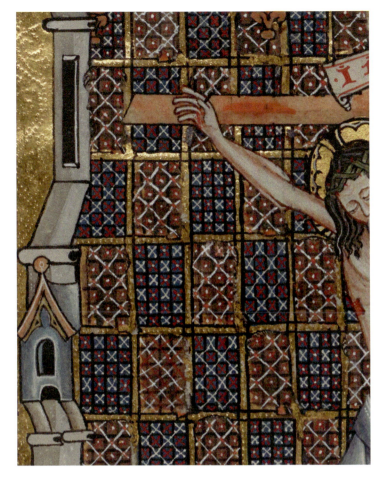

FIGURE 175A
Quadrant 1 of the Crucifixion, with traces of arms beneath overpaints. Summer Missal of Arnold of Rummen, Sint-Truiden (text), Ghent (decoration and illumination), c.1345–1350. Brussels, Koninklijke Bibliotheek/Bibliothèque royale de Belgique, Ms. 9217, fol. 115v, detail
PHOTO: KONINKLIJKE BIBLIOTHEEK/BIBLIOTHÈQUE ROYALE DE BELGIQUE

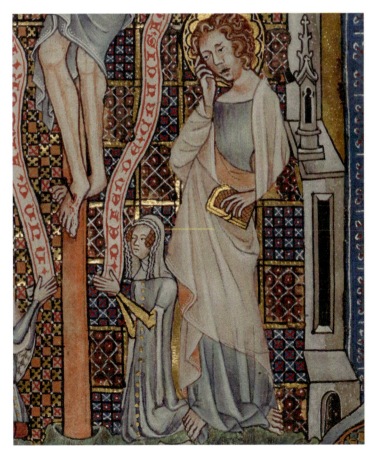

FIGURE 175B
Quadrant 4 of the Crucifixion, with traces of arms beneath overpaints. Summer Missal of Arnold of Rummen, Sint-Truiden (text), Ghent (decoration and illumination), c.1345–1350. Brussels, Koninklijke Bibliotheek/Bibliothèque royale de Belgique, Ms. 9217, fol. 115v, detail
PHOTO: KONINKLIJKE BIBLIOTHEEK/BIBLIOTHÈQUE ROYALE DE BELGIQUE

FIGURE 177A David harping: Compare to David in initial *A(d te)* on fol. 7r, Ms. 10 A 14. Artist 2. Liturgical psalter, Sint-Truiden (text), Ghent (decoration and illumination), c.1345–1350. Brussels, Koninklijke Bibliotheek/Bibliothèque royale de Belgique, Ms. 9427, fol. 14r, detail
PHOTO: KONINKLIJKE BIBLIOTHEEK/BIBLIOTHÈQUE ROYALE DE BELGIQUE

FIGURE 178 Initial *D*(*ixit*). Artist 2. Liturgical psalter, Sint-Truiden (text), Ghent (decoration and illumination), *c*.1345–1350. Brussels, Koninklijke Bibliotheek/Bibliothèque royale de Belgique, Ms. 9427, fol. 25r, detail
PHOTO: KONINKLIJKE BIBLIOTHEEK/BIBLIOTHÈQUE ROYALE DE BELGIQUE

FIGURE 181A   Stiff, barbed corkscrews. Artist 2. Liturgical psalter, Sint-Truiden (text), Ghent (decoration and illumination), *c*.1345–1350. Brussels, Koninklijke Bibliotheek/Bibliothèque royale de Belgique, Ms. 9427, fol. 45r, detail
PHOTO: KONINKLIJKE BIBLIOTHEEK/BIBLIOTHÈQUE ROYALE DE BELGIQUE

FIGURE 182A   Initial *S(alvum)*: divided image field. Liturgical psalter, Sint-Truiden (text), Ghent (decoration and illumination), c.1345–1350. Brussels, Koninklijke Bibliotheek/Bibliothèque royale de Belgique, Ms. 9427, fol. 100v, detail
PHOTO: KONINKLIJKE BIBLIOTHEEK/BIBLIOTHÈQUE ROYALE DE BELGIQUE

FIGURE 183A   Initial *E*(*xultate*): architecture of throne. Liturgical psalter, Sint-Truiden (text), Ghent (decoration and illumination), c.1345–1350. Brussels, Koninklijke Bibliotheek/Bibliothèque royale de Belgique, Brussels, Ms. 9427, fol. 124r, detail
PHOTO: KONINKLIJKE BIBLIOTHEEK/BIBLIOTHÈQUE ROYALE DE BELGIQUE

FIGURE 184
Initial *V(ix)* with humpbacked grotesque. *Dialogues of Gregory the Great*, Sint-Truiden, c.1350 (?)–1366. Liège, Bibliothèque de l'Université de Liège, Ms. 43, fol. 57r, detail
PHOTO: BIBLIOTHÈQUE DE L'UNIVERSITÉ DE LIÈGE

FIGURE 185
Initial *C(unctorum)* with John the Baptist in grisaille. *Passionarium 1*, Sint-Truiden, completed 1366. Liège, Bibliothèque de l'Université de Liège, Ms. 57, fol. 4r, detail
PHOTO: BIBLIOTHÈQUE DE L'UNIVERSITÉ DE LIÈGE

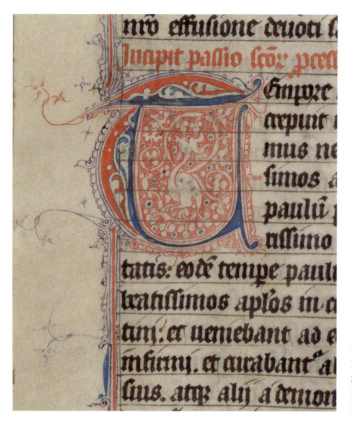

FIGURE 187
Initial *T(empore)* with humpbacked grotesque. *Passionarium 1*, Sint-Truiden, completed 1366. Liège, Bibliothèque de l'Université de Liège, Ms. 57, fol. 33v, detail
PHOTO: BIBLIOTHÈQUE DE L'UNIVERSITÉ DE LIÈGE

FIGURE 188   Initial *T(empore)* with humpbacked grotesque. *Passionarium 1*, Sint-Truiden, completed 1366. Liège, Bibliothèque de l'Université de Liège, Ms. 57, fol. 63v, detail
PHOTO: BIBLIOTHÈQUE DE L'UNIVERSITÉ DE LIÈGE

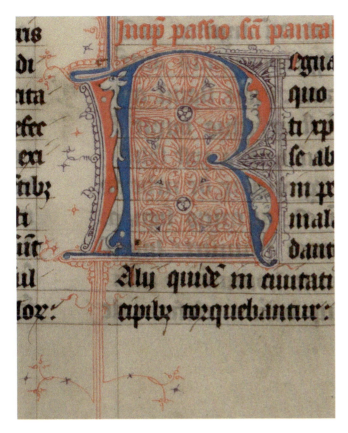

FIGURE 189
Initial *R(egnante)* with profile and ¾ heads in body of initial. *Passionarium 1*, Sint-Truiden, completed 1366. Liège, Bibliothèque de l'Université de Liège, Ms. 57, fol. 67v, detail
PHOTO: BIBLIOTHÈQUE DE L'UNIVERSITÉ DE LIÈGE

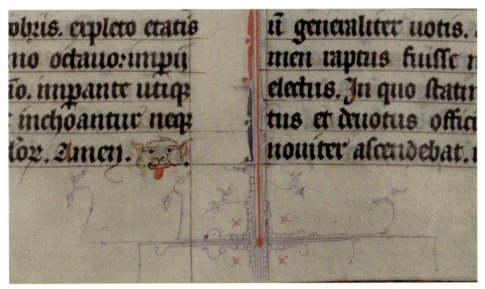

FIGURE 190 Flourishing in lower terminal complex. *Passionarium 1*, Sint-Truiden, completed 1366. Liège, Bibliothèque de l'Université de Liège, Ms. 57, fol. 220r, detail
PHOTO: BIBLIOTHÈQUE DE L'UNIVERSITÉ DE LIÈGE

FIGURE 191
Flourishing in lower terminal complex. *Passionarium 1*, Sint-Truiden, completed 1366. Liège, Bibliothèque de l'Université de Liège, Ms. 57, fol. 254v, detail
PHOTO: BIBLIOTHÈQUE DE L'UNIVERSITÉ DE LIÈGE

FIGURE 192 Flourishing in upper terminal complex. *Passionarium 1*, Sint-Truiden, completed 1366. Liège, Bibliothèque de l'Université de Liège, Ms. 57, fol. 256v, detail
PHOTO: BIBLIOTHÈQUE DE L'UNIVERSITÉ DE LIÈGE

FIGURES 375

FIGURE 193A
Initial *G*(*loriose*). *Passionarium 2*, Sint-Truiden, completed
c.1366. Liège, Bibliothèque de l'Université de Liège, Ms. 58,
fol. 2r, detail
PHOTO: BIBLIOTHÈQUE DE L'UNIVERSITÉ DE LIÈGE

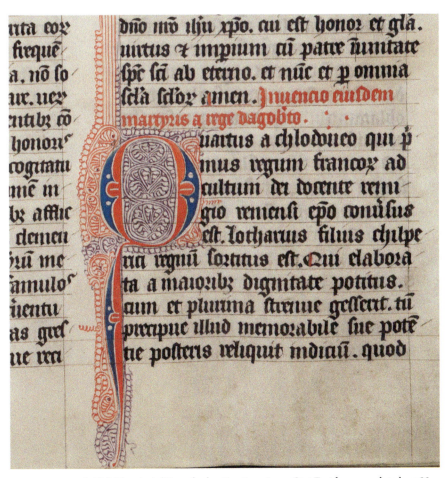

FIGURE 194   Initial *Q*(*uartus*), *littera duplex*. *Passionarium 2*, Sint-Truiden, completed *c*.1366.
Liège, Bibliothèque de l'Université de Liège, Ms. 58, fol. 12r, detail
PHOTO: BIBLIOTHÈQUE DE L'UNIVERSITÉ DE LIÈGE

FIGURE 196A

Initial *Q(uoniam)* with leaf face. *Speculum historiale 1*, Sint-Truiden, completed 1350. Liège, Bibliothèque de l'Université de Liège, Ms. 60, fol. 1r, detail

PHOTO: BIBLIOTHÈQUE DE L'UNIVERSITÉ DE LIÈGE

FIGURE 197A

Initial *D(eus)* with van Myrle and St. Trudo. *Speculum historiale 1*, Sint-Truiden, completed 1350. Liège, Bibliothèque de l'Université de Liège, Ms.60, fol. 17r, detail

PHOTO: BIBLIOTHÈQUE DE L'UNIVERSITÉ DE LIÈGE

FIGURE 198A
Initial *A(b anno)* with van Myrle and St. Trudo; gorgon in initial body. *Speculum historiale 2*, Sint-Truiden, completed 1352. Liège, Bibliothèque de l'Université de Liège, Ms. 61, fol. 1r, detail
PHOTO: BIBLIOTHÈQUE DE L'UNIVERSITÉ DE LIÈGE

FIGURE 199
Initial *D(ubitare)* with humpback grotesque. Gregory the Great, *Homilies on the Gospels*, Sint-Truiden, 1350 (?)–1366. Liège, Bibliothèque de l'Université de Liège, Ms. 138, fol. 36r, detail
PHOTO: BIBLIOTHÈQUE DE L'UNIVERSITÉ DE LIÈGE

FIGURE 200A Initial *S(acerdos)* with priest at the elevation. Loppem/Bruges Antiphonal, Ghent (?), *c.*1345. Bruges, Openbare Bibliotheek, Ms. SVC 10a, fol. [3r], detail. On loan from Stichting Jean van Caloen
PHOTO: OPENBARE BIBLIOTHEEK

FIGURE 201A
Initial *S*(*i oblitus*) with two clerics. Loppem/Bruges Antiphonal, Ghent (?), *c*.1345. Bruges, Openbare Bibliotheek, Ms. SVC 10a, fol. [4r], detail. On loan from Stichting Jean van Caloen
PHOTO: OPENBARE BIBLIOTHEEK

FIGURE 202
Initial *N*(*otam*) with pen flourishing. Loppem/Bruges Antiphonal, Ghent (?), *c*.1345. Bruges, Openbare Bibliotheek, Ms. SVC 10a, fol. [5v], detail. On loan from Stichting Jean van Caloen
PHOTO: OPENBARE BIBLIOTHEEK

FIGURE 203 Initial *D*(*Cum* [sic]) with Descent of the Holy Spirit. Loppem/Bruges Antiphonal, Ghent (?), c.1345. Bruges, Openbare Bibliotheek, Ms. SVC 10a, fol. [6r], detail. On loan from Stichting Jean van Caloen
PHOTO: OPENBARE BIBLIOTHEEK

FIGURE 204
Initial *S*(*cio*) with pen flourishing. Loppem/Bruges Antiphonal, Ghent (?), c.1345. Bruges, Openbare Bibliotheek, Ms. SVC 10a, fol. [8v], detail. On loan from Stichting Jean van Caloen
PHOTO: OPENBARE BIBLIOTHEEK

FIGURE 205   Initials with pen flourishing. Loppem/Bruges Antiphonal, Ghent (?), c.1345. Bruges, Openbare Bibliotheek, Ms. svc 10a, fol. [11v], detail. On loan from Stichting Jean van Caloen
PHOTO: OPENBARE BIBLIOTHEEK

FIGURE 206A   Initial *F(rater)*, with St. Jerome; frizzy pen flourishing. *Biblia*, Latin text with *Epistole* and *Prologi Hieronymi* and *Interpretationes*, Paris, c.1350. Stockholm, National Library of Sweden, Ms. A 165, fol. 2r, detail
PHOTO: NATIONAL LIBRARY OF SWEDEN

FIGURE 207 Incipit of Leviticus, with Moses kneeling before the Lord in initial *V(ocavit)* and gorgonesque grotesques in initial stem and bowl. *Biblia*, Latin text with *Epistole* and *Prologi Hieronymi* and *Interpretationes*, Paris, c.1350. Stockholm, National Library of Sweden, Ms. A 165, fol. 45v, detail
PHOTO: NATIONAL LIBRARY OF SWEDEN

FIGURE 208 Incipit of Psalm 38 (39) with King David in initial *D(ixi)* and gorgonesque conjoined heads in initial stem. *Biblia*, Latin text with *Epistole* and *Prologi Hieronymi* and *Interpretationes*, Paris, c.1350. Stockholm, National Library of Sweden, Ms. A 165, fol. 278r, detail
PHOTO: NATIONAL LIBRARY OF SWEDEN

FIGURE 209A
Soldier with facial rendering comparable to rendering in KBR 9217.
The Romance of Alexander, Tournai, 1338–1344. Oxford, Bodleian Library, Ms. Bodley 264, fol. 20v, detail
PHOTO: BODLEIAN LIBRARIES, UNIVERSITY OF OXFORD. HTTPS://DIGITAL.BODLEIAN.OX.AC.UK/. CREATIVE COMMONS LICENCE CC-BY-NC 4.0

FIGURES 385

FIGURE 210   Incipit of Christmas with gorgonesque grotesques in body of initial *H(odie)*. Loppem/Bruges Antiphonal, Ghent (?), c.1345. Bruges, Openbare Bibliotheek, Ms. svc 10a, fol. [2r], detail. On loan from Stichting Jean van Caloen
PHOTO: OPENBARE BIBLIOTHEEK